OUR FOREFATHERS

THE GOTHONIC NATIONS

OUR FOREFATHERS

THE GOTHONIC NATIONS

A
MANUAL OF THE ETHNOGRAPHY OF
THE GOTHIC, GERMAN,
DUTCH, ANGLO-SAXON, FRISIAN AND
SCANDINAVIAN PEOPLES

by

GUDMUND SCHÜTTE, Ph.D.

VOLUME II

CAMBRIDGE
AT THE UNIVERSITY PRESS
1933

CAMBRIDGE
UNIVERSITY PRESS

University Printing House, Cambridge CB2 8BS, United Kingdom

Published in the United States of America by Cambridge University Press, New York

Cambridge University Press is part of the University of Cambridge.

It furthers the University's mission by disseminating knowledge in the pursuit of education, learning and research at the highest international levels of excellence.

www.cambridge.org
Information on this title: www.cambridge.org/9781107677234

First published 1933
First paperback edition 2013

A catalogue record for this publication is available from the British Library

ISBN 978-1-107-67723-4 Paperback

To the memory of

DAME BERTHA PHILLPOTTS NEWALL

Published with the aid of subventions from the Carlsberg Fund and the Rask Ørsted Fund

CONTENTS

IV. §§ 209–210. The Dutch secondary sub-group

V. §§ 211–235. The North-west Gothonic sub-group

VI. §§ 236–248. The ancient intermediate peninsular sub-group or branch

ILLUSTRATIONS

PREFACE

The second volume of this work can only lay claim to the same modest value as its predecessor, so far as the preciseness of its particulars is concerned.

To make it quite satisfactory in this respect, its various parts ought to have been worked out by as many separate experts. I have not been able to obtain such authoritative collaboration; but Dr Schönfeld, who revised the first volume, has also given valuable help with the greater part of the second, and he has contributed largely to the contents of the Frisian chapter. In addition, the following chapters have been revised by specialists: the East Gothonic, German, and Erulian by Professor Rudolf Much of Vienna; the Anglo-Saxon by Professor Zachrisson of Uppsala; the Scandinavian and Danish by Dr Marius Kristensen of Copenhagen; the Gautic, Gotlandic and Svionic by Dr Rolf Nordenstreng of Uppsala; the Gotlandic by Professor Setälä of Helsingfors; the Norwegian by Dr Gustav Indrebö of Oslo. Various particulars concerning Scandinavian types of farmsteads have been supplied by Halvor Zangenberg of Lyngby, Sigurd Erixon of Stockholm, and Halvor Vreim of Oslo, experts on architectural history. I owe my sincere thanks to them all for their valuable assistance.

My chief aim has been to provide a methodical framework, showing how the detailed information expected in an ethnic manual *should be arranged.* The details themselves are of very unequal quality, sometimes being based upon my own special researches, sometimes upon manuals of recognised value: for it is impossible for one man to cover satisfactorily the whole of the ground required to fill out my scheme. Some of the facts which 'everybody knows' are, in practice, so often ignored that at last they run the risk of being totally forgotten. I, on the contrary, have endeavoured to collect them all and to put them into their right place in the whole scheme.

Owing to the relatively large number of specialists who have revised this work and have contributed numerous literary references, I have given up the practice of marking by an asterisk the works which I quote on the authority of the revisers. But I point out the chapters where I am especially indebted to my various contributors.

The *sequence of paragraphs* corresponds to that of the paragraphs in the Indo-European part, and to that of the chapters in the Gothonic part I. However, owing to the lack of expert collaboration, I here only work out four points of the above sequence, viz. 'Names', 'Sub-divisions', 'Ethnic Position', 'History'. On the other hand, I add a paragraph dealing with 'Legendary Traditions'.

The classical 'Names' of groups and tribes are not quoted with MS readings, as the reader will find all necessary particulars in Schönfeld's *Wörterbuch der altgermanischen Personen- und Völkernamen*, 1911. For scientific literature before 1911 I generally refer to the same work, which is, in reality, indispensable to any student of Gothonic ethnology. On the other hand, I add some particulars. Such additions are, for example, the old Scandinavian tribal names which are excluded from Schönfeld's collection because they are not exemplified in classical literature. Further, I add foreign spellings, eponymous forms, ethnic place names, etc., in order to illustrate more fully the onomastic development and to connect it with the point of view of ethnology.

As regards 'Sub-divisions', I have taken great care to avoid the arbitrary scheme of arrangement prevailing in most of the existing manuals. A systematic scheme of sub-division may easily tempt an author to be too categorical. Thus the reader will often find the different Gothonic tribes assigned respectively to the Vandili, Erminones, Istaevones, Inguaeones, and Hilleviones, as if we were no less well informed about these than about the local districts in Yorkshire and Norfolk. But such a use of the groups dating from the epoch of the ancient Mannung Genealogy is fatally misleading, and I have therefore felt obliged to give up this system with its deceptive categorical headings. Some examples will illustrate how I endeavour to avoid illusory statements.

§§ 141–144 deal with 'the Bastarnic Sub-group or Branch', leaving thus its exact rank in the classification open to doubt.

§§ 145–147 deal with 'the West Gothonic Linguistic Sub-group'. I state emphatically that the current name of 'Westgermanen' is merely philological, without any value in political history.

§§ 148–152 introduce the Germans and Dutch as 'the South Gothonic Sub-group', which I put in place of the group of 'Westgermanen', as the latter is imaginary in true political history. It is a grave fault of nearly all ethnologies and similar manuals that a paragraph dealing with the Germans and Dutch before their separation is omitted.

§§ 153–155 define the Erminones as a 'sub-group' which was almost extinct at the beginning of German history, and should therefore be avoided as an item within the practical classification of Gothonic tribes.

The identification of the Erminones with the Swabian branch is shown to be a theory which cannot be satisfactorily proved.

§§ 195–202 deal with 'the Marsic Branch, and the Chatthi, Ubii, and Bruchteri'. Though Tacitus, *Germ.* 2, in set terms co-ordinates the Marsi and the Gambrivii as German branches, it seems to be regarded as a matter of course that the Marsi are subordinate to the Gambrivii or Istaevones. I have reaffirmed the statement of Tacitus, placing the Marsi as co-ordinate with the Gambrivii or Istaevones. Moreover, I associate with the Marsi a number of West German tribes which are in the current system arbitrarily represented as Istaevones. But, as classical authorities confirm neither the one theory nor the other, I avoid a heading which might give a false idea of their relationship as an established fact; I simply write: the Marsic Branch, and the Chatthi, etc.

§§ 209–210 introduce 'the Dutch Secondary Sub-group'. From a modern point of view, as a separate nationality, the Dutch must claim their place in the system; but, in the ancient linguistic pedigree, they are only an offspring of the South Gothonic Sub-group, and their name 'Dutch' originates from the fact that in the Middle Ages they were regarded as Germans. Therefore §§ 209–210 can only briefly explain their ethnic position, and the other particulars must be given under the headings of the various German tribes from which they originate.

§§ 211–235 deal with 'the North-west Gothonic Sub-group', embracing Anglo-Saxons and Frisians. I prefer this term to 'Anglo-Frisians' or 'Inguaeones'. The first of these latter names leaves out the Saxon element, and the second is entirely misleading, as it cannot be proved that the Saxons and Frisians ever belonged to a sub-group called Inguaeones, while, on the other hand, the Inguaeonic community temporarily embraced Scandinavian tribes such as the Danes and Sviones.

§§ 236–248 introduce an 'Ancient Intermediate Peninsular Sub-group', embracing the Jutlanders and Varines. The current systems which describe the ancient Jutlanders categorically either as 'Anglo-Frisians' or as 'Scandinavians' are misleading, as we know in reality almost nothing about their ethnic characteristics before the Migration Age. The scope of Joh. Schmidt's 'wave theory' demands the existence of an intermediate domain between the Saxons and Danes, and no doubt the Jutlanders must once have been the connecting link. This link was lost when the Angles and Saxons emigrated in the fifth century, and those Jutlanders who remained in the country were united with the

Danes. Thus the intermediate sub-group has left no perceptible trace in modern times.

§§ 249–281 deal with 'the North Gothonic or Scandinavian Sub-group'. I pay no attention to the name of 'Hilleviones', which is by several scholars arbitrarily conceived as a synonym of Scandinavians.

The paragraphs representing the 'Ethnic Position' ought to form a main element of Vol. II. However, the particulars given in the paragraphs concerned may be open to several objections. Such a careful delineation of the Gothonic ethnic individualities has never before been attempted, and it is therefore to be expected that the first attempt will reflect the lack of preceding foundations.

The paragraphs dedicated to 'History', in a complete manual of ethnology, ought to give the ancient history of the sub-groups or tribes concerned in full. The present work, however, does not pretend to give so much. Its detailed representation of the ethnic development is generally limited to that age in which prehistory meets with the full dawn of history. I discuss the first emerging of the ethnic individuality and its first distinct efforts to assert itself—details which are by historians often more or less superficially worked out. But as soon as the well-known chain of historical events begins, I stop the detailed research, referring the reader to standard works such as L. Schmidt, *Geschichte der deutschen Stämme*; Hodgkin, *Italy and her Invaders*; Villari, *The Barbarian Invasions*, etc. I only try to emphasise the main points of ethnic importance, and I give some more detailed accounts if it is a question of the establishment of lasting ethnic frontiers or of the disappearance of a nation.

The paragraphs dealing with 'Legendary Traditions' should not be regarded as attempting to cover the ground of Wilh. Grimm's *Deutsche Heldensage*. I wish merely to draw the reader's attention to the acknowledged or possible representatives of historical tribes and persons, as the sum total of such figures enables us to realise the relative importance of the single ethnic individualities.

The English of the author's MS has been revised by Miss Winifred Husbands, B.A., of University College, London.

I conclude my work with the wish and hope that my attempt to create the first Anglo-Saxon Manual of Gothonic Ethnology may soon lead to the publication of a co-operative manual on the scale of the great Encyclopaedias.

ESKJÆR, 1932

G. S.

THE GOTHONIC NATIONS

I. §§ 112-144. THE GOTHIC OR EAST GOTHONIC SUB-GROUP

A. §§ 112–115. *THE SUB-GROUP AS A WHOLE*

§ 112. Names.

1. Lat. Vandili (Pliny, IV, 99), Vandilii (Tac. *Germ.* 2), the same word as 'Vandals'; perhaps originally a toponymic derived from a place name (cp. § 136, 2).

2. Gr. Γότθοι (Procopius, *Bell. Vand.* I, 2, p. 178); in more recent academic usage 'Goths'.

3. Germ. Ostgermanen, in modern academic terminology; the same as 'East Gothonic nations'.

Scarcely at any time have the peoples forming this section themselves used a native collective name.

German neighbours are most likely responsible for the use of the name Vandili (cp. Paulus Diaconus, I, 7, who relates a story which makes the Vandals neighbours of the Langobards on the lower reaches of the Elbe).

Goths, as used by Procopius, is quite suitable as a practical collective name, since the Goths created the national church and literary language of the East Gothonic nations. In grammatical works, Gothic stands as the solitary representative of the entire sub-group, as its other dialects are practically unknown.

The German term Ostgermanen is often extended so as to include the Scandinavians. This usage is misleading and should be avoided.

Lit. Loewe, *Gliederung*, 36; Kossinna, *Indogerm. Forsch.* VII, 308; Bremer, § 89; Kauffmann, I, 401.

§ 113. Sub-divisions.

(1) Goths and Gepidae, (2) Rugians and Sciri, (3) Burgundians, (4) Lugii and Vandals, (5) Bastarnae.

We have no classical evidence for the constituents and sub-divisions of this sub-group as a whole, and linguistic evidence is also quite inadequate. The sub-division just made must therefore only be understood as a rough and ready arrangement for practical purposes.

§ 114. Ethnic Position.

The East Gothonic sub-group is a linguistic fact, but history throws only a feeble light on its extent.

1. Pliny, IV, 99, presents the first sub-group of the Gothonic nations thus: 'Vandili quorum pars Burgundiones, Varinne, Charini, Gutones'. Here we have the sections, Goths and Burgundians, from our list in § 113; the Charini are apparently the Harii (Tacitus), a tribe of the section Lugii; to this same section belongs originally the sub-group, Vandals. The fifth unit on my list, the Bastarnae, on the other hand, are distinguished by Pliny as a special sub-group co-ordinate with the Vandals. Varinne = Varini (Tacitus) stand outside these, as they belong to the Anglo-Jutish tribes. Müllenhoff (*Germania Antiqua*, 93) would erase Varinne as a doublet for Charini, but the name does really seem to have stood in an original source, a geographical list, from which Ptolemy (II, 11, § 9 and III, 5, § 8) has taken two sets of doublets: Auarpoi, Burguntes = Auarinoi, Frugundiones (cp. the author's book *Ptolemy's Maps*, 132 and Fig. 24).

2. Tacitus, *Germ.* 2, after naming the three Gothonic sub-groups Ingaevones, Erminones, Istaevones, continues: 'quidam ut in licentia vetustatis pluris deo ortos plurisque gentis appellationes Marsos, Gambrivios, Svebos *Vandilios* affirmant eaque vera et antiqua nomina'.

3. Procopius says in his *Vandalic War*, I, 2, p. 178 A, B:

Γοτθικὰ ἔθνη πολλὰ μὲν καὶ ἄλλα πρότερόν τε ἦν καὶ τανῦν ἔστι, τὰ δὲ δὴ πάντων μέγιστά τε καὶ ἀξιολογώτατα Γότθοι τέ εἰσι καὶ Βανδίλοι καὶ Οὐισίγοτθοι καὶ Γήπαιδες....οὗτοι ἅπαντες ὀνόμασι μὲν ἀλλήλων διαφέρουσιν, ..., ἄλλῳ δὲ τῶν πάντων οὐδενὶ διαλλάσσουσι. λευκοί τε γὰρ ἅπαντες τὰ σώματά εἰσι καὶ τὰς κόμας ξανθοί, εὐμήκεις τε καὶ ἀγαθοὶ τὰς ὄψεις, καὶ **νόμοις** μὲν **τοῖς αὐτοῖς** χρῶνται, ὁμοίως δὲ τὰ ἐς τὸν θεὸν αὐτοῖς ἤσκηται. τῆς γὰρ **'Αρείου δόξης** εἰσὶν ἅπαντες, **φωνή** τε αὐτοῖς ἔστι **μία, Γοτθικὴ** λεγομένη. καί μοι δοκοῦν ἐξ ἑνὸς μὲν εἶναι ἅπαντες τὸ παλαιὸν ἔθνους, ὀνόμασι δὲ ὕστερον τῶν ἑκάστοις ἡγησαμένων διακεκρίσθαι.

'There were many Gothic nations in earlier times, just as also at the present, but the greatest and most important of all are the Goths, Vandals, Visigoths, and Gepidae....All these, while they are distinguished from one another by their names, as has been said, do not differ in anything else at all. For they all have white bodies and fair hair and are tall and handsome to look upon and they use the same laws and practise a common religion. For they are all of the Arian faith and have one language called Gothic; and, as it seems to me, they all come originally from one tribe and were distinguished later by the names of those who led each group.'

Yet the following tribes are occasionally designated as Gothic: Rugians (Procopius, *ibid.* III, 2, p. 470), Sciri and Alani (*ibid.* I, 1, p. 308), Burgundians (Agathias, I, 3), Eruli (Zonaras, III, 23, p. 590). The Eruli are North Gothonic, and the Alani as Iranians do not belong to the Gothonic nations; both of these, however, may possibly have been much Gothicised by intercourse with the Goths.

4. East Gothonic *tribal names* are again found in *Scandinavia*: (*a*) Gutar in Gotland; (*b*) Rygir in Rogaland, Norway; (*c*) inhabitants of Burgendaland, Bornholm; (*d*) inhabitants of Vendill, Sweden (cp. Wendle in Vendill, Jutland).

Bremer, § 85, adds the Gautic -greotingi (Jordanes, III, 22) = Gothic Greutungi, and Loewe, *Gliederung*, 43, attaches importance to the equation, Norwegian Holm-Rygir = East Gothonic (H)ulme-rugi (Jordanes, IV, 26). The first equation is, however, rather doubtful, and in the case of the Holm-Rygir we have to deal with a mediaeval transference to Norway of an East Gothonic name found in poetry.

5. Gothic has its own unmistakable distinctive stamp, sharply distinguished from both North and West Gothonic. This marks what scanty evidence we have concerning the language of the other branches of the East Gothonic sub-group. The most striking characteristics of the language are: the preservation of Gothonic *z* as a sibilant (cp. Goth. *weis* = H.G. *wir*, O.N. *vér*, 'we'). We notice the Gothic *z* or *s* in glosses and personal names from the fifth and sixth centuries, such as Burgundian Sigi*s*-mundus, Sigi*s*-ricus, hendino*s*,[1] Vandalic Gi*z*e-ricus, Gei*s*e-ricus, Hildi-ri*x*. (The German examples in *z* written *s*, such as Aflim*s*, Vatvim*s*, (H)ario-gai*s*os, are derived from the period before the decisive division amongst the Gothonic languages. Objection has been taken to names such as Vandalic Visim*a*r, Burg. Godom*a*r, where East Gothonic might be expected to show the development from *-mǣr* over *-mēr* to *-mīr* (cp. Kögel, *Zeitschrift*, XXXVII, 225; Much, *Indogerm. Anz.* IX, 201 note 2). But apart from the fact that we may here be dealing with another word altogether—perhaps Goth. *Wisu-marhs—

[1] The ending *-os* may possibly be due to the Greek nationality of the author Ammianus (though he writes in Latin).

it must be remembered that names of princes are not very reliable material: we can imagine that intermarriage would lead to the adoption of a foreign name with foreign phonetic form.) A negative fact is the absolute absence of the West Gothonic type of personal names in *-berht* (as in Scandinavian) (cp. Meyer-Lübke in *S.B. d. Wien. Akad. phil.-hist. Kl.* CXLIX, 2, 20: 'Die bei den anderen Germanenstämmen so ungemein beliebten Berht-Namen scheinen den Goten völlig zu fehlen'; cp. p. 57).

6. According to Brunner and Ficker, a uniform juridical type unites Goths, Burgundians, Scandinavians, Angles, Varini, Langobards, and Frisians. I have no means of checking this theory, and at any rate it does not clearly distinguish an East Gothonic sub-group. On the other hand, an East Gothonic community is indicated by the vocabulary of terms used for denoting various officials.

(*a*) Goth. *reiks* 'chieftain', early obsolete in the other Gothonic languages, is still so current in the Wulfilan texts that there seems to be no trace of a diminished use. The fifth-century Vandal royal title **Vandala-rix* (Luxorius, III, 21)[1] also points to the continued use of this word; cp. the Gothic loan word *rikys* in Prussian. On the other hand, the North and West Gothonic expression, 'king', is lacking in the Wulfilan texts and may have assumed another signification (cp. Lithuanian *kuningas* 'priest', i.e. heathen priest). Certainly it must be admitted that the Slavs have received the word *kunęgu* 'prince', from some East Gothonic tribe. The lexical material is too fragmentary to allow of quite decisive conclusions.

(*b*) Goth.-Vand. *garding* 'domesticus', e.g. *Leg. Visigoth.* II, tit. 1, 1, and Vict. Tunnun. ap. Roncallius, II, 364 (cp. Zeuss, 46; Wrede, *Sprache der Wandalen*, 87).

(*c*) Goth. *þusundifaþs* = Vand. 'millenarius' or 'chiliarchus'.

(*d*) The military division into detachments of 500 is exemplified amongst the Visigoths, Taifali, and Vandals (*Leg. Visigoth.* IX, 2, 1, etc.; Zosimus, II, 31, 3; cp. Schmidt, I, 36, 292, *Gesch. d. Wandalen*, 40, and *Die germ. Hundertschaftsverfassung* in *Vierteljahrsschrift f. Sozial- u. Wirtschaftsgeschichte*, 1928).

(*e*) Goth. *sinista* 'senator' = Burg. *sinistus* 'high priest', literally 'eldest' (Ammianus, XXVII, 5, § 15).

7. The Gothic national church of Arian creed, with its national literary language and national alphabet, came, in the end, to include all the Christian members of the East Gothonic sub-group except the

[1] Vocative Vandala-rice.

Goths of the Crimea. Some German-speaking members such as the Langobards also attached themselves to it, but these were in a dwindling minority. This bond of faith is emphasised by Procopius; when he calls the language of the sub-group Gothic, he is undoubtedly referring to the language of the church, which, amongst all the members of the sub-group, was of course Gothic.

The eighth point will consist of archaeological evidence. Kossinna, *Zeitschr. f. Ethnologie*, 1905, 369, takes the ornamentation found on certain lance heads to represent a decorative style common to East and North Gothonic nations. Kauffmann, I, 295, describes the use of 'fire pits' as a custom derived from Scandinavia, especially from Bornholm, which becomes characteristic for East Germany (cp. Almgren's map of the types of graves, *Mannus*, VIII, 291). But I express no opinion concerning these phenomena; moreover, they give no clear definition, uniting, as they do, both North and East Gothonic nations.

Undoubtedly the East Gothonic nations were originally only a Scandinavian section (cp. the common tribal names Goths, Rugians, Burgundians). After they had migrated south across the Baltic they quickly developed their own distinctive stamp, whence the 'Vandili' known to Pliny and Tacitus. The special characteristics of this sub-group for the moment show themselves most clearly in a passivity over against a series of common North and West Gothonic linguistic developments. But after their migration still further south, however, in the fourth century, the East Gothonic nations evolved their national church, literary language, and alphabet, produced the first written laws and the first common Gothonic heroic poetry. Thereupon they were called the Gothic sub-group by Procopius, who emphasises the distinctive stamp of their language and civilisation.

Lit. Zeuss, 403 (73 and 81 the erroneous equation: Istaevones=East Gothonic sub-group); Grimm, 464, etc.; Wackernagel and Binding, *Gesch. d. burgund. roman. Königreichs*, 329 seq.; Wrede, *Sprache der Wandalen*, 105, 109, 112; *idem*, *Sprache der Ostgoten in Italien*; Ficker, *Mitteil. des Instituts f. österreich. Geschichtsforschung*, II, Suppl. 1887, 455 seq.; *idem*, *Untersuchungen*, 1891; v. Amira, *Literaturblatt f. roman. Philologie*, 1888, 1–4; *idem*, *Götting. Gelehrt. Anzeiger*, 1892, No. 7; Maurer, *Kritische Vierteljahrsschrift*, XXXI, 190; Kögel, *Zeitschrift*, XXXVII, 223; Kossinna, *Die ethnolog. Stellung der Ostgermanen* in *Indogerm. Forsch.* VIII, 276; *idem*, *Zeitschr. f. Ethnologie*, 1905, 369; Much, *Goten u. Inguäonen* in *Beiträge*, XVII, 178; *idem*, *Stammeskunde*, 3rd ed. 115 seq.; *idem*, in Hoops, II, 180; Bremer, §§ 85, 87–92; Loewe, *Gliederung*, 25 seq.; Chadwick, *Encycl. Brit.* s.v. *Goths, Language*; Schmidt, I, 29, 49; Jellinek, *Gesch. der got. Sprache*, §§ 8–10.

§ 115. History.

The East Gothonic nations have nothing resembling a common history, yet phases of general importance may be pointed out in the story of their development.

Their primaeval station is reflected by the position of inhabitants of the Scandinavian regions: Gutar, Rygir, and the denizens of Burgendaland. On their migration south across the Baltic the same grouping may be observed, the Goths to the east, Rugians and Burgundians further west.

About 200 B.C. the Sciri and Bastarnae break through to the Black Sea as the first Gothonic tribes to play an active part in history. The Sciri belong to a series of tribes with names of the Short type—Rugi, Lugoi, Harji, *Dunoi, Buroi—extending from the Baltic to the Carpathians, a circumstance which speaks for an almost simultaneous colonisation of this region on the part of the individual tribes (cp. O.N. Harfaþa fjǫll 'the Carpathians', adopted before the Gothonic Sound Shift).

The German King Maroboduus' kingdom included East Gothonic tribes like the Luioi (Lugii) (Strabo, VII, 290), but it only lasted a short time, collapsing in A.D. 17 (Tac. *Ann.* 44, 62).

The participation of the Romans in the Prussian amber trade from the time of Nero on brought no little civilisation to the East Gothonic nations (cp. Pliny, XXXVII, 45).

During the Marcomannic war, c. A.D. 170, the Vandals forced their way into the country of the Κοιστοβῶκοι Dacians, who at that time extended through Poland as far north as and including Setidava round about the present Thorn (see Ptol. III, 5, § 21, II, 11, § 28, and the author's book *Ptolemy's Maps*, 113, 143, and *Beiträge*, XLI, 28). From now on they wander south and south-westwards, the Vandals towards Transylvania, the Goths to the Caucasus; the Goths harry Asia Minor and Greece on their Viking expeditions.

The Hunnish storm c. A.D. 370 forced the stream west, the Goths to Italy, Southern Gaul and Spain, and the Vandals to North Africa. The East Gothonic sphere of occupation hereafter extends from the mouth of the Weichsel and the Caucasus to Gibraltar and the Atlas Mountains. The great political achievements of the Migration Age belong, one might say, altogether to the East Gothonic nations who lead also from the point of view of civilisation (see § 114, 7). In the epic court guide of the Migration Age the Goths were appointed to the permanent position of No. 2, immediately after the Huns.

But the glory departed as swiftly as it came. By c. A.D. 566 all the East Gothonic states, with the exception of the Visigothic, were broken, and even that met its fate in 711. In the meantime the East Gothonic homeland was claimed by Avars, Baltic peoples, and Slavs. The last remnants of an East Gothonic language went under in the seventeenth century in the Crimea.

It may be convenient to give a survey of mediaeval or modern names of places or tribes which reflect the various members of the East Gothonic sub-group.

In the homeland: the Prussian region Gudden, and Lithuanian Gudai, i.e. White Russia, originally meaning Goths; Lett. Wid-semne, Germ. Wit-land, the region of the Gothic Vidivarii; Szlązaci in Silesia, the Silingi; O.N. epic place name Dun-heiðr 'heath of the Lugoi *Dunoi'.

In the colonial sphere: Gotia, bishopric in the Crimea; mountain Gotul in Roumania; Gossen-sass in Tyrol, 'seat of Goths'; various Godie in Venezian regions; Mont-gueun, Mor-godou in Southern France; Gepidasco, Zebedo, etc., in Northern Italy; Burgunt-hart, now Birkert near Carlsruhe, 'Burgundian wood'; Bourgogne or Burgundy in France; Tifauge in Western France < Theifalia; Gandalon in Southern France < *Vandalo; Andalusia in Spain < el Andalos, a headland from which the Vandals set out for Africa.

B. §§ 116–127. *THE GOTHIC BRANCH*

§ 116. Name.

1. Goth. *Gutans (in the runic inscription of Pietroassa 'Gutaniowihailag'; the interpretation of the form is questionable),[1] Gut-þiuda (calendary); O.E. Gotan; O.N. Gotar, Gotnar, Got-þjóð, Goð-þjóð; O.Swed. runic Kutar, read *Gutar;[2] Lat. Gutones (Pliny, first century),

[1] Cp. Rieger, *Zeitschr. f. deutsche Phil.* vi, 321; Loewe, *Idg. Forsch.* xxvi; Grienberger, *Arkiv*, xiv, 125; v. Friesen, *Om runskriftens härkomst*, 28; Cosijn, *Verslagen en Mededeel. d. k. Akad. van Wetensch.* 2. R., 7, 354; Meissner, *Zeitschrift*, lxvi, 54; lxvi, 213 seq.; Vendryes, *Indogerm. Forsch.* xlv, 367.

[2] Early Danish Gotte, Gotter (cp. Gothersgade in Copenhagen, pronounced Gottersgade) perhaps originates from a literary form, Lat. Gotti.

Gotones (Tacitus, first century), Gothones, Goti, Gotti, Gothi; Spanish Godos; O.Fr. Gotz; Gr. Gutones? (Pytheas, fourth century B.C., cited by Pliny), Γύθωνες (Ptolemy, second century), Γότθοι (Procopius, sixth century, etc., an abbreviation of Gut-þiuda), Γόττοι; O.Russ. Gъte, Gotje (Nestor), Gotъthi (*Legend of St Constantine*, i.e. Goth. Gut-þiuda); Circassian Gut; Tartarian Kut; Arabian Qut (in Spain). Personal name: vulg. Goth. Thiudi-goto (metathesis of Gut-þiuda). Epic place name, Latinised: Gothi-Scandza (Jordanes, see § 119). Prussian region Gudden; Lithuan. Gudai, i.e. White Russia (a form possibly introduced into Baltic before the Gothonic Sound Shift, but perhaps rather at a later epoch through the medium of Finnish).[1] Epic territorial names: O.N. Gotna-land, Goð-lǫnd, Goð-heimar (confused with 'the country of the gods'). Bishopric in the Crimea, abolished in 1786, Russ. Gotia. Place names: Muntele Gotuluĭ and Pîrîul Gotuluĭ in Transylvania (cp. Diculescu, *Die Gepiden*, 192; *Die Wandalen*, 50). Gossensass in Southern Tyrol (by Steub interpreted as *Gozzōno-sāz 'seat of Goths'; the correctness of this equation is shown by Much in *Der Sammler, Unterhaltungs- u. Literaturbeilage der Münchener Augsburger Abendzeitung*, 1926, No. 62). Numerous Godie in Venezia (cp. Bertoni, *L' elemento germanico nella lingua italiana*, 23). Lat. Mors Gothorum, Fr. Mor-godou, place of a Gothic defeat in Southern France. Lat. Mons Gothicus, Fr. Mont-gueun in Southern France (cp. Longnon, *Les noms de lieu de la France*).

The name Goths is found again in Gotland. It is probably connected with the verb 'to pour', Goth. *giutan*, participle *gutans*. But bearing in mind Langenfelt's warning (*Anthropos*, XIV/XV, 303), we should be on our guard against the current fanciful interpretations starting out from this root, such as 'pourers out of seed' and 'stallions' for example, or Noreen's 'poured out people'. In anticipation it is to be expected that the tribal name originates in a place name, in this case most likely a water name.

[1] The derivation of Gudden and Gudai from the Goths is usually rejected by philologists, but this theory is supported with good arguments by Güntert, *Über die Ursache der germ. Lautverschiebung* in *Wörter und Sachen*, X, 15. Lately, H. Jacobsohn has suggested that the name of Goths may have been introduced into Lithuanian through the medium of Finnish, see *Altgermanisches* in *Zeitschrift*, LXVI, 226 seq. Cp. K. Buga, *Kalba ir senovė*, I, 67; Senn, *Germ. Lehnwortstudien*, 76; Karsten, *Germanen*, 156; *idem*, *Zeitschrift*, LXVII, 253 seq.

If, as has been so often assumed, the Goths have a variant title (produced by gradation or 'Ablaut') in the tribal name, Gautar, it is tempting to derive it from the river Göta-elf (Gaut-elfr). I agree with Noreen in thinking it quite possible that this river may have been called plain Gaut in spite of Finnur Jónsson's assertion that the river is named after the tribe (*Danske Studier*, 1921, 41).

Lit. Grimm, 435 (erroneous equation Goths = Getae); Du Cange, s.v. *Goti*; Bezzenberger, *S.B. d. Altertumsgesellsch. Prussia*, 1900 (on the name of Gudden); Schütte, *Om Racenavnet* in *Norden*, 1904–5; *idem*, *Oldsagn om Godtjod*, 172 seq.; *idem*, *Publications of the Soc. for the Advancement of Scand. Study*, Illinois, 1912, 88; Noreen, *Upsala Univ. Årsskrift*, 1905, *Program*, 2, p. 5 note; Schmidt, I, 50; Schönfeld, s.v. *Gutones* (with lit.); *idem*, in Pauly-Wissowa, s.v. *Goti*; Much in Hoops, s.v. *Goten*; Streitberg, *Gotisches Elementarbuch*, §§ 5–7; Jellinek, *Gesch. der got. Sprache*, § 1; Sobolevskij, *Archiv f. slav. Phil.* XXXII, 309 seq.

2. O.E. Hrǽdas, Hréð-gotan (*Widsith*, ll. 120, 57); O.Gautic Hraiþ-gutar (inscription of Rök); O.N. Hreið-gotar, Reið-gotar. Country: O.N. Reið-gota-land. Ocean: O.Gautic Hraiþ-marr. The syllable Hraiþ- is obscure. Most scholars regard the Hrǽdas as identical with the Ostrogoths; others identify them with the Vidivarii on the mouth of the Weichsel. In our opinion, Hrǽdas and Hréðgotan are old poetical denominations of the Gothic nation as a whole. The later Icelandic tradition, e.g. *Skjǫldunga Saga*, transplants Reiðgotaland to Jutland.

Lit. (*a*) Hrǽdas identical with Ostrogoths: S. Bugge, *Efterladte Arbejder*, 58; Lindroth, *Svensk humanistisk tidskrift*, II, 209 seq.; Pipping, *Om runinskriften på Rökstenen*, 22; *idem*, *Rökstensinskriften ännu en gång*, 15; Brate, *Österg. run.* 236; *idem*, *Svensk humanistisk tidskrift*, III, 33 seq.; Johannson, *þiaurikʀ miʀ Hraiþkutum* (*Acta Phil. Scand.* VII, 97). (*b*) Localised in Prussia: v. Friesen, *Rök*, 39 seq., 43 seq., 83, 96, 109, 113 seq., 132 seq.; v. Grienberger, *Anglia*, XLVI, 352. (*c*) A collective name of the Goths: Schütte, *The Problem of the Hraidgoths* (*Acta Phil. Scand.* 1933). On the identification of Reiðgotaland with Jutland see v. Friesen, *Rök*, 125 seq., and Finnur Jónsson, *Arkiv*, XXVI, 86 seq. For further literature see Chambers, *Widsith*, 252.

§ 117. Sub-divisions.

1. (*a*) Lat. Visi (Trebellius, *Hist. Aug. v. Claudii*, c. A.D. 300), Vesi (Sid. Apollinaris), Wisi-gothae (Cassiodorus, *Var.* III, 1), Visi-gothae, Vese-gothae; Vulgar Lat. Guisi-gotae (Cassiodorus, MS M[a], twelfth century); Gr. Οὐισί-γοτθοι (Procopius). Visi is an original form and not a contraction (cp. Wehrle, *Zeitschr. f. deutsche Wortforsch.* VIII, 334, and Schönfeld); the Compound is a later expansion (cp. above, I,

157). The interpretation is uncertain. (*a*) Ablavius in Jordanes, XIV, 82, already takes Visigoths to mean 'the western Goths', (*b*) but the possibility of connexion with the Gothonic adverb *wisu* 'well' might also be envisaged. Yet, according to Langenfelt (cp. § 116), a geographical interpretation is to be preferred. The final homestead is Spain.

Lit. (*a*) Zeuss, 407; Falk and Torp, s.v. *Vest*; Much in Hoops, IV, 429, 513. (*b*) Streitberg, *Indogerm. Forsch.* IV, 300; *idem, Gotisches Elementarbuch*, 4th ed. § 5 (later withdrawn); Schönfeld, s.v. For the tradition see Hodgkin, I, i, 100 seq.

(*b*) Lat. *Tervingi (*Not. dign. Or.* VI, 20), *Tirvingi (Trebellius, *Hist. Aug. v. Claudii*, 6, c. A.D. 300), Thervingi (Ammianus); a surname of the Visigoths. Cp. the 'Tyrfingr' of the *Lay of Angantýr*, which seems there to stand for the territory of the Gothic King Angantýr, but which in the prose is taken to mean a sword. Interpretations: (*a*) The current theory refers Tervingi to a Gothonic word **terwa(n)* 'tar', **terwia-* 'resinous wood'; cp. Gothic *triu* 'tree', Cymric *derw* 'oak', and the Slav. tribe Drevljane 'treemen, woodmen'. (*b*) Frantzen is of the opinion that the pair, Tervingi and Greutungi, reflect the O.N. juxtaposition *torf ok grjót* 'turf and stone'. (*c*) The possibility of derivation from the river Drweca (Germ. Drewentz) in Eastern Prussia must also be taken into consideration, though it is not very likely. According to Holger Pedersen, the Polish form Drweca seems to derive from an original *Druontia which might be compared with the Gaulish Druentia, now Durance; but as this again may have something to do with the current British river name Derventio, a connexion with the Gothic Tervingi is perhaps not absolutely excluded (cp. Stokes in Fick's *Vergleich. Wörterbuch*, IV, 157).

Lit. (*a*) Zeuss, 407; Schönfeld, s.v.; Much in Hoops, IV, 514. (*b*) Frantzen, *Zeitschr. f. vergleich. Sprachwiss.* XLIII, 330. For the tradition see Hodgkin, I, i, 101. For the question of Tyrfingr see Neckel, *Beiträge zur Eddaforschung*, 258, 264; Symons, *Die Lieder der Edda*, III, 385.

2. (*a*) Lat. Austor-goti (Trebellius, *Hist. Aug. v. Claudii*, 6, c. A.D. 300), Ostro-gothi, -ae (Claudianus); Gr. Γότθοι (Procopius). Proper name: Goth. Ostro-gotha; O.E. East-gota; Langobard (f.) Austri-gusa. The diphthong in *austor-* is the literary Gothic form, whereas the monophthong in *ostro-* represents the later and more vulgar dialect; the *-o* of the ending, for older *-a*, is influenced by the *o* of the first syllable, according to later Gothic sound laws (cp. our article in *Arkiv*, XXXIII, 29). **austra* may be interpreted as (*a*) 'eastern' or (*b*) 'radiant'. The

first interpretation is found in Ablavius quoted by Jordanes, XIV, 82; (*b*) might serve as the analogy of Visi 'the well born'. Final home: Italy.

Lit. (*a*) Zeuss, 409; Wehrle, *Zeitschr. f. deutsche Wortforsch.* VIII, 334; Much in Hoops, III, 388, IV, 429, 513. (*b*) Streitberg, *Indogerm. Forsch.* IV. 300; *idem*, *Gotisches Elementarbuch*, 4th ed. § 5 (later withdrawn); Schönfeld, s.v. For the tradition see Hodgkin, I, i, 100 seq.

(*b*) Lat. *Greutungi, Grutungi (Trebellius, *Hist. Aug. v. Claudii*, 6, c. A.D. 300), Greuthungi (Ammian.), Greothingi (Hydatius, Contin.), Grauthungi (*Hist. Aug. v. Probi*); Gr. Γρόθιγγοι (Zosimus, fifth century A.D.), a surname of the Ostrogoths. Legendary Gothic hero: O.N. Gizurr Grýtinga liði 'leader of the Greutungi' (*Lay of Angantýr*). Proper name: O.H.G. Griuzing (Förstemann, 2nd ed. I, 675). The spelling *eu*, *au*, *u* is possibly due to gradation. The root in O.N. Grýtingar must be Gothonic **greut-*, O.N. *grjót* 'stone', and there is no known Gothonic root **greuþ-* extant, in spite of the constant spelling with *th* in the classical sources. However, this spelling might perhaps be supported by a derivation from the Prussian place name Graudenz, Polish Grudziądz, on the Weichsel (cp. Güntert, *Wörter u. Sachen*, X, 15). It is not necessary to assume original identity with the Gautic -greotingi in Jordanes, III, 22; the name might easily have come about as a toponymic for a stony district here and there.

Lit. Zeuss, 407; Hodgkin, I, i, 101; Bremer, § 85; Schönfeld, s.v.; Ihm in Pauly-Wissowa, s.v.; Much in Hoops, III, 389; Langenfelt, *Anthropos*, XIV/XV, 309 (Vienna, 1920).

(*c*) O.E. Amulingas, O.N. Ǫmlungar; a surname of the Ostrogoths. Epic personal name: O.H.G. Amulung. Derived from Amali, the Ostrogothic royal family.

Lit. Schönfeld, s.v. *Amal*; Much in Hoops, III, 389.

(*d*) O.E. Mǽringas; O.Swed. runic inscript. *Mæringar (gen. pl. Marika, *Rök Inscription*); O.H.G. Mērānare (*Regensb. Gl.*, *Zeitschrift*, XII, 415); Med. Lat. Mer-gothi (Notker's *Boëthius*, Preface: 'Theodorich rex Mergothorum et Ostrogothorum'). The forms are surnames of the Ostrogoths (cp. Notker). Epic place name: O.E. Mǽringaburg (*Deor's Complaint*). Derived from Gothic *mērs* 'famous' (in *vaila-mērs*)? According to Heinzel the name may emanate from the supporters of the Ostrogothic King Theodoric Valamer, who were called Valameriaci (see Liberatus, *Breviar. Nestorianorum et Eutychianorum*, ed. Garnerus,

XVIII, 125, sixth century). Johannson identifies the great Theodoric's epic residence Mǽringaburg with Μαρεβοῦργος (Procopius, Περὶ κτισμάτων, IV, § 6) near his historical residence Novae in Moesia.

Lit. Heinzel, *S.B. d. Wien. Akad. phil.-hist. Kl.* CXIX, 9; Bugge, *Kgl. Vitterh. Hist. och Antiq. Akad. Handl.* XXXI, 3, 22; Much in Hoops, III, 389 Johannson, *Acta Phil. Scand.* VII, 28, cp. Patzig, *Dietrich von Bern*, 33 seq.

(*e*) Med. Lat. Wala-gothi, Guala(n)-guti (*Generatio regum et gentium*), which comes from the sixth century; a surname of the Ostrogoths (?). Either (*a*) the Goths of 'Welschland' or Italy, or (*b*) identical with the above-mentioned Valameriaci; Much compares Frideschotten in the poem of *Kudrun*, i.e. 'King Fridebrand's Scots'.

Lit. (*a*) Müllenhoff, II, 280, III, 329; Much in Hoops, III, 389. (*b*) Heinzel, *S.B. d. Wien. Akad. phil.-hist. Kl.* CXIX, 10; Much, *l.c.*

3. Lat. Vidi-varii (Jordanes, V, 17, § 6). Personal name: Lat. Viduarius (king of the Quadi, Ammianus, XVII, 12, § 21, fourth century, or *Vidu-harius ?); O.H.G. Wit-war (*Mon. Germ. Libr. Confratr.* I, 249). Place name: O.H.G. Wit-land (Alfred's *Orosius*); L.G. Wid-land; Lett. Wid-semne; Liv. Vidu-maa (-semne, -maa, i.e. 'land'), that is Livland. The initial element probably belongs to Lith. *vidus* 'central, inner', but the Goths undoubtedly understood it as meaning 'wood, forest' (cp. *Widsith*, l. 119 seq., where Hrǽdas = Vidivarii guard the Wistlawudu, 'the wood of the Weichsel'). The final element is Gothonic *-warjôz* 'men'. Home according to Jordanes: the islands in the delta of the Weichsel.

Lit. Zeuss, 668; Müllenhoff, II, 346; Schönfeld, s.v.; Much in Hoops, s.v.

4. Gr. Γότθοι οἱ Τετραξῖται from Gr. τετραξός 'quadruple'. That this is a corruption of the place name Ταμάταρχα, as suggested by Loewe, is hardly probable. Home: Tamatarcha, the modern peninsula of Taman, east of the Sea of Azov. The Tetraxitae may be reckoned as forming a sub-division along with the Goths of the Crimea who have no old name of their own (Erulian origin can hardly count as proved in spite of Loewe, 29 seq., 71 seq.).

Lit. Massmann, *Zeitschrift*, I, 345; Loewe, 22 seq.; Much in Hoops, s.v.

5. Lat. Gothi minores, the so-called Moesian Goths. Home: Lower Moesia, round about Nicopolis.

Lit. Jordanes, LI, 267; Walafrid Strabo, *De rebus ecclesiasticis*, 7; Loewe, 250 seq.; Much in Hoops, s.v.

6. O.E. Gifeþas (or -an, *Widsith*, l. 60), Gefþas (or -an, *Beowulf*, l. 2404); N.H.G. Gepitzen? (Aventin, *Sämtl. Werke*, ed. Riezler, IV, 1160; the form is perhaps an arbitrary reconstruction by Aventin); Lat. Gipedae (Vopiscus, *Hist. Aug. v. Probi*, 18, 2, about A.D. 300), Gipedes (Trebellius, *Hist. Aug. v. Claudii*, 6, 2), Gipides, Gepidae, Gebidi, etc.; M.Lat. Zepidae (Sid. Apollinaris, *Carm.* VII, 322, Codices), Gebeteos (*Generatio regum et gentium*); Gr. Γήπαιδες (Procopius, etc.), Γίπαιδαι (Joann. Lyd. Mag.). Eponymous ancestor: M.H.G. Gibeche (*Nibelungenlied*, str. 1343, Bartsch). Personal name: O.H.G. Gebetho (A.D. 717), Gebizo (?eleventh century, see Förstemann, I, col. 632). Islands: Got. Geped-ojos (Jordanes, XVII, 96), i.e. the Weichsel Delta. Places in Lombardy, Ital. Coguzo Gepidasco (A.D. 996, document of Otto III), Zebedo, Zevedo, Zevio. The O.E. forms of the name are most reliable, and refer it to the root of the verb 'to give'. Diculescu reads the name with long ē and connects it with M.H.G. *gæbe*, O.N. *gæfr* 'acceptable, agreeable', but it seems preferable to connect it with O.E. *gifede*, O.L.G. *gibedig* 'concessus, felix'. The form with *p* is not original, but it is not simply a bad spelling by southern copyists (cp. the interpretation given by Jordanes, XVII, 95: 'lingua eorum pigra *gepanta* dicitur...gepanta pigrum aliquid tardumque designat'). Gepides would correspond literally to Lat. *hebetes* 'the lazy' (Much), but this interpretation is rejected by Diculescu who explains *gepanta* as present participle of **gipan*, Norw. *gipa* 'to yawn'. We must regard Gebidae as the true vernacular form, and Gepidae as a corruption due to neighbouring peoples. On the classification of the Gepidae as a Gothic tribe see § 118. Localisations: (1) home, Geped-ojos, the Weichsel Delta; (2) later realm, Dacia or Gipidia (cp. Diculescu's map, p. 76); (3) scattered colonies, Zebedo, etc., in Northern Italy (cp. Bertoni).

Lit. Förstemann, II, 638 (with lit.); Müllenhoff, II, 400; Much, *Zeitschr. f. deutsche Wortforschung*, I, 322; *idem*, in Hoops, s.v.; Kossinna, *Westdeutsche Zeitschr.* X, 109; Schönfeld, s.v.; Bertoni, *L' elemento germanico nella lingua italiana*, 23; Diculescu, *Die Gepiden*, 7–13.

Survey of the various types of names.

Generally speaking, Short Simplexes appear earlier than Compounds: Gutones first century, Austor-goti third century, Gut-þiuda sixth century, etc.; Visi third to fourth century, Vese-gothae fifth century; Hrǽdas, *Widsith*, alongside of Hréþ-gotan, Hraiþ-gutar, etc., *Rök Inscription*, *Edda*, etc.

A Derivative type like Gebidae conveys an impression of antiquity. The ending *-ing*, *-ung* makes its first appearance c. A.D. 300 in the names of two Gothic sub-divisions, Tervingi and Greutungi. The later forms Mǽringas and Amulingas belong to the same stratum.

The first Compound is Austor-goti, c. A.D. 300, at that time still an isolated example. Later follow Vese-gothae, Wala-goti, Mer-gothi, Hréþ-gotan, Gut-þiuda, Vidi-varii.

§ 118. Ethnic Position.

The Goths' claim to count as a special branch of the East Gothonic nations is proved by several facts.

1. Although in the first century A.D. the Goths form a united whole without sub-divisions mentioned by name, after the year A.D. 300 sources reveal to us a particularisation into about half a dozen proper names (see § 117, Nos. 1–6).

2. The name Gut-þiuda like Sví-þjóð undoubtedly symbolises the rank of a more distinguished tribal community; we have a trace of the same element in Angel-þéod, Sæx-þéod, where it constantly appears in association with greater units. Gut-þiuda is not exemplified earlier than the sixth century, but that this form was used earlier is implied by the abbreviation Gotthi.

3. The use of Compound tribal names from the fourth century on distinguishes the Goths from the Lugian-Vandalic branch, where it cannot be definitely proved. (On the other hand we find Compounds among the Rugians and Burgundians.)

4. The affinity of the Gepidae with the Goths is emphasised by Jordanes, XVII, 95: 'sine dubio ex Gothorum prosapie et hi trahunt originem'. A third part of the Goths' emigrant ships falls to them, and Geberic the king of the Goths calls them 'propinqui' (*ibid.* 99).

5. Tacitus, *Germ.* 43, characterises the Gothic-Rugian nationality thus: 'rotunda scuta breves gladii et erga reges obsequium'. Here the Goths are not distinguished from the Rugians, but it may be assumed that the description in question opposes the Goths not only to their West Gothonic neighbours, but also to those East Gothonic tribes of the Lugian branch with whom Tacitus has been dealing immediately before. (It must, however, be added that the monarchical system of government was not ever so deeply rooted amongst the Goths as we may gather from Tacitus' words; we hear of republican constitution in Ammianus,

XXXI, 4, § 4, where Athanaric is called 'Thervingorum judex'; cp. Schmidt, I, 95.)

6. Jordanes, III, 23, mentions the 'stabilitas' and 'tarditas' of the Goths. The Gepidae are always characterised by him as still more steady and slow. Correspondingly, Isidore in his *Origines*, 9, 2, derives their name from *pes* 'foot'. All this seems to indicate that the chief arm of the Goths was the infantry. In contrast to this the Vandals were decidedly an equestrian people (cp. for example Dexippus, *Exc.* ed. Bonn, 19–20 ; see Diculescu, *Die Wandalen*, 13).

Very little more can be said, apart from the copious archaeological material on which I shall not enter on account of its somewhat problematic nature. It is easy enough to describe Gothic civilisation as a whole (cp. Schmidt, I, 278), but it is difficult to point out features which might be peculiar to it and not shared in common with other East Gothonic tribes.

§ 119. Early History of the Goths.

If Goths = Gauts and should be derived from the river Götaelf (cp. § 116) we have here a hint at prehistoric expansions from the river Götaelf east through Götaland to the island of Gotland. The hypothesis is doubtful however. At all events legend unmistakably assigns the primitive home to Scandinavia.

The Goths are met with for the first time in history in Prussia in the first century A.D. The possibility that the immigration may have taken place *before* the Gothonic Sound Shift must be taken into consideration, as the Baltic peoples may have adopted the tribal name in the form *Ghud- whence Lith. Gudas 'Russian'; the original Russians were indeed Gothonic people (cp. Güntert, *Wörter u. Sachen*, X, 15). However, the *d* may also originate from a Finnish intermediate form (cp. Jacobsohn in *Zeitschrift*, LXVI, 226).

The historical home is reflected in a mass of geographical details found in Gothic legend.

Gothi-Scandza (Jordanes, IV, 28) is the name of the country of the Goths south of the Baltic (cp. Scatenauga as the name of the Langobards' home on the Elbe). An interpretation *Gutisk-andja or *Gutisk-andeis 'Gothic shore' has been suggested; thus Grienberger, *Zeitschrift*, XXIX, 173 note; Much in Hoops; Schönfeld in Pauly-Wissowa, *Goti.* In agreement with Kossinna, *Indogerm. Forsch.* VII, 288, I must reject this explanation as too artificial, too 'linguistic'. There are no examples of such a use of the adjectival ending *-isk* in Old Gothonic. We must rather abide by the traditional form containing the name of Goths without a derivative ending.

Conrad Celtis in the fifteenth century and later the Danzig scholar Klüver would identify Gothi-Scandza with Gyddanizc, Gdansk, the Polish name of Danzig. This identification seems rather questionable and at least requires that the sounds have been largely mutilated in Polish. On the other hand, the syllable Gyddan-, as well as the name of the neighbouring port Gdynia or Gdingen, may very well be derived from the same word as the Prussian Gudden and the Lithuanian Gudai, i.e. the name of the Goths.

Ojum (Jordanes, XVII, 27) = the delta of the Weichsel, Gothic *Aujōs (dat. *Aujōm), 'the islands', a name of the Short Simplex type.

Spesis (Jordanes, XVII, 96), a part of the delta; also Short Simplex type.

O.E. Ylfing in Alfred's *Orosius* is the present river Elbing, that is 'little river'. The name lived on after the Goths had become extinct.

Intercourse with the Baltic tribe Galindai (Ptol.) is hinted at by the Gothic personal name Galindo in Spain (cp. Much in Hoops, II, 304).

Reminiscence of peaceful relations with the Baltic peoples, the Aestui, seems to be proved by Jordanes, V, 36, where these are described as 'pacatum hominum genus omnino'. Baltic is full of Gothic loan words, e.g. Prussian *rikys* 'chieftain', and the Gothonic *-haim* type of place name in Dirschkeim in Samland.

Jordanes, IV, 26, makes mention of early Gothic victories over (H)ulmerugi and Vandals, but nothing can be ascertained concerning these.

The journey asserted to have been made by Pytheas to the amber coast of the 'Gutones' (Pliny, XXXVII, 35) must rest on a misunderstanding due to a confusion of this coast with the *Jutish* amber coast.

The amber trade, however, brought about early contact with southern neighbours; this explains loan words such as original Celtic *kēlikn* 'tower, upper storey', Dacian (?) *sipōneis* 'disciple', Celto-Latin (?) *peikabagms* 'palm tree'.

The Goths were governed by kings (Tac. *Germ.* 43). Gothic legend preserves no remembrance of a primitive period without kings.

Soon after A.D. 1 the Marcomannic King Maroboduus founded his great Swabian kingdom in Bohemia, which extended at least near to the Baltic. Schmidt, I, 52, denies that it included the Goths: 'Die häufig ausgesprochene Behauptung dass sie zum Reiche...gehört hatten ist unbegründet; sie stützt sich lediglich auf Strabo wo statt des überlieferten Βούτωνας Γούτωνας gelesen wird. Gegen ein Abhängigkeitsverhältnis von den Markomannen scheint die Tatsache zu sprechen, dass Katwalda vor dem Könige bei den Goten Schutz suchte und von diesen unterstützt im Jahre 19 n. Chr., den Sturz Marbods herbeiführte. Unter den Butonen Strabos hat man daher eher die Βατεινοί des Ptolemäus (im östlichen Böhmen) oder die Burgunden zu verstehen'.

Like Schönfeld in Pauly-Wissowa I am unable to acknowledge the force of these arguments. In my opinion Maroboduus ruled a Baltic tribe in East Prussia at any rate—the Sudinoi, i.e. Strabo's Sibinoi—and in that case the Goths scarcely escaped his sway. The fact that Tacitus takes the Goths to be Swabians seems to be most naturally explained by the assumption of a temporary dependence on the Swabian kingdom. At all events, however, the conquered tribes became independent again after Maroboduus' defeat in A.D. 17, and in the year 19 the Marcomannic outlaw Catvalda returned from the Goths and expelled Maroboduus from Bohemia (Tac. *Ann.* 44 and 62).

In the time of Nero the Romans formed close commercial connexions with the Prussian amber coast (Pliny, XXXVII, 45; cp. Tac. *Germ.* 45). Finds of Roman coins are especially associated with the first two centuries A.D. (cp. Friedrich, *Zeitschr. d. hist. Gesellsch. f. Posen*, XXIV, 236, 246, and Stjerna, *Essays on Beowulf*, 65). From now on Latin *f* is not changed to the Celtic substitute *p* as in *peika*, but is adopted unaltered, for example *faskja*. A word like *lukarn* 'taper, candle', Lat. *lucerna*, reaches Gotland through Gothic mediation. The influence of Gothic commerce on both sides of the Baltic is shown by the common linguistic developments: *i* and *u* appear as *æ* and *å* before a vowel in Gothic, Danish and Swedish (cp. Gothic Suehans, Jordanes, O.Swed. Svéar, over against Sviones, Tacitus, O.N. Svíar, Gothic *bauan*, O.Swed. *bóa*, but O.N. *búa*, 'to dwell'); the article *sa sō þata* is closely bound up with the pronominal adjective 'same', cp. vol. I, § 33.

Sten Konow is of the opinion that traces of the Goths are to be found in two Buddhist inscriptions in Junnar from about the year A.D. 150 (see *Journal of the Royal Asiatic Society*, 1912, 392 seq., and *Maal og Minne*, 1912, 69 seq., with notes by Magnus Olsen; cp. Premerstein,

Zeitschrift, LX, 72). It certainly cannot be denied that it seems a little bold to attempt to identify the Gatana of the inscription with Goths, Gothic *Gutans, since it is difficult to account for the rendering of Gothic *u* by *a*. Yet the assertion of Quintus Metellus Celer that, when pro-consul in Gaul, he accepted some 'Indian' merchants as a present from a king in Germany, lends colour to the theory (cp. Mela, V, 36; Pliny, II, 170). Taking one thing with another, the evidence seems to point to old commercial connexions between India and Eastern Germany (however cp. Much, *Ulixes in Germanien* in *Wörter u. Sachen*, XII, 342).

In Ptolemy, III, 5, § 8, the Goths still occupy their old historical home east of the mouth of the Weichsel as neighbours of the Galindai and Sudinoi, the Baltic tribes of Galinditae and Sudovitae. The last-mentioned names speak for a Ptolemaic source with fresh and accurate data (cp. the author's book *Ptolemy's Maps*, 109).

Gothic loan words in Slavonic, like *useręgъ* 'ear-ring', show that the Slavs were influenced by Gothic civilisation (cp. vol. I, § 56).

Ptolemy's description from c. A.D. 150 represents the situation before the migration. Just about this time, however, was ushered in the thorough-going revolution which was to transform the country of the Goths and its neighbouring territories—the great migration of peoples. The first warning was the outbreak of the Marcomannic war in A.D. 165. Julius Capitolinus, *Hist. Aug. v. M. Ant.* XIV, 14, describes it thus: 'Victualis et Marcomannis cuncta turbantibus, aliis etiam gentibus, quae pulsae a superioribus barbaris fugerant, nisi reciperentur, bellum inferentibus'. The 'superiores barbari' who chased their neighbours to the frontiers of Rome may have been the Goths.

The migration from the country of the Goths was accompanied by a change of name. Up to this time the district round the delta had been called *Aujos 'the islands' (in Jordanes, IV, 27, Ojum); now the Gepidae thronged in, in place of the Goths, and parts of the islands were given the name Gepidojos (*ibid.* XVII, 96).

The Spali, whom the Gothic emigrants conquered (*ibid.* IV, 28), may have been invaders on Slavonic soil; in Old Slavonic there is a word *spolinъ* 'giant' (see Much in Hoops, II, 305).

The first encounter with the Romans is recorded during the reign of the Emperor Caracalla, 211–217 (*Hist. Aug. v. Carac.* X, 6); possibly the Goths had now reached the regions of the Danube on their incursions. From this time on, Gothic History is so well documented that reference may be made to Schmidt, Hodgkin and other compendia. The following more important data may be noted.

In A.D. 253 and the following decades, Goths and Eruli starting from the Crimea ransack the coasts of the Black Sea and the Archipelago with Viking expeditions. The Gotthograikoi living in the district of Opsikion on the north coast of Asia Minor probably come from these invasions (see Loewe, 1 seq.).

In 269 the Emperor Claudius defeats Ostro- and Visigoths at Naissus, the modern Nish in Serbia.

About 274 the Emperor Aurelius expels the Goths from Thrace and Moesia but cedes Dacia to them.

In 325 an orthodox Gothic bishop takes part in the Synod of Nicaea (see Loewe, I, 210).

About 340 the Visigoths' Arian apostle Wulfila, translator of the Bible into Gothic and creator of the Gothic literary language, is active in Dacia. In 348 owing to Athanaric's persecution, he leads his flock over into Roman territory to Moesia where they live henceforth in peace as subjects of Rome; this branch of the group is known by the name Moesian Goths.

§ 120. History of the Ostrogoths Proper.

About A.D. 350 Ermanaric of the Amali founds an empire among the Ostrogothic nations in South Russia after their separation from the Visigoths. According to tradition, as represented by Jordanes, XXIII, 116, his power extended to the Baltic and to Merens and Mordens, i.e. the Finnish tribes Merja and Mordwa living in the Volga district. The names Merens and Mordens are obviously Gothic accusative forms and are thus derived from genuine Gothic tradition. Yet it is conceivable that Ermanaric's so-called sway over these tribes is an epic exaggeration and that the notion of his power has been worked up from a fragment reflecting the Gothic range of view.

About A.D. 370 the invasion of the Huns reaches Europe. Ermanaric commits suicide. His successor Vinithari becomes a Hunnish vassal, attempts to conquer the Antes, that is, Circassians, on his own but is attacked and slain by the Huns by the river Erac, i.e. the Greeks' Erax, also known as Phasis. Schmidt, I, 108, would reject this tradition in Jordanes as a fiction of Cassiodorus, but its genuineness is defended with strong arguments by Olrik, *Danske Studier*, 1914, 9 seq. It was in consequence of this collision with Asia that even at the end of the fifteenth century Gothic villages were found on the Caucasus side of the Straits of Azov.

In 451 the Ostrogoths take part as vassals in the unfortunate battle between the Hunnish King Attila and the Roman governor Aëtius and the Visigoths in Gaul.

In 453 the Ostrogoths and the other Gothonic vassals rebel against Attila's sons and emancipate themselves. Three brothers of the Amali share Pannonia. Valamer establishes himself on the territory between the river Scarniunga and the Aqua nigra, Thiudimer on Lake Pelsois (Balaton, Plattensee), Vidimer between the two (Jordanes, III, 268).

In 488 Thiudimer's son, Theodoric the Great, who had previously been on an expedition to Constantinople and Epirus, comes to an agreement with the Emperor Zeno and attacks the East Gothonic conqueror of Italy, Odovacar, slays him in 493 and founds a Gotho-Roman kingdom.

In 496, after their defeat by the Franks, some of the Alemanni take refuge under Ostrogothic rule (Ennodius, *Panegyr.* 15; Cassiodorus, *Var.* II, 41, XII, 4; Agathias, I, 6). The area incorporated embraced Switzerland (Schmidt, I, 299). Theodoric attempts to form an alliance against the Franks with the Eruli, Varini and Thuringians (Cassiodorus, *Var.* III, 3).

In 508, after the defeat of the Visigoths in Gaul by Franks and Burgundians, Theodoric annexes the southern part of Burgundy, Provence. During his regency for the young Visigothic King Amalaric, Ostrogoths and Visigoths are once more united under one sceptre.

From 534 to 555 the Ostrogoths are conquered by the Eastern Romans.

People living under Gothic law are still to be met with in Italy in the seventh century, e.g. in Brescia, A.D. 769 (cp. Brunner, *Deutsche Rechtsgeschichte*, I, 271). The place name Godie is still frequently met with in Venezia (cp. Bertoni, *L' elemento germanico nella lingua italiana*, 26). Gossensass reflects a Gothic colony in Southern Tyrol. The names of the runes in a ninth-century Salzburg MS testify to the existence of a Gothic language in Noricum, but these remains are not necessarily Ostrogothic.

§ 121. History of the Visigoths Proper.

In 378–379 the greater part of the Visigothic people retreats before the Huns into Roman territory, where they are incited to rebellion and inflict the great defeat of Adrianople on the Romans. The Emperor Valens is killed; his successor Theodosius finally pacifies the Goths.

In 385, after his death, they harry Greece and Illyricum, and break into Italy.

In 408 the Visigothic King Alaric takes Rome.

In 412 his successor Athaulf settles down under Roman supremacy in South Gaul. Afterwards, in the name of Rome, he makes war on Vandals and Swabians in Spain.

In 429 fifty thousand Visigoths follow the Vandals to North Africa (Possidius, *Vit. August.* 28).

In 451 the Visigothic King Theodered, together with the Roman governor Aëtius, checks the Hunnish king's victorious expedition in Gaul.

In 466 Euric (Evarix) throws off the yoke of Rome. He enlarges his kingdom at expense of Romans and Burgundians in Gaul, Romans and Swabians in Spain, and soon becomes the *de facto* ruler of the peninsula.

In 507 Euric's successor Alaric falls fighting against the Frankish King Chlodowech who, as a Roman Catholic, is supported by the native clergy against the Gothic and Arian heretics. The Visigoths lose all their Gaulish territory with the exception of Septimania between the Rhône and the Pyrenees. Provence goes over to the Ostrogothic King Theodoric, who, in the meantime, becomes regent in Spain as the young king's guardian.

In 587 (589) the Church Congress at Toledo abolishes Arianism as the established church of the Visigoths.

In 711 the Visigothic King Roderic falls at Xeres de la Frontera fighting the invading Arabs, who conquer the whole country except the Asturian and Galician frontier mountains.

Lit. (to Eastern and Western Goths). Zeuss, 134, 401 seq.; Müllenhoff, II, 73; Wietersheim-Dahn; Hodgkin; Bremer, § 87 seq.; Nerman, *Goternas äldsta hem*, *Fornvännen*, 1923, 165; Rappaport, *Die Einfälle der Goten*; Much, *Stammeskunde*, 3rd ed. 115 seq.; *idem*, in Hoops, s.v. *Goten*, *Ostgoten*, *Westgoten*; Villari, *Le invasioni barbariche in Italia* (Transl. *The Barbarian Invasions in Italy*); Barrière-Flavy, *Les arts industriels*, ch. *Visigoths*; Schmidt, *Allg. Gesch. d. germ. Völker*; *idem*, *Gesch. d. deutschen Stämme*, I; Meeson Beck and Freeman, *Encycl. Brit.* s.v. *Goths*; Schönfeld in Pauly-Wissowa, Suppl. s.v. *Goti*; Kauffmann, II, 87–89, 91.

§ 122. History of the Gepidae Proper.

About 200 the delta of the Weichsel, deserted by the Goths, is invaded by the Gepidae and is henceforward known as Gepid-ojos (Jordanes, XVII, 96; cp. IV, 27).

About 250 the Gepid King Fastida attacks the Goths in Dacia, but is repulsed (*ibid.* XVII, 97).

About 267 the first invasion of the Gepidae into Roman territory is recorded in *Script. hist. Aug. v. Probi*, 18, 2, *v. Claud.* 6, 2.

In 409 the Gepidae take part in the expedition of the Vandals and Quadi to Gaul (Hieronymus, *Ad Ageruchiam* (Migne, *Patr. Lat.* XXII, 1058)).

In 451 the Gepid King Ardaric (probably = *Hardureiks[1]), Attila's vassal, is the chief counsellor on the Hunnish expedition into Gaul (Jordanes, XXXVIII, 200).

In 453 Ardaric leads the rebellion against Attila's sons, and wins the greater part of Dacia (L, 259 seq.) (boundaries: the Carpathians and the river Olt on the east, Teiss on the north and west, the Danube on the south; see Diculescu, *Die Gepiden*, Map, 76).

In 567, after several decades of war with the Langobards, the Gepidae go under. The Langobards are helped by the Avars, to whom they cede Dacia and Pannonia on migration to Italy (Paulus Diaconus, I, 27).

In 568 hordes of the Gepidae accompany the Langobards to Italy, where their villages are still known to Paulus Diaconus; they betray themselves even now by names such as Zebedo, Zevedo, Zevio (cp. Bertoni, *L' elemento germanico nella lingua italiana*).

A ninth-century MS from Salzburg mentions the remnants of the Gepidae in Hungary: 'De Gepidis autem quidam adhuc ibi resident' (*Mon. Germ. SS.* XI, 9).

Lit. Zeuss, 436; Müllenhoff, II (see Index); Wietersheim-Dahn (see Index); Schmidt, I, 305; Much in Hoops, s.v.; Ihm in Pauly-Wissowa, s.v.; Kauffmann, II, 91; Diculescu, *Die Gepiden.*

§ 123. History of the Vidivarii Proper.

About 440–450 Wulfhere and Wyrmhere are guarding the frontiers of the Hrǽdas in the wood of the Weichsel against 'Attila's people' (*Widsith*, ll. 119–122). As we have pointed out in the *Acta Phil. Scand.*,

[1] Wulfila's -*u* becomes vulgar Gothic -*a* in unstressed syllables, cp. Friþ*a*-reik- in the Calendar. *H*arda*-rīk is besides influenced by vowel assonance.

Hrǽdas is used here as a collective name, a synonym of Goths, and does not indicate a special Gothic sub-tribe. The *Lay of Angantýr* localises the battle with the Huns in Dunheiðr, probably identical with the area round about the *Lugi Duni in Silesia (see § 137, 4) and near Myrkviðr, i.e. the Hercynian wood (cp. Miriquidui, i.e. Erzgebirge, *Mon. Germ. SS.* v, 807). It ends in a defeat for Ormarr (Wyrmhere), and the Huns ravage Gotþjóð.

About 550 the Vidivarii, who have inherited the delta country of Gepid-ojos after the migration of the Gepidae, assert themselves once more 'ex diversis nationibus ac si in unum asylum collecti' (Jordanes, XVII, 96). Here we see a Gothic place of retreat in the conflict with advancing eastern neighbours.

In the ninth century, when Wulfstan visits the country (cp. Alfred's *Orosius*), the Goths have been absorbed by the Prussians, although individual Gothic place names are still remembered such as the river name Ylfing, i.e. Elbing.

Lit. Müllenhoff, II, 13, 345; Much, *Zeitschrift*, XXXIII, 4; *idem*, in Hoops, s.v. *Vidivarii*; Schütte, *Arkiv*, XXI, 30; *idem*, *Oldsagn om Godtjod*, 63; *idem*, *Ptolemy's Maps*, 113; *idem*, *The Problem of the Hraid-goths* (*Acta Phil. Scand.* 1933); Chambers, *Widsith*, 221, 252; Heusler in Hoops, s.v. *Hunnenschlacht*; Johannson, *Acta Phil. Scand.* VII, 102, 111, etc.

§ 124. History of the Gothi Minores, the Moesian Goths Proper.

In 348 Bishop Wulfila flees across the Danube from the Visigothic chieftain Athanaric and founds the colony of Gothi minores at Nicopolis in Moesia (Auxentius, 207; Jordanes, LI, 267).

In 398 and 492–497 Gothic and Bessic troops in the Imperial army fight the rebels in Isauria in Asia Minor. The connexion with the Bessi from Thracia shows that Gothi minores are meant.

About 550 the Moesian Goth Jordanes describes his countrymen as a numerous and pacific people of agriculturalists suffering from the incursions of the Slavs (LI, 167).

Between 824 and 849 Abbot Walafrid Strabo is writing *De rebus ecclesiasticis* in Reichenau, the seventh chapter of which mentions Wulfila's translation of the Bible into Gothic and alludes to the continuation of Gothic worship about Tomi: 'Getae...in Graecorum provinciis commemorantes nostrum id est Theotiscum sermonem habuerint....Et fidelium fratrum relatione didicimus apud quasdam Scytharum gentes maxime Tomitanos eadem locutione divina hactenus recitari officia'. Later the Gothi minores are absorbed by the Slavs.

Lit. Zeuss, 429; Loewe, ch. v; Much in Hoops, s.v. *Gothi minores*; Hampe, *ibid.* s.v. *Jordanes.*

§ 125. History of the Gothi Tetraxitae and Eudusiani Proper.

In 548 the Tetraxitae in Tamatarcha east of the Straits of Azov ask the Emperor Justinian for a Catholic bishop (Procopius, *Bell. Got.* IV, 4). They conclude a firm alliance with their neighbours the Uturguric Huns, and put a standing army of two thousand men into the field (*ibid.* 18).

Εὐδουσιανοί, speaking a Gothic and 'Tauric' language, are mentioned by the *Periplus Pontus Euxini* as living on the Caucasus coast (*Fragm. hist. Graec.* V, 182). 'Tauric' perhaps means Alanic.

About 941 and 1094 Swedish Russian kings like Igor and Oleg (Ingvar and Helgi) temporarily annexed Tmutarakan, that is Tamatarcha. The Russian *Lay of Igor* mentions 'Gothic girls on the coast of the blue sea' (Loewe, 37).

In 1484 the Sultan Bajazet the Second conquers the 'Gotticae gentis... reliquiae usque ad Circassos dispersas' (Peucer, *Chron. Carionis*, IV, 187).

In 1778, after having subsequently submitted to the rule of Uturgurs, Khazars, Russians, Kumans, Circassians, Tartars, Mongols, Genoese and Turks, the descendants of the Tetraxitae ultimately come under Russia. The Jesuit Mondorf, when travelling in Turkey, appears to have met a Circassian living on the Caucasus coast who spoke a language resembling German. Loewe does not regard this piece of information as altogether unlikely (p. 54 seq.).

Lit. Zeuss, 430; Loewe, 19 seq.; Much in Hoops, s.v. *Tetraxiten.*

§ 126. History of the Goths of the Crimea Proper.

In 325 mention is made of a Catholic bishop from the Crimea.[1]

About 500 the Goths of the Crimea of their own free will attach themselves to the East Roman kingdom and put three thousand men into the field (Procopius, *De aedific.* III, 7, p. 267). In the course of

[1] But, according to Patsch, *Kleine S.B. d. Akad. in Wien*, Bd. 208, 2, p. 25, the see of Theophilus, 'Gothia', is not the Crimea, but Dacia.

time they came to have dealings with various powers, Russians, Huns, Khazars, Petchenegs, Tartars and Genoese.

In 1475 the Crimea is annexed by the Turkish Sultan Mahomet (Peucer, *Chron. Carionis*, IV, 186).

In 1595 the Fleming Busbeck, the ambassador of the German Emperor, describes his meeting (between 1560 and 1562) with an envoy of the Crimean Goths in Constantinople and notes down glosses of his language (cp. *De legationis Turcicae epistolae quatuor*, IV, 135).

In 1778 Tartar persecutions drive the Christian Tartar-speaking Goths into Russian territory, where they found Mariupol and twenty villages which are still to be seen there.

In 1786, after the death of the Metropolitan Ignatius, the bishopric of Gotia is abolished. Herewith ends the story of the Goths.

Lit. Zeuss, 432; Massmann, *Zeitschrift*, I, 345; Loewe, ch. iv; Much in Hoops, s.v. *Krimgoten*; Tomaschek in Pauly-Wissowa, s.v. *Krimgoten*.

§ 127. Legendary Traditions.

The Goths, as heroes of the great Migration Age, belong to the flower of the Gothonic epic aristocracy. The Huns were certainly number one, but the Goths constantly come second; thus in the O.E. epic catalogues of *Widsith*, I and II, in the O.N. *Lay of Angantýr* (*Hervararsaga*), and in various O.N. catalogues of a less important character (cp. the author's dissertation *Oldsagn om Godtjod*, 105 seq., and his article *Vidsid* in *Arkiv*, XXXVI, 8).

In England and Scandinavia, 'Goths' became the name of the 'Gothonic folk' (cp. *Widsith's* 'eþel Gotena', l. 109, and the Eddic *Got-þjóð). But examples of this terminology are rare, and Scandinavian poetry soon transformed the name into a vague metaphorical alternative for 'heroes' or 'warriors' (see Egilsson, *Lex. Poet.* 2nd ed. (Finn. J.), s.v. *Gotnar*). Moreover, the epic Got-þjóð of the *Lay of Angantýr*[1] was confused with the mythical Goð-þjǫð 'the folk of gods'; a conjectural *Got-heimar in Southern Russia would correspondingly have become Goð-heimar 'homes of the gods', though the popular origin of this term is denied by Heusler, *Abh. d. preuss. Ak. d. Wiss.* 1908, 50. Even non-Gothonic nations remember the Goths, as do the Russians in their *Lay of Igor* (cp. the Gotъthi in the *Legend of St Constantine*). The Circas-

[1] Got þioda K, Götuþjóða A, Göt þióda C, Gautu þiodar R, Gauta þjódum J, cp. Heinzel, *S.B. Wien. Ak. ph.-h. Kl.* CXIV, 471.

sians in the nineteenth century still remembered the defeat of their king Bakssan by the people Gut (see Olrik, *Danske Studier*, 1914, 12 seq.; cp. vol. I, § 68). The Italians changed the name of Goths into an abusive term, expressing 'northern barbarians'; hence 'the Gothic style', originally signifying a barbarian, non-Roman taste (cp. also 'Gothic script', a mediaeval name for the Gothonic runes).

The sub-tribes Tervingi and Greutungi seem to be reflected in the Norse tale of Angantýr, i.e. of A(g)ëtius, the ally of the Visigoths against the Huns. Angantýr has a famous sword Tyrfingr and a companion Gizurr Grýtingaliði, i.e. 'leader of the Greutungi'.

Gothic legends perhaps contain traditions which may rival the *Mannung Genealogy* (vol. I, § 10) in point of age, for we must at least consider the possibility that the leader of the Gothic emigration from Scandia, Berig (Jordanes, IV, 25), is identical with the Cimbrian chieftain Boiorix, 101 B.C., who led the first historical emigration from Scandinavia (cp. the author's article in *Danske Studier*, 1913, 178). At all events, after the third century A.D., numerous Gothic heroes crop up: Ostrogotha and his son Unven (Engl.); Vidigoia (Engl., Germ., Scand.); Ermanaric with the persons of the Sunilda episode (Engl., Germ., Scand.); Thiudimer (Germ., Scand.); his son Theodoric the Great (Engl., Germ., Scand.); Amalaberga (Germ.); Vitigis (Germ.); Wyrmhere-Ormarr (Engl., Scand.); Wulfhere-Wolfhart (Engl., Germ.). Walther of Aquitania in the German legend is undoubtedly a Visigoth, perhaps King Valja. The Gothic hero Hildebrand (Germ.), the most famous and faithful among King Theodoric's followers, is probably identical with the general Helba, Hebba, Ebba, Ibba, whom Theodoric in the year 508 sent to Gaul where he fought successfully against Franks and Goths (cp. Much, *Rüdiger von Pechlarn*, a lecture delivered to the Academy of Sciences in Wien on 31 May 1913, p. 4). Ermanaric and Theodoric became the central figures of the earliest Gothonic epic cycles, rivalling even Attila. The last Gothic person in legendary tradition is princess Brunehild of Spain, †613, temporary regent of Burgundy and residing at Worms, unjustly accused of having murdered the noble Frankish king Sigebert. Though her identity with the valkyrie Brynhild is not admitted by numerous scholars, she is at least known as a powerful witch in French legends, and her memory still survives in the Chaussées and Tours de Brunehaut (cp. the list given by Kurth, *Hist. poétique des Mérovingiens*, 426).

The number of more subordinate Gothic heroes is legion; we can only refer to the works of Heinzel and Matthaei cited below.

Gothic epic place names are frequent, often however incorrectly localised owing to the extinction of the Gothic nationality.

(*a*) English examples: Wistla-wudu, 'the wood of the people on the Weichsel', described as the old inheritance of the Hréð-goths, *Widsith*, l. 120; Witland, the region of the Vidivarii, Alfred's *Orosius*, probably with High German *t* for *d*; Ylfing, the river Elbing, *ibid.*; Mǽringa Burg, the capital of Theodoric the Great, *Deor's Lament*.

(*b*) German examples: Mērān, the land of the Mērānare or Mǽringas, i.e. Ostrogoths; Raben, i.e. Ravenna, in the poem *Raben-Schlacht*, described as the scene of the great battle between Theodoric and Odovacar; Bern, i.e. Verona, another scene of Theodoric's activity.

(*c*) Scandinavian examples: (H)reiðgotaland, in the *Hervararsaga*, still correctly identified with Poland, but otherwise misplaced in Jutland, etc.; Hraiþmarr, the Baltic? or the Adriatic?, from the *Rök Inscription*; Ernar herað and Árheimar, localities in the *Hervararsaga*; Dunheiðr, *ibid.*, the region of the *Lugi Duni; Danparstaðir, *ibid.*, the bank (Goth. *staþs*) of the river Danpr, the Dnieper; Danr and Danpr, possessing splendid halls, *Rigsþula*, str. 48, i.e. the regions about Don and Dnieper, but later erroneously brought into connexion with King Dan in Denmark; Harfaða fjǫll, *Hervararsaga*, the Carpathian mountains; Myrkviðr, *ibid.*, i.e. Miriquidui, the Hercynian wood; Goðheimar, *Ynglinga Saga*, chs. 10, 15, perhaps for *Gotheimar.

Lit. W. Grimm, *Heldensage*; Müllenhoff, *Zeugnisse u. Excurse zur deutschen Heldensage*, *Zeitschrift*, XII, 253, 413; V. Rydberg, *Undersökningar i germanisk mytologi*; W. Müller, *Mythologie der deutschen Heldensage*; Heinzel, *Über die Hervararsage* and *Die ostgot. Heldensage*, *S.B. d. Wien. Akad. phil.-hist. Kl.* CXIV, CXIX; Much, *Zeitschrift*, XXXIII, 1 seq.; Kurth, *Hist. poétique des Mérovingiens*; Symons, *Grundriss*, 2nd ed. II, i, 1 seq.; Kögel, *Gesch. der deutschen Literatur*, I, 146; Jiriczek, *Deutsche Heldensage* (*Samml. Göschen*, 3rd ed. 1918); *idem*, *Deutsche Heldensagen*, I; Matthaei, *Die bairische Hunnensage*, *Zeitschrift*, XLVI, 1 seq.; Schütte, *Angantykvadets Geografi*, *Arkiv*, XXI, 30; *idem*, *Oldsagn om Godtjod*, 163 seq.; *idem*, *Nibelungsagnet*, *Arkiv*, XXIV, 1 seq.; *idem*, *De ældste gottonske Sagnhelte*, *Danske Studier*, 1913; *idem*, *The Journal of Engl. and Germ. Philology*, XX, 291; Heusler, *Abh. d. Preuss. Ak. d. Wiss. phil.-hist. Kl.* 1908, 50 seq.; *idem*, *Heldennamen in mehrfacher Lautgestalt*, *Zeitschrift*, LII; *idem*, in Hoops, s.v. *Dietrich*, *Heldensage*, *Hunnenschlacht*; Boer, *Die Sage von Ermanarich*, *Germanist. Handbibliothek*, X; Chambers, *Widsith*; Chadwick, *The Heroic Age*; Olrik, *Goter og Tjerkesser*, *Danske Studier*, 1914, 9 seq.; Bruinier, *Die germanische Heldensage* (*Aus Natur u. Geisteswelt*, No. 486, ch. viii).

C. §§ 128–131. *THE RUGIANS, SCIRI, AND TORCILINGI*

§ 128. Names.

1. (*a*) O.E. *Ryge (*Widsith*, see 1 (*b*)). O.E. also *Rugas (dat. Rugum, *Widsith*); Lat. Rugii (Tacitus, first century A.D.), Rugi (fourth century seq. and Jordanes, etc.); M.Lat. Rogi (Paulus Diaconus); Gr. *Ῥοῦγοι (Ῥοῦβοι, Priscus), Ῥογοί (Procopius). Personal name: Hunno-Gothic Ruga, Rugila (*Chron. Gall.* v, 587 and 589, IV, 112 and 116), Gr. Ῥούγας (Socrates), Ῥοῦας (Priscus); Lat. Ruge-mirus (a Visigoth). Geographical names: Gr. Ῥούγιον (Ptolemy, second century A.D.); Langobard Rugilanda (*Origo Langobard.*); O.N. epical Rog-heimr (in Pomerania ?[1]). Etymology uncertain. If the name indicates a personal quality, it must be called obscure. (The signification 'yellow' has been suggested, cp. *rugi* 'rye'.) If it is geographical, as most of the Scandinavian tribal names are, it may be derived from a Scandinavian word *ryg-* 'stone' and would then come from the Norwegian Rogaland. Home: (1) Rugion in Pomerania or Western Prussia; (2) Rugilanda in Austria; (3) Italy.

Lit. Müllenhoff, II, 66, IV, 493, 620; Holz, *Beiträge zur germ. Altertumskunde*, I, 45, 59; Kossinna, *Anzeiger*, XVI, 5; *idem*, *Westdeutsche Zeitschr.* IX, 207; Loewe, *Gliederung*, 33; Schmidt, I, 327, 332 note; Schönfeld, s.v. *Rugi* (with lit.), *Ruga*, *Rugila* (*Appendix*); Rappaport in Pauly-Wissowa, s.v.; Much in Hoops, s.v. *Rugier*.

(*b*) M.Lat. Rugini (Bede, v, 9, eighth century); Gr. *Ῥουγίλωνες (Μουγίλωνες, Strabo, VII, 290, first century A.D.), *Ῥουγίκλειοι (*Ῥουτίκλειοι, Ptol. II, 11, § 7, second century A.D.), i.e. 'the smaller Rugians'. Zeuss proposes to alter Rutiklioi into *Turkilioi = Turcilingi, and his conjecture is accepted by Müllenhoff and even admitted as possible by Schönfeld, but rejected by Much with good reason. The alteration seems too forced. We have no other trace of the Turcilingi before the sixth century, and the type *-ling* looks secondary. The alteration of a Γ for a T is slight. Rugians appear in the same vicinity about A.D. 100, and a diminutive form with the element *-l* may be conjectured from Strabo's Mugilones.

[1] Rügenwalde in Pomerania is a learned 'emendation'. Rügen for Ruja (papal letter from 1177), Dan. Rø or Re is perhaps a L.German form originating from the native Wendic name of the inhabitants, Rujani. They are also called Runi, Rani, in O.N. Rængjar.

Lit. Zeuss, 155; Müllenhoff, III, 319, IV, 53, 494; Schmidt, I, 327; Schönfeld, s.v. *Rugi, Mugilones, Ruticlii* (with lit.); Schütte, *Beiträge*, XLI, 6; *idem, Arkiv*, XXXIII, 35; *idem, Ptolemy's Maps*, 18; Much in Hoops, s.v. *Rugier*, Μουγίλωνες, Ῥουτίκλειοι, *Torcilingi*.

(*c*) Vulg. Goth. *Hulmä-Rugīs; O.E. *Holm-Ryge (dat. Holm-Rycum, *Widsith*); O.N. Holm-Rygir (in Norway); Lat. (H)ulme-Rugi (Jordanes, IV, 26), i.e. 'the Rugians of the Islets', designating the people in the delta of the Weichsel. The O.N. form Holm-Rygir is not a survival from a primaeval period when the Norwegian and East Gothonic Rugians formed a unity, as Loewe believes, but simply a rather late borrowing from Gothic poetry.

Lit. Zeuss, 484 note 2; Grimm, 469; Müllenhoff, II, 400; Loewe, *Gliederung*, 33; Schmidt, I, 326; Schönfeld, s.v. *Ulmerugi*; Much in Hoops, s.v. *Rugier*.

2. Lat. Sciri (Scyri, Pliny, first century A.D.); Gr. Σκίροι (*Psephisma* on Protogenes, *CIG*. 2058 B, c. 190 B.C.), Σκύροι (Zosimus, fifth century A.D.). Etymology: Goth. *skeirs* 'sheer, pure', alluding to racial descent. Home: about the Weichsel (Pliny, IV, 97); later in Austria, Pannonia, Italy. Zeuss, Schmeller, Grimm derive the noble Bavarian family of Schyren or Scheiern in the district of Hōsi from the Sciri.

Lit. Zeuss, 156; Schmeller, *Bayerisches Wörterbuch*, III, 390; Müllenhoff, *Nordalbing. Studien*, I, 163; Grimm, 466; Much, *Zeitschrift*, XLI, 138; *idem*, in Hoops, s.v.; Schönfeld, s.v.; Schütte, *Ptolemy's Maps*, 17.

3. Lat. T(h)orcilingi, T(h)urcili(n)gi (Jordanes, sixth century A.D.). Obscure. Not identical with 'Rutikleioi' (Ptol., see 1 (*b*)). Final home: Italy.

Lit. Zeuss, 155; Müllenhoff, III, 319, IV, 494; Schmidt, I, 350; Schönfeld, s.v. *Thorcilingi*; Schütte, *Beiträge*, XLI, 6; *idem, Ptolemy's Maps*, 18; Much in Hoops, s.v. *Torcilingi*.

§ 129. Ethnic Position.

No ancient historian or law codex states that there existed a special branch embracing Rugians, Sciri and Torcilingi. These tribes may be called supernumerary members of the East Gothonic sub-group, who are neither Goths, nor Burgundians, nor Lugians. Owing to occasional co-operation at certain times, they may most conveniently be considered under a common heading.

The Rugians shared some characteristics of the Goths (cp. Tac. *Germ.* 43: 'rotunda scuta, breves gladii et erga reges obsequium', i.e. 'round shields, short swords, and obedience to kings'). During the Migration Age the Rugian monarchy increased in power, for their conquests in the Danube regions do not appear as 'folkland', but were directly under the kings (cp. Eugippius, *Vita Severini*, ch. 42 and 44; see Schmidt, I, 5 and 332).

The Hjadning myth, dealing with the everlasting fight of Hagena and Heoden, probably represents a local Rugian hero worship (see § 131).

Both Rugians and Sciri adopted the Arianic form of Christianity propagated by the Goths. Eugippius describes the Rugians as rather fanatic anti-Catholics.

Lit. Schmidt, I, 332; Rappaport in Pauly-Wissowa, s.v. *Rugi*; Much in Hoops, s.v. *Rugier*.

§ 130. History.

Like the Goths, Rugians are found both north and south of the Baltic. Even the prefix Holm- accompanies them in both places, but we must beware of drawing wrong conclusions from this fact. The Norwegian form Holm-Rygir is not primaeval, as Loewe maintains (*Gliederung*, 33), nor is Much right in assuming that the Rugians must come from another region than the Norwegian district of Rogaland, because its naked coast does not justify the epithet 'insular' (see Hoops, IV, 4; cp. Much's article in *Volk und Rasse*, 1930, 199, wherein he has himself withdrawn the theory). The epithet 'insular' is simply borrowed from Gothic poetry, just as (H)reiðgotaland was transferred to Jutland, when the Gothic nationality disappeared from Prussia.

If not the compound, perhaps the simple form Rugi may shed light upon the presumable homestead: the connexion with O.Dan. *ryge* 'stone' would imply Scandinavian origin rather than North German.

After settling on the coast of Pomerania, the Rugians obtained the surname 'insular', derived from the islands at the mouth of the Weichsel (cp. Jordanes, IV, 26: 'sedes (H)ulmerugorum, qui tunc oceani ripas insedebant'). Tac. *Germ.* 43, describes the place of the Rugii somewhat vaguely as 'protinus ab Oceano', but the sequence 'Lygii, Gotones, Rugii' is sufficiently clear: as the Lygii occupy Silesia and Posen, and the Goths the Weichsel Delta, we must localise the Rugians beside them farther north and west, i.e. in Pomerania. This is the place of Ptolemy's Rugion and *Rugikleioi, and even the traditions of the Hjadning myth point towards the same region: the hero Hagena in *Widsith*, l. 21, is called King of the Holm-Ryge, and the battle against his opponent Heoden takes place at Hithinsö, the present island of Hiddensee near Rügen (Saxo, 240). The island was perhaps a sanctuary of a Rugian Hjadning worship (cp. the Swedish personal name Hiþin-dis, i.e. 'Heoden's priestess').

The Sciri, whom Pliny, IV, 97, places about the Weichsel, accidentally open the Gothonic political history owing to their participation in a Scythian attack on the Greek colony Olbia c. 190 B.C. (*CIG.* 2058). Their 'Galatian' companions on that occasion are often conceived as the Bastarnae, but may also have been true Celts (cp. the Celtic town Noviodunum on the mouth of the Danube). The Sciri themselves appear as 'Galates' in the dictionary of Stephan of Byzance.

A victory of the Goths over the Hulme-Rugi is recorded by Jordanes, IV, 26, but the time of the event is uncertain.

In the first century of our era, we can find traces of tribal subdivisions: beside the Rugii appear the *Rugilones or *Rugikleioi, i.e. 'smaller Rugians'. The *Rugilones formed part of the ephemeral realm of King Maroboduus in Bohemia for the first two decades of our era (Strabo, VII, 290).

Owing to the increase of the amber trade in the first century A.D., the Romans obtained some information concerning the weapons and the monarchical constitution of the Rugians (Tac. *Germ.* 43).

The emigration of the Rugians from the coast of the Baltic can only be traced by means of numismatic evidence: Roman coins cease to appear in Pomerania after the age of Constantine (d. 337) (see Kühne, *Balt. Studien*, XXVII, cp. Schmidt, I, 5, and 327).

The Rugians and Sciri appear on the stage of political history at the beginning of the Migration Age, according to a document of about A.D. 300, *Gentes barbarae* (*Geogr. Lat. minores*). It places the Sciri among the nations menacing the Middle and Lower Danube regions, viz. Taifali, Vandals, and Goths, whereas the Rugians together with Eruli and Saxons appear among the assailants of Britain. Müllenhoff in his *Altertumskunde*, III, 312, removes the Rugians and Eruli to the vicinity of the Sciri, because all three nations had their chief basis of operations in easterly regions, and Rugians are never heard of on western shores. He may be right in this, but the Eruli raided Gaul at least as early as A.D. 289 (cp. Mamertin, *Panegyr. Maxim.* ch. 5, etc.), and we are not obliged to accept the *argumentum e silentio* concerning the Rugians, for the ethnic statistics of the annals from North-western Europe are anything but reliable: the Geatic raiders of *Beowulf* emerge and disappear like a shooting star, whereas the Anglian conquerors of England are completely ignored by Roman writers of the Migration Age! We must here remark that the German legend localises the battle of the Rugian King Hagena and his opponent Heoden in the channel of Hedinsee at the mouth of the Scheld—a fact which perhaps favours the assumption of Rugian expeditions to western shores; but perhaps it is only a reflection of Viking raids in later times. Cp. Symons, *Kudrun*, XLIII. These arguments are of course quite hypothetical, but they must at least be discussed and refuted, before Müllenhoff's view can be regarded as proved.

Jordanes, XXIII, 116, mentions Rogas beside the Finns, Aestii, Slavs, and Eruli, subjugated by the Gothic King Ermanaric about A.D. 350. The ending *-as* is probably the secondary vulgar pronunciation for the literary Gothic plural *-ōs*, as in the Baias of the Anonymus Ravennas for lit. Goth. *Bajōs. Rogas would then be *Rugōs, i.e. Rugians. But the entire list of names is so badly presented that we cannot rely upon it.

Both Rugians and Sciri, at any rate, were subjugated by the invading Huns c. 370. Huns, Carpi (Dacians) and Sciri, c. 381, attacked Moesia Inferior, but were repelled (Zosimus, IV, 34; cp. Schmidt, I, 351). Huns and Sciri were again defeated in Thracia 408–9 and partially transplanted to Asia Minor (Sozomenus, IX, 5). This colony represents the furthest extent of Scirian expansion towards the south-east.

For particulars concerning the further movements of Rugians and Sciri, which are generally of minor importance, see Schmidt.

Both tribes were fighting for Attila when he was defeated in Gaul A.D. 451 (cp. Sid. Apollinaris, *Carm.* VII, 1, 321), and took part in the revolt against his sons in Pannonia (Jordanes, L, 261). The Rugians afterwards obtained Noricum Ripense, the present Nieder Oesterreich, henceforth called Rugilanda. The Sciri occupied the present Moravia and Slovakia. The East Romans admitted bands of Rugians into their territory near Bizye and Arcadiopolis in Thracia, and of Sciri close by (Jordanes, L, 266). The conversion of both tribes to Arianism probably took place about this time.

After the Ostrogoths had voluntarily left Pannonia in 471, the Rugian King Feletheus extended his dominion from the river Enns to the Pannonian frontier near Klosterneuburg, and commanded the northern border of the Danube as well. He seems to have inherited the regions of the Sciri who had been dispersed by the Ostrogoths in 469. The Roman provincials of Noricum, who were abandoned by the illusory Imperial government, suffered sorely from the inroads of the Rugians and from the outburst of their Arianic fanaticism, but found a prominent spiritual leader in St Severin (cp. Eugippius, *Vita Severini*, and Schmidt, I, 328).

In 476 the Scirian mercenary Odovacar, general of Sciri, Rugians, Torcilingi and Eruli in the Roman army, dethroned the Emperor Romulus Augustulus. After Rugian plots, originating in Constantinople had repeatedly disturbed the peace, Odovacar conquered Rugilanda in 488 and transported most of its inhabitants to Italy. The deserted country was inherited by the Langobards (cp. *Vita Severini*, ch. 44, and *Origo Langobardorum*). The Ostrogothic King Theodoric conquered and killed Odovacar at Ravenna, 493. The Gothic-Roman war caused the Rugians to proclaim their leader Eraric as King of Italy in 541, and the Goths partially recognised him, but he was soon murdered (Procopius, *Bell. Got.* III, 2 seq.). His people finally shared the downfall of the Goths, 555 (cp. Schmidt, I, 321 seq.).

Gothic names of runes in a ninth-century MS from Salzburg may perhaps be attributed to a Rugian residue, cp. p. 20. A rather questionable theory suggests that the noble Bavarian family of Scheiern in the district of Hōsi may descend from the Sciri (cp. the literature cited in § 128, 2). Loewe, *Gliederung*, 33, suggests that various German places named Rugiheim might perhaps indicate colonies of Rugians; as a matter of fact, the Rhenish *-heim* is often compounded with obvious ethnic elements: Langobardon-heim, Brizzen-heim alias Brittanorum villa, etc. (cp. our monograph in the Danish *Geografisk Tidskrift*, 1918).

Kluge, *Grundriss*, 1st ed. I, 781, regards the English place names Surrey, Eastry and Westry as indications of Rugian colonies; but later editions have withdrawn the suggestion. We are probably to interpret Suþryge as Suþr-yge 'southern islands'. Cp. O.E. Sceden-ig, i.e. Scadinauja; the latter example shows that the element *-ig* need not mean 'island' in the exact sense of that word. (Much also suggests the possibility that the *-yge* may be the Aujones of Tacitus.)

In Pomerania and the neighbouring regions, the Rugians and Sciri, if any of them were left, were absorbed by the invading Slavs after the sixth or seventh century. An echo in German epic will be considered in § 131.

The name of the Rugians in Latin literature was perhaps sometimes transferred to the Russians. This has been assumed to be the case in the tariff of Louis the Child (*Mon. Germ. Leges*, III, 480 (*Raffelstädter Zollurkunde*)), issued c. A.D. 904: 'Sclavi vero, qui de Rugis vel de Boemanis mercandi causa exeunt, ubicunque juxta ripam Danubii vel ubicunque in Rotalariis vel in Reodariis loca mercandi optinuerunt' (cp. Waitz, *Deutsche Verfassungsgeschichte*, 2nd ed. IV, 72; Dümmler, *Gesch. des ostfränk. Reichs*, 2nd ed. III, 533; Schmidt, I, 332). However, the name Rugi in these surroundings cannot mean Russians. It must mean 'inhabitants of Rugilanda'. The use of it is a historical tradition, corresponding to the expression Boemani (Bohemians), i.e. Czechs.

Lit. **Zeuss**, 61, 154, 484, 489; **Müllenhoff**, II, 4, III, 312, IV, 494; **Wietersheim-Dahn**; **Dahn**, *Urgesch. der german. roman. Völker*, I, 575; **Hodgkin**, II, viii, III, iv–vi; **Villari**, *Le invasioni barbariche in Italia* (Transl. *The Barbarian Invasions*); **Much**, *Stammeskunde*, 3rd ed.; *idem*, in **Hoops**, s.v. *Rugier*, *Skiren*, *Torcilingi*; **Rappaport** in **Pauly-Wissowa**, s.v. *Rugi*, and VIII, 1160; **Kauffmann**, II, 90; **Karsten**, *Die Germanen*, 79.

§ 131. Legendary Traditions.

The surname, Goth. (H)ulme-Rugi, O.E. *Holm-Ryge, O.N. Holm-Rygir, is recorded exclusively in epic legends and poems and is possibly a poetical expression. After the Slavonic invasion had expelled it from the south of the Baltic, it was annexed by the Norwegian Rygir (cp. our article in *Zeitschrift*, LXVII, 132).

A famous myth of probably Rugian origin is the Hjaðningavíg or cycle of Hild. The everlasting battle of dead warriors, resuscitated by the Valkyrie Hild, may symbolise the traditional succession of recurring offerings to some local deity; cp. the Swedish personal name Hiþin-dís, 'Heoden's priestess', alluding to the Hjadning myth. A sign indicating ritual origin is the alliteration of the names of the chief persons and localities in *H*, an analogy of the four classes of victims offered in the Danish temple of Hleiðr (horses, hounds, hawks and *hanar*, i.e. 'cocks') (see vol. I, § 100). Cp. the Rugian King Hagena, his daughter Hild, his opponents Heoden and Heorrenda, leaders of the Heodeningas or Hjaðningar. Localisations: land of the Holm-Ryge (*Widsith*), Hithinsö (Saxo = the present Hiddensee near Rügen); Háey (Snorri), and the channel of Hedinsee near the battlefield of the German legend (cp. Frings in *Zeitschrift*, LXI, 192). It is the agreement of the English and Danish traditions as regards the Pomeranian locality that speaks in favour of Rugian origin.

The tribal name of the Sciri did not survive, as did that of the Holm-Ryge. But in compensation, the Scirian King Odovacar won a lasting remembrance in epic, owing to the fact that he put an end to the West Roman Empire. His fight with Theodoric the Great is recorded in the German legend of Otachar and Dietrich von Bern. Theodoric's long siege of Odovacar's fortress Ravenna has become the theme of a separate poem, the *Rabenschlacht.* Though Odovacar was a brave warrior, an honest man, and the victim of his conqueror's perjury, the legend treats the murdered hero quite unjustly, calumniating him as a forsworn traitor, the accomplice of Ermanaric (cp. Schmidt, I, 163).

We may finally consider the *Chronicon imperatorum et pontificum Bavaricum* (*Mon. Germ. SS.* XXIV, 221 seq.), dealing with the ethnic revolution of Eastern Germany during the Migration Age. The chronicle certainly mentions neither Rugians nor Sciri, but as it describes the fates of the ancient Rugian coast regions, we may with good reason refer to it here. After recording how the Slavs or 'sons of Cham' have gradually advanced their frontiers from the river Dnieper to the Weichsel, the chronicle goes on with the following words: 'Filii autem Japheth..., tirannidem filiorum Cham sustinere nolentes, navigio ad inferiores occidentis insulas venerunt et eas possederunt, videlicet Hiberniam, Brittanniam, Hislandiam, Frisiam et Sueciam. Cetere insule, scilicet Dacia, Norwegia, Gotlandia et alie a filiis Japhet, Sclavis locum dando, a Ruzia usque ad Rhenum possesse sunt'.

The author exaggerates the effect of the Slavonic invasion, regarding it as the origin of all Gothonic settlements in Scandinavia, Britain, and the Netherlands. But he seems to preserve a tradition that tells us how, owing to Slavonic pressure, the last Gothonic inhabitants of the Southern Baltic coast left their native regions by ship. It is also more than likely that these emigrants would have tried to conquer the Danish islands and Gotland before joining the raiders of Britain and of the Netherlands. The Rugians, who possessed those coast regions and islands which served as the last strongholds of the retiring Gothonic population, must have been the chief participators in such movements.

Lit. (*a*) **Hjadning myth. W. Grimm,** ***Heldensage*****, 3rd ed. 370–380, 494; P. E. Müller's ed. of Saxo,** ***notæ uberiores*****, 153; Bugge,** ***Home of the Eddic Poems*****, I, 94, II, 130; Symons,** ***Grundriss*****, 1st ed. II, 51 (2nd ed. III, 711);** ***idem, Kudrun*****, 2nd ed.; Kögel,** ***Gesch. d. deutsch. Literatur*****, I, 1, 170; Olrik,** ***Sakses oldhistorie*****, II, 191; Jiriczek,** ***Deutsche Heldensage (Samml. Göschen)*****, 163; Robertson,** ***Hist. of Germ. Literature*****, 72; Chambers,** ***Widsith*****, 100 seq.; Schütte,** ***Vor mytiske Kongerække*****, 17. (*b*) Legend of Odovacar. W. Grimm,** ***Heldensage*****, 27, 36, 41, 321, 392; Symons,** ***Grundriss*****, 1st ed. II, 44, 2nd ed. III, 689; Jiriczek,** ***l.c.*** **102. (*c*) The Slavonic invasion. Schütte,** ***Racenavnet*** **in** ***Norden*****, 1904, 143;** ***Oldsagn om Godtjod*****, 167 seq.**

D. §§ 132–135. *THE BURGUNDIANS*

§ 132. Names.

1. (*a*) O.E. *Burgend or *Burgende or *Burgendas or *Burgendan (*Widsith*, dat. Burgendum, cp. Gr. Βουργοῦντες); M.H.G. Burgonden (*Nibelungenlied*); O.N. Borgundar (*Edda*, cp. Lat. Burgondiones); Lat. Burgondiones (Pliny, first century A.D.) [Burgundiones in the archetypes of Pliny and Jordanes], Burgundii (Ammianus, fourth century); M.Lat. Burgundzones (Jordanes); Fr. Bourguignons; Gr. Βουργοῦντες (Ptolemy, second century A.D.), Βούργουδοι (Zosimus, fifth century), Βουργουντίονες (Olympiodorus), Βουργουζίωνες (Socrates). Personal name, fem.: O.H.G. Purcunt. Territorial names: O.E. Burgenda-land 'land of the Burgundians', i.e. Bornholm (Alfred's *Orosius*); Langobard Burgund-aib, in Eastern Germany (*Origo Langob.*); O.H.G. Burgunt-hart, now Birkert, 'Burgundian wood' (near Heppenheim); Fr. Bourgogne (Burgundy). Etymology: *Burgundz 'the steep country', cp. O.Ind. *bṛhánt* 'high'. The name might also be interpreted as 'the country with numerous hills', cp. O.N. Eikund, O.Dan. Ekund 'the island of oaks'. However, the first interpretation agrees best with the nature of Bornholm, whence the nation must derive. We may compare the Norwegian toponymic *Borgyndir, inhabitants of Borgund. The equation with the Celtic Brigantes (Hirt, *Beiträge*, XVIII, 514) is phonetically acceptable, but the derivation from the place name is preferable. An erroneous learned etymology is given by Orosius, VII, 32, 12: 'atque ita etiam nomen ex opere praesumpsisse, quia castra per limitem habitacula constituta *burgos* vulgo vocant'. Ihm in Pauly-Wissowa (1899), R. Kiepert in *Formae Orbis Antiqui*, Fig. XXIV (1911), and Much in Hoops, II, 103 (1913–15) separate the Burgundians from the Φρουγουνδίωνες of Ptol. III, 5, § 8. With Schönfeld, 57, and Schmidt, I, 267, we cannot accept this view, as the parallel between the Ptol. Auarinoi-

Frugundiones-Finnoi and the Ptol. Auarpoi-Burguntes-Finnoi indicates that this is an example of Ptolemy's usual arbitrary duplicates; cp. our monograph *Ptolemy's Maps*, Fig. 24, where the existence of two Ptolemaic prototypes with some thirty duplicates each is shown. Homes: (1) Bornholm (prehistoric); (2) Burgundaib in Middle or South-eastern Germany; (3) the Middle Rhine valley with Burgunthart; (4) Burgundy.

Lit. Ducange, s.v.; Ihm in Pauly-Wissowa, s.v.; Stjerna, *Bidrag till Bornholms befolkningshistoria*, 132; Schmidt, I, 367, 372; Schönfeld, s.v. (with lit.); Much in Hoops, s.v.; Förstemann, s.v.; Schütte, *Arkiv*, XXIX, 34; Karsten, *Die Germanen*, 78; Diculescu, *Die Gepiden*, I, 86 (on Φρουγουνδίωνες).

(*b*) M.Lat. Burgundo-farones (*Passio Sigism.*, *Mon. Germ. SS. Merov.* II, 333), Burgunde-farones ('Fredegar', *ibid.* II, 148; cp. 141, 143). Personal name: Frankish Burgunda-fara. *far-* reappears in the Angl. Lindisfaran, and is the most typical mark of East Danish sub-tribes, such as Sjællands-farer; cp. § 215, A, § 259, A 6. Much compares Gr. τηλέ-πορος 'far-going'.[1] The names with this element normally belong to coasts and islands, and thus probably indicate seafaring populations.

Lit. Waitz, *Deutsche Verfassungsgeschichte*, 3rd ed. II, 1, 168; Schütte, *Danske Studier*, 1914, 32; *idem*, (Norw.) *Hist. Tidsskrift*, 1917, 36.

(*c*) O.H.G. Burgund-ari (*Summarium Heinrici*). Compounded with *-warja* 'man'.

Lit. Förstemann, s.v.

2. M.Lat. Gundebadingi (Ducange, s.v.), Guntbadingi (*Mon. Germ. SS.* III, 74). A secondary patronymic like Merovings, Agilolfings, etc. It designates the Burgundians as the people living under the law of King Gundobad (d. 516), the 'Loi Gombette'.

Lit. Ducange, s.v.; Grimm, 704; Schütte, *Blandinger udg. af Univ. Jubil. Dan. Samf.* II, 124.

3. M.Lat. Scanadabii or Scathaoarii might be added, the alleged original name of the Burgundians after their emigration from Scandinavia, according to the *Passio Sigism.* ch. 1. But the forms look like learned fictions. On the other hand, a certain popular basis for the assertion is perhaps not absolutely excluded (cp. on Gothi-Scandza and the Langobard Scatenouge, § 73).

[1] On the other hand, the existence of a Langobard word *fara* 'district, tribe, family', should also be noticed.

§ 133. Ethnic Position.

The rank of the Burgundians as co-ordinate with Goths and Lugians is less distinct, in so far as they have no sub-divisions. Nevertheless, we regard this rank as sufficiently verified, for the following reasons.

1. The Burgundians are never classified as a sub-division of another East Gothonic branch. Jordanes, XVII, 97, distinguishes them from Goths and Gepidae. History also generally shows the Burgundians acting on their own account.

2. The compound Burgunda-fara may be regarded as a distinction of political rank, equivalent to the Gothic Gut-þiuda. In Danish, Anglian, and Langobardic certainly, the element *-far* only expresses sub-divisions. But when the same element appears in an absolutely isolated position within the East Gothonic group, we must assume that here it indicates a higher rank.

3. In the *Widsith* catalogue, I, the Burgundians are the first Gothonic people mentioned after the Goths. They are placed before the Finns and even before the subjects of the Roman Emperor.[1] In *Widsith*, II, the Goths open the list of Gothonic nations, but are not here honoured by descriptive verses; the Burgundian Gúþhere is the first sovereign who is distinguished in this way (cp. our monograph *Oldsagn om Godtjod*, 105).

4. The Law of King Gundobad made the national individuality of the Burgundians an established fact, as appears also from their surname, Gundebadingi.

5. The political and juridical nomenclature of the Burgundians seems to have possessed an individual stamp, as we gather from terms like *hendinos* 'king, chieftain', and *vitti-scalc* 'policeman'. The element *-fara*, even if shared by Danes and Angles, was a privilege of the Burgundians within the East Gothonic sub-group.

6. The phonetic stamp of Burgundian is distinctly East Gothonic as appears from the preservation of Gothonic *z* (written *s*): Ais(a)berga A.D. 491 (*CIL.* XII, 2384), and from the *s* developed from Gothonic

[1] The Báningas, who precede the Burgundians, are of uncertain origin. Báningas-Burgende form a traditional couple, as we see from the *Origo Langobardorum*: Baynaib, Burgundaib. The preference given to the Báningas in *Widsith* is a consequence of the rules of alliteration: the Báningas with their king Becca must stand in the first half of the line, and the Burgende with the non-alliterating Gifica in the second.

z: Sigis-mundus (and *hendinos* (Ammianus, XXVIII, 5, § 14); the ending here, it is true, might be due to the Greek author who notes down the word). On the other hand, the royal Burgundian name Godomar might seem to betray that Gothonic $\bar{æ}$ in Burgundian had not shared the Gothic development into $\bar{e}$ (sometimes written *ei* or *i*), but had become $\bar{a}$, as in Scand., Anglo-Saxon, and German (cp. Kögel, *Zeitschrift*, XXXVII, 225 seq.; Much, *Indogerm. Anzeiger*, IX, 204 note 1). The conclusiveness of this observation seems to us problematic, as royal intermarriage might easily introduce foreign forms (cp. on the similar case of the Vandalic royal name Visimar, § 114, 5). But as the Burgundians were for about a century settled amidst German populations, we could not be astonished if this proximity had affected the language.

Lit. Wackernagel in Binding, *Gesch. des burgund. rom. Königreichs*; Bremer, § 95; Much, *Stammeskunde*; *idem*, in Hoops, s.v.; Kossinna, *Indogerm. Forsch.* VII, 282; Barrière-Flavy, *Les arts industriels*, I, 343; Schmidt, I, 378.

§ 134. History.

Starting from Burgendaland, i.e. Bornholm, in prehistoric times, the Burgundians settled on the opposite coast of Germany. They seem to have been pushed towards the south by the Rugians who occupy the coast in historical times (cp. Tac. *Germ.* 43, 'protinus ab Oceano Rugii'; Ptol. II, 11, §§ 12 and 7, Rugion and *Rugikleioi on the coast; Jordanes, IV, 26, (H)ulmerugi on 'Oceani ripas').

The time when the Burgundians began their migration towards the south may be deduced from the fact that Roman coins in Posen and thereabout became considerably rarer from the time of Antoninus Pius (130–161) (cp. Friedrich, *Zeitschr. d. hist. Gesellsch. in Posen*, XXIV, 236; Schmidt, I, 368). Before 250 a severe defeat was inflicted upon the Burgundians by the Gepidic King Fastida (Jordanes, XVII, 97).

Οὐρουγοῦνδοι, whom Schmidt, I, 368, is probably right in regarding as Burgundians, assist the Goths on their maritime raids beyond the Black Sea from 250 on (cp. Zosimus, I, 27, 31; Mamertin, *Genethl. Maxim.* ch. 7).[1] But cp. also Diculescu, *Die Gepiden*, I, 22 seq.

During the general Gothonic onslaught on Rome about 260, the

[1] Zeuss, 694, identifies the Urugundoi with Strabo's Asiatic Urgoi, the Urogoi of Priscus. But a confusion is not likely, as the Burgundians were scarcely known before that time, and the termination *-und* is not a current type in Asia or South-eastern Europe.

Burgundians on the track of the Alemanni began to advance against the Roman Limes east of the Rhine, provisionally settling about the Upper Main. They were repulsed from the Danube in 278 (Josephus, I, 67 and 68), from the Alemannic colonies west of the Limes in 268 (*Panegyr. Maxim.* ch. 5; *Panegyr. Genethl. Maxim.* ch. 17). Ammianus mentions frontier stones of Burgundians and Alemanni, and the dispute of both tribes about the salt sources in the Main-Neckar region (XVIII, 2, § 15, XXVIII, 5, § 11). The *Gentes barbarae* (*Geogr. Lat. minores*, 128) mentions the Cati and Sueui as neighbours of the Burgundians.

Incited by the Vandalic-Swabian migration to Gaul, the Burgundians in 406 conquered the provincial capital Mainz (cp. Hieronymus, *ad Ageruchiam*, epist. 123). King Gundahar as a Roman mercenary in 411 tried to put on the throne the usurper Jovinus (Olympiodorus, *fragm.* 17).

About 415 the Burgundians west of the Rhine became Roman Catholics (Orosius, VII, 32, § 12), as did those east of the river in 430 (Socrates, *Hist. Eccl.* VII, 30).

In 436 the Hunnic mercenaries of the Roman governor Aëtius killed Gundahar, his whole family, and 20,000 (?) warriors (cp. Prosper Aquitan. ad an. 435; Hydatius, ch. 108, 110; *Chron. Gall.* ch. 118; Sid. Apollinaris, *Carm.* VII, 234 seq.). The survivors became Roman subjects in Savoy (*Chron. Gall.* ch. 128), and again independent after the murder of Aëtius in 454. They were successful against the Alemanni who, after temporarily occupying Besançon and Langres (cp. Anarid, cit. by Anonym. Ravennas, IV, 26), had lost those regions before 479 (cp. Castorius, cit. *ibid.* IV, 27, and Gregory of Tours, II, 23; see Schmidt, I, 378). At the same time, the Burgundians extended their dominion into Provence, in good agreement with the Roman inhabitants. The vicinity of the Goths caused the renewed spreading of Arianism.

Gundobad, who became king in 474, ordered the Burgundian law to be codified ('Loi Gombette'). He was unwise enough to assist the Franks in ruining the Visigoths in Gaul, 507 (Isidore, *Hist. Goth.* ch. 36), and the Ostrogothic King Theodoric the Great then annexed Provence. Gundobad's son Sigismund (516–536) tried to escape ruin by adopting the creed of Rome, but though this action procured him saintship, it could not save him from being captured and murdered by the Frankish King Chlodomer, 523 (Marius Avent. ad an. 523; Gregory of Tours, III, 6; *Passio Sigism.* ch. 8–9). Sigismund's brother Godomar avenged him by killing Chlodomer in the battle at Véséronce (Marius and Gregory, *ibid.*), but finally succumbed in 534 (Marius ad an. 534; Gregory of Tours, III, 11).

In 537–538 Transrhenish Burgundians and Alemanni invaded Italy, on the initiative of their Frankish masters (Procopius, *Bell. Got.* II, 12). This is the last individual action of the Burgundians.

Their diaspora in Burgundy were soon absorbed by the more numerous native Gallo-Romans, whereas the colonies east of the Rhine about Burgunthart, and perhaps also some Burgundian districts of Western Switzerland, were Germanised.

The ancient home of the Burgundians in Eastern Germany was occupied by the invading Slavs, and no onomastic trace of the earlier inhabitants survived.

Lit. Zeuss, 133, 465; Grimm, ch. xxiv; Stjerna, *Bidrag till Bornholms befolkningshistoria*, 132 seq.; *idem*, *Origine scandinave des Burgondes* (*Congr. Arch. de France*, 1906, 281); Kjær, *Bornholmske Samlinger*, 1907, 144; Blume, *Die germ. Stämme zwischen Oder u. Passarge*, 204; Binding, *Gesch. des burgundisch-romanischen Königreichs*; Wietersheim-Dahn, *Gesch. d. Völkerwanderung*; Hodgkin, II, 110, III, 323 seq.; Ihm in Pauly-Wissowa, s.v.; Schmidt, I, 367 seq.; Much in Hoops, s.v.; Benjamin in Pauly-Wissowa, s.v. *Gundobadus*, *Godomarus*; Seeck, *ibid.* s.v. *Gundiocus*; Kauffmann, I, 296, II, 92; Longnon, *Les noms de lieu de la France*, I, 130, 196; Murat, *Les noms de lieu germaniques en* -ens *ou* -ans, -enges *ou* -anges *dans les pays de domination burgunde* (*Revue de linguistique romane*, IV).

§ 135. Legendary Traditions.

Twice in history Burgundians tried to create Roman emperors, and one emperor was killed by a Burgundian prince. Apart from that, the political importance of the nation is not great, but its epic rank is all the more remarkable. Both catalogues of *Widsith*, as we noted above, record the Burgundians as the next great Gothonic power after the Goths. The Nibelung Legend contains four indubitable Burgundian kings whose names are mentioned together in the preface to Gundobad's law, viz. Gibica, Gudomarus, Gislaharius, Gundaharius. The catastrophe of Gundahar, 436, forms the final drama of the Legend. The fall of a Frankish prince, Sigebert's uncle, in the battle against Godomar, 524, is reflected in the Eddic version that represents the Burgundian Gottormr as the slayer of the Frankish hero Sigurd. Gottormr combines two historical persons: firstly, he is the older Godomar, mentioned in Gundobad's law; and, secondly, as the slain murderer of the Frankish hero, he is the younger Godomar who succumbed to the Franks, 534. The revengeful Burgundian princess Chrodehild, King Chlodowech's queen, who brings about the ruin of her own native country, is generally supposed to be reflected in the Burgundian princess Kriemhild in the German version. Moreover, we have suggested an equation of St Sigismund and the epic Sigmund of the Edda (prose, *Frá dauða Sinfjǫtla*). The decisive likeness appears in the fact that Sigismund's second wife, by means of drink, compasses the death of her noble stepson Si... (Sigisric, Sinfjǫtli), while her husband remains more or less passive and is afterwards seized by wild despair. As this is the first tale of the 'bad stepmother' in Gothonic history and legend, the parallel cannot possibly be accidental. The validity of the equation is by no means affected by the fact that there exists a mythical Sigmund, who, as leader of the dead men's host, reveals himself as the god Woden in disguise. For it is a well-known fact that mythical and historical namesakes tend to coalesce, as we see, e.g., in the case of the god Fróði friðgóði and the mortal King Froda the Hadobard.

The popularity of the Burgundian heroes may be explained by the greatness of the political catastrophes of 436 and 523–534. For further particulars we refer to our English monograph cited below.

Lit. Epic manuals of W. Grimm, Raszmann, Jiriczek, Bruinier; Zinnow in v.d. Hagen's *Germania*, 1843, 23; Bugge, *Home of the Eddic Poems*, 288; Symons, *Grundriss*, 2nd ed. III, 658; Matthaei, *Zeitschrift*, XLVI, 1 seq.; Schütte, *Arkiv*, XXIV, 1 seq.; *idem*, *Journal of Engl. and Germ. Philology*, XX, 201 seq.; Heusler, *Zeitschrift*, 1910, 100, 111; *idem*, *Die Heldenrollen im Burgundenuntergang*, in *S.B. d. Akad. d. Wiss. Berlin, phil.-hist. Kl.* 1914; *idem*, in Hoops, s.v. *Burgundensage* and *Heldensage*; Chambers, *Widsith*, 58, 191.

E. §§ 136–140. *THE LUGIAN OR VANDALIC BRANCH*

§ 136. Names.

1. Lat. Lygii (Tacitus, first century A.D.), *Lugiones (Lupiones, *Tab. Peuting.* fourth century); Gr. Λῦιοι (Strabo, first decade A.D.), Λοῦγοι (Ptolemy, second century), Λύγιοι (Dio Cassius, third century), Λογίωνες (Zosimus, fifth century). Personal name: Lat. Lugius, Cimbr. chieftain, second century B.C. (Orosius, V, 16, 20); Lugius, *CIL.* XII, 4468, in Narbonne; Lat. Logus, an Ermundure in Carnuntum, *CIL.* III, 14359, 4. Obscure. A toponymic? The various modern attempts at interpretation

seem quite unsatisfactory, owing to the lack of insight in the leading principles of primaeval ethnic nomenclature. Leaving the etymology apart, we must mention the possibility that the Lugians are originally identical with the Norwegian Há-leygir in Há-logaland, and that their name survives in the Wendic district of Łužica, Germ. Lausitz.

Lit. Müllenhoff, IV, 564 (on the delivery); Kauffmann, I, 403; Schönfeld, s.v. (with lit.); Koht, (Norw.) *Hist. Tidsskrift*, IV R, 6 B; Magn. Olsen, *Hedenske Kultminder*, 263; Much in Hoops, s.v.; Schütte, *Beiträge*, XLI, 34; *idem*, (Norw.) *Hist. Tidsskrift*, V R, 4 B, 6; *idem*, *Ptolemy's Maps*, 113; Langenfelt, *Anthropos*, XIV/XV, p. 310; Güntert, *Wörter u. Sachen*, IX, 131.

2. Lat. Vandili (Pliny, first century A.D.), Vandali (normal spelling), Wandali, Vanduli (*Tab. Peuting.* fourth century); M.Lat. Euandali, Guandali; Gr. Οὐάνδαλοι (Dio Cassius, third century A.D.), Βανδῆλοι, Βάνδηλοι (Dexippus, etc., third century), Βανδίλοι (Zosimus, fifth century), pronounced resp. Vandêloi, Vandiloi.[1] Royal title: Vandalic Vandala-ricus (Luxorius, *ep.* 1112, 1). Eponymous name: O.N. Vandill, an epic 'sea-king'. Personal names: Lat. Wandal-(h)arius, Ostrogothic king; Ostrogoth. Wandil. Mountain: Οὐανδαλικὰ ὄρη (Dio Cassius, LV, 1), i.e. the Riesengebirge. Headland: Arab. al Andalos, whence the Span. territorial name Andalusia. Probably derived from a locality. Swed. Vendel, O.N. Vendill, in the province of Upland, signifies (*a*) a lake, (*b*) its outlet, (*c*) the surrounding district. The same territorial name occurs in N. Jutland, O.N. Vendill, Dan. Vendsyssel; the projecting extremity of this county, the Skaw, might suggest the derivation from Goth. *vandus*, O.N. *vǫndr* 'twig'. The Vandals may have sprung either from the Swedish or the Danish Vendill. With Schönfeld and Bremer, § 89, we regard the shifting derivation *-il*, *-al*, *-ul* as an organic gradation of vowels ('Ablaut'), against Meyer-Lübke, *S.B. d. Wien. Akad. phil.-hist. Kl.* CXLIX, 2, 89.

Lit. Zeuss, 57, 443; Grimm, 475; Müllenhoff, IV, 128; Bugge, *Zeitschr. f. deutsche Philol.* IV, 197; Hellquist in Johannsson's *Beitr. z. griech. Sprachkunde* (*Upsala Univ. Årsskrift*, 1890), 118, 149; *idem*, *Etymolog. bemerkningar*, Gefle, 1893, IX (the theory withdrawn, *Arkiv*, XXV, 199, cp. Schütte, *ibid.* XXXIII, 70); Stjerna, *Essays on Beowulf*, III, *Arkiv*, XXI, 71; Schönfeld, s.v.; Much, *Wörter u. Sachen*, IV, 170; *idem*, in Hoops, s.v. On the O.E. Wen(d)le or Wendlas cp. Müllenhoff, *Beowulf*, 89; Much, *Beiträge*, XVII, 210; Chambers, *Widsith*, 208; Güntert, *Wörter u. Sachen*, IX, 131.

1 The identity of the Wenle of *Widsith* is questionable: Vandals or Scandinavians?

The question whether the names Lugians and Vandals coincide or not will be discussed in § 138, 1–3.

§ 137. Sub-divisions.

The synopsis below is arranged with approximate direction from north to south, beginning with the Lugian tribes and ending with the Vandals and their neighbours.

1. Lat. Lygii Eluhecones, Helvecones (MSS of Tacitus, first century A.D.); Gr. Αἰλουαίωνες (Ptolemy, second century A.D.). A toponymic? Root O.H.G. *elo*, gen. *elwes*, 'reddish brown' (Müllenhoff, Much). Kauffmann compares the Scand. Hilleviones (Pliny, IV, 96), which is, however, an unreliable ἅπαξ λεγόμενον. We may rather compare the Celtic Helvii, Helvetii; *h* is a Latin parasite, as in Helvecones. Müllenhoff would correct *-econes* into *-aeones*; Much and Schönfeld defend the spelling of Tacitus. Home: about the present Posen (Ptol. II, 11, § 9).

Lit. **Müllenhoff,** IV, 562 (*Zeitschrift,* IX, 248); **Schönfeld,** s.v. *Elvecones* (with lit.); **Much in Hoops,** s.v. *Helvecones*; **Kauffmann,** I, 250 note 6, 400 note 8; **Rappaport in Pauly-Wissowa,** s.v. *Helvecones*; **v. Kienle,** *Wörter u. Sachen,* XIV, 514.

2. Lat. Lygii Harii (Tacitus, first century A.D.); ? Charini (Pliny). ? Personal name: Lat. Harius (a 'frumentarius', *CIL.* VI, 3052). Etymology: Goth. *harjis*, 'army, flock'; the same element occurs in Celt. Koriondoi, Tri- and Petrocorii, '3 armies', '4 armies'. Schönfeld doubts whether Tacitus wrote Harii or Arii; but if Pliny's Charini refers to the same tribe, the initial must be *h*. Much identifies an epic tribe, O.E. Herelingas, Germ. Harlungen, and the possibility may be admitted. Home: beside No. 1 (Tac. *Germ.* 43).

Lit. **D'Arbois de Jubainville,** II, 351; **Panzer,** *Neujahrsbl. d. bad. hist. Komm.* 1904; **Schönfeld,** s.v. (with lit.); **Much in Hoops,** s.v.; **Rappaport in Pauly-Wissowa,** s.v.

3. (*a*) Lat. Lygii Manimi (Tacitus, first century A.D.); (*b*) Gr. Λοῦγοι Ὀμανοί (Ptolemy, second century A.D.). Obscure. Zeuss, 124, separates (*a*) from (*b*); otherwise they are generally identified. We have suggested a possible corruption: Ὀμανοί = Strabo's Bastarnic tribe Ἄτμονοι (cp. § 142, 2). Home: beside No. 1 (Ptol. II, 11, § 10).

Lit. **Schönfeld,** s.v. (with lit.); **Much in Hoops,** s.v. *Manimi* and Λοῦνοι; **Schütte,** *Beiträge,* XLI, 34; *idem, Arkiv,* XXXIII, 35; *idem, Ptolemy's Maps,* 113.

4. Gr. Λοῦγοι οἱ *Δοῦνοι (Λοῦγοι οἱ Ἰδοῦνοι, Ptol. II, 11, § 10, in *Cod. Vatic.* 191, which is preferred by Mommsen and C. Müller; otherwise Διδοῦνοι). So-called 'town', in reality a duplicate of the tribal name, Gr. Λουγί-δουνον (Ptol. *ibid.* § 13). Territorial name: O.N. Dun-heiðr (*Lay of Angantýr*). Obscure. A toponymic? Schmidt regards the tribal name as an arbitrary Ptolemaic construction from the Celtic town name Lugidunon; but Ptolemy's error is in reality in the opposite direction, as the tribal name is supported by the epic battlefield Dun-heiðr. The two names belong to a series of duplicates betraying two Ptolemaic prototypes. Much compares the Thracian tribe Thynoi, and it does not seem altogether unlikely that the Lugians might have inherited such a name from Daco-Thracian aborigines. Home: south of the Omanoi (Ptolemy).

Lit. Much, *Zeitschrift*, XXXIII, 8; *idem*, in Hoops, s.v. Δοῦνοι; Schmidt, I, 354; Schönfeld, s.v. *Diduni* (with lit.); Schütte, *Arkiv*, XXI, 39; *ibid.* XXXIII, 34; *idem*, *Beiträge*, XLI, 34; *idem*, (Norw.) *Hist. Tidsskrift*, 1917, 15; *idem*, *Ptolemy's Maps*, 113 and Figs. 19–20.

5. Lat. Lygii Helisii (Tacitus, first century A.D.). Obscure. Zeuss and others assume a Latin parasitic *h*, as in Helvecones, for *Elisii. As the name only occurs once, we might prefer to emend it into *Halisii (cp. Betavi, *CIR.* 20003 for the normal Batavi, and the present form Betuwe, exemplified from the eleventh century onwards).[1] For the conjectural form *Halisii would agree with the epic Hælsingas, mentioned in *Widsith*, l. 22, beside the Swabians and the East Gothonic Rugians. Moreover, we might compare the town Kalisia (Ptol. II, 11, § 13), the present Polish Kalisz, the important centre of a county on the frontier of Eastern Germany. The initial *K* might represent the pronunciation of the neighbouring Dacians, inherited by the Poles. Home: between the Manimi and the Naharvali, i.e. the Silesians (Tac. *Germ.* 43). The place would be exactly in the vicinity of Kalisz.

Lit. Zeuss, 124 note 3; Müllenhoff, IV, 560; Schönfeld, s.v.; Much in Hoops, s.v.; Schütte, *Beiträge*, XLI, 34; *idem*, (Norw.) *Hist. Tidsskrift*, 1917, 11; *idem*, *Ptolemy's Maps*, 112; Langenfelt, *Anthropos*, XIV/XV, 310.

6. Lat. Buri (Tacitus, first century A.D.); Gr. Λοῦγοι Βοῦροι (Ptolemy, second century A.D.), Βοῦρροι (Dio Cassius, third century). Place name:

[1] We suppose an analogous erroneous Tacitean *e* for *a* in Reudigni for *Randingi =O.E. Rondingas. Cp. § 237, 2.

Dac. Buri-dava, *Tab. Peuting.*='town of the Buri'?, which is by C. Müller, ed. of Ptol. I, 444, plausibly referred to the Burroi of Dio Cassius. We have proposed emending Ptolemy's Κουρίωνες (II, 11, § 11), and Βουργίωνες (III, 5, § 8), into *Buriones, i.e. Buri; if this correction is not acceptable, the two forms, which do not occur elsewhere, must be abandoned as being of no value. The name may be a toponymic connected with O.E. and O.N. *búr* 'building, house'. Otherwise it is generally referred to Goth. *baur*, O.N. *burr*, O.E. *byre* 'son'; so Much, Schönfeld, etc., but according to Langenfelt, a toponymic interpretation must be preferred (cp. *Anthropos*, XIV/XV, 303). Home: south of the mountain Askiburgion (Ptol. II, 11, § 10); the presumable colony of the Buridavensioi is situated in Middle or Northern Dacia (*ibid.* III, 8, § 3).

Lit. Schönfeld, s.v.; Much in Hoops, s.v.; Schütte, *Beiträge*, XLI, 32, 33; *idem*, *Arkiv*, XXXIII, 34; *idem*, *Ptolemy's Maps*, 112; v. Premerstein, *Zeitschrift*, LX, 72; Krahe, *Indogerm. Forsch.* XLVII, 324.

7. Lat. Lygii Naharvali (or Nahanarvali?, Tacitus, first century A.D.). Obscure. Home: probably in Silesia at the sanctuary of Limis, Λίμιος ἄλσος (Ptol. II, 11, § 13).

Lit. Schönfeld, s.v. (with lit.); Much in Hoops, s.v.; Langenfelt, *Anthropos*, XIV/XV, 312; Löwenthal, *Beiträge*, XLVII, 286, XLIX, 634.

8. (*a*) O.H.G. Hartunge; O.N. Haddingjar; Lat. Hasdingi (Cassiodorus, sixth century), Asdingi; Gr. Ἄστιγγοι (Dio Cassius, episode of the second century A.D.). Eponymous heroes: O.N. tveir Haddingjar. Etymology: Gothonic **hazd*- 'hair'. Originally perhaps a dynastic name (of the Naharvali?), it later embraces one of the two Vandalic sub-tribes. Home: (1) probably at the Silesian sanctuary of Limis (cp. under 7); (2) the Spanish province of Galicia; (3) Baetica; (4) Northern Africa; (5) Western Asia.

Lit. Grimm, 448; Müllenhoff, IV, 487, 572, 581; Wrede, *Sprache der Wandalen*, 42 (*Quellen u. Forschungen*, Strasb. LIX, with lit.); Ihm in Pauly-Wissowa, s.v. *Asdingi*; Schmidt, I, 357; *idem*, *Gesch. d. Wandalen*, 5; Schönfeld, s.v. *Hasdingi*; Helm, *Altgerm. Religionsgesch.* I, 323; v.d. Leyen, *Deutsche Literaturgesch.* 34, sp. 2187; Magnus Olsen, *Hedenske Kultminder*, 247; Much in Hoops, s.v. *Hasdingen*; Schütte, *Ptolemy's Maps*, 100.

(*b*) Lat. Silingi (Hydatius, etc., fifth century A.D.); Gr. Σιλίγγαι (Ptol. *Cod. Vatic.* 191, second century A.D.); Polish derivative Szlązaci 'Silesians'. Personal name: Erul. Silenga (*Chron. Gothanum*). Territorial name:

M.Lat. Silesia. Name of river: Czech. Sleza (Germ. Lohe, near Breslau). The Silingi are the second sub-tribe of the Vandals; Slav. *-ęz* in Silesia regularly corresponds to Gothonic *-ing*, as in *knęz* 'king'. The name is probably derived from a locality. Kossinna compares Silund, Selund, names of islands in ancient Denmark, but the form is not quite identical with Siling-, and the geographical distance is considerable. Better in both respects is the derivation from the Silesian river Sleza < *Silinga; the root Sil- occurs frequently in European names of rivers, and also as the name of a Swedish lake. On the other hand, we may certainly admit the possibility that the river might have been named after the tribe, not the reverse. Home: Silesia; later Baetica in Spain.

Lit. **Kossinna,** *Indogerm. Forsch.* VII, 281; **Schönfeld,** s.v. (with lit.); *idem,* in **Pauly-Wissowa,** s.v.; **Much in Hoops,** s.v.; **Schütte,** *Blandinger udg. af Univ. Jubil. Danske Samfund,* II, 123; **Much,** *Altschlesien,* I, 117 seq.; **Noreen,** *Fornvännen,* 1920, p. 38; **Langenfelt,** *Anthropos,* XIV/XV, 311; **Löwenthal,** *Beiträge,* XLVII, 290, LIV, 317.

9. Lat. *Taifuli (Taifruli, *Nomina provinciarum,* fourth century A.D., *Geogr. Lat. Min.* 128, 22), Taipholi, Taifali (Ammianus, fourth century, etc.), Thaifali (Mamert. *Genethl.*); Gr. Θαΐφαλοι (Zosimus, fifth century). Territorial name: M.Lat. Theiphalia; Fr. Tifauge. Obscure. The initial sound may be either *t* or *th*, but the territorial name speaks in favour of the latter, as the local tradition in Gaul would probably have preserved the true pronunciation. *-fal* might be Gothonic **falh-* 'plain' (?), as in Germ. Westphalia; but the alternation of *-al* and *-ul*, as in Vandali, Vanduli, according to Diculescu, points towards a derivative ending. Diculescu identifies the Thaifali with 11, the Lacringes. Colonies: (1) Southern Dacia (Muntenia and Oltenia); (2) Greater Phrygia (Asia Minor); (3) Northern Italy about Modena, Reggio, and Parma; (4) Theiphalia in Western Gaul, now Tifauge.

Lit. **Zeuss,** 432 (with lit.); **Schönfeld,** s.v.; **Much in Hoops,** s.v.; **Diculescu,** *Die Wandalen,* 13 (*Mannus-Bibliothek,* No. 34).

10. Lat. Victuali (Julius Capitolinus c. A.D. 300), Victoali, Victohali (Victobali). Obscure. The first element looks like the word 'wight' that appears in Gothonic and Celtic personal names. Much, however, compares the Cymric personal name Gweith-gual < *Viktovalos 'battle-strong'. Müllenhoff, II, 82 and 327, Much in Hoops, III, 417, and Diculescu, identify the Victuali with the Hasdingi. The identification is

rejected by Schmidt, *Gesch. d. Wandalen*, 8 note 5. Colony: Western Dacia.

Lit. Schönfeld, s.v.; Much in Hoops, s.v.; Diculescu, *Die Wandalen*, 13 (*Mannus-Bibliothek*, No. 34); Löwenthal, *Beiträge*, XLVII, 286, XLIX, 63.

11. Lat. Lacringes (*Script. Hist. Aug. v. M. Ant.* c. A.D. 300, episode of the second century); Gr. Λάκριγγοι (Dio Cassius, third century). Obscure, probably a toponymic. Diculescu identifies them with 9, the Thaifali. Home: somewhere on the northern frontier of Dacia.

Lit. Schönfeld, s.v.; Much in Hoops, s.v.; Diculescu, *Die Wandalen*, 14 (*Mannus-Bibliothek*, No. 34); Löwenthal, *Beiträge*, XLVII, 285, LI, 290.

Survey of types of names.

The Short types are represented first of all by the collective name of Lugoi, traceable two centuries B.C. through the Cimbric personal name Lugius, and further by Harji, Buri and *Duni; the equation of Manimi and Omanoi, if correct, would correspondingly point towards an original *Mani. All of these belong to the first century A.D.

Long Derivative types are: Vandili, Elvecones, Manimi, Helisii, Naharvali, first century A.D.; Hasdingi, Silingai, second century A.D. The collective name of Vandili may originate from a place name, belonging to the class of 'large district names, designated by Long Derivative types', cp. § 79. Silingai seems to originate from a local Silesian river; that is to say, its genesis belongs to the secondary stratum. Also the position of the Hasdingi and Silingi as sub-divisions of Vandali suggests a secondary formation.

To the above collection of Long Derivative types, we may still add three more, if we are right in regarding the Thaifali, Victuali and Lacringes as Vandalic tribes, and if Thaifali and Victuali are not Compounds.

Apart from the last-mentioned possibility, Compounds do not occur.

§ 138. Ethnic Position.

The existence of a Lugian branch is sufficiently verified. A still larger currency is of old attributed to the name of Vandals. Now the question is whether the two communities must be separated. In our opinion, they are rather identical.

1. The quality of a collective community appears at the first glance from the seven Lugian sub-divisions enumerated either by Tacitus, *Germ.*

43, or by Ptolemy, II, 11, § 18. It must be noticed that Tacitus represents his five Lugian tribes in set terms as selected from a larger number: 'latissime patet Lygiorum nomen, in plures civitates diffusum; valentissimas nominasse sufficiat'.

2. The denomination of Vandals was at least equally comprehensive, since Pliny, IV, ch. 99, attributes it to the entire East Gothonic group, and also Tacitus, *Germ.* 2, knows its use as a collective name of the same rank as, e.g., Swabians.

3. A coincidence of Lugians and Vandals seems to appear in some cases. The Lygii Naharvali of Tacitus, according to their religious institutions, seem to be continued by the Hasdingian Vandals (cf. § 137, 7, 8). As inhabitants of Silesia, the Hasdingian and Silingian Vandals have Lugian neighbours towards the north and south, viz. Helvecones, etc., and Buri, and probably also towards the east, viz. the Helisii (about Kalisz); thus the Vandals occupy the position of a connecting link between the Lugian extremities. Finally, Gothic and Langobardian primaeval legends speak of Vandals, where we should rather have expected Lugians, if the two names signified different communities. Thus we must assume identity.

4. Tacitus' description of the Goths (*Germ.* 43) seems to imply that the contrasting Lugians were distinguished by angular shields, long swords, and republican constitution. The original constitution of the Vandals partly corresponds to this: according to the *Origo Langobardorum* they were governed by dukes.

5. The worship of the dioscures called Alci (Tac. *Germ.* 43) may have been a temporary national religion of the Lugian-Vandalic branch, like the worship of Nerthus among the Angles and Jutes, and the worship of the 'regnator omnium deus' among the Semnones as the connecting link of all Swabian tribes. The sanctuary probably was situated at the 'grove of Limis' (Ptol. II, 11, § 13), no doubt on the isolated Silesian mountain of Sobotka or Zobten. The priests with 'female dress', i.e. long, floating hair, Gothonic **hazd-*, seem to be identical with the Vandalic dynasty of Hasdingi, reflected in epic legends by the German twins called Hartunge and by the Scandinavian 'tveir Haddingjar'. The dioscures Alci may also be reflected by the epic couple of Vandalic dukes, Ambri and Assi (*Origo Langobardorum*, 1 seq., and Paulus Diaconus, I, 7). The last-mentioned author gives a duplicate of the same episode in ch. 11, where the rôle of Ambri and Assi as conquered

enemies of the Langobards is played by the mysterious-looking people of the Assi-piti, who are perhaps the 'Assi pethi' 'both Assies'.[1] In later times the Hasdingian worship may have been adopted in parts of Scandinavia (cp. the Norwegian valley of Haddingja-dalr), but in ancient times the religion was probably limited to the Lugian-Vandalic branch (cp. Much, *Wandalische Götter*).

6. The Vandals are described as trained horsemen (cp. Dexippus, Exc. ed. Bonn, 19, 20). So also the Thaifali (Zosimus, II, 31). This quality is different from Gothic warfare which put the stress on the infantry (cp. Diculescu, *Die Wandalen*, 13).

7. The Victuali and Lacringes take part in the Marcomannic war, together with the Buri and Vandali (cp. Julius Capitolinus, XXII, 1 and 173). There seems to be a large participation of Lugian-Vandalic tribes, whereas the Goths can at the best be traced in those 'superiores barbari', *ibid.* 14, who cause the movements of their southern neighbours.

Lit. Members of the branch: Bremer, § 93; Schmidt, I, 354; *idem*, *Gesch. d. Wandalen*, 4; Much in Hoops, s.v. *Lugier*, *Wandalen*; Kauffmann, II, 6; Diculescu, *Die Wandalen*, 13. Dress: Schmidt, *Gesch. d. Wandalen*, 195. Antiquities: Kossinna, *Zeitschr. f. Ethnologie*, XXXVI, 404; Blume, *Die germ. Stämme u. Kulturen zwischen Oder u. Passarge* (*Mannus-Bibliothek*, No. 8); Kauffmann, I, 295. Constitution: Brunner, *Deutsche Rechtsgeschichte*, I, 121, 126; Schmidt, I, 36, 365; *idem*, *Gesch. d. Wandalen*, 41. Religion: Müllenhoff, IV, 487, 572; Helm, *Altgerm. Religionsgesch.* I, 321.

§ 139. History.

A questionable echo of the Lugians in Norway, Há-leygir, has been mentioned in § 136. Namesakes of the Vandals are the Wendle or Vendilenses in the Jutlandic Vendill, and the inhabitants of the homonymous Swedish district. Genetic relations between the Vandals and one of these tribes are not unlikely. We have seen in vol. I, § 79, that Long types like *Wandiliz are frequent in the early Gothonic nomenclature of larger districts, and it was probably from one such that the Λοῦγοι adopted the additional name of Vandili.

After settling on the south coast of the Baltic, the Lugians occupied the larger part of the Oder basin. They or their kinsmen seem to have

[1] Helm, *Altgerm. Religionsgesch.* I, 326, and Magnus Olsen, *Hedenske Kultminder*, 250, rediscover the dioscures in the Hasdingian chieftains Raus and Raptos, Dio Cassius, LXXI, 12, § 1, i.e. 'Reed' and 'Rafter'; but these are undoubtedly historical.

reached the Carpathian mountains before the Gothonic Sound Shift (cp. O.N. Harfaða fjǫll; see Much, *Zeitschrift*, XXXIII, 1 seq., and in Hoops, s.v. Δοῦνοι; Schütte, *Arkiv*, XXI, 40). We may connect this movement with the appearance of the Sciri and Bastarnae near the Black Sea about 200 B.C. The wandering Cimbri, before appearing in the Alps, 113 B.C., may have passed the Lugian territory in Eastern Germany, since one of their leaders was called Lugius.

A comparison of Tacitus, Pliny, and Ptolemy shows the sequence of Lugian tribes on the line north-south with approximate certainty. (1) Harji, as northern wing, Tac., the Charini of Pliny, beside coast tribes like the Goths. (2) Elvecones, Tac., the Elvaiones as northern wing, Ptol. (where the Harji are omitted). (3) Manimi, Tac., Omanoi, Ptol. (4) *Dunoi, Ptol., with the epic localisation Dunheiðr near the Myrkviðr (the Hercynian wood) according to the *Lay of Angantýr*. (5) Helisii, Tac., with capital ?? Kalisia, Ptol., south of the *Dunoi, the present Kalisz. (6) Naharvali, Tac.; their presumable sanctuary Λίμιος ἄλσος is by Ptol. misplaced north-west of Kalisia instead of south-west, where the mountain Sobotka is situated. (7) Silingai, Ptol., quite misplaced towards the west; their correct localisation is indicated by the territorial name of Silesia, and more exactly by the river Ślęza east of the Sobotka; their south frontier appears as the Vandalic mountains (Dio Cassius, LXXVII, 20). (8) Buri south of the 'montium jugum', Tac., and Buroi south of the Askiburgion, Ptol.; cp. the presumable colony Buri-dava in Dacia (Ptol., *Tab. Peuting.*). If we are right in correcting Burgiones (Ptol. III, 5, § 8) into *Buriones, the Buri would also have advanced farther east along the Carpathian chain, since they are here registered among 'Sarmatian' tribes.

Non-Gothonic neighbours were: Dacians in Poland and south of the Carpathian mountains; Pannonian and Celtic survivals in the mountains south of the Buri; Sarmates in the Hungarian plains farther south.

The Lugians, according to Strabo, VII, 290, became subjects of King Maroboduus' great Swabian Empire in the first decade of our era, but regained their independence through the defeat of this prince in A.D. 17 (Tac. *Ann.* II, 45). Lugian forces assisted the Ermundures in conquering the Quadic King Vannius in Moravia A.D. 50 (*ibid.* XII, 29). The Roman amber trade, which increased considerably during the reign of Nero (cp. Pliny, XXXVII, 45), even affected the Lugian territory, though only because it was on the trade route. On the frequent occurrence of Roman coins of the first two centuries of our era cp. Friedrich, *Zeitschrift der hist. Gesellsch. v. Posen*, XXIV, 236, 246. About A.D. 86 the Lugians with some Roman support fought the Swabians in 'Mysia' (Dacia?) (Dio Cassius, LXVII, 5, § 2); we may perhaps connect this undertaking with the appearance of the Buridavenses in Dacia. The Southern Lugians (Buri) allied with the Dacians against Rome, but did not support them effectively during Trajan's war of conquest A.D. 105 (Dio Cassius, LXVIII, 8).

Various Lugian tribes took part in the Marcomannian war. At the outset, 166, Buri and Victuali assisted the Marcomans against Rome, being pressed towards the south by remoter barbarians (Julius Capitolinus, *Hist. Aug. v. M. Ant.* ch. 22). About 170 the Hasdingian chieftains Raus and Raptos asked for admission into Roman Dacia (Dio Cassius, LXXI, 12, § 1). The governor Clemens declined it, but allowed them to leave wives and children provisionally on Roman soil, while the warriors set out to conquer the independent Dacian tribe of the Koistobokoi. The attack proved successful and caused the Koistobokoi, in their turn, to invade Thracia and Greece. 18,000 Koistobokoi sought shelter in Roman Dacia A.D. 180 (Dio Cassius, LXXII, 3). The town of Piroboridava seems to have been founded by the emigrant King Pieporus or Petoporus (cp. our monograph *Ptolemy's Maps*, 100, 142). Here the question arises: where was the region of the said Koistobokoi? Müllenhoff, II, 91, Schmidt, I, 357, and Diculescu, *Die Wandalen*, 2, without discussion assume that it was situated on the upper Teiss. But they are contradicted by Ptolemy, III, 5, § 9, where the independent Koistobokoi are placed in Poland and designated as *Transmontanoi (Tranomontanoi), in contradistinction to their emigrated section in Roman Dacia. Certainly it would seem more natural for the emigrated Hasdingi to attack a tribe near Roman Dacia than to return through the Carpathians in order to invade Poland; and no doubt Ptolemy is often guilty of quite erroneous localisations. However, Koistobokoi are not otherwise heard of on the Upper Teiss; from this inland region they could not have undertaken a maritime raid on Greece; the addition of 'transmontanoi' expressly places them north of the Carpathians; the Ptolemaic town of Setidava (Ptol. II, 11, § 13) proves the extension of Dacian territory towards the Lower Weichsel; generally, the section of the Ptolemaic map due north of the Carpathians is of superior quality; and finally Ptolemy is supported by Ammianus who mentions Costobocae in Western Scythia beside the Alani Europaei (XXII, 8). Consequently, the theory of the modern ethnographers must be rejected. For reasons unknown to us, the Hasdings must have returned to Silesia; perhaps because the best chance of success was an attack on the neighbouring Koistobokoi in co-operation with their own countrymen in the homeland. But soon after the Hasdings suffered a crushing defeat by another Lugian (?) tribe, the Lacringes (Dio Cassius, 11, § 6), and, as Schmidt remarks (II, 184 note 2), the conquest of Northern Dacia cannot have been lasting, for in 180 the Hasdings appear in the vicinity of Quadi, Buri, and Sarmates, i.e. south of the Moravian mountains (Dio Cassius, LXXII, 2). The Buri alternately assisted the Romans and the Quadi (*ibid.* LXXI, 18, LXXII, 3). At the final conclusion of peace, in 180, both Vandals (i.e. Hasdings) and Buri seem to have been on good terms with Rome, since the Marcomans and Quadi were pledged to abstain from hostilities against them. All the Gothonic tribes concerned were forbidden to settle within a space of 400 stadia from Roman Dacia.

Lugian and Vandalic raids of lesser importance into Roman territory are mentioned in the years 248, 270, 278.

The *Tabula Peutingeriana* still records the *Lugians and Buri together with the Vandals; the two former appear beside the Sarmates, and the Vandals beside the Marcomans. In the annals of history, however, the Lugians disappear after 278 and the Buri earlier still, after 180. The Hasdingi and Silingi survive, forming together the Vandalic nation, and probably absorbing the rest of the Lugian branch, with the exception of the Thaifali, who allied with the Visigoths.

After the Goths had, about 260, occupied Transylvania and successfully repulsed an attack of the Gepidae, the Vandals in 290 supported a fresh attempt of the latter, but they were beaten by the Goths, who were in their turn assisted by the Thaifali (Mamertinus, *Genethl. Maximiani*, § 17).

Later, the Vandals temporarily succeeded in occupying the disputed region (cp. Jordanes, XXII, §§ 113–114): 'quo tempore erant in eo loco manentes, ubi nunc Gepidas sedent, juxta flumina Marisia (Mureş, Marosch), Miliare (Schnelle Körös) et Gilpil (Schwarze Körös) et Grisia (Criş, Körös) [et *Tisianus] (Weisse Körös), qui omnes supradictos excedet'. The Victuali, who are identified with the Vandals by Diculescu, about the same time were situated east of the Teiss, where they received some fugitive Sarmates (Ammianus, xvii, 12). But about 335 King Visimar, of the Hasdingian dynasty, was defeated by the Gothic King Geberic, and fell. The survivors of the defeated people were received by the Romans as 'federates' in Pannonia (Jordanes, xxii, 115). Schmidt, *Gesch. d. Wandalen,* 15 seq., rejects the report of Jordanes as fictitious, but Diculescu defends it with good arguments (*Die Wandalen,* 26). In Pannonia, the Vandals were converted to Christianity by the Goths and became fanatic Arians.

The Thaifali, in agreement with the Goths, had occupied Southern Dacia, i.e. the present districts of Muntenia and Oltenia (cp. Diculescu, *Die Wandalen,* 16). Their eastern frontier appears from the description given by Ammianus, xxxi, 32, § 7, of the defensive wall constructed by Athanaric against the Huns: 'a superciliis Gerasi fluminis (from the river Siret) adusque Danubium Taifalorum terras praestringens muros altius erigebat'. The words *ibid.* xvii, 13, § 20 show that the district extended westwards to the Banat. Thaifalic prisoners of war about 332 were transported as colonists to greater Phrygia (cp. Symeon Metaphrastes, *Biography of St Nicolaus,* 17 (Migne, *Patrologia Graeca,* 116, p. 337)). About 377 Athanaric ejected the Sarmates situated in Caucalandensis locus, i.e. perhaps in Coca in Muntenia (Ammianus, xxxi, 4, § 13). The Thaifali shared their fate (cp. Ambrosius, *in Lucam,* x, 10). After invading Moesia and being beaten by the Romans, some were transplanted to the surroundings of Modena, Reggio and Parma in Northern Italy (Ammianus, xxxi, 39), others to Western Gaul, where the *Notitia dignitatum Occ.* xlii, 65, mentions a 'praefectus Sarmatarum et Taifalorum' about Poitiers, and where the name of a district Theifalia persists to this day as Tifauge.

Henceforth the annals of the Vandals almost exclusively concern the rich and well-known history of their states on Roman soil. We give only an outline, referring to the standard manuals.

406–408. Migration of Vandals, Alani and Quadic Swabians along the Danube through Northern and Southern Gaul into the Iberian Peninsula. The Alani obtain the provinces Carthaginiensis and Lusitania, the Silingi Baetica, the Hasdingi and Swabians Galicia.

416. The Visigothic King Valja beats the Alani and exterminates the Silingi. The latter are replaced by the Hasdingi, who begin to act as pirates.

429. Geizeric, King of Hasdingi and Alani and of some Gothic

followers, conquers Roman North-west Africa except Carthage. His Gothonic and Alanic people, according to a census (Victor Vit. I, 2), number 80,000. Rome has to acknowledge the Vandals as 'federates'. See page 447.

439. Geizeric annexes Carthage and ravages Sicily.

442. The conclusion of peace makes the Vandals sovereign masters of: (1) Mauritania Abaritana, (2) Zeugitana, (3) Byzacena, (4) Gaetulia, (5) Numidia proconsularis, i.e. (1) (probably) the region of Tangier, (2–4) Tunisia, (5) Eastern Algeria, the environs of Bona.

455. After the murder of the Emperor Valentinianus, Geizeric declares himself absolved from the peace treaty, plunders Rome (2 June) and annexes Tripolis.

c. 475. The Vandals command the Pithyuses, the Baleares, Corsica, Sardinia, and Sicily. Half of Sicily is granted to Odovacar on payment of a tribute.

477–484. Under Geizeric's successor, Huneric, the persecution of the Roman Catholics culminates. A royal edict literally copies the Imperial measures against heresy, only replacing 'Arians' by 'Roman Catholics'. The patriarch Cyrila tries to enforce the use of the Vandalic language at a synod.

532–534. Conquest of the Vandals by Belisarius, the general of the Emperor Justinianus. King Geilamer is captured.

536–539. Unsuccessful rebellion of the Vandals and Mauri. From this time, the Vandals in Africa cease to exist as a nation. The remnants are to a great extent transplanted to oriental regions.

The European remnants of the Vandals sent ambassadors to King Geizeric in Africa, asking their emigrated brothers to resign the inherited 'right of remigration'. The supplicants urged that only the full, undisputed possession of the paternal soil could inspire them to defend it vigorously against the assailing barbarians. But the assembly of the Vandals in Africa would not give up the chance of a retreat in case of bad fortune. This report of Procopius, *Bell. Vand.* I, 22 (cp. 3), has been disputed, e.g. by Dahn, *Urgesch. f. germ. roman. Völker*, I, 205, but there seems to be no reason for rejecting it, as Gothonic analogies occur (cp. Freytag, *Bilder aus der deutschen Vergangenheit*, I, 65; Platner, *Forsch. zur deutschen Gesch.* XX, 165; Seelmann, *Jahrbuch d. Vereins f. Niederdeutsche Sprachforsch.* XII, 30; Schmidt, *Gesch. d. Wandalen*, 17; Schütte, *Oldsagn om Godtjod*, 85).

It is questionable where the European Vandals concerned were situated. Freytag places them in Silesia, while Schmidt suggests the region about the river Teiss. We are inclined to prefer Freytag's view, for onomastic traces of pre-Slavonic inhabitants are not as frequent about the Teiss as in the vicinity of Silesia. Such traces are: Silesia with river Ślęza; the epic Dunheiðr; Kalisz; Jeseníky or Gesenke ('Ash-mountain'), i.e. Ἀσκιβούργιον ὄρος (Ptol.), with river Oskava; Bieskiden, the mountain of the Biessoi (?); O.G. Miriquidui, O.N. Myrkviðr; Stregun or Striegau on a homonymous river may be Stragona (Ptol. II, 11, § 13). Němči or Nimptsch on the river Ślęza may perhaps indicate an ancient stronghold of a Gothonic residue, as the name appears already at the close of the tenth century, before these regions had been colonised by the Germans. Epic traditions know of Gothonic tribes fighting unsuccessfully against foreign invaders in these regions—the Goths against the Huns, the Langobards against the Bulgars. There were also German legends or myths of Hasdingian Vandals defeated by the Slavs (cp. § 140), but they give no hint as to the time when the Gothonic element succumbed to the invaders.

Lit. Zeuss, 127, 455; Müllenhoff, II, 92; Wietersheim-Dahn, *Gesch. d. Völkerwanderung*; Hodgkin, II, ii, III, 593 seq.; Much, *Zeitschrift*, XXXIII, 9 seq.; *idem*, in Hoops, s.v.; *idem*, *Altschlesien*, I, 117; Pflugk-Harttung, *Hist. Zeitschrift*, LXI, 69; Schmidt, I, 354 seq.; *idem*, *Gesch. d. Wandalen*; Seeck in Pauly-Wissowa, s.v. *Geisericus*; Benjamin, *ibid.* s.v. *Hunericus*; Schönfeld, *ibid.* s.v. *Lugii* and *Silingae*; Diculescu, *Die Wandalen* (*Mannus-Bibliothek*, No. 34).

§ 140. Legendary Traditions.

The mythical couple of Hasdingi are the main representatives of the Vandals in Gothonic legends, Germ. Hartunge, O.N. tveir Haddingjar.

Otherwise the Vandals, in spite of their famous conquest of Roman Africa, have only left few traces. King Alfred's translation of Orosius, when mentioning the migration to Africa, replaces 'Vandals' by 'Goths'.

The O.N. 'sea-king' Vandill seems to be a reflection of Vandalic sea-power; the eponymous signification of the name appears from the fact that Vandill is accompanied by a Vinnill, the representative of the Winnili or Langobards.

Heinzel, *Ueber die Hervararsaga* (*S.B. d. Wien. Akad. phil.-hist. Kl.* CXIV, 465, 468), identifies Geizeric with the epic Gizurr Grýtingaliði, the hardy counsellor of the Reidgothic King Angantýr. Though the

Grýtingar are Greutungi, Ostrogoths, the theory may be plausible. The conclusion of the legend reflects the battle in Gaul A.D. 451, Angantýr being the Roman governor A(g)ëtius, Hlǫðr the Frank Chlodio, Humli the Hunnic King Attila (Humbers rois des Hunus in Wace's *Brut*, l. 1331). This Armageddon might very well have contained a fourth grand hero of that age, the Vandal Geizeric. Though his rank and nationality had been obliterated, we should recognise a well-known side of his character, viz. his inclination for stirring up conflicts (cp. Jordanes, XXXIII, 168: 'ad sollicitandas gentes providentissimus, semina contentionum jacere, odia miscere paratus').

The Gothic battles of the *Hervararsaga* are fought partly on Vandalic ground, on the plain of the Lugoi *Dunoi near the Miriquidui.

The two mythical Vandalic brothers Hertnid and Herther in the German legend are represented as defenders of the Gothonic soil against the Slavs. One German poem, which is unfortunately lost, had the title *Der Wilzen sturm*, i.e. 'the storm of the Slavs called Veletabi'. Similar German legends were translated into Old Norse in the cycle called *Thidrekssaga*. They describe in a lengthy way the battles and victories of the invading Slavs, whose chief representatives are the eponymous King Vilcinus and King Osantrix (*-rix* a Vandalic form ?, cp. Gothic *reiks*).

Subsequent ages confused the extinct Vandals partly with the Winnili or Langobards, partly with the victorious Slavs or Wends (cp. 'Wandalus id est Winid', Steinmeyer and Sievers, *Glossen*, IV, 540, No. 389 (*Cod. Monacensis*, Cat. 14,429)). This incorrect terminology was certainly in most cases a learned 'ornament', but probably also occurred in popular speech.

Lit. Heinzel, *S.B. d. Wien. Akad. phil.-hist. Kl.* CXIV; Much, *Zeitschrift*, XXXIII, 1 seq. and LXII, 142; *idem*, in Hoops, s.v. Δοῦνοι; *idem*, *Wandalische Götter*; Schütte, *Arkiv*, XXI, 30; *idem*, *Oldsagn om Godtjod*, 110; Neckel, *Beiträge z. Eddaforschung*, 256; Symons, *Grundriss*, 2nd ed. III, 677; Heusler in Hoops, s.v. *Hunnenschlacht.*

F. §§ 141–144. *THE BASTARNIC OR PEUKINIC SUB-GROUP OR BRANCH*

§ 141. Names.

1. Lat. Bastarnae (*Res gest. Aug.* v, 52, tarn..., Tacitus), Basternae (inscr. and Pliny); M.Lat. Vasternae, Vasterni; Gr. Βαστάρναι (Eratosthenes, third century B.C., cited by Strabo, II, 93), Βαστέρναι. Mountains: Lat. Alpes Bastarnice, i.e. the Carpathians (*Tab. Peuting.* fourth cen-

tury A.D.). Fortress: Gr. Βαστέρνας (near Odessos, Procopius, *De Aedific.* IV, 11). Obscure. Derivative suffix as in Goth. *widuwairna* 'an orphan'.

Lit. Zeuss, 127; Ihm in Pauly-Wissowa, s.v.; Schönfeld, s.v. (with lit.); Schütte, (Norw.) *Hist. Tidsskrift*, 1917, 6 and 11; Much in Hoops, s.v.; Löwenthal, *Wörter u. Sachen*, VIII, 177; *Reallexikon der Vorgeschichte*, s.v.; Bauer, *S.B. d. Wien. Akad. phil.-hist. Kl.* CLXXXV, 2. Abt.; Jacobsohn, *Zeitschrift*, LXVI, 232.

2. Lat. Peucini (Pliny, Tacitus, first century A.D.), Peucenni (inscr.), Peuci (Trebellius, third to fourth centuries; Ammianus, fourth century); Gr. Πευκινοί (Strabo, first century A.D.), Πεῦκαι (Zosimus, I, 42, fifth century). Island: Gr. Πεύκη 'pine'. The ethnicon originates from the Greek name of a wooded island situated in the Danubian Delta (cp. Scymnus, *Geogr. Graec. Min.* I, 228, 789–790). The Gothonic islanders may have called themselves *Peukōz, whereas Peucini looks like a Latin or Graeco-Latin enlargement, perhaps formed in order to embrace the entire sub-group or branch. We do not understand why Holder registers the name as 'Celtic', as the root is Greek, and the suffix *-in* is extremely rare among the continental Celts, much rarer than among the Gothonic nations. Ptolemy's 'mountain Peuke' in Galicia, i.e. Lysa Gora, was no doubt artificially named by the author of his prototype E, a learned geographer who introduced a regular system of 'ethno-topic denomination', e.g. Wends with Wendic gulf and mountains (cp. our monographs, *Beiträge*, XLI, 41, and *Ptolemy's Maps*, 129, 130).

Lit. Zeuss, 127; Grimm, 461; Müllenhoff, IV, 536; Holder, *Altcelt. Sprachschatz*, s.v. *Peuce*; Much in Hoops, I, 178; *idem*, *Der Eintritt der Germanen* (*Germanistische Forschungen*); Tackenberg, *Die Bastarnen* (*Volk u. Rasse*, IV, 232).

§ 142. Sub-divisions.

1. Lat. *Sidones (Valerius Flaccus, *Argon.* VI, 95, first century B.C.; Sidonicae habenae, in a description of the Bastarnae); Gr. Σίδονες (Strabo, first century B.C.), Σίδωνες (Ptolemy, second century). Personal name: Quadic Sido (Tac. *Ann.* XII, 29; the brothers Vangio and Sido are obviously a couple with intentional ethnic nomenclature). Etymology: 'side', i.e. 'coast' or perhaps 'slope of a mountain'. It is superfluous with Holder to have recourse to a Celtic word for 'peaceful', and geographical etymologies are always preferable to constructions of the

fanciful speculative sort. Home: on the slopes of the mountains east of Germany (Ptol. II, 11, § 10).

Lit. Zeuss, 127; Grimm, 459; Müllenhoff, II, 325; Much, *Beiträge*, XVII, 136; *idem*, *Zeitschrift*, XXXIX, 37; *idem*, in Hoops, I, 177, 178, III, 190, IV, 171; Holder, *Altcelt. Sprachschatz*, s.v.; Schönfeld, s.v.; *idem*, in Pauly-Wissowa, s.v.; Schütte, (Norw.) *Hist. Tidsskrift*, 1917, 6; Westberg, *Thèse de l'acad. de St Pétersb.* VIII, 6, 5, p. 27 (erroneous equation: Sidones = Sitones = Issedones).

2. Gr. Ἄτμονοι (Strabo, VII, 306, first century A.D.). Personal name: Gr. Ἀτμών (a barbarian, *Etymologicum magnum*, ed. Gaisford, 1848, 715). Obscure. We have suggested an equation with the Lugian tribal name Ὀμανοί (Ptol.), but if Atmôn really belongs to Atmonoi, the suggestion scarcely holds good, as the root of Omanoi must be Man- (cp. the Tacitean form Manimi, see § 137, 3). Home: north of the Sidones, if the sequence Atmonoi, Sidones, Peukinoi in Peuke, is to be taken as indicating the relative positions; the localisation would agree with that of the Omanoi (Ptol. II, 11, § 10).

Lit. Zeuss, 127; Much, *Beiträge*, XVII, 36; Schönfeld, s.v.; Schütte, *Ptolemy's Maps*, 113. For Ἀτμών see K. Schmidt, *Berl. Phil. Wochenschrift*, XXVII, 1106.

3. Lat. Bastarnae, etc. (cp. § 141, 2). We suppose that the collective name originates from a sub-division. Ptolemy records Bastarnai, Sidones, and Peukinoi separately, a fact that is of course not strictly conclusive. Home: north-east of the Alpes Bastarnice (*Tab. Peuting.*), i.e. the Carpathian mountains.

4. Lat. Peucini, Peuci, etc. (cp. § 141, 2). Sub-division according to Strabo, VII, 306. Home: the island Peuke in the Danubian Delta (cp. Strabo, *l.c.*).

Survey of types of names.

We regard the Short type Sido, first century B.C., as older than the Long type Bastarna, though the latter appears in literature some two centuries earlier. The Sidones remained for a longer while unknown to the Greek geographers, owing to their position in a distant inland country, but this position is *primary* from the point of view of Gothonic expansion. The Bastarnae were early known as pioneers interfering with the Greek area on the Black Sea, but this position is *secondary* from the point of view of Gothonic expansion. The Gothonic forms Atmonoi and Peukines are too questionable to allow of chronological classification.

§ 143. Ethnic Position.

The rank of the Bastarnae as a Gothonic sub-group is stated by Pliny, IV, 99: 'Germanorum genera quinque. Vandili...Ingyaeones... Istriaones...Hermiones...quinta pars Peucini, Basternae'.

Strabo, VII, p. 306, supplements his evidence by mentioning three Bastarnic sub-divisions, the Atmonoi, Sidones, and Peukines.

The collective use of the names Bastarnae and Peucini is probably of Graeco-Latin origin.

We have no direct justification for questioning Pliny's view of the Bastarnae, but it must be noticed that their claim to form a separate sub-group co-ordinate with the East Gothonic, etc., stands and falls with his authority. If the problematic equation Atmonoi = Lugoi Omanoi could be supported by more solid evidence, we might be led to the conclusion that the Bastarnae were an offshoot of the East Gothonic group, and thus, at the best, a branch co-ordinate with Goths, Lugians, and so on.

Reasons why Pliny conceived the Bastarnae as a sub-group might be sought in their geographical isolation and in their intermixture with foreign races.

But whether we consider the Bastarnae as a 'sub-group' or as a mere subordinate 'branch', their susceptibility to foreign influences must be regarded as the most prominent feature of their national individuality, from the Gothonic point of view. Though Pliny unhesitatingly refers them to the 'Germanorum genera', and an inscription (*CIL.* VI, 4344) mentions an Imperial guard 'Nereus nat(ione) German(us) Peucennus', both Strabo and Tacitus notice that their Gothonic nationality had been made a matter of doubt. Strabo says: 'almost of Gothonic nationality'. And Tacitus describes the Peucini thus, *Germ.* 46: 'Peucinorum... nationes Germanis an Sarmatis ascribam, dubito...sermone, cultu, sede ac domiciliis ut Germani agunt. sordes omnium ac torpor procerum; connubiis mixtis nonnihil in Sarmatarum habitum foedantur...hi tamen inter Germanos potius referuntur, quia et domos figunt et scuta gestant et pedum usu ac pernicitate gaudent: quae omnia diversa Sarmatis sunt in plaustro equoque viventibus'.

The alleged laziness of the noblemen agrees with the statement of Dio Cassius, LI, 34, that the Bastarnae are addicted to drink—a well-known Gothonic inclination.

The handiness of the foot-soldiers is illustrated more fully by Livius, XLIV, 26, and Plutarch, *Aemilius Paulus*, 12. The Bastarnae had adopted the institution of 'parabatai', i.e. the runners who accompanied the horsemen in full course, clinging to the manes or bridles. The same custom exists among the Highland Celts of to-day, and is mentioned among some South-western Gothonic tribes (cp. Caesar, *Bell. Gall.* I, 48). Bastarnic bridles called 'Sidonicae habenae' are mentioned by Valerius Flaccus, *Argon.* VI, 95, a fact indicating that the combined Bastarnic arm of cavalry and 'parabatai' was well known among the Romans.

According to Furtwängler, *Intermezzi*, 68 seq., Bastarnic captives on the triumphal monument of Trajanus at Adamklissi in Moesia Inferior are represented with oval shields and with 'pig-tails' recalling the Swabian mode of dressing the hair; so, e.g., on the Metopes 4, 6, 37. According to Schmidt, I, 465, the Bastarnae represented on the column of Trajanus wear the same Swabian 'pig-tails'. We are, however, not quite convinced that the barbarians concerned are correctly identified as Bastarnae.

The constitution was republican, as among the Lugians, Germans, and Saxons. A plurality of princes is mentioned (cp. 'reges Bastarnarum', *CIL.* XIV, 3608; see Schmidt, I, 465). Perhaps expressions like 'reges' and 'Clondicus regulus' (Livius, XLIV, 26) are not so conclusive as Schmidt thinks; but, *a priori*, we must expect republicanism among the Bastarnae, as this constitution prevailed among their Lugian-Vandalic neighbours.

Lit. Zeuss, 127; Grimm, 458; Müllenhoff, II, 105 note 2, IV, 119, 512; Tomaschek, *Göttinger Gelehrter Anzeiger*, 1888, 301; Much, *Beiträge*, XVIII, 38; *idem*, in Hoops, s.v.; *idem*, *Germanistische Forschungen*, 10; Ihm in Pauly-Wissowa, s.v.; Kauffmann, I, 402; Schumacher, *Mainzer Zeitschrift*, IV, 1 seq. and 12; Brunner, *Deutsche Rechtsgeschichte*, 2nd ed. I, 183; Schmidt, I, 459, 464.

§ 144. History.

After the Teutones and 'Guiones' of Pytheas, fourth century B.C., the Bastarnae and Sciri represent the second stratum in Gothonic history, and as active players on the historical scene they are absolutely first.

The starting-point of the movement may be indicated by the position of the Sidones on the slopes of the Bohemian mountains. Hence the Bastarnae proper went down the Dniester to the Black Sea about 200 B.C. Pseudo-Scymnus, *Periplus Pontus Euxini*, v. 797, mentions them as 'newcomers' (ἐπήλυδες); his source must be the geographer Demetrius, who lived in Callatis near the Danube 200 B.C. (cp. Müllenhoff, II, 104). The migration chiefly affected Dacian territories.

'Galates', Sciri, and Scythians attacked the Greek colony of Olbia about 190 B.C. (*CIG.* 2058 B). The 'Galates' are perhaps Bastarnae.

After preliminary negotiations in 182, the Macedonian King Philip V in 179 caused the Bastarnae to attack the Illyrian tribe of Dardani; the Bastarnae were led by their 'regulus' Clondicus, who is the first known Gothonic person in history. They had mobilised 10,000 horsemen and 10,000 foot-soldiers; but the undertaking led to no conquest south of the Danube (cp. Livius, XXXIX, 34, 4 seq., XL, 5, 10, 57, 58; Polybius, XXV, 6; Plutarch, *Aemilius Paulus,* 11, 12; inscr. in Fiebiger-Schmidt, *Inschriftensammlung zur Gesch. der Ostgermanen,* No. 4). Afterwards they attacked the Greek colony of Istros at the mouth of the Danube (cp. inscr. *ibid.* No. 7). Probably their settlement on Peuke near the Celtic town of Noviodunon took place about this time.

Bastarnae fought Rome as mercenaries of the Bosporan King Mithradates, 88–61 B.C.; hence the 'Bastrenae' mentioned by Pliny, VII, 98, as conquered by Pompeius (cp. Schönfeld, 45). As allies of the Greek colonies, they defeated the proconsul Antonius at Istros 61 B.C. (Dio Cassius, XXXVIII, 10, LI, 26).

The powerful Dacian King Boirebistas must have subjected the Southern Bastarnae (cp. Schmidt, I, 461), but his death, 45 B.C., released them. Crassus repulsed their invasion of Macedonia 26 B.C.; the Romans advanced to the Danube and the Bastarnae of Peuke became their subjects (cp. Dio Cassius, LI, 23; Livius, *perioch.* 134; Victor, *Epit.* I, 7).

In 14 B.C. the Western Bastarnae (i.e. Sidones) were temporarily reduced to subjection by a Roman army starting from Carnuntum (cp. an inscr., Fiebiger-Schmidt, No. 8; Schönfeld, s.v. *Sidones*). The racial mixture already prevailing about the Dniester was increased when the Sarmatian tribe of Jazyges settled on the river Teiss, c. A.D. 60. The Bastarnae took part in occasional conflicts, as mercenaries or, as in the Marcomannic war 166–180, as enemies of Rome. They were fighting on the side of the Goths when they were defeated by the Emperor Claudius at Naissus (Nish) A.D. 269 (*Scr. hist. Aug. v. Claud.* VI, 1–2; Zosimus, I, 42, 1; cp. Rappaport, *Einfälle der Goten,* 84). About 100,000 Bastarnae were driven out by the Goths and received by the Emperor Probus in

Thrace A.D. 280 (*Scr. hist. Aug. v. Probi*, XVIII, 11; Zosimus, I, 71, 1). Diocletianus received another band in Thrace A.D. 295 (Eutropius, IX, 25).

From this time, the Bastarnae disappear from history, their name becoming a mere ornament of poetical and rhetorical phrases. Their last onomastic trace is the fortress of Basternas near Odessos, mentioned in a Byzantine chronicle A.D. 1188 (cp. Tomaschek in Pauly-Wissowa, s.v.).

Lit. Zeuss, 127, 442; Grimm, 458; Müllenhoff, II, 104 seq.; Wietersheim-Dahn, *Gesch. d. Völkerwanderung*, (see Index); Tomaschek, *Göttinger Gelehrter Anzeiger*, 1888, 300; Bremer, § 92; Ihm in Pauly-Wissowa, s.v.; Schmidt, I, 459 seq.; Much in Hoops, s.v.

II. §§ 145-147. THE WEST GOTHONIC LINGUISTIC SUB-GROUP

§ 145. Name.

Germ. West-Germanen. This is a learned philological term, following naturally from the use of the collective term 'Germanen', and dating from the beginning of the nineteenth century. Translations are used in Dutch and Scandinavian. In English, the corresponding form 'West Germans' in the sense of West Gothonic nations is rarely used, though it is found in Chambers' *Widsith* (1912) and in Stjerna's *Essays on Beowulf*, translated by Clark Hall (1912). The same difficulty seems to be felt about the use of the term in Italian, for Bertoni, *L' elemento germanico nella lingua italiana* (1914), uses the German form in quotation marks: 'westgermanisch' (p. 31).

§ 146. Sub-divisions.

{1. Germans ('Dutch' in American terminology, i.e. Germ. Deutsche).
{2. Dutchmen.

From the linguistic point of view often taken together as the 'German section' in a wider sense.

{3. Anglo-Saxons.
{4. Frisians.

From the linguistic point of view often taken together as the 'Anglo-Frisian section'.

§ 147. Ethnic Position.

The West Gothonic linguistic unity is an obvious and acknowledged fact, cp. §§ 32–34. Here we only emphasise some few criteria of ethnic importance.

1. Phonetics. The loss of final *-z*.

2. Grammar. Substitution of a form ending in *-i* (optative or aorist ?) for the 2nd pers. pret. indicative: O.E. *bude*, O.H.G. *buti*; cp. Goth. *baust*, O.N. *bautt* 'you ordered'.

3. Personal names. A favourite German and Anglo-Saxon type is *berht-* 'bright', which is avoided in North and East Gothonic[1] (cp. Meyer-Lübke, *S.B. d. Wien. Akad. phil.-hist. Kl.* CXLIX, 2, 20 and 57). However, it appears also to be a foreign element in Frisian names.

4. Place names. German and Anglo-Saxon types, some of which are found also in Frisian, are: 'Brook, Field, Ford, Hurst, Worth'. However, we do not know whether they were used in East Gothonic.

5. Names of offices. Germ. *her-zog*, O.E. *here-toga* 'duke'; O.H.G. *scult-heizo*; O.L.G. *skuld-hētio*; O.E. *scyld-háta*; O.Fris. *skelt-ā(ta)* 'sheriff'; O.L.G. and O.E. *scop* 'poet'.[2]

6. Religious names. Germ. *ostern*, Engl. *easter*; cp. the O.E. vernal goddess *Eostre*.

In face of such linguistic evidence, we are struck by the meagreness of other phenomena reflecting the ethnic community. First of all, the West Gothonic nations have no old collective name, corresponding to 'Vandili' alias 'Goths' for the East Gothonic nations, or to 'Danes', 'Northmen', 'Rus' for the North Gothonic nations. And whereas the ethnogonies cited by Pliny and Tacitus seem to recognise the unity of the Vandili, they know of two or three West Gothonic branches without any unity. Some German-Dutch-English-Frisian community of civilisation is certainly implied by the vocables given above, classes 3–6, but their number is not imposing, and several of them might be counterbalanced by Anglo-Scandinavian correspondences; beside the Germ.-Engl. *scop* 'poet' there is, e.g., the Engl.-Scand. *þyle-þulr*. History

[1] Bjartmarr in the *Hervararsaga*, III, does not count, as this saga deals largely with South Gothonic persons.

[2] Germ. *graf*, O.E. *gerēfa* (whence Engl. *sheriff*), Fris. *grēfa*, are usually taken as parallel forms, but this etymology is rejected by Kluge, *Etym. Wörterb.*; *graf* belongs to Got. *ga-grēfts* 'order', *gerēfa*, *girœba* is derived from *róf* 'number'.

records no West Gothonic commonwealth or common political action. The Gothic Church and literary language and script as symbols of the East Gothonic community (cp. Procopius) have no analogy in West Gothonic. The West Gothonic states were never—either voluntarily or by force—united under one ruler, as was Scandinavia during the Kalmar Union. It would be impossible to find a West Gothonic analogy of those old Icelandic statutes which treat Norwegian, Swedish, and Danish visitors as favoured guests, to be preferred to the 'foreign nations'. Nor would any of the West Gothonic languages have been acknowledged as a symbol of unity within the entire community, as the 'Danish Tongue' was taken to symbolise North Gothonic nationality. To sum up, the West Gothonic nations remain a philological category, and nothing more.

These negative facts ought to be emphasised, because the almost excessive use of the term 'Westgermanen' must inevitably produce the impression that the nations concerned formed of old a recognised unity similar to that of the creedsmen of the Gothic Church or the people speaking the 'Danish Tongue'. No idea could be more misleading. To make a neat distinction between the North and West Gothonic tribes, and to classify, e.g., the ancient Jutlanders as belonging to the one or the other category, would be a grave mistake. It would be taken as implying that the ancient Jutlander as a 'West Gothonic' citizen would have felt more familiar with the remote Bavarian or Upper Frank than with the neighbouring Dane. So we should be led to obviously absurd conclusions. The Jutlander of those days could neither love nor hate the 'Westgermanen', because the name did not yet exist and the ethnic category has never existed. The 'Westgermanen' are a creation of modern philologists, useful for grammatical purposes, but only a chimera in ethnic and political history.

For these reasons, we have designated the West Gothonic community vaguely as a 'linguistic sub-group', in order to indicate that it is, from the ethnic point of view, a somewhat hypothetical quantity, which must yet be kept separate so as not to confuse the methodical arrangement. If the 'West Gothonic sub-group' had really been equivalent to the East Gothonic, etc., the sub-divisions called Germans, Dutchmen, Anglo-Saxons, and Frisians, ought to have been registered as 'branches', parallel with the Goths, Burgundians, Vandals, etc., in the East Gothonic sub-group. But in our opinion such a scheme is not justified. From an ethnic point of view, the West Gothonic common denominator must be eliminated as imaginary, and the German, Dutch, Anglo-Saxon, and Frisian sections must be recognised as 'sub-groups', not as 'branches'. But, for historical reasons, we must treat Germans and Dutchmen as one in the earlier stages.

III. §§ 148–208. THE GERMAN-DUTCH OR SOUTH GOTHONIC SUB-GROUP

A. §§ 148–152. *THE SUB-GROUP AS A WHOLE*

§ 148. Names.

1. O.H.G. Theodiscun, Theotiscun; O.L.G. Thiudisca liudi; M.H.G. Diutsche, Tiu(t)sche, Tiutsch-man; M.L.G. Dudesche; M.Dutch Dietsche, Duutsche, Duitsche; N.H.G. Teutsche, Deutsche, Deutsch-länder; American-English Dutch; N.Frisian Tschösche; O.N. þjóð-verjar, þjóð-verskir menn; Dan. Ty(d)skere, Ty(d)sk-mænd; M.Lat. Theodisci, Theudisci, and (learned) Theutones, Teutones, Theutonici; Ital. Tedeschi, Todeschi; M.Fr. Tieois, Tyois, Tiches; Fr. Tudesques ('ancient Germans'). Name of country: H.G. Deutsch-land; O.N. þýð-verska; Lith. Tautà. Derived from Gothon. *þeuð-*, Goth. *þiuda* 'people'. The mediaeval derivation erroneously assumes that the Teutones of the fourth century B.C. were 'Deutsche' in the modern sense of the word. Colonies of them certainly survived in South-west Germany, and 'laeti Teutoniciani' appear in the *Not. dign. Occ.* XLII, 33, fourth century A.D., but a connexion with the name of 'Deutsche' can scarcely be assumed. On the other hand, there is a Gothonic adjective **þeuðisk-*, meaning 'popular', found both in Gothic and Old English. It is generally assumed that this term was originally applied to the popular idiom, as opposed to the learned language of the Roman Church, and that it later gave rise to a name for the nation. It was the Emperor Otto the Great (936–973) who first styled himself Rex Theutonicorum. It does not appear that 'Deutsche' had been used as a substantive before his time.[1]

[1] A noteworthy statement occurs in Freculph's *Chronicle*, ninth century A.D.: 'Scanza, de qua Gothi et ceterae nationes *Theotisci* exierunt'. The name of Theotisci here has a vague sense, to be interpreted both as 'Germans proper' and as 'Gothonic nations'. From the latter point of view, the evidence ought to have been cited in our vol. I, § 20.

Lit. Zeuss, 63; Grimm, *Grammatik*, 3rd ed. I, 12; *idem*, *Gesch. d. deutschen Sprache*, 789; *idem*, *Wörterbuch*, s.v.; Grimm and Rask in *Briefwechsel der Gebr. Grimm mit nordischen Gelehrten*, hrsg. v. E. Schmidt; Germ. dictionaries by Schmeller, Benecke, Lexer, Kluge; Verwijs and Verdam, *Middelnederl. woordenboek*; Frank van Wyk, *Etymol. woordenboek*; Wackernagel, *Gesch. d. deutschen Litt.* 2nd ed. I, 63, 70; Schütte, *Racenavnet og Racetanken*, in the periodical *Norden*, 1904–5; *Deutsche Erde*, IX, 76; te Winkel, *Grundriss*, 2nd ed. I, 785; Behaghel, *ibid.* 4th ed. II, § 1: Dove, *Studien zur Vorgeschichte des deutschen Volksnamens*; Howorth, (Engl.) *Hist. Review*, XXIII, 424; Neckel, *Germanen und Kelten* (*Kultur u. Sprache*, VI, 38 note 1); Braune, *Althochdeutsch u. Angelsächsisch* (*Beiträge*, XLIII, 436 seq.). Cp. vol. I, §§ 20 and 21.

2. Engl. Germans; Lat. Germani; Gr. Γερμανοί (N.Gr. pronounced: Yermani).[1] Originally the name of a Belgian tribe; later applied to the Franks. First instance in English 1552 A.D. (cp. Bradley in the *Oxford Engl. Dict.*).

Lit. See vol. I, § 19.

3. O.H.G. *Frankun (frenkisgiu zunga, Otfrid v. Weissenburg, eighth century),[2] i.e. the tribe of Franks.

Lit. Wackernagel, *Gesch. d. deutschen Litt.* 2nd ed. I, 63, 70; *Deutsche Erde*, IX, 79.

4. O.N. Saxar; Finn. Saksalaiset; Esthon. Saksad, Saksa-mēs, Saksa-kēle-mēs. Eponymous hero: O.N. Saxi, Sunnmanna gramr ('Saxon, king of the Southmen', *Goðrúnarkviða*, III, str. 6). Name of country: O.N. Sax-land; M.Fr. Sessuyne; Fin. Saksan-maa. Place name: M.Dan. Saxæ-gildæ-strætæ ('Street of the Saxon guild' in Lund, Scania). Originally the tribe of Saxons.

Lit. *Deutsche Erde*, IX, 79; Wiedemann, *Esthnisch-deutsches Wörterbuch*, s.v. *kēl* ('language').

5. O.N. Sunn-menn, i.e. 'South-men'. Cp. 4.

6. M.H.G. Al-mân (Walther von der Vogelweide, ed. Lachmann Kraus, 37, 7; the term is adopted from Italian and is an ironic imitation of this language); Engl. Al-maynes; Fr. Alle-mands; Ital. Ala-magni; Portug. Ala-mãos; Cymric Ell-myn; Pers. Turk. Al-man. Name of country: Fr. Alle-magne; Portug. Alle-manha. Originally the tribe of Alemanni.

Lit. See vol. I, § 22; *Deutsche Erde*, IX, 81.

[1] Zulu Geleman; Chinese Dji-ërh-man. See also page 447.

[2] Tartarian (in Russia) Ferengi.

7. Rouman. Şvobi; Czech Švaby; Serb. Švabaci; Magyar Svábok. I.e. the tribe of Swabians.

Lit. See § 158; *Deutsche Erde*, IX, 80.

8. Wend. Bavarski; Serb. Bavaraci. I.e. the tribe of Bavarians.

Lit. Schmeller, *Bayer. Wörterbuch*, s.v. *Bayern*; Haupt and Schmeller, *Volkslieder der Wenden*, I, 3; Schmidt, II, 211; *Deutsche Erde*, IX, 81; cp. § 167, 3.

9. Slav. Němici; Rouman. Neamţi; N.Gr. Nemetzi; Magyar Német; Morocc. Nemzaui; Turk. Nemsauji. Generally derived from a Slavonic word for 'speechless'. The derivation from the ancient German tribe of Nemetes can scarcely be admitted, owing to phonetic and historical reasons (see vol. I, § 16).[1]

Lit. See vol. I, § 16; Grimm, 780; *Deutsche Erde*, IX, 79 and 81; Gleye, *ibid.* VIII, 214, X, 24; Feist, *Wörter u. Sachen*, XI, 44; Rich. Huss, *Die Nemetes bei Feist* (*Zeitschrift f. deutsche Phil.* LV, 264).

10. Lith. Võkiečei; Lett. Vácietīs. Name of country: Lith. Võkietija; Lett. Vácija. Obscure. The name has been compared with Finn. Vuohjola, i.e. Gotland (?). Cp. § 268.

Lit. Šafarik, *Slav. Altertümer*, I, 414; Müllenhoff, II, 107.

11. Hebrew Aschenaz. It originally means the Ascanii or Phrygians, but later is applied to the Jews of Germany, or the Germans.[2]

The names 1, 2, 4, 6, 9, (10?) may also be used to mean the entire Gothonic group, while No. 3 may embrace all Christian Europeans, the 'Ferengi' of the oriental horizon. No. 5, Sunnmenn, is a vague northern name for southern races.

No. 1, Deutsche, is supposed to have been an old collective term, alluding to the spoken language.

No. 2, Germans, temporarily a name of the Franks, is of Belgian origin.

Nos. 3, 6, 7, 8 originate from particular German tribes: Franks, Alemanni, Swabians, Bavarians; Ba- in the latter name is the Celtic tribe name Boji.

[1] In Magyar, the word Nemet also expresses 'Gothonic', and according to Ballagi, *Deutsches u. ungarisches Wörterbuch* (1881), there seems to exist no other synonym. E.g. a student of Gothonic philology, Germ. *Germanist*, is called *német jogtanár*.

[2] As a matter of curiosity, we add some exotic names, recorded in *Deutsche Erde*, IX, 78 seq.: Morocc. Bruss, i.e. Prussians; Ki-Suaheli Wadathchi; Chinese Tē-kwo-jēn 'German Empire's Men'; Chinese Da-goa 'Great Nation'; Sioux 'The People with the difficult language', and 'The honest people from beyond the great water'.

No. 4, Saxons, comes from the ancestors of the English nation, who have been Germanised in the ninth century.

Nos. 9, 10, 11 are names of obscure origin, given by foreigners.

As literary terms, Nos. 1, 2, 6, and 9 are most current.

§ 149. Sub-divisions.

A. Ancient division. Pliny, IV, 99; Tac. *Germ.* 2 and 38–43; Strabo, VII, 290; cp. Caesar, *Bell. Gall.* I, 51.

1. Erminones; Pliny, 'mediterranei'; Tacitus, 'medii'; embracing:
   - (*a*) Swabians proper, Pliny:
     - (*α*) Semnones, Strabo (Tacitus, '*caput Sveborum*') > the later North Swabians.
     - (*β*) Quadi, Strabo, Tacitus > the later Portuguese Swabians.
     - (*γ*) Later Alemanni > the present Schwaben.
   - (*b*) Marcomans, Caesar, co-operating with Swabians; Strabo, Tacitus, Swabians > the later Bavarians, with ancestral hero Ermin.
   - (*c*) Ermundures, Pliny (Strabo, Tacitus, Swabian); notice the initial element Ermun-; > the later Thuringians.
   - (*d*, *e*) Chatthi, Cherusci; their classification by Pliny as Erminones cannot be verified.
   - (*f*) Langobards; their classification by Strabo and Tacitus as Swabians seems somewhat questionable.
2. *Isteones, i.e. 'Cymbri', Pliny; Istaevones with presumable synonym Gambrivii, Tacitus > the later Franks with ancestral hero Istio.
3. Marsi; Tacitus > later absorbed by the Low Saxons.

B. Present division. Correspondences of the ancient branches with the chief dialects.

1. Swabians (Schwaben) < Alemanni. 2. Bavarians < Marcomans. 3. Thuringians and High Saxons < Ermundures. 4. Langobards (extinct). 5. Middle and High Franks and Hessians < Isteones and Chatthi.	High Germans.

6. Low Franks or Dutchmen < Isteones (including Franconised Saxons in Flanders).
7. Low Saxons or Niederdeutsche < Cherusci and Marsi (the Saxon-speaking population of Eastern Holland now counts as Dutch).

} Dutchmen and Low Germans.

C. Present division. More exact specification of dialects, according to Behaghel.

I. High Germans proper, Oberdeutsche.

1. 'Alemanni'. (*a*) Swiss and Alsatians; (*b*) Schwaben and Vorarlbergers.
2. 'Marcomans'. (*a*) Bavarians and Austrians; (*b*) Upper Pfälzers.
3. Upper Franks. (*a*) South Franks (Rhine-Neckar); (*b*) East Franks (Main-Saale).

II. Middle High Germans, Mitteldeutsche.[1]

4. Middle Franks. (*a*) Rhenish Franks; (*b*) Mosel Franks; (*c*) Ripuarians (about Cologne).
5. East Middle Germans, Ostmitteldeutsche. (*a*) Thuringians and High Saxons; (*b*) Silesians; (*c*) North Bohemians; (*d*) Inhabitants of Culmerland and Southern Ermeland in East Prussia.

III. Dutchmen and Low Germans, Netherlanders and Niederdeutsche.

6. Low Franks, partly of German, partly of Dutch nationality.
7. Low Saxons between the Zuider Zee and the Elbe, and in Holstein, South Slesvig, and Mecklenburg.
8. East Elbians, in Brandenburg, Pomerania, Posen, and Prussia.

Cp. the maps accompanying the following works: Kluge, *Von Luther bis Lessing*; Bremer, *Der grosse Brockhaus* (1929), s.v. *Deutsche Mundarten*; Behaghel, *Grundriss*, section *Geschichte der deutschen Sprache*, 1st ed. (1891) and 5th ed. (1928); W. Stammler, *Meyers Konversationslexikon* (1925), 536–537; Lecoutere and Grootaers, *Inleiding tot de Geschiedenis van het Nederlandsch*, 2nd ed. 240–241.

[1] From the linguistic point of view, we might add a group of European and American Jews, who form a separate nationality speaking a peculiar old dialect of Middle German called Yiddish.

The ancient division is fragmentary and problematical (cp. vol. I, § 27). Tacitus obviously exaggerates the size of the Swabian tribe, when he includes in it the Goths, the Angles, the Swedes, etc., and so his Svebi Langobardi may also be an error (though supported by Strabo and Ptolemy); that is to say, it may be simply a temporary political classification of Roman origin. Similarly, the Erminonic character of Pliny's Chatthi and Cherusci is open to doubt. Another obscure point is the position of the North Germans. The whole of the evidence is so controversial that it is hardly worth discussing.

The present division is into two sections, High German or 'Hochdeutsch' contrasting with Low German or 'Niederdeutsch'. The terminology varies, sometimes including Dutch within Low German, sometimes excluding it, cp. below, p. 77. Both High and Low German include Frankish sections; the majority of the Franks with the Low German dialect now constitute the separate Dutch nationality. Saxons also are found in both chief sections, but those of the High German state of Saxony are in reality Thuringian in origin, while those of Transylvania are Mosel Franks whose alleged Low German characteristics are limited to pronouns like *dat, wat* for *das, was*. In the Middle Ages, also, Bards (Langobards) and Swabians were included in both sections, but the High German Langobards have long since been Romanised; on the other hand, the use of the name Swabians only survives on High German soil. Further variations in the ethnic terminology will be mentioned in § 150, 5.

The frontier between High German (H.G.) and Low German (L.G.), as far as the High German Sound Shift is concerned, dates from the thirteenth century. It is generally called the 'Benrath Line', the name given to it by Wencker. It starts at the frontier of Walloon south of Limburg, passes Eupen (L.G.), Aachen (H.G.), Geilenkirchen, Erkelenz, Odenkirchen (all L.G.), and reaches the Rhine below Benrath (H.G.). From there the line bends towards the south-east, between Leichlingen-Burscheid (H.G.) and Solingen-Remscheid (L.G.), goes through Wipperfürt and Gummersbach, and reaches its southern extremity near Waldbröl (H.G.). Thence it continues eastwards, passing Olpe (H.G.), Freudenberg (L.G.), Berleburg, Frankenburg (H.G.), Sachsenberg (L.G.), Waldeck, Naumburg, Cassel, Heiligenstadt, Sachsa, Harzgerode (all H.G.). The line reaches the Elbe near Magdeburg (L.G.) and follows the river towards the east as far as Griebau and Wittenberg (H.G.); it passes

Luckau (L.G.), and finally reaches the western extremity of Polish territory at Schwerin (H.G.). A small High German enclave exists south of Cleve on the Lower Rhine, another round Klaustal in the Harz mountains; a larger isolated H.G. population occupies Culmerland and parts of Southern Ermeland in East Prussia.

On both sides of the Rhine, the frontier of High German almost coincides with that of the archbishopric of Cologne. This important see has contributed a good deal towards the spread of the High German type in an originally Low Frankish region (cp. Frings, *Das Alter der Benrather Linie*, *Beiträge*, XXXIX, 362).

From South-western Westphalia to the Elbe, the two linguistic sections generally meet at the ancient political frontier between Franks and Thuringians on the one side, and Saxons on the other. A High German Frankenburg and a Low German Sachsenberg still face each other to-day. The linguistic frontier between the Rhine and the Weser and between the Elbe and the Oder also fairly coincides with the frontier line of Frankish and Saxon architecture (cp. our map, Fig. 2). But High German has made several conquests, as in Sachsa, Marsfeld Eisleben, Merseburg, Halle, Bernburg, Köten, Dessau, Wittenberg. Bremer adds Frankfurt on the Oder, some districts north of the river Warte, and even the banks of the river Spree, so that Berlin ceases to be a H.G. enclave (cp. our map, Fig. 1, with a copy of the section concerned of Bremer's map). This conquest, however, has not yet been definitely established, and Behaghel does not accept it in the fifth edition of his map, published in 1928.

The division of High German between Middle and Upper German seems to be subject to some doubt. In earlier works, Middle German is taken as including High Frankish, Thuringian, High Saxon, and Silesian, while Upper German includes Alemannic and Marcomannic. So Kluge in *Von Luther bis Lessing*, Bremer in *Brockhaus' Konv. Lex.* and Behaghel in *Grundriss*, 1st ed. I, 534–535. But in his 5th edition, Behaghel separates South and East Frankish from Middle German and incorporates them with Upper German. The frontier starts from the French area west of Strassburg, passes between Saarburg-Lützelstein (M.G.) and Zabern-Ingweiler (U.G.), between Bitsch-Bergzabern-Rheinzabern (M.G.) and Reichshofen-Weissenburg-Mühlburg (U.G.), and crosses the Rhine between Germersheim (M.G.) and Philippsburg (U.G.); it goes on between Wiesloch-Ebersbach (M.G.) and

Waibstadt-Mosbach (U.G.), Amorsbach-Miltenberg (M.G.) and Buchen-Külsheim (U.G.), crosses the Main between Freudenberg (M.G.) and the mouth of the Tauber (U.G.), thence follows closely the west bank of the river as far as Lohr (M.G.) and Gemünden-Rieneck (U.G.), and passes between Brückenau-Kaltennordheim-Salzungen (M.G.) and Bischofsheim-Fladungen-Schmalkalden (U.G.); it goes along the crest of the Thüringer Wald towards the south-east; then again turns north-east, till the Saale is reached near Saalfeld; then east, crossing the Elster near Berga; then south, past Reichenbach, Auerbach, Falkenstein, Schöneck (all U.G.), and through the Erzgebirge into Western Bohemia; finally after passing Konstadt, Bleistadt, Schönlind, Neudeck, Schlackenwert, Duppau, Waltsch, Chiesch, Jechnitz, the line reaches the Czech area at Nečetin. The Northern German enclaves within the Czecho-Slovakian state are Middle German, those of Brünn are Middle Bavarian, and those of Budweis and Iglau are North Bavarian.

The following differences between Bremer's and Behaghel's schemes may further be noticed. Bremer regards the Bavarian Palatinate as Rhenish Frankish, whereas Behaghel incorporates its south-eastern extremity with South Frankish—a dialect which does not appear in Bremer's scheme. East Frankish according to Bremer (and Behaghel, 1st ed.) does not touch the Danube; but in Behaghel's 5th edition, the South Frankish dialect reaches the river opposite the Lech. Whereas East Frankish is by Bremer (and Behaghel, 1st ed.) regarded as Middle German, Behaghel's 5th edition unites both East and South Frankish with Upper German. The entire valley of the Lech south of Augsburg is Schwabian, according to Bremer; but according to Behaghel, § 133, the upper Lech valley is almost entirely Bavarian.

We accept Behaghel's altered scheme as correct. An important ethnic criterion is the use of the diminutive suffix *-l* in Upper German (incl. East and South Frankish) for *-chen* in Middle German and *-ken* in Low German (cp. Behaghel, § 130). This implies a certain intentional choice and may thus reflect ancient tribal divisions which have partially been effaced through secondary displacements. When this diminutive suffix occurs in regions which were not Frankish before A.D. 496, we may surmise that it betrays the survival of numerous Alemannic inhabitants after the conquest (cp. § 162).

W. Stammler's dialect map in Meyer's *Konversationslexikon*, 1925, differs from those of Behaghel and Bremer in Hungary where the enclaves west of Buda-Pest are represented as Middle German, not as Upper German.

The literary languages show a number of local types throughout the Middle Ages and even later. Each seat of government tried to impose its language on the district under its control. Important High German centres existed, e.g. in the Electorate of Saxony, in the Imperial residences Vienna and Prague, in Switzerland, and in the see of Cologne. There were Low Saxon centres in North Germany, and Dutch centres in the Netherlands. The High German church reformer Luther finally ensured the victory of High German among all populations that regard themselves as of German nationality. So only two literary types are left, viz. High German in Germany, Austria, and Switzerland, and Dutch in the Netherlands.[1] In the beginning of the nineteenth century, several Calvinistic churches in North-western Germany still used Dutch for their services, but nowadays the frontiers of states and of literary languages coincide.

From time to time, during and after the Middle Ages, observers have recorded the existence of German dialects. Though they contribute little positive to our knowledge, they show at least how far the contrasts were being realised.

An Icelandic abbot Nikulas in the twelfth century wrote an itinerary, published as *Alfrœði íslenzk* by the Samfund til Udgivelse af gl. nordisk Litteratur (No. 37). On p. 13 he describes the route of pilgrims going up the Weser. 'Thence it is a short distance to Nienburg (Nyioborg). Then follows Minden (Mundioborg). Now the tongues change. Thence it is two days' voyage to Paderborn (Pöddubrunni).' The localisation of the frontier is not correct, but the attention paid to linguistic phenomena is at any rate noteworthy.

The Bavarian poet Wernher the Gardener, thirteenth century, in the poem *Meier Helmbrecht* describes how a youth returning from abroad addresses his own people in Latin, French, Bohemian, Brabantic, and Saxon. One of them says, v. 744 seq.:

Als ich von im vernomen hān,	As I have heard from him,
so ist er ze Sahsen	he was born in Saxony
oder ze Brābant gewahsen.	or in Brabant.
Er sprach: 'liebe soete kindekīn';	He said: 'liebe soete kindekīn';
er mac wol ein Sahse sīn.	he may well be a Saxon.

[1] A third national literary type is the Yiddish of the Jews in Eastern Europe, England, America, etc. It is often written with Hebrew letters.

The father summons the young lad to speak German: 'sprich ein wort tiutischen!' (v. 759). Here the Saxon dialect is placed among the non-German tongues which are not understood by the Bavarians.

An East Frankish schoolmaster, Hugo von Trimberg, fourteenth century, composed a didactic poem *Renner* 'the Runner', wherein he characterises the High German dialects, v. 22,218 seq.:

Swāben ir wörter spaltent;	The Schwaben split their words;
die Franken ein teil sie valtent;	the Franks somehow fold them;
die Beire sie zezerrent;	the Bavarians distort them;
die During sie ūf sperrent.	the Thuringians expand them.

A Swiss schoolmaster, J. Helber, in 1523 speaks of three separate dialects used by the printers: (1) Mitteldeutsch, in Leipzig, Erfurt, Nuremberg, Würzburg, Frankfort, Mayence, Spires, Strassburg, and Cologne; (2) Donauisch, in Bavaria and Swabia proper; (3) Höchst Rheinisch, i.e. Swiss German.

The following early attempts at more exact observations concerning German dialects may be mentioned: Gessner, *Mithridates* (1555); *idem*, preface to Maaler, *Die Teutsch Sprach* (1561); Lazius, *De gentium aliquot migrationibus, sedibus fixis, reliquiis, linguarum initiis & immutationibus ac dialectis libri XII* (1557); Scaliger, *Diatriba de Europaeorum linguis* (1599); Schottel, *Ausführliche Arbeit von der Teutschen Haubt-Sprache* (1663).

Lit. On the early methodical ethnic and linguistic manuals of Zeuss, Grimm, Schleicher, Scherer, etc., cp. the bibliography of Raumer, *Gesch. der germ. Philologie*, 637 seq., and Paul, *Grundriss*, 2nd ed. I, § 31 seq.; Kluge, *Von Luther bis Lessing*; Socin, *Schriftsprache u. Dialekte im Deutschen*; Behaghel, *Deutsche Sprache* (*Grundriss*, 5th ed. with map and full bibliography); Kauffmann, *Deutsche u. niederländische Mundarten* (*Grundriss*, 2nd ed. I, v, with bibliography); Mentz, *Bibliographie der deutschen Mundartenforschung*; Bremer, *Ethnographie* in *Grundriss*, 2nd ed.; *idem*, *Deutsche Mundarten* in *Der grosse Brockhaus*, 15th ed. IV, with map, pp. 584–585 (the most specialised map existing); *ibid.* maps showing *Verkleinerungsformen* and *Neuhochdeutsche Diphthongierung*; Willy Pessler, map, *Die Hauptmundarten* in *Wörter u. Sachen*, III, 63; W. Stammler, map, *Deutsche Mundarten* in *Meyer's Lexikon*, 7th ed. III, 536–537; Lecoutere-Grootaers, *Inleiding tot de Taalkunde...van het Nederlandsch*, 237, with map *Kontinentaal Germaansch*, 240–241; Much, *Deutsche Stammeskunde*, 3rd ed.; O. Weise, *Die deutschen Volksstämme u. Landschaften*, 5th ed.; *idem*, *Unsere Mundarten* (with bibliography);[1] Wencker, *Sprachatlas des deutschen Reichs*;

[1] Characterises the Danish dialect of North Slesvig as 'German', a grave misrepresentation of facts. The same error disfigures Gerland, *Atlas der Völkerkunde* (1892), Fig. VII, and Robertson and Bartholomew, *An Historical Atlas of Modern Europe*, publ. by the Oxford Univ. Press (1924). The error has been corrected in Bartholomew's *An Advanced Atlas* (1930).

the contents summarised by Wrede, *Anzeiger*, XVIII–XXVIII, with a collective survey, *ibid.* XXV, 391. Linguistic anthology by Firmenich, *Germaniens Völkerstimmen*; Leopold, *Van de Schelde tot de Weichsel* (and for Dutch alone, van Ginneken, *Handboek der Nederlandsche taal*, I).

§ 150. Ethnic Position.

The existence of a German nationality is a linguistic and political fact which needs no further proof. In ancient times, however, it is latent. No classical authority refers to it; there exists no religious or poetical Germanism, no 'united Germany', and the limit between Germans and Anglo-Saxons is entirely confused.

The conception of early Germanism is made still more difficult by the absence of any attempt at an exact definition in the current manuals. The following observations, therefore, are merely preliminary.

1. The occurrence of the West Gothonic linguistic type may be a sufficient criterion, if Frisian or Anglo-Saxon origin is excluded on historical grounds. E.g., the element *-berht* ('bright') in names of the Portuguese Swabians excludes the possibility of Gothic origin (cp. Meyer-Lübke, *S.B. d. Wien. Akad. phil.-hist. Kl.* CXLIX, 2, 57), and compels us to assume that they were really Swabians proper, i.e. Germans. The same is true of the Portuguese royal name Berengaria, if it is genuinely Swabian; the Gothic form would be *Berengaisia or *Berengesia.

2. Common linguistic features distinguish German and Dutch from all other Gothonic languages, including Frisian and Anglo-Saxon. One such feature is the compulsory use of the prefix *ge-* in the past participle. A negative criterion is the absence of the Anglo-Saxon and Frisian palatalisation of *k* and *g*.

3. German and Dutch possess various names of offices in common: Germ. *graf*, Dutch *graaf* 'count'; Germ. *schöffe*, Dutch *schepen* 'judge lateral' (French *échevin*); Germ. *truchsess*, M.Dutch *drossāte* 'dapifer', 'steward'.

4. A typical German and Langobard name of office is *scherge* 'usher'.

5. The use of a German spoken dialect and of the German literary language characterises that entire community which we regard nowadays as German by nationality. But not all people speaking a German dialect are Germans by nationality; the Saxons of Eastern Holland count as Dutchmen, because they use the Dutch literary language.

Point 5 touches the somewhat perplexing variations in meaning of the terms 'Deutsch' and 'Dutch'. Gothonic *þeuðisk- 'popular' originally might be applied to Anglo-Saxon, to the language of the Netherlands, to German, and it is even found in Gothic. The mediaeval Netherlanders called their language Dietsc, later Duutsc, etc., whence the normal English signification of 'Dutch'. Similarly, the Germans called themselves Deutsch, i.e. 'Dutch' in the American-English sense of the word. Nederduitsch, Niederdeutsch, as contrasted with Hochdeutsch, might mean either Dutch or Low Saxon or both, and the synonym Nedderlendesch in the sixteenth century might include both sections. But after the Netherlands had formed a separate nationality and refused to accept Luther's High German literary language, they also ceased to use the name 'Dutchmen', which only remained in English; at the same time, Nedderlendesch ceased to be used for Low Saxon, Low German. The distribution of terms and dialects may be illustrated by means of a tabular survey.

'Nederland'

West	North-east
Dutch pol. nationality	Dutch pol. nationality
Dutch dialect	'Deutsch' (Saxon) dialect
Dutch literary language	Dutch literary language

'Deutschland'

West (L. Rhine)	Main area
'Deutsch' pol. nationality	'Deutsch' pol. nationality
Dutch dialect[1]	'Deutsch' dialect
'Deutsch' literary language	'Deutsch' literary language

Some further variations in the ethnic terminology may be considered. The North Germans and North-east Dutch speak a dialect called Saxon which is on German linguistic maps designated as German. The true Saxons, however, are those who came to England with the Angles, though the popular use of the name in this connexion persists only in the Celtic languages. The German Saxons include: (1) Saxons proper, who have been Germanised, but have kept their national name; (2) Frisians and Danes, who are equally Germanised and who have adopted the name of Saxons; (3, 4) Low Germans and High Germans who have kept their language, but have adopted the name of Saxons.

[1] So we must consider the so-called German dialect of the North-western Rhine Province.

The Langobards of Italy spoke a High German dialect, but never called themselves 'Deutsche', because they had migrated before this name assumed its collective signification. The *Chron. Salernitanum*, 978, certainly uses the phrase 'lingua todesca, quam olim Longobardi loquebantur', i.e. 'the Deutsch language, which the Langobards spoke in olden days' (cp. Bruckner, *Die Sprache der Langobarden*, § 2). But this statement may be due rather to the individual linguistic knowledge of the author than to a current Langobard terminology (cp. § 175).

The Jews, though speaking the German dialect of Yiddish, are not acknowledged as Germans unless they adopt the usual literary German language.

On the other hand, the North Frisians, though occasionally styling themselves and their language German, are not true Germans from the linguistic point of view.

There is no uniform *type of houses* in Germany. A common feature is the absence of the double-court plan, giving one yard for men and one for cattle, such as is found in Norway and Sweden. In numerous regions the houses have two storeys.

The following types may be observed (cp. the map, Fig. 2).

1. The 'compound house' ('einheitshaus, einbau'), uniting the dwelling-house, cattle stalls, and granaries under the same roof. The main entrance is from the gable end, not at the side, as in the English and Danish type. The Saxon house has one storey, the Alemannic and Bavarian ones have two. The main features of the Saxon type correspond to those of the Frisian 'hauberg', but the roof is constructed differently (cp. § 205, 4).

2. The Alpine-Bavarian 'double farmstead' ('paarhof'). A similar type is frequent in Denmark, especially in Western and Northern Jutland.

3. The 'T-house' ('dwarshus, krukhuis'), built in the shape of a T; it occurs on the lower Rhine both on German and Dutch soil. It may be compared with the 'gamma house', built in the shape of a Γ, which is found in Denmark; the Γ house appears on the Gautic island of Öland already in the Iron Age.

4. The Alpine-Bavarian irregular farmstead ('gruppenhof, haufenhof'), especially frequent in Kärnten and Steiermark. It is also found in Scandinavia, especially in West Gautland, Vermland, and North Norway.

5, 6. The Gotlandic, Norwegian, and Icelandic 'row farmstead' ('reihenhof'), and the Danish farmstead with three ranges (|‾‾|), do not seem to occur; at least, they are not mentioned in the current German manuals.

7. The Frankish yard, with isolated buildings placed irregularly, but enclosed by a regular wall. A 'Celtic-Frankish' and a 'Roman-Frankish' type are distinguished, but we have found no maps which represent their distribution.

8. The quadrangle ('vierkanthof') occurs in the Altmark (west of the Middle Elbe), in Eastern Bavaria, and in Oberösterreich. It is a type most characteristic of modern Denmark, including parts of South Jutland and the ancient Danish provinces Scania and Halland, and also occurs in Northern Sweden and Eastern and Northern Norway.

The distribution of the types of houses in Germany and the neighbouring countries is represented by Pessler (*Wörter und Sachen*, III, 64), and by Haberlandt (*Die Völker Europas*, 176–177). We have reproduced Haberlandt's map in a simplified form (Fig. 2). Pessler's and Haberlandt's maps are somewhat divergent (cp. our reproduction of Pessler's map of South-western Germany, Fig. 3; cp. also the map *Bauernhausformen* in *Der grosse Brockhaus*, 15th ed. IV, 624–625 (where, however, the Danish part of South Jutland is erroneously represented as belonging to the Saxon type)).

Chr. Ranck, *Kulturgeschichte des deutschen Bauernhauses* (*Aus Natur und Geisteswelt*, vol. 121), defines the main types of houses in Germany, as follows: 'Das Wesen dieser (ursprünglichen niederdeutschen) Form ist nirgends verwischt worden und ist selbst in dem scheinbar vom Hause des Niedersachsen ganz verschiedenen Organismus des friesischen Hauberges deutlich erkennbar. Es ist das Zusammenwohnen von Mensch und Vieh unter einem Dache und in einem Raume... Die Idee...ist jedenfalls höchst altertümlich' (p. 72).

'Als Merkmal der oberdeutschen Gruppe deutscher Bauernhausformen war die im ganzen Gebiete der Gruppe gleichartige, von den Räumen der Wirtschaft getrennte Wohnung bezeichnet worden' (p. 48).

'Der Hof mit mehreren getrennten und bald ohne jede Ordnung, bald um einen mehr oder weniger regelmässigen Hof zwanglos gruppierten Gebäude (möge) der "Haufenhof" genannt werden.[1] Er zeigt

[1] Also called 'Gruppenhof', 'group farmstead'.

deutlich seine Abstammung von der urgermanischen Hofanlage; seine Vertreter trifft man namentlich in Skandinavien und in den Alpen.

'Aus dieser Grundlage entwickelte der oberdeutsche Bauer...zwei weitere Gehöftformen,...das fränkische Gehöft und den "Einbau". Zum fränkischen Gehöft näherte er die einzelnen Hofbauten, Wohnung, Ställe, Scheune, Schuppen, einander und stellte sie um einen vierseitigen, meist rechteckigen Hof, der je nach der Zahl der vorhandenen Gebäude auf allen Seiten oder nur auf zwei oder drei Seiten von ihnen eingeschlossen war, wobei nach Behuf auch mehrere Gebäude unter einem Dache vereinigt wurden. Dieses fränkische Gehöft kommt...im ganzen mittleren Deutschland vor, von der Ruhr bis zu den Alpen, in Böhmen, Schlesien, Oberösterreich und Siebenbürgen. Manchmal steigert sich die Verbindung der einzelnen Gebäude so weit, dass sie an den Ecken des Hofes völlig miteinander verbaut sind und unter fortlaufendem Dache liegen' (p. 50).

'Die engste Verbindung von Wohnung, Stall und Scheune tritt aber ein, wenn alle drei unter einem Dache zum "Einbau" nebeneinander gelegt sind. Diese Einbauten finden sich vorzugsweise am Nordabhange der Alpen, im südlichen Bayern, im Elsass und im Schwarzwald, also in den alten Sitzen der Allemannen und Bajuvarier....Meist hat der Einbau noch weniger wichtige Nebengebäude, als Backhaus, Waschhaus u. dgl. um sich und nähert sich dann in seiner äusseren Erscheinung wieder dem "Haufenhofe"....Das Gebiet des Haufenhofes...finden wir in Innerösterreich, in Kärnten und in Steiermark' (p. 51).

The details of the single types of houses will be described in the paragraph 'Ethnic Position' under the special headings, Swabians, Marcomans, Franks, Low Germans, and so on.

Lit. There exist no works which try to define the characteristics of Germanism methodically from the point of view sketched above. The current linguistic and ethnological manuals generally forget to introduce a paragraph on the Germans as a whole; so, e.g., Zeuss, Behaghel, Bremer, Much, and Hoops' *Reallexikon*. We may, at most, find occasional scattered observations in various works cited in the lit. under the heading 'sub-divisions'. For particulars concerning the German house see the great manual published under the three headings: *Das Bauernhaus im Deutschen Reiche*, *Das Bauernhaus in Österreich-Ungarn*, *Das Bauernhaus in der Schweiz*.

§ 151. History.

As we mentioned in § 150, no German ethnic unity appears in ancient times. Perhaps the Swabians represent the Germans proper, while the tribes of North-west Germany may rather be Germanised aborigines (cp. the Chatthi with the Celt. Cassi).

The Swabian migration to Southern Germany and Eastern Gaul about 70 B.C. is the first known German movement.

In the first decades of our era, the Marcomannic King Maroboduus, after conquering Bohemia, tried to found a united Germany, consisting chiefly of Swabians, but including also members of the East Gothonic sub-group. He was opposed by the non-Swabian tribes of North-west Germany and defeated by their leader Arminius in A.D. 17. For some 500 years there was no further attempt to unite Germany.

After the break-up of Maroboduus' Empire, the republican constitution prevailed undisturbed in the larger part of the German territory; the model was probably adopted from Gaul, where republicanism was established in the second century B.C. The tribal district is called 'gau', as in Gothic; the West Germans use the same term as the Anglo-Saxons, 'hundred'.

Evidence shows that German civilisation contains the same element of loans from Celtic, Greek, and eastern sources as primitive Gothonic: *amt* ('office', Celtic) 'rich' (Celt.), *paida* ('leather jacket', Greek) 'hemp' (Scythian), 'silver'. The early Roman loan words, as we mentioned in vol. I, p. 101, are much more numerous than in Gothic. There are also several Roman words which are not found in Anglo-Saxon. Cp. for instance: (*a*) trade, payment: *decher* 'decade', *zins* (lit. *census*) 'taxation', O.H.G. *tehhamon* 'to pay tithes'; (*b*) house, kitchen, garden: *aduch* (dial.) 'aqueduct', *mauer* 'wall', *fenster* 'window', *speicher* 'store-house' ('spicery'), *schemel* 'stool', *zieche* 'pillow-case', *korb* 'basket', *schüssel* 'bowl', *kerze* 'candle', *tiegel* 'melting-pot', *eimer* 'pail', *pfister* 'baker', *weiher* 'pond', *kürbis* 'pumpkin', *wicke* 'vetch', O.H.G. *attarminza* 'ink'; (*c*) wine-dressing: *kelter* and *torkel* 'press', *trichter* 'funnel', *lauer* 'dregs'; O.H.G. *windemōn* 'to gather grapes'. From the Romans, the Germans also received some words of barbarian origin: *karch*, Celto-Lat. *carruca* 'carriage'; *pferd*, Celto-Lat. *paraveredus* 'horse'; *zelter*, Hispano-Lat. *thieldo* 'ambler'; O.H.G. *lorihhīn*, Hispano-Lat. *laurex* 'rabbit'.

After the conversion of the Goths to the Arian form of Christianity, in the fourth century, the Germans were subjected to their religious influence. One tribe speaking the German language, viz. the Langobards, became a member of the Gothic Church. Hence a number of ecclesiastical terms of Gothic or of exotic origin were introduced into German. Cp. Upper German *tult* < Goth. *dulþs* 'feast'; Germ. *barmherzig* 'merciful', *langmut* 'longanimity', both after Latino-Gothic models; *pfaffe* 'priest', *pfingsten* 'Whitsuntide', Bavar. *ertag* 'Tuesday', *pfinztag* 'Thursday', Graeco-Gothic terms; Germ. *samstag*, Goth. *sabbatō dags*, of Hebrew origin.

After 496, however, when the Franks adopted Roman Catholicism, the Gothic-Arianic line of German development was abandoned. From that time onwards, fresh elements from abroad come almost entirely from Rome and the Romance nations. The mutual relations of Romance and German civilisation grow so overwhelmingly rich that it is impossible to illustrate them here adequately by examples of loan words.

The beginnings of a recognised nationality properly called Germans have not yet been thoroughly investigated, but in reality seem to be sufficiently traceable.

The first rudimentary conception of Germans proper appears in the history of Dio Cassius, LXXI, 3, § 5, where he explains the title Germanicus given to the Emperor Marcus Aurelius after his victory over the Marcomans in A.D. 171; 'for the inland peoples', Dio adds, 'are by us called Germani'.

This statement, however, is rather a sort of compromise with the Roman triumphal style than a proof of Dio's own usual terminology. For in LIII, 12, § 6, he avowedly limits the name Germani to the inhabitants of Rhenish Belgium, and the territorial name Germania is by him exclusively applied to the districts west of the Rhine, except for the passage (LVI, 18), where Varus is called governor of Germania.[1]

To trace how the idea of Germans proper develops, we must start from Dio's limited terminology, and not from the vague beginnings of a more extensive conception. The same limitation is always found in the works of Claudianus, Agathias, Procopius, Venantius Fortunatus, Anonymus Ravennas (cp. our vol. I, p. 20).

Now, Rhenish Germania was occupied by the Franks and these, in the terminology of the authors cited, were the first people to be called by the name Germani. After their victory over the Alemanni in 496, the Franks temporarily united nearly all German-speaking and Dutch tribes

[1] When Kunze, *Die Germanen in der antiken Literatur*, II, 69, explains Dio's expression 'ἐς τὴν πολεμίαν', LVIII, 6, as meaning 'ἐς τὴν Γερμανίαν', he commits a serious mistake. Dio could only have written 'ἐς τὴν Κελτικήν' (as e.g. in LVI, 25).

of the homeland. Charlemagne completed the work by conquering even the Langobards in Italy and the Saxons, including their German-speaking fellow-citizens, 772–804.

It was a natural and necessary consequence that the Franks, as creators of a united Germany, should supply also the collective ethnic term. As a matter of fact, the name Franks was used for the Germans proper. So Otfrid von Weissenburg, ninth century, sings 'in the Frankish tongue'. And, in Latin literature at about the same time, a similar meaning was given to the synonym of Franks, viz. Germani.

Of the two synonymous terms, Franks and Germani, the Latin one persisted, and since 1552 has also been adopted from Latin literature into popular English.

The native term Franks was outstripped by the synonym Deutsche, which first appears in Germany in A.D. 788, and then in an edict of Charlemagne dated 813. It is Latinised as Theotonici, and first officially recognised by the Emperor Otto the Great (936–973) in his title of 'Rex Theutonicorum'. The political idea of Germanism is later expressed by the formula 'Römisches Kaiserreich Deutscher Nation'.

The Migration Age considerably enlarged the German *national area* towards the west and south, but at the same time Bohemia, the present state of Saxony, and all German regions east of the Elbe were lost to the Slavs

The next centuries witnessed the loss of the diaspora on Romance soil, viz. the Swabians in Portugal, the Langobards in Italy, the Varisti in Eastern Gaul, the Franks in the interior of Gaul. The advance of the Slavs still continued west of the Middle Elbe, favoured by the Frankish policy, and in 804 they annexed East Holstein from the Saxons.

Yet such losses were more than compensated by the steady gain of Germanism in the Rhenish regions and south of the Danube. Numerous Gallo-Romans had survived in the Mosel valley, in the mountains of the Palatinate, and in the Schwarzwald, etc. All these were gradually swallowed up. German wood-cutters and agriculturalists began clearing the mountain forests in the Alps and the Vosges, entering Italy both through the Tyrol and the Valais. Salzburg and the larger part of the Romance Tyrol were also Germanised.[1]

[1] It is, however, a great error, when v. Erckert, *Wanderungen und Siedelungen* (1900), represents the Germanisation as completed in the lower Mosel valley c. A.D. 500, in Salzburg c. 600, in the Tyrol c. 800.

The first great German movement towards the east caused the conquest of the Saxons (772–804) and the extinction of the Anglo-Saxon nationality on the continent. In the tenth century, the advancing Slavs and Magyars were stopped. Germanism gradually reconquered from the Slavs the lost areas east of the Elbe with the exception of Lausitz and the interior of Bohemia, and gained besides large parts of the ancient East Gothonic territory. As on the Romance frontiers, large mountain forests were cleared in the Böhmerwald, Erzgebirge, Riesengebirge, etc. German colonies spread among Russians, Magyars, Roumanians, Baltic nations, and Esthonians.

A north-westward and northward movement was also going on. The Frisian part of Groningen adopted the Low Saxon dialect and Germanism absorbed all Frisian areas along the North Sea coast from the river Ems to Husum in South Jutland, with the sole exception of some few thousands of Frisian-speaking people in Saterland and on Heligoland. Further, the Danes were driven back in South Jutland, though only slowly and in a limited area. From the thirteenth century onwards, the North German Hansa League established its boards of trade in London and in various Scandinavian towns; Visby on Gotland entered the League, the municipality of Stockholm was dominated by its Hanseatic members, and in Bergen, the leading mercantile centre of Norway, the board of the Hansa formed a practically autonomous city.

Since the thirteenth century, however, or since the Roman Catholic reaction against Lutheranism and Calvinism, the progress of Germanism has no longer been general. The Franco-German linguistic frontier has become stationary; at some points, however, French is advancing. On the Italian, Slavonic, and Magyar frontiers, German is only holding its own. It has especially suffered grave losses in the Venetian Alps and in the Southern Tyrol. Germanisation is still at work among some smaller neighbours, such as the Rhaeto-Romans in the Grisons, the Lithuanians in East Prussia, the Wends in the Lausitz, the Frisians and Danes in the German part of South Jutland. The Hansa colonies in Scandinavian towns have long since ceased to exist, but they are to some extent compensated by the waves of modern German emigration which reach Scandinavia as well as the countries overseas.

After the wars of independence against Spain 1568–1648, when Holland became independent, the inhabitants gave up the designation 'Dutch' = Germans, and since that time they have formed a separate Netherlandic nationality.

The total number of German-speaking people is about 90 millions (according to Brockhaus and Meyer).

(*a*) **States of chiefly German nationality:**	
Germany (1925)	61,000,000
Austria (1925)	6,370,000
Switzerland (1920)	2,750,000
(*b*) **Surrounding states which contain provinces with German nationality:**	
Belgium	100,000
Italy (Tyrol)	250,000
France (Alsace-Lorraine, 1910)	1,600,000
Poland (1921)[1]	1,059,000
Czechoslovakia (1921)[1]	3,200,000
(*c*) **Scattered colonies:**	
Denmark	20,000
Norway (1920)	4,200
Sweden (1920)	4,500
Great Britain (1921)[2]	12,300
Holland (1920)	5,600
France (apart from Alsace-Lorraine) (1921)	82,000
Hungary (1920)	520,000
Jugoslavia	750,000
Roumania	716,000
Baltic States	210,000
Russia and Siberia, more than	1,000,000
Syria, East Asia	20,000
South Africa	30,000
U.S.A., about	8-10,000,000
Canada	300,000
Mexico and various South American States	20,000
Argentina	130,000
Chile[1]	30,000
Brazil	600,000
Australia	100,000
	Total c. 90 millions

Lit. Zeuss; Grimm; Kluge, *Von Luther bis Lessing*; Socin, *Schriftsprache u. Dialekte im Deutschen*; Behaghel, *Die deutsche Sprache*; *idem*, *Deutsche Sprache* (*Grundriss*, 5th ed.); Bremer, *Ethnographie* (*Grundriss*, 2nd ed.); Much, *Deutsche Stammeskunde* (3rd ed. *Sammlung Göschen*, 126); Schlüter, *Deutsches Siedlungswesen*, in Hoops, I; Priebsch, *German Language* (*Encycl. Brit.* 1910). The national statistics and the history of national struggles are dealt with by R. Böckh, *Der Deutschen Volkszahl u. Sprachgebiet*; Schiern, *Nyere historiske Studier*;

[1] The official figure is supposed to be too low.

[2] In 1911 the figure was 53,300.

Dominian, *The Frontiers of Language and Nationality in Europe* (published by the American Geographical Society, with maps); *Deutschtum im Ausland* (*Der grosse Brockhaus*, 15th ed. p. 717); Carl Petersen and Otto Scheel, *Handwörterbuch des Grenz- u. Ausland-Deutschtums*; Periodicals: *Deutsche Erde, Das Deutschtum im Ausland, Der Kampf ums Deutschtum, Muttersprache.*

Maps and Atlases. K. Bernhardi, *Sprachkarte von Deutschland* (1844); Berghaus, *Physikalischer Atlas* (1848, 3rd ed. with *Ethnographischer Atlas* by Gerland, cp. footnote on p. 75); Nabert, *Wandkarte*; Kiepert, *Übersichtskarte der Verbreitung der Deutschen in Europa*; Langhans, *Alldeutscher Atlas*; v. Erckert, *Wanderungen u. Siedelungen der germanischen Stämme bis auf Karl den Grossen*; ethnographical maps in the atlases published by Wagner and Debes and Velhagen and Klasing and in André's *Handatlas*, 7th ed. (maps No. 31, 32, 41, 45, 47, 49, 60, 63, 67, 83); maps in *Der grosse Brockhaus*, 15th ed. vol. IV, viz. *Sprachverteilung*, pp. 664–665; *Das Deutschtum in Europa*; *Verbreitung des Deutschtums*; *Das Deutschtum in den Vereinigten Staaten von Amerika*, pp. 720–721; ethnographical maps of Middle Europe, published by the British Staff (1925). Institutes for the study of the German nationality abroad have been established in Stuttgart and Marburg.

§ 152. Legendary Traditions.

Although the Gothonic genetic myths dating from classical times afford no general representations of the Germans proper, such figures appear in mediaeval times, especially in Scandinavia, e.g. the eponymous Saxi, Sunnmanna gramr 'Saxon, king of the Southmen', in the *Goðrúnarkviða*, III, str. 6; King Granmar of Suðrmannaland in the *Ynglinga Saga*, 36, transferred to the Swedish Södermanland (?); Scatus, Alemanniæ satrapa in Saxo's history, p. 24.

The Gothic King Theodoric the Great becomes the standard representative of Germany in Danish ballads, whereas, according to native legends, the German Emperor, Frederick Barbarossa, sleeping in the mountain Kyffhäuser, will once resurge and save his country from distress.

The *Chronicon imperatorum et pontificum Bavaricum* (*Mon. Germ. SS.* XXIV, 222 seq.), of the thirteenth and fourteenth century, summarises the history of the Theutonici after the close of the great Migration Age—the ravages of the Huns, the invasion of the Slavs, and the German reconquest. Theutonici here means 'Teutons' in the modern English sense (Gothonic nations); but the chronicle of course deals chiefly with the author's countrymen, the Germans. In spite of its late date, it contains valuable ethnic traditions, preserved in no other sources.

An epic account of the Slavonic invasion was given in the poem called *Der Wilzen Sturm*, but unfortunately only the title has been preserved.

B. §§ 153–155. *THE ERMINONIC BRANCH, AND VARIOUS SOUTH GERMAN TRIBES OF INDISTINCT POSITION*

§ 153. Name.

Lat. Hermi(n)ones (Mela, III, 32; Pliny, IV, 99; Tac. *Germ.* 2, first century A.D.). Eponymous hero: O.Germ. Irmin, Irmino; M.Lat. Ermenus, Ermeno (*Generatio regum et gentium*). Gothonic *ermin-* means 'grand, mighty'; the Latin *h* is a secondary addition. Cp. O.E. *eormenláf* 'great legacy'. Müllenhoff compares Gr. ὄρμενος, participle of ὄρνυμι 'I lift up'. Erminones is a Simplex; the theory that it is a contraction of Bremer's conjectural Compound *Ermun-swǣbōz must be rejected as contrary to the general laws of development[1] (cp. the analogous case of Saxons and Sax-nōt, vol. I, § 75 and § 217, 1).

Lit. Zeuss, 75; Grimm, 825; Müllenhoff, IV, 116; *idem, Zeitschrift*, XXIII, 1 seq.; *idem*, in Schmidt's *Allg. Zeitschr. f. Geschichte*, VIII, 209; Rieger, *Zeitschrift*, XI, 181; Kossinna, *Indogerm. Forsch.* VII, 304; Mogk, *Grundriss*, 3rd ed. III, 315; Holtz, *Beiträge zur germ. Altertumskunde*, 43; Bremer, § 81 (note), § 216; Schönfeld, s.v. *Herminones*; Much in Hoops, II, 182; Haug in Pauly-Wissowa, s.v.; Kauffmann, I, 250 note 9; Löwenthal, *Beiträge*, XLV, 256 seq.; J. de Vries, *Tijdschrift van Nederl. Taal- en Letterkunde*, LI, 302.

§ 154. Sub-divisions.

Pliny, who characterises the Erminones as 'mediterranei' (cp. 'medii', Tacitus), enumerates four sub-divisions (IV, 99):

1. Svebi, Swabians, on the Lower Elbe; later in Schwaben on the Danube (§§ 156–164).
2. Hermunduri, in Thuringia (§§ 178–181).
3. Chatthi, in Hesse (§§ 195–202).
4. Cherusci, in Northern Germany, between the Svebi and Chatthi (§§ 206, 208).

Various tribes of indeterminate position may be added. Some of them appear as Swabians, but they do not seem to belong to the Swabians proper. Others are never classified as belonging to any of the German branches, but they somehow appear in company with the Swabians. And to all of them the Plinian adjective 'mediterranean' is applicable.

[1] Much in Hoops, II, 182, suggests a similar Compound *Ermin-aiwaniz, but, as he informs me privately, he has now withdrawn this suggestion.

5. Marcomans or Bavarians; ancestral hero Ermin. Homes: (1) the Marca, i.e. the South German frontier-wood about the Main; (2) Bohemia; (3) Bavaria and Austria (§§ 165–169).

6. Varisti alias Naristi. Homes: (1) Stadewanga on the river Regen; (2) Pagus Warascus in Burgundy (§§ 170–172).

7. Scudingi who accompany the Varisti to Burgundy (§ 170, 2).

8. (*a*) Lat. Marsigni (Tacitus, first century A.D.); (*b*) Gr. Μαρουίνγοι (Ptol. II, 11, § 11 bis). Two isolated names never mentioned elsewhere, and no doubt identical. If the Latin spelling is to be preferred, the name would probably originate from the tribal name Marsi, like that of the Marsaci in the Dutch district of Marsum. Phonetic reasons seem to exclude Möller's identification of the Μαρουίνγοι with the O.E. Myrgingas. Home: (*a*) beside the Buri on the eastern side of Bohemia (Tac. *Germ.* 43); (*b*) beside the *Buriones (Κουρίωνες) and Bohemia (Ptolemy, *l.c.*).

Lit. Möller, *Das altengl. Volksepos*, 26; *idem*, *Anzeiger*, XXII, 152; Schönfeld, s.v. *Marsigni* and *Marvingi* (with lit.); Much in Hoops, s.v. *Marsigni* and Μαρουίνγοι; Schütte, *Beiträge*, XLI, 33; *idem*, *Arkiv*, XXXIII, 35; *idem*, *Ptolemy's Maps*, 112.

9. Lat. Vangiones (Caesar, first century B.C.); M.Lat. Gwangiones; Gr. Οὐαγγίονες (Ptolemy, second century A.D., and miswritten Οὐαργίωνες). Personal name: Quadic Vangio (Tac. *Ann.* XII, 29). Capital: Lat. Vangiones, Vangionas, i.e. Worms. The name originates from O.G. *wang*, O.N. *vangr* 'field'. Much's identification with the O.E. Wóingas (*Widsith*) is not probable and has been withdrawn by himself. The monstrous Ptolemaic form 'Vargiones' that still disfigures R. Kiepert's *Formae Orbis Antiqui* (1911) ought to disappear. The original home may have been in the east, as the personal name Vangio appears among the Quadi in Moravia, accompanied by Sido, which originates from the East Gothonic Sidones; position after 58 B.C. west of the Middle Rhine, about Worms.

Lit. Much, *Beiträge*, XVII, 94 seq., 107 seq.; *idem*, *Zeitschrift*, XXXIX, 35; Schönfeld, s.v. (with lit.); Schütte, *Beiträge*, XLI, 36; *idem*, *Arkiv*, XXXIII, 35; *idem*, *Ptolemy's Maps*, 123; Howorth, *Engl. Hist. Review*, XXIII, 627; Neckel, *Neue Jahrbücher*, II, 147; Löwenthal, *Wörter u. Sachen*, X, 180.

10. Celto-Lat. Nemetes (Caesar, first century B.C.); Gr. Νεμῆτες (Ptolemy, second century A.D.). Personal name: Celto-Lat. Nemetialis. Eponymous goddess: Celt. Nemetona. Capital: Celto-Lat. Nemetes; M.Fr.

Nymaie (Jacques de Guise, *Hist. de Hainault*, fourteenth century, i.e. Spires). The name, according to the current theory, originates from Celt. *nemeton* 'sanctuary', which has been adopted into some Gothonic dialects, e.g. Frisian; d'Arbois de Jubainville and Much prefer the Irish signification, *nemed* 'noble', but a toponymic is more probable. On the similar-sounding Slavonic name for the Gothonic or German people, Němici, see vol. I, § 16; if the identification with this name were correct, it would imply a position originally to the east (cp. the couple Vangio and Sido under No. 9). Home after 58 B.C.: west of the Middle Rhine, about Spires.

Lit. Zeuss, 220; *idem*, *Gram. Celt.* 759; Grimm, 497, 780; *idem*, *Mythologie*, 614; Müllenhoff, IV, 395; Much, *Beiträge*, XVII, 107; *idem*, in Hoops, s.v.; d'Arbois de Jubainville, *Les noms gaulois*, 146 seq.; Holder, *Altcelt. Sprachschatz*, s.v.; Schönfeld, s.v. (with lit.); Ihm, *Jahrb. d. Altertumsfreunde im Rheinland*, LXXXIII, 16; Janko, *Wörter u. Sachen*, I, 103; Schachmatow, *Archiv f. slav. Phil.* XXXIII, 84; v. Keussler, *Deutsche Erde*, 1911, 182; Schmidt, II, 143; Kluge, *Urgermanisch*, 52 (*Grundriss*, 3rd ed. II); Howorth, *Engl. Hist. Review*, XXIII, 628; Dottin, *La langue gauloise*, 128; Maver, *Einfluss der vorchristl. Kulte a. d. Topon. Frankreichs*, pp. 41 seq.; Feist, *Wörter u. Sachen*, XI, 441, Pokorny, *ibid.* 304; Huss, *Zeitschr. f. deutsche Phil.* LIV, 164; Janko, *Teuthonista*, VIII, 127.

11. Lat. Tri-boci (Caesar, first century B.C. and inscr.), Tri-boccus, Tre-bocus sing. (inscr.); Gr. Τρί-βοκχοι (Strabo, first century A.D.), Τρι-βόκοι (Ptolemy, second century). Town: Lat. *Tri-boci (Tribunci, Ammianus, XVI, 12, § 58). As the name reappears in the Maritime Alps, it would seem to be Celtic; the first element is the numeral 'three', known from Celtic, Thracian, and Gothonic tribe names. German names of mountains and woods such as Melibokon and Albuch might seem to make a Gothonic etymology possible, but the Alpine 'Triboci' certainly favours a Celtic derivation. Home after 58 B.C.: Lower Alsace; Triboci are also found near Marbach on the Neckar (*CIL.* XIII, 6448).

Lit. Mabillon, *De arte diplomatica*, 507; Zeuss, 220; Grimm, 497; Müllenhoff, IV, 394; Glück, *Die bei Caesar vorkommenden kelt. Namen*, 158; Holder, s.v.; d'Arbois de Jubainville, *Les noms gaulois*, 222; Bremer, *Indogerm. Forsch.* IV, 22; Howorth, *Engl. Hist. Review*, XXIII, 627; Much, *Beiträge*, XVII, 107; *idem*, in Hoops, s.v.; Schönfeld, s.v.; Feist, *Germanen u. Kelten in d. antiken Überlieferung*, 19 note 4; Dottin, *La langue gauloise*, 128.

12. Lat. Arma-lausi (*Tab. Peuting.* fourth century), Armi-lausini (e.g. *Excerpt.* Jul. Honor., in *Geogr. Lat. Min.* 40, 6). Derived from Gothic *arme-lausa* 'sleeveless gown' (Isidorus, *Etymologiae*), whence an ethnic nickname has been formed. In the Roman army an ἀρμελαύσια

was worn by the train soldiers (Mauricius, XII, 1). Miller, *Itin. Roman.* p. 615, combines the name with the river Armata. Home: on the Upper Danube (*Tab. Peuting.*).

Lit. Grimm, 499; Ihm in Pauly-Wissowa, s.v.; Schönfeld, s.v. (with lit.); Much in Hoops, s.v. and IV, 430.

§ 155. Ethnic Position.

Our knowledge of the Erminones is inconclusive, as their community had already ceased to play any part in political history before the beginning of our era. The problem generally is not very eagerly discussed; Hoops, e.g., has no article *Erminonen or *Herminonen.

Bremer, §§ 82 and 216, identifies the Erminones with those Tacitean Swabians who must be regarded as real Germans. He may be right, but then Pliny's classification of the Chatthi and Cherusci among the Erminones must be rejected as erroneous.

In order to ascertain the position of the Erminonic community, we must try to build upon coinciding evidence from various authorities.

1. Pliny: Erminones are 'mediterranei' (cp. Tac. *Germ.* 2: Erminones are 'medii'). Their position among the surrounding branches or sub-groups can be illustrated as follows:

West	North	East
	Inguaeones (Pliny, Tac.)	
Istuaeones (Pliny, Tac.) (Gambrivii, Tac.) (Marsi, Tac.)		Vandili (Pliny, Tac.) Bastarnae (Pliny)
	Middle Erminones (Pliny, Tac.)	

Mela, III, 3, 32, apparently disagrees, as his Erminones are not 'mediterranei', but 'ultimi Germaniae'. But his idea of Germania may simply represent an older, more rudimentary scheme which ignores the Vandili or East Gothonic nations; if so, the Erminones actually are the extreme eastern inhabitants of his Germania.

2. Pliny: Branch No. 1 of the Erminones are the Svebi, that is to say the Swabians proper, not including, e.g., the Ermundures. Strabo, VII. 290: the Semnones are stated to be a large tribe of the Svebi. Tac. *Germ.* 29: the Semnones are named as Svebi No. 1 and as the 'Sveborum caput', that is to say, as the Swabians proper. These Semnones occupy exactly the 'mediterranean' position of the Erminones. Mela's Ermi-

nones, mentioned in the vicinity of the Cimbri, must necessarily be identical with the Semnones.

3. Pliny: the Ermundures are the Erminonic branch No. 2, co-ordinate with the Svebi. Strabo, *l.c.*, Tac. *Germ.* 41: the Ermundures are Svebi, but not 'Sveborum caput'. Onomastic criterion: the prefix Ermun- confirms the Erminonic nationality; local traditions after Strabo and Tacitus never refer to the Ermundures alias Thuringians as Swabians—that is to say, they are not Swabians proper.

4. Strabo, *l.c.*, Tac. *Germ.* 82: the Marcomans are Svebi, but not 'Sveborum caput'. Onomastic evidence: local traditions derive the Bavarian descendants of the Marcomans from 'Armenia', i.e. from the Erminones, but never refer to them as Swabians—that is to say, they are not Swabians proper.

The remaining tribes of the interior or south of Germany either appear as Swabians or in co-operation with the Swabians. The most important incidents are summarised below.

5. Caesar, *Bell. Gall.* I, 51: Svebi, Marcomans, Vangiones, Nemetes, and Triboci jointly invade Gaul about 70 B.C. Co-operation of the Erminonic branches 1 and 3.

6 Strabo, VII, 290: the Marcomannic King Maroboduus in Bohemia about A.D. 1 establishes an Empire which extends up to and includes the Svebi Semnones and must consequently have included the *Ermundures. Co-operation of the Erminonic branches 1, *2, and 3.

7. Tac. *Ann.* II, 63: the Ermundures eject Catvalda who has usurped the Marcomannic throne, A.D. 19. If this may be regarded as participation in a Marcomannic civil war, it may count as a co-operation of the Erminonic branches 2 and 3.

8. Tac. *Ann.* XIII, 57: the Ermundures inflict a crushing defeat on the Chatthi in A.D. 58. This catastrophe may explain why Pliny regards the conquered Chatthi as Erminonic.

9. Julius Capitolinus, *Scr. Hist. Aug. v. M. Ant.* 22, A.D. 165–180; the first of the belligerent German tribes enumerated are: Marcomans, Varisti, Ermundures, and Quadic Swabians. Co-operation of the Erminonic branches 1, 2, and 3. (The friendly relations between the Semnones and the Quadic Swabians appear from Dio Cassius, LXXI, 20.)

Points 1–4 seem to be confirmed by the political proceedings 5–9 which represent a sort of Erminonic solidarity, though the name Erminones does not appear in political history. At any rate, the members of the group never appear to have taken different sides, fighting each other with the obstinacy of mortal enemies.

For exactly similar reasons, we must reject Pliny's assertion that the Erminones include the Cherusci. For the Cherusci were hereditary enemies of the Swabians who were Erminones (cp. Caesar, *Bell. Gall.* VI, 10: 'silvam..., quae adpellatur Bacenis..., pro nativo muro objectam, Cheruscos ab Svevis...injuriis incursionibus prohibere'). Further, it is well known that the Cherusci were the chief enemies of Maroboduus' Marcomannic-Swabian Empire half a century after Caesar's time.

Similarly, the Chatthi, who were bitter enemies of the Ermundures, cannot have been true Erminones (cp. Tac. *Ann.* XIII, 57). However, as we suggested above, the decisive victory of the Ermundures may temporarily have reduced the beaten nation into the position of an Erminonic vassal state.

After the second century, the Erminones cease to exist as an ethnic category, for the branches of the group—Swabians, Ermundures, and Marcomans—act from that time forward as separate and distinct tribes. But the memory of Ermin as ancestor of the Bavarians still survived till mediaeval times.

C. §§ 156–164. *THE SWABIAN BRANCH*

§ 156. Name.

O.H.G. Swābā, Swāpā; M.H.G. Swāben; N.H.G. Schwaben (dial. pron. Schwauben); O.L.G. Swevon; M.L.G. Swav-ee (*Sachsenspiegel*); O.E. *Swǽfe or *Swǽfas (dat. pl. Swǽfum, *Widsith*); O.N. Sváfar; Lat. Svevi (Caesar, first century B.C.); Svebi (Nepos, first century B.C., cit. by Pliny; Tacitus, first century A.D.); Svaebi (*CIL.* VI, 32,806); Svabi (*Vict. Not. Num.* 96, 89, fifth century); Svavi (Jordanes, sixth century);[1] Portug. Svevos; Rouman. Şvobi; Gr. Σοήβοι (Strabo, first century A.D.); Σουῆβοι (Plutarch, second century; Dio Cassius, third century); Σύηβοι (Ptolemy, second century); Σούαβοι (Procopius, sixth century); Gotho-Gr. Σουΐβοι (Sozomenus, sixth century, three times); Czech. Švaby; Serb. Švabaci; Magyar Svábok. Eponymous hero: O.N. Sváfnir. Valkyrie: O.N. Sváfa. Personal name: Visigoth. Svabila (Fourth Council of Toledo, A.D. 633; Dahn, *Könige der Germanen*, VI, 443); O.E. Suǣb-

[1] A verse cited by Paulus Diaconus, III, 19, refers Svavus to the Latin word *suavis* 'sweet'. It dates from about A.D. 578.

hard; O.H.G. Swāb-beraht; O.N. Swāba-harjaʀ (Inscr. of Rö, and in the Zealandic place name Svogerslev). Territorial names: O.H.G. Suābo-rīchi (Otfrid); Swāb-ouwa (*Origo Swevorum*); dial. Schwoba-land, Schwåbe-land; O.N. Sváfa-land. Place name: Portug. Svevos (five villages).[1] Obscure. The Gothonic vowel ǣ becomes ā in German, ē in the Gothic of Ulfila, ī in later Gothic (cp. the Σουῆβοι of Sozomenus). Schönfeld's rejection of the well-authenticated form is unjustified; the form Svavi of Jordanes simply is a loan from German (cp. the Gothic personal name Svabila). The terminal *-ee* in M.L.G. Swav-ee seems to be Gothon. *-aiw*, as in Ing-aevones, etc. In Roumanian, Czechian, and Magyar, the name Swabians becomes the collective name for Germans (cp. § 148, 7).

Lit. Schönfeld, s.v. *Svevi* (with lit.); *idem*, in Pauly-Wissowa, s.v. *Suebi*; Much in *Beiträge*, XVII, 48; *idem*, in Hoops, s.v. *Sueben*; Kauffmann, I, 238 note 4. Geogr. survivals: Jungfer, *Über Personennamen in den Ortschaften Spaniens u. Portugals*, 19. Collective use: *Deutsche Erde*, IX, 80; Kauffmann, I, 410 note 11.

§ 157. Sub-divisions.

1. Lat. Svebi, i.e. 'Swabians proper' (Pliny), that is the Svebi Semnones, 'Sveborum caput' (Tacitus, first century A.D.), otherwise Nor-savi (King Theodebert's letter to Justinian, c. A.D. 547, *Mon. Germ. Epist. Merow.* I, 133), Nordo-squavi (*Ann. Mettens.* ad an. 748, *Mon. Germ. SS.* I, 330); Gr. Σέμνωνες (Strabo, first century B.C.), Σέμνονες (Ptolemy, second century A.D.). Personal name: Gr. Σέμνων (a Lugian, Zosimus, fifth century). The origin is disputed. Much compares the O.N. goddess Sjǫfn, Sjǫmn, *Gylfaginning*, c. 36, whose name is *ibid.* derived from an O.N. noun *sjafni* 'love'. Moreover, Much refers the name to O.Swed. *safer* 'placidus', O.E. *sibb* 'kindness', O.H.G. *sibb(i)a* 'kindred'. Zeuss, Bremer, Schönfeld, and Magnus Olsen derive it from a root **semn-* 'collective'; Olsen compares O.N. Samnangr 'the firth of the comrades' (?). Müllenhoff interprets the name as 'feathered, with linked limbs', alluding to the Semnonic worship (Tac. *Germ.* 39). Much rejects the latter interpretations as 'unannehmbar'. We are inclined to prefer the interpretation 'collective', as it would agree with the generally toponymic character of Gothonic tribe names. Grimm compares the mountain

[1] The name of the Law of Schwabenspiegel is formed in the sixteenth century by Goldast in imitation of *Sachsenspiegel*.

Semanus, but this has a long ē, whereas the *e* of Semnones is short; besides, the *n* in Semanus is probably of Latin origin, as in Sinus Codanus, Silva Marciana, etc. Bremer and Schönfeld identify Semnones with Sibinoi (Strabo, VII, 290); but the latter form is not verified, and we prefer to identify it with Ptolemy's duplicates Seidinoi and Sudinoi. Home: north-east of the Lower Elbe; later, in the district of Swevon, west of the Middle Elbe; emigrated Semnones form the tribe of Alemanni (cp. § 158, V).

Lit. Zeuss, 130; Grimm, 493; Müllenhoff, IV, 459, 531 (with lit.); Bremer, *Zeitschrift*, XXXVII, 9; *idem*, *Zeitschr. f. deutsche Philol.* XXII, 251; Förstemann, s.v. *Suevi*; Schönfeld, s.v. *Suevi* (with lit.); *idem*, in Pauly-Wissowa, s.v.; Schütte, *Beiträge*, XLI, 8, 39; *idem*, *Arkiv*, XXXIII, 35; *idem*, *Ptolemy's Maps*, 25, 126; Much in Hoops, s.v. *Sueben* and *Semnonen*; Magnus Olsen, *Norske Gaardnavne*, XI, 515; *idem*, *Stednavnestudier*, 12; Güntert, *Wörter u. Sachen*, IX, 131.

2. Lat. Svebi Quadi (Tacitus, first century A.D.); Gr. *Κοαδουοί (Κολδουοί, Strabo, first century B.C.), Κούαδοι (Ptolemy, second century A.D.). Probably a toponymic derived from Gothon. **kwada-*, M.H.G. *quat* 'dirt, mire', and referring to the marshy stretches along the river March in Moravia. Grimm compares Dutch *kwaad* 'evil', but it has an original Gothon. *æ*, not *a*. Home: Moravia and Nieder Oesterreich; later (as Svevi) in Portugal and Galicia.

Lit. Grimm, 506; Kluge, *Etym. Wörterbuch*, s.v. *Kot* ('dirt'); Kögel, *Anzeiger*, XIX, 8; Brugmann, *Indogerm. Forsch.* V, 375; Schönfeld, s.v. (with lit.); Much in Hoops, s.v.; Zachrisson, *Studier tillägnade Ax. Kock*, 493; Premerstein, *Zeitschrift*, LX, 71.

3. Lat. Brisigaui (*Not. dign.* fifth century A.D.), that is 'inhabitants of the district of Breisgau'; O.H.G. Brisa-gowe. The name originates from the capital Breisach, Celt. Brisiakos. The epic collar, O.N. Brísinga men (O.E. Brosinga mene, *Beow.* l. 1199), is by Müllenhoff interpreted as 'treasure of the Brisigaui', but Much objects that O.N. *brísingr* is a word for fire (cp. O.N. *brísa* 'to burn'). Home: Breisgau in South-western Baden.

Lit. Müllenhoff, *Zeitschrift*, XXII, 304, XXX, 220; Much, *Der germ. Himmelsgott*, 54; Schönfeld, s.v. (with lit.); Mogk in Hoops, s.v. *Brísinga men.*

4. N.H.G. Riesser; Lat. *Raeto-varii (Raeto-barii, *Not. dign. Orient.* V, 17, fifth century A.D.). Ptolemy's Χαιτούωροι, II, 11, § 11, probably confuses *Raetovarii with the Chattvarii of a Rhenish map. The name

means 'Rhaetian men'. Home: in the Roman province of Rhaetia; O.H.G. Rezi; N.H.G. Riess (cp. Germ. *riessling*, 'Rhaetian wine').

Lit. Schmeller, *Bayer. Wörterb.* s.v. *Riess*; Schönfeld, s.v. (with lit.); Schütte, *Beiträge*, XLI, 37; *idem*, *Ptolemy's Maps*, 119.

5. (*a*) Lat. Svebi Nicretes (cives Sveba[e] Nicreti(s), *CIL.* XIII, 2, 633); in inscriptions often abbreviated S.N.; (*b*) Nictrenses (*Not. gentium*, fourth century A.D.); (*c*) Gr. *Νικρίωνες? (Νιτρίωνες var. 'Ιγκρίονες, Ptolemy, second century A.D.). 'Inhabitants of the Neckar valley.' Capital: Lat. Lopodunum; O.H.G. Lobedunburg (with district Lobedungou); Germ. Ladenburg. Most inscriptions of the Nicretes originate from the environs of Ladenburg and Heidelberg. See page 447.

Lit. Schönfeld, s.v. *Nictrenses* (with lit.); *idem*, s.v. *Incriones*; *idem*, in Pauly-Wissowa, s.v. *Svebi*, col. 577; Zangemeister, *N. Heidelb. Jahrb.* III, 1; Wirtz, *Bonner Jahrb.* CVIII, 197; Much in Hoops, s.v. *Neckarsweben* and *Nicer.*

6 or 7. (*a*) (an Alemannic sub-tribe). Lat. Svebi Euthungi (matribus Svebis Euthungabus, *CIL.* XIII, 8225); Iuthungi (Alemanni, Ammianus, XVII, 6, § 1, fourth century A.D.); Iotungi, Iutugi, Uitungi; Gr. 'Ιουθοῦγγοι (Dexippus eight times, third century A.D.). Personal name: O.Bavar. Eodunc, Iedunc (cp. O.N. Iuþingar). Perhaps derived from Gothon. *euð-*, O.N. *jóð* 'kindred, descent', but cp. Zachrisson, cited in § 237, 5). The Iuthungi may be descendants of the Eudoses co-operating with the Swabians of Ariovistus in Gaul, 58 B.C. (cp. § 239, 5). Home: South-western Germany; the inscription cited is from Cologne.

Lit. Zeuss, 146, 312; Grimm, 500; Müllenhoff, IV, 460, 578; *idem*, *Zeitschrift*, X, 562; Much, *Beiträge*, XVII, 85; *idem*, in Hoops, s.v. *Juthungen*; Schönfeld, s.v. *Euthungae* and *Iuthungi*; *idem*, in Pauly-Wissowa, s.v. *Iuthungi.*

(*b*) Germ. Linzgauer; Lat. Lentienses (an Alemannic sub-tribe, Ammianus, XV, 4, § 1, XXXI, 10, §§ 2, 4, fourth century A.D.). Lentienses is a Latin toponymic of a Rhaetian place name in Linzgau, east of tbe Boden Lake.

Lit. Holder, *Altcelt. Sprachschatz*, s.v. *Lentienses.*

(*c*) Lat. Bucino-bantes (an Alemannic sub-tribe, Ammianus, XXIX, 4, § 7, fourth century A.D.). The name has been derived from the O.G. Buchonia 'the beechwood', but rather belongs to Germ. *gebück(e)* 'defensive hedge', cp. Grimm, *Wörterb.* IV, 1a, 1879 seq.; *-bant* is 'county' (cp. Brabant in the Netherlands and Belgium); the toponymic appears in Tu-bantes and O.H.G. Destar-benzon (pl.), and in the adjective *elibenzo* 'alien, from other regions'. The form *-bant*, however, is not typically Alemannic, but Frankish (cp. § 184, 17). Home: north-east of Mayence.

Lit. Schönfeld, s.v. (with lit.); Ihm in Pauly-Wissowa, s.v. *Buconia*; Much in Hoops, s.v.; v. Ginneken in *Onze Taaltuin*, I, 84 seq.

(*d*) Lat. Ala-manni, Ale-manni, etc., see under vol. I, § 22. Etymology: 'All men', as already stated by Asinius Quadratus (cp. Agathias, I, 6: ''*Ἀλαμανοὶ...ξύγκλυδές* [var. *ξυνήλυδές*] *εἰσιν ἄνθρωποι καὶ μιγάδες, καὶ τοῦτο δύναται αὐτοῖς ἡ ἐπωνυμία*': 'the Alemanni are a mixed race, formed from many peoples, and hence their name'). Cp. also the Gothic noun *ala-mans*, O.H.G. *ala-mannida*, Dan. *al-minding*, 'common, commonwealth'. On their descent from the Semnones (Suidas) see § 150, v, 1. For their being identified with Swabians see Paulus Diaconus, II, 15: 'Swaviam, hoc est Allamannorum patriam'; Walafrid Strabo, *Mon. Germ. SS.* II, 2: 'Quia mixti Alamannis Svebi partem Germaniae ultra Danubium...obsederunt, antiquorum vocabulorum veritate ab incolis nomen patriae derivemus et Alemanniam vel Sveviam nominemus. Nam cum duo vocabula, unam gentem significantia, priori nomine nos appellant (Romani), sequenti usus nos nuncupat barbarorum'. The West Romance languages later enlarge the term Alemanni so as to embrace all Germans (cp. § 148, 6), and the mediaeval Italian Alamagna means the entire Gothonic group (cp. vol. I, § 22). Home: South-western Germany, later also Switzerland.

Lit. Zeuss, 303; Grimm, 498; Bremer, § 221; Ihm in Pauly-Wissowa, s.v.; Schönfeld, s.v.; Förstemann, s.v. (with lit.); Much in Hoops, s.v. Collective sense: *Deutsche Erde*, IX (*Die Namen der Deutschen*); Schütte, *Racenavnet* (*Norden*, 1904–5, 127, 128).

§ 158. Ethnic Position.

That the Swabian branch exists with various sub-divisions is an undisputed fact, but its extent is open to some doubt (cp. the statements which follow).

1. Strabo, VII, 290. The Swabians extend from the Rhine beyond the Elbe, embracing Semnones, Langobards, Ermundures, Marcomans, Quadi. To the Swabian King Maroboduus' Empire belong: the East Gothonic nations and the 'Sibinoi' (the Baltic tribe of Sudinoi, Ptol.). Cimbri, Chauchi, Cherusci, Chatthi are excluded.

2. Tac. *Germ.* 28 seq. The Swabians embrace Semnones, Langobards, Ermundures, Marcomans, Quadi, Naristi, Marsigni; and moreover

Angles (!), Varines (!), Eudoses (!), etc.; the East Gothonic nations (!), the Swedes (!!), Balts (!!!), and the Sitones who are probably the Finns (!!!). Cimbri, Chauchi, Cherusci, Chatthi, etc., are excluded.

3. Ptol. II, 11, § 8 seq. The Swabians extend from the Rhine beyond the Elbe, embracing Semnones, Langobards, and Angles (!). Not only are Cimbri, Chauchi, Cherusci, and Chatthi excluded, but also most of the Swabians of Tacitus, viz. Marcomans, Quadi, Varisti, Marvingoi, *Varines, and *Eudoses (Fundusioi).

We notice various important points of agreement. (*a*) Strabo and Ptolemy agree that the Swabians extend from the Rhine beyond the Elbe; Tacitus does not mention the Rhine, but agrees with the extension beyond the Elbe. (*b*) All three declare that Semnones and Langobards are Swabian. (*c*) Strabo and Tacitus include Ermundures, Marcomans, Quadi. (*d*) Tacitus and Ptolemy also include Angles. (*e*) Strabo, Tacitus, and Ptolemy exclude Cimbri, Chauchi, Cherusci, Chatthi. (*f*) Tacitus *begins* his Swabian list with Semnones, Langobards, and Anglo-Jutic tribes, whereas Ptolemy emphasises the Swabian origin of Semnones, Langobards, and Angles by excluding the remaining Swabians.

Yet though our authorities agree in part, they seem to represent a rough and inaccurate Roman hypothesis rather than a definite knowledge of facts from the Gothonic standpoint.

The extent of the Swabian branch, as given by Tacitus, is obviously exaggerated into a learned fiction, and even if he is supported by Ptolemy, that does not make his statement reliable: the Swabian Angles of Tacitus and Ptolemy are as fictitious as the 'Swabian Swedes', for the Angles were not Germans at all.

Even the threefold authority of Strabo, Tacitus, and Ptolemy does not always inspire faith. Schmidt, I, 428, doubts the Swabianism of the Langobards, and Schönfeld in Pauly-Wissowa, s.v. *Suebi*, 578, absolutely denies it. We are inclined to agree with him, for Langobard civilisation, legends, and history seem to betray no Swabian nationality.

The alleged Swabianism of the Langobards probably originates from the fact that they belonged temporarily to Maroboduus' Empire, and similarly we may explain the 'Svebi Anglii', who would only by accident have been forgotten in the list of Maroboduus' subjects (cp. A. Riese, *Die Sueben, Westdeutsche Zeitschrift*, IX, 339); we regard Bremer's objections (§ 215 note 1) as not justified.

Another explanation of the exaggerated extent of the Swabians may be surmised from an individual theory of Tacitus, *Germ.* 38. He there emphasises the 'pig-tail' as a national mark of all Swabians, and so he may have taken for Swabians some other nations who happened to share this conspicuous fashion.

Lately we have become aware of a noteworthy theory which has been set forth by F. Frahm in *Klio*, XXIII, 181. He maintains that the name of Germani originates from the well known regions about the Northern Rhine and was thence by the Romans gradually extended towards the east; the name of Swabians originally was used by the Romans as a collective designation of the more easterly tribes that were less known to them. In the course of time, Germani came to embrace all of the Gothonic nations, but Swabians remained as the name of a subordinate group, and the divergence between the ancient and later terminology gave rise to a certain fluctuation and vagueness of the ethnic categories. The description of the Jutlandic population may serve as an example. The Cimbri, though not belonging to the ancient Germani of the Rhenish regions, had been early known and had chiefly acted on western scenes; therefore they were attributed to the Germanic section and were regarded as non-Swabian; but their close neighbours, the Eudoses, Angles, etc., occupied regions which remained unknown to the Romans till the beginning of our era and which were by Tacitus characterised as belonging to the 'secretiora Germaniae'; therefore the tribes mentioned are attributed to the Swabian section. Thus the development of classical geography leads to the establishment of an imaginary distinction between the inhabitants of Jutland.

Having criticised the classical authorities, we must try to extract the sum total of trustworthy evidence, verified either by their mutual agreement or by additional criteria.

I. Semnones, 'Sveborum caput', i.e. North Swabians.

1. Strabo, Tacitus, and Ptolemy all speak of Svebi Semnones. The position is emphasised, for Strabo mentions them as the only 'big nation' among the Swabians; Tacitus puts them first on the list, 'vetustissimi et nobilissimi Sveborum...Sveborum caput'; Ptolemy selects them as one of the three divisions of the Swabians; their fame is shown by his wrong spelling of a Gaulish tribe in Italy, Semnones being written for Senones (III, 1, § 44).

2. Tacitus says that the Semnones possess the central sanctuary of all the Swabians, and they themselves lay claim to sacred majesty.

3. Dio Cassius shows that the political schemes of the Quadic Swabians recognise the Semnones as the ancestral stock (cp. under II); and that the Alemannic Swabians are also derived from the North Swabians, i.e. Semnones is a legend surviving among their descendants (cp. under V).

4. The name of Swabians outlasts that of Semnones: Nordo-Squavi, Swevon, Swav-ee.

II. Quadi, i.e. Semnones, i.e. Swabians in Portugal.

1. Dio Cassius, LXXI, 20, says that the Quadi, beaten by Marcus Aurelius, plan to (r)emigrate to the Semnones—that is to say, they recognise them as their ancestral stock, the 'Sveborum caput'. Cp. our dissertation *Oldsagn om Godtjod*, 84–87, on the analogous cases of the Saxons, Vandals, and Erules.

2. Strabo, VII, 290, and Tacitus, *Germ.* 42, in set terms represent the Quadi as a Swabian sub-tribe. One king, Vannius, alternately rules the 'Quadi' and the 'Swabians' (Tac. *Ann.* II, 88, XII, 29), and this interchanging use of the names goes on for centuries. However, if Swabians in South-eastern Germany are mentioned, the Quadi are always meant, and never Marcomans, Varisti, etc.[1]

3. Hieronymus, *ad Ageruchiam*, ep. 123, enumerates the Quadi among the Pannonian invaders of Gaul in A.D. 406. This is the last recorded use of the local name. In Spain and Portugal, only Swabians are spoken of, but their identity with the Quadi is indubitable. Here, as everywhere, the collective name outlasts the local name.

4. Also the Quadi of the Danubian homeland after the fourth century call themselves Swabians..

III. Nicretes, i.e. Swabians, i.e. Alemanni.

1. The inscription *CIL.* XIII, 2, makes use of the term Sveba Nicretis (cp. Zangemeister, *N. Heidelb. Jahrb.* III, 1).

2. The Nicretes are situated in mediaeval Alemanni, that is Swabia.

[1] Cp. Köstlin, *Die Donaukriege Domitians*, 81. L. Schmidt's objections, II, 174, are not justified. A solitary exception is when Ammianus, XVI, 10, § 20, distinguishes the Euthungi as Swabian in contrast to the Quadi.

IV. Euthungi, i.e. Swabians, i.e. Alemanni.

1. The inscription *CIL.* XIII, 8225, makes use of the term Svebae Euthungae.

2. Ammianus, XVII, 6, § 1, says that the Iuthungi are a sub-tribe or the Alemanni.

3. The Euthungi are situated in mediaeval Alemannia, that is Swabia.

V. Alemanni, i.e Semnones, i.e. Swabians.

1. Fragm. ap. Suidam: '*οἱ Γερμανοί* (i.e. *Φράγγοι*), *οἱ ἀμφὶ τὸν Ῥῆνον ποταμόν εἰσιν, οἱ κατέθεον τὴν γῆν τῶν Ἀλβανῶν, οὓς καὶ Σήνωνας καλοῦσιν*': 'the Franks, who are situated about the Rhine and have occupied the soil of the *Alemanni, who are also called *Semnones'. 'Albanoi' is a current Greek distortion (cp. Schönfeld, s.v. *Alamanni*), and the Gaulish Senones are substituted for *Semnones (cp. the opposite mistake, Semnones for the Gaulish Senones in Italy, Ptol. III, 1, § 44).[1]

2. *Origo Swevorum*, a vernacular legend, derives the Alemanni in Swabouwa from North Swabians (who are again identical with the Semnones, 'Sveborum caput'). Cp. *Zeitschrift*, XVII, 51 seq.

3. Paulus Diaconus, II, 15: 'Swaviam, hoc est Allemannorum patriam'. Similarly Walafrid Strabo, *Mon. Germ. SS.* II, 2 (cited on p. 96).

4. The name Alemanni disappears after the Middle Ages and only the name Swabians remains, the modern Schwaben.

It is manifest that the Swabian origin of the Semnones, Quadi, Nicretes, Euthungi, and Alemanni, is not merely a Roman fiction, but is verified by tribal nomenclature and national traditions. These are the Swabians proper, whereas the Swabian origin of the other alleged members of the branch is not so well verified.

Tacitus, *Germ.* 38, conceives the 'pig-tail' as a national mark of the Swabians. But he admits himself that it was imitated by other nations; Furtwängler believes that it is to be found among the Bastarnae in Eastern Europe, and a similar way of dressing the hair was used by the Setesdøler in Norway till the nineteenth century. So this test is not conclusive.

The religion common originally to all Swabians is recorded by Tacitus, *Germ.* 39: 'Vetustissimos se nobilissimosque Sveborum Semnones me-

[1] L. Schmidt's objections, II, 238, are not justified.

morant. fides antiquitatis religione firmatur. stato tempore in silvam auguriis patrum et prisca formidine sacram omnes eiusdem sanguinis populi legationibus coeunt caesoque publice homine celebrant barbari ritus horrenda primordia. est et alia luco reverentia: nemo nisi vinculo ligatus ingreditur, ut minor et potestatem numinis prae se ferens. si forte prolapsus est, attolli et insurgere haud licitum; per humum evolvuntur. eoque omnis superstitio respicit, tanquam inde initia gentis, ibi regnator omnium deus, cetera subjecta atque parentia'.

The worship of the 'regnator omnium deus' among the Semnones of the first century A.D. shows that their religion had not yet submitted to the hegemony of Woden. But who was the god whose name Tacitus does not mention? He is generally identified with the ancient god of heaven, Týr; so e.g. Much in Hoops, IV, 165. It is probable that the Swabians worshipped Týr (cp. Schwabian *ziestac* 'Tuesday', instead of Bavarian *ertag* and North-west German *dingsdag* 'the day of Mars Thingsus').[1]

But we believe that the words of Tacitus contain the key to another interpretation. He emphasises that the worship of the Semnones represents the 'initia gentis', the dominion of the united Swabians, whereas the emigrated members of the tribe are subordinate. Thus the stress is to be put on the word *omnium* 'of all', and the universal god may simply be the eponymous Semno 'the united'. The rite of linking his worshippers' hands and feet may allude to the same idea. Cp. local gods such as Saxnōt 'treasure of Saxons' (?), Gautatýr 'god of Gauts', Yngvifreyr 'the Freyr of the Inguaeones', etc.[2]

Later, owing to south-western influence (cp. Mercurius in inscriptions of the Vangiones, Nemetes, Triboci), Woden was introduced even among the Swabians. Columbanus in the ninth century found the Alemanni near the Boden Lake feasting round a huge bowl of beer in worship of Woden (cp. *Vita Col.*, *Mon. Germ. SS. Merov.* IV, 102). The Alemannic clasp from Nordendorf shows the runic names Wodan and Donar (cp. Henning, *Deutsche Runendenkmäler*, 87 seq., Wimmer, *Aarbøger*, 1894, 14).

The Svebi Euthungi adopted the worship of 'matres', which other-

[1] The alleged surname of the Swabians, Cyuuari 'worshippers of Týr', is only an error for Suuabi. Also Ciesburc for Augsburg is erroneous. Cp. Miedel, *Blätter f. d. bayr. Gymnasial-Schulwesen*, LII, 268, and Mogk in Hoops, s.v. *Týr*.

[2] However, G. Neckel, *Neue Jahrbücher für Wissenschaft u. Jugendbildung*, II, 139 seq., regards the 'regnator omnium' as identical with Mercurius, i.e. Woden.

wise does not occur on Swabian territory. It is common to Gauls and Rhenish Germans.

The Quadi worshipped the naked sword (cp. Ammianus, XVII, 12, § 21, speaking of an oath sworn in A.D. 358: 'eductisque mucronibus, quos pro numinibus colunt, juravere'). They must have adopted this rite from their Sarmatic neighbours and allies, whose Alanic kinsmen shared it (cp. Hodgkin, II, 30). It was of Asiatic origin, known among the Hiong-nu (Huns) (*ibid.* 14), and among the Huns of Attila (*ibid.* 84).

The Swabians described by Caesar, *Bell. Gall.* IV, 2, and I, 8, were most dexterous horsemen. The cavalry of Ariovistus consisted of 6000 men, each of whom was accompanied by his attendant foot-soldier who was able to follow the horse in full gallop when holding its mane. The Alemanni of the fourth century had the same combination of the two arms (Ammianus, XVI, 12, § 21). Such attendant foot-soldiers, in Greek called 'parabatai', were a Gaulish institution which we have already noticed among the Bastarnae. Their occurrence seems to betray a considerable influence from Gaul. The Quadi have adopted the Sarmatian scale armour of horn.

The Swabian constitution is not directly mentioned by Tacitus, but as a republic seems to be the normal type of government of his Germani, and a monarchy the exception, the implication seems to be that the Swabians were as republican as the other Germans, and as the Saxons and Lugians.

But the sources at our disposal only record a republic among the Langobards whose Swabian nationality seems to be questionable. Otherwise, the few entries available would rather seem to speak in favour of a monarchy. Cp. Metellus Celer (Pliny, II, 170), 'rex Sveborum'; Dio Cassius, LXVII, 5, § 3, Masyos, a king of the Semnones, c. A.D. 85; *Widsith*, l. 22, Witta, a king of the Swabians; Saxo, 170, a king of the 'Saxons', who are the original Swabians (*Widsith*), fights King Uffo. Cp. also King Vibilius of the Ermundures who belong to the Swabians of Tacitus, *Ann.* XII, 29. The plurality of Alemannic 'reges et regales et regulos' (Ammianus, XVIII, 2, § 13) certainly gives a somewhat different impression (cp. Schmidt, II, 307), but at any rate does not indicate that republicanism prevailed exclusively.[1] We hold that a certain inclination

[1] We do not take into account here such instances as the Marcomannic King Maroboduus, and the Quadic King Vannius, for in the states founded through conquest of non-Gothonic soil a kingdom would easily be introduced even among people with republican traditions, cp. the Saxons in England.

for monarchical government distinguished the Swabians from the North-western Germans, as from the Saxons and Lugians.

The peculiarities of the single tribes cannot be compared, owing to the early disappearance of the Semnones and Quadi. Widukind, *Mon. Germ. SS.* I, 634, distinguishes the laws of the North Swabians, i.e. Semnones, from those of the Saxons; but he fails to inform us whether the North and South Swabian types agreed. The names of the Swabians in Portugal are largely Gothicised—a fact which cannot surprise us; yet some specimens of Compounds in *-berht* and *-gar* betray their German origin (cp. § 150, 1).

The Alemanni or Schwaben, who afford the sole marks of Swabianism in later times, remain.

1. The dialect called 'Alemannic' or Schwäbisch, is the one chief branch of Upper German. According to Behaghel, we must add South and East Franconian as originally Alemannic (cp. § 149).

2. The Alemannic-Schwäbisch type of place names seems to favour the derivatives ending in *-ingen* and to avoid the favourite Frankish compounds ending in *-heim*; when the suffix *-heim* appears on Alemannic ground, we are inclined to regard these place names as a consequence of Frankish colonisation or of Frankish influence. The district names ending in *-bara* are typically Alemannic, and also the Compounds ending in *-huntari* with names of persons: Albuines-, Perahtoltes-, Focholtes-para, Goldines-, Hatten-, Muntariches-, Suercen-huntari; they are frequent round the Upper Neckar and Danube in the same regions as abound in names ending in *-ingen* (see Spruner-Mencke, *Handatlas des Mittelalters*, No. 35). On these somewhat controversial points see our monograph, *Frankisk Kolonisation paa allemannisk Grund*, *Geogr. Tidskrift*, 1918, 191, and the objections of Bückmann in *Petermanns Mitteilungen*, 1922, 13.

3. The Alemanni possess their own type of law. A *Pactus Alamannorum* is issued in the seventh century, the *Lex Alamannorum* under Duke Lantfrid (709–730) (cp. Rietschel in Hoops, III, 153).

4. The type of Alemannic-Schwäbisch archaeological remains is commented upon by Schmidt, II, 297.

5. The Schwaben, according to Meitzen's researches, share with the Bavarians and the High German Franks the Upper German type of the Gothonic 'Gewanndörfer', see Schlüter's map in Hoops, I, 482, s.v. *Deutsches Siedlungswesen.*

6. The ancient Semnonic-Swabian house had the square form, cp.

Dietr. Schäfer, *Das Bauernhaus im Deutschen Reiche*, 6: '(Die) Hausurnen (mögen) für das ganze semnonische Gebiet (zu beiden Seiten der mittleren Elbe von Harz und Unstrut bis nach Mecklenburg hin) das viereckige Haus schon für das zweite und dritte Jahrhundert belegen'.

The modern Swabian-Alemannic house is described by Bernh. Kossmann, *ibid.* 286 seq., as follows: 'Verwickelter (i.e. more complicated than in the case of the Frankish type) liegen die Verhältnisse bei den Bezeichnungen "schwäbisches" und "alemannisches" Haus....Nachdem... nunmehr mit dem Worte "Schwaben" im allgemeinen das Volk Württembergs bezeichnet wird, und im Königreich Württemberg noch am deutlichsten die Herrschaft des einst sehr weit verbreiteten "gestelzten" Hauses nachgewiesen werden kann, und da ferner die Bauweise mit Stallung unter der Wohnung von Osten her in den Schwarzwald eindrang, so werden wir immerhin mit einem gewissen Recht unter "schwäbischer Anlage" ein Gehöft bezeichnen dürfen, bei welchem sich im "gestelzten Hause" die Stallung im Unterraum befindet'.

(The term 'gestelzter Bogen' means 'stilted arch'. Cp. Muret Sanders, *Encyklopäd. Wörterbuch, Englisch-Deutsch.* The *Concise Oxford Dictionary* explains 'stilted' as a construction 'with pieces of upright masonry between imposts and feet of the true arch'. A description of the 'stilted' house is given by O. Gruber, *Deutsche Bürger- u. Ackerbürgerhäuser*, p. 39 seq.)

'Für die Bezeichnung "alemannischer Bau" werden wir dann das mehr oder weniger gestelzte Wohnhaus erhalten, an welches sich Stallung und Tenne direkt anschliessen; dieses Gebäude steht mit der Traufseite an der Strasse.'

'Im Gegensatz zu den fränkischen, schwäbischen und alemannischen Bauernhäusern, bei welchen eine *nachträgliche* Zusammenfassung von Wohn- und Ökonomieräumlichkeiten stattfand, befindet sich das *Schwarzwald-* und das *Hotzenhaus.* Ersteres, mit Giebel gegen die Strasse stehend, ist hervorgegangen aus der Viehhütte, ebenso wie das "*sächsische Haus*".[1] Über den Ursprung des Hotzenhauses lassen sich zurzeit nur Vermutungen aufstellen; dasselbe ist mit der Traufseite parallel zur Strasse gestellt.'

[1] Cp. Ranck, *Kulturgesch. des deutschen Bauernhauses*, 60: 'Häuser des Schwarzwaldes, deren eigentümliche Erscheinung durch die mächtigen und namentlich über den abgewalmten Giebeln weit vorspringenden Dächer bedingt wird'.

'Die Häuser gegen Basel hin zeigen...in der Rheinebene vielfach—je mehr nach Süden um so mehr—sogenannten alemannischen Charakter, Haus- und Wirtschaftsgebäude unter *einem* Dach, und liegen mit der Traufe an der Strasse.'

'Etwa von der Murg an südwärts, also von einstiger politischer Grenze des alemannischen Staatsgebietes und der jetzt noch deutlich bemerkbaren Sprachgrenze zwischen fränkischer und alemannischer Mundart an, zeigen bis hinauf nach Tüllingen alle Dörfer am Rande des Gebirges um so ausgeprägtere alemannische Art, je weiter sie im Bergland liegen.'

'Auch in die grossen Seitentäler des Rheins, trotzdem sie von altersher starke Verkehrsstrassen waren, konnte die fränkische Bauweise nicht weit eindringen; es beginnen die alemannischen oder Schwarzwaldhäuser gleich beim Austritt des Tales aus dem Hügelland.'

'In den der Rheinebene zunächst liegenden Dörfern des Hügellandes nördlich der Murg zeigen die Häuser vielfach schwäbischen Typus. Die Stallungen liegen im Untergeschoss des Wohnhauses, der Giebel des Hauses ist aber der Strasse zugekehrt. Da diese schwäbischen Bauernhäuser stets einen mehr oder weniger geschlossenen Hof haben, sehr häufig mit Torbogen und Eingangspforte in der Hofmauer, so ist der Einfluss fränkischer Bauart nicht von der Hand zu weisen.'

(p. 292.) 'Das, was der oberschwäbische Bauer an Wohnung, Ställen und Scheunen nötig hat, ist in der Regel unter einem riesigen Strohdach vereinigt. Als freistehende oder später angebaute Anhängsel treffen wir höchstens Wagenschuppen, Speicher, Backöfen, die aber gegenüber der grossen Masse des Hauptgebäudes ganz in den Hintergrund treten (Einheitstypus).'

The 'compound house' also occurs in Switzerland, in the Berner Mittelland, cp. Ranck, *Kulturgeschichte des deutschen Bauernhauses* (*Aus Natur und Geisteswelt*, CXXI, 60): 'Einbauten mit ihren gewaltigen, "steilen Schindeldächern" ').

Beside the 'compound house', Switzerland possesses specimens of the irregular farmstead (*ibid.* 52: 'Das zur Gehöftform des Haufenhofes gehörende Alpenhaus der Schweiz...(hat) eigentlich einen Hof in unserm Sinne überhaupt nicht, denn Stall und Scheune liegen meist sehr entfernt vom Wohnhaus....Das Wohnhaus des Alpengehöftes ruht auf einem steinernen, mehr oder weniger tief in die Erde gegrabenen Unterbau, dem "Underhus"....Auf dem Underhus erhebt sich die immer zweistöckige eigentliche Wohnungsanlage, die manchmal zwei Familien dient').

7. The type of Alemannic-Schwäbisch archaeological remains is commented upon by Schmidt, II, 297.

Lit. Zeuss, 57, 94; Grimm, 482; Wislicenus, *Gesch. d. Elbgermanen*; Müllenhoff, IV (see Index); Baumann, *Schwaben u. Alamannen, ihre Herkunft u. Identität* (*Forsch. z. deutschen Gesch.* XVI); A. Riese, *Die Sueben* (*Rhein. Musäum*, N.F. XLIV, 331 and 488); Kossinna, *Die Sweben*, *ibid.* IX and X; Kauffmann, *Gesch. d. schwäb. Mundart*, XXV; *idem*, *Altertumskunde*, I, 38, 68; Herm. Fischer, *Geogr. d. schwäb. Mundart*, III; Bruckner, *Die Sprache der Langobarden*, 26; Bremer, § 213; Schmidt, I, 428, II, 140, 237; Much, *Stammeskunde*; *idem*, in Hoops, s.v. *Alamannen, Quaden, Semnonen, Sweben*; Feist, *Germanen u. Kelten in d. antiken Überlieferung*, 32 seq.

§ 159. History of the Swabians, collectively.

About 100 B.C. the Swabians were probably limited to the regions on the Middle Elbe, the 'initia gentis', the area of the Semnones, 'Sveborum caput'. But they were then advancing against the Celts, and also against the North-west Germans (cp. Caesar, *Bell. Gall.* IV, 1, 3 and 4). The North-west German tribe of Ubii was made tributary to them, but seized any opportunity of allying with the Romans (*ibid.* IV, 3). In 38 B.C. the Swabians again attack the Ubii (Strabo, IV, 194).

The Helvetian Celts after 100 B.C. abandon their regions north-east of the Upper Rhine, henceforth called the 'Helvetian deserts' (Ptol. II, 11, § 6). About 60 B.C. the Marcomans (and perhaps the Quadic Swabians) drive out the Celts from Bohemia (Tac. *Germ.* 42; Strabo, VII, 304 and 313). At the same time, Ariovistus with his Swabians, Marcomans, etc., acts as mercenary general in the Gallic civil wars and becomes the lord of Eastern Gaul through the victory at Magetobriga in 61 B.C. (Caesar, *Bell. Gall.* I, 31). The Vangiones occupy the region of Worms, the Nemetes the surroundings of the river Spira, now Speyer, and the Triboci, Northern Alsace with the capital Brocomagus, now Brumt. In 58 B.C. Swabian newcomers, commanded by Cimberius and Nasva, menace the Moselle valley. Caesar, however, repulses Ariovistus from Gaul in 58 B.C., and Cimberius and Nasva beat a retreat (cp. *ibid.* I, 37, 51, 54).

The Vangiones, Nemetes, Triboci henceforth were Roman subjects, separated from the Swabians, who had emigrated to the Main valley and thereabouts, whence they had ejected the North-west German tribes of Usipii and Tenchteri in 58 B.C. (*ibid.* IV, 1 and 4).

The mountains in Middle Germany called Bacenis separated these emigrant Swabians from the Cherusci, *ibid.* VI, 10: 'pro nativo muro objectam Cheruscos ab Svevis Svevosque ab Cheruscis injuriis incursionibusque prohibuere'. Large borderlands south of the Main, probably including Bohemia, were left unpeopled; *ibid.* IV, 3: 'circiter milia passuum sexcenta agri vacare dicuntur'. West of the Swabians dwelt the Ubii (*ibid.* and II, 35), and the Chatthi (cp. Velleius, II, 109).

After the death of the Dacian potentate Boirebistas in 45 B.C. the Sarmatian tribe of Iazyges annexed the West Dacian plains between the Danube and the Teiss (cp. Pliny, IV, 80), probably by agreement with the Quadic Swabians, who appear a little later settled in Moravia as the inseparable allies of the Sarmates.

Rome and the Swabians of the Main valley had insignificant conflicts in 55, 53, 51 B.C. (Caesar, *Bell. Gall.* IV, 16, VI, 9, 10, 29, VIII, 45), and 38, 30, 11 B.C. (Dio Cassius, XLVIII, 49, LI, 21 and 22, LIV, 32). In 9 B.C. Drusus inflicted a serious defeat on the Swabians and Marcomans (Dio Cassius, LV, 1; Florus, II, 30, 23; Orosius, VI, 21, 15), and transplanted some of them to Gaul (Suetonius, *Aug.* 21) (perhaps these are those Swabians who received shipwrecked German deserters from Roman Britain 83 A.D., Tac. *Agricola,* 28; cp. Schmidt, II, 159). Tiberius in A.D. 5 menaced the Svebi Semnones on the Lower Elbe (Velleius, II, 106).

Owing to the Roman pressure, Maroboduus about A.D. 1 led the Marcomans into deserted Bohemia. His rapidly growing empire embraced the northernmost Swabians, the Semnones, and probably also the south-eastern outpost of Swabians, the Quadi. Therefore, it seems that the Romans designated his empire as Swabian. But with Maroboduus' defeat in A.D. 17, this embryonic 'united Swabia' ceased to exist.

Henceforth, in the annals of Roman politics, the name Svebi appears for a time as occupying two positions only. The one is the angle between the Rhine and Danube, where we meet with the Svebi Nicretes as Roman subjects about Lopodunum (Ladenburg), and the Svebi Euthungi as independent enemies menacing Rhaetia. The other and more important position is the present Moravia, where the Svebi alias Quadi appear now as vassals of Rome, now as dangerous enemies, e.g. in the Marcomannic war, 166–180. In 406 some of the latter Swabians leave their country and start for Gaul; in 411 they establish a kingdom in the Iberian Peninsula, but both here and on the Middle Danube, their survivals soon disappear.

The North Swabians or Semnones play a part in the O.E. legends of the Migration Age, but during the Middle Ages their remnants disappear, being absorbed by the German Saxons.

Only the South-western Swabians or Alemanni survive to this day. After having conquered the Agri Decumates, North-west Rhaetia, Alsace-Lorraine, and Switzerland from the Romans, they are themselves conquered by the Franks in 496, but in spite of large territorial losses still maintain their ethnic and political individuality. Swabian farmers and wood-cutters take part in German colonisation; they cross the Vosges into French territory, and the Alps into Piedmont. After the eleventh to twelfth century, large Swabian colonies are established among Slavs, Magyars, and Roumanians as far east as Transylvania. After the Reformation, this advance is partly turned into a retreat.

The political name of Schwaben ceased to be used after the sixteenth century; the Great Duchy of Württemberg may be called the most direct heir of the Swabian political individuality.

Roumanian, Serbian, and Magyar languages use 'Swabian' to mean German; cp. Allemand in French (cp. § 149, 7).

§ 160. History of the Semnones Proper, that is the North Swabians.

The position of the Semnones is indistinctly defined by the classical authorities and a subject of dispute among modern scholars. The question is whether they were situated east or west of the Elbe.

1. Augustus, *Res gestae*: 'Classi...ad solis orientis regionem...navigavit...Cimbrique et Charydes et Semnones et ejusdem tractus alii Germanorum populi per legatos amicitiam meam et populi Romani petierunt'. The 'tractus' of the Semnones is described as north-eastward, lying beyond the frontier of Rome. The frontier was the Elbe.

2. Velleius, II, 106, who speaks as an eye-witness, says that the Romans, after subjecting the Cherusci and Chauchi and crushing the resistance of the Langobards (in Bardengau), reached 'Albim, qui Semnonum Hermundurorumque fines praeterfluit'. That is to say: from the frontier of the new province, which was on the Elbe, Velleius could see the frontier of the Semnones and Ermunduri which was on the eastern bank of the river. It seems to have been not far up the Elbe, for the report goes on: 'eodem...classis...subvecta...Caesarique se junxit'.

3. Strabo, VII, 290, describing the extension of the Marcomannic King Maroboduus' kingdom, first mentions some East Gothonic tribes such as the Lugians and *Rugians (Mugilones), and then goes on: *καὶ τῶν Σοήβων αὐτῶν μέγα ἔθνος, Σέμνωνας....τὸ τῶν Σοήβων ἔθνος διήκει γὰρ ἀπὸ τοῦ 'Ρήνου μέχρι τοῦ Ἄλβιος· μέρος δέ τι αὐτῶν καὶ πέραν τοῦ Ἄλβιος νέμεται, καθάπερ Ἑρμόνδοροι καὶ Λαγκόβαρδοι*: 'and a large tribe of the Swabians, the Semnones....The nation of the Swabians... extends from the Rhine towards the Elbe. Some of them even extend beyond the Elbe, as for instance the Ermunduri and Langobards'. Here, the Semnones are not in set terms placed 'beyond the Elbe', but they are at least mentioned in connexion with East Gothonic tribes which undoubtedly occupy this position. The Elbe, in the epoch A.D. 5–9, was the frontier between Rome and Maroboduus: on its western bank there were no Semnones, for no collision between them and Rome is mentioned; the Semnones, as Maroboduus' subjects, belonged to the eastern bank of the frontier river.

4. Ptolemy, II, 11, § 6, places his Syeboi Semnones east of the Middle Elbe. The authority is not very reliable, as his Syeboi Langobardoi and Syeboi Angeiloi are so absurdly displaced. But if we carry back the Langobards to their true home, the Bardengau in Eastern Hanover, the continuation of that movement will place the Semnones still farther east of the Elbe than they are already situated. In no wise is the evidence of Ptolemy reconcilable with the placing of the Semnones west of the river.

5. Vibius Sequester, *De fluminibus*, 2 (ed. Bursian), says: 'Albis Germaniae, Svevos a Cheruscis dividit'. Svevi here probably means Semnones. The evidence certainly is late and long after the event, but we have no reason to doubt that it is a quotation from a report dating from the time when the Romans knew the Lower Elbe through eye-witnesses such as Velleius. According to Bursian, p. 1, the author has almost exclusively used sources not later than the first century A.D. (Vergilius, Ovidius, Lucanus, Statius, Silius Italicus).

6. *Origo Swevorum* (*Zeitschrift*, XVII, 51 seq.) is a native Swabian legend recording how the emigrants from the northern island of Swevia first landed in Slesvig and then passed through Holstein. The primaeval station Holstein fairly agrees with the position deduced from the classical authorities, that is, north-east of the Lower Elbe.

7. *Widsith*, ll. 43–44, describes a battle on the frontier of Angles and

Swabians. Saxo's Danish version, p. 170 seq., places it on the frontier of Slesvig and Holstein, Angles being replaced by the Danes (in possession of Angel), and Swabians being replaced by the Saxons. This is putting the original Swabians in the same position as in the *Origo Swevorum*, i.e. north-east of the Lower Elbe.

Though the evidence cited is more or less vague, one thing is clear: there is absolutely no trace of Semnones west of the Elbe. Thus it is inconceivable how Bremer, § 218, can arrive at the opposite conclusion. He rejects the evidence that does not suit him (cp. § 219: 'Das späte Zeugnis des Vibius Sequester kann nichts besagen'). He places the frontier of the Semnones and Ermunduri west of the river and suggests that the Semnones might have been driven from the western bank by Drusus in 9 B.C. or have abandoned it for fear of Tiberius in A.D. 5 (cp. Bremer's map, 868–869). All this is fancy.

It remains to discuss whether the Semnones occupied in historical times any part of the Baltic coast. This must be denied. Between them and the coast, Ptolemy twice places the Varines (Οὐίρουνοι and Αὔαρποι, II, 11, § 9) and our authority, otherwise unreliable, is here supported by the religious and juridical cohesion of Angles and Varines, and by modern place names such as Warnow (cp. § 237, 4). So we must assume that the Semnones in historical times extended from Eastern Holstein along the Lower Elbe to the Ermunduric frontier, which may be conjectured to be about the mouth of the river Havel. They had no other access to the sea than by the Elbe.

The Semnones formed a powerful state, regarding themselves as the origin and head of all the Swabians; ambassadors from the emigrant tribes attended the feasts in their central sanctuary (Tac. *Germ.* 39, quoted p. 100).

The Swabian conquerors fighting in Southern Germany during the last century B.C., in spite of Bremer's denial, p. 934 (last line), must have included Semnones, since even Jutlandic tribes such as the Eudoses and Harudes took part in the movement (Caesar, *Bell. Gall.* I, 51 and 31).

In A.D. 5 Tiberius faces the Semnones with his joint army and navy, but does not pass the Elbe (Velleius, II, 106–107). The Semnones ask for the Emperor's friendship, Augustus, *Res gestae*, but soon afterwards join the hostile Empire of the Marcomannic King Maroboduus in Bohemia.

During the conflict between Maroboduus and the Cheruscian leader

Arminius in A.D. 17, they, together with the Langobards, desert Maroboduus and join his opponent (Tac. *Ann.* II, 44).

In A.D. 92 a Semnonic King Masyos, together with a famous witch (Germ. '*ganna*'), makes a journey to Rome in order to negotiate with the Emperor Domitian (Dio Cassius, LXVII, 5, § 3). These guests obviously are the authorities of Tacitus for what he says of the Semnonic commonwealth in his *Germ.* 39, published in A.D. 98. He describes the great sacrifices offered to the 'regnator omnium deus' and the prominent political position of the nation, which regards itself as the head and motherstock of all Swabians and receives embassies from them during the religious feasts.

As a matter of fact, the Quadic Swabians during the Marcomannic war planned to remigrate to the Semnones (cp. Dio Cassius, LXXI, 20).

About the beginning of the third century, a south-westward movement causes the colonisation of the Main region, where the Semnones appear as Alemanni. Suidas, s.v. *Keltoi*, states that 'Σήνωνες' and 'Αλβανοί' are identical. Though the names are distorted, owing to learned misconceptions, there is no reason to doubt with Schmidt, II, 238, that Semnones and Alemanni are meant.

Henceforth, the name of the Semnones disappears. Their descendants appear again in North Germany during the Migration Age as North Swabians. The Frankish king Theodebert (534–548) subjects them (cp. his letter to Justinian, *Mon. Germ. Epist. III, Epist. Merow. et Karol. aev.* I, 133: 'feliciter subactis Thoringiis..., Norsavorum itaque gentem').

In 568, when the Saxons took part in the migration of the Langobards to Italy, the Franks transplanted the North Swabians to the evacuated region south of the river Bode (cp. Gregory of Tours, V, 15 (and hence again Paulus Diaconus, II, 6, III, 7, and 'Fredegar', III, 76); Widukind, I, 14).

In 572, however, the disappointed Saxons return and claim their former homes. The two tribes destroy one another to such an extent that finally there is room for both. The Swabians maintain their own laws, different from the Saxon type (Widukind, *l.c.*), but like the Langobards of Bardengau are gradually assimilated with their Low German neighbours.

In 748 the Frankish *Major domus* Pippin subjugates those 'Saxons who are called Nordosquavi' (*Ann. Mettens.* ad an.). He is assisted by the Slavs, who henceforth advance west of the Elbe.

The district of Swevon survives till the eleventh century, and the *Sachsenspiegel*, codified in the thirteenth century, still remembers the descent of several Saxon families from the tribe of 'Swav-ee'.[1]

Lit. Zeuss, 130, 362, 457; Grimm, 492; Müllenhoff, II and IV (see Indices); Seelmann, *Jahrbuch des Vereins f. niederdeutsche Sprachforschung*, XII, 2 seq., 39 seq.; Herm. Möller, *Anzeiger*, XXII, 137, 145 note; Bremer, § 218 seq.; Schmidt, II, 139, 236; Much in Hoops, s.v. *Semnonen*; Schönfeld, s.v. *Semnones*.

§ 161. History of the Quadi or Portuguese Svevi Proper.

On the descent of the Quadi from the Semnones and on the synonymous character of the names Quadi and Swabians in South-eastern Germany see § 158, II. The identity of the Quadi and the Middle Danubian Swabians may further be concluded from the fact that for centuries the same two names appear alternately in close connexion with the Pannonian Sarmates—a circumstance which is not sufficiently noticed in historical and ethnographical manuals.[2]

A companionship of Quadi and Vangiones in the army of Ariovistus is perhaps reflected by the name of a Quadic prince Vangio.

About 60 B.C. the Quadi probably take part in the Marcomannic action against the Celts of Bohemia.

After the death of the Dacian potentate Boirebistas, the Aryan tribe of Sarmates or Iazyges annexes the West Dacian plains between the Danube and the Teiss (Pliny, IV, 80); the Quadic Swabians later appear settled in Moravia, probably on agreement with the Sarmates.

The name Quadi first appears in Strabo's Geography miswritten as Κολδούων and then on a medal of Tiberius (cp. Cohen, *Descr. hist. des monnaies, frappées sous l'empire romain*, I, 204). Their King Vannius is established as vassal of Rome in Moravia (Tac. *Ann.* II. 63).

In A.D. 20 they are reinforced by the followers ('comitati') of the exiled kings Maroboduus and Catvalda from Bohemia, chiefly Marcomans (*l.c.*). Vannius reigns 'inter flumina Marum et Cusum' (*l.c.*). Pliny says, IV, 80: 'Superiora autem inter Danuvium et Hercynium saltum usque ad Pannonica hiberna et Carnunti Germanorumque ibi confinium

[1] The alleged 'Swabians' near Antwerp, mentioned by Venant. Fortunatus, *Carm.* IX, 1, 75, etc., are fictitious. Their real name is Zeeuwen, the toponymic of the province of Zeeland. Cp. Schönfeld in Pauly-Wissowa, s.v. *Suebi*, col. 567 (with lit.).

[2] Schmidt does at least notice in passing the cohesion of the Quadi and Sarmates, II, 194.

campos et plana Iazyges Sarmatae, montes vero et saltus pulsi ab his Daci ad Pathissum amnem. A Maro, sive Duria est a Svebis regnoque Vanniano dirimens eos, aversa Bastarnae tenent aliique inde Germani'.

These two statements have been differently interpreted. To begin with, we must state that a continuation of the ancient names may be expected, as many of the more important rivers in these regions appear till this day with their original names: March, O.H.Germ. Maraha, Czech Morava, is the Marus; Gran, Czech Hron, is the Granua; Regen, Czech Řezna, the Regnus; Kamp and Cham, Czech Kouba, Kuba, are the rivers of the Adrabai Kampoi and Parmai Kampoi. Now Mommsen, *Röm. Gesch.* v, 196, has proposed to identify Cusus with the present Gusen, which flows into the Danube near Linz. But Much in Hoops, s.v. *Cusus*, objects that the river mentioned must be situated *east* of the Marus. A more plausible theory is set forth by Ernst Schwarz, *Zur Namenforschung u. Siedlungsgeschichte in den Sudetenländern* (*Prager Deutsche Studien*, Heft 30, 24 seq.); *idem*, *Zeitschr. f. Ortsnamenforschung*, VII, 200 seq. (cp. Králiček, *Die Donauvölker Altgermaniens* (*Jahresber. der deutschen Oberrealschule in Brünn*, 1896–1897)). Schwarz points out that a streamlet debouching into the Waag near Sillein is in the modern Slowack language called Kysuča, that is, 'the little Cusus'; consequently, Cusus seems to be the ancient name of the Waag. The name Cusus must have had a long *ū*, which is normally reflected by the Slavonic *y*; Much refers it to the root of the Greek κῦμα 'high waving water' and suggests that the German name Waag may have been an old translation of the Pannonian name. See page 447.

Lit. Müllenhoff, II, 322; Schmidt, II, 172; Tomaschek in Pauly-Wissowa, s.v. *Cusus* and *Duria*; Kauffmann, I, 334 note 7; Much in Hoops, s.v. *Duria*, *Marus*, and *Quadi*.[1]

The non-Gothonic neighbours of the Quadi were the *Cotini*, Celtic iron-workers on the frontier of the Sarmates (Tac. *Germ.* 43); the probably Celtic *Kampoi* (see above); cp. the mediaeval region of Champ-richi on the western river *Campus; *Rakatai* near the

[1] In *Arkiv*, 1919, 357, we have proposed to identify Duria with an affluent of the Marus, Czech Dyje, Germ. Thaya. The Czech form could certainly not have been developed directly from Duria, but we might suppose an intermediate Celtic or Pannonian form. As we do not know the phonetics of either language, the suggestion cannot be proved, but the possibility may at least be considered.

Marus[1]; *Osi* close by, neighbours of the Sarmates, a tribe of Pannonian nationality (Tac. *Germ.* 43); *Dacians* in the Carpathian mountains, e.g. *Biessoi*, namesakes of the Thracian Bessi, and possibly reflected by the mountains now called Bieskides.

The most powerful non-Gothonic neighbours were the *Sarmates* or *Jazyges*, invaders like the Quadi themselves. Curiously enough, we are ignorant of the circumstances which led the two nations to an entente lasting for several centuries. We can only note some fragmentary indications of their cohesion. Various alliances but no mutual wars of theirs are recorded. They share the tribute paid by the Cotini and Osi, probably on friendly agreement (cp. Tac. *Germ.* 43: 'partem tributorum Sarmatae, partem Quadi ut aligenis imponunt'). The Quadi adopt the Sarmatian scale armour of horn (Ammianus, XVII, 12, § 1), and the worship of the sword (*ibid.* § 21).[2]

Vannius reigns successfully for 30 years, supported by his Sarmatian cavalry, and heaping up treasures through wars of rapine. But in A.D. 51 his nephews Vangio and Sido, aided by Lugians and Ermundures, dethrone him. The Emperor Claudius refuses help, but receives Vannius and his followers in Pannonia (Tac. *Ann.* XII, 29–30). Hence we may derive the town Cusum, *Tab. Peuting.*, near Peterwardein, named after the Quadic frontier river Cusus, and perhaps Teutoburgion, the modern Dálya (Ptol. II, 15, § 3).[3] Vangio and Sido then reign together, 'most commendably faithful to Rome' (Tacitus, *l.c.*). The increase of the amber trade under Nero (Pliny, XXXVII, 45) influences the Quadi, whose territory faces the great mercantile centre of Carnuntum. For a century the Quadi alternately act as vassals or as invaders in insignificant wars (see Schmidt, II, 172 seq.). We are, however, emphasising instances of their joining with the Sarmates. In 69 Sido and Italicus, 'reges Sveborum' (notice the Latin name Italicus), serve as mercenaries of Vespasian side by side with Sarmates (Tac. *Hist.* III, 5, 21, 33); in 89 'bellum Marcomannorum Quadorum Sarmatarum', inscription of Baalbek (cp. Schmidt, II, 173); in 92 'expeditio Svebica et Sarmatica', 'bellum

[1] Müllenhoff, II, 96, 331, traces the Rakatai in the Czechian Rakušane, 'Austrians'. But this identification is scarcely correct. The Czechian name derives from the castle of Raabs on the river Thaya, A.D. 1112 called Ratgoz, whence the O.Czech. nom. *Rakusi, now Rakousy, 'Austria'. It seems to mean 'the people of the chieftain Rātgōz'. Cp. Steinhauser, *Archiv f. slav. Philol.* XLII, 246.

[2] On Gothon. **Bainingōz*, i.e. Sarmates; see page 447.

[3] Rather founded by Quadi than by Teutones (113 B.C.), as suggested by Schmidt, II, 8.

Svebicum item Sarmaticum', inscription, Dessau, 1017 and 2719. Tacitus, in A.D. 98, describes the Quadi as Roman vassals and adds, *Germ.* 42: 'now they even tolerate foreign kings', i.e. probably Sarmates.

The peace is disturbed by the great Danubian war of 166–180, in which the Quadi and Sarmates play chief parts. Julius Capitolinus, 22, enumerates the enemies: 'Marcomanni, Varistae, Hermunduri et Quadi Svebi, Sarmatae, Lacringes et Buri, etc.'; we notice the copula 'et' which separates the Quadi from the Gothonic tribes, whereas they are not separated from the Sarmates. Similarly, 17, 10: 'bellum cum Marcomannis, Hermunduris, *Sarmatis, Quadis*'. After repulsing the invaders from Pannonia, 166, the Emperor Marcus Aurelius introduces Furtius as king of the Quadi (Dio Cassius, LXXI, 13, § 3); the name which is the Ossetian *furt* 'son', Ind. *putra*, is Sarmatian.[1] In 170 Germani and Jazyges, i.e. Quadi and Sarmates, menace the capital of Dacia, Sarmizegethusa (inscr. Dessau, 1098, 371). After beating the Quadi on their own soil, Marcus Aurelius compels them to abstain from alliance with the Marcomans and Sarmates (Dio Cassius, LXXI, 11). The Celtic Coteni in the interest of Rome revolt against the Quadi and Sarmates, but then desert their Roman allegiance and, as a punishment, are transplanted to Roman Pannonia (*ibid.* 12). The Quadi drive out the pro-Roman Furtius, but Marcus Aurelius beats them near Gran which appears as a Quadic river (*Γρανούα*, Marcus Aurelius, Εἰς ἑαυτόν, ch. 1). They are forced to deliver up their anti-Roman King Hariogaiz and receive Roman garrisons (cp. the archaeological finds at Stampfen, Surany, Zelic, *CIL.* III, 4659, IV, 11352, 11303, 3750, 11076; further at Oberleiserberg in Nieder Oesterreich. Cp. Herbert Mitscha Märheim and Ernst Nischer Falkenhof, *Der Oberleiserberg* (*Mitteil. d. prähist. Kommission d. Akad. d. Wiss. in Wien*, II, No. 5, 392 seq.)). The Sarmates are conquered in the next year (Dio Cassius, LXXI, 16–17). After a fresh revolt in 177, the Quadi try to remigrate to the Semnones (i.e. their ancestors, the 'caput Sveborum'), but are prevented by Rome (*ibid.* 20). The Sarmates are bought over (*ibid.* 18–19). After the Emperor's death in 180, his son Commodus, contented with Roman suzerainty, causes the garrisons to retire and only maintains the 'no man's land' directly beyond the Danube. The diets of Marcomans and Quadi were to be

[1] Schönfeld, *Acta Phil. Scandinavica*, III, 89, throws doubt on our assumption, we do not see on what grounds. Compounds with the same element appear among the Scythian names in Herodotus.

attended by Roman officials and both nations had to renounce hostilities against those neighbours who had previously been pacified, viz. Sarmates, Buri, and Vandals. Thirteen thousand Quadi had to enter the service of Rome; the sum total of Roman captives and deserters delivered up by the Quadi during the war was 63,000 (Dio Cassius, LXXII, 1–2).

Two marks of beginning Latin influence appear on Ptolemy's map of the Quadic soil. The one is Felicia, probably to be supplemented, castra; the other is Singone, which seems to contain the same (Illyrian?) word as in Singi-dunum, but has assumed the Latin locative form, so frequent on Roman itineraries, and indicating that there was a good deal of mercantile intercourse on that route. Yet the Quadi still remain troublesome, whereas the Marcomans almost disappear from history after the end of the war. Quadi and Sarmates invade Pannonia in 255 (Eutrop. IX, 8; *Scr. hist. Aug. v. Probi,* V, 2); both are repulsed by Aurelian in 270 (*Scr. hist. Aug. v. Aurel.* XVIII and XXXIII, 4); both by Numerianus 284 (cp. Schmidt, II, 194), both by Constantius 357 and 358 (Ammianus, XVI, 10, § 20, XVII, 12, §§ 12–14). Among the Quadi who give hostages are Viduarius[1] and Agilimund. The conquered Quadic chieftain Arahari in 358 appears with a Sarmatian vassal Usafer and as ruler of the 'Transjugitani', probably beyond the mountains of Tatra.

In 365–370 the Emperor Valentinian restores the forts beyond the Danube (cp. the archaeological finds between Gran and Waitzen and near Pest, *CIL.* III, 3761, 3766, 3769–72, 4668, 10574, 10681, 10684–85). The Quadic King Gabinius who protests is murdered. Quadi and Sarmates then invade Pannonia, but are beaten in 375, and the forts are completed (Ammianus, XXIX, 6, § 5, XXX, 3, §§ 1, 5, 6). About 390 Ammianus regards the Quadi as pacified, 'natio parum formidanda' (XXIX, 6, § 1).

In 406, however, Rome is terrified by the 'Quadus, Wandalus, Sarmata, Halani, Gipedes', invading Gaul (Hieronymus, *ad Ageruchiam,* ep. 123). After this the Quadi appear as Swabians only.

In 411 the invaders force the passage of the Pyrenees and the Emperor Honorius admits them as 'federates', the Swabian King Ermeric receiving Galicia (Hydatius, ch. 11; Orosius, VII, 40, § 10, 41, § 7, 43, § 14). Bracara becomes their first capital (cp. Sallet-Regling, *Handb. d. Kgl. Museums zu Berlin, Antike Münzen,* p. 127). The sanguinary rivalry of the Vandals ends with their departure for Africa in 429. The

[1] Perhaps belonging to the Gothic tribal name Vidi-varii.

heathen Swabian King Rechila annexes Merida in 439, Sevilla, the entire Baetica and Carthaginiensis in 441 (Hydatius, *Cont.* 121–123). Rechihar, who reigned from 448, adopts Roman Catholicism; he is conquered and executed in 456 by the Visigothic King Theodered who fights under Roman authority (Hydatius, *Cont.* 170, 172, 173–175, 178); but the Swabian kings soon regain their kingdom, including Portugal. Remismund, who became king in 460, adopts the Gothic-Arian creed (Hydatius, *Cont.* 188–207, 219–220, 223, 226, 230–232). Under Miro, who became king in 570, the final conversion to Roman Catholicism takes place (Joh. Biclar., ad an. 583, 584), and the final overthrow of the Swabian state follows in 585, when the Visigothic King Lubigild dethrones King Audica (Joh. Biclar., ad an. 583–585).

The Swabian dynasty and nobility in the Iberian Peninsula soon became more or less Gothicised, cp. the names ending in *-a*, and also the *-i* in Miro, cp. Schönfeld, 36, 186, *idem*, in Pauly-Wissowa, s.v. *Suebi*, col. 575. Romanism soon absorbed their Gothonic nationality, which left only a few traces such as the name 'Suevos' of certain villages.

The Swabians left in Moravia follow the Hun Attila to Gaul in 451 and take part in the Gothic revolt against his sons in 453 (Jordanes, L, 261).

In 467 the Swabian King Hunimund raids Dalmatia, but is beaten by the Ostrogoths near the Balaton Lake. Allied with *Sarmates*, Sciri, Rugians, and Gepides, he unsuccessfully attacks the Goths on the river Bolia in Pannonia, 469 (Jordanes, L, 274–279).

In 480 a Hunimund—according to Schönfeld different from the above-mentioned king—surprises Passau and kills its feeble Roman garrison (Eugippius, *Vita Severini*, 22).

About 530 the Swabians are subjugated by the Langobard King Wacho (*Origo Langob.* 4; Paulus Diaconus, I, 21).

In 568 Swabians and *Sarmates* accompany the Langobards to Italy, where their villages still exist in the ninth century (Paulus Diaconus, II, 26). This is the last record of the curious cohesion between Quadi and Iranians.

The Swabian country between the rivers Gran and Morava is occupied by the Avars in 568 and peopled by their Slavonic vassals.

Lit. Zeuss, 117, 123, 364, 462; Grimm, 505; Müllenhoff, II, 322, IV, 185, 455, 479, 519; Bremer, § 241; Much, *Stammeskunde*, 3rd ed. 109 seq.; *idem*, in Hoops, s.v. *Quaden*; Schmidt, II, 167, 221; map in *CIL.* III suppl. (1902); Meyer-Lübke, *Roman. Namenstudien*, I (*S.B. d. Wien. Akad. phil.-hist. Kl.* CXLIX); Jungfer, *Über Personennamen in d. Ortsnamen Spaniens u. Portugals*, 19; Schönfeld in Pauly-Wissowa, s.v. *Suebi*, 5 *b*.

§ 162. History of the Alemanni or Schwaben Proper.

The South-west Germans, called Alemanni or Schwaben, are originally Semnones (cp. Suidas; see § 158, V), but reinforced by various outsiders: Teutones 113 B.C., Jutlanders such as the Cimbri 113 B.C., *Eudoses (Iuthungi ?) and Harudes 58 B.C.; further by the Nemetes (with a Celtic name), 70–58 B.C., and the Bucinobantes (with a Frankish name), fourth century. Hence the name of 'All-men', meaning a 'confederated and mixed people' (Asinius Quadratus, cp. § 157, 7).

Their first onset compels the Helvetian Celts to leave the Schwarzwald, the 'Helvetian deserts' (Ptol. II, 11, § 6). Then Ariovistus unsuccessfully attacks Gaul, 70–58 B.C. The Vangiones, Nemetes, Triboci maintain their conquests west of the Rhine, but become Roman subjects; the others retire east of the Rhine (Caesar, *Bell. Gall.* I, 53).

Inscriptions record various colonies, mostly east of the river: Teutones at Miltenberg, Cimbri also at Miltenberg and at Heidelberg, Svebi Nicretes on the Neckar, Svebi Iuthungi at Cologne, Triboci at Marbach; the last-named perhaps came with a succession of Gaulish settlers in the first century A.D. (Tac. *Germ.* 29).

Ariovistus' second wife was Celtic (Caesar, *Bell. Gall.* I, 53). Celtic civilisation soon absorbed the Vangiones (?), Nemetes, and Triboci, and the greater part of the regions on both sides of the Schwarzwald (cp. Tacitus, *l.c.*), where inscriptions mention colonists of various Gaulish tribes: Senones, Mediomatrici, Caturiges, Cubi (or Bituriges), Sequani, Boji (cp. Stälin, *Württemberg. Gesch.* I, 32–62). The capital of the Svebi Nicretes, Lopodunum, the modern Ladenburg, is Celtic; the Teutones appear with the Celtic spelling Toutoni (*CIL.* XIII, 6610), and the god Woden has Celtic surnames: Cissonius, Visucius, Alaunus.

The Swabians north of the Main, more remote from the influence of Celtic civilisation, enter into conflicts with Rome, 55, 53, 51, 38, 30, 11 B.C. (cp. § 159). The victory of Drusus in 9 B.C. seems to efface them. Bremer, § 226, enumerates those Roman generals who failed to meet them, viz. Tiberius A.D. 4–6 (Velleius II, 105 seq.); Germanicus 14–16 (Tac. *Ann.* I, 50, 55, II, 7, 25, 41; Strabo, VII, 292); Galba 41 (Dio Cassius, LX, 8, § 7); Pomponius 50 (Tac. *Ann.* XII, 27); Swabians are also absent from the wars of 58 and 69 (Tac. *Ann.* XIII, 56–57; *Hist.* IV, 37, 70). Bremer hence concludes that the Swabians must have evacuated the Main region, but such a conclusion is not justified. The Romanised

Dacians or Thracians survive till the present time as Roumanians; though the name Roumanians has no mediaeval history, the continuity is established beyond all doubt. Similarly, the Swabians of the Main region, though temporarily obscured, later appear as Se(m)nones alias Alemanni and survive till the present day as Schwaben.

Meanwhile, the Emperors Claudius and Vespasian build forts east of the Rhine (cp. *Mainzer Zeitschr.* IV, 10, VI, 31). The governor Clemens, 73–74, incorporates the Transrhenish 'Germania superior' (cp. Dessau, *Inscr. select.* 987, 990, 991) as a tithe-paying border-land, 'Agri Decumates' (Tac. *Germ.* 29). The frontier wall or 'Limes' is completed by Hadrian, i.e. before A.D. 138, and the population is soon Romanised (cp. Schmidt, II, 164 seq.).

In 166, at the outset of the Marcomannic war, 'Celts', i.e. Swabians, attack Rome beyond the Rhine (Dio Cassius, LXXI, 3). According to Schmidt and Schönfeld, the emigration to the Semnones, planned by the Quadi in A.D. 178 (Dio Cassius, LXXI, 20), would indicate that the Semnones were then evacuating their country and moving towards the south-west, where they were soon to reappear as Alemanni (cp. Schmidt, II, 237, and Pauly-Wissowa, s.v. *Semnones*). We cannot admit these conclusions as correct. The plan of the Quadi was a 'remigration justified by political disasters', as we know from Erulian, Vandalic, and Saxon analogies (cp. our monograph *Oldsagn om Godtjod*, 84–87, and Freytag, *Bilder aus der deutschen Vergangenheit*, I, 65, 66). It does not imply evacuation on the part of the Semnones.

In A.D. 213 Alemanni are mentioned (Victor, *Caes.* XXI, 2; *Spartianus*, X); the Emperor Caracalla fights them (Dio Cassius, LXXVII, 13, § 4). The new name probably indicates a league of Swabian and non-Swabian elements, and the attacks on Roman territory now become continuous, e.g. from 233 to 238 (cp. Schmidt, II, 242 seq.), and a violent onset after the capture of the Emperor Valerian by the Persian King Sapor in 260. Lack of archaeological discoveries denotes the decay of Roman dominion (cp. the synopsis given by Schmidt, II, 246–248). Invading Alemanni are four times repulsed from Italy between 260 and 271 (Zosimus, I, 37; Victor. *epit.* XXXIV, 2; Dexippus, 682 *a*, 684 *a*; Zosimus, I, 49, § 1). After the murder of Aurelian in 275, Alemanni and Franks conquer sixty Gaulish cities (*Hist. Aug. v. Taciti*, III, 4; *v. Probi*, XIII, 14). Probus pacifies Gaul in 277, repulses Burgundians, Vandals, and Lugians from Rhaetia, and rebuilds Roman forts on the Neckar (*v. Tac.* VII, 4; *v. Probi*,

XIII, 14; Zosimus, I, 67–69). Maximian and Diocletian defeat Alemanni and Burgundians in the Agri Decumates, 286–291, but only Wiesbaden is maintained as a Roman fortress (cp. Mamertinus, *Panegyr. Max.* ch. 7, *Genethl. Max.* 5, 7, 16).

The Alemanni are being pressed towards the Rhine by the Burgundians, from whom the Limes separates them (Ammianus, XVIII, 2, § 15); about 286 Burgundian vanguards west of the Limes are repulsed by the Alemanni (Mamertinus, *Genethl. Max.* 17). Both nations claimed the salt springs, probably at Schwäbisch Hall (Ammianus, XXVIII, 5, § 11).

The Alemanni are repeatedly repulsed from Gaul and Switzerland by Constantine the Great (see coins, Schmidt, II, 263). After his death in 337, Saxons, Franks, and Alemanni conquer a continuous area of Belgium and Gaul, extending some 30 miles west of the Rhine. The Alemanni take Mayence, Worms, Spires, Selz, Brumt, Zabern, Strassburg, all forts east of the Rhine (Ammianus, XVI, 12, § 5). Iuthungi are repulsed from Rhaetia (cp. § 163).

In 357 seven Alemannic kings under Chnodomar camp near Brumt, claiming the cession of Alsace, but Julian repulses them with great glory (Ammianus, XVI, 12 seq.; Julian, *epist. ad Athen.*). In 359 he dictates the peace near the so-called Palas, i.e. the Roman Limes, now the frontier of Alemanni and Burgundians (Ammianus, XVIII, 2, § 15). Bucinobantes near Mainz, Brisigavi in Breisgau, Lentienses in Linzgau on the Boden Lake, Raetovarii and Iuthungi in Rhaetia north of the Danube, all appear as Alemanni (cp. § 157, 6, 7 (*b*), (*c*), § 163).

After the death of Julian in 363, Alemannic invaders reach Châlons-sur-Marne, while others go on raiding Alsace and Rhaetia. Roman counter-attacks are undertaken. So in 378 Gratian ravages the Lentienses (Ammianus, XXXI, 10); this is the last expedition of a Roman Emperor into German territory (cp. Schmidt, II, 287).

Stilicho re-establishes the Roman frontier on the Rhine (Claudian, *IV cons. Hon.* 439, *laud. Stilich.* I, 20, 189 seq., 216 seq., II, 186 seq.).

About 400 Franks replace the Alemanni north of the Main, while Burgundians occupy the region between the Main and the Neckar. The Alemannic raids beyond the Upper Rhine increase. No Roman coins of a later date than this are found in Augst near Basel and in Windisch (cp. Schultheiss, *Archäol. Anzeiger*, 1910, 362, 1911, 389).

Yet in 410 the Alemanni are still called Transrhenish (cp. Sozomenus, IX, 13, and Renatus Profuturus Frigeridus, cit. by Gregor. Tur. II, 9).

In 430 Aëtius repulses the Iuthungi from Rhaetia (*Chron. Gall.* 452, 106; Hydatius, 93; Sid. Apollinaris, *Carm.* VII, 233); later, they appear as Alemanni or Schwaben.

In 436 the Burgundian catastrophe benefits the Alemanni who regain the regions on the Neckar. They do not seem to have taken part in Attila's expedition to Gaul in 451.

In 454 the murder of Aëtius makes them masters of the long desired Alsace.

In 458 their invaders are repulsed on the Campi Canini near Bellinzona (Sid. Apollinaris, *Carm.* V, 373). About 470 they raid the Danubian city of Passau, even menacing Lorch (Eugippius, *Vit. Severini,* 19, 25, 27, 31).

In 479 they reach Troyes near Paris (*Vita S. Lupi Boll. Jul.* 7, 81).

About 470 the Alemannic territory embraces Langres, Worms, Spires, Zabern, Strassburg, Basel, Besançon, Mandeure, Zürich, Bregenz, and probably Ascapha (Aschaffenburg) and Uburzis (Würzburg), according to the Gothic geographer Athanared cited by Anon. Ravennas, IV, 26 (but cp. the doubts expressed by Schmidt, II, 291). The river Lech forms the frontier against South-western Bavaria.

After 480 Langres, Besançon, and Mandeure are occupied by the Burgundians (Gregor. Tur. II, 23, and Castorius, cited by Anon. Ravennas, IV, 27; cp. Schmidt, I, 378). The Alemanni attack the Frankish territory as far north as Zülpich (Gregor. Tur. II, 37).

But the year 496 puts an end to their attacks and their independence. The Frankish King Chlodowech destroys their power in a bloody battle, in which their king falls. Western Alemannia is subjugated, while other Alemanni submit to the Gothic King Theodoric the Great (Gregor. Tur. II, 30; Ennodius, *Panegyr. Theod.* XV, 72; and Theodoric's letter in Cassiodorus, *Variae,* II, 41). Theodoric's name appears in a 'Theodoricopolis' in Switzerland (Anon. Ravennas, IV, 26); on the extension of Gothic rule see Schmidt, II, 299, and Hodgkin, III, 342, 353. Hodgkin, referring to v. Schubert, *Die Unterwerfung der Alamannen* (1884), says: 'Eastern Switzerland, Western Tyrol, Southern Baden, and Württemberg, and South-western Bavaria, probably formed this new [Gothic] Alamannia....Against a consensus of first-rate authorities [such as Theodoric, Agathias, Ennodius], the mere silence of a writer like Gregory counts for very little'.

In 536, however, the Gothic King Vitigis cedes his Alemannic possessions to the Franks as the price of their help against the Byzantines. The treacherous ally, King Theodebert, then causes Alemannic marauders to raid both Goths and Byzantines, 536–539 (Procopius, *Bell. Got.* I, 13, II, 12, 25; Cassiodorus, *Variae*, XII, 7, 28; Paulus Diaconus, II, 2).

The catastrophe of 496 deprived the Alemanni of large areas. This ethnic revolution is not questioned, but its extent is a matter of controversy. Opinions especially differ concerning the fate of Alsace. An old author, Ermold Nigellus (*Mon. Germ. SS.* II, 517), in set terms states the existence of a Frankish colony in Alsace:

> Terra antiqua, potens, Franco possesso colono, cui nomen Helisaz Francus habere dedit.

But the current theory limits the Frankish colonisation to the districts now speaking the Frankish dialect and excludes the later Duchy of Alemannia because of its Alemannic dialect. So Witte, *Zur Geschichte des Deutschtums im Elsass*; *idem*, *Deutsche Geschichtsblätter*, III, 153, 209; Bremer, § 211; Cramer, *Römisch-germ. Studien*, 142; Schmidt, II, 316.

Others maintain that the place names ending in *-heim* indicate Frankish colonisation within the Duchy of Alemannia, while those ending in *-ingen* would generally represent the Alemannic residue. So Arnold, *Ansiedlungen und Wanderungen deutscher Stamme*; Tourneur-Aumont, *L'Alsace et l'Alemanie*; Schliz in *7. Bericht des Hist. Vereins Heilbronn*, 4 seq.; Schütte, *Geogr. Tidskrift*, 1918, 191, with map. We may especially quote G. Wolfram in Petersen and Scheel, *Handwörterbuch des Grenz- u. Auslanddeutschtums*, s.v. *Elsass u. Lothringen*: 'Die Franken sind unter Chlodwig als Eroberer in das Gebiet eingedrungen. Um aber das neu gewonnene Land halten zu können, sind...an den wichtigen Römerstrassen mehr oder weniger fränk. Krieger in den vorhandenen alemann. Siedelungen als Besatzung u. Herren zurückgeblieben oder haben an diesen Verkehrswegen neue Siedelungsplätze geschaffen. Die alemann. Siedelungen werden nach den fränk. Herren umgenannt, neubesiedelte Plätze erhalten den Namen ihres Besitzers. So entstehen die Orte auf -heim, die durchweg, soweit sie der ältesten Zeit angehören, als Herrensiedelungen angesehen werden müssen.... Die Alemannen sind zum grössten Teil in dem von den Franken unterworfenen Gebiete sitzen geblieben. So erklärt es sich auch, dass Oberelsass u. Unterelsass bis zum Hagenauer Forst die alemann. Sprache gewahrt haben. Wenn sich in Lothringen (where the names ending in

-ingen predominate) der fränk. Dialekt allmählich durchgesetzt hat, so erklärt sich das ungezwungen aus dem Einfluss der staatlichen Territorialbildungen u. den Verkehrsbeziehungen, die durch die Vogesen nach dem alemann. Stammlande zu abgeschnitten waren, die Verbindung aber mit dem moselfränk. Gebiet öffneten. Immerhin zeigen in Lothringen auch jetzt noch zahlreiche alemann. Reste im Dialekt...die alte Stammesverwandtschaft oder Zugehörigkeit'.

Steinbach, *Studien zur westdeutschen Stammes- u. Volksgeschichte* (*Schriften des Instituts für Grenz- u. Auslanddeutschtum*, Univ. Marburg, Heft 5), represents a sort of intermediate point of view. On p. 66, he states: 'die bekannte Tatsache, dass beide Endungen (*-ingen* u. *-heim*) gemeingermanisches Sprachgut sind, dass aber der Süden eine Vorliebe für -ingen, der Norden eine solche für -heim entwickelt hat....Wir dürfen ...ohne Bedenken annehmen, dass die fränk. Eroberung und Kolonisation des Elsass für die Ortsnamengruppierung von Bedeutung gewesen ist....Durch die engere Zugehörigkeit der elsässischen Ebene zum Frankenreich wurden diese Gebiete in stärkerem Masse in den Kulturbereich der nördlich anstossenden Gebiete hereingezogen. Es brauchte keine Umnennung stattzufinden; denn die Namengebung war noch im Zustand des Werdens. Es ist aber auch nicht einmal nötig, an die besonderen politischen Beziehungen zu denken. Die Sprachkarten lehren uns deutlich genug, dass geradezu keilförmig der Kultureinfluss aus der Maingegend zu allen Zeiten nach dem Oberrhein vorstösst, wobei die Gegend östlich des Schwarzwalds beim Süden bleibt'.

The problem may best be illustrated by a synopsis showing the occurrence of the types of place names within the different provinces.

Local district	Chief district	Local dialect	Chief dialect	Predominant type of place names
1. Schwaben and Switzerland	Alemannia	Alemannic	Upper German	-ingen
2. South Baden	—	—	—	-ingen
3. Alsace	—	—	—	-heim
4. Middle Baden	—	—	—	-heim
5. Middle Baden	Franconia	Frankish	—	-ingen (-heim)
6. Middle Baden	—	—	Middle German	-heim
7. Lothringen	—	—	—	-ingen
8. Luxemburg	—	—	—	-ingen

Cp. also Schiber's map in *Die fränk. u. alemann. Siedlungen in Gallien.*

The main point of controversy is the conclusiveness of the dialect spoken in modern times. Witte, Bremer, and Schmidt maintain that the names ending in *-heim* within the Alemannic dialect area are no sure test of Frankish colonists, and, on the other hand, the names ending in *-ingen* within the Frankish dialect area would be no sure test of Alemannic aborigines. Yet we believe that these scholars are mistaken (cp. Wolfram's words cited above on p. 122). The present dialect is no absolutely reliable test of the original nationality. For example, the inhabitants of the Flemish coast now speak a Frankish dialect, though history shows that they were to a great extent Saxons; and this Saxon origin is betrayed by the very fact that their favourite place names end in *-inghem* and *-ton* (cp. Taylor, *Words and Places*, 89). The dialect spoken by the outposts of a nation ('enfants perdus') will easily adopt the general character of the predominant kindred dialect in the vicinity, but the types of place names remain as indelible survivals of the original stock.

Supposing that the names ending in *-ingen* in Lothringen and Luxemburg originate from the Alemannic expansion after 454, both districts were doomed to be Franconised after the catastrophe of 496 (cp. Wolfram's words cited above). On the other hand, the presumably Frankish inhabitants of places with names ending in *-heim* in Alsace and Middle Baden would naturally be absorbed by the contiguous Alemannic element east of the Rhine after they had been incorporated in a Duchy of Alemannia.[1] As to the Frankish districts registered under No. 5, they occupy an intermediate position: their chief dialect is Frankish, but still they belong to the Upper German section, because they side in essential points with Alemannic and Bavarian (cp. § 149). This mixture of types is illustrated by the partly promiscuous occurrence of names ending in *-ingen* and *-heim*.

In order to ascertain the extent of Frankish colonisation on Alemannic soil, all the ancient place names should be investigated. The *-heim* suffix is frequently accompanied by Frankish elements such as *-apa*, *-lar*, *-strut*, *-horst*, *Mahlberg*. For example, the dense stratum of names ending in *-heim* in Alsace and Middle Baden contains a *Mahlberg* ('law-court hill') and is fringed by long lines of names ending in *-strut* and

[1] In the seventh century Alsace still formed a separate Duchy, cp. Stälin, *Württembergische Geschichte*, I, 179 and 223.

-horst, so as to leave no doubt of its Frankish origin (cp. our sketch map in *Geogr. Tidskrift*, 1918, 200).[1]

Finally, also, the types of architecture observed by Meitzen may be worth noticing (cp. the map in this work, Fig. 3). In Alsace and Baden, the names ending in *-ingen* fairly coincide with the Alemannic type of house, the names ending in *-heim* with the Frankish. A few surviving names ending in *-ingen* and Alemannic houses appear in the mountains east and west of the Rhine, as on a common line of retreat. The isolated mountain of Kaiserstuhl, projecting north of Breisach, forms a barrier which has stopped the advance both of the names ending in *-heim* and of the Frankish type of house.

Our suggestions have been rejected by Bückmann in *Petermanns Mitteilungen*, 1922, 13, but we cannot admit his objections as conclusive.

The Duchy of Alemannia first appears in 587, with a Duke Leudefred (cp. 'Fredegar', IV, 8). Its real vernacular name is Schwaben, and the subordinate districts are: Schwaben proper, Southern Baden, Alsace, and Switzerland.

After 600 the inhabitants are converted to Christianity. The *Pactus Alamannorum* in the seventh century still reflects the existence of paganism which has disappeared in later codes (cp. Schmidt, II, 322 (with lit.)).

In compensation for their losses to the Franks, the Alemanni are during the Middle Ages constantly advancing in the Alps. They reach Upper Wallis in the ninth century, first colonise the mountain slopes and then assimilate the population of the valley east of Sion, who, about 1500, according to Sebastian Frank, still spoke French. From Wallis the 'free Walsers' during the thirteenth century spread to Montafon in Vorarlberg and to the Grison valleys of Davos, Rheinwald, Schams, Madris, where some of them are placed by the Hohenstaufen Emperors as guards of the St Gotthard Pass. Finally the Walsers, passing the Pass of Splügen, reach the valleys of Pommat in Italy and Bosco in Canton Ticino, and beyond Monte Rosa, the valley of Gressoney in Italy. The Gressoney people are called in French Silvières, 'Foresters'. Such Alemannic colonies have Germanised the Bernese Alps, the entire

[1] Cp. Bethge who points out in *Wörter u. Sachen*, VI, 14 seq., that the settlements ending in *-heim* represent frequently a methodical Frankish colonisation that went on till the Carlovingian epoch.

Vorarlberg, and the northern Grisons. At the present day, German is retreating in Wallis and south of the Alpine crest, but still advancing in the Grisons. A large field for expansion was opened to the Alemanni, when Magyar kings during the Middle Ages began to establish German colonies throughout Hungary and Transylvania. But though they have made the name of Schwaben general in these regions, they now to a great extent speak the Bavarian-Austrian dialect (cp. Herm. Schmidt, *Das Deutschtum in Rumpfungarn*).

In 1268 the last duke of Schwaben, Konradin, died. A league of Schwabian towns continued the idea of a political Swabia till c. 1550. The Peace of Westphalia in 1648 separated Alsace and Switzerland from Germany. Württemberg, a kingdom from 1806 to 1918, is the most direct heir of ancient Schwaben. The tribal name Schwaben holds its own, though within a diminished area, and among the south-eastern neighbours of Austria and Hungary replaces the collective name of Germans. The synonym Alemanni, which has completely disappeared from popular German, occupies a similar position in foreign languages: in French it means Germans, and in mediaeval Italian it may also express Gothonic nations.

Lit. **Zeuss, 303; Grimm, 495; Wietersheim-Dahn,** *Gesch. d. Völkerwanderung*; **Stälin,** *Württembergische Geschichte*; **Bremer, §§ 221–223; Ihm in Pauly-Wissowa, s.v.** *Alamanni*; **Behaghel,** *Wörter u. Sachen*, **II, 42;** *idem*, *Gesch. d. deutschen Sprache*, **§§ 86–100 (***Grundriss*, **5th ed. with copious lit. on the displacements of the linguistic frontiers); Schmidt, II, 163 seq., 236 seq.**

§ 163. History of the Iuthungi and Raetovarii Proper.

Certain individual features make it advisable to present the Iuthungi separately side by side with the Alemanni.

The Jutlandic *Eudoses in the army of Ariovistus are probably their ancestors (cp. § 237, 5, § 244), for it is hard to believe that the solitary element Eud-, Euth- could appear twice in the Rhine area without indicating some close connexion between the owners of the names. Their Jutlandic origin would explain why the Iuthungi emphasise their claim to a national individuality (Dexippus, *fragm.* 24).

But in South-west Germany, the Iuthungi must of course soon coalesce with the Germans surrounding them. So an inscription (*CIL.* XIII, 3225) is dedicated to the 'mothers of the Euthungian Swabians', and Ammianus, XVII, 6, § 1, calls the Iuthungi 'pars Alamannorum'.

The *Tabula Peutingeriana* erroneously places the Iutugi, that is the Iuthungi, north of the Danube between Regensburg and Vienna (cp. Müllenhoff, III, 217, and Schmidt, II, 252). All historical evidence points to a more westerly position: they worship the Swabian Mothers in Cologne and raid Rhaetia, Vindelicia, Noricum.

Rome recognised the Iuthungi as 'federates' (Dexippus, *fragm.* 24). In 270 they invade Italy; again in 271 together with Alemanni (cp. Dexippus, *ibid.*; Zosimus, I, 49, § 1). In 358 and 383 they invade Rhaetia (Ammianus, XVII, 6, § 1; Socrates, V, 11, § 2; Ambrosius, *epist.* 18, 21); in 430 Noricum and Vindelicia (Hydatius, 93; Sid. Apollinaris, *Carm.* VII, l. 233). After their defeat by Aëtius in 430 they disappear from history.

As neighbours of Rhaetia, they are probably identical with the mercenaries called *Raetovarii (*Not. dign. Or.* V, 17), and their descendants would be the present Riesser, a Schwabian population in the district of Riess, O.H.G. Rezi. The region comprises parts of ancient Rhaetia north and south of the Danube (cp. Schmeller, *Bayerisches Wörterb.* s.v. *Riess*; Steinhauser, *Teuthonista*, VI, 100). The change of Iuthungi into Raetovarii would correspond to that of Marcomans into Baivarii, and of Jutes into Cantvarii.

Lit. Zeuss, 312; Müllenhoff, III, 217; Wietersheim-Dahn, *Gesch. d. Völkerwanderung*, Index; Bremer, § 223; Schmidt, II, Index; Much in Hoops, s.v. *Juthungen* and *Raetobarii*; Schönfeld in Pauly-Wissowa, s.v. *Iuthungi*.

§ 164. Legendary Traditions.

Swabians, probably Semnones, appear in O.E. and O.N. legends. King Sváfnir of Sváfaland and the Valkyrie Sváfa in the *Helgakviða Hjörvarðssonar* are eponymous.[1] *Widsith*, l. 22, names Witta, King of the Swabians, as connected with the persons of the Hjaðning Legend. The Anglian King Offa maintains the frontier against the Swabians (*ibid.* ll. 43–44); Saxo's Danish version replaces them by Saxons, an almost unavoidable change, as all Germans are in old Scandinavian called Saxons. If the Myrgings as companions of the Swabians (l. 44) are to be identified with them, the famous epic King Eadgils (l. 93) would be of Swabian nationality. He may again be identified with the so-called 'Swede' Athisl, an antagonist of Offa's father (Saxo, 162 seq.; cp. Chambers, *Widsith*, 159, with lit.).

[1] Much in Hoops, IV, 107, suggests that the O.N. goddess Sjǫfn, *Gylfaginning*, 36, might be an eponymous expression of the Semnones.

Origo Swevorum, written in the thirteenth century, contains fragments of genuine North Swabian traditions, though confused with literary borrowings from Widukind's *Saxon History*. The 'region of Swabia' as the cradle of the nation is the Gothonic ancestral home, the 'island of Scandinavia'. Its King Rodulf may reflect the Skjoldung King Hroðulf, known from *Widsith*, *Beowulf*, and Norse sagas. Holstein and the region west of the Middle Elbe reflect successive stations of the Semnones. After this the legend goes on with traditions of the Alemanni who settle in Swabouwa in Southern Germany. As their neighbours appear: Wilzen, that is the Slavs in Mecklenburg, Wilheri, perhaps the Winnili (i.e. Langobards), and Burgundians. The Burgundian King Adilfolch seems to have a fictitious name, but the reference to fierce battles with the Burgundians corresponds to historical facts, the memory of which is only preserved in fragmentary records (cp. Schmidt, I, 378).

Eulalius Kiburger, fifteenth century, and the so-called *Ostfriesenlied* concoct a tale of Swyzers who have immigrated from Sweden. Apart from learned fancies, these fables seem to echo the narrative of the *Origo Swevorum*.

The most popular Alemannic legend deals with the Harlung brothers in Breisgau, Ambrico and Fridilo. Eckehard writes in *Chronicon Uraugiense*, twelfth century, p. 157: 'Est autem in confinio Alsatiae castellum vocabulo Brisach,...quod fertur olim fuisse illorum qui Harelungi dicebantur'. Associated with the cycle of Ermanaric, the Harlung lays were sung in Germany and England and even reached Scandinavia.

'Fredegar', II, 40, relates that an Alemannic invader Wibil on his way to Italy about A.D. 260 burnt down the provincial capital Aventicum in Switzerland, the present Avenches; its German name is Wifflisburg, i.e. 'Wibil's borough'. The author seems to be a native of the vicinity. A Norse saga also records the tale of the raid, but here Wibil is obliterated and replaced by the famous Danish Viking Ragnar Lodbrok who is said to have ravaged Gaul and Italy; perhaps Alemanni and O.N. *askmenn* 'Vikings' were confused. The Icelandic pilgrim Nikulas of Þverá on passing 'Vifilsborg' about 1150 commented upon the Norse legend (cp. *Alfræði íslenzk*, publ. by Kalund, pp. 14 and xix, and Roth, *Archiv f. Schweizerische Geschichte*, 1860, 77; Krusch in *Mon. Germ. SS. Merow.* II, 64; Schütte, *Danske Studier*, 1913, 181).

Lit. (*a*) **North Swabians: Müllenhoff,** *Sagen der Herzogt. Schleswig, Holstein u. Lauenburg*, No. 400; *idem*, *Zeitschrift*, XVII, 51 (*Origo Swevorum*), XXIII, 139,

170; *idem*, *Beovulf*, 99; Bugge, *Studier ov. de nordiske Gude- og Heltesagn*, II, 263 seq., 302 seq. (transl. as *Home of the Eddic Poems*); Schütte, *Oldsagn om Godtjod*, 170, 201; Chambers, *Widsith*, 194. (*b*) Schwaben, Alemanni: W. Grimm, *Heldensage*, Index, s.v. *Harlungen*; Müllenhoff, *Zeitschrift*, XII, 304, No. 13, 26, 65; *ibid.* XXX, 217; Symons, *Grundriss*, 3rd ed. III, 685; Jiriczek, *Deutsche Heldensagen*, I, 99; *idem*, *Deutsche Heldensage* (*Sammlung Göschen*), 121.

D. §§ 165–169. *THE MARCOMANS OR BAVARIANS*

§ 165. Names.

1. Lat. Marco-manni (Caesar, first century B.C.), Marco-mani; Gr. Μαρκο-μάνοι (Strabo, first century B.C.), Μαρκο-μανοί, Μαρκο-μαννοί. Place name: Lat. Marco-mannia (now Marmagne, in Allier, Cher, Côte d'Or, Sâone et Loire, and Marmaigne in Mayenne; see Longnon, *Les noms de lieu de la France*, p. 134). The name is compounded of Germ. *mark* 'marginal wood', 'borderland', and 'men'. Wissowa points out that the spelling with one *n* is normal in classical orthography. In the ninth century the name is used to indicate 'Men of Den-*mark*' (see § 258, 3); cp. also the O.N. Marka-menn, but *Markir* here means 'the Woods', and the ending *-a* is genitival. Home: (1) the *Marca of the Main region, i.e. Silva Marciana, *Tab. Peuting.*; (2) Bohemia; (3) Bavaria and Austria.

Lit. Zeuss, 114; Grimm, 502; Müllenhoff, II, 300, IV, 478; Schönfeld, s.v. *Marcomanni*; Much in Hoops, s.v. *Markomannen*; Wissowa, *Götting. Gel. Anz.* 178, 662 seq.; Möller, *Indogerm. Forsch.* XXXIII, *Anz.* 53.

2. Goth. *Bajōs; vulg. Goth. Bajas (Anon. Ravennas, IV, 18, seventh century A.D.); a territorial term, but equivalent to Celt. Boji, ancient inhabitants of Bohemia. The statement of Jonas of Bobbio in his *Life of St Eustasius* is perhaps of learned origin: 'Bojos, qui nunc Bavocarii vocantur', see Mabillon, *Saec.* 2, 117; the *Vita S. Salabergae*, *Boll. Sept.* 6, 521, refers the identification of Boji and Baicarii to Orosius.

Lit. Zeuss, 386, 379; Holder, *Altcelt. Sprachschatz*, s.v. *Boji*, 471, 472; Much in Hoops, I, 156.

3. O.H.G. Bei-erā, Peig-irā, and (sing., corrupted by false etymology) Bauc-ver; M.H.G. Beire; N.H.G. Bayern, Baiern; Bavarian-Austrian dial. Boarn; dial. of Vienna and Kärnten Bár; O.E. Bæg-eras, Bæg-ware (Alfred, *Orosius*, 16); O.N. Bei-arar, Bæj-arar; M.Lat. Bai-varii, Bai-vvarii, Bai-oarii, Bai-bari, Bag-vvarii, Pag-arii, Bog-ari, Baug-varii, Bauc-veri, Bavo-carii, Boi-oarii, Ba-vari, Ba-bari, Wai-ocarii, Wa-wari

(for quotations see Förstemann, II, 1, 512 seq.); M.Fr. Bai-viers, Ba-viers; Ital. Ba-bieresi; Czech. Ba-vori; Wend. Ba-varski; Sloven. Pari, Parezi, Ba-varizi. Country: N.H.G. Bayern, Baiern, O.N. Beiara-land; Gr. Βαγιβαρεία (Constant. Porphyrog. *De admin.* 30), Βαϊ-ούρη (*idem*, *De caerem. aulae Byz.* II, 398); Czech. Bavory, Bavorsko. Etymology: 'Bojic men', i.e. inhabitants of Bohemia, the home of the ancient Boji. The *Monum. Boica*, VII, 375, gives a mediaeval etymology: 'Baucveri ex proprie etymologia lingue nomen sumpserunt. *Baugo* enim apud illos corona appellatur. *Wer* autem *vir*. Hinc Baucver coronatus vir appellatur'. This wrong interpretation 'Crowned men' is of popular origin, as appears from the frequent spelling Baucveri, used by Isidore as early as the sixth century; compare the normal Gipedes 'lazy' for Gibides 'gifted', § 117, 6. According to Schönfeld, 'Lateinisches *ai* (in Bai-) ist...der genaue Reflex des germ. *ai*', but he is mistaken. Goth., Celt., Gr. *ai* in Latin is transcribed *ae*, as Celt. and Gr. *oi* is transcribed *oe* (cp. Moenus, Boeotia). The Latin Bai-, Boi-, indicates Baj-, Boj-, cp. such spellings as Boiio-durus, Boiio-rix (Holder, *Altcelt. Sprachschatz*), and Baucveri, Bagibareia, Bægware, etc. The town Bojóduron in Vindelicia became Bojotro, *Bojtro, whence perhaps the somewhat questionable territorial name Boiten-gow, and the name of the brook Beider-bach (cp. Böcking, *ad Not. dign.* II, 751; C. Müller, *ed. Ptol.* II, 12, § 4; and Holder, *l.c.*, s.v. *Boiodurum*). However, a collateral form with Gothon. Bai- also existed; it appears in M.H.G. Bē-heim.

Lit. Zeuss, 364 seq.; *idem*, *Die Herkunft der Bayern*; Schmeller, *Bayerisches Wörterbuch*, I, 218; Grimm, 781; Müllenhoff, II, 96; Holder, *Altcelt. Sprachschatz*, s.v. *Boii* and Appendix; Schönfeld, s.v.; Much in Hoops, s.v.; *idem*, *Baiwarii* (*Neues Archiv der Ges. f. ält. deutsche Geschichtskunde*, XLVI, 385); Förstemann, s.v.; Schmidt, II, 211; Skok, *Zeitschr. f. Ortsnamenforsch.* IV, 224. On the pers. name Βαϊάγενα see Fiebiger, *Beiträge*, XLII, 331. Collective sense: *Deutsche Erde*, IX, 81 (cp. § 148, 8).

§ 166. Sub-divisions.

No sub-tribes of the Marcomans or Bavarians are recorded. But the *Lex Baiwariorum* enumerates five noble families, viz. Hōsi, Thrōzzā, Faganā, Hāhilingā, and Annionā (probably to be read *Annion, cp. v. Kralik, *Die deutschen Bestandteile der Lex Baiuvariorum*, in *Neues Archiv der Ges. f. ält. deutsche Geschichtskunde*, XXXVIII, 42), whose wergeld is double, as was that of the ducal dynasty of Agilolfings. These privileged families perhaps represent ancient clans. The silence of the annals is no serious objection, as the records of the Marcomans are very fragmentary. And the vague idea of 'privileged clans' is all we could expect to survive of ancient sub-tribes at the time of the Lex.

Lit. **Zeuss, 371; Schmidt, II, 218; Much in Hoops, s.v.** *Baiern.*

§ 167. Ethnic Position.

Descent from the Erminones is reflected by the derivation from 'Armenia' in a Tegernsee MS, De origine Noricorum (Pez, *Thesaur. anecdot.* III, 3, 492) (cp. Riezler, *Baierische Gesch.* I, 18; Massmann, edition of *Kaiserchronik,* III, 476; Schütte, *Oldsagn om Godtjod,* 168, 186).

Tacitus, *Germ.* 42, and Strabo, VII, 290, register the Marcomans as Swabians, but history shows that they do not belong to the Swabians proper. They normally appear *in company with* the Swabians (so Caesar, *Bell. Gall.* I, 51; Florus, II, 30, § 23; Ptol. II, 11, § 11); but neither in inscriptions nor in annals do the Marcomans or Bavarians designate themselves Swabians. Riese, *Rhein. Mus.* N. F. XLIV, 331 seq., 488, denies that they are Swabians at all, but Kossinna is of different opinion (*Westdeutsche Zeitschr.* IX, 199 seq., X, 104 seq., 293 seq.).

The identity of Marcomans and Bavarians, though sometimes denied, seems obvious. If an important ancient tribe name disappears and is replaced by a new one which is accompanied by no traditions of immigration from abroad, the identification of their owners becomes almost certain. Notice the fact that the Marcomans came from the 'home of the Boji', and that the Bavarians are the 'Bojic men' (cp. the presumable analogy of the Iuthungi > *Raetovarii, now Riesser, § 163).

The position of the Bavarians in mediaeval and modern Germany is easily defined. They form one of the four High-German branches, co-ordinate with Schwaben, Thuringians, and Franks. Their dialect belongs to the Upper German section, and they possess a national law codex, *Lex Baiwariorum.*

Lit. **Zeuss, 364;** *idem, Die Herkunft der Bayern;* **Müllenhoff, IV, 120 (criticised by Much in Hoops, s.v.** *Baiern***); Brunner,** *Deutsche Rechtsgesch.* **2nd ed. I, 454; Rietschel in Hoops, s.v.** *Lex Bajuvariorum.*

The type of the Bavarian-Alpine house (cp. the map of German types of houses, Fig. 2), with the very broad front and the low roof, two storeys, and entrance at the gable end, seems to be of pre-German origin, according to Meitzen, I, 453. An almost identical type occurs among the Basks (cp. Haberlandt, *Die Völker Europas,* Fig. 258, p. 445).

Aug. Thiersch says in *Das Bauernhaus im Deutschen Reiche*, 301: 'Der einheitliche Volkscharakter des besonders über Österreich weit verbreiteten bajuwarischen Volksstammes ist nicht nur in Sprache und Sitte, sondern auch in der Bauart des Hauses ausgeprägt'.

'Gemeinsam ist dem ganzen Alpengebiet das Alleinstehen des Hauses, welches unter *einem* Dach Wohnung, Stall und Scheune vereinigt; das Einheitshaus (the "Compound house").'

'Die Einteilung des zweigeschossigen Hauses ist diese: den vorderen, der Sonne zugekehrten Teil des Hauses nimmt die von Lauben umgebene Wohnung ein; an diese schliesst sich unmittelbar der Stall, zuletzt der Schupfen an. Über dem Stall liegt der Stadl (für Getreide und Heu) mit der Tenne, zu welcher man auf einer Rampe oder Brücke (Stadlbrucken) hinauffährt, sowie der Heu- und Getreideboden. Ein flachgeneigtes, mit Steinen beschwertes Legschindeldach deckt das Ganze und schützt, weit vorspringend, Lauben und Wände des Hauses vor der Nässe der Regengüsse'.

The domain of the Bavarian-Alpine 'Compound house' is defined thus by A. Dachler in *Das Bauernhaus in Österreich-Ungarn*: 'Es herrscht im Tiroler Unter-Inntale westlich bis Innsbruck, sowie in den Seitentälern, weit nach Bayern hinaus, im oberen Rienz- und Drautale, nach Süden bis Ampezzo, im westlichen Ober-Kärnten, und zwar im oberen Gail- und Mölltale, in Salzburg, nördlich des Passes Lueg, im sogenannten Flachgau, im nördlichen Pinzgau zwischen Saalfelden und Unken, im Gebiete des Mond-, Wolfgang- und Attersees, ein grosses Stück nach Oberösterreich hineinreichend, in einem kleinen Teile der nordwestlichen Steiermark und in einem grossen Teile im Salzburger Lungau, vermischt mit dem Haufen- bezw. Paarhof bei bayerischem Wohngebäude'.

Chr. Ranck says in *Kulturgeschichte des deutschen Bauernhauses* (*Aus Natur und Geisteswelt*, CXXI, 51): 'Meist hat der Einbau noch weniger wichtige Nebengebäude, als Backhaus, Waschhaus u. dgl. um sich und nähert sich dann in seiner äusseren Erscheinung...dem Haufenhofe'.[1]

A 'Compound house' with entrance at the middle of the long side, as in England and Denmark, occurs in South-western Bavaria.

A 'double farmstead' ('Paarhof'), as in West Jutland, is frequent in the Middle Tyrol and in Western Kärnten.

[1] The irregular farmstead, in German also called 'Gruppenhof'.

The irregular farmstead ('Haufenhof' or 'Gruppenhof'), known from West Gautland, Vermeland, and Northern Norway, predominates in Kärnten and Steiermark.

A 'quadrangle' as in Denmark, but with two storeys, predominates in Eastern Bavaria along the Danube, and in Oberösterreich.

§ 168. History.

The name Marco-manni denotes settlers in the *Marca or Silva Marciana about the river Main. It is the first heavy Compound in Gothonic ethnic nomenclature, perhaps formed just before Caesar's time to designate emigrants of the track of the Cimbric and Swabian movements.

About 60 B.C. the Marcomans eject the Celts of Bohemia, the Boji (Strabo, VII, 313; Tac. *Germ.* 42; cp. Niese, *Zeitschrift*, XLII, 160; Schmidt, II, 141).

In 58 B.C. the Marcomannic and Swabian attack on Gaul is repulsed by Caesar (cp. § 159).

In 9 B.C. Drusus defeats the Swabians of the Main region, and then the Marcomans (Dio Cassius, LIV, 33, § 2; Florus, II, 30, § 24).

Between A.D. 1 and 6 the Marcomans, whose country is partially inherited by Ermundures (Dio Cassius, LV, 10, § 2), retire to Bohemia, led by Maroboduus (Velleius, II, 108). The Celtic iron-working Cotini survive in the valley of the Gran, the Parmai Kampoi on the Bavarian river Cham, and the Adrabai Kampoi on the river Kamp in Nieder Oesterreich. Maroboduus' anti-Roman League (Velleius, *l.c.*) is joined by the Semnonic Swabians and the Langobards (Tac. *Ann.* II, 45), and by the 'Λουίους, Ζούμους, Βούτωνας, Μουγίλωνας, Σιβίνους' (Strabo, VII, 290) (read: Lugians, ..., Gutones, Rugilones, Sudini). The so-called 'Swabian' Angles were probably included, according to Tacitus and Ptolemy, and those Ermundures who retired east of the Elbe for fear of Rome (Strabo, *l.c.*), for they are the necessary link between Bohemia and the Semnones. On the inclusion of the Goths and Sudini (?), see § 119. Maroboduus' southern frontier was about 200 Roman miles from the Alpine crest, i.e. about the present Budweis in Bohemia; his infantry numbered 70,000 men, his cavalry 4000, trained according to Roman methods which he had studied in Italy (Velleius, II, 109). The preventive war planned by Augustus in A.D. 6 is frustrated by the Dalmatian rebellion and by the victory of the Cherusci over Rome, A.D. 9. In

A.D. 17, however, the Cheruscian leader Arminius falls out with Maroboduus, who is deserted by the Semnones and Langobards and driven back to Bohemia. In 19 Maroboduus is deposed by the returned outlaw Catvalda, who soon suffers the same fate at the hands of the Ermunduric King Vibilius. Bohemia becomes a vassal state of Rome. Both exiled monarchs take refuge in Italy, while their followers are received by the Roman vassal Vannius, king of the Quadi (Tac. *Ann.* II, 44 seq.; cp. § 161). Some insignificant wars with Rome follow, but the Marcomans are quiet vassals when Tacitus writes his *Germania*, A.D. 98 (cp. ch. 42).

Between 166 and 180 the Marcomans become famous through the 'Bellum Marcomannicum', as Julius Capitolinus calls it. Their King Ballomar is among the first assailants (Dio Cassius, LXXI, 8), and Marcomans together with Quadi invade Italy in A.D. 169 (Ammianus, XXIX, 6, § 1; Dio Cassius, LXXI, 3, § 2). The Marcomans are beaten in 172 and 179 (Julius Capitolinus, XXI, 10; Dio Cassius, LXXI, 33). The peace of 180 restores Roman suzerainty. The national diets are to be under supervision; 10,000 warriors enter the Imperial army; a 'no man's land' is established along the frontier, 300 stadia broad (cp. Dio Cassius, LXXII, 2). After this, the Marcomans are little heard of.

About 215, stirred up by the Emperor Caracalla, they quarrel with the Vandals (Dio Cassius, LXXVII, 20, § 3).

In 256 the Emperor Gallienus establishes the Marcomannic King Attal in Pannonia and receives his daughter Pipa or Pipara as a concubine (*Hist. Aug. v. Gallieni*, 21; Victor, *Caes.* XXXIII, 6, *epit.* XXXIII, 1).

A defeat in 299 is the last-known military action of the Marcomans (*Cons. Constant.* a. 299; Victor, *Caes.* XXXIX, 43).

In 397 a Catholic Marcomannic Queen Fritigil causes her husband to settle on Roman soil as a federate (Paulinus, *Vit. Ambros.* 36), and a 'gens Marcomannorum' under the command of a tribune appears in Upper Pannonia and Noricum (*Not. dign. Occ.* XXXIV, 24). Marcomannic mercenaries serve in Italy and Africa about 410–420 (*ibid.* VII, 38, 183, 198, 199). Their forces probably take part in Attila's attack on Gaul, 451, and the Gothic revolt against his sons, 453.

In the sixth century the Bavarians appear, filling the place of the Marcomans (cp. Jordanis and Isidore). The self-conscious etymology 'Baucveri = crown-men' (Isidore, XIII, 21) seems to imply some political force, yet the annals remain silent: the Bavarians do not rival the Alemanni, Quadi, Goths, Rugians, Erules, Thuringians, and Langobards as raiders of the Danubian regions. Perhaps the Marcomannic colonisation took place on friendly agreement with the Romans (cp. above regarding Attal and Fritigil).

After 496, when Theodoric the Great extends the Gothic dominion over the Southern Alemanni, he may have added Bavarian regions. The letter of the Frankish King Theodebert to Justinian seems to indicate that they were included: after the Goths have in 536 ceded their Transalpine possessions, Frankish rule extends from the Ocean to Pannonia.

About 555 a Catholic duke Garibald of the Agilolfing dynasty appears as a Frankish vassal (Paulus Diaconus, I, 21; Gregor. Tur. IV, 9); allied with the Langobards, he vainly tries to emancipate himself in 589 (Paulus Diaconus, III, 30).

A series of rival nations in the regions round the Danube gradually vanish or withdraw. The Rugians in Rugilanda, i.e. Austria, are scattered by Odovacar in 488; their kinsmen, the Sciri, can be traced only in the Bavarian noble family of Scheiern (cp. § 128, 2). The Goths withdraw in 536, leaving only such traces as the names of runes in a Salzburg MS, Upper Germ. *tult* 'feast' and other religious terms, and a number of personal names such as Amalung, Amalfrith, Alarich, Alawiw, Sigifuns, etc. Frankish victories in 496 and 531 check the expansion of Alemanni and Thuringians; the river Lech remains the east frontier of the Alemanni, and the Bavarians become undisputed masters of the Nordgau about Regensburg, while East Franks replace the Thuringians as their neighbours north of the Danube. The Langobards, who had taken possession of Rugilanda in 488, and conquered the Erules in 505, occupy Bohemia during the reign of Wacho (d. 540) (*Chron. Gothanum*, p. 643), but emigrate to Italy in 568.

Thus the Bavarians are finally left as the unrivalled colonisers of the vast plains between the Lech and the Böhmerwald. The temporary survival of Roman populations appears from the place names Wallgau, Walchen, Strasswalchen, etc., probably also from numbers of forms ending in *-kirch* and *-zell*, for Christian missionaries would naturally settle among the surviving Romans. Persons of Roman nationality appear in Regensburg in the ninth century (cp. the use of the Celtic name of the town in documents: Ratisbona), in Ebersberg west of Munich in the eleventh century, in Salzburg in the eleventh and twelfth centuries (cp. Behaghel, *Gesch. d. deutschen Sprache*, § 101 (*Grundriss*, 5th ed.)). The southern neighbours of the Bavarians were the Breones in the Tyrol (cp. Venantius Fortunatus, *Vita Martini*, IV, l. 644). Though Romanised, these Rhaetian mountaineers retained their primitive vigour and became practically independent during the Migration Age. Then they became subject to the Bavarians who are masters of the Eisack and Upper Drau valleys about 590, and of Bozen about 600 (cp. Egger, *Archiv f. österreich. Gesch.* XC, 372). The early advance of Bavarian settlers in the Inn valley appears from place names ending in *-ing* which extend beyond Innsbruck and of which there are isolated examples south of the Brenner pass such as Sterzing.

About 685 the Bavarians unsuccessfully fight the Langobards of Trient (Paulus Diaconus, V, 36). About 670 Mais near Meran was the frontier between the two nations (cp. *Vita Corbiniani*, ap. Meichelbeck, XI, 35). The names Mezzo Tedesco and Mezzo Lombardo (Deutsch Metz and Welsch Metz) somewhat farther south still mark the frontier of those times. Bavarian settlers gradually advance along the Adige, cultivating the wooded sides of the valleys. Rather early—we do not know exactly when—they form the 7 and 13 Communes north of Verona (one family of colonists here can be traced back to the region of Benediktbeuern south of Munich), and even people the Monti Berici south-east of that town. These first German settlers in Italy are called Cembri, perhaps from Germ. *zimmerer* 'carpenters', but perhaps rather a learned term, originating from erroneous identification with the famous Cimbri.

While constantly advancing through the Tyrol under Frankish rule, the Bavarians are threatened in their rear by eastern invaders. The Avars about 560 reach Thuringia and conquer the Franks (Paulus Diaconus, II, 10; Gregor. Tur. IV, 23 and 29). They lay waste Bohemia (*Mon. Germ. SS.* XXIV, 222), and take possession of Pannonia, as the Langobards leave it in 568 (Paulus Diaconus, II, 7). The river Enns becomes the east frontier of Bavaria (Einhard, an. ad a. 791, *Mon. Germ. SS.* I, 177).

Slavs accompany the Avars everywhere and after fighting the Bavarians about 610 at Aguntum, now Innichen (Paulus Diaconus, IV, 39), occupy the valley of Pustertal almost up to the source of the river Drau.

In 630 the victory gained over the Franks by Samo, king of the Bohemian Slavs, menaces the Bavarian east frontier (cp. § 185, p. 176).

In 788 Charlemagne replaces the rebellious Duke Tassilo of Bavaria by a Frankish count.

In 799 Charlemagne overthrows the state of the Avars and sets up the Bavarian margravate of Austria.

In 894 the Magyar invaders succeed the Avars, occupying Pannonia as the allies of the German King Arnulf against the Slavs. The 'new Huns' raid Bavaria and even Switzerland, but are repulsed by King Henry the Fowler at Merseburg in 933, and by the Emperor Otto I on the river Lech in 955.

After this, the Bavarian expansion eastward and southward is no more interrupted by invasions. The slopes of the Böhmerwald are cultivated. Most of the Slovenes north of the Drau are absorbed. The Bavarians found a large enclave about Gottschee between Kärnten and Krain.

Whereas the Breonic valley of Stubay north of the Brenner must still have spoken Romance in the fifteenth century, to judge from the palatalised *c* before *o* in place names like Tschontschefrin, it was afterwards Germanised, and its fate is shared after the seventeenth century by the valley of the Rhaetian Venostes, the Vintschgau. During the Hohenstaufen period, the entire province of Friuli in Northern Italy is covered by German castles and towns, some of which still keep their German names, such as Solimbergo and Spilimbergo. Even the native noblemen are half Germanised; one of them, Thomasin of Zirclære, in the thirteenth century writes a German poem, *Der welsche gast* ('The Welsh Guest') (cp. Bongioanni, *Nomi personali germanici*, Udine, 1911).

After the downfall of the last prince of Hohenstaufen, 1268, German influence is forced back by the Italian language spreading in the Tyrol and North-eastern Italy. The religious and political emancipation of the Hussitic Czechs in Bohemia after 1409 is a similar Slavonic reaction, and the advance of German nationality generally has stopped on this side.

A kingdom of Bavaria existed from 1806 to 1918. On the Slavonic use of the term Bavarians to mean Germans see § 148, 8.

Lit. Zeuss, 114, 364 seq.; *idem, Die Herkunft der Bayern*; Grimm, 502; Müllenhoff, IV, Index (Baiern, Markomannen); Wietersheim-Dahn, *Gesch. der Völkerwanderung*, Index; Bremer, §§ 238–240 (with special lit. on the mediaeval colonies); Schmidt, II, 141 seq., 166 seq.; Much, *Stammeskunde*, 107 seq.; *idem*, in Hoops, s.v. *Baiern, Markomannen*; Kauffmann, I, 329 seq., II, 86 seq.; Behaghel, *Gesch. d. deutschen Sprache*, §§ 11–18 (*Grundriss*, 5th ed. with lit.); Nowak, *Quellen zur Gesch. der Bojer, Markomannen u. Quaden*; Krusch, *Neues Archiv der Gesellsch. f. ältere Geschichte*, XLVII, 31 seq.

§ 169. Legendary Traditions.

Bavaria's epic fame is small and lies beyond the English and Scandinavian horizon.

The *Origo Noricorum* (Pez, *Thesaur. anecdot.* III, 3, 492) deals with the descent of the Bavarians from the Erminonic ancestor Ermin, and their emancipation from the Roman suzerainty.

The poem *König Rother* celebrates Duke Garibald's daughter Theodelinde as the bride of a Langobard king. She appears as a princess of Constantinople with altered name and her historical lover Authari is replaced by his more famous successor Hrothari.

The *Nibelungenlied*, v. 1921 seq. (Zarncke), seems to reflect a slaughter of fugitive Bulgares in Bavaria by order of King Dagobert about 630 (*Mon. Germ. SS. Merov.* II, 157): Dankwart attacks a detachment of 'Huns' on the east frontier of Bavaria.

The Bavarians also record numerous legends dealing with the Huns and Goths in the regions round the Danube (cp. Matthaei, *Die bairische Hunnensage* (*Zeitschrift*, XLVI, 1 seq.)).

E. §§ 170–172. *THE VARISTAE AND SCOTINGI*

§ 170. Names.

1. (*a*) Lat. Varistae (Julius Capitolinus, fourth century A.D.); M.Lat. Waresci, Warasci; Gr. Οὐαρισταί (Ptolemy, second century A.D.). Personal name: Lat. Varistus (*CIL.* XIII, 4178). Territorial name: O.H.G. Warasch; M.Lat. Pagus Warascus. Obscure; cp. the tribe of Varini, and see under 1 (*b*). Home: (1) 'de pago...Stadevanga...circa Regnum flumen' (Egilbert, *Vita S. Ermenfredi, Boll. Sept.* 7, 117); (2) Pagus Warascus in Burgundy.

(*b*) Lat. Naristi (Tacitus, *bis*, first century A.D.; *CIL.* III, 4500, and X, 7200: Nar..ti); Gr. Ναρισταί (Dio Cassius, third century). Obscure.

The alternation of Var- and Nar- is well verified. Much has suggested a case of 'ethnic nick-name' (cp. Gebides-Gepides and Baivarii-Baucveri). The possibility is perhaps not excluded. He also suggests that Varistae and Naristi might have been two local sections of the same tribe. The ending *-ist* might perhaps originate from the Illyrian neighbours.

Lit. 1 (*a*) and (*b*). Schönfeld, s.v. *Varisti* (with lit.); Much in Hoops, s.v. *Naristi*; Jacobsohn, *Zeitschrift*, LXVI, 232; W. Steinhauser, *Das Illyrertum der Naristen* (*Wiener Prähist. Zeitschr.* XIX, 300 seq.).

2. M.Lat. Scotingi ('Fredegar', c. 24, *Mon. Germ. SS. Merov.* II, 130). Territorial name: O.Germ. Scodinga (*Vita S. Anatolii, Boll. Febr.* 1, 359), Scudingum (*Mon. Germ. SS.* I, 435); M.Lat. Comitatus Scudingius (*ibid.* I, 489, III, 373, 517). Obscure. Home: in Burgundy, beside the Waresci.

Lit. Zeuss, 584.

§ 171. Ethnic Position, History.

Tacitus, *Germ.* 42, represents the Naristi as Swabians. We cannot verify his statement. On geographical grounds the Naristi-Varistae and Scotingi may be placed among the Erminones who also included the Swabians.

The localisation by Tacitus near the Danube beside Ermundures and Marcomans agrees with Ptolemy, II, 11, § 11, and with the alleged origin from the banks of the river Regen (Egilbert).

Varistae take part in the Marcomannic war (Julius Capitolinus, 22). Rome receives 2000 of them in Pannonia A.D. 179 (Dio Cassius, LXXI, 21; *CIL.* III, 4500).

Egilbert's *Vita S. Ermenfredi* states that the Varistae were first beaten by the Burgundians, but afterwards conquered the environs of the river Doubs (fifth century ?). The Scotingi probably accompanied them. Their German nationality seems to have survived till the ninth century, but later they were Romanised.

Lit. Zeuss, 117, 584; Müllenhoff, IV (Index, s.v. *Varisti*); Much in Hoops, s.v. *Naristi.*

§ 172. Legendary Traditions.

Egilbert's migration legend contains more ethnic facts than do all the historical references. We notice three stages: the exactly localised primaeval home, the emigration and the conflict with the Burgundians, and the final establishment in Gaul, provisionally under Roman suzerainty. The adultery committed by the Varistic housewives with their slaves while the husbands are absent on military expeditions has a curious analogy in a Scythian legend reported by Herodotus, IV, 1 (cp. Schütte, *Oldsagn om Godtjod*, 201).

F. §§ 173–177. *THE LANGOBARDS*

§ 173. Names.

1. O.H.G. Lanc-parton; M.H.G. Lam-parten; O.E. Long-beardan (*Widsith*); O.N. Lang-barðar; Lat. Lango-bardi (Velleius ad an. A.D. 5), Longo-bardi (Hydatius, fifth century); Ital. Lom-bardi; Gr. *Λαγκό-βαρδοι (Strabo, first century B.C.), Λαγγο-βάρδοι, Λακκο-βάρδοι (Ptolemy, second century A.D.), Λαγγιο-βάρδοι (Dio Cassius, third century), Λογγί-βαρδοι (Agathias, sixth century). Personal name: O.H.G. Lanc-part. Country: O.H.G. Lancpartonolant; O.N. run. Langbarðaland; M.Dan. Lumerdi; Ital. Lombardia. Place name: O.H.G. Langbardon-heim; N.G. Lampertheim. Etymology, according to the *Origo Langobardorum*: 'Long beards', cp. the O.N. Langbarðr, which occurs in a myth dealing with Woden; further Isidore, *Etym.* II, 2, and *Etym. magn.* 225, 45.[1] Kögel proposes the etymology 'long halberds'. But the testimony of the native myth seems preferable, and Bruckner remarks that the national Langobard weapon according to legends and archaeological finds is no halberd, but a spear; cp. the national assembly called *gaire-thinx* 'spear-court'. The Compound Langobardi has several contemporary analogues, Marco-manni, Ermun-duri, Sugambri, Tu-bantes, Chatt-, Chas-, Angri-varii. These tribes extend from the Rhine to the eastern border of the Elbe; otherwise, Compound names for Gothonic tribes are almost unheard of in the first century of our era. The fashion probably started from Gaul which also supplied the model of the republican constitution prevailing among the Langobards as among their German neighbours and the Saxons.

Lit. Müllenhoff, IV, Index; Kögel, *Anzeiger*, XIX, 7; Bruckner, *Sprache der Langobarden*, 33 seq.; Blasel, *Die Wanderzüge der Langobarden*, 129 seq.; Schönfeld, s.v. (w. lit.); *idem*, in Pauly-Wissowa, s.v.; Much in Hoops, s.v.

2. M.Lat. Bardi (epitaph on Drochtulf, d. 572, Paulus Diaconus, III, 19; poem in *Cod. Vatic.* 5001, fol. 147; Adam Brem. *Mon. Germ. SS.* IV, 285; Helmold, 17, *Mon. Germ. SS.* XXI); Vardi-genae (*Chron. Salern.*, *Mon. Germ. SS.* V, 470). Territorial name: O.L.G. Bardun-gawe; N.G. Barden-gau. Place name: O.L.G. Bardan-wich; N.L.G. Bardo-wiek; O.E. Beardan-ea, Engl. Bardn-ey (Lincolnshire). Etymology: see No. 1. Blasel regards the short type Bardi as abbreviated, as it occurs only

[1] Widukind, II, 36 (*Mon. Germ. SS.* III, 446), distinguishes the shorter Saxon beard: the Langobards had 'prolixior barba, et haec contra morem antiquum'.

in poetry and much later than the Compound. Förstemann, Kluge, and Bremer defend the Simplex. As a rule, Simplexes are primary (cp. §§ 76, 77, and our article in the Norwegian *Hist. Tidsskrift*, 1917, 5 seq.). The name Bardi is closely related to the cradle of the nation and to one of its chief towns. It also lies behind the current poetical expression Heaðo-beardan 'warlike Bards'.

Lit. Grimm, 689; Förstemann, s.v.; Hammerstein-Loxten, *Der Bardengau*, 4; Kluge, *Literaturblatt*, XVI, 400; *idem*, *Zeitschrift f. deutsche Wortforschung*, VII, 141; Bremer, § 242 note 1; Blasel, see No. 1; Much in Hoops, III, 124; Schönfeld in Pauly-Wissowa, s.v. *Langobardi*.

3. M.Lat. Winniles, Winnolis, Guinniles (*Origo Langob.*), Winili (*Chron. Gothan.*), Winili, -oli, -uli (Paulus Diaconus), Winuli (Helmold). Eponymous figure: O.N. Vinnill (a 'sea-king' who appears beside Vandill, i.e. the Vandal). Obscure.[1] The name has been referred to O.L.Germ. *winnan* 'to fight'. The O.N. form Vinnill seems to show that the spelling with double *n* should be preferred. Helmold identifies Winuli, Wandali, Winithi (Wends) (cp. his ch. 2); this is of course a learned confusion, but the steady *-ul* in his Winuli seems to originate from a local popular tradition.

Lit. Zeuss, 57; Müllenhoff, IV, 462; Meyer, *Langob. Sprachdenkmäler*, Index, s.v.; Laistner, *Württemberg. Vierteljahrsschrift*, 1892, 25: Bruckner, *Sprache der Langobarden*, 322; Much in Hoops, s.v. *Langobarden*; *Zeitschrift*, LX, 120 seq.

§ 174. Sub-divisions.

The names Bardi or Langobardi or Winnili may be referred to the tribe in any of its dwellings. But in the mediaeval terminology, two sections were practically distinguished, viz.

(1) Bardi in Bardengau on the Elbe.

(2) Lango-bardi in Lombardy.

As we mentioned in § 173, 2, the O.E. name Heaðo-beardan originates from the Simplex Bardi, but the prefix is a merely poetical ornament, and does not indicate a sub-division. The Heaðo-beardan who appear separately in *Widsith* beside the Langobards (of Italy) are simply the Bards of Bardengau (cp. our article in *Zeitschrift*, LXVII, 129).

§ 175. Ethnic Position.

The nationality of the Langobards is disputed.

The statement that they are Swabians (Strabo, Tacitus, Ptolemy), as confirmed by their High German dialect in Italy, is accepted by Grimm,

[1] The assonance of the Celtic Venelli in Normandy must be mentioned.

Müllenhoff, Bremer, etc. But Bruckner derives them from the 'Anglo-Frisians', and Ficker, Schmidt, Kier, partially also Much, suggest Scandinavian origin.

The evidence of Strabo, Tacitus, and Ptolemy may indicate a certain co-operation with the Swabians during the first century A.D. But later this co-operation ceases, and the Langobards always act as an entirely separate commonwealth. There are no historical references to the Langobards in expressions corresponding to Svebi Euthungi, Svebi Nicretes, Quadi Svebi. Thus we cannot acknowledge them to be Swabians proper. The argument that in Italy they spoke a High German dialect is not conclusive; during their stay on the Danube, they would almost necessarily have adopted the dialect of the surrounding tribes.

The following ethnic criteria may be worth considering.

A. German or German and Saxon affinities.

1. Republican constitution, as among Germans and Saxons.

2. Office of *sculd-hais* 'sheriff', O.H.G. *scult-heizo*, Fris. *scelt-(h)ata*, O.E. *scyld-hǣta*.

3. Offices of *stōle-sāzo* 'judge', and *scario* 'usher', O.H.G. *stuol-sāzo*, *scario* (Germ. *scherge*).

4. Onomastic element *-aib* in Burgund-aib, Bayn-aib, cp. Hessian Weter-eiba, Wingart-eiba.

5. National dress, resembling that of the Anglisaxones (Paulus Diaconus, IV, 22). But the Saxones are distinguished by their shorter beards and long, floating hair (cp. Widukind who notes the difference, II, 36). The Langobard method of wearing the hair is more like the Frankish, as described by Sid. Apollinaris, *Carm.* V, l. 238 ('rutili quibus arce cerebri ad frontem coma tracta jacet, nudataque cervix'), whereas the long beard has an analogy among the Chatthi (Tac. *Germ.* 31).

6. Participation of Saxons in the Langobard conquest of Italy, under the title of 'amici vetuli', 'old friends' (Paulus Diaconus, II, 6). (But the Saxon and Langobard laws are irreconcilably different, *ibid.* III, 6.)

B. Anglo-Scandinavian affinities.

7. Common absence of certain typical German and Saxon elements of names such as *ermin-* and *-berht.* The early Langobard nomenclature shows no trace of them (cp. the Dukes Ebor and Agio and fourteen kings of various dynasties from Agilmund to Hrodwald incl.; ten ancestors

of Hrodwald; some thirty-six contemporary and earlier Langobards, mentioned by Paulus Diaconus). The element *-berht* enters with the descendants of the *Bavarian* Gundwald, viz. Haripert, Pertarid, Cuninc-pert, Liutpert. It is similar with the Angles and Jutes, whose earlier royal names do not include the elements *ermin-* and *-berht*, which are only introduced in Britain under Saxon influence.

8. Correspondences with Anglian, Scandinavian, Frisian, Burgundian, and Gothic laws, according to Ficker, *Untersuchungen*. We are not able to criticise Ficker's results, but we must emphasise the Langobard-Scandinavian affinities pointed out by Kier in his book *Edictus Rothari*, which has been too little noticed by the contributors to the discussion. He shows that various alleged Langobard-Saxon affinities, e.g. noticed by Bruckner, *Sprache der Langobarden*, 25 and 32, are in reality shared by the Scandinavians.[1] Special Langobard-Scandinavian affinities, observed by Kier, are: the use of *lex* (lit. 'law') for 'oath', 44 seq.; *(h)ariscild*, O.N. *her-skjǫldr*, lit. 'army-shield', for 'armed disturbance of peace', 126; *exercitus*, lit. 'army', for 'a number of four persons', 127 (cp. *Ed. Hrothari*, ch. 19: 'si quis cum exercitum...usque ad quattuor homines').

The sum total of the above observations seems to indicate that the Langobards occupied originally the position of a connecting link. Their republicanism associates them with German and Saxon standards, whereas, on the other hand, various juridical institutions seem to betray an inclination towards Scandinavia.

The majority of Langobard names of offices and institutions betray a marked individual type, not occurring among other Gothonic nations. Cp. *gaire-thinx* 'spear-court', i.e. national assembly; **marh-paiz* (*mar-pahis, marepais*) 'marshal'; **scilt-por* (*scilpor*) 'shield-bearer', i.e. royal guard; *mund-uald* 'guardian'. The term *aldius* 'freedman' is shared by the Bavarian juridical language, but here we are undoubtedly faced with a loan from Langobardian (cp. Bruckner, *Beiträge*, XVIII, 573). The entire terminology gives the impression of a national individuality, fairly co-ordinate with that of the Germans.

During their stay in Austria and Pannonia, the Langobards were in close touch with German tribes, viz. Quadic Swabians towards the south-east, Bavarians, Thuringians, and Schwaben towards the west. So it cannot surprise us that the Langobard language becomes completely

[1] We may add Langobard *ware-gango* 'stranger', O.L.G. **wari-gang* (Lex. Chamav.), O.E. *wǽr-genga*, which seems to reappear in O.N. *væringr*.

High German from the phonetic point of view. The vocabulary is less thoroughly Germanised, but even here the advance of German influence is traceable: we notice how the Bavarian immigrant, Prince Gundwald, introduces the element *-berht*, hitherto unknown among the Langobards, into the proper names.

In any case, the Langobards never seem to have called themselves 'Deutsche', i.e. Germans. If the *Chronicon Salernitanum*, *Mon. Germ. SS.* III, 489, mentions the former 'lingua todesca' of the Langobards, it is rather a learned philological remark than evidence of vernacular Langobard terminology. On the ancient southern frontier of Bavaria in the Tyrol, the Langobard boundary post or *metium* is still distinguished from the 'Deutsch' one, Ital. Mezzo Lombardo and Mezzo Tedesco, Germ. Welsch Metz and Deutsch Metz.

Lit. Zeuss, 109 note 1; Grimm, 690, 698; Müllenhoff, IV, 119; Bremer, § 242; Bruckner, *Sprache der Langobarden*, 24 and 32; Ficker, *Untersuchungen zur deutschen Rechtsgeschichte*; Kier, *Edictus Rothari*; Schmidt, I, 429; Much in Hoops, s.v.

§ 176. History.

The Langobards appear in A.D. 5 in the present Bardengau south of the Lower Elbe. The *Chronicon Gothanum* calls their home Scatenauga, repeating the name of the traditional Gothonic cradle, Scandinavia.

In A.D. 5 the Langobards are 'broken' ('fracti') by Tiberius, who has previously subjugated the Chauchi in Northern Hanover and then advanced to a point facing the frontier of the Semnones and Ermundures on the right bank of the Elbe (Velleius, II, 106). The Langobards retire north of the river (Strabo, VII, 290), but after the Roman defeat in A.D. 9 must have re-occupied the evacuated Bardengau. Like the Semnones, they did homage to the Marcomannic King Maroboduus in Bohemia, but in A.D. 17 they join his Cheruscian antagonist Arminius (Tac. *Ann.* II, 45).

In A.D. 47 Italicus, a Cheruscian protégé of Rome, is re-established as king by the Langobards (*ibid.* XI, 17). Tacitus in A.D. 98 describes them as a small, but eminently warlike nation (*Germ.* 40). Roman power never again extends as far as the Bardengau.

In A.D. 166 6000 Langobards and 'Obioi' together with Marcomans are repulsed from Pannonia. The enigmatic 'Obioi' are probably a branch of the Ubii surviving in North Germany (cp. Much, *Beiträge*,

XVII, 126 and in Hoops, s.v. Ὄβιοι; Loewe, *Indogerm. Anz.* XIV, 21; Schönfeld, s.v. *Obii*). *Dulgubnii from the vicinity of the Langobards also appear on the scene; they settled in Pannonia (cp. inscr. Domaszewski, *Röm. germ. Korr. Blatt*, III, 84; but cp. the doubts of Much in Hoops, s.v. *Dulgubnii*). The raid may have been a joint undertaking from Northern Germany (cp. Schmidt, II, 139), but not, as Schmidt thinks, insignificant ('bedeutungslos') and unconnected with the later migration. The Marcomannic war of 166 seq. denotes one great ethnic movement; it also gave rise to the Langobard raid, which may have been a sort of reconnaissance, as was the service of 5500 Langobards as Roman mercenaries against the Goths in Italy in 552, preceding the invasion of 568. If the reconnaissance of 166 had no immediate consequences, that is sufficiently explained by its unfortunate result.

Three legends record early stages of the Langobard migration, viz. (A) *Origo Langobardorum*, seventh century; (B) Paulus Diaconus, I, 11, eighth century; (C) *Chronicon Gothanum*, ninth century. They are to some extent parallel; (B) and (C) contain elements of (A), but with original and divergent details (cp. § 177). If we eliminate the irrelevant epic ornaments, we may obtain some trustworthy details of the route.

1. (C) Scatenauga, i.e. Bardengau. 2. (B) Scoringa, i.e. 'the Shore', probably the home of those maritime Bards (Heaðo-beardan) whose conflicts with the Danes in Zealand are described in *Widsith* and *Beowulf*. 3. (A) Land of the Vandalic Dukes Ambri and Assi, i.e. east of the Elbe. (B) Land of the Assipiti and Maurunga, i.e. (Maur)ungani patria Albis (Anon. Ravennas, IV, 18), beyond the Elbe. The Assipiti seem to have something to do with the Duke Assi in the other version. 4. (A) Golaida, Anthaib; Baynaib, i.e. Land of the epic Bánìngas (*Widsith*, l. 19). 5. (A) Burgund-aib, i.e. Land of the Burgundians, who appear on the Main about 260 and may have come thither from the vicinity of Bohemia. The stations Baynaib-Burgundaib, which are echoed by *Widsith's* 'Báningum...Burgendum', may coincide with the Langobard raid into Pannonia A.D. 166. Version (C) finally has a station Beo-winidi, i.e. Land of the Bohemian Wends, but this seems to belong to the sixth century.

After beating the Vandals (A) or Mauringians (B), the Langobards elect Agilmund as their king (A), (B), (C), *Ed. Hrothari*. He is overcome by Bulgarian invaders (B) (I, 16), probably the Huns (cp. Zeuss, 710 seq.; Much, *Zeitschrift*, XXXIII, 9 seq., LXII, 118 seq.).

In the fifth century, while neighbours of the Rugians in Oesterreich north of the Danube, the Langobards receive from them the Arian creed (cp. Schmidt, II, 436).

In 488 King Odovacar of Italy breaks up the Rugian state; the Langobards occupy Rugilanda for ten years, and then for three years 'Field', i.e. the present Alföld between the Danube and Theiss (A), (B), (C). They become vassals of the Erules.

About 505 the Langobards conquer the Erulian state ((A), (B), (C), and Procopius, *Bell. Got.* II, 14). The Langobard King Wacho (died c. 540), subjugates the Swabians (A), and occupies Beowinidi, i.e. Bohemia, where his palace was shown centuries after (C). His policy of intermarriage establishes relations with Thuringians, Gepidae, Franks and Bavarians (A), (B) (I, 21). An alliance with Eastern Rome denotes the increase of Langobard power (Procopius, *Bell. Got.* II, 22).

In 552 2500 free Langobards and 3000 slaves fight on behalf of the Roman general Narses against the Goths in Italy and so prepare the way for the future invasion (*ibid.* 26 and 33; Paulus Diaconus, II, 1).

In 567, with the aid of the Avars, the Langobard Knig Alboin, Audoin's son, overcomes the Gepidae (Paulus Diaconus, I, 27).

In 568 Alboin grants the conquered Pannonia to the Avars, yet reserving the right of remigration, and invades Italy, reinforced by Saxons, Gepidae, Swabians, Sarmates, Bulgares, and Avars (Paulus Diaconus, II, 26). The North Italian plains surrender at once, but the East Romans keep numerous fortresses along the coasts and on the river Po, and even some Western Alpine districts.

In 569 and 571 Langobard invaders are repulsed from Gaul, while the Franks in return invade the Tyrol (Marius Avent. ad an. 569; Paulus Diaconus, III, 8 seq.; Gregor. Tur. IV, 42).

In 572 Pavia is stormed (Paulus Diaconus, II, 27), and made the Langobard capital. The murder of Alboin in 572 is followed by an interregnum of 35 dukes (*ibid.* 30). The Langobards are now masters of North Italy, and are still advancing in Middle and South Italy.

About 580 the Duchy of Benevent is founded (*ibid.* III, 32, 33). However, the conquest remains incomplete, as it does not extend to Rome, Venice, Ravenna, Grado, Istria, the southern coasts and islands. Even small, isolated forts were able to brave the Langobards for decades; for instance Comacina on an island in the Lake of Como resisted till 588 (*ibid.* III, 27). The incompleteness of the conquest was eventually fatal to the Langobard power.

In 584 the kingdom is restored by Authari who marries the Catholic Bavarian Princess Theodelinda (*ibid.* 16).

In 644 the Langobard laws are codified by the vigorous conqueror Hrothari. Theodelinda's nephew Haripert, son of the Bavarian immigrant Gundwald, abolishes Arianism. Aistulf, 749–750, conquers Ravenna, but Rome is saved from capture by the Frankish ruler Pippin.

In 774 Charlemagne subjugates the Langobards, in spite of the brave resistance of their King Desiderius; only the Duchy of Benevent survived as a Frankish vassal state. Paul Warnefrid (Paulus Diaconus) (died 795) notes down the legends and annals of his nation.

By about 1000 the Langobard nationality had died out in South Italy (cp. Bruckner, *Sprache der Langobarden*, 11–14). It survived longer in Lombardy and is reflected by hundreds of place names ending in *-engo* or *-ingo*: Marengo, Ghislarengo (cp. Bavar. Geiselhöring), etc. Such names are also frequent in Canton Ticino and in the Val Leventina, and even occur in Tuscany. The Langobard origin, however, is sometimes questionable, e.g. in the case of Spedalingo, Casalingo, formed from Latin words. Another Langobard element is Fara, 'family', e.g. in Fara Gera d'Adda (see Bertoni, *L' elemento germanico nella lingua italiana*, 23).

The nationality of the epic Heaðo-beardan in North Germany has been much discussed. Onomastic considerations naturally have advocated an identification with the Bards of Bardengau. But Müllenhoff has identified the questionable people with the Erules, and Wessén lately has conceived them as the original Danes, whereas the so-called 'Danes' of *Widsith* and *Beowulf* would have been disguised Erules.

This whole discussion, however, starts from erroneous presuppositions. Müllenhoff and Wessén conceive the word Heaðo-beardan as an individual ethnic name used in prosaic speech, but they are mistaken. The name occurs exclusively in the poems *Widsith* and *Beowulf* and must be regarded as analogous with the form Heaðo-réamas in the same two texts. That is to say, *heaðo-* ('war') is merely a poetical addition to the prosaic names Bards and Raumar. There may have been a tendency towards constantly using the decorated poetical forms, as was the case with O.E. Holm-ryge, O.N. Holm-rygir, used for the Simplex Rugians. But we have no right whatever to regard the Heaðo-beardan as a separate national individuality, independent of the Bards.

Those Bards who appear in the poems as Heaðo-beardan seem to have been situated in Scoringa (Paulus Diaconus, I, 7), i.e. on the 'Shore', in the present Mecklenburg. About A.D. 500 they are governed by a King Froda, who is killed by the Danes. His son Ingeld marries a Danish princess and then takes revenge on her family (*Beowulf*, l. 2019 seq.). The Danish Kings Hróðgar and Hróðwulf finally destroy his power near the hall Heorot in Zealand (*Widsith*, l. 45). Afterwards they may have colonised the conquered region, introducing the place names ending in *-leben*. The coast region finally fell to the Slavs, and the settlements ending in *-leben* were transplanted south-west of the Middle Elbe (cp. §§ 180 and 260, B 5).

Lit. on the **Heaðo-beardan. Grimm**, 689; **Müllenhoff**, *Beovulf*, 31; **Bugge**, *Home of the Eddic Poems*, 151; **Binz**, *Beiträge*, XX, 174; **Chambers**, *Widsith*, 79, 82, 205; **Wessén**, *De nordiska folkstammarna i Beowulf* (*Kungl. Vitterh. och Antikv. Hist. och Antikv. Ak. Handl.* part 36, 2); **Schütte**, *Ethnische Prunknamen* (*Zeitschrift*, LXII, 133).

The Bards in Bardengau survive, but only as a Saxon sub-tribe. Charlemagne compels them to be baptised (*Ann. Lauriss.* ad an. 780). Numerous rebellious Bards are exiled in 804 (Einhard, *Vit. Caroli*, ch. 7). The invading Slavs touch the east frontier of Bardengau. Helmold in the twelfth century speaks of 'Bardi bellicosissimi'. He knows their surname Winuli, but confuses it partly with Vandals, partly with Wends (Slavs).

Lit. **Zeuss**, 94 seq., 109 seq., 471 seq.; **Grimm**, 682 seq.; **Müllenhoff**, IV (see Index); **Wietersheim-Dahn**; **Hodgkin**; **Bruckner**, *Sprache der Langobarden*; **Bremer**, §§ 242–243; **Schmidt**, I, 427; **Villari**, *The Barbarian invasions*; **Much** in **Hoops**, s.v.; **Schönfeld** in **Pauly-Wissowa**, s.v.; **Hartmann**, *Geschichte Italiens*; **Kauffmann**, II, 93.

§ 177. Legendary Traditions.

The prominent epic poetry of the Langobards is in accordance with their history (cp. Velleius, II, 106: 'gens Germana feritate ferocior'; Tac. *Germ.* 40: 'paucitas nobilitat'). They must have developed a rich poetry during the Migration Age.

Much in *Zeitschrift*, LXII, 120 seq. tries to prove that also the epic Myrgingas and Hundingas belonged to the Langobards.

Lamisio, 'the man from the pond' (Paulus Diaconus, I, 15), as mythical saviour of the nation recalls the Anglian ancestor Sceaf who comes from the sea (cp. Sceafa as king of the Langobards, *Widsith*, l. 32).

The Langobard migration is recorded in three versions of which (A) and (B) are obviously parallel.

(A) *Origo Langobardorum.* The Langobards are menaced by the superior forces of the Vandalic Dukes Ambri and Assi. Frea advises the Langobards to make their numbers appear greater by disguising their women as men with long beards. Thus they deceive Woden and obtain the victory. Released slaves (*aldones*) share their subsequent migration through Burgundaib, etc.

(B) Paulus Diaconus, I, 11–13. The Langobards are menaced by the superior forces of the Assipiti, but deceive them by pretending to have a larger number of men, including man-eaters with dogs' heads. After conquering Mauringa, they solemnly release several slaves in order to increase the number of warriors. They pass Rugiland, etc.

Parallel. (1) Enemies: A, Assi and his fellow; B, Assipiti. (2) Inferior number of Langobards. (3) Increase of number through addition of fictitious men, viz. women with hairy faces in A, beasts with hairy faces in B. (4) Emancipation of slaves. (5) Migration through the regions of various East Gothonic tribes.

The following ethnic details are worth noticing: the small Langobard number (A) and (B) (cp. Tacitus, 'paucitas nobilitat'), republicanism of the emigrants and their enemies (A); double leadership (A); Langobard worship and fashion of beard (A).

Version (C), the *Chronicon Gothanum*, with its partly fictitious route—through Western Germany!—stands apart. But it also contains trustworthy details such as the record of King Wacho's palace in Beowinidi, i.e. in Bohemia.

The sum total of legendary place names is considerable (cp. § 176).

The numerous heroes may be illustrated by some of the most striking names.

The emigrating Dukes Ebor and Agio come first in chronological order (second century A.D.?).

Agilmund follows next. His elevation to the throne and his tragic fate secure him a widespread fame (cp. *Edictus Hrothari*, *Widsith*, l. 117, and three Langobard migration legends). Agilmund killed by the Bulgares is by Much plausibly compared with the 'Gothic' King Angantýr defeated by the Huns in Eastern Germany according to the *Hervararsaga* (*Zeitschrift*, XXXIII, 9 seq.). A historical Agilimund appears among the Quadi near Bregetio A.D. 358 (Ammianus, XVII, 12, § 21), at a time which might agree with that of the Langobard king; it is perhaps not impossible that the latter might temporarily have fought among the Quadi, as Beowulf fought among the Danes.

King Tato's conquest of the Erulian King Hrodulf about 505 inspired the Langobards to rich poetry (Paulus Diaconus, I, 20). The *Thidreks-saga* records the fallen king as Rodolf, alias Rodingeir of Bakalar, but his conquerors are replaced by the Nibelung heroes (cp. Boer, *Zeitschrift f. deutsche Philol.* XXV, 443; Matthæi, *Zeitschrift*, XLIII, 305; Much, *Rüdiger von Pechlarn* (*Almanach der Akad. d. Wiss. in Wien*, LXIII, 509 seq.); Bertelsen, *Didrik af Berns Saga*, 42).

King Audoin who entered Pannonia in 546 appears in *Widsith* as Eadwine (ll. 74, 117).

King Alboin as conqueror of the Gepidae and East Romans is the most famous of all Langobard heroes, and is praised by Bavarians, German Saxons and Anglo-Saxons (cp. Paulus Diaconus, I, 27; *Widsith*, l. 70 seq.). His command to his wife Rosemunda to drink wine out of her own father's skull is very well known and is an illustration proving the state of Langobard civilisation!

King Authari's wooing of Theodelinda is recorded in the German poem *König Rother*, which has, however, replaced his name by that of his more renowned successor, Hrothari.

The loss of Langobard independence has no noteworthy echo, apart from some French legends dealing with King Desiderius (cp. Bédier, *Les légendes épiques*, II).

The tragic fates of the Bardic Kings Froda and Ingeld play a considerable part in English and Danish legends. The foreign origin of these heroes was soon forgotten and they then enter the list of legendary Danish kings.

Lit. W. Grimm, *Heldensage* (see Index, s.v. *Ruther*); Kögel, *Gesch. d. deutschen Literatur*, I, 115 seq.; Jiriczek, *Deutsche Heldensage*, 148 seq. (*Sammlung Göschen*); Symons, *Grundriss*, 2nd ed. III, 720; Olrik, *Danmarks Heltedigtning*, II, 37; Bugge, *The Home of the Eddic Poems*, 139, 157; Chambers, *Widsith*, 123 seq.; Wessén, *De nord. folkstammarna i Beowulf* (*Kungl. Vitterh. Hist. och Antikv. Akad. Handl.* XXXVI, 2); Kemp Malone, *Am. Journ. of Phil.* XLVII, 319.

G. §§ 178–181. *THE ERMUNDURES OR THURINGIANS*

§ 178. Names.

1. Lat. Hermun-duri (Velleius, Pliny, Tacitus, first century A.D.), Ermun-duli, Hermun-duli; Gr. *'Ερμόν-δοροι (Strabo, first century B.C.,

Εὐμόν-δοροι), Ἑρμούν-δουροι (Dio Cassius, third century A.D.), Ἑρμουν-δουλοί (*Diamerism*, third century). Etymology: 'the great, mighty Duri'. Concerning *ermun-*, *ermin-*, see § 153. *-duri* is obscure, probably the same as Thuringi; *þ* has become voiced in non-accentuated position ('Verner's Law'). Much compares the Celtic Turones at Tours. Home: (1) on both sides of the Middle Elbe; (2) Thuringia; (3) a temporary colony appears on the Upper Danube near Regensburg.

Lit. Zeuss, 102, 353; Grimm, 597; Müllenhoff, IV, 477; H. Möller, *Anzeiger*, XXII, 142 note 2; Bremer, § 43 note; *idem*, *Zeitschrift*, XXXVII, 11; Much, *Beiträge*, XVII, 36; *idem*, in Hoops, s.v. *Hermunduren* and *Thüringer*; Schönfeld, s.v. *Ermunduri*.

2. Gr. Τευριο-χαῖμαι? (Ptolemy, second century A.D.). A toponymic, meaning 'inhabitants of the home of the Teurii' (cp. Βαινο-χαῖμαι, Ptol.; Fin-(h)aithae, Jordanes). The root T(h)eur- might be a gradation ('Ablaut') of Thur- in Thuringians. On the other hand, the assonance might also be accidental. Teurio- possibly belongs to an I.E. stem *tauro-* 'mountain' (cp. Taurus in Asia Minor, Hohe Tauern in Austria). Home: west of the Bainochaimai, i.e. Bohemians (Ptol. II, 11, § 11).

Lit. Zeuss, 103; Grimm, 597; Schönfeld, s.v. (with lit.); Schütte, *Beiträge*, XLI and *Ptolemy's Maps*, Fig. 20; *idem*, (Norwegian) *Hist. Tidsskrift*, 1917, 24; Much in Hoops, s.v.

3. Gr. Τούρωνοι? (Ptolemy, second century A.D.). A questionable form not found elsewhere; perhaps for Thuringians, cp. the Celtic Turones at Tours; perhaps miswritten for the Toutoni on the Main. Home: south-west of the Teuriochaimai (Ptol. II, 11, § 11).

Lit. Zeuss, 121; Holder, *Altcelt. Sprachschatz*, s.v.; Schönfeld, s.v. (with lit.); Schütte, see No. 2.

4. O.E. þyringas (*Widsith*); M.H.G. Düringe, Dürgen, Dürck(e); Lat. Toringi (Sid. Apollinaris, fifth century), Turingi (Aethicus, about A.D. 500), Thuringi (Jordanes, sixth century), Thoringi (Eugippius, sixth century); Gr. Θούριγγοι (Malchus, fifth century), Θόριγγοι (Procopius, sixth century). Territorial name: M.H.G. Düringen, Dürgen-lant; M.Lat. Thuringia. Place names: O.H.G. Thuringo-heim, Germ. Dürkheim, Türk-heim; O.H.G. During-feld, Germ. Türkenfeld.

Lit. Schmeller, *Bayerisches Wörterbuch*, I, 620; Förstemann, s.v. *Thuring*; Much in Hoops, s.v. *Thüringer*, and the lit. cited under No. 1.

§ 179. Ethnic Position.

Pliny, VI, 99, represents the Ermundures as Erminones, co-ordinate with the Swabian branch. Strabo, VII, 290, and Tacitus, *Germ.* 39, reduce them to a Swabian sub-tribe. We prefer to follow Pliny, for history never represents them as Swabians.

Their Thuringian successors speak a dialect co-ordinate with Schwäbisch, Bavarian, and Frankish, and in the sixth century they possess a national kingdom. The type of the Thuringian village, according to Meitzen, is the so-called 'gewanndorf', resembling that of Hesse, Hanover, Holstein, Jutland, and the Scandinavian Peninsula, but different from the 'gewanndorf' of the Schwaben, Bavarians, and Franks (cp. Schlüter's map in Hoops, I, 482).

Thus, the rank of both Ermundures and Thuringians is equivalent to that of Swabians, Bavarians, Franks, etc.

The identity of Ermundures and Thuringians has been denied by Devrient and Herm. Möller, but is assumed by Zeuss, Grimm, Müllenhoff, Much, Bremer, Schönfeld, and Schmidt. We may consider some of the more important arguments in its favour.

1. The position of the Ermundures fairly coincides with that of the Thuringians of the Middle Elbe.

2. Settlers from both tribes are found in the same position on the Upper Danube (Dio Cassius, LV, 10 *a*; Anon. Ravennas, IV, 25).

3. The Ermundures on the Danube are granted their territory by the Emperor Augustus (Dio Cassius, *l.c.*), and the Thuringians some five centuries later claim to possess Thuringia as a gift from the same Emperor (Procopius, *Bell. Got.* I, 12). Though the locality is different, the same grant seems to be concerned (cp. Much, *Beiträge*, XVII, 76; Schütte, *Oldsagn om Godtjod*, 84; Schmidt, II, 342).

4. The Ermundures disappear from political history after A.D. 166 (and even before that date Ptolemy has replaced them by Teuriochaimai), but no emigration of Ermundures is recorded in the second century or later.

5. The Thuringians appear in both of the Ermunduric territories without any record of immigration from other regions, and claim to have possessed the land continuously since the days of Augustus.

These arguments, in our opinion, prove the identity of the tribes in question.

The type of Thuringian houses is Frankish. Cp. Dietr. Schäfer in *Das Bauernhaus im Deutschen Reiche*, 30: 'Das Haus ist jetzt das sogenannte fränkische. Das sogenannte Lutherhaus in Sonnenberg, das von Judenbach her an seine jetzige Stelle gebracht wurde, wohl eins der ältesten, wenn nicht das älteste thüringisch-fränkische Bauernhaus, ist einräumig'.

Lit. Zeuss, 102, 353, 374; Grimm, 596; Müllenhoff, IV, 477, 519; Wietersheim-Dahn, I, 177; Devrient, *Neue Jahrbücher*, VII, 422; *Hist. Vierteljahrsschrift*, VI, 14; Herm. Möller, *Anzeiger*, XXII, 142; Much, *Beiträge*, XVII, 58, 62, 75, 95, XX, 20; *idem*, *Stammeskunde*, 111 seq.; *idem*, in Hoops, s.v. *Hermunduren*; Bremer, §§ 228–237; Schmidt, II, 141, 329, 342; Schönfeld, s.v. *Ermunduri* and *Thuringi*; Kauffmann, I, 413.

§ 180. History.

The doubtful identification of the Turonoi, Thuringi, with the Celtic Turones at Tours obliges us to consider the possibility that the two tribes might originate from one primaeval clan; but we only mention this as an argument that has been brought forward.

Bremer, § 228, identifies the Ermundures with Caesar's Swabians, but we cannot recognise them as Swabians proper (cp. § 173). The pre-Christian annals only make it clear that the Ermundures are not yet settled south-west of the Middle Elbe. Drusus, 19–9 B.C., does not meet them when marching against the Cherusci from the Rhine to the Elbe and the Saale (Dio Cassius, LV, 55, §§ 1 and 2; Strabo, VII, 291). He defeats only Marcomans, Cherusci, Swabians, and Sugambri (Florus, II, 30, §§ 24 and 26; Orosius, VI, 21, § 12).

Scarcely, however, have the defeated Marcomans evacuated Thuringia, when the Ermundures appear on the Danube, taking possession of the empty soil by agreement with Rome, about A.D. 1 (Dio Cassius, IV, 10 *a*; cp. § 179, 3).

Strabo, VII, 290, says that the Ermundures retired to the right bank of the Elbe for fear of Rome, as did the defeated Langobards in A.D. 5. This is perhaps an exaggerating generalisation from the Langobard retreat (cp. Bremer, § 229), for the Ermundures had no conflict with Rome, nay, rather profited from her victory over the Marcomans.

The Roman army camping on the Elbe in A.D. 6 was in sight of the frontier between Ermundures and Semnones east of the river (Velleius, II, 106). As the Semnones joined Maroboduus' Bohemian state, the Ermundures also must have done so (cp. Schmidt, II, 326), but they did not side with him against the Cherusci in A.D. 17 (cp. Tac. *Ann.* II, 63: 'Maroboduo undique deserto').

In A.D. 19 the Ermunduric King Vibilius drives out Maroboduus' conqueror Catvalda (*ibid.*), and in 51 King Vannius of the Quadic Swabians (*ibid.* XII, 29) suffers the same fate.

In 58 the Ermundures totally defeat the Chatthi and conquer the valley of the Werra (*ibid.* XIII, 57).

Tacitus, writing in 98, calls the Ermundures a 'state faithful to Rome', and describes their privileged trade with the provincial capital Augusta Vindelicorum (*Germ.* 41). Ptolemy, II, 11, § 13, mentions a 'Bohemian' town Lupfurdon, i.e. 'the ford on the river Lup-'. Eastern Germany has only one river with a name similar to this, viz. the Luppe, which flows through Leipzig, and this town thus seems to be the ancient Lupfurdon which was perhaps a mercantile centre of the Ermundures.[1]

In 166 the peace is broken by the Ermundures—probably those on the Danube—as allies of the Marcomans (Julius Capitolinus, 22); perhaps this episode is the cause of a solemn Roman declaration of war against the 'populus Hermundolus', cited by Cincius, *De re militari* (Aulus Gellius, XVI, 4).[2]

After this the Ermundures disappear from history.

In the fifth century the Thuringians appear praised by Vegetius for their fine horses (cp. *Mulomedicina*, III, 6, § 3). Their appearance indicates an epoch of expansion. The Thuringians on the river Regen (Anon. Ravennas, IV, 25) may have driven the Varistae into Gaul (cp. § 171).

In 451 Thuringian warriors probably accompany the Huns to Gaul.

In 480 Thuringians ravage Passau and menace Lorch (Eugippius, *Vita Severini*, 27 and 31).

West of the Middle Elbe the Thuringians seem to have occupied ancient Cheruscian territories. The northern frontier of early mediaeval Thuringia is formed by the rivers Ohre and Aller, the western frontier by the river Werra. Widukind exaggerates when he makes their territory extend to the northern point of Hanover (I, 4). The companionship of Thuringians, Angles, and Varines, may indicate a sort of co-operation (cp. the *Lex Angliorum et Werinorum, hoc est Thoringorum*).

Thuringia's most powerful king was Bisin, who probably resided at Bisinesburg in Bisinstidi, now Bösenburg, in Besenstedt. His daughter

[1] Perhaps the name of the town, Slav. Lipsk, originates from a distorted form of Luppe.

[2] Holz, *Beitr. z. germ. Altertumskunde*, I, 75, maintains that Cincius lived in the early second century; cp. *ibid.* 43.

and his widow both married Langobard kings, and a later Langobard King Agilulf was of Thuringian origin (cp. Schmidt, II, 331).[1]

Bisin is succeeded by his son Irminfrid, whose two brothers are also styled kings. The Ostrogothic King Theodoric the Great summons the kings of Thoringi, Erules, and Varines to ally with him against the advancing Franks (Cassiodorus, *Variae*, II, 9). Schmidt, II, 341, maintains that the Rhenish colonists are meant, as the haughty tone of the letter would have been offensive to a powerful state like Thuringia. But obviously only powerful states were worth the trouble of addressing, and we know that Theodoric wrote equally haughtily to the southern Erules who did actually ally with him.

About 500 the Thoringi in the Rhine Delta submitted to the Frankish King Chlodowech (Gregor. Tur. II, 27; cp. Schmidt, II, 342). It may, however, be regarded as questionable whether these Thoringi are really Thuringian colonists.

About 510 Irminfrid marries Theodoric's daughter Amalaberga (Jordanes, LVIII, 299; Procopius, *Bell. Got.* I, 12), but this alliance does not prevent his fate.

In 531 he is conquered by the North Frankish Kings Theodoric and Theodebert and their Saxon allies (cp. Theodoric's letter to Justinian, *Mon. Germ. Epist. Merow.* I, 133; Venantius Fortunatus, *Carm. append.* I, III; Gregor. Tur. III, 7 seq.; Widukind, I, 9 seq.; and the *Quedlinburg Annals*). Defeated on the river Unstrut, Irminfrid still resists, but finally surrenders and is treacherously killed in 534 (Gregor. Tur. III, 8). Thuringia, south of the Unstrut and the Harz, becomes a Frankish province governed by dukes, while the north falls to the Saxons. The local High German dialect survives under Frankish rule. The Saxons drive out many of the natives, and the dialect becomes Low German, though a part of the Saxon country keeps the name of North Thuringgau. After 568 North Swabians replace the Saxons in the region henceforth called Swevon (cp. § 160, p. 112). The Thuringians on the Danube are absorbed by the Bavarians.

About 560 Thuringia is devastated by the Avars, and Slavs take possession of the evacuated regions, advancing as far west as the river Saale.

In many parts of Thuringia, there are numerous examples of the

[1] Schmidt's objections against Bückmann, II, 329, are not justified. Agilulf's nationality is stated by the *Edictus Hrothari* and the *Origo Langobardorum*.

remarkable place names ending in *-leben*, which seem to have their origin in a centre on the Danish islands. There is nothing extraordinary in the assumption that the Slavonic invasion might have pushed a population of Danish settlers from the coast of Mecklenburg towards the south-west. It is only strange that the number of names with this element *-leben* leaves almost no room for a national Thuringian type (cp. on this problem §§ 176 (conclusion) and 260, B, 5).

After the ninth century the steady Thuringian retreat ceases and is followed by a reconquest from the Slavs. Thuringian settlers gradually cultivate large wooded slopes in the Erzgebirge and in Western Silesia. Their dialect becomes predominant in the so-called Saxon electorate and in Silesia. Slavonic survives round Leipzig till after 1300, in Sachsen-Altenburg till the fifteenth century, and in the Lausitz to the present day. On the Thuringian-Saxon conquests from Low German see § 149, p. 72.

The High German literary language of Luther is chiefly based upon the governmental idiom of the Saxon electorate; however, it is not purely Thuringian-Saxon, but is influenced by the Austrian governmental office (cp. Behaghel, *Gesch. d. deutschen Sprache*, § 160 (*Grundriss*, 5th ed.)).

Lit. Zeuss, 97, 102, 353, 374; Grimm, 596; A. Kirchhoff, *Thüringen doch Hermundurenland*; Lippert, *Beiträge zur ältesten Gesch. der Thüringer* in *Zeitschr. des Vereins f. thür. Gesch.* XI, 239, XII, 73, XV, 1; Lorenz, *Die thüring. Katastrophe vom Jahre* 531 (*ibid.* XV, 335); Much, *Beiträge*, XVII, 58, 62, 75, XX, 20; *idem*, in Hoops, s.v. *Hermunduren* and *Thüringer*; Bremer, § 227 (with lit.).

§ 181. Legendary Traditions.

In epic the Thuringians rank moderately.

The eponymous ancestor Ermino may have been identified with King Irminfrid, whose legendary companion Iring is a symbol of the Milky Way.

On the long-lived tradition of an Imperial grant, see p. 132.

The Hunnish King Attila's supremacy over Thuringia is remembered in the *Nibelungenlied*, ch. XXXV seq.

A Thuringian prince Wód appears in *Widsith*, l. 30.

King Bisin of Thuringia is recorded in Frankish legends ('Fredegar'), whereas his so-called Queen Basina is foreign to Thuringian traditions according to Schmidt, II, 332.

King Irminfrid's downfall is the central point of the Thuringian drama. It is recorded by Gaulish Franks (cp. Gregory of Tours and 'Fredegar'), by High Germans (cp. *Nibelungenlied*, *Wolfdietrich*, etc.), by Saxons (cp. Widukind), by North Swabians (cp. *Origo Swevorum*, partly copied from Widukind). The German Nibelung Legend still preserves the memory of the alliance of Irminfrid and the Gothic Theodoric against the Gothonic rulers of Gaul. Berther in the legend of *Wolfdietrich* probably represents Irminfrid's brother Berthar, but then his nationality and actions have been forgotten (cp. the altered position of Amalaberga). Various non-Thuringian persons appear in the legend. The Gothic princess Amalaberga in the Saxon version is represented as Frankish. King Theodoric of Northern France is reflected partly as Hug-Dietrich, partly as Wolf-Dietrich.

Lit. W. Grimm, *Heldensage*, s.v. *Irmenfried, Irnfrit, Iring*; J. Grimm, *Mythologie*, 333; Jiriczek, *Deutsche Heldensage* (*Samml. Göschen*), 55, 72; von der Leyen, *Deutsches Sagenbuch*, II, 71 seq.; Schmidt, II, 332; Chambers, *Widsith*, 198; Kemp Malone, *Agilmund and Lamicho* (*American Journ. of Philology*, XLVII, 319 seq.); Bruinier, *Die germ. Heldensage* (*Aus Natur u. Geisteswelt*, 486), p. 64.

H. §§ 182–194. *THE ISTEONIC, GAMBRIVIAN, FRANKISH, OR NORTH-WEST GERMAN BRANCH*

§ 182. Names.

1. Lat. Istriones (Pliny, first century A.D.), Istaevones (Istvaeones or Isteones) (Tacitus, first century A.D.). Eponymous hero: Frank. Istio (Escio, Hisisio, etc., *Generatio regum et gentium*, sixth century). Obscure. Ending *-aevones* as in Fris-aevones? (cp. § 226); or *-aeones* (cp. Lat. *-ēji*)?

Lit. Schönfeld, s.v. *Istuaeones* (with lit.); Much in Hoops, s.v. *Germanen*; Kauffmann, I, 250 note 10; Schmidt in Pauly-Wissowa, s.v. *Istaevones*; Löwenthal, *Arkiv*, XXXII, *idem*, *Beiträge*, XLIX, 421 seq., LIII, 463; J. de Vries, *Tijdschr. v. Nederl. Taal- en Letterkunde*, LI, 302 seq.

2. Lat. Gambrivii (Tacitus, fifth century A.D.). It is a Rhenish tribal name, Gr. Γαμαβρίουοι (Strabo, first century B.C.), connected with Sugambri (cp. § 183, 1). The name originates from O.H.G. *gambar* 'courageous'. The ending reappears in Goth. *lasiws* 'feeble'.

Lit. Schönfeld, s.v. (with lit.); *idem*, s.v. *Hilleviones*; Much in Hoops, s.v. Cp. Sugambri, § 183, 1.

3. Lat. Germani (Hieronymus, *Vita Hilarion.* fifth century); Gr. Γερμανοί (Dio Cassius, LIII, 12, § 6, third century A.D.). Originally 'natives of Belgium'; enlarged significations 'Germans' and 'Gothonic nations' ('Germanen') (cp. vol. I, § 19).

Lit. F. Frahm, *Die 'Germanen' bei Poseidonios und Cäsar* (*Klio*, XXIII, 189 seq.).

4. O.G. Frankun, Franchon, Vrancun; Germ. Franken; O.E. Froncan; O.N. Frakkar; Lat. Franci (Theoclius, cit. by Vopiscus, third century A.D.); M.Lat. Francones; Gr. Φράγγοι (*Diamerismus*, third century A.D.; Procopius, sixth century), Φρακτοί (Libanius, fourth century, an arbitrary distortion). Secondary name: Germ. Franzosen, Franzmänner; Engl. Frenchmen; M.Lat. Franciscani; Fr. Français; Ital. Franceschi, Francesi; Czech. Francouci; Lith. Francusai; Lett. Špranzis, Špranzusis; Magyar Frantzus; Finn. Ranskan, Ranskalaiset; Turk. Ferenghi. Eponymous 'sea-king': O.N. Frakki. Place names: O.H.G. Franconofurt; M.Lat. Villare Francorum, Fr. Villers-Franqueun; Francorcamps, etc. The adjective *frank* means 'ferocious', according to the traditional interpretation (Isidore, *Etym.* IX, 2, 161; Ermold Nigellus, I, 344; cp. O.N. frakkr 'brisk'). The old etymology is preferable to the divergent guesses of modern philologists. The derivation from an alleged old adjective meaning 'free' should be avoided; this signification is secondary, arising from the position of the ruling Franks among the subjected Romans.

Lit. Schönfeld (with lit.); Much in Hoops, s.v.; Chambers, *Widsith*, 195; Schmidt, II, 433; Kauffmann, II, 108; Schmaus, *Geschichte u. Herkunft der...Franken*, 154 seq.; Longnon, *Les noms de lieu de la France*, I, 130 seq.

5. O.E. Mere-wioingas (*Beowulf*, l. 2922) or Merovings, a dynastic surname (cp. Scyldings for the Danes, Scilfings for the Swedes, Amulings for the Ostrogoths).

6. O.H.G. Charlingā (Notker, tenth century); M.H.G. Kerlingen, i.e. Carlovingians, another dynastic surname.

As No. 7, M.Lat. Hugones might be added, if we follow the *Quedlinburg Annals*, *Mon. Germ. SS.* III, 31: 'Hugo Theodoricus...id est Francus, quia olim omnes Franci Hugones vocabantur a quodam duce Hugone'. But as this statement stands quite by itself, we cannot regard it as trustworthy (cp. § 215, 6, on the Chauchi).

§ 183. Sub-divisions.

The members of the Isteonic branch are nowhere recorded. We here enumerate all North-west German tribes of which we have any record, except those belonging to the Marsic branch and the Chatthi (§ 195 seq.).

1. (*a*) Lat. Su-gambri (Caesar, first century B.C. and inscr.), Sy-gambri (Horatius, first century B.C. and inscr.), Si-gambri (Suetonius, second century A.D. and inscr.), Su-cambri, Sy-cambri, Si-cambri (second cen-

tury A.D. seq.); Gr. Σού-γαμβροι (Strabo, first century B.C.), Σύ-γαμβροι (Dio Cassius, third century A.D.), Σού-καμβροι (Appianus, second century A.D.). Etymology: 'well-courageous'. Prefix *su-* as in O.N. *sú-svǫrt* 'black thrush' (lit. 'quite black'), according to Holthausen. The model for the ethnic Compound is Celtic, for example Su-essiones in Gaul, now Soissons. On O.G. *gambar* see § 182, 2. Home: on the Rhine, between the affluents Lippe and Sieg; later, west of the Rhine.

Lit. Holthausen, *Indogerm. Forsch.* XX, 321; Falk and Torp, *Etym. Ordbog ov. norsk og dansk Sprog*, s.v. *Solsort*; Schönfeld, s.v. (with lit.); Much in Hoops, s.v.; Förstemann, s.v.

(*b*) Gr. Γαμαβρίουοι (Strabo, first century B.C., see § 182, 2).

(*c*) Lat. Cugerni (Tacitus, first century A.D. and numerous inscr.); Cuberni (Pliny, first century A.D. and inscr.). Obscure. A Compound Cu-gerni? Or a derivative ending as in Basternae? Home: west of the Rhine, south of the island of Betuwe. According to Bremer and other philologists a later name for the Sugambri west of the Rhine (cp. § 186).

Lit. Bremer, § 168; Schönfeld, s.v. (with lit.); Much in Hoops, s.v.; v. Wijk, *Tijdschrift v. Nederl. Taal- en Letterkunde*, XXI, 200 (on the alternation of *g* and *b*); Loewenthal, *Beiträge*, XLVII, 290.

2. (*a*) O.L. Frank Salon; Lat. Salii (Claudianus, fourth century A.D.), Zalii (inscr.); Gr. Σάλιοι (Julianus, fourth century A.D.). Eponymous figure: M.Lat. Sali-gastus (*Lex Sal., Preface*). Territorial name: O.L. Frank Sale-chaim (*ibid.*); Dutch Salland. Obscure, perhaps derived from O.H. Germ. *sal*, M.Dutch *salu* 'dirty'; Salland would then be 'bog', 'moor-land' (cp. Carnoy, *Verslagen...der Vlaamsche Academie*, 1925, p. 365; *idem, Origine des noms de lieux des environs de Bruxelles*, p. 346). Rübel suggests a combination with a 'fortified manor', *sala*, in the area of Salian settlement. Home: Salland, south-east of the Zuider Zee; later in Belgium and North-western Gaul.

Lit. Schmidt, *Allg. Gesch. d. germ. Völker*, 213 (with lit.); Schönfeld, s.v. *Salii* (with lit.); Förstemann, s.v. (with lit.); Schmaus, *Gesch. u. Herkunft der Franken*, 157; Rübel, *Die Franken*, 488; Much in Hoops, II, 82; Zachrisson, *Studia neophilologica*, I, 19; Mansion, *Handelingen v. d. Commissie v. toponomie en dialectologie*, VI, 281.

(*b*) M.Lat. Ni-wistrii (*Ann. Mettens.* ad an. 668), Neustri; meaning 'western', as distinguished from Austri 'eastern' (7 (*b*)). Neustria and Austria also occur in Italy (see Liutprand's Langobard Law, *Preface, de anno quinto*). *ni* seems to be a preposition of which there is no other example; we may perhaps compare O.Ind. *ni* 'downwards' (Germ. 'herab'), and the Engl. word *nether*. Home: the Salian part of Gaul.

Lit. **Zeuss, 349; Grimm, 529; Förstemann, I, 280, 2, 406.**

(*c*) M.L.G. Flæmen, Vlæmen, Vlaminge, Vlæminge; Dutch Vlamingen; O.E. Flandre (-an, -on); Engl. Flemings; O.N. Flamingjar; M.Lat. Flamingi (*Ann. Vedast.*), Flandri; Fr. Flamands; Ital. Fiamenghi. Territorial name: O.Frank Flandra (*Mon. Germ. SS.* III, 426, eighth century); M.Dutch Vlaendern (-en); Dutch Vlaanderen. Obscure. Home: Flanders, a district of Neustria. See page 447.

Lit. **Verwijs and Verdam,** ***Mid. Nederl. Woordenboek,*** **s.v.** ***Vlaemsch, Vlaender*** **and** ***Vlaminc*****; Much in Hoops, II, 82; Mansion,** ***Zeeuwensche Oud-Gentsche Naamkunde,*** **85 seq.;** ***idem, Bijdragen,*** **XV, 91.**

3. Lat. Chamavi (Tacitus, first century A.D.); Chamaves (Ausonius, fourth century); *Camavi (Camari, *Not. gent.*, fourth century); Gr. Καμαυοί (Ptolemy, second century A.D.), Χάμαβοι (Julianus, fourth century). Divine 'matres' of the tribe, Lat. Hamavehae (*CIL.* XIII, 7864). Country: O.L. Frank Hamaland. Colony: M.Lat. Pagus Commavorum, s. Amavorum in Burgundy. Obscure. *-av* is generally conceived as a derivative (cp. Celtic Pictavi); Grimm refers Chamavi and Batavi to Gothon. *-auj-* 'island', but here it is questionable whether the classical spelling justifies this interpretation. Home: (1) Hamaland in the province of Overijssel, later also extending south of the Rhine; (2) a colony in Burgundy.

Lit. **Zeuss, 582; Grimm, 530; Ihm in Pauly-Wissowa, s.v.; Schönfeld, s.v.** (with lit.); **Much in Hoops, s.v.**

4. O.E. Hæt-were (*Widsith*, l. 33), Het-ware (*Beowulf*, l. 2354, etc.); O.H.G. *Hazz-warā; Lat. Att-vari (Velleius, first century A.D.), Atthvarii (Ammianus, fourth century), *Catto-vari (Gallovari, *Not. gent.*, fourth century); M.Lat. Chat-varii (*Ann. S. Amandi*), Hat-varii (*Ann. Tiliani*), Hazz-oarii (*Ann. Fuld.*); Gr. Χαττ-ουάριοι (Strabo, first century B.C.). Territorial name: O.L.G. Hatterun. Colony: M.Lat. Pagus Attoariensis in Burgundy. The etymology of the first element is obscure. Its current derivation from the Chatti or Catthi is wrong, as this name has a Gothonic *þþ* or *tþ* (cp. O.H.G. Hassi, see § 195, 2 (*a*)), whereas Chatt-varii has Gothonic *tt* (cp. O.E. Hæt-were, O.H.G. *Hazz-warā). Perhaps the Chattvarii are the 'Men of Hattem' on the Zuider Zee (Hatheim an. 891, *Nomina geogr. neerlandica,* III, 120). Home:

(1) in Hamaland, south-east of the Zuider Zee; (2) later, between the Lower Lippe and Ruhr, and beyond the Rhine extending a little west of the Meuse; (3) a colony in Burgundy.

Lit. Zeuss, 582; Grimm, 576, 589; Ihm in Pauly-Wissowa, s.v. *Attuarii*; Schönfeld, s.v. *Chattuarii* (with lit.); Förstemann, s.v.; Much in Hoops, s.v.; Schütte, *Ptolemy's Maps*, 119, 121.

5. Lat. Ampsi-varii (Tacitus, first century A.D.), Amsi-vari (*Not. gent.*, fourth century); Gr. Ἀμψιανοί? (Strabo, first century B.C.). Territorial name: O.L.G. Emis-go. Etymology: 'Ems-men'. Home: (1) at the mouth of the river Amisia or Ems; (2) later, in Westphalia.

Lit. Ihm in Pauly-Wissowa, s.v.; Schönfeld, s.v. (with lit.) and s.v. *Campsiani*; Förstemann, s.v.; Much in Hoops, s.v.

6. Lat. Chas-varii (Tacitus, first century A.D.), Cas-varii (*Not. gent.*, fourth century); Gr. Κασ-ουάροι (Ptolemy, second century A.D.). Territorial name: O.L.G. Hasu-go. Etymology: 'Hase-men'. Home: (1) on the Hase, i.e. 'the Grey River'; (2) later, in Westphalia.

Lit. Zeuss, 113 note 1; Grimm, 588; Müllenhoff, IV, 427; Ihm in Pauly-Wissowa, s.v.; Schönfeld, s.v.; Förstemann, s.v.; Much in Hoops, s.v.

7. (*a*) M.H.G. Rīfere; Lat. Ripari (?) or Riparioli (?) (Jordanes, sixth century); M.Lat. Rib-varii (*Liber hist. Franc.* written about 727), Rip-varii; O.Fr. Rivers, Ruiers. Place name: M.H.G. Rīfere-schīt; Germ. Rüffer-scheid, Reiffer-scheid, 'boundary of the Ripuarians' (frequent). The name originates from Lat. *ripa* 'river-bank'. The ending *-varii* as in Nos. 4, 5, 6, means 'men'. But we must consider the possibility that it has replaced a Latin *-arii*. Schmidt, II, 456, denies that the Ripari of Jordanes, XXXVI, 191, whom he regards as inhabitants of a Gallo-Roman river-bank, are identical with the Ripuarian Franks; for, he says, the Franks are named quite separately in the list of Roman auxiliaries, A.D. 451. He may be right in so far as it is possible or likely that the Ripari of Jordanes are really a Gallo-Roman population and not Franks; but it is still possible that the Ripuarian Franks have taken the name of this population, just as the Anglo-Saxon Dornwære continue to be called after the name of the British town of Durnovaria (cp. our § 77, pp. 157 and 159).[1] Home: on the 'ripa' of the Rhine in the Moselle region.

[1] In *Anzeiger*, XXVIII, 17, we have suggested that the Ripuarians might be *Uzīp-warjōz, identical with the ancient Usipii. This interpretation would certainly claim a stress on the second syllable, not ordinary in Gothonic. But it is not absolutely excluded; cp. the Norwegian toponymic Danglinger < *Eiðánglingar.

Lit. Zeuss, 343; Grimm, 527, 781; Müllenhoff in Mommsen's ed. of Jordanes (see Index); Schmaus, *Gesch. u. Herkunft der Franken*, 154; Much in Hoops, I, 82; Förstemann, s.v.; Seeck in Pauly-Wissowa, s.v. *Riparienses*; Kluge, *Urgermanisch*, 227 (*Grundriss*, 3rd ed.); Riese, *Germania* (*Korrespondenzblatt*), III, 38 seq.; Feist, *Beiträge*, XLIV, 355 seq., 515; Schwarz, *Zeitschr. f. Ortsnamenforsch.* II, 195 seq.

(*b*) M.Lat. Austri, Austrasii, meaning 'eastern', contrasting with Neustri 'the western' (§ 183, 2 (*b*)). The ending *-asii* is probably Celto-Latin. Home: Eastern Gaul.

Lit. Zeuss, 349; Förstemann, s.v. *Austrasia.*

8. Lat. Tu-bantes (Tacitus, first century A.D.); M.Lat. *Tu-vantes (Tuvanies, *Not. gent.*, fourth century); Gr. *Του-βάντιοι (Του-βάττιοι, Strabo, first century B.C.), Τού-βαντοι (Ptolemy, second century A.D.). *tu* is perhaps a variant of 'two' (cp. Lat. *du* in *du-plex* 'double'). *-bant* is a typical Frankish word for 'county', e.g. occurring in Bra-bant; cp. No. 12. The assonance of No. 9, Tvi-hanti, is probably accidental. Home: (1) east of the Lower Rhine; (2) later, east of the Middle Rhine.

Lit. Zeuss, 88; Hirt, *Beiträge*, XXI, 139; Schönfeld, s.v. (with lit.); Förstemann, s.v.; Much in Hoops, s.v.; Löwenthal, *Beiträge*, XLIX, 415; Güntert, *Wörter u. Sachen*, IX, 131; v. Ginneken, *Onze Taaltuin*, I, 84 seq.

9. Lat. Tvi-hanti (*Inscr. Ephem.* VII, 1040). Region: O.L.G. Tvi-anti; Dutch Twente. Etymology: *tvi*, meaning 'two'; *hant* probably meaning 'county'. Home: east of the Zuider Zee; the contiguous district, Drente, has a similar name, O.L.G. Thre-ont, 'Three counties'.

Lit. Grimm, 593; v. Helten, *Beiträge*, XXVII, 152; *Nom. geogr. neerlandica*, V, 1 (on Drente); Schönfeld, s.v.; Much in Hoops, s.v.; Förstemann, s.v.; Huss, *Teuthonista*, V, 310 (cp. the lit. in No. 8).

10. Lat. Usipetes (Caesar, first century B.C.; Tacitus, first century A.D.), Usipii (Martialis, first century A.D.); M.Lat. Usiphi (*Not. gent.*, fourth century A.D.); Gr. Οὔσιποι, Οὐσίπιοι (Strabo, first century A.D.), *Οὐσίποι (Οὐίσποι, Ptolemy, second century A.D.), Οὐσιπέται (Dio Cassius, third century). Obscure. *us-* is perhaps a prefix as in Celtic Usluntioi (?), Ireland. Much explains the name as Celtic, meaning εὐίπποι. Home: (1) west of the Swabians in the Main region; (2) later, successively on the Lower and Middle Rhine.

Lit. Schönfeld, s.v. and s.v. *Vispi* (with lit.); Förstemann, s.v.; Kauffmann, I, 257 note 10, and 388 note 1; Much in Hoops, s.v. *Usipeter*; Löwenthal, *Beiträge*, XLV, 242; Feist, *Germanen u. Kelten*, 36.

11. Lat. Tencteri, Tenchteri (Caesar, first century B.C.); Gr. Τέγκεροι (Ptolemy, second century A.D.), Τέγκτηροι (Dio Cassius, third century A.D.). Obscure. Cp. the Gaulish Cambolectri. Companions of the Usipetes.

Lit. **Schönfeld, s.v. (with lit.); Förstemann, s.v.; Much in Hoops, s.v.; Kauffmann, I, 251 with note 1; Güntert, *Wörter u. Sachen,* IX, 131; Langenfelt, *Anthropos,* XIV/XV, 313; Löwenthal, *Beiträge,* XLVII, 291.**

12. Lat. Bucino-bantes, 'People of the hedged country'. Appear as Alemanni, but must originally have been Franks, as *bant* is a Frankish word (cp. § 157, 8).

13. Lat. Bructeri. Home: north of the river Lippe. Cp. the later Pagus Borahtra south of this river (see § 195, 4).

14. Lat. Chatti (Chathi), with sub-tribes Mattiaci, Batavi, Cannenefates. Home: Hesse, with colonies in the Rhine Delta (see § 195, 2 (a)).

Survey of types of names.

1. Short Simplexes: Salii, Flæmen, Austri.
2. Long Derivative types: Gambrivii, Cugerni, Chamavi, Us-ipites, Tenchteri.
3. Long Derivative types of Latin origin: Ripari.
4. Compounds: Su-gambri, Ni-wistrii, Us-ipii, Chatt-, Ampsi-, Chasvarii; secondary: Rip-varii (cp. the North German Angri-varii), Tubantes (cp. the so-called 'Alemannic' Bucino-bantes), Tvi-hanti.

Long Derivative types and Compounds predominate. Short Simplexes are rare; the very common adjective Austri 'eastern' in reality does not count. But the long forms may be enlarged Simplexes; e.g. from Gambrivii and Su-gambri we may deduce an original *Gambri.

§ 184. Ethnic Position.

The North-west German branch is a definite one, but its members are vaguely defined.

A. Branch of Isteones.

1. Pliny, IV, 99: 'Istriones proximi Rheno, quorum pars Cymbri' (cp. 'Sugambri...proximi Rheno', Caesar, *Bell. Gall.* VI, 35). Co-ordinate are: Vandili, that is, the East Gothonic tribes; Incyaeones, the Cimbri and Chauchi; Hermiones or mediterranei, including the Swabians, Ermundures, Cherusci, Chatthi.

2. Tacitus A, *Germ.* 2: 'Manno assignant...Istaevones'. Co-ordinate are: 'Ingvaeones proximi oceano (i.e. 'proximi oceano Cimbri', *ibid.* 37), Herminones medii'.

3. *Generatio regum et gentium*, sixth century: 'Istio...genuit Francus'. Co-ordinate are: 'Saxones, Thoringus, Bajoarius, Alamannus', etc.

B. BRANCH OF GAMBRIVII (CP. PLINY'S 'CYMBRI').

4. Tacitus B, *ibid.*: 'quidam...pluris deo (Manno) ortos...Gambrivios...affirmant, eaque vera et antiqua nomina'. Co-ordinate are: Vandilii (cp. Pliny); Swabians (part of Pliny's Hermiones); Marsi (corresponding to Pliny's Chatthi ?).

C. BRANCH OF GERMANI OR FRANKS.

5–10. Jordanes, Agathias, Procopius, Venantius Fortunatus, Anonymus Ravennas, and Suidas, all identify Germani with Franks (see § 19). The original Germani are inhabitants of Belgium.

11. Vopiscus, *Hist. Aug. v. Aurel.* 7: Franci occur near Mayence, A.D. 260; *idem, v. Probi*, 11: Franci in the 'invii paludes' of the Rhine Delta, A.D. 280.

12. *Tabula Peutingeriana*: 'Chamavi *qui et Franci (Quielpranci)'; Francia is mentioned side by side with Svevia and Allemannia.

13. Ammianus, XVII, 8 and XX, 10, ad an. 358 and 360; the Franks include: (*a*) 'Francos, eos videlicet quos consuetudo Salios appellavit'; (*b*) Chamavi; (*c*) (Ch)atthvarii (var. Ansivarii).

14. Zosimus, III, 6: 'τὸ Σαλίων ἔθνος, φράγγων ἀπόμοιρον'.

15. Mediaeval Franconia embraces: the Salian district of Neustria (incl. Flanders), Hamaland, Pagus Hattvariensis, Pagus Ripvariensis, Eastern Franconia (and Hesse).

16. The Frankish dialect type is spoken in the area referred to under No. 15 and is co-ordinate with Thuringian, Swabian, and Bavarian.

17. A typical Frankish element is *bant* 'county' (cp. O.H.Germ. *elibenzo* 'belonging to an alien tribe'), which may be compared with Swab. *-bara*, Hess. Langobard *-aib*, Fris. *-del*, Anglo-Sax. *-scire*, Gautic *-kind*, Norweg. *-fylki*, etc. It occurs after A.D. 55. The district where it is found as a place name lies between the following points: Bant, island facing the mouth of the Ems; Bucino-bantes near Mayence; Westrobant and Ostrobant (later Oostervant) on the Scheld; Brabant; Teisterbant and Swiftarbant on the Waal. In a part of this area,

the German element *-gau* 'county' is almost excluded from the place names; for example, one can see on Spruner-Mencke's map, *Handatlas des Mittelalters*, No. 32, an almost uninterrupted sequence of districts, starting from the vicinity of the ancient Tubantes: Bursibant, Tvihanti, Thre(h)ant, Salechaim or Salland, Felue, Batua, Flethetti, Germepi, Kinhem, *Marshem (Marsum), Testerbant, Bracbant, Karabant, Osterbant; there occurs only one 'Gau' amongst them, viz. Huitingoe on the mouth of the Meuse. It is well known that *-gau* is also common to both Saxons and Goths. Thus the replacing of this element by *-bant* marks the Isteonic-Frankish nucleus as a distinct individuality.

18. Frankish and Hessian names of rivers often end in *-apa*. This may be a Celtic loan word, but does not denote Celtic aborigines, as Müllenhoff believes, *Altertumskunde*, II, 209 seq. (with map) (cp. Bremer, §69; Schütte, *Anzeiger*, XXVIII, 14); Schnetz, *Zeitschr. f. Ortsnamenforsch.* VIII, 8 seq.

19. Various elements of place names are characteristically Northwest German, such as *mahlberg* 'law-court hill',[1] *-hlār* (of uncertain signification), *-horst* 'hurst' (also Frisian and Anglo-Saxon). Their limits towards the north have not been sufficiently investigated, but they are at any rate important means of tracing the Frankish expansion on Swabian-Alemannic soil (cp. Schütte, *Anzeiger*, XXVIII, 14; *idem*, *Geogr. Tidskrift*, 1918, 201 (criticised by Bückmann, *Petermanns Mitteilungen*, 1922, 13); Schnetz, *Das Lahr-Problem*, *Programm*, Lohr, 1915; *idem*, *Zeitschr. f. Ortsnamenforsch.* VII, 123. Förstemann, II, 1, 1513 on *-horst*; H. Jellinghaus, *Anglia*, N.F. VIII, 295 on *-hurst*).

20. The suffix *-heim* on ancient Swabian soil in our opinion marks the Frankish expansion, contrasting with the Swabian-Alemannic *-ingen*. This point is controversial (cp. §162, conclusion).

21. The Frankish 'reges criniti' are privileged to dress the hair in a certain way (Gregor. Tur. I, 9, etc.). The Vandalic Hasdingi or 'Hairy people' seem to have had a similar privilege, whereas the immediate neighbours did not observe the fashion; the Saxons and Chatthi were all 'criniti', and the Swabians had their 'pig-tail'.

22. The Franks possess a national law codex with almost identical expressions in the *Lex Salica*, *Lex Chamavorum*, and *Lex Ribuaria* (cp. Rietschel in Hoops, s.v. *Lex Salica* and *Ribuaria*).

[1] Cp. the Danish place name Māl-høg which is no doubt due to imitation of the Frankish model.

23. The Frankish nomenclature of offices, professions, etc., contains some expressions with an individual stamp similar to the Langobard ones: *thungin* 'president of the thing or law-court' (cp. Seeliger in Hoops, s.v. *thunginus*); *ragine-burg* (*Lex Sal.* and *Rib.*) 'judge lateral' (literally 'counsel-guarantee', Germ. 'rat-bürge'); *an(d)-trustio* 'member of the princely bodyguard'.

24. The Franks possess a special type of farmyard which has been adopted by numerous German and non-German neighbours in the east. It affords a chief means of distinguishing the Frankish and Saxon territory (cp. the detailed description below on p. 169 seq.).

The above evidence may be summarised as follows:

1–10. A North-west German branch has asserted itself ever since the dawn of history under the varying names Isteones, Gambrivii, Germani, and Franks. The synonyms are often identified or contrasted: Pliny: 'Istriones quorum pars *Sucambri'; Tacitus A: Istaevones; Tacitus B: Gambrivii; early mediaeval authors say that Germani is an ancient name of Franks.

4–16. The Isteonic-Gambrivian-Frankish branch undoubtedly embraces Sugambri or Gambrivii, whence comes one of the collective names; Salians or Neustri, one of the ruling tribes of France, with separate Lex; Chamavi, with separate Lex; Chattvarii; Ripvarii or Austri, the second ruling tribe of France, with separate Lex. On onomastic grounds we add Tubantes, with a typical Frankish element. The Bucinobantes equally must belong to the original nucleus of the Franks, though accidentally they appear as Alemanni in the solitary entry that records their name; they may have contributed to the genesis of the Ripuarians.

16–20. The linguistic evidence affords the best means of defining the position of mediaeval and modern Franconia. But as various points are controversial, we can here only present them as problems which urgently need more penetrating investigation. Fluctuation of limits appears as given in detail above: the dialects of the Middle Neckar and Upper Main belong to Franconia and pass for Frankish, but yet adhere to the Upper German type which reflects the Alemannic substratum.

21–24. The privileged royal fashion of hair-dressing, the territorial laws, and offices with solitary names such as *thungin*, *ragineburg*, and *anthrustio*, complete the national Frankish physiognomy by showing rudiments of an individual civilisation.

It remains to classify various tribes whose position is less distinct.

In our opinion, two varieties must be noticed. The one consists of what we may term 'outsiders', partly cultivators of borderland woods and deserts, partly homeless newcomers from abroad. Both of these sub-species would be easily absorbed by any surrounding well-established communities. In addition to these 'outsiders' of minor political rank, we notice some tribes which possess a marked ethnic individuality, but which in historical times are found only in the position of what may be termed 'decaying rivals'.

North German 'outsiders' of the borderer class are the Amsivarii, the Chasvarii, the Angrivarii, the Tvihanti; the element *-warja* originally is a typical mark of borderers, cp. Ripvarii, Raetovarii, Bajvarii. The Amsivarii and probably also the Chasvarii appear as exiled newcomers; to the same class belong the Usipii and Tenchteri from the interior of Germany. The exiled Amsivarii are received by the Tubantes (Tac. *Ann.* XIII, 55); the exiled Usipii and Tenchteri are received by the Sugambri (Caesar, *Bell. Gall.* V, 41); the Angrivarii—who are separated from the Cherusci by a large frontier wall (Tac. *Ann.* II, 19)—conclude with the Chamavi an offensive alliance against the Bruchteri (Tac. *Germ.* 33). Such relations show the growing of the ancient Isteonic or Gambrivian branch.

'Decaying rivals' are the Marsi, who appear as co-ordinate with the Gambrivii (Tac. *Germ.* 2), and possess a famous central sanctuary, the Temple of Tanfana (Tac. *Ann.* I, 51); the Chatthi, who are separated from the Isteones by Pliny, IV, 99, and whose Hessian descendants are even up to the present time regarded as somehow co-ordinate with Franks, Thuringians, etc.; the Ubii, who are the hereditary enemies of the Sugambri (Caesar, *Bell. Gall.* IV, 16–18); the Bruchteri, whose state is destroyed by the Chamavi and Angrivarii.

The areas occupied by the tribes mentioned are in the course of time either temporarily or permanently incorporated with Franconia.

Also other displacements of national boundaries have taken place. The Franks have absorbed Saxon and Frisian settlers in the Netherlands, and large Alemannic districts; on the other hand, the Saxons have annexed Salland, the Angrivarian region, parts of Hamaland and of the Pagus Hattvariensis; while the Bucinobantes are original Franks who appear as Alemanni. The alleged 'Saxons' of Transylvania are Franks from the Moselle valley; the alleged Dutchmen (i.e. 'Franks') in Salland, Drente, Overijssel, Groningen, etc., are Saxon-speaking people on ancient Frankish or Frisian soil.

The problem of the Hugones must here be discussed. As we mentioned in § 182, 7, the *Quedlinburg Annals* assert that the hero Hugo Theodoricus is named Hugo after an old synonym of 'all Franks', Hugones. *Beowulf*, l. 2915 seq., describes Hygelac's defeat when fighting against him 'among the Hugas...in Friesland', and states (l. 2502 seq.) that Dæghrefn, the champion of the Hugas, was not able to bring Hygelac's armour to the Frisian king. The Hugones have been identified with a well-known colony of Chauchi in the Rhine Delta (cp. also the county of Hugmerke in the prov. of Groningen). Combining such evidence, Much in Hoops, s.v. *Franken*, and Schmaus, *Gesch. u. Herkunft der Franken*, 144 seq., venture to assume that the Hugones, that is the Chauchi, are the nucleus of the Franks. We cannot accept this theory. *Beowulf* does not identify Franks and Hugas, but enumerates them with Hetware and Frisians as fellow-antagonists of Hygelac; and why, if the champion of the Hugas were a Frank, should he think of bringing his trophies to the Frisian king? In our opinion, the epic name of Hugo Theodoricus originates from the fact that Theodoric conquered a Hugleik among the Hugones; after posterity had forgotten the exact particulars, it conceived the Hugones as the people of Hugo Theodoricus and consequently changed them into Franks.

The later development of the Franks leads to a differentiation into three separate political powers.

1. The earliest Empire of the Franks, in Gaul, keeps up the national names of France and Français, though the German nationality of the ruling classes has long before been absorbed by the Gallo-Roman. Owing to the leading position of Frenchmen among the crusaders, the name Franks becomes the most current oriental name for Europeans.

2. After the Franks have in the ninth century united all surviving Gothonic tribes south of the Eider, their Latin synonym Germani assumes the signification of 'Germans', and the state of Germania (i.e. Franconia) becomes 'Germany'. The vernacular name Franks sometimes is used as a synonym of 'Germans', but only temporarily (Otfrid).

3. The North-west Frankish section of the Germans after the close of the Middle Ages dissociates itself from Germany as a separate Dutch nationality, with its own literary language and a church of a national

stamp, in the independent states of the Netherlands and Belgium. Its headquarters are almost identical in position with those of the ancient Isteonic branch.

Finally, the above-mentioned Frankish type of farmstead must be described; cp. Ranck, *Kulturgeschichte des deutschen Bauernhauses* (*Aus Natur und Geisteswelt*, CXXI), p. 61: 'Das Wesen des fränkischen Gehöftes...besteht in der planvollen Anordnung der Wirtschaftsgebäude um einen vierseitigen, meist rechteckigen inneren Hof, der an denjenigen Stellen, wo er nicht von Gebäuden begrenzt ist, durch Mauern oder Zäune vom Nachbar getrennt ist. Alle Gebäude des Gehöftes sind nur von diesem Hof aus zugänglich, nach aussen haben sie meist nicht einmal Fenster, bis auf die Stube des Wohnhauses, die fast immer an der Dorfstrasse so gelegen ist, dass der Bauer von ihr aus sowohl den Hof als auch die Strasse übersehen kann. Wie diese fränkische Hofanlage... entstanden ist, ob nach den Bedürfnissen der fränkischen Bauern allmählich entwickelt, oder von den Franken...in Anlehnung an gallisch-römische Vorbilder ausgebildet, ist zweifelhaft. Wir wissen nur, dass die Landgüter des Frankenkaisers Karls des Grossen aus der grossen Zahl ihrer Einzelgebäude zu schliessen noch Haufenhöfe waren, dass aber etwa 300 Jahre später deutsche aus der Maingegend stammende Kolonisten die in ihrer ganzen Eigenart entwickelte fränkische Hofanlage nach Pommern verpflanzten'.

Whereas Ranck is inclined to assume a development on a national line, M. Haberlandt believes to observe traces of Roman influence (cp. *Die Völker Europas*, 448): 'Schon in der Antike zum Stockbau für das Hauptgebäude fortgeschritten, ist die Villa rustica auch in Frankreich für die Gehöftebildung massgebend geworden, und es unterliegt keinem Zweifel, dass die sogenannten fränkischen Gehöfte in Nordfrankreich, Belgien und Holland, vorzugsweise aber auf südwest- und mitteldeutschem Boden angelegt und von hier seit etwa dem 11ten Jahrhundert als vorzüglicher Kolonistentyp bis in die Sudetenländer und Ungarn verbreitet, diesem Stamm zuzuzählen sind'.

The frontier of the Frankish type against the Saxon generally coincides with the frontier between Middle German and Low German (cp. our map, Fig. 2). However, the Frankish type has conquered the Low German region about the Harz mountain, and the Middle German colony in

Eastern Prussia has introduced that type throughout the province. On the other hand, the Saxon type predominates in the Dutch regions Veluwe, Utrecht, and South Holland, though the dialect is Frankish. The 'T house' or 'dwarshuis', in North Brabant called 'krukhuis', which is according to Schrijnen (I, p. 55) a variety of the Saxon type, is the normal type in the Betuwe and further found along the Ijssel and Vecht, in het Land van Maas and Waal, and as far west as de Langstraat; it also prevails in the northern part of the German Rhine Province. The Frisian 'hauberg' or 'stelphoeve' survives in North Holland, the ancient West Friesland, and also occurs in some insular districts in the Rhine Delta (see p. 283).

A distinction is made between two varieties of the Frankish type. According to Schrijnen, *Nederlandsche Volkskunde*, 2nd ed. I, 59 seq., the 'Celtic-Frankish type' predominates in Holland south of the Rhine (except South Limburg), in Flanders, Antwerpen, Brabant, and especially in Belgian Limburg; isolated examples occur in the Betuwe, Veluwe, Utrecht, South Holland, and Southern North Holland. The 'Roman-Frankish type' is found in South Limburg, Belgian Limburg, East Flanders, Brabant, Hainaut, districts of Namur and Liège, and beyond the Middle Rhine through Middle Germany as far east as Silesia and Transylvania. But as the distinction is omitted on the German maps at our disposal, we have not been able to give its particulars on our map (Fig. 2).

Concerning the important frontier between the Frankish and Alemannic type we may quote some statements from *Das Bauernhaus im Deutschen Reiche*.

K. Statsmann, p. 247: 'Am verbreitetsten, insbesondere im Unterelsass und im nördlichen Sundgau des Oberelsasses (Rheinebene und Nachbargebiete) ist die sogenannte fränkische Hofanlage'.

Bernh. Kossmann, p. 286: 'Die genaue Durchforschung der Dörfer in der Rheinebene zeigte, dass in diesem ganzen Gebiete bis hinauf nach Basel, östlich bis in das Gebirge gehend, die fränkische Bauweise vorherrschend ist, also das Haus mit dem Giebel an der Strasse steht, und die anderen Gebäude des Anwesens—mehr oder weniger zusammengebaut—um einen geschlossenen Hof liegen'. (Concerning the Alemannic type south of Basel see quotation on p. 105.)

p. 262: 'Im Badischen (findet sich, z.t.)...sog. fränkische Anlage.... Nördlich und nordöstlich vom Schwarzwald (hat) die sog. fränkische Hofanlage, die im Mittelalter und in der Renaissancezeit sich weit ausbreitete, allem Anschein nach...nicht die Alleinherrschaft erobert'.

Lit. **Müllenhoff,** IV **(see Index, s.v.** ***Franken*****); Bremer, § 157 seq.; Much in Hoops, s.v.** ***Franken*****; Schmidt,** II, **393, 433.**

§ 185. History of the Franks, collectively.

The original position of the North-west German tribes may be considered in relation to the whole system of their tribal names. The North Sea coast from the Eider to the Zuider Zee is occupied by important non-German tribes with names of the Short Simplex type, viz. Saxones, Chauchi, Frisii. Their southern frontier is fringed by German borderers of the secondary type *-varii*, viz. Angri-, Chas-, Amsi-, Chatt-varii. The headquarters of the North-west German branch obviously cannot be placed in the eastern dominion of these *-varii*, the middle basin of the rivers Weser and Ems, which must be regarded as a secondary settlement. But on the Zuider Zee, between the Frisians and the Franks called Chatt-varii, there appears one German representative of the Simplex type, viz. the Salii, the most important tribe of the Frankish branch. And south of them we may conjecture that there was an original tribe of *Gambri, the prototype of the historical Gambrivii (cp. Su-gambri), whose name came to be used as a synonym of the collective name Isteones. To the same vicinity belong the old Frankish tribe of Chamavi, and the Tubantes whose name affords the first example of the typical Frankish element *-bant*. To sum up, the claim of the south-eastern corner of the Zuider Zee is based on a series of onomastic and historical facts: it supplies the Simplexes *Gambri and Salii, the collective name of Gambrivii, the first instance of *-bant*, and from its narrow area originate the three most important West Frankish tribes, viz. Salii, Chamavi, and Chattvarii. If we accept the above-mentioned region as the original home of the North-west German group, the further development appears as a series of quite natural radiations. The continuous chain of *-varii*—Amsi-, Chas-, Angri-varii—represents an expansion which advances in the desert borderlands, between the Frisians-Saxons on the one hand, and the Bruchteri-Cherusci on the other hand. The movement of the Usipii and Tenchteri from the Lower Rhine up the Middle Rhine is a second radiation from the same centre (whereas their earlier migration from the Main region to the Lower Rhine does not belong to this survey: before they were received by the Sugambri, they did not belong to the North-west German branch).

Finally, we notice how the Frankish type *-bant*, first exemplified on the Lower Rhine, first century A.D., appears in the fourth century on the Middle Rhine in the name Bucinobantes near Mayence.

It is worth noticing the pronounced eastward expansion of the early North-west Germans, for all their neighbours advance in more or less opposite directions. Moving in a southward direction, the Chauchi drive out the Amsivarii and advance to the vicinity of the Chatthi. Westward, the Ermundures conquer the Chatthic regions west of the river Werra; the Swabians in the Main region drive out the Usipii and Tenchteri and menace the Moselle region. North-westward, the Usipii and Tenchteri (before joining the North-west German branch) attack the Menapii on the Lower Rhine; Chatthi emigrate from Hesse to the Rhine Delta (Batavians, Cannenefates); the Marsi in the Ruhr region seem to have dispatched the Marsaci to the Rhine Delta; the Bruchteri, with head-quarters on the river Lippe, descend the river Ems. This expansion in a direction contrary to that of its rival neighbours is one of the most remarkable tests of the North-west German national individuality.

The Sugambri or Gambrivii, to whom the North-west Germans owe one of their collective names, are the earliest political champions of this branch, leaders of an anti-Roman faction that in 55 B.C. is reinforced by the Usipii and Tenchteri from the interior of Germany (Caesar, *Bell. Gall.* IV, 16 and 18, V, 41).

Till 55 B.C. the Belgian Celts named Menapii still partially maintain their hold on the eastern bank of the Lower Rhine which the Usipii and Tenchteri strive to possess. After Caesar's conquest of Belgium about the same time, the Roman territory reaches the Rhine and even acquires vassals beyond it. Apart from the temporary incorporation of almost the whole of North Germany (A.D. 4–9), a Roman borderland beyond the Rhine exists from 12 B.C. till about A.D. 260 (Dio Cassius, LIV, 32 seq.; Tac. *Ann.* XIII, 54; *Not. gent.*). In spite of mutual Roman and German inroads across the Rhine after Caesar's time, this river and the Ijssel for centuries form a stationary frontier.

In 8 B.C. Tiberius transplants 40,000 Sugambri west of the Rhine (Tac. *Ann.* XII, 39; Suetonius, *Aug.* 21; *idem, Tiber.* 9; Strabo, IV, 194); perhaps these are the Cugerni between Batavia and Cologne (Pliny, IV, 106). But the frontier of nationalities is not affected by the change, as the transplanted people are soon Celticised or Romanised. From this moment, the Sugambri disappear from the scene of action, and the Isteones-Gambrivii for centuries have no political centre.

In A.D. 41 the Chauchi appear as pirates on the Belgian coast (Suetonius, *Claud.* 24). This attack signalises the beginning of an expansion which also affects the North-west Germans. In A.D. 58 the Chauchi drive out the Amsivarii, who appear in the Rhenish regions. The exiled people are decimated or dissipated by the Chatthi and Cherusci (Tac. *Ann.* XIII, 55 and 56). The Chasvarii, who appear later in Rhenish regions, are probably also driven out by the Chauchi. The Angrivarii, no doubt yielding to the pressure of the same Chauchi, shortly before 98 ally with the Chamavi and conquer the Bruchteri who lose their entire territory north of the river Lippe (cp. Tac. *Germ.* 33).

The anti-Roman rebellion of the Batavian chieftain Civilis, A.D. 69–70, is often represented as a political manifestation of the North-west German branch, but such an idea is not justified. The presumable representatives of this branch—Sugambri, Chamavi, Chattvarii, Chasvarii, Tubantes, etc.—are all conspicuous by their absence; the Usipii and Tenchteri as immigrants from the interior of Germany do not count as true North-west Germans; and a leading part is played by the Bruchteri, who are known as avowed antagonists of the North-west German tribe of Chamavi.

Difficult to explain is the fact that the Frankish place name Machlinium 'law-court', of which the present Mechelen or Malines is an instance, appears already in the second century A.D., traceable in an inscription dedicated to the matronae Mahlinehae (see Schönfeld, s.v.). From this circumstance it appears that there must have been some Frankish colonisation in North-western Belgium as early as the second century, but we do not know its origin or its extension.

During the reign of Gallienus (260–268), Rome loses the military borderland east of the Rhine, comprising the districts of the Chasvarii, Tubantes, and Usipii (*Not. gent.*).

The collective name of Franks appears about 258 (Theoclius, cit. by Vopiscus, *Hist. Aug. v. Aurel.* 7, 1 and 2). Provisionally the branch embraces: Chamavi (*Tab. Peuting.*), Salians (Zosimus, III, 6; Ammianus, XVII, 8, § 3) and Chattvarii (Ammianus, XX, 10, § 2). Procopius, *Bell. Got.* I, 12, places its original home in the Rhenish marshes; this location agrees with the Francia of the *Tab. Peuting.* and with the fact that the first historical exploits of the Franks are adventurous raids on the Mediterranean. We must reject the view of Schmidt who places the nucleus of the Franks among the Bruchteri (II, 434); as enemies of the Chamavic Franks, they can only be regarded as secondary members of the tribe.

In 259 the Franks invade Gaul and Spain, destroy Tarragona, and, after procuring ships, even reach Africa (Victor, *Caes.* 33, 3; Eutropius, IX, 8, § 2; Orosius, VII, 22, § 7, 41, § 2). Their sphere of action in Gaul and Belgium is shown by deposits of coins (cp. Schmidt, II, 438–439).

In 277 Franks captured by the Emperor Probus in Gaul are placed as colonists in Thracia, but escape by ship and after raiding the Mediterranean reach their homes in 279 (Zosimus, I, 67 and 71; *Hist. Aug. v. Prob.* 18).

About 286 Frankish and Saxon pirates are raiding the Channel (Eutropius, IX, 21). Constantius subjugates Frankish settlers in Batavia and Northern Belgium (*Paneg. v. Max. et Constantio*, IV, 2, VI, 5, 6); from colonies of captives we may derive the Pagi of Chamavi and Chattvarii on the frontier of Gaul and Helvetia (Zeuss, 582). A defeated league of Bruchteri, Chamavi, Tubantes, and Alemanni, is mentioned by Nazarius, *Paneg. Constantin.* 18; we here notice the Bruchteri in Frankish surroundings, a symptom of their subsequent Franconisation.

After 350 Franks and Alemanni conquer the borderlands west of the Rhine, extending their territory by some 300 stadia in places (cp. Julianus, *Ep. ad Athen.*; Libanius, II, 24, 71, 251; Zosimus, III, 1; Ammianus, XVI, 12, § 5 seq.). The Franks storm Castra Herculis, Qualburg, Tricensima (Vetera), Neuss, Cologne, Bonn, Andernach, Bingen, and menace Paris, but are defeated by Julian in 356 seq. In 358 he allows Salian Franks to remain as settlers in Toxandria, a place name which survives in the name of a village, Tessenderloo in Belgian Limburg (Ammianus, XVII, 8, § 3). Other Salians, driven out from the Batavian island by the 'Kouadoi', i.e. Chauchi, are received in Northern Belgium (Zosimus, III, 6).[1] Julian repulses the Chamavi (Julianus, *Ep. ad Athen.* p. 280; Ammianus, *l.c.*), and punishes Chattvarian raiders, 360 (Ammianus, XX, 10, § 2).

After the death of Julian, 363, Frankish and Saxon raiders again trouble the Belgian coasts and borderlands.

In 380 the Alemannic King Macrianus, an ally of the Romans, attacks the Frankish King Mallobaud, but is defeated (Ammianus, XXX, 3, § 7) and the Franks conquer the Alemannic territory north of the Main (Schmidt, II, 449). The nationality of the area concerned seems to have

[1] L. Schmidt, II, 447, corrects 'Kouadoi' into Chamaboi, but we prefer the current interpretation, for it is not likely that the Chamavi would have attacked their Frankish kinsmen.

been somewhat fluctuating, for the people of Macrianus, the Bucinobantes, though said to be Alemanni (Ammianus, XXIX, 4, § 7), have a typical Frankish name.

In 388, during a Roman civil war, the Frankish dukes Gennobaud, Marcomer, and Sunno, raid Belgium. In return, the Roman general Arbogast, of Frankish birth, invades the regions of the Bruchteri and Chamavi, 392–393 (Sulpicius Alexander, cit. by Gregor. Tur. II, 9). He also touches the mountains of the Amsivarii and 'Chatti'; Schmidt proposes to read *Chattvarii, as the Pagus Hattvariensis extends later to the mountains or hills on the south frontier of the Bruchteri. In the sources which we follow the Bruchteri appear as Franks, governed by Marcomer; this fact illustrates the growing expansion of the Frankish community.

During the next two decades, the Franks remain quiet. They even try to prevent the Vandals and their companions from invading Gaul in 406 (Orosius, VII, 40).

After 412 the Roman civil wars invite the Eastern Franks to fresh hostilities. Treves is sacked four times by them, 412–440 (Salvian. *De gub. Dei*, 130), and they begin to settle west of the Rhine.

In 428 the Roman governor Aëtius repulses the Eastern Franks beyond the Rhine (*Chron. Gall.* ad an. 428). Meanwhile, Chlodio succeeds in founding a firmly established dynasty of 'reges criniti' among the Salian Franks who herewith finally cease to be a republic (Gregor. Tur. II, 9). Chlodio advances towards the south, but is repulsed by Aëtius near Arras (Sid. Apollinaris, *Carm.* V, 211).

The invasion of the Hunnish King Attila in 451 divides the Franks, who, disunited by a dynastic strife, fight both for the Huns and Romans (cp. Jordanes, XXXVI, 191, and Sid. Apollinaris, *Carm.* VII, 324).

The murder of Aëtius in 454 immediately gives fresh life to the Frankish expansion. Chlodio annexes Cambray and advances towards the Somme (Gregor. Tur. II, 9). The Ripuarian Franks occupy the environs of Cologne—probably about 460—and of Treves (cp. Schmidt, II, 458).

The political relations continue to vary: the Salian Franks alternately appear as vassals and as independent allies of Rome. Their king Childeric in 463 and 469 assists the Romans in repulsing the Visigoths near the Loire, and then in pacifying the Saxon pirates on the islets opposite this river (Gregor. Tur. II, 18; *Ann. Andegav.* ad an. 469). Childeric dies in 482 as a pagan.

In 486 his son Chlodowech annexes the last remaining West Roman territory, after conquering the governor Syagrius at Soissons and killing him (Gregor. Tur. II, 27). Chlodowech's conversion to Roman Catholicism procures him the aid of the Church against pagans and Arian Goths. Through wiles, assassinations, and open murders, he disposes of all rival Frankish kings. He conquers Alemannia in 496 (§ 162), and Visigothic Gaul in 507, except Septimania on the Mediterranean (Gregor. Tur. II, 30 and 37; Isidore, *Hist. Got.* 36 (§ 121)). His sons subjugate Thuringia and Burgundy, 530–534 (§§ 181, 135); even Bavarians, North Swabians, and Saxons submit. During the wars of Ostrogoths and Eastern Romans, the Franks make predatory expeditions into Italy. In 536 the Ostrogoths cede to the Frankish King Theodebert their Alemannic possessions, of which Switzerland is the most important (§ 120). Thus the Franks unite Germany and in addition master the Burgundians and sections of Gothic, Frisian, and Saxon tribes. Systematic colonisation accompanies the Frankish conquests; especially, the defeated Alemanni are driven from large parts of the Rhine and Main valleys (§ 162).

If the development of the Franks from 400 to 550 approaches steadily towards a climax in this direction, the area of their national community is quite as constantly retreating on the north-eastern flank, being forced back first by the Chauchi and later by their kinsmen, the Saxons, whose colonies are extended to Flanders. The conflict with the north-eastern neighbours goes on for centuries with alternating success.

About 526 the Frankish King Theodebert repulses the Scandinavian Viking Hugleik (Hygelac) from the Pagus Hattvariensis (Gregor. Tur. III, 3). In 555 Chlotar fights Saxons and Danes (*ibid.* IV, 10; Venant. Fortunatus, *Carm.* IX, 1). A joint invasion of Saxons and Danes is repulsed by Sigebert's army in 565 near the river Bordaa, i.e. the present Boorne in Friesland (*ibid. Carm.* VII, 7, 51). Childebert in 595 subjugates the rebel Varines by the aid of the Slavs ('Fredegar', IV, 15, *Mon. Germ. SS. Merov.* II, 127); this co-operation of Franks and Slavs is repeated for centuries to the detriment of the Gothonic element in Northern Germany. In 630 the Frankish power is seriously checked through the defeat of Dagobert by the Frankish emigrant Samo, king of the Czechian Slavs ('Fredegar', IV, 68, *Mon. Germ. SS. Merov.* II, 155). Thuringia, supported by the Slavs, throws off the Frankish suzerainty (*ibid.* 77 and 87). In 689 the Franks annex Western Friesland, including the territory of the ancient Marsaci and Cannenefates.

In 697, on the other hand, the Saxons subjugate the Bruchteri and uproot the beginnings of the Christian mission there (Bede, v, 11). In 714 the Frisians reconquer West Friesland. In 715 the Saxons invade the Pagus Hattvariensis (cp. *Ann. Amandi, Tiliani, Petaviani, Mon. Germ. SS.* I, 6), and they are also advancing at other points.

Looking at the history as a whole up to about 715, a decrease of the Frankish expansion is shown, and an increase of the Chauchic-Saxon: Chauchic conquests from the Amsivarii, Chasvarii, Angrivarii, and Salii, have been taken over by the Saxons; Saxons have incorporated the Bruchteri and Tvihanti and partially conquered the Thuringians, Hessians, Chamavi, and Chattvarii.

But soon after 715 the tide definitely turns; this is especially the case after 732, when the famous victory of Charles Martel over the Arabs at Tours has averted the danger threatening from the south. In 719 the Franks reconquer West Friesland; in 734 Pippin II subjugates the Middle Frisians; in 748, with Slavonic aid, he subjugates the North Swabians (*Ann. Mett., Mon. Germ. SS.* I, 320). During the years 772–804 Charlemagne, helped repeatedly by the Slavs, breaks down the resistance of the fanatically heathen Saxons. The regions evacuated by them are to a great extent colonised by Franks and other Germans (cp. Rübel, *Die Franken, ihr Eroberungs- und Siedlungssystem im deutschen Volkslande*, 484; Bethge, *Wörter u. Sachen*, VI, 14 seq.). Eastern Holstein is granted to the Slavs. In 774 Charlemagne conquers the Langobards, in 775 the East Frisians, in 788 the rebellious Bavarians, in 796–799 the Avars in Pannonia.

Meanwhile, the Frankish expansion meets with a fresh check from the north, viz. the Viking raids. After 789 the Danes, as allies of the Saxons, begin to invade the Frankish coasts. In 811 the Eider is recognised as frontier between Franconia and Denmark, but a Frankish army as early as 815 invades Jutland, and the Viking raids go on, finally leading to the establishment of a Norman state in Gaul, in 911.

The Franks in the interior of Gaul are soon Romanised, but in Flanders and along the Rhine they absorb both the Gallo-Roman survivors and the Gothonic settlers—Saxons, Frisians, and Alemanni. The Lower Moselle valley spoke Romance till the tenth century (cp. Behaghel, *Gesch. d. deutschen Sprache*, § 86 (*Grundriss*, 5th ed.)); its

Germanisation is chiefly due to the broad wedge of German colonists in Luxemburg and Lorraine, probably Franconised Alemanni.

Frankish settlers, chiefly from Flanders, have led the German colonisations on Slavonic soil since the twelfth century; hence, e.g., the territorial name of Fläming in Brandenburg. Franks and Saxons in Eastern Germany have coalesced into the mixed North German stock.

The extreme vanguards of the Franks towards the south-east are the so-called 'Saxons' of Transylvania.

The westward advance of the Frankish nationality ceases with the later Middle Ages. Romanism has reconquered parts of French Flanders and of Lorraine, and has still a firm hold in the civilisation of Belgium and Luxemburg.

In the overseas colonies—South Africa, Eastern Asia, and America—the Frankish branch is chiefly represented by its Netherlandic offshoot, now forming the separate Dutch nationality (cp. §§ 209–210).

Lit. Rübel, *Die Franken*; Th. Frings, *Rheinische Sprachgeschichte* (in Aubin, Frings, etc., *Geschichte des Rheinlandes*).

§ 186. History of the Sugambri Proper.

Gamabriuoi and Sugambri are enumerated by Strabo, VII, 291, as separate tribes in the same vicinity. Tacitus also uses the names with two distinct meanings, Gambrivii as a collective name (*Germ.* 2), and Sugambri as a tribal name (*Ann.* II, 26, etc.). We may assume that Tacitus' terminology is the more correct: that is to say, Gambrivii is not a local tribal name, but the collective name, formed from the root of (Su-)Gambri. English bears a similar relation to Angles.

Strabo, *l.c.*, places the Sugambri on the coast. This location certainly is not correct, for apart from this reference they only appear as an inland tribe. But it may perhaps point to the position of their earlier home; at least, Strabo's other notes on the maritime tribes contain some trustworthy particulars which are not recorded in other sources (on the *Kaulkoi and the navy of the Bruchteri).

Caesar places the Sugambri on the Rhine opposite the Belgian tribe of Eburones, i.e. south of the river Lippe (*Bell. Gall.* VI, 35). Towards the north the neighbours are also Belgians, viz. the Menapii on the right bank of the Rhine (*ibid.* IV, 4). German neighbours towards the south are the Ubii in the Westerwald (*ibid.* IV, 18), and towards the north-east the Marsi and Bruchteri. On their rear, the Sugambri may have been in contact with their close kinsmen, the Chamavi and Chattvarii near the Zuider Zee, but otherwise they seem to project far south of the Isteonic region, as an isolated vanguard among non-Isteonic communities.

In 55 B.C. the Sugambri become the leaders of the German resistance against Rome. Both antagonists repeatedly cross the river. The Sugambri are reinforced by the remnants of the Usipii and Tenchteri who were destroyed by Caesar in Belgium (*Bell. Gall.* IV, 16, 18, 19). The Ubii, on the other hand, as hereditary enemies of the Sugambri, apply to Caesar for assistance (Dio Cassius, XXXIX, 48), and constantly remain pro-Roman, or at least neutral. Similarly, in 12 B.C., the Chatthi refuse to enter a league of Sugambri, Cherusci, and Swabians against Rome and are therefore furiously attacked by the Sugambri (Dio Cassius, LIV, 33). Later they join the league.

In 17 B.C. the Sugambri defeat the Roman general Lollius in Belgium (*ibid.* LIV, 20).

In 8 B.C. Augustus succeeds in pacifying the Sugambri, partly by means of imprisoning their ambassadors (*ibid.* LV, 6). The king (or ἡγεμών, Strabo, VII, 291) Maelo surrenders (Augustus, *Res gestae*, VI, 3). Forty thousand (?) Sugambri are transplanted to the Roman territory west of the Rhine (Dio Cassius, LV, 4; Suetonius, *Aug.* 21, *Tib.* 9). It is generally assumed that they appear here as Cugerni, though the identity is never stated by contemporary sources. Those who remain east of the Rhine henceforth play no part in history, while the Cugerni join the rebellion of the Batavian Civilis, A.D. 69–70 (Tac. *Hist.* IV, 26, V, 16, 18). Cohorts of Sugambri and Cugerni exist till the third century (cp. Müllenhoff, IV, 615), but their members probably cease to be natives of the tribes from which they were named. In Roman literature, the name of Sugambri becomes merely ornamental. The Sugambri east of the Rhine remain German, while their western colony is soon more or less Romanised and then re-Germanised at the close of the Migration Age.

Lit. Zeuss, 83, 326; Grimm, 519; Müllenhoff, IV (see Index); *idem*, *Zeitschrift*, XXIII, 26; Zippel, *Deutsche Völkerbewegungen*, 13; Bremer, § 188; Much, *Stammeskunde*, 77 seq.; *idem*, in Hoops, s.v.; Schmidt, II, 393.

§ 187. History of the Salians or Neustrii Proper.

Salland is situated east of the Zuider Zee and together with the Chamavic district forms presumably the original home of the primaeval

Isteonic community whose expansion seems to have been chiefly eastward. The Salii are not mentioned before the close of the third century A.D. They then appear as a part of the Franks and as pressed by the Saxon tribe of Chauchi[1] who are pushing them from Salland into the hitherto Roman island of Batavia (Zosimus, III, 6, § 2).

About 286 the Franks, i.e. chiefly Salians, begin raiding the Belgian coast as pirates beside the Saxons (Eutropius, IX, 21).

In 358 the Salians, ejected from Batavia by the Chauchi, are received by the Emperor Julian in Northern Belgium (Zosimus, *l.c.*). Other Salians are by him allowed to settle in Toxandria in Belgian Limburg (Ammianus, XVII, 8, § 2).

Chlodio, who establishes a firm monarchy among the Salians, enlarges their area in Northern Belgium, but is defeated by the Roman governor Aëtius about Arras (Sid. Apollinaris, *Carm.* V, 211). After the murder of Aëtius in 454, Chlodio annexes Cambray and advances to the river Somme (Gregor. Tur. II, 9). Henceforth, the history of the Salians becomes identical with the general history of the Franks in France.

The *Lex Salica* is codified in the fifth or sixth century. As masters of Gaul the Salians are generally called *Neustrii*. The original Salland has adopted a Saxon-German dialect, while the Salians have absorbed the Saxon colonies in Flanders.

Lit. Zeuss, 329; Grimm, 528; G. Kurth, *La frontière linguistique en Belgique et dans le nord de la France*; Bremer, §§ 171–174; Much, *Stammeskunde*, 90; *idem*, in Hoops, s.v. *Salier*; Schmidt, II (see Index); Aubin, *Kulturströmungen u. Kulturprovinzen in den Rheinlanden*, p. 35 seq.; Dez Marez, *Le problème de la colonisation franque* (*Acad. royale de Belgique, Cl. des lettres, Mém.*, 2. Série, IX, 1926).

§ 188. History of the Chamavi Proper.

The Chamavi originally are situated south-east of the Zuider Zee, south of the Salians. In the first century B.C. they temporarily reach the Rhine and settle in a district which is later occupied by Tubantes, Usipii, Frisians, and Amsivarii, and finally maintained by the Romans as a military borderland (Tac. *Ann.* XIII, 55); on the question of time see Bremer, § 175.

The Chamavi are Roman subjects from A.D. 4 to 47.

About A.D. 97 they ally with the Angrivarii against the Bruchteri and

[1] 'Κούαδοι.'

conquer their western territory (Tac. *Germ.* 33). The mediaeval Chamavic district, i.e. Hamaland between Rhine, Ijssel, and Lippe, chiefly consists of what was once Bruchterian territory.

The words 'Chamavi *qui et Franci' (*Tab. Peuting.*) seem to indicate that the name of Franks originates from the vicinity of the Chamavi.

In 294 or 295 Chamavi and Frisians are driven from Batavia (*Paneg. Constantio,* VI, 5, VII, 4, VIII, 3, 8, 9). Prisoners are settled as colonists in Gaul, cp. the Pagus Commavorum or Amavorum on the Saone and the Doubs (Zeuss, 582; Schmidt, II, 442).

In 358 the Chamavi invade Belgium, pressed in their rear by the Saxon tribe of Chauchi, and are repulsed by Julian (Ammianus, XVII, 8, § 5; Julianus, *Ep. ad Athen.* 280).

In 392 the Romans invade the Chamavic district (Sulpicius Alexander, cit. by Gregor. Tur. II, 9). A cohort of Chamavi serves in the orient about 400 (*Not. dign. Or.* XXXI, 61); this is the last trace of their political activity under the tribal name.

The *Lex Francorum Chamavorum* is codified about 800, but only contains some few original additions to the text of the *Lex Salica.* Also the district of Drente seems to have acknowledged the Chamavic law (cp. Schmidt, II, 464).

The mediaeval Hamaland represents only the southern part of the ancient Chamavic territory, and about 700 the larger part of Hamaland is annexed by the Saxons and adopts the Saxon-German dialect.

Lit. **Zeuss, 91, 326, 334, 582; Grimm, 530; Müllenhoff,** IV **(see Index); Bremer, § 150, 5, §§ 175–177; Much,** ***Stammeskunde,*** **81 seq.;** ***idem,*** **in Hoops, s.v.; Ihm in Pauly-Wissowa, s.v.; Schmidt,** II, **422, 463.**

§ 189. History of the Chattvarii Proper.

In A.D. 4 the Chattvarii are situated east of the Cannenefates, west of the Bruchteri (cp. Velleius, II, 105). Perhaps they are the 'Men of Hatheim' (cp. § 183, 4). The place of Hatheim, now Hattem, opposite Salland, would agree very well with the assumption that the region surrounding the mouths of the rivers Ijssel and Vecht is the original home of the Isteones alias Franks.

Tiberius conquers the Chattvarii, A.D. 4 (Velleius, *l.c.*).

Constantius, after repulsing invading Franks from Belgium A.D. 294 or 295 (cp. § 185), seems to have transplanted Chattvarii to Eastern Gaul together with the Chamavi (cp. Zeuss, 582).

In 360 Julian leads an expedition from Tricensima in Belgium against the 'Attuarian Franks' (var. Ansivarian). As the region is described as mountainous, we notice that the Chattvarii occupy now the same place as in the Middle Ages, viz. the Pagus Hattvariensis, extending from the river Lippe to beyond the Ruhr, south-west of the Bruchteri.

In 392 the Chattvarii are again attacked by the Romans, if we are to adopt Schmidt's reading *Chattvarii for the Chatti of Sulpicius Alexander (cp. § 199).

After the collapse of the Roman dominion, they extend their area to the western border of the Meuse.

About 526 the Scandinavian Viking Hugleik is defeated and killed in the Pagus Hattvariensis (Gregor. Tur. III, 3).

In 715 the Saxons annex the eastern part of the Pagus, which henceforth speaks Saxon-German. The Hattvarians west of the Rhine now speak the Salian dialect.

Lit. Zeuss, 99, 336, 341, 582; Grimm, 589; Müllenhoff, IV, 399, 551, 593; Bremer, §§ 181–184; Much, *Stammeskunde*, 80; *idem*, in Hoops, s.v.; Ihm in Pauly-Wissowa, s.v. *Attuarii*; Schmidt, II, 421.

§ 190. History of the Amsivarii and Chasvarii Proper.

The Amsivarii and Chasvarii originally inhabit respectively the Emsgau on the river Ems, and the Hasegau on the river Hase.

In 12 B.C. Drusus probably subjects both tribes. The Amsivarii remain faithful to Rome during the campaigns of Tiberius and Germanicus and refuse to join the anti-Roman league of the Cheruscian chieftain Arminius.

About A.D. 50 they are exiled by the Chauchi, and in A.D. 58 refused admission into the Roman military borderland on the Lower Rhine. After being temporarily received by the Usipii and Tubantes, the Amsivarii are finally almost destroyed by the Chatthi and Cherusci (Tac. *Ann.* XIII, 55–56).

The Chasvarii have probably been driven out by the Chauchi at the same time as the Amsivarii, but are received by the Romans into the military borderland beside the Usipii and Tubantes, in North-west Hesse or thereabouts.

About 260, during the reign of Gallienus, the Roman dominion over these tribes comes to an end (*Not. gent.*).

Towards 400 the Amsivarii still supply mercenaries to Rome (*Not.*

dign. Occ. v, 40). In 392 they are involved in a Roman expedition against the Bruchteri (Sulpicius Alexander, cit. by Gregor. Tur. II, 9). On this occasion, the Amsivarii appear as Franks. Both they and the Chasvarii belong to the branch of the Franks called Ripuarians.

Lit. (*a*) **Amsivarii: Zeuss, 90, 341; Müllenhoff, IV, 419, 424, 435, 551; *idem*, *Zeitschrift*, IX, 237; Bremer, § 150, 2; Much, *Stammeskunde*, 85 seq.; *idem*, in Hoops, s.v.; Ihm in Pauly-Wissowa, s.v.; Schmidt, II, 91.** (*b*) **Chasvarii: Zeuss, 113; Grimm, 588, 628; Müllenhoff, IV (see Index); Bremer, § 201; Much, *Stammeskunde*, 86; *idem*, in Hoops, s.v.; Ihm in Pauly-Wissowa, s.v.; Schütte, *Ptolemy's Maps*, 119, 121; Schmidt, II, 416.**

§ 191. History of the Tubantes Proper.

The element *-bant* characterises the Tubantes as belonging to the nucleus of the Isteonic-Gambrivian-Frankish branch.

They first appear as transitory settlers in the Roman military borderland north of the Lower Rhine—after the Chamavi, and before the Usipii (Tac. *Ann.* XIII, 55).

In A.D. 14 the Tubantes assist the Usipii and Bruchteri in assailing Germanicus after the destruction of the Marsic sanctuary (*ibid.* I, 51).

In 58 the Tubantes, like the Usipii, Tenchteri, and Bruchteri, try to help the exiled Amsivarii (*ibid.* XIII, 56).

The Tubantes seem to have accompanied the Usipii to Hesse, and after A.D. 83 to have shared their partial subjection to Roman dominion in the military borderland.

About 260, during the reign of Gallienus, both tribes regain their independence (*Not. gent.*).

In 321 Tubantes, Bruchteri, Chamavi, Alemanni, etc., appear as members of an anti-Roman league (Nazarius, *Paneg. Constantino*, 18). Tubantes serve as Roman mercenaries about 400 (*Not. dign. Or.* VI, 10; *Occ.* V, 28). Like the Usipii and Tenchteri, they help to form the Ripuarian Franks.

Lit. **Zeuss, 88, 305; Grimm, 592; Müllenhoff, IV, 43, 549; Bremer, § 202; Much, *Stammeskunde*, 79; *idem*, in Hoops, s.v.; Schmidt, II, 405 seq.**

§ 192. History of the Usipii and Tenchteri Proper.

The Usipii and Tenchteri are tribes from the interior of Germany, probably belonging to the same stock as the Marsi, Chatthi, Ubii, and Bruchteri. Owing to the large district separating them the Usipii are not hereditary enemies of the Isteones-Gambrivii, as are the immediate neighbours such as the Chatthi, Ubii, and Bruchteri. Thus, the common antagonism to Rome soon brings about an alliance between the Isteones-Gambrivii and the exiled Usipii and Tenchteri. But though the alliance leads to a fusion of the exiled tribes with the Isteones-Gambrivii, or Franks, the ancient kinship with the Chatthi and Bruchteri does not seem to have been completely forgotten. The Usipii and Tenchteri seem to have occupied the position of an intermediate link.

About 56 B.C. the Usipii and Tenchteri are driven from the interior of Germany by the Swabians (Caesar, *Bell. Gall.* IV, 1). In 55 they annex the area of the Belgian Menapii on the right border of the Lower Rhine, are repulsed from Belgium by Caesar, and received by the Sugambri (*ibid.* 4, 15, 18; Dio Cassius, XXXIX, 47 seq.). The Usipii are situated north of the river Lippe (*ibid.* LIV, 31, 33).

In 38 B.C., when the Ubii are transplanted west of the Rhine, the Tenchteri seem to have taken over parts of their territory, i.e. the region south of the Ruhr.

In 17 B.C. the Sugambri, Usipii, and Tenchteri defeat the Roman general Lollius in Belgium (*ibid.* LIV, 20).

In 12 and 11 B.C. Drusus attacks the Sugambri and subjugates the Usipii and Tenchteri (*ibid.* LIV, 32, 33; Livius, *perioch.* 140). Florus, II, 30, § 23, writes: 'Drusus primos domuit Usipetes, inde Tencteros percurrit et Cattos'. Drusus started from Batavia (Dio Cassius, *l.c.*), and the list of Florus gives a sequence of tribes along the Rhine to Hesse inclusive.

In 8 B.C. the Usipii and Tenchteri take possession of parts of the evacuated Sugambric territory.

The revolt of Arminius in A.D. 9 again makes both tribes independent.

In A.D. 14 the Usipii, Bruchteri, and Tubantes try to take vengeance on Germanicus for the destruction of the Marsic temple of Tanfana (Tac. *Ann.* I, 51). The Usipii and Tenchteri, like the Bruchteri, seem to have belonged to the 'amphictyony' of the Marsi, and this ancient religious community persisted even after the two exiled tribes had entered the political commonwealth of the Isteones-Gambrivii.

During their stay north of the river Lippe, the Usipii try to colonise the Roman military borderland north-east of the Lower Rhine, but in vain.

In A.D. 58 the exiled Amsivarii, who make the same attempt, are vainly assisted by the Usipii, Tenchteri, and Bruchteri (Tac. *Ann.* XIII, 55, 56). We notice the continued solidarity of Usipii, Tenchteri, and Bruchteri.

In 69–70 both Usipii and Tenchteri support the rebellion of the Batavian chieftain Civilis against Rome. The Usipii on this occasion appear to be fighting side by side with the Chatthi and Mattiaci (Tac. *Hist.* IV, 37), and thus seem to have emigrated to Hesse. We notice the continued solidarity of 'Bructeri Tencterique' (*ibid.* 21 and 77); the two tribes form one wing of the united army.

In 83, when the Emperor Domitian organises the Roman military borderland in Hesse, sections of the Usipii again become Roman subjects; but Tacitus in 98 still enumerates both Usipii and Tenchteri among the independent tribes (*Germ.* 32). He praises the trained cavalry of the Tenchteri.

About 260, during the reign of Gallienus, the Usipii of the Roman borderland in Hesse regain their independence (*Not. gent.*).

Later, both Usipii and Tenchteri seem to have been absorbed by the Ripuarian Franks.

Lit. **Zeuss**, 88, 89; **Grimm**, 533; **Müllenhoff**, IV (see Indices); **Much**, *Beiträge*, XVII, 80, 88, 137, 146; *idem*, in **Hoops**, s.v.; **Holz**, *Beitr. z. germ. Altertumskunde*, I, 8, 17, 68, 71; **Bremer**, §§ 196 and 203; **Schmidt**, II, 405 seq., and **Index**.

§ 193. History of the Ripvarii or Austrasii Proper.

The tribe of Ripuarians has its origin in remnants of Sugambri, Amsivarii, Chasvarii, Tubantes, Usipii, and Tenchteri. Apart from some insignificant ramifications into the Westphalian inland, the area occupied by these tribes is chiefly limited to the eastern 'ripa' of the Rhine, and the Frankish dialect area of to-day observes the same limitation on its eastern front. As a name of the Franks, Riboarii appears for the first time in the *Liber hist. Franc.*, written about 727.

Incursions of Franks into the western 'ripa' begin to grow frequent towards the close of the third century (cp. *Paneg. Maximian.* x, 7, XI, 5, etc.).

In 321 a league of Frankish and Alemannic tribes is repulsed (Nazarius, *Paneg. Constantin.* 18).

After 350 the Eastern Franks occupy the entire western bank of the Rhine from Vetera (Xanten) to Bingen, including Cologne, but they are defeated by Julian, 356 seq. (see p. 174).

In 380 the Frankish King Mallobaud conquers the Alemannic territory north of the Main (Ammianus, XXX, 3, § 7).

In 392–393 the Romans invade the Frankish regions, in order to avenge an invasion of Belgium (see § 185).

In 406 the Franks try to prevent the Vandals and Swabians from invading Gaul (Orosius, VII, 40).

Between 413 and 440 the Franks four times sack Treves. In 428 they are repulsed by Aëtius (see § 185).

About 460 they finally occupy Cologne, and temporarily Treves with its environs (see § 185).

About 496 the Frankish King Sigebert repulses the invading Alemanni at Zülpich (Gregor. Tur. II, 37). After the victory of the Salian King Chlodowech the Eastern Franks take over parts of the annexed Alemannic territory.

In 511 Sigebert is assassinated by his own son at Chlodowech's instigation, and the latter is chosen as king in his place.

The Carlovingian dynasty is of East Frankish origin, but at the time of its ascension to the throne, both sections of the Franks had long been united.

Within the state of France, the Eastern Franks often form a subordinate kingdom, Austrasia; the inhabitants are called Austri or Austrasii.

The leading tribe of the Austrasii assumes the name of Ripvarii, of which change examples occur after 727, and its territorial law is codified in the eighth century as the *Lex Ribuaria.*

The Pagus Ripvariensis generally covers the area of the Middle Frankish dialect, and the frontier is marked by the place names Reiferscheid, Rüfferscheid, Riescheid, Rescheid, i.e. 'Ripuarian frontier'. We cannot agree with Ramisch, *Deutsche Dialektgeographie*, I, 67, and Schmidt, II, 462, that the frontiers of these areas are irreconcilable. At least, Bremer's territorial map in his *Ethnographie*, pp. 868–869, compared with his *Karte der deutschen Mundarten* in *Der grosse Brockhaus*, IV (1929), seems to show a general agreement. Riescheid (*bis*), Reiferscheid, Rieferat on the line Barmen-Sieg fairly coincide with the Frankish-Saxon frontier; Reiferscheid in the Westerwald with the Frankish-Hessian. The five instances between Adenau and Schleiden on the northern slopes of the mountain Eifel certainly lie behind the south frontier of the Pagus Ripvariensis, but the dialect seems to be found correspondingly further south just here. The frontier line of these places (Reiferscheid, etc.) seems to date from a temporary expansion of the Alemanni. Before 496 their vanguards had already reached Zülpich in the plain north of the Eifel, when they were stopped by King Sigebert. The five place names (Reiferscheid) on the Eifel obviously mark the vicinity of the most advanced northern settlements of the Alemanni, for south of this line we notice frequent instances of the typical Alemannic place names ending in *-ingen*, e.g. Hönningen (on the eastern border of the Rhine), Kesseling, Hönningen, Bettingen, Büllingen (near Malmedy on the frontier of the French language). South of Büllingen, a continuous stratum of place names ending in *-ingen* extends throughout Luxemburg and Lothringen. The temporary bar, established by the Alemanni in the Eifel against Frankish expansion, is emphasised by the fact that the percentage of Gallo-Roman place names increases remarkably south of the Eifel; as we mentioned above, French was spoken in the Lower Moselle valley till the tenth century. But after the great victory of the Franks in 496, the territory of the victorious nation would naturally grow, and so the Pagus Ripvariensis advanced south of the frontier line designated by the five place names (Reiferscheid, etc.).

The dialect of the Ripuarians is High German, but with a strong inclination towards the Low German type. The so-called 'Saxons' of Transylvania are Frankish colonists from the Moselle region.

For particulars concerning the distribution and frontiers of dialects in the Pagus Ripvariensis and the Moselle valley see Bremer.

Lit. Zeuss, 343, 578; Bremer, §§ 192-193; Seeck in Pauly-Wissowa, s.v. *Riparienses milites*; Schmidt, II, 458 seq.

§ 194. Legendary Traditions.

Franks alias Merewioingas alias Kerlings play an enormous part in Gothonic legends, as heirs of the West Roman Empire. Though Huns and Goths occupy a more important position in the epic 'Almanach de Gotha the Franks beat all records as regards the number of characters. First of all, in our opinion, they supply the chief characters and incidents of the Nibelungen Legend, the *Iliad* of the Gothonic nations. Space here only allows of a limited selection of instances.

Frakkar, i.e. Franks, is a synonym of 'warriors' in the Scandinavian poetical language.

The Isteonic eponymous figure Istio, ancestor of the Franks, appears with his brothers Ingo and Ermin in the Frankish *Generatio regum et gentium*, sixth century—mere names certainly, but still signs of ethnogenic traditions (cp. Müllenhoff, II, 325, and our monograph *Oldsagn om Godtjod*, 185).

A mythical hero Ansegis, the same as the Saxon ethnic hero Ansehis (Anon. Ravennas, V, 31), appears disguised as the Trojan 'Anchises' as ancestor of the Carlovingian dynasty in the *Gesta Episcop. Mettensium*, written by Paulus Diaconus about 787. The learned confusion starts from the use of the name Ansegis in the Carlovingian family (cp. Rydberg, *Undersökningar i germ. mytologi*, I, 40, 85, 754, and our monograph *Oldsagn om Godtjod*, 161, *Vor mytiske Kongerække*, 25).

The bull Quinotaurus as Merovingian ancestor ('Fredegar', III, 9) reflects a bull worship, adopted from the Gauls (cp. § 96).

Aëtius alias Egetius alias Aequantius (so in Nennius) is generally regarded as the model for Angantýr, the conqueror of the Huns in the *Hervararsaga*. Angantýr's Gothic nationality reflects the alliance of Aëtius with the Visigoths. His antagonist Attila is called Humli, who is 'Humbers rois des Hunus' in Wace's *Roman de Brut*, which deals with the same subject. Humli's Gothic ally corresponds to Attila's Ostrogothic vassals. Angantýr's counsellor Gizurr, 'leader of the Grýtingar', reflects the surname of the Ostrogoths, Greutungi, but his name Gizurr and his eagerness in stirring up the conflict seems to echo the Vandalic King Geizeric, who has thus suffered a national displacement. Angantýr's stepbrother and rival Hlǫðr is the Frankish King Chlodio, who was defeated by Aëtius in 428 and whose neutrality in 451 seems to have been doubtful; their alleged kinship reflects the historical fact that Aëtius had adopted a Frankish prince. The names Incgenþéow and Hliþe (*Widsith*, l. 116) seem to point to the existence of the same legend in England; later English fables make King Humbers drown in the river Humber (cp. Grundtvig, *Danm. Folkeviser*, II, 637; Heinzel, *S.B. d. Wien. Akad. phil.-hist. Kl.* CXVII and CXIX; Much, *Zeitschrift*, XXXIII, 9 seq.; Schütte, *Arkiv*, XXI, 30; Chambers, *Widsith*, 46, 48, 220; Heusler in Hoops, s.v. *Hunnenschlacht*; Bruinier, *Die germ. Heldensage*, 70).[1]

Aegidius, the successor of Aëtius, is recorded in a legend of a national Frankish stamp (Gregor. Tur. II, 12, and 'Fredegar', III, 11). Here, King Childeric is dethroned by the Franks owing to his debauches, and the Roman Aegidius chosen in his place; but Childeric's friend Wiomad

[1] On the demonic Hagen of the Nibelungen Legend as a possible echo of Aëtius cp. our monograph in the *Journ. Engl. and Germ. Phil.* XX, 304.

causes Aegidius to forfeit his credit among the Franks because of his tyranny, and so they at last restore the exiled king. The 'delivery from Roman slavery' is a typical feature in tales of the rise of Gothonic states during the Migration Age (cp. our monograph *Oldsagn om Godtjod*, 208).

Childeric's wife Basina has a symbolic dream of three Merovingian generations, viz. lions, wolves, and hounds. The first part of the dream is not represented in epic; the 'lion' is perhaps formed in assonance with Chlodjo, Hlojo. The 'wolves' are the epic Wülfings or Ylfingar; the 'hounds' are the epic Hundingar (cp. our article, *Journ. Engl. and Germ. Phil.* xx, 312 seq.).

Childeric's son Chlodowech, founder of France, only seems to survive as a 'walking gentleman', King Hlǫðvér, in the Eddic legend of Wayland Smith (cp. 'Hlǫðvér's halls' in *Goðrúnarkviða en forna*, str. 25). He must, however, have impressed the epic mind more deeply; it is necessary to search for him under some disguised name. Above all, it seems undeniable that his wooing of the Burgundian princess Chrodehild (Gregor. Tur. II, 28) is echoed by Attila's love story (cp. Bugge, *Home of the Eddic Poems*, 276, 282; Voretzsch, *Zeitschrift*, 1909, 50; Schütte, *l.c.* 310 seq.).

Theodoric of Austrasia, a bastard of Chlodowech's, and Theodebert, a bastard of Theodoric's, are the leading 'wolves'. The German Wülfing Legend gives both the symbol of wolves and the illegitimate birth. Theodoric appears as Hug-Dietrich,[1] a name drawn from his famous conflict with the Viking Hugleik in the country of the Hugas. Theodebert, the real hero of the battle, is called Wolf-Dietrich. The fight with Hugleik is recorded in *Beowulf*. The Scandinavian echo of the historical actions is dim, but the rivalry of the Ylfingar and Hundingar, i.e. 'Wolves' and 'Hounds', is still traceable (cp. W. Grimm, *Heldensage*, see Index (*Hug-Dietrich, Wolf-D., Wölfinge*); Bugge, *Home of the Eddic Poems*, 82, 184; Schütte, *l.c.* 312 seq.).

Charibert, Chlodowech's grandson, who died in 567, seems to be the Eddic Hervarðr, a Hunding (cp. Schütte, *l.c.* 314).

The fall of Sigebert's uncle while fighting against the Burgundian Godomar is traceable in the Edda: the Frankish hero Sigurd is killed by the Burgundian Gottormr (cp. W. Grimm, *l.c.* 13, 35; Schütte, *l.c.* 317).

Gunthram of Burgundy, who died in 593, is exactly reproduced in the weak and unwarlike King Gunther of Burgundy in Part I of the

[1] But Hug-Dietrich also reflects Chlodowech; cp. Schneider, *Die Gedichte und die Sage von Wolfdietrich*.

Nibelungenlied (in Part II, Gunther is the genuine Burgundian and really heroic King Gundahar, who died in 436; cp. Schütte, *l.c.* 319 seq.).

Gunthram's brother Chilperic in Tournay (Doornick), Sigebert's slayer, as to his residence and actions is reproduced in Hagen of Troneje (or Troneck), Sigfrid's slayer, but may have coalesced with A(g)ëtius (cp. Schütte, *l.c.* 319).

Sigebert of Austrasia (Rhenish Franconia), who died in 575, is Sigfrid or Sigurd of Rhenish Franconia, the champion of the Nibelungen Legend. As Wolf-Dietrich's fame arose from his victory over a northern Viking, so the poet Venantius Fortunatus celebrates a victory won by Sigebert's army over Danes and Saxons, and a similar exploit of Sigfrid's is fully recorded in the *Nibelungenlied.* Sigebert's Queen Brunehild, when residing at Worms as regent of Burgundy, is executed in 613 on the false charge of having murdered him; her likeness to the epic Brünhild, the queen of Burgundy, in spite of inevitable alterations, is obvious (cp. Schütte, *l.c.* 318 seq.).

Dagobert, the last gallant Merovingian, defeated by the heathen heirs of the Huns in Eastern Germany in 630, corresponds to the epic Dankwart who succumbs to the Huns of Attila (cp. Schütte, *l.c.* 325).

The name of Nibelungs first emerges in the Carlovingian dynasty (cp. Müllenhoff, *Zeitschrift*, XII, 290, 293; Schütte, *l.c.* 326).

Charlemagne becomes a favourite champion in all Gothonic literatures, but no longer counts as really Gothonic, since he represents Romance poetry.

Lit. W. Grimm, *Heldensage*; Müllenhoff, *Die merovingische Stammsage* (*Zeitschrift*, VI, 430); *idem*, *Die austrasische Dietrichsage* (*ibid.* 435); Bugge, *Home of the Eddic Poems*; Jiriczek, *Deutsche Heldensage*, 4th ed. (*Samml. Göschen*), 163; Symons, *Grundriss*, 2nd ed. III, 671; Voretzsch, *Zeitschrift*, LI, 39; Schütte, *Arkiv*, XXIV, 1 seq.; Bruinier, *Die germ. Heldensage*, 69 seq.

I. §§ 195–202. *THE MARSIC BRANCH, AND THE CHATTHI, UBII, AND BRUCHTERI*

§ 195. Names.

1. Lat. Marsi (Tacitus, first century A.D.); Gr. Μάρσοι (Strabo, first century B.C.). Personal name: Frank. Marso. Place name: (??) O.G. Merse-velt, Germ. Mörsfeld (in Hesse). Obscure. Home: east of the Silva Caesia, O.G. Heisiwalt (Tac. *Ann.* I, 50); north of the river Ruhr.

There is presumably a colony in the Rhine Delta, the Marsaci (cp. § 196, 1 (*a*)).

Lit. **Zeuss, 86; Grimm, 618; Hirt,** ***Beiträge,*** **XVIII, 513; Schönfeld, s.v. (with lit.); Much in Hoops, s.v.; Förstemann, s.v.** ***Marsi*** **and** ***Marso*****; Löwenthal,** ***Beiträge,*** **XLVII, 289 seq.**

2. (*a*) Lat. Chatti (Pliny, Tacitus, first century A.D.; Suetonius, second century A.D.); Catthi (Velleius, first century A.D.; Tac. *Ann.* XII, 27 and 28, XIII, 56 and 57, all codices; Juvenalis, Suetonius, Florus, Julius Capitolinus); Catti (Statius, Eutropius, Orosius); Cazzi, Caththi (Julius Honorius, *Geogr. Lat. Min.* XXXII, 11); Gr. Χάττοι (Strabo, first century B.C.), Χάτται (Ptolemy, second century A.D.). Obscure. No doubt identical with O.G. Hassi, Germ. Hessen; perhaps also with Celt. Cassi, Tri-caꝫꝫes, Tri-castini (now Troyes, Trois-châteaux), etc. Frequent spellings such as Catthi, Cazzi, etc., prove that the dental consonant is an aspirate. Divergent forms such as Chatti do not affect this conclusion, for the classically 'correct' orthography did not tolerate two aspirates beside each other as in Chatthi; it must be either Chatti or Catthi (cp. our article in *Arkiv*, XXXIII, 26). The Frankish tribal name Chatt-varii has nothing to do with the Chatthi, as its dental is an original Gothonic *tt* (cp. O.E. Hætwere). Home: Hesse. A colony in the Rhine Delta (cp. § 196, 2 (*b*) and (*c*)).

Lit. **Schönfeld, s.v. (with lit.); Much in Hoops, s.v.; Kauffmann, I, 246 note 6, 415 note 5; Schmidt, II, 362; G. Wolff,** ***Chatten, Hessen, Franken*****; Zachrisson,** ***Studier tillägn. Ax. Kock,*** **492.**

(*b*) O.G. Hassi, Hessi (*epist.* Bonifatii, *Mon. Germ. epist. Merow. et Karoli I*, No. 101, No. 43, A.D. 732–755); Germ. Hessen; M.Lat. Hassi, Hessi, Hassones, Haessones, Hessones, Hessiones, Hassingi. Personal name: Ostphal. Hassio. Region: O.G. Hessun, Germ. Hessen; M.Lat. Hassia, Hessia, Hassonia. Place name: O.G. Hessi-heim (near Worms).

Lit. **Förstemann, s.v.** ***Chatti*****; Schoof,** ***Der Name Hessen*** **(*****Hessenland,*** **XXX, 1).**

3. Lat. Ubii (Caesar, first century B.C., Tacitus, first century A.D., etc.); Gr. Ὄβιοι? (Dio Cassius, LXXI, 3, third century A.D.). Obscure. Home: Hesse, on the river Lahn; later west of the Rhine, with capital Cologne.

Lit. **Müllenhoff, IV, 395 (with lit.); Schönfeld, s.v. and s.v.** ***Obii*** **(with lit.); Loewe,** ***Indogerm. Anz.*** **XIV, 21; Förstemann, s.v.; Much in Hoops, s.v. and s.v.** ***Obioi*****; Zachrisson,** ***Studier tillägn. Ax. Kock,*** **493.**

4. Lat. Bructeri (Velleius, first century A.D.), Bructeres (Pliny, second century A.D.), Bruch(t)eres (*CIL.* v, 8768, c. A.D. 400), Bruteri (Nazarius, fourth century), Burcturi (*Tab. Peuting.*, fourth century); M.Lat. Bricteri (Gregor. Tur., sixth century); Boruct-varii (Bede); Borthari (ep. Gregor. III, c. an. 738); Porahtani (*Act. Sanct.*); Gr. Βρούκτεροι (Strabo, first century B.C.), *Βουράκτεροι (Βουσάκτεροι, Ptolemy, second century A.D.). Personal name: O.L.G. Borhter (*Trad. Corbej.*). Region: O.L.G. Borahtra gowe. Place name: L.G. Brochterbeck (near Tecklenburg). Obscure. The Frisian island of Burcana or Borkum may be compared. Home: north of the river Lippe; later, south of the river.

Lit. Bremer, § 194; Schönfeld, s.v. (with lit.); Much in Hoops, s.v.; Kauffmann, I, 405 note 6; Förstemann, s.v.; Schmidt, II, 416; Löwenthal, *Beiträge*, XLVII, 291.

§ 196. Sub-divisions.

1. (*a*) Lat. Marsacii (Pliny, first century A.D.), Marsaquii (*CIL.* VI, 3263), Marsaci (Tacitus, first century A.D.). Nymphs: Lat. Matres (M)arsacae and Maxacae (*CIL.* XIII, 8630; *CIR.* 208). Region: M.L. Frank. Mars-um < *Mars-heim. Derived from Marsi with Celtic suffix *-ac* (cp. 2 (*a*), Mattiaci). Home: Marsum in the province of South Holland.

Lit. Grimm, 619; Holder, *Altcelt. Sprachschatz*, s.v.; Bremer, *Indogerm. Forsch.* XIV, 365; Much in Hoops, s.v.; Förstemann, s.v. and s.v. *Marsum.*

(*b*) (?) Lat. Marsigni (Tacitus, first century A.D.); Gr. Μαρουίνγοι (Ptolemy, second century A.D.). Derived from Marsi with Gothonic suffix *-ing*, if the Latin spelling is correct. Home: beside the Buri in the vicinity of Bohemia (Tac. *Germ.* 43).

Lit. Schönfeld, s.v. (with lit.); Much in Hoops, s.v.

2. (*a*) Lat. Mattiaci. Personal name: O.G. Mattio (Swabian, Schumacher, *Altertümer unserer heidn. Vorzeit*, v, 375). Capital of the Chatthi, Lat. Mattium, probably the present Metze; cp. the region of Matfeld, north-west of Mattium. Baths: Lat. Aquae Mattiacae; Gr. Ματτιακόν (Ptolemy), now Wiesbaden. Obscure; of Celtic origin? The ending *-ac* is Celtic, as in Marsaci. Chatthic sub-tribe with home about Mattiakon in Hesse-Nassau.

Lit. Zeuss, 98 note 1; Müllenhoff, IV, 592; Much, *Beiträge*, XVII, 90; *idem*, *Zeitschrift*, XLI, 116; *idem*, *Stammeskunde*, 77; *idem*, in Hoops, s.v.; Bremer, § 170; Holder, *Altcelt. Sprachschatz*, s.v.; Kauffmann, I, 288; Förstemann, s.v.; Braune, *Indogerm. Forsch.* IV, 348; Streitberg, *ibid.* v, 87; Kropatschek, *Röm.-germ. Korrespondenzbl.* IV, 76; Riese, *Germania*, IV.

(*b*) Lat. Batavi (Caesar, *Bell. Gall.* IV, 10, interpolation?; Pliny, Tacitus, first century A.D., numerous inscr.), Batabi (Lucanus, first century A.D.), Batai (*CIL.* III, 8752, 8761, 8776), Betavi (*CIR.* 2003, and *CIL.* III, 3681 from Poetovio, Petovio, now Pettau); M.Lat. Patabi (*Tab. Peuting.*), Vatavi (MSS of Caesar, Pliny, etc.); Gr. Βατάβοι (Plutarch, Ptolemy, second century A.D.), Βατάουαι (Ptolemy), Βατάοι (Zosimus, sixth century). Region: O.L. Frank. Batua; Dutch Betuwe; Gr. Βαταούα, Βαταβία (Dio Cassius, third century A.D.). Place name: Celt. Βατανό-δουρον (Ptolemy; the accentuation is Celtic); Lat. Batavium (Pliny, etc.), M.Lat. Batavis (*Not. dign.*), O.H.G. Pazauwa, Germ. Passau, Czech. Pasov. River: M.Lat. Patabus (*Tab. Peuting.* i.e. Waal). Obscure. The strange *e* in Betavi may perhaps have been borrowed from the Pannonian town Petovio where the one sample of inscriptions with this form has been found. On the other hand, it might be referred to the modern Dutch form Betuwe which is, however, not exemplified earlier than the eleventh century. The ending *-av* is generally regarded as a suffix, as in Celt. Pictavi. The insular shape of the Betuwe certainly seems to suggest a Compound ending with *-auj* 'island', but the neighbouring Chamavi have the same ending without being situated on an island. The Batavi are a Chatthic sub-tribe with home in the Betuwe.

Lit. Schönfeld, s.v. (with lit.); Much in Hoops, s.v.; Förstemann, s.v.; Kluge, *Etym. Wörterb. d. deutschen Sprache*, s.v. *Au*; Muller, *Nomina geogr. neerlandica*, VIII, 112 seq.

(*c*) Cannenefates (Pliny, first century A.D.), Canninefates (Tacitus, first century A.D.), Cannanefates, Canafates (inscriptions), etc. Region: O.L. Frank. Kenne-hem, O.Fris. Kinne-hem, Dutch Kennemerland, with toponymic, O.M.L. Frank. Kennemare. Obscure. *-fat* looks like Goth. *-faþs* 'man' as in *brūþ-faþs* 'bride-groom', but the firm *t* of *-fates* does not agree with this word which has *d* in the cas. obliq. Besides, the element *-faþs* seems to be exclusively East Gothonic. And the final *e* of Cannene- would be difficult to explain. The Cannenefates are a Chatthic sub-tribe with home in the province of North Holland.

Lit. Schönfeld, s.v. (with lit.); Much in Hoops, s.v.; Förstemann, s.v.; Löwenthal, *Beiträge*, XLIX, 423.

Survey of the types of the tribal names.

We notice a characteristic contrast between the old more important tribe names of the Simplex type, and the names of secondary sub-tribes with various long types: Marsi, Chatthi as contrasted with Marsaci, Mattiaci, Batavi, Cannenefates.

§ 197. Ethnic Position.

The above-mentioned tribes are generally without much consideration attributed to the Isteonic-Gambrivian-Frankish branch. So the Marsi by Bremer, § 199; Schmidt, II, 398; the Chatthi by Bremer, §§ 158, 205[1]; the Ubii by Bremer, § 169; Schmidt, II, 425; the Bruchteri by Bremer, § 194; Schmidt, II, 434. Bremer says in § 205: 'Die Zugehörigkeit der Chatten zu der fränk. Stammesgruppe ist sicher bezeugt', and Schmidt says on p. 434: 'Seinen Ausgang scheint der Frankenname und damit die Stammesbildung...speziell von den...Brukterern genommen zu haben.'

We admit that the tribes concerned have temporarily or permanently been united with the Franks. But as a conception of the *original* distribution of ethnic communities the current opinion is as misleading as possible. It summarily characterises as Frankish a series of tribes that appear at the outset of their history in most marked opposition to the community of the later Franks.

1. The Marsi claim the rank of an ancient and important branch, co-ordinate with the Gambrivii, Swabians, and Vandili (Tac. *Germ.* 2). This high rank is emphasised by the fact that they possess the central national sanctuary of Tanfana (Tac. *Ann.* I, 51); cp. the similar central sanctuary of the Semnones, the 'Sveborum caput' (Tac. *Germ.* 39).

2. The Chatthi are separated from the Isteones-*Sugambri by Pliny, IV, 99. When he classifies the Chatthi as Erminonic, he may be mistaken; but perhaps he had solid reasons for stating that their ethnic connexions were rather eastward than westward. Chatthic fashion of dressing the hair, as described by Tacitus, *Germ.* 31, is different both from the Frankish and the Swabian fashion. In 11 B.C. the Chatthi refuse to join the anti-Roman league of the Sugambri and on that account are furiously attacked by them (Dio Cassius, LIV, 33). In A.D. 58 the Chatthi and Cherusci without mercy decimate and scatter the exiled Amsivarii, another North-west German tribe (Tac. *Ann.* XIII, 56).

3. The Ubii are hereditary enemies of the Sugambri (Caesar, *Bell. Gall.* IV, 16–18).

4. The Bruchteri are defeated and driven out by the allied Chamavi and Angrivarii (Tac. *Germ.* 33).

[1] But not by Schmidt, II, 347.

5, 6. The Usipii and Tenchteri originally are separated from the Sugambri, Chamavi, etc., by a large intervening territory which is occupied by the avowed enemies of these tribes, viz. the Chatthi, Ubii, Bruchteri, etc. Consequently the Usipii and Tenchteri cannot possibly have belonged to the Isteonic-Gambrivian branch from the beginning, and even after joining it in 55 B.C. they keep their ancient religious and political relations with the Marsi, Chatthi, Bruchteri, etc.

7. The religious community of Tanfana embraces Marsi, Bruchteri, Usipii, and Tubantes (Tac. *Ann.* I, 51). The last-mentioned tribe according to the form of its name must be Isteonic-Gambrivian (cp. § 184, 17); but we notice that the most important tribes of this branch are omitted, viz. Sugambri, Chamavi, Chattvarii, Chasvarii, etc.

8. The rebellion of Civilis, A.D. 69–70 (Tac. *Hist.* IV, 12 seq.), is supported by Marsaci 56, Chatthi 37 (incl. Batavi 12, Cannenefates 15, Mattiaci 37), Bructeri Tencterique 21, Usipii 37, Frisians and Chauchi 79. The only Isteonic-Gambrivian people taking part are the Cugerni 26, if we are right in identifying them with the transplanted Sugambri. We notice the complete absence of the Chamavi, Chattvarii, Chasvarii, Tubantes, etc.

To summarise the evidence of points 1–8, it is clear that the Marsi-Chatthi, etc., and the Isteones-Gambrivii are two distinctly separated communities, hostile to each other, and often unwilling to consider the idea of an alliance, even if the question is one of defence against the great common enemy, Rome. Only the Usipii and Tenchteri occupy the position of an intermediate link.

9. A common characteristic of the Marsi, Chatthi, etc., is their relatively high standard of civilisation. The Marsi possess a 'celeberrimum templum', some sort of building which is by Germanicus levelled with the earth (Tac. *Ann.* I, 51), whereas the Germans generally possess no temples (cp. Tac. *Germ.* 9). The Chatthi have a military organisation with almost Roman training (*ibid.* 32). The Ubii from the beginning of their history constantly appear as peaceful and pro-Roman (Caesar, *Bell. Gall.* IV, 3–8 seq.). The Bruchteri possess a regular navy (Strabo, VII, 290). The Usipii and Tenchteri are keen agriculturists (Caesar, *Bell. Gall.* IV, 1), and Tacitus praises the trained cavalry of the Tenchteri, a mode of warfare of probably Gaulish origin (*Germ.* 32).

It remains to consider the evidence of Tacitus concerning the subtribes of the Chatthi. *Hist.* IV, 2: 'Batavi...pars Chattorum'; *Germ.* 29:

'Chattorum quondam populus'; *Hist.* IV, 15, on the Cannenefates: 'origine, lingua, virtute par Batavis'; *Germ.* 29, on the Mattiaci: 'similes Batavis'. The Marsaci probably are a sub-tribe of the Marsi, who have emigrated to the Rhine Delta together with the Batavi.

The general history of the Marsi, Chatthi, etc., till the beginning of the Middle Ages shows an almost uninterrupted decay of their ethnic individuality; this is owing to the expansion of Franks, Frisians, and Saxons (cp. § 185). Most of the tribes here dealt with are Franconised.

However, it is worth noticing that the descendants of the Marsaci and Cannenefates for a time avoid Franconisation by joining the Frisian federation. A co-operation of Cannenefates and Chauchi appears even during the piratic activity of Gannascus in A.D. 47, and the same tribes plus Marsaci and Frisians co-operate during the Batavian rebellion, 69–70. The fusion is merely political, for as members of the Frisian federation the Marsaci and Cannenefates still keep their non-Frisian idiom. So we may regard their position as a temporary survival of the ancient Marsic branch though their nationality is disguised.

The descendants of the Chatthi in Hesse, similarly, though after the Middle Ages they coalesce with the Franks, are not regarded as entirely Frankish. Up to the present time the Hessians, in the popular conception of German tribes, occupy a position in some degree co-ordinate.

As the Thuringians, the Hessians have adopted the Frankish type of house. Cp. Hans Lutsch, *Das Bauernhaus im Deutschen Reiche*, 223: 'Das Bauernhaus unserer ganzen Landschaft hat dieselbe Lage auf dem Gehöfte—hess. "Bünde" oder "Binde", im Hanauischen "Benne" geheissen—und im wesentlichen denselben Grundriss wie das Thüringens. Mit den Wirtschaftsgebäuden umschliesst es einen Wirtschaftshof. Das Wohnhaus selbst steht in der Regel mit dem Giebel nach der Strasse, mit der Langseite nach dem Hofe, dessen Hintergrund die Scheuer einnimmt....Nur im Westerwalde haben Wohnhaus, Stall und Scheuer meist ein gemeinsames Dach, das auf der hinteren Langseite fast bis zum Gelände herabläuft und unter dem niederen Teile den sogenannten "Niederlass" bildet'.

Lit. There exists no literature, as the position of the tribes here dealt with has hitherto been ignored.

§ 198. History of the Marsi, Chatthi, Ubii, and Bruchteri, etc., till c. A.D. 100.

A Marsic branch, co-ordinate with the Isteonic-Gambrivian, existed at the beginning of our era (Tac. *Germ.* 2). We do not know whether at one time it embraced the Chatthi, Ubii, Bruchteri, Usipii, and Tenchteri, but we may confidently assume that these tribes were at least closely associated with it. The region occupied by them lies between the Weser, Main, and Middle Rhine and towards the north reaches of the Lower Ems. Their German neighbours are: the Cherusci and Swabians in the east, the Isteones-Gambrivii in the west; their non-German neighbours: the Chauchi and Frisians on the North Sea, and the Celts west of the Rhine who were later Romanised. The religious centre of the area described is the Marsic sanctuary of Tanfana, situated east of the Silva Caesia, the O.Germ. Heisiwalt, i.e. between the rivers Lippe and Ruhr (cp. Tac. *Ann.* I, 50).

In 56 B.C. the Usipii and Tenchteri are driven from their domiciles by the Swabians and appear on the Lower Rhine, where they join the political community of the Isteones-Gambrivii, yet without abandoning their religious solidarity with the Marsi (cp. Caesar, *Bell. Gall.* IV, 1 and 16).

After 55 and before 12 B.C. the Chatthi in Hesse occupy the island of Batavia in the Rhine Delta (cp. Schmidt, II, 369). The Marsaci probably about the same time have emigrated from the Marsi to the mouth of the Rhine.

In 38 B.C. the Ubii are transplanted to the Roman territory west of the Rhine (Strabo, IV, 194; Tac. *Germ.* 28). The Chatthi take possession of parts of their evacuated area about the river Lahn, acting on an agreement with Rome (Dio Cassius, LIV, 36, § 3); other regions perhaps fell to the Tenchteri.

After 12 B.C. the tribes here dealt with submit to Rome, either peacefully or compelled by force to do so.

In A.D. 9 those situated east of the Rhine, except the Mattiaci, regain their independence, owing to the revolt of Arminius. The Marsi, Chatthi, and Bruchteri take part in this war of liberation and in the subsequent campaigns (Tac. *Ann.* I, 56, 60; cp. II, 25).

In A.D. 14 Germanicus destroys the central temple of Tanfana and breaks the power of the Marsi, in spite of the assistance offered him by the Bruchteri and Usipii, etc. (*ibid.* I, 51). He invades their territory again in A.D. 16 (*ibid.* II, 25), and they retire to the interior of Germany (Strabo, VII, 290).

In 58 the Chatthi suffer a crushing defeat at the hands of the Ermundures to whom they lose their eastern territories (*ibid.* XIII, 57).

In 69 and 70 the Batavian chieftain Civilis unsuccessfully revolts against Rome, supported by Marsaci, Chatthi, Cannenefates, Mattiaci, Ubii, Bruchteri, Usipii, Tenchteri, Frisians, and Chauchi, but by none of the central Isteonic-Gambrivian tribes (Tac. *Hist.* IV, 12 seq.).

The Roman Limes protecting the borderland in the Taunus region is restored by Vespasian.

About 97 the Bruchteri are conquered by the Chamavi and Angrivarii and driven out from their territory north of the river Lippe (Tac. *Germ.* 33).

The above summary of historical facts sufficiently shows the declining power of the tribes concerned.

The destruction of the temple of Tanfana in A.D. 14 and the campaigns of Germanicus A.D. 15–16 put an end to the history of the Marsi.

The German nationality of the Marsaci, judging from the form of their name, seems to have been exposed early to strong Celtic influence.

The Batavi after their unsuccessful rebellion are totally under Gallo-Roman or Roman influence.

The Ubii, who have dwelt on Roman soil since 18 B.C., are soon entirely absorbed.

The Mattiaci, whose territory is repeatedly reduced to a Roman borderland, are in a similar situation. Notice the Celticised form of their name!

The Bruchteri after their defeat in 97 are reduced to temporary insignificance. When they are again heard of, they appear as Franks, A.D. 292–293 (Sulpicius Alexander, cit. by Gregor. Tur. II, 9). In 697 their territory is annexed by the German Saxons.

Thus the Marsi and their companions, far from consolidating their amphictyony into a national kingdom like that of the Franks, move in the opposite direction. About A.D. 100 their religious and political commonwealth seems to be completely dissolved. The Chatthi only to a certain extent maintain a continued national individuality.

Lit. On the Marsi cp. Bremer, § 199; Schmidt, II, 398; Kornemann, *Neue Jahrbücher*, XXV, 53 seq. As we mentioned in § 197, there exists no general literature on the entire community of tribes.

§ 199. History of the Chatthi and Mattiaci Proper.

The original centre of the Chatthi seems to lie on the river Adrana, the present Eder, where their capital Mattium is situated, probably the present Metze (Tac. *Ann.* I, 56). From Mattium, the sub-tribe of Mattiaci derives its name. Owing to internal dissensions, parts of the Chatthi (viz. the Batavi and Cannenefates) early emigrate to the Rhine Delta (Tac. *Hist.* IV, 12 and 15).

In 38 B.C. the Chatthi take possession of the evacuated Ubian region on the river Lahn (cp. Dio Cassius, LIV, 36, § 3).

In 12 B.C. the Chatthi refuse to enter the anti-Roman league of the Sugambri and are attacked by them, but later join the league for fear of the Roman fortifications (*ibid.* 20 and 33).

In 9 B.C. Drusus conquers both tribes, and the Chatthi evacuate the Ubian territory (*ibid.* 33, § 3).

Only the Mattiaci keep their settlements south of the Taunus and generally remain pro-Roman (Tac. *Germ.* 29).

In A.D. 6 Hesse is a Roman military base (Velleius, II, 109). The Chatthi take part in the war of liberation in A.D. 9 and in the subsequent campaigns (Tac. *Ann.* I, 56 and 60); the Mattiaci also regain their liberty.

In A.D. 17 Germanicus burns Mattium, the Chatthic capital (Tac. *Ann.* I, 56).

Dissensions with the Cherusci follow (*ibid.* II, 88, XII, 27 and 28), and inroads into Gaul, and Roman counter-attacks A.D. 40–50 (*ibid.*).

In 58 the Chatthi and Cherusci scatter the exiled Amsivarii (*ibid.* XIII, 56). In the same year the Chatthi suffer a crushing defeat at the hands of the Ermundures, who conquer the eagerly disputed salt springs near the river Werra (*ibid.* 57); the frontier thus established separates the dialects of Hessians and Thuringians to the present day.

In 69 the Chatthi and Mattiaci support the anti-Roman revolt of the Batavian chieftain Civilis (Tac. *Hist.* IV, 37). Vespasian after their defeat repairs the Roman Limes in the Taunus region. The Mattiaci as Roman subjects are soon almost completely Romanised. Their name still appears in the lists of Roman mercenaries about A.D. 400 (*Not. dign. Or.* 5, 12, etc.; *Occ.* 5, 20, and in inscr.).

In 83 and 89 Domitian invades the Chatthic territory (Dio Cassius, LXVII, 4, § 1; Suetonius, *Dom.* 6; Frontinus, I, 1, § 8, and inscr.; see Schmidt, II, 355).

In 85 the Chatthi successfully interfere in the internal dissensions of the Cherusci (Dio Cassius, LXVII, 5, § 1).

In 162 the Chatthi invade Germania Superior and Rhaetia, in 170 Germania Superior and Belgium (*Hist. Aug. v. Marc.* VIII, 7 and 8; *v. Did. Jul.* I, 8).

In 213 they fight Caracalla (Dio Cassius, LXXVII, 14).

About 260, during the reign of Gallienus, the Romans lose the Limes district in Hesse (*Not. gent.*). However, the Burgundians, Alemanni, and Franks dispute the possession of this territory with the Chatthi. The Bucinobantes in Hesse about 357 (Ammianus, XXIX, 4, § 7) have a Frankish name, but belong to the Alemannic federation. In 380 the disputed region is conquered by the Frankish King Mallobaud (*ibid.* XXX, 3, § 7).

In 392–393 'Chatti' are named among the Franks, but if we follow Schmidt, this is an error for *Chattvarii.

The forms Cazzi or Caththi in the geographical excerpts of Julius Honorius in the fourth century foreshadow the appearing of the Hassi or Hessians; we notice how the 'classical' orthography of the name is getting obliterated, while the true German pronunciation is asserting itself. The disappearance of the name from history for more than three centuries must indicate a period of political decline.

In 496 the Hessians as Frankish subjects profit by Chlodowech's victory, for from this time onwards they are able to advance in the Main regions at the expense of the conquered Alemanni. On the other hand, the Hessians are losing ground to the advancing Saxons, who conquer the region due north of Cassel (cp. Spruner-Mencke, *Handatlas des Mittelalters*, No. 33). Henceforth, the 'Francorum pagus...Hassi' (Poeta Saxo ad an. 774), or 'Pagus Hessi Franconicus', is distinguished from the 'Pagus Hessi Saxonicus' (cp. Falke, *Cod. Trad. Corbej.* ad an. 1017). To the present day, the dialect in the region annexed by the Saxons is called Engrisch-Hessisch, as analogous with the dialect Hessisch-Thüringisch in that region which was annexed from the Chatthi by the Ermundures in A.D. 58 (cp. Bremer's dialect map in *Der grosse Brockhaus*, s.v. *Deutsche Mundarten*).

The name of the Hessians in its post-classical form first appears in a letter of Pope Gregory III in A.D. 720. Though they are sometimes called in general terms Franks, e.g. in contrast with Saxons in *Dipl. Caroli M.* ap. Falke, p. 377, they are to the present day often regarded as co-ordinate with Franks, Thuringians, Swabians, etc.

In 1265 the larger part of Hesse is united to form a county, which later develops into the electorate and the Grand-Duchy of that name. The present republic of Hesse is the only state which represents a German tribal district with unbroken continuity from classical to modern times.

Lit. (*a*) Chatthi: Zeuss, 37, 94, 345; Grimm, 565; Müllenhoff, IV (see Index); Bremer, §§ 158, 205–209; Schmaus, *Geschichtl. Herkunft der Franken*, 10 seq.; Kauffmann, I, §§ 52 seq., 56 (p. 358), p. 71, II, § 100 (p. 153); Much in Hoops, s.v.; Schmidt, II, 347 seq. (*b*) Mattiaci: Zeuss, 98; Grimm, 581; Müllenhoff, IV (see Index); Bremer, § 170; Much in Hoops, s.v.; Zangemeister, *CIL.* XIII, 2, p. 406 seq.; Schumacher, *Mainzer Zeitschr.* VII, 77 seq.; *idem, Prähist. Zeitschr.* VI, 279 seq.

§ 200. History of the Batavi and Cannenefates Proper.

Both tribes are descendants of the Chatthi (Tac. *Hist.* IV, 12 and 15). Owing to internal dissensions, they emigrate to the Rhine Delta. The Batavians occupy the Betuwe, and the Cannenefates the Kennemerland (cp. § 196, 2 (*b*) and (*c*)). The *Bell. Gall.* of Caesar mentions the Batavi as settled there before 56 B.C., but this must be an anachronism, introduced by a copyist. For Caesar never met the Batavians, nor does Strabo mention them some decades later (cp. Stolle, *Wo schlug Cäsar die Usipeter und Tenkterer*, 1; Klotz, *Cäsarstudien*, 36 seq.; Holmes, *Caesar's Conquest of Gaul*, 2nd ed. 453, 691; Schmidt, II, 348). The name of the town Batauóduron indicates that the inhabitants were to a large extent Celticised.

In 12 B.C. Drusus uses Batavia as a Roman military base (Dio Cassius, LIV, 31).

In A.D. 4 Tiberius subjugates the Cannenefates (Velleius, II, 105).

After 69–70, when the revolt of Civilis has been suppressed, the Batavians and Cannenefates remain Roman subjects and are more or less Romanised.

In 294 invading Franks are repulsed. They appear settled in Batavia about 358 (cp. § 185).

Batavian auxiliaries fight the Alemanni in Gaul in 366 (Zosimus, IV, 9), the Goths at Adrianople in 379 (Ammianus, XXXI, 13, § 8), and still appear about 400 in the *Not. dign.* (Schönfeld, 46), but they must be regarded as people of Roman nationality. The town of Passau derives its name from a Batavian garrison, cp. *Not. dign. Occ.* XXX, 220.

The Batavians, after the close of the fourth century, are re-Germanised, i.e. Franconised.

The Cannenefates disappear, leaving only a trace in the territorial name Kennemerland.

Lit. (*a*) **Batavi: Zeuss, 100, 389; Grimm, 580; Müllenhoff, IV (see Index); Bremer, §§ 166–167; Kauffmann, I, 57; Blok, *Gesch. d. Niederlanden*, I, 36 seq.; Much in Hoops, s.v.; Schmidt, II, 367 seq. (*b*) Cannenefates: Zeuss, 102; Grimm, 586; Müllenhoff, IV, 399, 532, 593; Bremer, §§ 158, 179; Blok, *Gesch. d. Niederlanden*, I, 38, 44 seq.; Much in Hoops, s.v.; Schmidt, II (see Index); Muller, *Nom. geogr. neerlandica*, VIII, 112 seq.**

§ 201. History of the Ubii Proper.

Situated on the river Lahn, the Ubii are attacked by the Swabians and made tributary to them (Caesar, *Bell. Gall.* IV, 3). After 55 B.C. they appear as pro-Roman (*ibid.* 16), and assist Caesar against the Sugambri (*ibid.* 19).

In 38 B.C. the Ubii are transplanted to the Roman territory west of the Rhine (Strabo, IV, 194; Tac. *Germ.* 28). Their new area includes Gelduba in the north, now Gellep or Gelb, near Kaiserswert (Tac. *Hist.* IV, 26; cp. Müllenhoff, II, 230), and reaches Tolbiacum in the west, now Zülpich (Tac. *Hist.* IV, 79).

In A.D. 50 the Emperor Claudius founds Colonia Agrippina, the present Cologne; this new capital contributes largely to Romanising the Ubii, who often call themselves Agrippinenses (cp. Tac. *Ann.* XII, 27).

In 70, compelled by anti-Roman kinsmen, they join the Batavian rebellion of Civilis, but they desert him again as soon as his fortune declines (Tac. *Hist.* IV, 77 and 79).

About 98 the Ubii still show that they remember their German origin (Tac. *Germ.* 28), but in the subsequent century they are completely Romanised.

In 157 the name of Ubius appears for the last time (*CIL.* V, 5050).

In 166 'Obioi' and Langobards invade Pannonia (Dio Cassius, LXXI, 3); perhaps these are remnants of Ubii from the interior of Germany. After the fifth century the Ubian territory is re-Germanised by the Ripuarian Franks.

Lit. **Zeuss, 83, 87; Grimm, 527; Müllenhoff, IV (see Index); Bremer, § 169; Much in Hoops, s.v. *Obioi*; Schmidt, II, 425.**

§ 202. History of the Bruchteri Proper.

The Bruchteri appear sub-divided into two sections, the greater and lesser Bruchteri (Strabo, VII, 291; Ptol. II, 11, §§ 6 and 9). They extend from the southern border of the Lippe to the Lower Ems (Strabo, VII, 290, 291). Their eastern frontier on the Teutoburger Wald is indicated by the place name Brochterbeck near Tecklenburg.

In 12 B.C. their navy is defeated by Drusus on the river Ems (Strabo, VII, 290).

In A.D. 4 they are subjugated by Tiberius (Velleius, II, 105).

In A.D. 9 the revolt of Arminius again restores their liberty, and they take part in the subsequent campaigns.

In 14, after the destruction of the temple of Tanfana by Germanicus, the Bruchteri and Usipii assist the Marsi against him (Tac. *Ann.* I, 51). In the next year Germanicus invades their country (*ibid.* I, 60).

In 58 the Bruchteri try to assist the exiled Amsivarii against the Romans (*ibid.* XIII, 56).

In 69 the Bruchteri join the rebellion of the Batavian Civilis (Tac. *Hist.* IV, 21). The so-called Veleda, a wise woman (cp. O.Irish *fili* [gen. *filed*] 'poet', Vendryes, *Bulletin de la soc. de linguist.* XXII, 25), becomes their religious leader (Tac. *ibid.* IV, 61).

In 77 there must have been fresh troubles, for the Veleda about that time is made prisoner (Statius, *Silvae*, I, 4, l. 89 seq.; cp. Schmidt, II, 419).

About 97 the Bruchteri are beaten by the allied Chamavi and Angrivarii and lose all their territory north of the Lippe (Tac. *Germ.* 33).

In 321 the Bruchteri again are heard of. They appear as members of a Frankish-Alemannic league against Rome (Nazarius, *Paneg. Constantino*, 18).

Towards 400 they are mentioned as Roman mercenaries (*Not. dign. Occ.* V, 39).

In 392–393 their territory is invaded by the Romans (Sulpicius Alexander, cit. by Gregor. Tur. II, 9). They now appear as Franks.

In 697 they are subjugated by the Saxons who uproot any germs of Christianity among them (Bede, V, 11). They are still mentioned by Bishop Aribo of Freising (died 782) (cp. *Vita S. Emmerami, Boll. Sept.* 6, 483). The district of Borahtra Gowe existed even longer.

Lit. Zeuss, 92, 94, 328, 340, 350; Grimm, 531; Müllenhoff, IV (see Index); Holz, *Beiträge zur germ. Altertumskunde*, I, 7; Bremer, §§ 194-195; Kauffmann, I, 64; Much in Hoops, s.v.; Schmidt, II, 416.

J. §§ 203–208. *THE GERMAN SAXON OR NIEDERDEUTSCH BRANCH*

§ 203. Names.

No ancient collective name exists, and the earliest mediaeval one is not native, but borrowed from non-German neighbours.

1. Germ. Sachsen; L.G. Sassen. Language: L.G. *sassesche sprake.* Country: L.G. Sassenland (cp. § 148, 4 and § 215, 1).

2. Germ. Niedersachsen; L.G. Nedersassen 'Low Saxons'.

3. L.G. (sixteenth century) *Nedderlender. Language: L.G. Nedderlendesch, 'Netherlanders, Lowlanders'.

4. Germ. Niederdeutsche 'Low Germans'.

5. Germ. name of language: Plattdeutsch 'Low German'.

Lit. Lasch, *Mittelniederdeutsche Grammatik*, 5 seq.

§ 204. Sub-divisions.

A. Ancient Division.

1. Lat. Cherusci (Caesar, first century B.C.), Cerusci (Tacitus, first century A.D., MSS), Cerisci (Julius Honorius, fourth century), Herusci (Nazarius, fourth century); Gr. Χηροῦσκοι (Strabo, first century B.C.), Χαιρούσικοι (Ptolemy, second century A.D.), Χεροῦσκοι (Dio Cassius, third century). Country: Gr. Χερουσκίς (*ibid.*). Place name: O.L.G. Herskes-gebutle?, L.G. Harxbüttel near Brunswick. Possibly derived from Gothon. **heru* 'sword', or from **herut* 'hart, stag'. Ending as in Rhaet. Rugusci, Ligur. place name Tarusco, Belgian Caranusca; cp. Lat. *coruscus* 'radiant', *coruscare* 'to butt with horns'. Home: between the Middle Elbe and the Middle Weser.

Lit. Schönfeld, s.v. (with lit.); Much in Hoops, s.v.; Ihm in Pauly-Wissowa, s.v.; Förstemann, s.v.

2. Lat. Fosi (Tacitus, first century A.D.). Obscure. Leibnitz, Zeuss, Grimm, derive Fosi from the river Fuse, an affluent of the Aller. Grimm later objects that tribal names are never derived from rivers such as Danube, Elbe, Rhine, Weser, and Müllenhoff interprets Fuse as *Funsa 'the rapid'. We still prefer the etymology of Leibnitz; geographical coincidence weighs more heavily than etymological guesses. Grimm's objection is wrong. There are a great many similar Norwegian toponymics such as Begnir from the river Begna. Primaeval Germans would naturally

have formed similar names, though a later fashion certainly replaced them by compounds like Amsi-varii, Chas-varii, etc. Home: beside the Cherusci, probably on the river Fuse.

Lit. **Zeuss, 108; Grimm, 574 and 782; Müllenhoff, IV, 443; Schönfeld, s.v. (with lit.); Much in Hoops, s.v.; Ihm in Pauly-Wissowa, s.v.; Förstemann, s.v.; Schmidt, II, 138; Schütte, (Norw.) *Hist. Tidsskrift*, 1917, 14; Löwenthal, *Beiträge*, XLVI, 190; *idem*, *Wörter u. Sachen*, x, 106.**

3. Lat. Dulgibini (Tacitus, first century A.D.), inscr. Dulg(ubniorum, see p. 213); Gr. Δουλγούμνιοι (Ptolemy, second century A.D.). The word *dulg-* is known in Gothonic, but the sense differs: Goth. *dulgs* 'guilt'; O.N. *dolgr* 'enemy, elfish spirit'. The ending is as in Goth. *fraistubni* 'temptation', cp. the Belg. tribal name Geidumni, and the Gaulish Consoramni at Conserans. The alternation of *ƀn* and *mn* is well known in Gothonic. Home: in Eastern Hanover, south of the Langobards (Ptol. II, 11, § 9).

Lit. **Schönfeld, s.v. (with lit.); Much in Hoops, s.v.; Ihm in Pauly-Wissowa, s.v.; Förstemann, s.v.**

4. Lat. Angri-varii (Velleius, Tacitus, first century A.D.); M.Lat. Angrarii, Angarii; Gr. Ἀγγρι-ουάριοι (Ptolemy, second century A.D.). Region: Germ. Engeren in Westphalia. The analogy of Amsi-varii and Chas-varii suggests derivation from a stream Angara, mentioned by Förstemann, but this is only a brook, whereas the Amisia and Hase are well-known rivers. The current etymology 'Meadow-men' is only to be accepted if 'Meadow', O.Germ. Angar, is conceived as an individual place name; for all other ancient compounds ending in *-warja* start from place names or tribal names, not from a simple appellative. Home: east of the Upper Ems and about the Middle Weser.

Lit. **Grimm, 629, 783; Ihm in Pauly-Wissowa, s.v.; Schönfeld, s.v. (with lit.); Much in Hoops, s.v.; Förstemann, s.v. and s.v. *Angara*; Knoke, *Der Angrivarierwall* (*Mannus*, XVIII, 3).**

B. Mediaeval Division of Tribes.

1. M.Lat. Ost-falahi 'People of the eastern plain' (?). Home: Eastern Hanover, chiefly the Cheruscian district together with some Swabian and Thuringian areas.

2. M.Lat. Angrarii, Angarii, i.e. Angri-varii (see § 204, 4). Home: the Weser basin, i.e. the ancient Angrivarian district, together with the district of the Bardi, parts of Hesse, and some non-German areas,

viz. the Chauchic in Northern Hanover, and the Saxon in Holstein or Nordalbingia.

3. Germ. West-falen, West-falinger; M.Lat. West-falahi 'People of the western plain' (?). Home: Westphalia, chiefly consisting of areas annexed from other German tribes, viz. Bursibant, Tvihanti, *Thre-(h)anti, Chamavi, Salii, Chattvarii (all Isteonic), Amsivarii, Chasvarii (Isteonic?), Bruchteri, and Marsi.

C. Modern Division of Dialects.

1. Ostphalian, almost coinciding with the district of the Ostfalahi.
2. Northern Low Saxon, in Northern Hanover, in Bardengau, Ostfriesland, Holstein, Southern Slesvig, and Mecklenburg (all except Bardengau originally non-German).
3. Engrisch, in the southern part of the Angrarian district, together with the region of Engeren in Eastern Westphalia.
4. Westphalian, in the larger part of Westphalia, and a similar Saxon dialect in Eastern Holland including the originally Frisian part of Groningen.

Lit. **Zeuss, 388; Bremer, § 152; Much in Hoops, I, 374.**

§ 205. Ethnic Position.

The genesis of the North German individuality is wrapped in oblivion. We know of no ancient collective name, and no evidence as to religious or political co-operation. The mediaeval name and the federation of Saxons start from a non-German nation.

The Cherusci may claim the leading place among the ancient North Germans. Pliny, IV, 99, enumerates them among the Erminones, coordinate with Swabians, Ermundures, and Chatthi. The alleged ethnic unity cannot be verified, but the juxtaposition with Swabians, etc., seems to denote that the Cherusci may claim a similarly high rank, whereas we observe, on the other hand, that they are separated from the Isteones, i.e. Franks. That the unity with Swabians and Chatthi is no very close one appears from Caesar, VI, 10, and Tac. *Ann.* XII, 28, where the hereditary animosity of the Cherusci and the tribes mentioned is stated; notice especially Tacitus on the Chatthi: 'cum quis aeternum discordant'.

The Fosi may be regarded as a sub-tribe of the Cherusci, as they share in their political ruin (Tac. *Germ.* 36). The position of the Dulgibini is quite vague.

The Angrivarii originally seem rather to be North-west Germans than North Germans. A large frontier wall separates them from the Cherusci (Tac. *Ann.* II, 19); the element *-warja* shows them to be united with the Frankish tribes of Chattvarii and Ripvarii; and they ally with the Frankish Chamavi against the Bruchteri (Tac. *Germ.* 33). But as the final place of the Angrarii denotes that they are one of the three leading Saxon tribes, it is safest to consider them under the heading of North Germans.

The growth of the united North Germans is indubitably due to the Saxons and Chauchi. The expansion partly rests on warlike conquests, in spite of Schmidt's denial (II, 59). But the enlarged Saxon republic at any rate is promoted by the voluntary tendency towards union.

Saxons and Langobards in 568 co-operate on the basis of their 'ancient friendship' (Paulus Diaconus, II, 6). Though the friendship could not reconcile the divergence of Saxon and Langobard law in Italy (*ibid.* III, 6), we may assume that it still facilitated the fusion of the Bardengau with the Saxon state. The alleged 'ancient friendship' recalls the alliance of Cherusci and Langobards against Maroboduus in A.D. 17 (Tac. *Ann.* II, 45); the Cherusci, from the territorial point of view, are almost identical with the Saxons of 568. It seems that the declining Cherusci were gradually absorbed by the Chauchi who advanced 'in Chattos usque' (Tac. *Germ.* 35); and that the Chauchi later assumed the name of their Saxon kinsmen. In a manner similar to the Cherusci and Langobards, the Angrivarii also may have entered the Saxon union.

After the fusion of the North Germans and the Chauchi-Saxons has grown to be an accomplished fact, the features of the national individuality are easy to observe.

1. The language is Low Saxon. The mediaeval terminology is somewhat vague, for it often gives the name of Saxon to Dutch and German dialects which do not share the High German sound shift. Cp. Melis Stoke, *Rymchroniek*, I, ch. 5, 41–65, where it is stated 'dat al lant beneden Nimaghen wilen Nedersassen hiet', i.e. 'that all land south of Nymwegen was once called Lower Saxony', and *Chronicle of St Denis* (Bouquet, *Recueil des hist. de la France*, V, 252): 'De celle gent (the Saxons) sont né et estrait, si comme l'on dit, li Brabançon et li Flamene, et ont encore celle meismes langue'. On the other hand, the orthographical distinction between Dutch and true German Saxon is sometimes fictitious, as in the case of Dutch *zes* and Saxon *ses* 'six', for both languages in

reality pronounce *zes*. But there are certain more fundamental marks of distinction, and the line of demarcation generally coincides with the west frontier of the Saxons after their last conquests about the beginning of the eighth century. Some illustrative proofs of Saxon identity may here be given.

(*a*) In Saxon, as in O.English and Frisian, the verbal persons 1, 2, 3 plur. are not distinguished: O.L.Sax. *bindad,* O.E. *bindað,* O.Fris. *bindath,* cp. O.H.Germ. *bintamēs, bintat, bintant,* and Dutch *wij binden, julli bindt, zij binden* 'we, you, they bind'.

(*b*) In Saxon, as in English and Frisian, nasals are lost before *s* and *þ*: O.L.Sax. *ūs, mūþ,* O.E. *ús, múþ,* O.Fris. *ūs, mūtha*; cp. H.Germ. *uns, mund,* and Dutch *ons, mond* 'us, mouth'. However, not all dialects of Low Saxon share this development. The place names ending in *-mutha* 'mouth' thus become a sure means of tracing the past or present extension of the more definitely Saxon tribes. Cp. Ijsselmuiden, Genemuiden in Salland, Muiden, Leimuiden in North Holland, Masamuda in North Brabant (?), Arnemuiden in Zealand, Dixmuiden in West Flanders, Anaimuthiun in Hanover, Angelmude near Münster, Rammuthe near Altena, Backemude near Meppen, Müden near Celle and on the Aller in the Pagus Muthiwide; on the other hand: Ijsselmonde, Rupelmonde, Dendermonde in East Flanders, Dortmund in the district of the Bruchteri, Münden in Waldeck and in Saxon Hesse at the junction of the Werra and Fulda (cp. Bremer, § 146; Kloeke, *Zum Ingwäonismenproblem* (*Festschrift Borchling*, p. 338 seq., especially p. 356)).

2. The *Lex Saxonum* and the *Sachsenspiegel* represent an individual type of national law.

3. The keeping of a republican form of government by the Saxons is remarkable. No other Gothonic nation preserves the republican constitution so faithfully.

4. The Saxons possess their own type of house, viz. the 'hall-house', lodging men and cattle under one roof. The same absence of distinction between the lodgings of men and cattle characterises the Danish farmstead, whereas the Gauts and Sviones introduce a strict separation (cp. Sigurd Erixon in *Ymer*, 1922, 263).

Meitzen in *Das deutsche Haus*, 10, describes the Saxon house as follows (transl. by Sidney Oldall Addy, *The Evolution of the English House*, 79): 'Its chief characteristic is that it unites in one body the space necessary for a very considerable establishment under one and the same roof, and therefore represents an extremely large building. Its ground plan is that of a basilica with nave and aisles. The middle always forms the so-called "floor" (*diele*), which is entered at the gable end through a large gate, and which goes through the whole house as far as the dwelling rooms at the end. Owing to the want of an exit this floor is used for backing wagons out....In the forms of the Frisian and Saxon house generally in use the horses and cows are always so placed on both sides of the "floor" that they are foddered from it. Over the "floor", over the cattle stalls, and over all other rooms up to the ridge of the roof the corn harvest and hay harvest are stored on boards and poles laid between the joists. In the Saxon house the back ground of the "floor" ends in a low hearth, on both sides of which are the bedsteads of the family arranged in a kind of narrow and rather high cupboards, whilst over against them, and near them, the men-servants sleep over the horses, and the maids over the cows. To the right and left of the hearth extends the space used for the household, which is uninterrupted as far as the two opposite side walls of the house. This part of the house is lighted by high and broad windows, and on either side a glass door forms an exit into the open air. Usually, too, the well is inside the house at the side of the hearth'.

'Thus the master of the house can superintend the whole management of the household from the hearth and his bedstead, and hear every sound. So he exercises the fullest supervision, and so long as the smoke of the great hearth fire, which had no chimney, permeated the whole building, insects and the bad stench of the cattle were driven away, so that not till the most recent times was the need felt for building additional rooms behind the hearth-wall.'

A chief characteristic of the Saxon house, distinguishing it from the Frisian 'hauberg' and the Danish house, is the construction of the roof. Cp. Fr. Saeftels, ***Haubarg und Barghus, die friesischen Grosshäuser an der schleswig-holsteinischen Westküste***, p. 3 seq.:

'(Den grundlegenden Unterschied des friesischen und sächsischen "Einbaus") verdeutlicht erst recht die beiderseitige Ständer-Ausbildung und ihre Beziehung zum Dach....Der Dachverband in beiden Hausformen ist schon im wesentlichen so verschieden, dass durch einen Vergleich beider auch an dieser Stelle nur die besondere Eigenart und Kühnheit gerade der friesischen Eigenschöpfung herauskommen kann. Das Sachsenhaus hat nämlich Ständer in ausgesprochen enger Ständerstellung, so dass immer ein Ständer auch einem Sparren entspricht, mithin jeder

Sparren mit dem auf einem Ständer liegenden Deckenbalken richtig zu einem Gebilde abgezimmert ist und mit ihm zusammen gerichtet wird. Die Ständer stehen dann dementsprechend höchstens 2 bis 2,20 m auseinander, ein Mass, das auch auf der grossen Diele für die Standbreiten des Viehs gut ausgenützt werden kann. Der von Ständer zu Ständer laufende Längsverband einer jeden Dach-Längsseite, also die Pfette, hat zwischen den Ständern keine Last mehr aufzunehmen, da ja jeder Sparren unmittelbar auf einen Ständer zu liegen kommt. Sie kann also im Querschnitt schwach gehalten werden'.

'Demgegenüber hat der Haubarg möglichst wenig Ständer, bei also nur einem Vierkant auch nur vier Ständer. Diese Beschränkung auf eine geringe Anzahl Ständer ergibt dann ebensoweite Feldbreiten wie Feldtiefen, sie löst den ganzen Stuhl von der Anzahl und Anordnung der Sparren los, sie schafft ein starkes vierbeiniges—bei mehr als einem Vierkant ein sechs- oder achtbeiniges—inneres Bockgerüst, dessen Längsträger, also die Pfetten, hier "Schunk" genannt, auf ihre ganze Länge durch alle Sparren des Ober- und Unterdaches belastet werden, mithin jetzt genügenden Querschnitt aufweisen müssen und dessen Querträger nicht auf den Ständern aufliegen, sondern als "Stichbalken" zwischen die Ständer gesetzt, durch dieselben ganz hindurchgezapft und verkeilt sind, jedoch selbst keine unmittelbare Dachlast aufzunehmen haben.... Auf den Schunken und den Legbalken liegen nun die Dachsparren auf, die in der ganzen ersten Zeit auf ihnen meist "gestossen" wurden....Im Oberdach sorgen ausserdem Hahnenbalken in jedem zweiten bis dritten Sparrenpaar für gute Sicherung des Firstes....Somit trägt der Stuhl beim Haubarg mehr als drei Viertel der gesamten Dachlast, was bei dem nassen und stürmereichen Wetter Eiderstedts viel sagen will.'

The Saxon type of house generally predominates in the regions speaking Saxon dialects. Its frontier against the Frankish type between the Rhine and the Weichsel to a great extent coincides with the frontier between Low German and Middle German. In Holland, the Saxon type is found, not only in most of the provinces speaking Saxon—Drente, Overijssel, part of Gelderland—but also in regions speaking Dutch (Low Frankish), such as the Veluwe, Utrecht, and South Holland. It has been adopted by a part of the Saxonised Eastern Frisians, and by the Saxonised Danes of Schwansen in South Jutland. On the other hand, the Frankish type has been introduced among the Saxons of the Harz region, and among the mixed Saxon-Frankish inhabitants of Eastern Prussia. The 'haubarg' survives among the Saxonised Frisians in Groningen and in Eastern Friesland between the rivers Ems and Weser; besides, it has been adopted by the Saxons in Dietmarschen. A quadrangle, perhaps of Frankish origin, has developed in the region of Altmark, west of the Middle Elbe. The Danish quadrangle and the Danish 'compound house' survive in the Saxonised region of Angel in South Jutland. The map in *Der grosse Brockhaus* (1929), IV, 624–625, representing the whole of South Jutland as belonging to the Saxon type, commits a grave error which ought to have been avoided. Cp. Willy Pessler, *Das altsächsische Bauernhaus*, 113 seq.; Chr. Ranck, *Kulturgeschichte des deutschen Bauernhauses* (*Aus Natur und Geisteswelt*, CXXI), 70 seq., and *Das Bauernhaus im Deutschen Reiche*; Schrijnen, *Nederlandsche Volkskunde*, 2nd ed. I, 40 seq.

Lit. Rietschel in Hoops, s.v. *Lex Saxonum*; Pessler, *Ethno-geographische Wellen des Sachsentums, Wörter u. Sachen*, I, 49 (with map); *idem, ibid.* III, 64 (map).

§ 206. History of the Cherusci, Angrivarii, and Dulgibini.

The area occupied by the ancient North Germans lies between the Teutoburger Wald, the Thüringer Wald, and the Middle Elbe. There is no mountain or river marking a boundary towards the north, but in this very direction the linguistic contrast is most pronounced, for the northern neighbour is the non-German nation of Chauchi. The north-eastern neighbours are: the Langobards in Bardengau, south of the Elbe; the eastern: the Swabians (Semnones) and Ermundures east of the Middle Elbe (cp. Vibius Sequester, *De fluminibus*, 2 (ed. Bursian): 'Albis Germaniae, Svevos a Cheruscis dividit'; cp. § 160, 5); the southern: originally the Swabians (Semnones), later partly replaced by Ermundures, beyond the mountain Bacenis, i.e. the mediaeval Buchonia (cp. Caesar, *Bell. Gall.* VI, 10 on the frontier of Cherusci and Swabians); the south-western: the Chatthi on the river Adrana; the western: the Bruchteri on the river Lippe (cp. the Brochterbeck in the region of the Teutoburger Wald); and the north-western: the Amsivarii and Chasvarii on the rivers Ems and Hase, later replaced by Chauchi.

A large frontier wall separates the Cherusci and Angrivarii east of the Middle Weser near the mountains Deister and Süntel (Tac. *Ann.* II, 19).

In 12 B.C. Cherusci and Sugambri ally against Rome (Dio Cassius, LIV, 33, § 2).

In 11 Drusus reaches the Weser (*ibid.*), and repulses the Cherusci at Arbalo (Pliny, XI, 18; Florus, II, 30, § 24).

In 10 he penetrates the regions occupied by the Swabians on the Main, the Marcomans, and the Cherusci from the Weser to the Elbe (Dio Cassius, LV, 1); he reaches the mouth of the Saale (Strabo, VII, 291).

In A.D. 1 the general Domitius Ahenobarbus advances from the Danube, passes the Middle Elbe, and through the Cheruscian territory reaches the Rhine (Dio Cassius, LV, 10 *a*).

In A.D. 4 Tiberius subjects the Cherusci (Velleius, II, 185).

In A.D. 9 the Cheruscian Arminius, formerly a Roman officer, stirs up the great revolt of the Northern and North-western Germans. His kinsman Segest remains pro-Roman (Tac. *Ann.* I, 55 and 60; Strabo, VII, 292), and so do the Chauchi, Frisians, and Amsivarii, while the Marcomannic King Maroboduus observes neutrality (Velleius, II, 119). The governor Varus and his army are routed in the Teutoburg Forest (*ibid.* 117; Dio Cassius, LVI, 18 seq.; Tac. *Ann.* I, 61). All Roman forts in the interior of Germany are stormed except Aliso on the river Lippe which is left inviolate for a time (Velleius, II, 120; Zonaras, X, 37). Augustus abandons the interior of Germany, but still maintains his dominion over the coast.

In 14–15 Germanicus and Arminius fight near the Weser (Tac. *Ann.* I, 49 seq.).

In A.D. 17 the rivalry of Arminius and Maroboduus comes to a head (*ibid.* II, 44–46). Arminius is deserted by Inguiomer, but reinforced by deserters from Maroboduus' camp, viz. Langobards and Semnones. Maroboduus is worsted and driven back to Bohemia.

In 21 Arminius is murdered (*ibid.* 88). In 47 his pro-Roman kinsman Italicus becomes king of the Cherusci; he is dethroned, but with Langobard aid re-established (*ibid.* XI, 16–17).

About 85 the pro-Roman successor Chariomer is expelled by the Chatthi, but regains his throne (Dio Cassius, LXVIII, 5).

The Chatthic victory seems to have broken up the Cherusci and Fosi (Tac. *Germ.* 36). Henceforth despised as 'inertes et stulti', the Cherusci disappear from history and their name becomes merely a learned ornament of later panegyrics. Parts of their area fall to the Ermundures, viz. the North Thuringgau, while the Chauchi advance to the vicinity of the Chatthi in Hesse (Tac. *Germ.* 35). The survival of Cherusci in the region of Hersi north of Hesse (Förstemann, II, 1, 351) is questionable. Another example of assonance in the place names is Herskesgebutle near Brunswick, A.D. 1007, contrasted with a Thuringesgibutli close by; it might perhaps denote the ancient frontier of Cherusci and Thuringians (cp. Förstemann, s.v.; Much in Hoops, s.v. *Cherusker*).

The alliance of Angrivarii and Chamavi about A.D. 97, and their conquest of the Bruchteri (Tac. *Germ.* 33), must be mentioned here for the sake of making this survey complete, though it is questionable whether the ancient Angrivarii are true representatives of the North Germans.

Dulgibini may have taken part in the Langobard raid into Pannonia in A.D. 166 (cp. 'region. Dulg.' in an inscription from Bregetio, v. Domaszewski, *Röm. germ. Korrespondenzblatt*, III, 85; Schmidt, II, 139; it is, however, doubted by Much in Hoops, s.v.).

Lit. Zeuss, 105, 108; Müllenhoff, IV (see Indices); Kauffmann, I, §§ 65 and 69; Schmidt, II, 95; Much in Hoops, s.v.

§ 207. Legendary Traditions.

The champion Arminius survived in poetry at least for a century (cp. Tac. *Ann.* II, 88: 'caniturque adhuc barbaras apud gentes'). It is the first verified evidence of Gothonic epic-historical poetry. As Arminius' kinsman Segimund has a namesake in the family of the Nibelung hero Sigfrid, this hero is identified with Arminius by Jellinghaus, H. L. Hanna, and others. But the mediaeval Gothonic legends contain no traces which can be verified of historical persons earlier than the Gothic heroes Ermanaric and Vidigoja of the fourth century A.D. And if historical prototypes of Sigmund and his son Sigfrid are searched for, the kings Sigismund and Sigebert in the sixth century are much more probable, because their age marks the culmination of the inspiration and production of Gothonic epic. Cp. also Behaghel's important onomastic observation, *Beiträge*, XLIV, 156: 'es ist ausgeschlossen, dass um die Zeit des Arminius ein Germanenname auf *-frethus* ausgegangen ist'.

Lit. Kögel, *Gesch. d. deutschen Litt.* I, 112; Jellinghaus, *Sigfrid-Arminius* (1894); Beneke, *Siegfried und die Varusschlacht*; H. L. Hanna, *Siegfried-Arminius, Journ. Engl. and Germ. Phil.* XIX, 439 seq.; Symons, *Grundriss*, 3rd ed. III, 654; Matthaei, *Beiträge zur Gesch. d. Siegfriedsage*; Jiriczek, *Deutsche Heldensage*, 77; Schütte, *Journ. Engl. and Germ. Phil.* XX, 300.

§ 208. History of the German Saxons.

Preliminary episodes are the conquests of the Chauchi on Amsivarian soil before A.D. 58 (Tac. *Ann.* XIII, 55) and their expansion on Cheruscian soil to the vicinity of the Chatthi before A.D. 98 (Tac. *Germ.* 35). In 358 the 'Saxons called *Chauchi', having conquered the Salian district on the Zuider Zee, begin attacking Batavia (Zosimus, III, 8, § 1).

In 531 the Saxons appear as successors of the Chauchi in Hanover and help the Franks in their destruction of Thuringia (cp. Widukind, I, 9 seq.). The Saxon part of the booty embraces North Thuringgau, Suevon, Frisonoveld, Hassagau, Hardagau, Deringgau. The Thuringian noblemen are destroyed, while the peasants are allowed to remain as *lāti*, i.e. tenant farmers (cp. *Sachsenspiegel*, III, 44, § 3).

After their alliance in 531 the mutual relations of Franks and Saxons for centuries form a series of alternating Frankish supremacy and Saxon emancipation.

In 556 Saxon raiders are repulsed west of the Rhine near Deutz (Gregor. Tur. IV, 16 and 17).

In 565 Saxons and Danes invade Friesland.

In 568 Saxon settlers in Thuringia as 'ancient friends' accompany the Langobards to Italy (Paulus Diaconus, II, 6). We suggested above that these 'ancient friends' are descendants of the Cherusci who have assumed the name of Saxons. Disappointed, however, they return in 572 and try to expel the North Swabians whom the Franks have meanwhile introduced into the region they have evacuated. So many are killed on either side that there is room enough left for both (Gregor. Tur. V, 15).

At an unknown epoch the Saxons conquer from the Chatthi or Hessians the 'Pagus Hessi Saxonicus'.

In 697 the territory of the Bruchteri is annexed and all trace of Christianity exterminated (Bede, V, 11).

In 715 the Saxons raid and annex the eastern part of the Pagus Chattvariensis (*Mon. Germ. SS.* I, 6); their annexation of Twente and of the larger part of the Chamavian district may be fairly contemporary.

Frankish counter-attacks after 738 are not decisive.

In 752 the Saxons invade Thuringia and destroy more than 30 churches (cp. a letter of Bonifatius, *Mon. Germ. ep. Merov.* I, No. 108).

From 772 to 804 the crusades of Charlemagne at last break the independence and also the heathen fanaticism of the Saxons. These well-known facts cannot be related at length here. By seizing their territory and driving out large numbers of the conquered people, Charlemagne stamps out the Anglo-Saxon element in its chief strongholds, Holstein and North-eastern Hanover, replacing it by German settlers, chiefly of Frankish origin. The Germanisation of the Saxon noblemen and of the colonies interspersed throughout Northern Germany is henceforth only a question of time. Cp. Schönfeld, *Historiese gramm. van het Nederlands*, Introd. § VI.

Meanwhile, the Slavs are advancing in Eastern Germany as a consequence of the disastrous Hunnish inroads in the fifth century.

In 804 their north-westward expansion culminates when Charlemagne grants Eastern Holstein to them (cp. Einhard, *Mon. Germ. SS.* I, 191: 'Saxones transtulit in Franciam et pagos transalbianos Abodritis dedit'). They occupy also the western border of the Elbe from Bardengau to Magdeburg.

On their track follow the Magyar raiders.

In 933 Henry the Fowler stops them at Merseburg. He vigorously fights the Slavs, and in 936 tries to establish a Saxon margravate in Southern Slesvig, but without lasting success.

About 1150 most of the converted Slavs along the Baltic relapse into paganism, driving out the German counts and missionaries. Holstein is so cruelly ravaged that more than 600 families (approximately 5000–6000 people) emigrate to the Harz region for fear of the invaders (Helmold, I, 26).

About a century later the fanatical resistance of the heathen Slavs is finally broken and an immense current of North German settlers, mixed with Franks and Frisians, floods the reconquered regions east of the Elbe.

In the thirteenth century, North German crusaders conquer Livonia, Curland, and Esthonia. Prussia is conquered by South German princes, but chiefly colonised by North Germans. A narrow borderland in South Jutland is also colonised by its German neighbours, while the Hanse merchants spread Germanism throughout Scandinavia.

The North Germans reconquer for the Gothonic nationality all the lost area between Hanover and Western Prussia, and beyond the Weichsel a limited region corresponding to that of the ancient Goths. They have absorbed the Anglo-Saxons remaining on the Continent, half of the

Frisians, and a small section of the Scandinavians, and parts of various German-speaking tribes: Langobards, Swabians, Thuringians, Franks, and Chatthi.

In modern times the progress of North German towards the east has generally ceased. The North German dialect is also constantly losing ground to Middle German, and it has practically ceased to be a literary language, being since the Reformation replaced by High German in Germany, and by Dutch in Eastern Holland.

So-called Saxons who are not in reality such are the inhabitants of the late Kingdom of Saxony and the German colonies in Transylvania. On the Saxons who are Dutchmen speaking Low German, and on the use of the name Saxons to embrace all Germans, see § 150, 5 and § 148, 4.

IV. §§ 209–210. THE DUTCH SECONDARY SUB-GROUP

§ 209. Names.

1. Dutch Nederlanders; French Neerlandais (since 1550).

2. Dutch Nederduitsche, and language Nederduitsch (sixteenth century).

3. Engl. Dutch, Dutchmen, literally the German word Deutsche 'Germans' (see § 148, 1). Language: M.L. Frank. Dietsc.

Lit. E. Verwijs, *Taalkund. Bijdr.* I, 217; te Winkel in *Grundriss*, 2nd ed. I, 785; Verdam, *Uit de Geschiedenis der Nederl. taal*, 4th ed., 161; Van der Meer, *Hist. Gramm. d. niederl. Sprache*, I, p. xxix; Verwijs and Verdam, *Nederl. Woordenboek*, p. 5 seq.

§ 210. Ethnic Position.

The differentiation of a separate Dutch nationality from the common German-Dutch stock is so late that the study of its growth does not come within the scope of the present work, which pays greater attention to ancient and early mediaeval times. We shall here only point out some facts which seem to indicate that rudimentary germs of a Dutch nationality may already be observed at quite an early date.

The area of the present Netherlands since primaeval times seems to be a most productive source of national individuality.

The earliest Gothonic nationality with a distinct individual character—the Frisians—develops east of the Zuider Zee.

Due south of this area, in Salland or thereabout, lies the original home of another old, though less pronounced individuality, that of the Isteones, the later Franks.

And next to it, in the Rhine Delta, follows a filial settlement of the Marsi and Chatthi, with an equally marked individual type. The island of Batavia fosters the revolt of Civilis (A.D. 69–70) which unites Marsaci and Chatthic settlers with Frisians, Chauchi, and Belgians, in a common federative movement (already in 47 the Cannenefate Gannascus had co-operated with Chauchi). This is an anticipation of the 'greater Netherlands'. Remarkably enough the federal movement is not shared by the Isteones (the later Franks); it seems as if their abstinence foreshadows the later political frontier between the Netherlands and Germany.

During the Migration Age the federation formed by Civilis is repeated on a smaller scale: the descendants of the Marsaci and Chatthi in Marsum and Kennemerland unite with the Frisians to form a 'greater Friesland' which embraces a great part of the marshes of the present Netherlands and lasts till the eighth century.

But at the same time the Rhine Delta gives rise to the state of the Salian Franks, the germ of the present France. And this powerful political rival succeeds in preventing the rise of a united state of Netherlands under the banner of the Frisian water-lily.

Finally, in the sixteenth century, the Netherlands foster a type of religious Reformation which is in contact with that of Switzerland and France, but separated from that of Lutheran Germany. And whereas all Lutheran Protestants and at last even the Swiss Calvinists, and the German Catholics, adopt Luther's High German dialect as their literary language, the Dutch Calvinists and Catholics obstinately keep their Low Frankish dialect also for religious and literary use. The religious feeling underlying the linguistic differentiation becomes especially manifest when we observe that a series of Calvinistic parishes in North-west Germany use Dutch as their religious language till towards the middle of the nineteenth century.

The religious and linguistic differences, together with the political self-esteem fostered during the long wars of independence against Spain, result in the historical Treaty of Westphalia recognising the Dutch Netherlands as a sovereign state. This is the official recognition of a Dutch nationality.

The calculation of the number of people speaking Dutch, Flemish or the Boer patois is rather vague, as the census of South Africa in this century does not distinguish the various nationalities of the 'White Men'. The following figures are given:

Holland (1930)	c. 8,000,000
Belgium (1920)	3,790,867
Java and Madura ('Europeanen' 1926)	170,000
Cape Colony (1891)	230,000
Natal (1908)	13,000
Oranje (1890)	c. 67,900
The former German South-west Africa	c. 500

In 1899 there were counted some 645,000 Boers, but this figure was no doubt too high. The entire number of the Dutch, Flemings, and Boers may be about 11,000,000.

Lit. te Winkel, *Geschichte der niederländ. Sprache* in *Grundriss*, 2nd ed. I, 781 seq. (with lit.); van Ginneken, *Handboek der Nederlandsche taal* (2nd ed.); van Ginneken and Endepole, *De regenboogkleuren van Nederlands taal*; Lecoutere-Grootaers, *Inleiding tot de geschiedenis van het Nederlandsch* (3rd ed.). All the works cited contain dialect maps; van Ginneken's *Handboek* contains a colonial map, *Nederlandsch diaspora*, pp. 206–207. Linguistic anthology in van Ginneken's *Handboek*, in Firmenich, *Germaniens Völkerstimmen*, and in Leopold, *Van de Schelde tot de Weichsel.*

V. §§ 211–235. THE NORTH-WEST GOTHONIC SUB-GROUP

A. §§ 211–218. *THE SUB-GROUP AS A WHOLE*

§ 211. Names.

The sub-group has no old or popular name. Its classification is merely philological.

Its supposed ancient name, Inguaeones, or 'Ingwiaiwen' in Bremer's spelling, rests merely on Pliny's isolated evidence, IV, 99: 'Ingyaeones, quorum pars Cimbri, Teutoni, ac Chaucorum gentes', the Saxons being surmised to be the missing link between the Cimbri and Chauchi. This assumption of a missing link is quite hypothetical, as the details of Pliny's lists are anything but trustworthy; cp. § 197, 2 and § 205 dealing with his probably incorrect classification of the Chatthi and Cherusci as Erminones. On the other hand, since the earliest native evidence includes the Danes and Swedes among the Inguaeones, in order to defend the restriction of the name Inguaeones to Anglo-Saxons and Frisians, curious attempts have been made to reject such evidence. Thus Kögel declares, *Gesch. d. deutschen Litt.* I, 57 note, that the Inguaeonic Danes of *Beowulf*, ll. 1045 and 1322, are not really Danes, but pre-Danish Anglo-Frisians! And Müllenhoff, *Nordalbingische Studien*, I, 127, says of the eponymous hero Inguo: 'fälschlich rühmten sich die schwedischen Ynglingar, von ihm abzustammen' (cp. the objections of Rieger 1859 and Kossinna 1897 against such arbitrary theories). The original extension of the name Inguaeones is so vague that the term cannot be used in the systematic classification of the Gothonic peoples. Its use in linguistic and historical manuals is all the more misleading as no cultural or political bond unites the Anglo-Saxons and Frisians (cp. § 213). The term has also been rejected in Much's *Deutsche Stammeskunde* (cp. Siebs, who states in *Grundriss*, 2nd ed. I, 1154, that it is 'nicht ratsam, von einer ingvaeonischen Sprache zu reden').

A learned synonym of the erroneous term 'Ingwiaiwen' is 'Anglo-Friesen'. This cannot be recommended, as it neglects the Saxons, a most prominent part of the community. Cp. Siebs, *Grundriss*, 2nd ed. I, 1154: 'Die Bezeichnung "anglofriesisch" ist durchaus zu vermeiden, denn sie verleitet zu der falschen Auffassung, dass nur (oder doch vornehmlich) die Sprache der Angeln in näherer Beziehung zum Friesischen stehe'.

We prefer to use the term North-west Gothonic nations which is rendered justifiable by the establishment of the Anglo-Saxons in England and Scotland.

Lit. Rieger, *Zeitschrift*, XI, 178; Kossinna, *Indogerm. Forsch.* VII, 308 seq.; Schütte, *Anzeiger*, XXVIII, 9; *idem*, *Smaaskrifter udg. af Selsk. f. germ. Filologi*, No. 14, ch. 4; Chadwick, 61 seq.; Much in Hoops, s.v. *Germani*, § 18.

§ 212. Sub-divisions.

1. Anglo-Saxons.

(*a*) Island Saxons (in England; the continental Saxons now speak Low German or Dutch).

(*b*) Chauchi (to-day speaking either Frisian or Low German).

(*c*) Angles (those in Angel in South Jutland spoke Danish till the nineteenth century, but now speak Low German). From this tribe comes the name, O.E. Englalond, Engl. England, French Angleterre.

(*d*) Jutes, comprising Kentishmen in Kent, Wihtwære on the Isle of Wight, and Meanwære in Hampshire. (The Jutes in Jutland speak Danish.)

2. Frisians, in Holland, Hanover, Oldenburg, Heligoland, South-western South Jutland (nowadays to a great extent speaking Dutch in Holland, Low German in Germany).

Lit. Sweet, *Dialects and Prehistoric Forms of Old English* (*Trans. Phil. Soc.* 1875–76, 643); Bremer, § 121 seq.; Siebs, *Grundriss*, 2nd ed. I, 1154–1155.

§ 213. Ethnic Position.

The nameless community constituting the ancient North-west Gothonic sub-group is to be recognised almost solely by linguistic phenomena (see the synopsis given by Siebs, *l.c.* 1154).

Cp. some examples of the contrast with Gothic, German, and Scandinavian.

1. Change of ǣ into ā (in common with pre-literary Scandinavian, cp. run. Marila), differing from Low German which keeps ǣ till the tenth century (cp. Bremer, *Beiträge*, XI, 1, 27).

2. Retrograde change of ā into ǣ, except before certain consonants:

O.Engl.	O.Fris.	Goth.	O.H.G.	O.Norse	
hwǽr, hwér	hwēr	—	hwār	hvár	'where'

3. Change of ă into ǣ or ĕ in certain cases, not caused by following palatal sounds:

O.Engl.	O.Fris.	Goth.	O.H.G.	O.Norse	
dæȝ	dei	dags	tag	dagr	'day'
æcer	ekker	akrs	acker	akr	'acre'

4. Change of ǣ (Gothonic ǣ) into ō before nasals:

O.Engl.	O.Fris.	Goth.	O.H.G.	O.Norse	
móna	mōna	mēna	māno	máni	'moon'

5. Change of ă into ŏ before nasals[1]:

O.Engl.	O.Fris.	Goth.	O.H.G.	O.Norse	
lond	lond	land	lant	land	'land'

6. Change of final West Gothonic *a* into *e*:

O.Engl.	O.Fris.	Goth.	O.H.G.	O.Norse	
tunȝe	tunge	(tuggō)	zunga	tunga	'tongue'

7. Early palatalisation of *g* and *k* before palatals:

O.Engl.	O.Fris.	Goth.	O.H.G.	O.Norse	
ȝiestran	jærsne	gistra-	gestaron	í-gǽr	'yesterday'
dæȝ	dei	dags	tag	dagr	'day'
næȝel	neil	nagls	nagal	nagl	'nail'
Engl.	Fris.				
edge	edz	—	eck	egg	'edge'
church	tsiarke	—	kirihha	kyrkja	'church'

[1] Only Anglian and East Frisian, not Saxon and West Frisian.

Palatalisation[1] is typical of English and Frisian, and has also been recognised as a racial test in the popular saying: 'Butter and *cheese* is English and Fries', which is supposed to be pronounced the same in both languages.[2] This palatalisation often appears in place names; cp. the English pronunciation Stounhendž for Stonehenge, and Frisian Grins, Harns, Frentsjer, Snits for Groningen, Harlingen, Franeker, Sneek. Such palatalised forms are an important means of tracing the area over which extended the ancient nationality; e.g. the name of the town Celle in Hanover is derived from an ancient Saxon Kielle, i.e. L.G. *kelle*, Germ. *quelle*, O.N. *kelda* 'well', and it thus betrays that the inhabitants once spoke Anglo-Saxon (cp. Bremer, § 146, 3); Butseghem, W. Flanders, in the tenth century was written Bucingehem. Cp. Schönfeld, *Historiese grammatika van het Nederlands*, XXVII, XXX. Similarly Peize (earlier Pedge), south of Groningen, reflects the ancient Frisian nationality.

If other than linguistic tests should be deemed necessary, we might mention the heathen fanaticism of Saxons and Frisians as a common racial feature, also shared by Wends, Prussians, and Esthonian Finns.

Lit. The current dogma of 'Inguaeonism' is represented by Zeuss, 71, Grimm, 829, Müllenhoff, IV, 120 seq., and *Nordalbingische Studien*, I, 11 seq.; Bremer, § 82 seq., § 121 seq.; Schmidt, II, 1 seq.; *idem*, in Pauly-Wissowa, s.v. *Ingvaeones*; Kauffmann, I, 402. A more intermediate view is advocated by Schütte, *Var Anglerne Tyskere?* (*Sønderjydske Aarbøger*, 1900); *idem*, *Anzeiger*, XXVIII, 9 seq.; *idem*, *Smaaskrifter udg. af Selsk. f. germ. Filologi*, No. 14, ch. 4; *idem*, *Arkiv*, XXXIII, 38, XXXVI, 169; Chadwick, *Origin of the Engl. Nation*, 61 seq.; *idem*, in Chambers' *Encycl.* s.v. *English*; Neckel, *Beiträge*, LI, 1 seq.; Kloeke, *Zum Ingwäonismenproblem* (*Festschrift Borchling*, 338 seq.). For linguistic details see Sweet, *Dialects and Prehistoric Forms of Old English* (*Trans. Phil. Soc.* 1875–76, 308 seq.); Murray, *Encycl. Brit.* 9th ed. s.v. *English*; Siebs, *Zur Gesch. der engl. fries. Sprache*; *idem*, *Grundriss*, 2nd ed. I, 1154 seq.; Bremer, § 121 seq.; *idem*, *Indogerm. Forsch.* IV, 24, 27, 31; Morsbach, *Anglia*, *Beiblatt*, VII, 324 seq.; Heuser, *Altfries. Lesebuch*, § 1 seq.

B. §§ 214–225. *THE ANGLO-SAXON BRANCH*

§ 214. Names.

1. O.E. Seaxe, Seaxan, Sæx-þéod (cp. § 215).

2. O.E. Ongol-Seaxan (Athelstan: 'Ic Æþelstán, Ongol-Saxna cyning', see Birch, *Cart. Sax.* II, 410); O.G. sing. Engel-Saxo (Einhard, *Vit.*

[1] This phenomenon is often called 'zetacism' by German philologists.

[2] The similar palatalisation in Scandinavian dialects is of much later date.

Alcuin, Mon. Germ. SS. IV, 193); M.Lat. Angli-Saxones (Paulus Diaconus, IV, 22), Angul-Saxones (Asser's *Life of King Alfred*, ed. Stevenson, 148).

3. O.E. Engle (*Sax. Chron.* ad an. 473), Angel-cyn, Angel-þéod; Engl. English, Englishmen (cp. § 237, 1).

The collective term 'Saxons' for Anglo-Saxons is used by the Celts. The combined form Anglo-Saxons is first used by the Langobard scholar Paulus Diaconus, not as the name of a united nation, but simply signifying 'Saxons in England', in contradistinction to 'German Saxons'; though occurring in O.E. the term never grew popular. As a name of the nation as a whole, it appears for the first time in the nineteenth century (the adjective 1840, the substantive 1853, *Oxf. Dict.*). Its use is and remains merely literary. Engle, English, became the popular name among the English themselves for the whole nation, but it again lost much of its popularity owing to political feeling: the Anglicised Welshman, Scotchman, Manxman, Irishman, and the citizen of U.S.A., will never suffer himself to be called an Englishman. If he does not claim to be a Celt, he is, at most, an Anglo-Saxon. But he will at least admit that his *language* is English; denominations such as Scotch or American can only express dialects of English, not the language itself, as equivalent to French, German, etc.

It is worth noting that in the mediaeval terminology of the University of Paris, the 'English Nation' included both Scandinavians and Germans. This expression was probably used for want of a recognised name denoting the 'Gothonic nations'. It was only a practical way of enlisting students from the less important countries. But such makeshift expressions are certainly the germs of definite tribal names, and for this reason we ought perhaps to have mentioned 'English' in our list of synonyms of the Gothonic Nations, vol. I. In Cymric poetry, Eingl is sometimes used to denote the East Anglian Danes (cp. § 258, 7).

Lit. Freeman, *Norman Conquest*, 2nd ed. 523; Chadwick, 55; Hoops, I, 89.

§ 215. Sub-divisions.

A. Division on the Continent.

1. O.E. Seaxe (dat. Seaxum, *Widsith*; cp. Middel-Seaxe, *Sax. Chron.* 658), Seaxan (*Orosius*; Alfred's *Bede*, I, 861, V, 914; *Sax. Chron.* 885); Sæx-þéod (Layamon's *Brut*, I, 14494); O.Fris. Saxa; O.H.G. Sahsun;

Germ. Sachsen; L.G. Sassen; O.N. Saxar; Lat. Saxones (Eutropius, fourth century A.D.); O.Fr. Seissons; Gr. Σάξονες (Ptolemy, second century A.D.); O.Cymric Saeson; Bret. Saozon; Gael. Sassanaigh; Sloven. Šavizi (Schmeller, *Bayer. Wörterbuch*, II, 217); Finn. Saksalaiset; Magyar Szászok. Eponymous prince, O.N. Saxi Sunnmanna gramr (*Goðrunarkviða*, III, str. 6). Personal names: O.E. Seax-wulf, Seax-mund, etc. God: O.E. Seax-néat; O.L.G. Sax-nōt 'Saxon treasure'. Country: Germ. Sachsen; L.Germ. Sassenland; O.N. Saxland; Lat. Saxonia (anonymous letter, Caspari, *Briefe, Abhandlungen u. Predigten*, p. 3, c. A.D. 420 (?); cp. Egger, *Byzantion*, v (1929–30), 29); O.Fr. Sessuyne; Gr. Σαξονείη (inscription of Theodosius in the Macedonian town Stobi, now in Drenovo, c. A.D. 390; cp. Egger, *ibid.* p. 9 seq.); cp. Gael. Sasunn 'England'. Place names: Germ. Sachsenberg; M.L. Frank. Sax-haven, M.Lat. Saxi-portus, now Hulst; Breton Sauzon on the island of Guédel or Belle-Île. The legend derives the name of Saxons from O.E. *seax* 'a dagger or short sword', the alleged national weapon of the tribe (Nennius, § 48; Widukind, I, 7). Zachrisson in *Studier tillägnade Axel Kock*, p. 492, proposes a derivation from a topographical element *sax*, identical with Lat. *saxum* 'rock'; this element, e.g., occurs in the name of a village, Glad-sax, situated on a steep hill in Eastern Scania (cp. Hellquist, *Svensk etym. ordbok*, s.v. *Sax* and *saxare* (see § 266)).[1] Saxones is original, not an abbreviation of a *Sahsaganautas, conjectured by Fick (*Ilias*, 562), and Laistner, *Württemberg. Vierteljahrsschrift*, 1892, 29 (cp. Much in Hoops, IV, 62). Concerning the enlarged signification 'Germans' see § 148, 4. Home: Western Holstein and the 'Saxon islands' (Ptol. II, 11, §§ 7 and 16); later in Germany south-west of the Elbe, with scattered settlements in Flanders, Normandy, Brittany, and Noirmoutiers west of the mouth of the Loire.

Lit. Schmeller, *Bayer. Wörterbuch*, II, 217; Zeuss, 150; Grimm, 609 (identification with Scyth. Sakai?); Müllenhoff, IV, 164; Wietersheim-Dahn, *Gesch. d. Völkerwanderung*, I, 180; Much, *Stammeskunde*, 92; *idem*, in Hoops, s.v.; Kluge, *Zeitschr. f. deutsche Wortforschung*, VIII, 142; Schönfeld, s.v.; Förstemann, s.v.; Schmidt, II, 37; Hoops, I, 89; Langenfelt, *Toponymics in English*, 49; Karsten, *Die Germanen*, 148; Wagner, *Teuthonista*, IX, 42.

2. Gr. Σιγούλωνες (Ptolemy, second century A.D.). Obscure. Etymologically Sigulones cannot be connected with No. 3, Secgas, according to Wadstein whose opinion is accepted by Zachrisson. Wadstein compares

1 Perhaps also in Bol-saxen, a bank in the Cattegat.

Fris. *sil* 'drain' < **sihil* (but Sillende in South Jutland originates from a different word, as it is in Thegan's *Vita Hludov.* 25, written Sinlendi). Home: north of the Saxons, approximately in the present North Friesland (Ptol. II, 11, § 7).

Lit. Seelmann, *Jahrb. des Vereins f. niederd. Sprachforschung*, XII, 43 note 1; Detlefsen, *Hermes*, XLVI, 309; Schönfeld, s.v.; Much, *Beiträge*, XVII, 199; *idem*, in Hoops, s.v. Σιγούλωνες and *Dänen*, § 5; v. Friesen, *Röstenen*, 70; Wadstein, *Fil. Samfundet i Göteborg Minnesskrift*, 1925, 190; cp. Zachrisson, *Studia Neophilologica*, II, 62 on **sīg-* in an English place name.

3. O.E. *Secgas, Secgan (*Widsith*, l. 62: 'mid Seaxum ic wæs ond Sycgum'; l. 31: 'Sæferð (wéold) Sycgum'; *Finnsburg Lay*, l. 42: 'Sigeferð, Secgena léod'). Mythical ancestors: O.E. Ge-secg and And-secg, son and grandson of Seaxnéat (East Sax. *royal pedigree*, Florence of Worcester, ed. Thorpe, I, 250). According to Zachrisson the tribal name is identical with the O.E. word *secgas* 'men' (corresponding to Lat. *socii*).[1] In his opinion, Secgan in the *Finnsburg Lay* is the correct form, whereas Sycgas in *Widsith* is a Kenticism with *y* as an inverted spelling for *e* (Sigeferð, *Finnsb. Lay*, is likewise the correct form and Sæferð, *Widsith*, is corrupt. The identity of Sæferð the Sycg and Sigeferð the Secg is obvious; Möller shows that one person in the MSS of Bede is alternately called Saeberchtus and Sigberchtus). On the difference between Secgas and Sigulones see under No. 2. The home of the Secgas is unknown, but both *Widsith* and the East Saxon royal pedigree seem to indicate that they lived in the immediate vicinity of the Saxons.

Lit. Zeuss, 151 note 2; Müllenhoff, *Beovulf*, 684; Möller, *Altengl. Volksepos*, 86; Kögel, *Gesch. d. deutsch. Litt.* I, 164; Much, *Beiträge*, XVII, 199; *idem*, in Hoops, s.v. Σιγούλωνες; Chambers, *Widsith*, 199 (with lit.); Zachrisson, *Studier tillägn. Axel Kock*, 492; Wadstein, *Fil. Samfundet i Göteborg Minnesskrift*, 1925.

4. O.E. Ymbre (*Widsith*, l. 32, next to Sæferð Sycgum); ? Lat. Ambrones (Orosius, fifth century A.D.); ? Gr. Ἄμβρωνες (Plutarch, *Marius*, 19, first century A.D.; history of the second century B.C.). Place name: ?? Ombersetene gemære (Birch, *Cartular. Saxon.* 817, 462, in Worcestershire; cp. on the element *-sæte* in ethnic compounds, p. 233). Obscure. Zachrisson suggests that Ymbre may be a Kenticism for *Embre, i.e. Ambrones (cp. Sycgas for *Secgas). Nennius, § 63, says: 'Paulinus

[1] Another derivation must at least be mentioned. There exists an O.E. word **secg* (Gl. *segg*), meaning 'sea', appearing in the well-known compound *gár-secg*. A possible connexion with this word ought to be considered.

Eboracensis archiepiscopus...non cessavit baptizare omne genus Ambronum', and *MS. Corp. Christ. Camb.* 139, thirteenth century, adds: 'Id est Aldsaxonum'. The legendary British King Uther Pendragon scornfully says of the Saxons: 'vocabant me semimortuum Ambrones isti', Sigbert Gemblac. ad an. 466. We may suggest literary descent from the ill-famed Ambrones of the Cimbric raid, or that the Ambrones of Nennius are the *Umbrones, i.e. Northumbrians (cp. Chadwick, 56). On the other hand, a survival of the Ymbre of *Widsith* in legendary traditions is not impossible. The home is in the vicinity of the Saxons, but its exact position is a matter of controversy. (*a*) Lappenberg: island of Fehmarn, O.Dan. Imbræ, Ymbræ; (*b*) Thorpe: Ambria, Ammeri, now Ammerland, west of the Weser; (*c*) Ettmüller: island of Ambrum or Amrum, west of Slesvig, with the population called Amrings.

Lit. Zeuss, 147 seq.; Grimm, 638; Lappenberg, *Hist. England*, 101; Müllenhoff, II, 114, 118; *idem*, *Beovulf*, 95; C. Müller, ed. of Ptolemy, III, 5, § 8; Holder, *Altcelt. Sprachschatz*, s.v. *Ambrones*; Hirt, *Beiträge*, XXI, 155; *Die Indogermanen*, 164; Laistner, *Württemberg. Vierteljahrsschrift*, 1892, 27; Siebs, *Zur Gesch. d. engl. fries. Sprache*, 15; Much, *Beiträge*, XVII, 9; *idem*, *Götting. Gelehrt. Anzeiger*, 1901, 458 note 1; *idem*, *Stammeskunde*, 96; *idem*, in Hoops, s.v. *Ambrones*; Schmidt, II, 25; Chambers, *Widsith*, 200; Schütte, *Beiträge*, XLI, 43; *idem*, *Ptolemy's Maps*, 133; Noreen, *Fornvännen*, 1920, 27. Home of the Ymbre: (*a*) Lappenberg, *Hist. England*, 177; Siebs, *l.c.* 17; (*b*) Thorpe, *Cod. Exoniensis*, 516; Müllenhoff, *Nordalbing. Studien*, I, 159; *idem*, *Zeitschrift*, XI, 283; (*c*) Ettmüller, *Vidsidh*, 18; Much, *Stammeskunde*, 101; *idem*, in Hoops, s.v. *Ambrones*; *idem*, *Zeitschrift*, LXII, 134 (on the incorrectness of the derivation from Fehmarn).

5. Lat. Chauchi (MSS of Suetonius, second century A.D., and Claudianus, fourth to fifth century), Chauci (Lucanus, Pliny, Tacitus, first century A.D.), Cauchi (Velleius, first century A.D., Suetonius, Claudianus), Haci (*Tab. Peuting.*, fourth century), Cauci (Julius Honorius, fourth century), Gr. Καῦκοι (Strabo, first century B.C.), Καῦχοι (Ptolemy, second century A.D.), distorted Κούαδοι (Zosimus, fifth century). Imperial title: Lat. Cauchius (A.D. 41, Suetonius, *Claud.* 24). The etymology is clear from the phonetic point of view; the sounds of the name are the same as those of Goth. *hauhs* 'high'. But the question is what does it mean? It might be 'high men', but a geographical interpretation seems preferable, either 'people of the mounds' (cp. Zachrisson, *Studier tillägn. Axel Kock*, p. 492), or 'people of the high woods'. Homonymous are: the Celt. Kaukoi (perhaps the Irish Ui Cúaich, cp. Pokorny, *Zeitschr. f. celt. Phil.* XI, 169); the Kaukones in Peloponnese and Asia Minor; cp.

also the Dacian Kaukoensioi Ptol. in Caucalandensis locus (Ammianus, XXXI, 4, § 13). The spelling with initial or final *c* or *k* is irrelevant; classical orthography allowed only Chauci or Cauchi or Cauci (cp. on the Chatthi, § 196, 2 (*a*)). The true Gothonic form only appears in MSS with what would have been termed bad orthography. Home: Northern Hanover (cp. Ptol. II, 11, § 7).

Lit. **Müllenhoff**, *Nordalbing. Studien*, I, 157; **Much**, *Korrespondenzblatt d. Ges. f. Anthropologie*, XXIX, 113; *idem*, *Stammeskunde*, 73, 90; *idem*, in **Hoops**, s.v. *Chauken*; **Schönfeld**, s.v. (with lit.); **Förstemann**, s.v.; **Ihm** in **Pauly-Wissowa**, s.v.; **Boissevain**, ed. **Dio Cassius**, LIV, 32; **Chambers**, *Widsith*, 68 note 2; **Schmidt**, II, 38; **Schütte**, *Arkiv*, XXXIII, 25; **Löwenthal**, *Beiträge*, XLV, 250; LV, 318; *idem*, *Zeitschr. f. Ortsnamenforsch.* VI, 77.

6. O.E. Hugas (*Beowulf*, l. 2502); M.Lat. Hugones (*Quedlinburg Ann.*, *Mon. Germ. SS.* III, 31); Gr. **Καοῦλκοι* (*Καθύλκοι* Strabo, first century B.C.), *Καλούκωνες* (Ptolemy, second century A.D.). We may also compare Lat. Caynones, var. Cauiones, Caybones, Chaibones (Mamertinus, about A.D. 300). Eponymous king: M.Lat. Huga rex Francorum (*Quedlinburg Ann. l.c.*). Epic surname: M.H.G. Hug-Dietrich. Region: O.L.G. Hugmerke, O.Fris. Hum-merze, N.Fris. Humsterland. The above tribal names seem to designate the 'lesser Chauchi' of Ptolemy, II, 11, § 7. Hugas as compared with Chauchi shows the same vocalic and consonantal changes as Germ. *hügel* 'hill' compared with Goth. *hauhs* 'high' ('Ablaut' and 'Verner's Law'). The spellings Cayn-, Cayb-, Caui- of Mamertinus (ed. Baehrens, 1911) point to an original Cau-, and Cauiones might easily have dropped an O.E. ȝ (cp. Strabo's *Λούιοι* for Lugii, and Priscus' *Ῥοῦας* for Rugas). If not the same as the *Caugiones, this enigmatic name cannot be identified. Strabo's distorted *Καθύλκοι* is corrected into **Καοῦλκοι* by all scholars; it is obviously a diminutive form meaning *Chauchli. Ptolemy's *Καλούκωνες* starts from the same base, but is modelled on the name of a tribe within the Roman Empire, viz. the tribe of Calucones in Rhaetia (Pliny, III, 136; Ptol. II, 12, § 2; cp. the author's monograph *Ptolemy's Maps*, 25). Home of the 'lesser Chauchi': in Hanover west of the Weser (Ptol. II, 11, § 7); the Frisian district of Hugmerke represents a movement westward; Pliny mentions Chauchi as settled already in the first century A.D. on the islets west of the Vlie, (IV, 101), possibly the Hugas of *Beowulf*.

Lit. (1) **Hugas**: **Ettmüller**, *Vidsidh*, 16; **Grimm**, 675; **Rieger**, *Zeitschrift*, XI, 186; **Much**, *Stammeskunde*, 90; *idem*, in **Hoops**, s.v. *Chauken* and *Franken*; **Schönfeld**, s.v. *Chauchi*; **Chambers**, *Widsith*, 68; **Schütte** (Norw.) *Hist. Tidsskrift*,

1917, 16; objections by Loewe, *Indogerm. Forsch.*, *Beiblatt*, XIV, 22. (2) Hugmerke: Richthofen, *Untersuch. üb. fries. Rechtsgeschichte*, II, vol. 2, 754; Weiland, *Festgabe f. Georg Hanssen* (1889), extract, p. 29. (3) Cauiones: Zeuss, 152, 477; Grimm, 473; Much, *Zeitschrift*, XXXIX, 50; *idem*, in Hoops, s.v. *Chabionen*; Tomaschek, *Anzeiger*, XXIII, 125; Schönfeld, s.v. *Chaibones*. (4) Kaulkoi and Kalukones: Schönfeld, s.v. (with lit.); Förstemann, s.v.; Much in Hoops, s.v.; Krahe, *Indogerm. Forsch.* XLVII, 325; W. de Vries, *Nom. geogr. neerland.* VIII, 24 seq.

B. Division in Britain.

Bede, I, 15, enumerates three sections, viz.:

1. Saxons—orientales, meridiani, occidui.
2. Angles—orientales, mediterranei, Mercii, Nordhumbri.
3. Jutes—Cantvarii, Vectvarii.

They may be divided according to dialects, as follows (cp. Siebs in *Grundriss*, 2nd ed. I, 1154, and Brandl, *Abh. d. Preuss. Akad. d. Wissenschaften*, No. 4, with map; for references to the single names cp. Bosworth-Toller, *Anglo-Saxon Dictionary*; cp. Kluge's map (*Grundriss*, 2nd ed. I, 1008–1009), reproduced as Fig. 5, and the dialect map drawn by Ellis, Fig. 7, of the present work).

1. *Saxons.*

The Southern dialect.

(*a*) South Saxons, in the kingdom of Sussex. Suðseaxe, Alfred's *Bede*, Praef. 74; Suðseaxan, *ibid.* I, 880, V, 2225; *Sax. Chron.* 1038. Country, on Suð Seaxna londe, *ibid.* 773.

(*b*) West Saxons or Gewisse in the kingdom of Wessex. Westseaxe, Alfred's *Bede*, Praef. 65; *Sax. Chron.* 514, 871, 1015; Westseaxan, Alfred's *Bede*, I, 880, V, 2227; *Sax. Chron.* 1016. The surname Gewisse is identical with Goth. *gawiss* 'connecting link', *gawidan* 'to combine'. Asser, *Life of King Alfred*, Preface, wrongly represents the name as Cymric. The alleged form Gegwis may have existed, but is only the Cymric pronunciation of the Anglo-Saxon name.

(*c*) Hwicce is a kingdom corresponding to Worcestershire, Gloucestershire, and parts of Warwickshire. Alfred's *Bede*, II, 2; Lat. Huiccii, *Bede*, IV, 23. Place names: Whichford in Warwickshire, Wychwood on the borders of Oxfordshire. Brandl, on the authority of Florence of Worcester, regards Hwicce as Cymric, but this opinion is scarcely justified (cp. Zachrisson in *Studia Neophilologica*, II, 62). The dialect is southern, but contiguous to a western dialect which is perhaps the original dialect of the Hwicce.

The Eastern dialect.

(*d*) Middle Saxons in Middlesex belonging to the East Saxon kingdom. Middel Sexe, Alfred's *Bede*, I, 15; Birch, *Cartular. Sax.* I, 297.

(*e*) East Saxons in the kingdom of Essex. Eastsexe, Alfred's *Bede*, *Praef.* 65; Eastseaxan, *ibid.* III, 2322.

2. *Angles.*

The Northern or Northumbrian dialect (*which again is the source of Lowland Scotch*).

(*a*) Dere in the kingdom of Deira. Dere, Alfred's *Bede*, II, 107; gen. Dera, *ibid.* 1546, Dearne, *Sax. Chron.* 643; M.Lat. Deiri, *Bede*, II, 1. Place name: O.E. Dera-uuda 'Wood of the Dere' (Beverley, Co. York). O.E. sources normally write Der-, whereas Bede's Latin text has Deir-, perhaps owing to the fictitious Latin etymology 'de ira'. The name is Cymric, Deur. The Dere are said to be Angles, but their earliest royal names are almost identical with those of the East Saxons.

Lit. Miller, *Place Names in the English Bede*, 22; *Sax. Chron.* Index; Ekwall, *Engl. Place-Name Society*, I, 21.

(*b*) Beornice in the kingdom of Bernicia. Alfred's *Bede*, III, 492. The name is Cymric, Birneich < *Briganticia, derived from the British tribe of Brigantes.

Lit. Miller, *Place Names in the English Bede*, 22; Ekwall, *l.c.*

The Eastern dialect.

(*c*) East Angles in the kingdom of East Anglia. East Engle, Alfred's *Bede*, I, 883. Sub-divided into Northfolk and Southfolk and speaking the East Saxon dialect.

The Midland dialect.

(*d*) Middle Angles in the kingdom of Middle Anglia. Middel Engle, Alfred's *Bede*, I, 883; *Sax. Chron.* 653. *Vide ibid.* Index.

(*e*) South Angles in South-western Mercia. Súþ Engle, Simeon of Durham, A.D. 1130 (cp. Plummer's *Bede*, II, 30).

(*f*) M(i)erce (*Sax. Chron.* 655, 872) or Mirce or Myrce (Alfred's *Bede*, 483, 25) in the kingdom of Mercia. Gen. Mearca, *Sax. Chron.* 449, M(i)ercna, Alfred's *Bede*, III, 2855 (on the mixed declension see Sievers,

Angelsächs. Gramm. 3rd ed. § 264, p. 138, § 276, note 3, p. 145). Sub-divisions: *Nordmierce, Alfred's *Bede*, III, 2905; Súðmercna ríce, *ibid.* III, 2901. The name means 'inhabitants of a wooded borderland' (cp. the place name Marcis among the Saxon colonists in Gaul (*Not. dignitatum*)). It 'is very remarkable as it is one of the last native names formed with the suffix *-i* in England' (Langenfelt).

Lit. Miller, *Place Names in the English Bede*, 23; *Sax. Chron.* Index; Langenfelt, *Toponymics*, 43.

(*g*) Gyrwan, forming a principality about the Wash. Alfred's *Bede*, IV, 1111; M.Lat. Guruii (Miller, *Place Names in the Engl. Bede*, 38, 50). The name belongs to O.E. *gyrwe* 'fen' and means 'the marsh-dwellers', see Zachrisson, *Englische Studien*, LXII, 105 and ref. (Brandl regards it as Cymric. Holger Pedersen in a letter to the author proposes to interpret it as the plural of Cymric *garw* 'rough'.)

Lit. Hoops, II, 343; MacClure, *British Place-Names*, 178 footnote 2; Birch, *Cartular. Sax.* III, 203; Chadwick, 9; Ekwall, *Anglia, Beiblatt*, 1922, 116; Stenton, *Engl. Place-Name Society*, I, 1, 47.

(*h*) Lindisware or *Lindisfaran in the kingdom of Lindsey. Lindissi, Lindissæ (Bede), Lindesse (*Sax. Chron.* 838, 873), with the capital Lindon (Ptol.); Lat. Lindum colonia, now Lincoln; Lindisware, *Sax. Chron.* 678 (O.Fr. Lindesware, Gaimar, 1460); *Lindisfaran (gen. Lindesfarona), *Tribal Hidage*. Ekwall says: 'The name is no doubt derived from Lindon with a British suffix; we may compare Loidis, the old form of Leeds. Lindon means "the pool" or "the lake", and refers to the pool formed by the Witham in Lindon'. The author is of the opinion that Lindisfaran is the original form of the tribal name, see discussion on pp. 231–232.

Lit. Stevenson, *Asser's Life of King Alfred*, 242; Miller, *Place Names in the Engl. Bede*, 31, 54; Ekwall, *Engl. Place-Name Society*, I, 1, 21.

3. *Jutes.*

The Southern dialect.

(*a*) Centingas, Cantwære, Kentishmen, in the kingdom of Kent. Centingan, Thorpe, *Diplomatar. ævi Saxonici*, 551; sub-divisions, East-Centing, *Sax. Chron.* 1009, West-Centingas, *ibid.* 999.[1] Cantware,

[1] Centingas corresponds to the Celtic tribal name Cantiaci in Anonymus Ravennas, ed. Pinder and Parthey, p. 428.

Alfred's *Bede*, 2, 38, gen. Cantwarena, Birch, *Cartular. Sax.* 799–801, 297; sub-divisions, East Cantwarena and West Cantwarena, Kemble, *Cod. Dipl.* 965–993, 1288. Kentysshmen, Kentischemen, Trevisa's *Transl. of Polychronicon*, VIII, 574, V, 265, 355. Speaking the Saxon southern dialect.

(*b*) Wihtware and Meanware, on the Isle of Wight and on the river Meon in Hampshire,[1] respectively, together forming a separate state. Wihtware, *Sax. Chron.* 449; Wihtsætan, Alfred's *Bede*, I, 877 (the latter form does not occur in the *Sax. Chron.* before A.D. 800). Gen. Meanwara, Alfred's *Bede*, IV, 1922; Kemble, *Cod. Dipl.* 826, 1038. Speaking the Saxon southern dialect.

Lit. On Wihtware, Stevenson, *Asser's Life of King Alfred*, 172; Chadwick, 22 footnote. On Meanware, MacClure, *British Place-Names*, 182 footnote.

No less than thirty-four 'tribes' are enumerated in the O.E. *Tribal Hidage* (cp. Goodall, *Zeitschrift für Ortsnamenforschung*, I, 39). But only territory belonging to Mercia is assessed in detail and the synopsis leaves out names just as important as those which it puts in, e.g. the Jutes called Meanwære and Merswære, the Gedingas in Middlesex, the Tonsetan on the banks of the Severn, the Defnesetan, Dornsetan and Sumursetan, i.e. the People of Devon, Dorset and Somerset, and the West Hecanas in Herefordshire (cp. Kemble, *The Saxons in England*, I, 81). Some of the tribes mentioned are of great importance, such as the Merce (Myrcna) with 30,000 hides, or the West Saxons with 100,000. Others are little more than village communities, with only 300–600 hides.

The distribution of toponymics is examined by Langenfelt in his valuable monograph, *Toponymics in English*. The following types occur:

1. *-ing* (Langenfelt, 55 seq.). This favourite Gothonic type is not very frequent in names of territorial populations in England; examples are:

[1] The Celtic form of the name Meon probably was Masona. This appears from a comparison between two lists in Anonymus Ravennas, p. 425, representing the same route from Exeter towards the east:

Isca Dumnaniorum	Milidunum	Apauna ri(vu)s	Masona
(I)sca Do(mno)niorum	Moriduno	Alauna silva	

Milidunum-Moriduno is known from the *Itinerarium Antonini* as Muriduno, from the *Tab. Peuting.* as Ridumo. *Alauna rivus is the river Alaunos of Ptolemy, and Alauna silva is the New Forest in its vicinity. The following station, Masona, consequently must have been situated on the river Meon. The *s* has been lost according to Cymric sound laws, as in Trent < Tris-antona.

Centingas, Fifburgingas, Gedingas, Hertfordingas, Lindisfarnelondingas, Westmoringas. But it is all the more frequent among the inhabitants of towns and villages, e.g. Ealdingetuningas; Langenfelt records some fifty-five examples. The elements of the names are almost exclusively Gothonic; derivation from a Celtic word, as in Centingas, Eoforwicingas, Lindisfarnelondingas, is rare. Still more rarely examples of the Gothonic type are found among Celtic populations: Dalreadingas in Dalriada in Ireland and Scotland, Lidwicingas, the Letavici in Brittany, normally called Lidwicce (it seems to be more frequent in names of exotic peoples: Mofdingas, i.e. Moabites; Sercingas, i.e. Saracens; Seringas, i.e. Syrians or Chinese).

2. *-hǽme*? (Langenfelt, 95). Kemble, *Cod. Dipl.* 842, 17[II]: 'in loco celebri qui vocatur Andredeseme', derived from the Brit. town Anderida; *ibid.* 986, 221[III]: 'usque Awelburhe heme diche'. Langenfelt adds: 'It seems as if *-hǣma* was used here as an independent cp.-element, meaning "inhabitant"'. But in the other thirty-six examples collected by Langenfelt, the independent character of the element *-hǽme* does not seem obvious. E.g., Uppinghǽma gemǽra need not mean 'the boundary of the inhabitants of Upping'; the author supposes rather that the inhabitants of Uppingham in Rutlandshire are meant.

3. *-ge*. The territorial element *-gawi* 'district' is common to Saxon, German, and Gothic, and a corresponding German toponymic Brisigavi is exemplified already in the *Notitia dignitatum*, about A.D. 400. English examples are probably Súðrige, inhabitants of the county of Surrey, and Eastrige in Eastry. Langenfelt suggests that the same element is found in Ohtgaga, Noxgaga (Birch, *Cartular. Sax.* I, 297), but these names have also been explained as Cymric, containing a word **kagi* 'hedge' (Goodall, *Zeitschr. f. Ortsnamenforschung*, I, 39).

4. *-folc* 'people'. This very rare element, known from the Jutlandic district Wændlefolk and the Gautic Vifolka härad, supplies the names of the two sub-divisions of East Anglia, Norðfolc and Súðfolc.

5. *-faran* (Langenfelt, 98). There is only one authentic example of this element, an element which is frequent among the Danes and also occurs among the Burgundians: Lindisfaran on the island of Lindisfarena éa, now Farne Island; it is exemplified almost exclusively in genitive forms: Lindisfarena, Lindisfarene, Lindisfearona, etc. (Alfred's *Bede, Praef.* 109; III, 230, 2414, 2855, V, 3315, 3334); Lindisfarne-londinga(s) (Skeat, *The Gospel acc. to St John*, 188; for other instances see Miller,

Engl. Place Names in Bede, 35, 54). In the *Tribal Hidage* the same genitive form Lindesfarona is used with reference to the inhabitants of the kingdom of Lindisse, who are otherwise constantly called Lindis*ware*. The author believes that Lindisfaran is the original form and that it was replaced by Lindisware, because the element *-faran* was so extremely rare. The element *-ware*, on the contrary, was frequent in the south of England (cp. Langenfelt's examples from Kent, London, Sussex, Hampshire, Dorset), and was also used in the names of some Celtic populations (cp. Manware on the Isle of Man, and Niðware, i.e. Picts (and O.N. Mylverjar, i.e. inhabitants of Mull)), but Langenfelt gives no examples from the whole of the coast between Edinburgh and Lincolnshire. It may therefore be assumed that Lindisfaran was in Lindisse altered into Lindisware in imitation of the numerous South English models. Besides, the frequent use of this important Lincolnshire toponymic might cause a mechanical change of the sounds *-sfar* into *-svar* (cp. the English pronunciation of *sphere* as *svīr*). But in Northumberland the element *-ware* was little used, and the present form Farne Island shows that the syllable *-far* in Lindisfaran was distinctly felt as a separate element. Thus it is easily understood how the ancient form of the name was here preserved. As to the etymology, it is easy to account for a place with the Celtic name *lindon* 'lake' on the mainland, as in Lincolnshire; but it is a little difficult to understand how the inhabitants of Farne Island should be called 'Lake-men', as this tiny island has hardly room for a lake worth speaking of. Finally, as Ekwall remarks (see quotation p. 229), the form Lindis- seems to contain a Celtic derivative suffix, and it is extremely difficult to understand how the same suffix could be employed both in Lindisware and in Lindisfaran, if these two names had nothing to do with each other. Thus it must almost necessarily be concluded that the Lindisfaran were colonists from Lindisse.

6. *-ware* 'men' (Langenfelt, 88). The element is originally West German, but after the Migration Age is adopted by all other Gothonic nations (cp. vol. I, p. 159). It often occurs in South England in connexion with Gothonic place names, but equally often with Celtic ones: Cantware, Doferware, Lundenware, Tenetware, Wihtware. In numerous cases, it indicates foreign peoples: Rómware, i.e. Romans; Etelware, i.e. Italians; Manware, i.e. Manxmen; Niðware, i.e. Picts. In the case of Dornware (or Dornsætan, men of Dorset), it comes from the British place name Durnovaria.

7. *-sǽtan* or *-sǽte* 'settlers' (Langenfelt, 82; Schram, *Zeitschr. f. Ortsnamenforschung*, III, 202). This element first appears in the classical German place name Furgi-satis (Ptol.). It occurs also in Friesland and Scandinavia. From an ethnic point of view it requires closer examination. A remarkably large number of the examples collected by Langenfelt belong to the mixed Saxon-Celtic borderlands; cp. the following list:

Hiisǽtan on the island of Ioua (the so-called 'Iona').

Elmedsǽtan in a British kingdom, existing until the seventh century (cp. the district Elfet in Wales).

W(r)ocensǽtan in the British town Viroconium, the destruction of which is deplored in a Welsh poem.

Dúnsǽtan, British population; name compounded with British -**dūnon*.

Wentsǽte in the British region Gwent (cp. *Angelsächs. Gesetze*, 378, 9: 'Hwílon...hyrdon into Dúnsǽtan').

Magesǽtan in the same region; British *-magos* 'field'.

Wilsǽtan < British river name Wiley.

Dornsǽtan, synonym of Dornwære < British *Durnovarii in Durnovaria, Durngueir.

A detailed survey of the historical data in connexion with the local sub-divisions is given by Palgrave. The demarcations, especially of the ecclesiastical dioceses, are examined by Brandl. Further local details are collected in the *Victoria History of the Counties of England* (1900–1914).

Lit. F. Palgrave, *The Rise and Progress of the English Commonwealth*, see section *Proofs and Illustrations* (*Coll. Hist. Works*, VI–VII); Kemble, *The Saxons in England*, I, 81; J. R. Green, *A Short History of the English People* (with chronological maps illustrating the Anglo-Saxon Heptarchy); Sweet, *Dialects and Prehistoric Forms of English* (*Trans. Phil. Soc.* 1875–76); *Early English Pronunciation* (with dialect maps); Siebs, *Zur Geschichte der engl. fries. Sprache*; *idem*, in *Grundriss*, 2nd ed. I, 1154; Chadwick, ch. IV (with map, pp. 10–11); A. Brandl, *Zur Geographie der altengl. Dialekte* (*Abh. d. Preuss. Akad. d. Wissenschaften*, 1915, No. 4 (with map)); *Encycl. Brit.* 11th ed. s.v. *Lincolnshire*, *Middlesex*, *Wight*; F. G. Meeson Beck, *ibid.* s.v. *Bernicia*, *Deia*, *East Anglia*, *Essex*, *Hwicce*, *Kent*, *Sussex*.

§ 216. Ethnic Position.

The existence of an Anglo-Saxon individuality needs no proof. Yet both the origin of the community and the question of its extent will require some consideration. One naturally begins with the Saxons.

(*a*) Ancient Tests of Saxon Individuality.

1. The (Anglo-)Saxon language, though first cousin to Frisian, is separated from this language in certain important points (cp. § 228, 2). It is never in popular speech identified with Frisian, nor does there exist any authentic term which may alternately mean Saxon or Frisian. As regards the phenomenon of 'Breaking', (Anglo-)Saxon is more closely related to Scandinavian than to Frisian.

2. The god Saxnōt indicates that there was a national Saxon amphictyony, analogous to that of the Frisian Baduhenna (?), the Vandalic dioscures, the Swabian 'regnator omnium deus', the Isteonic Thingsus, the Marsic Tanfana, the Anglo-Scandinavian Nerthus.

3. The Saxon law is not of the same type as that observed by Ficker as being common to Frisians, Angles, Varines, Scandinavians, and Goths (cp. his *Untersuchungen*, §§ 7, 8, 1714, etc.; the author is not in a position to criticise this observation).

4. The Saxon law makes no distinction between the wergeld of the free and the freed man. In the Danish legend of Helgi (Saxo, p. 81), the continental Saxons also originally shared this peculiarity which is unique among the Gothonic nations (cp. Chadwick, 76).

5. The Saxon division of land has the individualistic term 'shire', analogous to Frisian *dēl*, Alemann. *bara*, Frank. *bant*, Hess. Langobard *aib*, Langobard Anglo-Dan. *fara*, Anglo-Scand. *folk*, Norweg. *fylki*, Gautic *kind*.

(*b*) Frisian Affinities.

6. The linguistic phenomena mentioned in § 213.

7. Chauchi and Frisians co-operate during the revolt of Civilis (cp. the 'flagrantissima cohors...e Chaucis Frisiisque composita', Tac. *Hist.* IV, 79). The champion of the Hugas (Chauchi minores) is a subject of the 'Frescyning' (*Beowulf*, l. 2503). Hug-merke, i.e. the western borderland of the Chauchi minores, belongs to mediaeval Friesland, and so does most of their territory. Even sections of the Chauchi majores appear as mediaeval Frisians. It seems that half of the Chauchi became Saxons, and half of them Frisians.

(*c*) German Affinities.

8. The linguistic phenomena mentioned in vol. I, § 33 and § 148, i.e. the West Gothonic type (cp. **skuldi-haitō* 'sheriff', *gawi-* 'county' (also Gothic)).

9. Saxon-German elements of personal names such as *ermin* and *-berht* (cp. § 147).

10. The Saxon-German feast of 'easter', Germ. *ostern*.

11. Saxon-German republican government, contrasting with kingship among Frisians, Angles, and Scandinavians.

12. The Saxon-German profession of *scop* 'poet'.

13. Saxon-German place names ending in 'ford', 'field', 'hurst', 'worth', 'brook', 'strood', etc. (see Jellinghaus, *Anglia*, XX).

(*d*) Scandinavian Affinities.

14. The phenomenon of 'Breaking' in O.E. *meolc, Heodeningas* corresponds to O.N. *mjǫlk, Hjaðningar*, contrasting with non-broken vowels in Frisian, Gothic, and German (see vol. I, § 31). For lexical relationships, see Hoops, I, 87.

15. The Saxon-Scandinavian profession of *þyle, þulr* 'poet'.

16. Saxon-Scandinavian place names ending in 'fleet'; Saxon-Jutlandic-Gautic place names ending in 'sike'; Saxon-Danish place names ending in 'ore' and 'well'; Saxon-Svīonic-Norwegian place names ending in 'town'.

17. Saxon-Danish political co-operation against the Franks from the sixth to the ninth century. The joint Viking raid of 'Cauiones' (probably the Chauchi) and Erules in A.D. 289 seems to precede this co-operation.

Points 1–5 sufficiently illustrate the marked individuality of the Saxons, whereas the following ones represent their relationship to various neighbours. Our general impression confirms the observation of Joh. Schmidt that Anglo-Saxon occupies an intermediate position between German and Scandinavian. According to Jordan's examination of the vocabulary, the West Saxon dialect inclines towards Frisian and German Saxon, and the Anglian towards Scandinavian (cp. Hoops, I, 88).

Leaving the general Anglo-Saxon type in Britain, we turn to the much discussed problem of how far this type really embraces the Angles and Jutes from the beginning of their history.

It is a current dogma that the Anglo-Saxon character of the Angles in Britain proves the Anglo-Saxon character of the continental ancestors, not only of the Angles, but even of the Jutes from Angel to the Skaw.

Some of the more important arguments in support of this theory may be considered.

(*a*) Pliny, IV, 99: the Ingyaeones embrace Cimbri and Chauchi, i.e. in Jutland and Hanover.

(*b*) King Wǽrmund of the continental Angles has a name with a Saxon *ǽ* instead of Scand. *á* (cp. Saxo's Vermundus (but O.Icelandic Vármundr)); Wǽrmund's son Offa, the Uffo of Saxo, has a non-Scandinavian medial *ff* (cp. Chadwick, 142).

(*c*) A local Anglian and East Frisian development changes *ă* before nasals into *ŏ*. This peculiarity has been taken to denote an Anglo-Frisian community of speech.

(*d*) The Jutish dialect of Kent has certain apparently Frisian features, such as the palatalisation *ē̆* of *ū̆*, where other dialects have *ȳ̆* (cp. Möller, *Altengl. Volksepos*, 88).

(*e*) The Anglian section of Britain is larger than the Saxon and the superiority of the Angles gave rise to the national name. Consequently the Saxons were inferior, both in numbers and influence, and it seems hard to explain how under such circumstances they would have been able to Saxonise the Angles.

These, in our opinion, are the most noteworthy arguments in favour of ancient Jutland's being Anglo-Saxon.

(*f*) A sixth point is the archaeological evidence of the burial places in Kent. Thurlow Leeds says, *Archaeology of the Anglo-Saxon Settlements*, 127–128: 'It may here be said...that it is in Frankish territory that the origin of most of the Kentish culture must be sought....Indeed, it is probably...a small section of it (the Rhineland) and that the most northerly, and therefore the nearest to the sea. This area lies along the Rhine between Coblenz and Düsseldorf, stretching eastwards into the Eifel district, together with a narrow strip on the opposite bank'. This observation, certainly, would represent the Kentish Jutes as Germans rather than as Anglo-Saxons, but, at any rate, it does not support the theory of Scandinavian affinities.

The best point is (*b*), for it gives some definite data concerning the dialect spoken by the kings of Angel. And yet its evidence must not be overrated, for Saxo's 'Anglo-Saxon' form Vermundus is counterbalanced by the Warmundus of the *Vitae duorum Offarum* which agrees with O.N. Vármundr.

Pliny's evidence is not trustworthy (cp. vol. I, p. 39), and at any rate it is too isolated to allow definite linguistic conclusions to be drawn. The religious, constitutional, and epic traditions and customs of Angel point to affinity with the Danes and not with the Saxons, a fact already observed by Grundtvig a century ago (cp. the particulars in § 238). The Jutes of Kent did not share the Saxon system of wergeld (Chadwick, 77).

The Anglian and East Frisian *o* in *lond* cannot be adduced as evidence of a primaeval 'Anglo-Frisian' community, for the Saxons, who occupy the territory between the two tribes, do *not* share the development. Besides, the original form *land* was still used by the Angles when they settled in Britain. The earlier texts have *a*, all later texts have *o* (Anglian) or *a* and *o* (West Saxon, Kentish) (cp. Bülbring, *Altengl. Elementarbuch*, 123). Zachrisson hence concludes that, if there is a common development, it can only have taken place *after* the Angles left home, as a result of mercantile intercourse with the Frisian populations beyond the sea.

Concerning the Kentish and Frisian palatalisation *ē̆* instead of the ordinary *ȳ̆*, we refer to Chadwick, 67: 'As early Kentish also had *ȳ̆*, and as *ē̆* does not make its appearance for about four hundred years after the invasion, there does not seem to be much probability of a historical connection between the Frisian and Kentish changes. Indeed, if they must be consorted, it would seem more probable to attribute the fact to intercourse between Kent and the Netherlands at a later period. As a matter of fact, the early Kentish texts show no dialectical peculiarities which do not occur also either in Midland or West Saxon texts'.

As to point 5, which we may call the statistical argument, we shall examine it more particularly below. Provisionally, we will take for granted that it is conclusive, and that the Angles of Angel spoke Anglo-Saxon, as may also be inferred from the royal names Wærmund and Offa.

This admission, however, only concerns that part of Jutland lying south of the Firth of Flensborg. The language of the Jutlanders farther north is not involved.

According to Joh. Schmidt's ingenious 'Wave Theory', which, on the whole, gives the most satisfactory account of linguistic relations in the ancient Gothonic world, we must assume a gradual, almost imperceptible transition from the one Gothonic sub-group to the other. The ancient Jutlanders must have formed a linguistic bridge between the north and the north-west; to define their dialect as pronounced Anglo-Saxon and distinct from Danish, as Bremer does, is not sound philology. Moreover, if people speaking an intermediate dialect like the ancient Jutlandic happened to participate in great ethnic movements of their southern neighbours, it is not difficult to imagine the inevitable result. One century was sufficient to Romanise the Normans settled in France, so that, when conquering England, they did not introduce their native Scandinavian, but a foreign language, French. As the Jutlandic companions of the Saxons had not to adopt a non-Gothonic language, but only to accommodate their own dialect to that of their kindred neighbours, a generation or two would be sufficient to bring about an almost complete fusion.

We shall here enter into a discussion of what we have termed the *statistical argument*, as regards the Jutes. After settling in Britain the Jutes were quite submerged by the overwhelming majority of Saxons surrounding them; a single glance at the map is sufficient to show this. But the Jutish settlers were not only *surrounded*; the Saxons were even *interspersed* among them. The well-known legendary landing-place of the Jutes on the coast of Kent is the island of Thanet, and its vicinity is characterised by three rivers or channels, the Swale, the Stour, and the Wantsumu. Besides, there is in Kent another Swale and a Swallow (cp. Wallenberg, *Kentish Place Names*). The three names mentioned seem to be an echo, not from Jutland, but from *Holstein* and *Mecklenburg*, where we find a Schwale, two rivers Stör, and a Wanse, Wandsbeck. The same names are found all over England, a Swale in Berkshire and in North Riding, Yorkshire (cp. a Swell in North Riding), Stour in Essex, Dorset, Gloucester, Worcester, Wensum in Norfolk (cp. Wansbeck in Northumberland). This can hardly be due to coincidence; these river names seem to betray the invaders' nostalgic memory of their ancient home. But nowhere do the three names appear in such close and obvious conjunction as among the Jutes in Kent. Hence we must almost necessarily draw the conclusion that the large majority of Hengest's and Horsa's followers were not Jutes but Saxons. As for the Jutes of the Isle of Wight, they were exterminated in A.D. 686 by the West Saxon King Cædwalla (Bede, IV, 16). Such circumstances made the Saxonising of the Jutes in Britain a mere question of time.

What is in reality a similar view is pronounced by Thurlow Leeds on p. 137. After defining the invaders of Kent as 'the more northerly members of the Rhenish Franks', he says: 'It does not exclude the possibility that the leaders of the immigrants may have been Jutes from Jutland; the genealogy is certainly no more than that of the ruling house, and the name which the settlers bore may quite well have sprung from the traditions surrounding that house'.

To sum up, if we consider the intermediate position of the ancient

Jutlandic language, the overwhelming majority of Saxons surrounding the Jutes in Britain, and the names of rivers in Kent derived from Holstein, the Saxon dialect of these Jutes becomes a very feeble argument in favour of Anglo-Saxon nationality among the Jutes on the Continent. To proclaim the Anglo-Saxon character of ancient Jutland on such grounds is, to say the least of it, to exaggerate the importance of imaginary evidence.[1]

Some remarks concerning the earliest Jutlandic inscriptions may be added. We do not lay emphasis on such evidence, both because the date is somewhat controversial and because inscriptions on movable objects may have been taken from their place of origin. But for the sake of making this survey complete such phenomena must be mentioned. The most vital point concerns the preservation or loss of final *-z*; and here the Jutlandic inscriptions show the North Gothonic retention of the *-z*, whereas the West Gothonic loss of *-z* does not occur. Cp. Hlewagastiz Holtingaz (or HlewagastiR HoltingaR) on the inscription of Gallehus in North Slesvig, dated by v. Friesen in Hoops, IV, 13, as about A.D. 400–425, and contrasting with the absence of *-z* in the forms of early German inscriptions from the Migration Age such as Godahi(l)d (Bezenye), *runa* (Freilaubersheim), Wodan, þonar, Leubwini (Nordendorf). It is obvious that the runic inscriptions give no evidence of special affinity between the Jutlandic dialect and Anglo-Saxon.

Further fragmentary material is provided by the most ancient Jutlandic names of persons. We are here considering the Jutish and

[1] In a letter to the author, Prof. Zachrisson makes the following remarks concerning the Kentish river names: 'I have examined the river names you mentioned: Stör, Schwale and Wandsbeck (Witte gives Wantesbeke 1296—Wandse—Eilbek bei Hamburg), and I find the correspondence with the Stour, Swale and Wantsum in Kent most remarkable. Of these Wantsum is certainly Germanic from O.E. *wændsum*, *wandsum* "winding" as in Wensum, Norfolk. Swale in Kent and in Berkshire and N. Riding, Yorkshire may also be Germanic (**suel-* "to move"), although the same root occurs in English river names which are certainly Keltic. The Stour (also in Essex, Dorset, Gloucester, Worcester (cf. Sturkel in Dorset and Styric in Cambridge from the same root)) has generally been looked upon as Keltic as there are two rivers Stura in Italy. But the Keltic form ought to have given O.E. *Stīre not Stūre. For this reason the name is probably Germanic at least in Kent, or a Germanic adaptation of a Keltic name. It has been objected that the *u* in the Germanic river name (Stör, etc.) is probably short, whereas *u* in O.E. Sture is long, but it is quite possible to assume forms with a long and a short vowel from this root: I.G. **st(h)a-* "stand, be stiff" (cf. Swed. *stor*, dial. *stur*, Dutch *stoer* "big, powerful"). The meaning would be a big or considerable river'.

Anglian names collectively, as representing the Jutlandic stock. Our sources are various ancient legends, runic inscriptions, and the earliest dynastic names in genealogies including the first generations after the conquest of Britain.

A. Jutes. (*a*) Gefwulf (*Widsith*, l. 26); (*b*) Wihtgils, Hengest, Horsa, Eoric (*Genealogy*, Kent); (*c*) Húnláf, Ordláf, Gúþláf, followers of Hengest (*Lay of Finnsburg*, ll. 1143, 1148); (*d*) Amleth, Frovin, Wigo (Saxo, 138, 162); (*e*) Hlewagastiz (Gallehus), Wolþuþewaz (Thorsbjerg).

B. Auiones. Oswine (*Widsith*, l. 26).

C. Wendle (in Vendsyssel ?). Wulfgár (*Beow.* 348).

D. Angles. (*a*) Waþolgéat, Wihtlæg, Wǽrmund, Éomǽr (*Genealogy*, Mercia); (*b*) Titmon, Trygils, Hróþmund (*Genealogy*, East Anglia); (*c*) Wegbrand, Angangéat (*Genealogy*, Bernicia); (*d*) Cueldgils, Ceadbed (*Genealogy*, Lindsey).

The affinities in the above collection are perhaps not very obvious, but in most cases they seem to point towards Scandinavian. The three names ending in *-láf* represent a favourite Scandinavian type; Frovin corresponds to the Skjoldung princess Fréawaru (*Beow.*); Hróþmund is the namesake of a Skjoldung prince (*ibid.*); Cueldgils contains a typical Scandinavian element, known from O.N. Kveldulfr. Wǽrmund, on the other hand, seems to have namesakes only in Germany (cp. the modern family-name Wahrmund); but such cases seem to be in a minority.

More important than such positive affinities is this negative point: there occur no names with the typical non-Scandinavian elements *ermin-*, *berht-*, and *bald-*. Saxo's Jutlandic traditions contain one single instance of Erm-, viz. Ermuthrud (Hermuthruda), the queen of the Anglian King Viglek (Wihtlæg, 161), and she is not a native, but comes from abroad ('Scotland').

Scarcely, however, are the Jutes and Angles established in Britain, than the West Gothonic forms suddenly emerge on a large scale. Cp. (1) Jutes: Eormenric, Æthelbert, Egbert, Earconbert, Eadbald. (2) Angles: (*a*) Mercians: Æthelbald; (*b*) East Anglians: Æthelbert, Sigebert; (*c*) Northumbrians: Eadbert, Osbert. Though Mercian princes still adopt Scandinavian names from the legends, such as Wigláf and Alewih, it is obvious that the royal nomenclature has been subjected to a radical revolution. And this can be due to *Saxon influence* only.

Here we may compare the fate of the Scandinavians settled in

Normandy. When they arrived there the invaders of course bore Scandinavian names and some of them have survived to this day, such as An(s)quetil. But the leading chieftains almost at once adopted the West Gothonic type current among the Romanised Franks. So the conqueror Hrolf was baptised Hrodbert, and other favourite names in his family were Richard and Wilhelm, all of avowedly non-Scandinavian type. Also Celtic names such as Brian might occur. When we observe this change from one national type of name to another taking place in historical times as a consequence of denationalisation, we can hardly doubt that the same thing happened in the case of the Anglian chieftains settled as leaders among the Saxon populations of Britain.

We had arrived above at the *a priori* conclusion that a weak minority like the Jutes *must* have been absorbed by the surrounding Saxons, and we believe that we have now discovered at least *some* traces of the process.

As to the Angles, our theory may perhaps invite contradiction. What we call the statistical argument may seem at first sight to be against it. The Anglian territory is larger than the Saxon, and it has therefore been concluded that the Angles cannot have been Saxonised. We believe that this *a priori* conclusion is far from being a sound one.

History shows the Saxons changing the whole of North Germany into Saxony, and founding colonies in Italy, Flanders, Normandy, Brittany, and on the islets opposite the Loire, while the Angles can only point to insignificant and short-lived colonies in Thuringia and (?) about the Rhine Delta. Roman annals from the third to the fifth century abound in references to Saxons raiding the Channel and the East British coasts as far as the Orkneys; the Angles in these stories are conspicuous only by their absence. The Roman military government in Gaul as in Britain organises a Litus Saxonicum, no *Litus Anglicum; the 'Saxon' district includes East Anglia. The Celts of Britain designate all the invaders as Saxons and do not know the collective use of the name Angles.

All this evidence gives the impression that the Saxons largely outnumbered the Angles.

But how, then, could the name Angles oust that of Saxons as a designation of the united nation? We believe that we can solve this apparent riddle by a series of important observations.

1. The Saxons were republicans, the Angles were monarchists. Thus, when the political current of the time caused the Saxons to adopt a

monarchy, they were handicapped by the absence of families with royal rank. The consequence was that only one of their states produced a national dynasty, derived from the native god Seaxneat, viz. the East Saxon. Otherwise the Saxon states introduce into their genealogical trees the Anglian mythical ancestor, Woden—that is to say, have recourse to Anglian candidates for their early kings. The most powerful state, the West Saxon, is notorious in that it owns a dynasty which springs from the same stock as that of the Angles in Bernicia (cp. Chadwick, 60), whereas parallel traditions of Saxo's, p. 163, enable us to identify the West Saxon ancestors Freawine and Wig with the Jutlandic princes Frovin and Vigo. Chadwick, on p. 301, summarises his view upon the dynastic preponderance of the Angles thus: 'In subjection to them was a numerous population, presumably of Saxon origin. With the course of time this subject population would naturally tend to predominate, while the descendants of the Angli would dwindle into a military aristocracy'.

2. King Æthelbert of Kent before 595 became lord of the Southern and Eastern Saxons and of all Anglian states south of the Humber (cp. the map in Green's *Short Hist. of the Engl. People* (1890), I, 30). As his own people, the Jutes or Kentishmen, were only a small minority, he could not call his state Jutish or Kentish. His Saxon subjects were also relatively few, and the independent West Saxons were his most powerful rivals. The majority of his subjects were Angles, and so quite naturally he was styled 'King of the Angles', e.g. in letters from the Roman Church after 601. Here Angles became a collective designation, including Jutes and Saxons.

3. The Angles, being the tribe in England in which monarchy was most firmly established, were also the creators of the English epic court literature, which almost entirely ignores the Saxons (cp. our statistical proofs showing the absence of the Saxons, *Journ. Engl. and Germ. Phil.* 1912, No. 4, 23 seq.).

4. The Angles—and the Kentish Jutes—created the English Church, while the Southern Saxons remained heathen for almost a century longer. The pun on the 'Christian Angles' became a symbolic watchword for the conversion of the nation (Bede, II, 1). Half a century after the conversion of the last heathen Saxons, Bede wrote the history of the mission. An Anglian by birth, he of course glorified the Anglian metropolis of York and accepted the traditional collective use of the national

religious name; and the fame of his work again contributed largely to the final supremacy of this name.

5. The Christian Anglo-Saxons, already accustomed to the supremacy of Anglian priests, naturally felt and emphasised their difference from the continental Saxons who had fallen into ill repute because of their remaining heathen for centuries longer. The contrast between Anglians who were Christians, and Saxons who were heathen fanatics, which at one time was noted in Britain, was later insisted on as distinguishing the united Anglo-Saxons from their continental kinsmen. This circumstance certainly discouraged the British Saxons from emphasising their own national name, which had in international use fallen into disrepute because of its association with the abominable savagery of paganism. They were henceforth compelled to prefer the name of Angles as a safeguard against being confused with their former brethren (cp. Hoops, I, 94).

6. During the Viking Age a local contrast between Engla lagu and Dena lagu was created in Middle Britain. Here again the Angles represented Christianity, whereas the neighbours were originally heathen. Though the opponents of Christianity are not in this case Saxon, yet the traditional connexion between the ideas of the Anglian and English Church is reinforced (cp. Hoops, *l.c.*).

7. The Angles, as creators of the English epic poetry and of the English Church, also exercised a predominating influence upon the English literary language till the time of Egbert of Wessex.

This sequence of observations sufficiently explains how and why the Gothonic people of Britain came to be called Angles and not Saxons. First of all the Saxons excluded the use of their own name through their heathen fanaticism. The consequence was not to be wondered at. The strange thing is that there should have existed, here, as in German Saxony, such a degree of fanaticism as to prove a dead weight in the competition for higher civilisation. Fortune had bestowed on the Saxons a port like London, and that part of the British coast most directly facing the Continent. But a century of obstinate paganism delayed the development of civilisation among the South Saxons so much that the Angles, though less favoured by natural conditions, got ahead of them and secured for the name 'English' an inalienable supremacy.

The early history of the name 'English' includes the story of the genesis of an Anglo-Saxon nation. On the Continent there had existed no political Anglo-Saxon community. The Angles, though perhaps speaking a dialect chiefly of Saxon stamp, had no close political, constitutional, religious or epic relations with the Saxons, but had rather affinity with the Danes; therefore their continental history comes under another heading, that of the Jutlandic tribes. With the Jutes it must have been similar, and even after their language had been Saxonised in England, they kept their own system of wergeld different from the Saxon type (cp. Chadwick, 77).

It was their *isolation* in the island of Britain that caused the fusion of Angles, Jutes, and Saxons into the united nation of English (later also called Anglo-Saxons).

After their amalgamation they received two infusions of Scandinavian blood, from the Vikings, and from the Normans, the former speaking Scandinavian, the latter speaking French.

As a final result of these infusions and of this isolation, the position of English among the Gothonic languages has suffered a considerable displacement. Almost every conspicuous mark of West Gothonic grammar has been lost; the syntax has grown almost more akin to Scandinavian than to German; the West Gothonic stock of words is rivalled by Scandinavian and is even outnumbered by French loans, while the scientific language has become chiefly Latin and Greek. At the same time, the vocabulary of the Scandinavian languages on the Continent has approximated to the German. Thus if at one time English and German were united and separated from Scandinavian, the present arrangement is that German and Scandinavian are united, and English separated from both.

Lit. Zeuss, 495 seq.; Grimm, 642 seq., 658 seq.; Müllenhoff, IV (see Index, s.v. *Angelsachsen, Ingvaeonen*); *idem, Nordalbing. Studien*, I, 111 seq.; *idem, Beovulf*, 58; Grundtvig, *Haandbog i Verdenshistorien*, II, 203 (2nd ed. 220); Kemble, *The Saxons in England*; R. G. Latham, *The English Language*, 5th ed.; Sweet, *Dialects and Prehistoric Forms of English* (*Trans. Phil. Soc.* 1875–76); Murray, *Encycl. Brit.* 9th ed. s.v. *English Language*; Beddoe, *The Races of Britain*; Weiland, *Die Angeln* (*Festgabe f. Georg Hanssen*); Erdmann, *Die Heimat...der Angeln*; Siebs, *Zur Gesch. d. engl. fries. Sprache*; *idem*, in *Grundriss*, 2nd ed. I, 1154; Bremer, §§ 121, 122, 129; Much, *Zur Stammeskunde der Altsachsen* (*Correspondenzblatt der Deutschen anthropolog. Gesellschaft*, 1898, 113); *idem, Stammeskunde*, 95; *idem*, in Hoops, s.v. *Sachsen*; Schütte, *Var Anglerne Tyskere?* (*Sønderjydske Aarbøger*, 1900); *idem*, in *Smaaskrifter udg. af Selsk. f. germ. Filologi*, No. 13, IV, §§ 1–21; *idem, Arkiv*, XXV, 314, 320; H. Bradley, *The Making of English*; Chadwick, *The Origin of the Engl. Nation*, ch. IV; *idem, Encycl. Brit.* s.v. *Britain*; Hoops, s.v. *Angelsachsen*; Chambers, *Widsith*, 66 seq.; la Cour, *Sønderjyllands Historie*, I, 189 seq.

The various types of Anglo-Saxon houses are described by Sidney Oldall Addy in *The Evolution of the English House* (*Social England Series*, edited by Kenelm D. Cotes).

A very old type of simple form is rectangular, with triangular end walls, and with a roof which reaches the ground; it is the ordinary form of old Icelandic country houses (cp. Addy, p. 17 seq.): 'In whatever part of England we look for examples of the smaller or humbler domestic house or cottage we shall find that an old method of construction prevails. These buildings were erected in "bays", the house of one "bay" being the simplest form. The principle of construction of the house of one bay was simple. Two pairs of bent trees, in form resembling the lancet-shaped arches of a Gothic church, were set up on the ground, and united at their apexes by a ridge-tree. The framework so set up was strengthened by two tie-beams and four wind-braces, and was fastened together by wooden pegs. The bent trees or arches were placed at a distance of about sixteen feet apart, and the space included between them was known as a "bay". Thus the "bay" formed a sort of architectural unit, for the building of one "bay" might be increased indefinitely in length by adding other "bays" '.

'These couples or pairs of bent trees were anciently known as "forks"....They were also known as "gavels" or "gavelforks", but this term can only be strictly applied to the "forks" at the two ends of the building, which thus acquired the name of "the gable end".'

'The "forks" were also known by other names. They are now popularly called "croks", "crucks", and "crutches", and a building erected in this way is now said to be "built on crucks". In some old surveys these "crutches", which were intended to support the building, are described as "couples" or "couples of syles" or "siles". The distinction which in old documents is made between "couples of syles" and "gavelforks" arose from the fact that the "syles" were straight, whilst the "gavelforks" intersected each other at the top. Usually all the "forks" were curved....'

'The oldest of these buildings had no upper storey, and the walls were made of wattle-work plastered over with clay or mud. Sometimes they were covered by planking resting on the "crucks" and laid parallel to the ridge. Bede tells us that Bishop Eadberht removed the wattles from a church built in this way, and covered the whole with lead, both the roof and the walls themselves. Again, according to Malmesbury, an old church at Glastonbury was covered with lead from the summit to the very ground. In Iceland the shieling was built with one main beam as a ridge-pole, and this rested on the two gable ends. The door of these buildings was in one of the gable ends. A house at Scrivelsby, near Horncastle, popularly known as "Teapot Hall", is an excellent example of a building of this kind. It is built of two pairs of straight "crucks", which extend from the four corners of the house to the ridge-tree, and which support the ridge-tree, the framework being further strengthened by the addition of wind-braces. The length, breadth, and height of the building is 19 feet respectively. The doorway is in the south gable end, and a small "outshot" building, whose roof is considerably below that of the main building, projects from the opposite gable end. This "outshot", built of wood, and coeval with the house, contains the buttery and scullery, the buttery being, as is usually the case, in the north-west. From the floor of the "outshot" a ladder goes up to the bedroom above....The walls, which are about six inches thick, are composed of wooden studs, with twigs or branches of trees interwoven, the whole being overlaid with mud and plaster. The sides are thatched with straw down to a point a little below the bedroom floor. From this point grey slates extend to the ground. The roof of the "outshot" is rounded, and thatched with straw. The fireplace, which may be in its original position, is of brick, and it, as well as the chimney, is of more recent date than the rest of the house....A house of this kind was formerly known as a booth, and it is interesting to notice that the size of the booth in the 14th century was about the same as that of the house which we are now examining.'

A more developed type of building is the 'hall', the 'hall-house' or the 'fire-house', Icel. *eld-hús* (cp. Addy, p. 59 seq.); it unites dwelling-house, barn, and stables under one roof. 'A very large number of English farmhouses still exist in which the dwelling-house, barn, and stables are combined under one and the same roof.'...'In the 16th century the word fire-house was...used as a synonym for the better kind of dwelling-house....In larger country houses the fire-house or hall was often in the centre of the building, with the women's apartments consisting of the "chamber" and buttery at one end and a barn or combined barn and ox-house at the other. The main entrance to the building was a passage which divided the "fire-house" from the ox-house or barn, and which was the threshing-floor. This passage was known by various names. Anciently it was called the "floor" or the "threshold", a word which means "threshing-floor", because in ancient times the floor at the entrance was for threshing. It was sometimes called the "entry". Doors opened out of this passage both into the "fire-house" and into the barn, or ox-house.'

'The main difference between the combined house and "shippon" as still found in England, and the German dwelling (the Saxon house, cp. our § 205, p. 208) lies in the position of the "floor" or barn floor. In the German dwelling the great doors are at the gable end of the building, and the "floor" extends longitudinally from the great doors through the building as far as the hearth-wall. But in the English buildings the great doors, otherwise the great barn doors, are at one of the sides, and the threshing-floor intersects the building transversely so as to separate the dwelling-house from the "shippon". In the English, as well as in the German, building, the corn harvest appears to have been stored in the "balk" above the cattle, and to have been thence thrown down upon the "floor" to be threshed. On one side of the "floor" of the typical old English farm-building is a wall reaching up to the joists of the "balk", and dividing the "floor" from the "shippon". On the other side of the "floor" the wall goes up to the ridge-tree, and behind this last-named wall the chimney-stack of the "house-place" or fire-house is often found....In Lancashire the "balk" has a complete partition wall, and is called the "scaffo'd", hay being thrown through a hole in such wall called the "scaffo'd hole" (pp. 85–86).'

Whereas the position of the entrance differs from that of the Saxon house, it corresponds to that of a Jutlandic type of house (cp. p. 308).

English courtyards containing several buildings are mentioned in mediaeval documents. 'In 1392 the Prioress of Nun Monkton took a lease of property at Nun Stainton and in it convented to repair the buildings of the messuage, viz. "a house called the fire-house, containing five couples of syles and two gavelforks, and another for grain containing three couples of syles and two gavelforks, and another storehouse for grain containing one couple of syles and two gavelforks, a little to the west of the said fire-house containing three couples of syles and two gavelforks" (p. 59).'

'In the twelfth century the manor house of Sandon, in Essex, consisted of a hall, a bower, and a latrina. Adjoining it were ample storehouses for grain, an ox-house, a washhouse in which clothes were trodden in vats by the feet, a brewery, a pig-cote, and a hen-house (p. 129).'

'The buildings of these manor houses were so arranged as to form a quadrangle or courtyard (p. 132).'

'In the houses of the wealthy stone was used at an early period, we do not know how early....Where in existing houses the lower part of the wooden framework is filled in by stone or bricks, such houses are said, in common phraseology, to be "half-timbered"....The oldest way was to weave twigs or brushwood in and out the posts. After that came laths, which were fitted into "slots" in the posts by a process known as "shooting". In a house at Warrington examined by the author, wattle and daub, stone and brick are filled into the woodwork of different parts (p. 109).'

'Although stone, slates, straw, reeds, rushes, and other materials were used for roofing, yet moss or turf, on account of its cheapness, was much used for farm-buildings and the cheaper kinds of houses. In the fifteenth century the turf used for this purpose was known in the north of England as "dovet", and it seems to have been laid on a foundation of ling or heather. Turf roofs were common amongst the Romans. In Iceland the roofs of farm-buildings are still covered with "green fresh grass-covered turves", as they were long ago. Old accounts often mention the heather and the moss which were used for covering or thatching buildings (p. 127).'

Lit. Innocent, *The Development of English Building Construction*; Thomas Wright, *Homes of Other Days*; J. A. Gotch, *Growth of the English House*; *idem*, *The English Home*; W. H. Godfrey, *The Story of Architecture in England.*

§ 217. History of the Saxons and Chauchi on the Continent.

The tribal names of a short Simplex type—Saxones, Chauchi, Ymbre, Secgan—denote a primary settlement.

Ptolemy, who draws his information from the discoveries of the Roman naval expedition in A.D. 5, places the Saxons 'on the back of the neck of the Cimbric Chersonese', II, 11, § 7, cp. his § 16.

The Ymbre, *Widsith*, l. 32, are perhaps the classical Ambrones (cp. add. to Nennius, § 63: 'genus Ambronum...id est Aldsaxonum'). Whether they belong to the island of Ambrum west of Slesvig is open to question (cp. § 215, 4). The greater Chauchi (Ptol. *l.c.*) dwell between the Elbe and the Weser; the lesser Chauchi west of the Weser, i.e. extending to the district of Hug-merke, 'the borderland of the Hugas or lesser Chauchi' (cp. § 215, 5 and 6).

Their neighbours are: north-east, Jutes and Angles; east, Semnonic

Swabians; south-east, Langobards; south, Cherusci, Angrivarii, Amsivarii; south-west, Isteones (Franks); west, Frisians.

The earliest historical allusion to them would be in connexion with the Cimbric raid, in 113–101 B.C., that is, if the Ambrones are Saxons. They contribute largely to the victory gained over the Romans at Arausio in 105 B.C. (Orosius, V, 16), and are involved in the disaster of the Teutones at Aquae Sextiae in 102 B.C. (Plutarch, *Marius*, 19).

In 12 B.C. the Roman navy visits the Chauchi (Dio Cassius, LIV, 31). In A.D. 5 they submit to Tiberius (Velleius, II, 106). Roman garrisons appear even after the defeat of Varus, e.g. A.D. 14 (Tac. *Ann.* I, 38); Chauchi serve under Germanicus against Arminius in A.D. 15 (*ibid.* I, 60).

In 41 and 47 Chauchic pirates are repulsed from Belgium (Suetonius, *Claud.* 24; Tac. *Ann.* XI, 18); hence perhaps their settlements on the islands west of Vlie (Pliny, IV, 101). In 47 Claudius withdraws the Roman frontier to the Rhine Delta (Tac. *Ann.* XI, 19).

In A.D. 58 the Chauchi drive the Amsivarii from the Emsgau on the river Ems (*ibid.* XIII, 55), and probably also the Chasvarii from the Hasegau.

In A.D. 70 a united cohort of Chauchi and Frisians supports the Batavian rebellion against Rome (Tac. *Hist.* IV, 79).

In 98 the Chauchi have become neighbours of the Chatthi in the interior of Germany (Tac. *Germ.* 36); this expansion on Angrivarian-Cheruscian soil, however, is merely political, as the German nationality persists.

In 170 pirates from the Elbe are repulsed from Belgium (*Hist. Aug. v. Did. Jul.* 1, 7).

In 289 Maximian repulses 'Chauiones' and Erules from Gaul (Mamertin, *Paneg. Maxim.* 5, *Genethl.* 7). We propose to read *Chaugiones, that is the Hugas or lesser Chauchi. Their alliance with Erules anticipates the later Saxon-Danish co-operation (cp. § 215, 6).

In 286 the Saxons appear as raiders of the Channel. A coast-guard along the 'Litus Saxonicum' has to be established against them (Eutropius, IX, 21).

Chauchi and Saxons are pressing the Franks towards Batavia and Belgium (cp. § 185).

In 308 'Chauiones' join a league of Franks and Alemanni against Rome (Nazarius, 18); the reading Vangiones is wrong, as this tribe was Romanised long before this. Constantius frustrates the attack.

About 355 the 'Saxon tribe of Kouadoi', i.e. Chauchi, has conquered Salland and is attacking the exiled Salian Franks in Batavia, but is repulsed by Julian in 358. Schmidt would read *Chamaboi (II, 37; cp. *Hist. Vierteljahrsschrift*, 1911, 2 seq.); but the Chamavi were not Saxons at all. We here notice the transition from Chauchi to Saxons; only the epic poetry preserves the ancient name as Hugas.

In 365 the indefatigable Saxon pirates reach Scotland, in 391 the Orkneys (cp. Ammianus, XXVI, 4, § 5; Pacatius, *Paneg. Theodos.* 5); Theodosius only temporarily subdues them. A more effective defence of the 'Litus Saxonicum' is arranged, in Belgica II between the Scheld and Seine, in the Tractus Armoricanus between the Seine and Loire, and in Britain from the Wash to Portsmouth (*Not. dign. Occ.* XXXVIII, 3, § 7, XXVII, 2, § 14). The name probably indicates 'a shore exposed to Saxon inroads', but may also imply permanent Saxon settlements on outlying headlands and islets (cp. below, p. 255, on the presumably Saxon place names Marcis and Locus Hornenis in the *Not. dign.*). The Angles, and the Jutes, raiding Thanet and Wight, probably take part in these expeditions.

In 451 Saxon auxiliaries from Gaul serve under the Roman governor Aëtius against Attila (Jordanes, XXVI, 191).

In 464 and 469 the Saxon Adovacar, from his lair on the islets opposite the mouth of the Loire, sets out to besiege Angers. Romans and Franks beat him and conquer his insular home, but he is left in peace and even allies with the Franks (Gregor. Tur. II, 18, 19).

In 475 the Saxons from the isles ravage the Bay of Biscay, but are conquered by the Gaulish coast-guard Namatius, in Visigothic service (Sid. Apollonius, *epist.* VIII, 6, § 13). After this they are pacified and absorbed (cp. the Breton place name Sauzon on the island of Guédel (Belle-Île)).

During the following centuries the decline of the Saxon nationality on the Continent and its fusion with Roman and German civilisations take place.

The Franks as heirs of Rome soon bring into subjection all the Saxons west of the Rhine. Chlodowech or his successors seem to have settled Saxons and Frisians in the various Rhenish Sachsenheim and Friesenheim after the defeat of the Alemanni in 496 (cp. Britzenheim, the Villa Brettanorum near Mayence, Förstemann, II, 577; this indicates that the settlers included Bretons, i.e. the neighbours of the Saxons in Gaul).

In 578 King Chilperic orders the Saxons of Bayeux to attack Brittany, but they are defeated (Gregor. Tur. v, 26). Their territory Autlingua appears as Otlingua Saxonica in a document of 843 (*Mon. Germ. Capitul. Reg. Franc.* II, 275). They were absorbed by Roman civilisation.

The Saxons of Flanders remain Gothonic, but are Franconised and now speak Dutch. Hulst, north-west of Antwerp, in the fourteenth century is named Saxhaven or Saxiportus.

In Germany the true Saxons and the German natives can scarcely be distinguished from each other.

Those Saxons who assisted the Franks in ruining Thuringia between 531 and 534 may be regarded as non-German. Widukind's legendary narrative emphasises the national contrast by placing the Thuringians in the position of the Britons of Nennius as victims of the awful 'seaxes'. And the place names along the ancient Thuringian frontier abound in non-German palatalisations (cp. Bremer's survey in his § 146, 3). The distribution of examples indicates that a pronounced linguistic barrier existed here for centuries after the conquest.

The final conflict between Saxons and Franks was religious rather than national. But certainly the religious fanaticism of the Saxons was again a racial and non-German feature. And the headquarters of Saxon resistance were almost identical with the domain of the pure non-German Saxons, viz. Holstein and North-eastern Hanover. Here Charlemagne waged his most merciless war of extermination against the champions of heathendom. Thus, in 804, he banished 10,000 inhabitants to Gaul and Germany (Einhard, *Vita Caroli M.* 7); the *Chron. Moissac.* ad an. 804 mentions transplanted inhabitants of Wi(g)modia, Hostingavi, and Rosogavi, and Saxones ultra Albiam. As the Slavs obtained Eastern Holstein, Einhard (*ibid.*), and about 1150 expelled some thousands more (Helmold, I, 96), it is no wonder that the old Saxon nationality has been completely rooted out on the Continent. Its last distinct survivals do not appear in Holstein or in Northern Hanover, but near Merseburg, traceable in the personal names of Thietmar's *Chronicle*, eleventh century, and in the *Merseburg necrologies* and *Glosses* (cp. Bremer's § 145).

Other Saxons joined the East Frisians for a time, but even they have now been Germanised.

Lit. Wietersheim-Dahn (see Index); Krom, *De populis Germanis...Anglo-saxonumque migrationibus*; Lot, *Les migrations saxonnes* (*Revue hist.* CXIX, 39);

idem, *Revue historique*, CXIX seq.; Prentout, *ibid.* CVII, 285 seq.; Longnon, *Les noms de lieu de la France*, 178 seq.; Schmidt, II, 33, 46 seq.; Much, *Zur Stammeskunde der Altsachsen* (*Correspondenzblatt der Deutschen anthropolog. Gesellschaft*, 1898, 113); Mansion, *Le problème saxon* (*Bull. bibliogr. et pédag. du Musée Belge*, XXIX, 5 seq.); Schönfeld, *Hist. gramm. van het Nederlands*, § VI (with lit. XLIV).

§ 218. Nature of the Saxon Conquest in Britain.

There exist two different theories concerning the nature of the conquest. According to the one there was no continuity between the ancient British civilisation and the new Saxon. According to the other, the extinction of the Britons in numerous regions was less radical, and a corresponding continuity of elements from their civilisation may be observed.

Haverfield says (*Romanisation*, 86): '...destruction came...on the population. During the long series of disasters, many of the Romanised inhabitants of the lowlands must have perished. Many must have fallen into slavery, and many may have been sold into foreign lands. The remnant, such as it was, doubtless retired to the west. But, in doing so, it exchanged the region of walled cities and civilised houses, of city life and Roman culture, for a Celtic land'.

Collingwood says (*Roman Britain*, 100): 'By extinction, I do not mean that the population was literally wiped out. I mean that the towns were destroyed and left desolate, the country-houses looted and burnt, and the population driven into the forests, there to subsist as best it could. The raiders wanted loot rather than blood, and though impoverished and in danger of starving, the great mass of the Britons must have survived. But the most Romanised classes perished utterly, and those who survived can only have been the villagers, who were not Romanised enough to rebuild the Romano-British civilisation again from the foundations'.

An opposite view is held by Foord, *The Last Age of Roman Britain*, Weigall, *Wanderings in Roman Britain*, and Zachrisson, *Romans, Kelts and Saxons in Ancient Britain* (*Skrifter utg. av Kgl. Human. Vetenskaps-Samfundet i Uppsala*, XXIV, 12, 31 seq.). The latter says, on p. 31: 'It is in itself improbable that all the Roman towns should have lain waste and deserted during the peaceful period between the battle of Mount Badon and the onslaught of Ceawlin. We are distinctly told that Ceawlin conquered the three towns of Bath, Gloucester, and

Cirencester....Nor can we conclude from Gildas' account of Britain in the middle of the fifth century that Roman civilisation and the knowledge of the Latin language had been utterly lost. Gildas writes excellent Latin and is well acquainted with the Latin poets and the Roman Christian historians. He calls Latin *nostra lingua*, and refers to the Britons as *cives*, i.e. citizens of the Roman Empire....Roman names were borne by many of the British rulers, such as Ambrosius Aurelianus..., Constantine of Damnonia, and Aurelius Caninus, who were contemporary with Gildas, Condidan or Candidianus, who fell in the last decisive fight between the Britons and the Saxons, and there appear also many such names in the Keltic genealogies'....'The fact that Gregory the Great in 601, writing to Augustine, indicates London and York as the most appropriate seats of the chief English bishoprics (*Hist. Eccles.* I, 29), in connection with Bede's (731) reference (*ibid.* II, 3) to London as *multorum emporium populorum terra marique venientium*, does not bear out Haverfield's assertion (*Romanisation*, 84) that these towns had been entirely depopulated during the early Saxon occupation'.

According to Zachrisson's examination of place names (p. 56), 'the Keltic element is well represented in Lancashire, Derbyshire, Staffordshire, Worcestershire, Gloucestershire, Wiltshire, and Dorset. A few safe instances occur in Oxfordshire and Buckinghamshire, but to the east of this area there are very few safe survivals'. (P. 59) 'names, in which Welsh *coed* and *crug* appear as Chet, Church or Creech, i.e. with a palatalised *k*, have a special claim to the attention of the historian. For phonetic reasons these names can only occur in areas with a mixed Saxon and Keltic population, where the English tongue was replacing the native language, and where the Saxons must have been permanently settled before the sound-change that turned *k* into *ch* had ceased to operate. This can hardly have been much later than the seventh century'.

We quite agree with Zachrisson's arguments. And we may even add that though he draws the boundary line marking the eastern limit of Celtic elements through the middle of England, there may be found survivals still farther east.

In the east of England it seems to have been inhabitants of towns rather than rural populations that survived. The Anglo-Saxon invaders generally avoided the towns, and, if they did not utterly destroy them, some of the citizens might succeed in maintaining themselves there. Thurlow Leeds says, *Archaeology of the Anglo-Saxon Settlements*, 21: 'In the matter of the Roman towns there is no reason to suppose that in some of them at least, some measure of communal life has not survived unbroken from Roman times. The evidence for this seems particularly strong in the case of London, where the customary law, notably that of inheritance, which came into being during the Roman domination, still remained in force'. Cp. p. 53: 'The Roman system of partition as to one third to the wife, one third to the children, and one third as the testator willed, survived down to the reign of George I'. Cp. Bede's description of London as an important 'emporium', cited above.

As to York, its honorary Roman surname 'Municipium' was still remembered at the time of Bede (III, 1) and the same seems to have held good of St Albans (Verulamium), according to the Welsh form of its name (Cair Mincip, Nennius, § 76).

Strangely enough, the Romano-British element is especially strong in a district where it would seem, *a priori*, to have been first in danger of extinction, viz. in Kent. Here, a number of towns in close proximity—in fact, all the more important ones—preserved their ancient names for a considerable time, or even till the present day. And some of the forms seem to betray the existence of a bilingual population. For instance, the British name of the Kentish capital, Durovernum, survives for a time as Dorwitceastre (read *Dorwicceastre), whereas the town is in Anglo-Saxon called Cantwarabyrig, now Canterbury, a name which may also have a British origin, as it re-appears in Welsh as Cair Ceint. The island of Thanet, Brit. Tanatis, has an additional name Ruoihin (Nennius, § 43) which appears as Ruym in later times. Nobody would imagine a phonetic connexion between Hrofæscæstræ, the present Rochester, and the ancient British Durobrivae, and yet it exists, as appears from the form Hrofireui A.D. 604 (Birch, *Cartular. Saxon.* 3, *Textus Roffensis*). The British name was pronounced Duróbrivae, with a strong stress on *ó*; later, the contracted form *Drróbrivae was by the Saxons understood as Hrofireui, owing to a strange, but not incredible change of sound (cp. Zachrisson, *l.c.* 81). As the Saxon form starts from the Celtic pronunciation Duróbrivae, and not from the Latin, Durobrívae, it betrays the survival of a Celtic element till after the conquest. The full list of surviving British names in Kent will be commented upon in § 220.

The evidence of the place names seems to be contradicted by that of archaeology, for no English region contains so many ancient Anglo-Saxon burial places as Kent (cp. the map drawn by Thurlow Leeds (our Fig. 7, reproduced from the above-mentioned monograph *Archaeology*, 19)). But we must assume that the contradiction is merely apparent. The position would have been much the same as in Dalmatia, where the Romance nationality of the important towns persisted after the open country had been occupied by the Slavs.

Lit. Engl. Place-Name Society, vol. I, Part 1 (containing Mawer and Stenton, *Introduction to the Survey of Engl. Place-Names*; Ekwall, *The Celtic Element*; Stenton, *The English Element*; Crawford, *Place-Names and Archaeology*); Mawer, *Problems of Place-Name Study*.

§ 219. The Roman Defensive System and its Influence upon the Process of the Conquest.

In order to trace more exactly the beginning and early progress of the conquest, it is important to discuss the problems of the Roman system of coast defence and especially of the term Litus Saxonicum (cp. the lit. cited in § 217).

Lot, *Les migrations saxonnes* (*Revue historique*, CXIX, 39), maintains that the Litus Saxonicum, as a common territorial denomination in Gaul and Britain, does not mean 'coasts colonised by the Saxons'. 'Dans la grande île, comme sur le continent, le Litus Saxonicum c'est le rivage, qu'il faut défendre contre les Saxons.'

However, he admits: 'Deux localités seulement de la *Notitia dignitatum*, Marcis et Grannona, sont suivies de l'indication *in litore Saxonico*. Il est impossible de ne pas remarquer aussitôt, que la première certainement, la seconde vraisemblablement, sont situées en des régions ou près de régions colonisées par les Saxons'....'À défaut de renseignements annalistiques, la toponomastique, en nous montrant dans les environs de Boulogne quarante-deux localités terminées en *-incthon*,[1] nous révèle une occupation saxonne.' He might have added that this settlement appears already from the names in the *Notitia*, for Marcis, the present Marck in the Pas-de-Calais (Lot, *l.c.*), is a Saxon name, the same as Mercia. Similarly, the harbour at the mouth of the Somme called Locus Hornensis is a Saxon 'horn', i.e. 'headland'.[2] Further, we know of

1 Cp. Taylor, *Words and Places*, p. 87 seq. (with map on p. 87).

2 Horn frequently appears as the name of headlands and peninsulas in Zealand, Funen, and Jutland.

Saxons settled on the islands facing the mouth of the Loire, A.D. 463, that is, twenty-five years before Gaul ceased to be under Roman rule. Cp. the place name Sauzon, i.e. 'Saxon' on the Breton island Guédel or Belle-Île. (The Saxons in the Norman district Bessin may also have been established there in Roman times.)

The invaders may for a time have been subjected more or less effectively to Roman rule; this, we may assume, was the case with the Saxon colonists about Marck and Horn in Flanders, when these two places were incorporated in the Roman system of defence. But the more outlying settlements, especially on islets such as Guédel and the Île de Noirmoutier facing the mouth of the Loire, may easily have evaded the control of the Roman coast-guards.

The position, in spite of Lot's assertions, cannot have been different in Britain. In any case, the preliminary settlements of the Saxon pioneers must have been even more extensive than in Gaul, where the vicinity of larger Roman garrisons must always to a certain extent have handicapped them.

A settlement of the same sort as Marck and Horn is perhaps the fortress Othona on the Litus Saxonicum in the present Essex. In Anglo-Saxon it is called Yþanceaster, and the Latin spelling *th*, as compared with the O.E. *þ*, may point towards Gothonic origin. It is certainly possible that this appearance is misleading, but such an assumption requires that we accept a series of rather questionable hypotheses. First, the Latin spelling must incorrectly have introduced *th* for *t*; secondly, the O.E. form must—accidentally (!)—contain a similar incorrect spelling *þ*; and, finally, the substitution of O.E. *y* for Lat. *o* is difficult to explain (from a hypothetical Lat. form *Othonia or *Othina?). Consequently, we must admit the possible existence of an early Saxon colony, like Marck and Horn on the Gaulish side of the Channel. We must then assume that the construction of the fortress for a time brought the colonists into subjection. A legendary instance is the statement of Nennius that the Jutish invaders of Kent landed on the island of Thanet, whereas those of Hampshire no doubt first took possession of the Isle of Wight. Neither of these islands was protected by fortresses and consequently they lay open to invasion, like Guédel and the Île de Noirmoutier. The Jutish chieftain Hengest in the legend opens the way for the whole conquest. This circumstance may show that the Jutes, though inferior in numbers to the Saxons, had been active among the first invaders; as a matter of fact, their possession of the two islands mentioned seems to indicate that they were the very first to conquer and settle in the land. But the presence of the numerous fortresses in Kent hampered their progress. The decisive blow was struck by the Saxons and Angles who entered Britain at more accessible places.

In order to make out which places were most accessible, we must consider what may be learnt from the distribution of the past and present names of Roman fortifications. The main question is whether the names ending in *-caster*, *-chester*, *-cester* may be taken to supplement the list of Roman coast fortresses given in the *Notitia dignitatum*.

Allen Mawer, *English Place-Name Society*, I, Part 2, p. 14, denies that they may be so taken. He says that *castra* is 'used independently in O.E. to denote a large city or town. It may have this sense in the names of some of the towns and cities famous in Roman times..., but its wide use in place names and the size and character of many of the places, indeed the great proportion of them, show that there it is used of any site whatever on which fortifications of any kind, or the remains of such, were to be found. There is no doubt also that the term is applied to sites in which the defensive works were of pre-Roman origin'.

Cp. also Crawford in *Engl. Place-Name Society*, I, 1, 145: '(*ceaster*) was not, as the older antiquarians believed, a direct inheritance from the Romano-British society. Bede makes this quite clear....But it was also used in the north of England and in Southern Scotland of earthworks of native construction'.

We cannot, however, admit Mawer's view as correct. It may hold good of various smaller *castra*, but in the majority of cases these names occur at important points of the Roman defensive system, viz. (1) along the Litus Saxonicum; (2) along the Picts' Wall; (3) along the great military roads (cp. map, Fig. 9).

Consequently, in order to investigate the beginnings of the Anglo-Saxon invasion, we may use the names ending in *castra* to supplement the *Notitia dignitatum*.

We enumerate first the fortresses of the Litus Saxonicum and some additional *castra*. Some of the names exist in Welsh forms, which is perhaps an indication that the ancient nationality was not immediately lost. The names are: *Brannodunum* (Brancaster, Caer Bran); *Garianonum* (Caister near Yarmouth); *Dommocceastre* (Dunwich); *Camalodunum* (Colchester, Cair Colun); *Othona* (Yþanceaster); *Caster*; *Lon-*

dinium (Lundenceastre, Cair Lundein); *Durobrivae* (Rochester, Cair Graig); *Regulbium* (Reculver); *Rutupiae* (Reptacæstir, Richborough); *Durovernum* (Dorwitceastre, Cantwarabyrig, Cair Ceint); *Dubris* (Dover); *Lemanus portus* (Lymne); *Anderida* (Andredsceaster, Andredes(h)eme, now Pevensey); *Portus Adurni* (on the river Adur). Farther west, beyond the defensive system of the Litus: *Regnum* (Cissanceaster, Chichester); *Porchester* (Cair Peris); *Venta* (Winchester, Cair Guent).[1]

The coast of the Channel west of Portsmouth has only a few *castra*—*Durnovaria* (Dorchester, Durngueir), and *Isca* (Exeter, Cair Legion guar Usic)—but its more remote position seems to have favoured the survival of British nationality for a while (cp. the transition of the river name *Trisantona through *Trihantona into Trent, a relatively late Welsh development).

Finally we notice about sixteen *castra* along the Picts' Wall (Welsh Guaul) and on both sides of it; and even here there are Welsh forms on the North Sea coast: *Penguaul* (Gael. Cenail, O.E. Peneltun, now Wallsend, Nennius, MS K, § 23); *Metcaud* (Farne Island, Nennius, § 63); *Cair Weir* (Wearmouth?, *Myvyrian Archaiology*, 388).

If the above-mentioned regions were protected by *castra*, we can now fairly imagine the process of the invasion.

The Channel was the old high road of the invaders. Here the Saxons and Erules are operating since A.D. 286–289, and we may add the Jutes, for the legendary tradition names them as the *first* invaders of Britain, and this statement is confirmed by their possession of Thanet and the Isle of Wight, outlying unprotected islets which were the first natural strongholds of an invader coming from the south-east. In A.D. 368, according to Ammianus, XXVII, 8, § 7, Theodosius repulses pirates menacing London. Here probably Jutes from the invaders' haunt on Thanet are meant. There may also have been good chance of invasion along the unprotected coast west of Portus Adurni—Sussex, Hampshire, etc.

However, the strong row of fortresses along the 'Saxon coast' from Camalodunum to Portus Adurni largely hampered the progress of the invasion. The main blow was not struck from this side, but farther north; this fact is also stated by Thurlow Leeds, *Archaeology*, X, and accepted by Zachrisson. The invaders seized the opportunity of entering

[1] For Welsh forms see Nennius, ed. Stevenson, Index, s.v. *Cair*.

the long entirely unprotected coast between the 'Saxon coast' and the Picts' Wall. Or rather, East Anglia and a part of Essex may also have lain open, as the fortresses Brannodunum and Garianonum were too isolated to protect this long coast.

The above-mentioned fact appears beyond all doubts from the distribution of inscriptions and from statements in the historical annals.

After 360 Roman inscriptions in Northern Britain become rare, owing to the frequent invasions (cp. Winckelmann, *Geschichte der Angelsachsen*, 15).

In A.D. 365 Ammianus writes, XXVI, 4: 'Picti, Saxonesque et Scotti et Atacotti Britannos aerumnis vexavere continuis'.

In A.D. 391 Pacatius sings, *Panegyr. Theodos.* 5:

> maduerunt Saxone fuso
> Orcades, incaluit Pictorum sanguine Thule.

Claudianus, *De IV. cons. Honorii*, 31, says about Theodosius:

> Illius effectum curis, ne tela timerem
> Scotica, ne Pictum tremerem, ne litore toto
> prospicerem dubiis venturum Saxona ventis.

About A.D. 400 Sidonius Apollinaris sings, *Carm.* VII, l. 88:

> victricia Caesar
> signa Caledonios transvexit adusque Britannos,
> fuderit et quamquam Scotum, et cum Saxone Pictum.

In 429 St Germanus obtains a miraculous victory over the Saxons and Picts near Verulam (St Albans), according to the *Vita Germani* which is regarded as trustworthy by Chadwick, 39. The incident shows that Britain was at that time in the power of the natives as far north as St Albans. But the negative conclusion is equally obvious: the country beyond this point was already lost, at least East Anglia and the north-eastern coast. We may imagine St Germanus' line of defence going from Colchester, Yþanceaster, Dommocceastre through Werlamacæstre to Manchester or Chester.

Our assumption is supported by a Welsh legendary tradition, mentioned by Taylor, *Words and Places*, 212: 'There is a high probability that Maes Garmon near Mold was the scene of the famous Alleluia victory, which was obtained by St Garmon over the Picts'. The battle itself, in spite of Taylor's words, is perhaps rather an imaginary echo of that of St Albans, but the legend still may reflect the historical fact that North-eastern Britain was at the time of St Germanus left defenceless against the Picts who were even able to menace Wales. The amount of devastation in middle Britain appears from the nomenclature, as this region was by the invading Angles called Mercia, 'Woodland'.

Whereas the above evidence concerning the north-east of Britain is only vague and indirect, another Welsh legendary tradition directly deals with the fate of this region. Nennius in § 38 describes a Saxon expedition which precedes the establishment of Hengest in Kent:

'Et dixit Hencgistus ad Guorthigirnum: "Invitabo filium meum cum fratrueli suo..., ut dimicent contra Scottos; et da illis regiones quae sunt in aquilone, juxta murum, qui vocatur Guaul". Et jussit, ut invitaret eos, et invitati sunt Octha et Ebissa cum quadraginta ciulis. At ipsi, cum navigarent contra Pictos, vastaverunt Orcades insulas, et venerunt et occupaverunt regiones plurimas ultra Mare Fre(ne)sicum, usque ad confinium Pictorum.'

As this is the only echo of the conquest of the north in legend, we may assume that in this region the Anglo-Saxon conquest was no such sanguinary war of extinction as in the south. The regions next to the Picts' Wall had probably been devastated and half unpeopled by the Picts before the Saxons and their companions came there. Consequently, there was plenty of ownerless land for fresh settlers. Moreover, the Frisian and German—perhaps also Saxon—mercenaries along the Picts' Wall had already introduced a strong Gothonic element among the population. It is true the Roman garrisons were gradually withdrawn after 383, but, owing to intermarriage with the natives, they may have procreated a semi-Gothonic population which remained to defend the country against the invading Picts and Scots (cp. Wadstein, *Norden och Västeuropa*, 36). As a matter of fact the foreign garrisons have contributed to the nomenclature of North Britain in ancient times: a fort of the Picts' Wall is called Hunnum, denoting a Hunnish garrison.[1] We may thus assume that the borderland population consisted of mixed national elements, and to this population the Saxons, if they entered the country in a peaceful way, would be much more welcome than the hereditary enemies, the Picts and Scots. And the Saxons may really have carried out the pact which they are said to have made with the British king of Kent, to defend the country against those hereditary

[1] *Not. dign. Occ.* XL, 37; Onno, Anon. Ravenn. 437, 15, now Halton Chesters, cp. Haverfield, *County Hist. of Northumberland*, vol. x, Appendix.

enemies. Then they may gradually have absorbed the surviving Celtic natives in much the same way as the descendants of English colonists in later times absorbed the Lowland Scots. That such a process took place may be inferred from the fact that two of the North English kingdoms have British names, viz. Bernicia and Deira. Otherwise, however, the absorption of the natives must have been quick and complete; on the coast between the Picts' Wall and Brancaster all British names of settlements have disappeared, and even in Welsh traditions there are no such additional Welsh names as Caer Bran for Brancaster or Penguaul for Wallsend.

So much for the north-eastern coast of England. In the south-east the development is quite different, as appears both from legends and place names. Till towards 445 the violent attacks of the invaders, supported by their strongholds on Thanet and the Isle of Wight, had not been able to break the resistance of the fortresses along the 'Saxon coast'. But about 445 the catastrophe finally takes place; Kent, Sussex, and Essex are conquered. In spite of great slaughter the Romano-British population of the important towns must have survived, for their names are preserved and London even continues traditions of Roman law.

The distribution of the *castra* and other Romano-British onomastic survivals fairly well coincides with the evidence of history and legend. But the question is how far this collective evidence is also supported by the distribution of early Anglo-Saxon burial places and place names. It must be admitted that the agreement is not complete.

The map drawn by Thurlow Leeds in *Archaeology*, 19, shows a dense collection of Anglo-Saxon burial places and barrows in Northumberland west and south-west of Flamborough Head. It is accompanied by a repetition of the North German river name Swale (Schwale, an affluent of the Lower Elbe and of the Wernitz). On the coast north and south of Flamborough Head there occur besides two streamlets named Skerne, repetitions of the East and West Jutlandic river name Skern (the *sk* instead of Engl. *sh* may be due to the influence of Scandinavian settlers in the Viking Age). This field of Anglo-Saxon settlement corresponds fairly well to the legendary establishment of Octha and Ebissa south of the Picts' Wall. But we might certainly have expected a more intensive and widely extended colonisation in these entirely unprotected regions.

Fairly numerous burial places also cover the coast and the interior of East Anglia and the northern part of Essex. Repetitions of Holsteinic river names occur: Wensum in East Anglia, Stour between East Anglia and Essex. A rather early conquest of this region might beforehand be expected, as its projecting coast has an exposed position and was insufficiently protected by the fortresses Brannodunum and Garianonum. We have seen above that in 429 the invaders had advanced as far south of East Anglia as St Albans.

We then enter Kent where we are struck by the enormously high number of Anglo-Saxon burial places; no other county is so completely covered by them. Correspondingly, there occur three repetitions of river names from Holstein or thereabout: Swale, Wantsumu, and Stour, all facing Hengest's legendary stronghold, the islet of Thanet. The intensity of the settlement consequently is greater than in Northumberland, although the latter region was colonised earlier according to the legend reported by Nennius.

Between Kent and Sussex there is a gap entirely bare of ancient Anglo-Saxon burial places. This fact agrees with the *Saxon Chronicle* according to which the south-western part of the 'Litus Saxonicum' was unconquered as late as 491.

In Sussex there is a narrow, but very dense collection of burial places. The evidence of the *Saxon Chronicle* again agrees, as Sussex was conquered next after Kent.

The Isle of Wight, finally, has three burial places. A repetition of a Holsteinic river name occurs on the opposite coast, Stour. The number of burial places is below the rate of Kent, though not quite low in relation to the area of the island. We might certainly beforehand have expected a higher figure, because the island had an exposed position and was not protected by fortresses.

Remarkably enough, a certain midland or rather western region of England is more densely covered by Anglo-Saxon burial places than the south coasts and even parts of the east coast. It is the area between the Trent, Severn and the Upper Thames. Again here there occur two repetitions of the Holsteinic river name Stör, Stour. Thurlow Leeds in *History*, x, points out that the settlement has chiefly advanced from East Anglia along the military road called the Icknield Way, O.E. Icenan hild-wæg.[1] From this distribution it appears that the higher or lower number of burial places gives no absolute indication as to the chrono-

[1] 'Military road of the Iceni'? The road starts from the region of the ancient British tribe called Iceni.

logical sequence of the settlement: for before settling in the middle or west of England the Anglo-Saxon invaders must undoubtedly have passed those eastern districts which they left bare or almost bare of burial places.

Beside archaeology and river names also some ancient types of names of settlement must be examined. Seebohm in *The English Village Community*, 256–257, has drawn maps representing the percentage of local names ending in *-ham* and in *-ing* without further suffix, according to the *Domesday Book* (cp. Figs. 7 and 8 of the present work). This sort of evidence partly confirms, partly disagrees with that of archaeology.

The distribution of the names ending in *-ing* agrees remarkably well with that of the burial places in South-eastern England. Kent has the highest percentage (4); then follow Surrey and Essex (3); then Sussex (2 ?, the figure is not readable); Norfolk (2); Suffolk ($1\frac{2}{3}$); Cambridge, Hertford, Berks (all 2). The latter three counties correspond to the Icknield Way with its dense collection of burial places. On the other hand, there is little correspondence with the archaeological map in Western and Northern England. The Isle of Wight is blank.

Again, the distribution of *-ham* differs essentially from that of *-ing* in the south-east. Here Essex shows the highest percentage, 30. Then follow Suffolk and Norfolk with 18 and 16 respectively as a second group. The third group is represented by Surrey with 13, Sussex with 12, Cambridge and Kent with 10—a rather low position of Kent, only one-third of the figure of Essex. The western and northern counties show lower figures, partly corresponding to the distribution of *-ing*. The Isle of Wight again is blank.

It is not easy to account for the disagreement of the various sorts of evidence. As regards East Anglia and Essex, we are inclined to prefer the evidence of the names ending in *-ham*. The badly protected coast of East Anglia naturally must have been conquered earlier than the well-protected coast of Kent. We also believe that the gradual decline of *-ham* and *-ing* towards the west is easier to understand than the remarkably high percentage of Anglo-Saxon burial places in Western England. On the other hand, it is extraordinary that the Isle of Wight is quite blank and that there is such a low percentage of ancient Anglo-Saxon place names in Northumberland which was early conquered according to both history, legend, and archaeology. Perhaps we may assume that it is due to devastations during the Viking Age. We may here refer to

Taylor's map, *Settlements of the Celts, Saxons, Danes and Norwegians in the British Isles* (*Words and Places*), which is certainly not very trustworthy, but may still somehow give an idea of the distribution of national elements. According to his map, Scandinavian place names are predominant along the whole coast from the river Tees to the Wash, and this fact would mean to say that the percentage of Anglo-Saxon nomenclature has been correspondingly reduced. Cp. Ekwall, *Engl. Place-Names in -ing* (*Skr. utg. av Kgl. Hum. Vetenskaps-Samfundet i Lund*, VI, 116): 'There is every reason to believe that Old Engl. names have been replaced on a large scale by Scandinavian ones'; p. 117: 'The comparatively small number of *-ings* may be due to the strong Scand. influence'. In such a way we may perhaps account for the low figures for *-ing* and *-ham* in the north of England. But it must be left to future researches to examine how the obscure points may be made clear.

To conclude this paragraph, we may shortly point out how Britain disappeared from the southern horizon. After the Roman legions had been withdrawn, first in 383 from North Britain, subsequently also from South Britain, the island and its population were rapidly forgotten. Though Belisarius offered it to the Goths in 537 as an Imperial dominion (!), Procopius, who relates the story in his *Bell. Goth.* II, 28, has only dim and fabulous ideas of this once flourishing province of his own state (cp. § 225).

In the paragraphs to follow, we shall regard the progress of the conquest in the single parts of England.

Lit. Stenton, *Engl. Place-Name Soc.* I, 2, 50 seq. (on names ending in *-ingas*); Mawer, *Problems of Place-Name Study*, p. 113 seq. (on *-ing*, *-ingham*, etc., with lit.); Ekwall, *Engl. Place-Name Soc.* I, 2, 55 (*The Scandinavian Element*); Smith, *ibid.* V (*The Place-Names of North Riding of Yorkshire*).

§ 220. The Conquest of Kent.

If the legend represents Kent as the first district attacked by the invaders, it is true in so far as the island of Thanet, like the Isle of Wight, is one of those outlying places which became their natural strongholds. But the unprotected coasts north of the Wash must have succumbed much earlier than the mainland of Kent, as we may infer also from the legend of the expedition of Ebissa and Octha (cp. § 219). Kent was the last station of the Roman legions before leaving Britain, and its strong row of fortresses must for a while have barred the entrance into the interior. As to the date of the conquest, we can hardly make use of Bede's chronology and the unreliable entries of the *Saxon Chronicle.* But a trustworthy date is given by the *Vita Germani*, according to which St Germanus obtained a miraculous victory over the Saxons and Picts near Verulam (St Albans) in 429 (p. 17) and made a second visit to Britain about 440. But immediately after, the *Chronica Gallica* ad an. 442 says: 'Brittanniae usque ad hoc tempus variis cladibus eventibusque (vex)atae in dicionem Saxonum rediguntur'. Gildas says that even after that time the Britons obtained reinforcements from Rome, but in 446 they asked in vain. Bede, I, 13, quotes their letter to Aëtius, dated 446.

According to Bede, I, 15, the Jutish conqueror of Kent, Hengest, first came as a mercenary at the invitation of the British King Vortigern and, according to Nennius, § 31, Hengest's place of resort was the island of Thanet. There is no reason to doubt these traditions; Vortigern, O.E. Wyrtgeorn, is a true British name containing the element *tigern*- 'chieftain', and Thanet was a natural landing-place and protected by no fortress. Moreover, that the invasion started from this corner is shown by the three river names Stour, Swale, and Wantsum, which are repetitions of names found in Holstein, viz. Stör, Schwale, and Wanse. At the same time, they betray that the majority of Hengest's followers were not Jutes, but Saxons from Holstein (cp. 238).

Ekwall says, *Engl. Place-Names in -ing*, p. 20: 'Names in -ing are... by far most frequent in Kent'. Cp. p. 107 (on *-ing*), p. 152 (on *-ingham*).

Nennius and the *Saxon Chronicle* mention several battlefields which may in part be fictitious, but which in part also originate from old traditions. In the first battle, according to Nennius, § 43 seq., Hengest is driven back to Thanet. The second takes place on the river Derguentid, presumably the Darent; the third on Rit Hergabail, 'the ford of the horses', where Hengest's brother Horsa is killed; the fourth is fought near the Lapis Tituli on the Gaulish Sea, where the natives are victorious.

After the final conquest, there must still have remained a considerable number of Britons in the towns, for the British nomenclature still survives, more or less undisturbed, and there appear various double or triple names which seem to betray the existence of a bilingual population.

The first stronghold of Hengest preserves the British name Thanet and has besides the name Ruoihin (Nennius, § 43). The latter name also appears in later times as Ruym (cp. Palgrave, *Rise and Progress of the English Commonwealth*, I, 326, II, 450, 869 (*Coll. Hist. Works*, VI–VII)).[1]

Rutupiae or Ritupis is by the Saxons called Reptacæstir. Zachrisson is inclined to look upon this name as a Kentish form with *e* for *y*, derived from a Romano-British Rutupis (> *Rypta-, Repta-). As has been shown by Prof. Ritter and Dr Wallenberg, Kentish *e* for *y* may date back to the eighth century (cp. *Vermischte Beiträge*, p. 204, resp. p. 56). The modern form Richborough (c. 1500) is due to an earlier Retteburg (i.e. Repta + *burh* instead of *-ceaster*), Retesbrough, with the development of *-ets* to *-ich* or so-called inner sound substitution.

Duróbrivae becomes Hrofireui (A.D. 604), whence the enlarged Saxon form Hrofe(s)ceaster, now Rochester. An additional Welsh name is Caer Graig.

Regulbium, now Reculver.

Dubris, now Dover.

Lemanis, now Lymne.

The name Anderida, in the south of Kent, still survived in Saxon times as Andredesceaster or Andredes(h)eme; the neighbouring wood on the border of Kent and Sussex was called Andredesleag.

The name of the Kentish capital Durovernum survived for a time as Dorwitceastre (read *Dorwicceastre). Its additional name Cantwara-byrig, Canterbury, corresponds to the Welsh Cair Ceint. According to Bede, I, 26, a church near Canterbury was found in a serviceable state in A.D. 595, i.e. some 150 years after the conquest; its preservation seems to indicate that it had been continuously used by the inhabitants.[2]

§ 221. The Conquest of Hampshire and Sussex.

The geographical position of the Isle of Wight might *a priori* lead to the conclusion that it had been conquered as early as other outlying islands, such as Guédel, l'Île de Noirmoutier, and Thanet. However, according to the archaeological evidence the conquest here is later (cp. Leeds, *The Archaeology of the Anglo-Saxon Settlements*, 51, Zachrisson,

[1] Palgrave in the original edition cites a charter of A.D. 694, but, according to the note in the *Coll. Works*, p. 869, Ruym is not found in the printed editions of that charter (Kemble, *Cod. dipl.* No. XXXVII, and Birch, *Cartular. Saxon.* No. 86); 'it would appear to have been added by the compiler of the *Chronologia* here cited from Twysden under the name of W. Thorn'.

[2] Prof. Phillips maintains that a non-Saxon racial type, with dark hair and low stature, is frequent in Kent, cp. Grant Allen, *Anglo-Saxon Britain*, 57.

Romans, Kelts, and Saxons, 19, and the map designed by Leeds, reproduced as Fig. 7). But in other respects the Isle of Wight seems to stand in the same relation to the opposite coast of Hampshire as the island of Thanet to that of Kent. In both places the island, out of reach of the fortresses of the coast defence, serves as a stronghold for the invaders. In both places the leading chieftains are Jutes. In both places they mark their place of landing by introducing from Holstein the name of the river Stör (Stour in Kent and Dorset), an indication that the majority of the followers were Saxons. Further progress may have been rather slow, as the British element seems to have survived for a considerable time in the neighbouring region of Dorset, the country of the *Durnovarii, O.E. Dornwære, and also in Wiltshire (cp. the note on the river name Trent, p. 258, and the statements of Zachrisson cited on p. 253).

Ekwall says, *Engl. Place-Names in -ing*, p. 20: 'Names in *-ing* are... by far most frequent in Kent. It is a curious fact that Southern Hants has fairly many examples; this reminds us of the fact that the district was first taken possession of by Jutes'. On *-ing* in Sussex, *ibid.* p. 109. Cp. Mawer-Stenton, *Engl. Place-Name Society, Sussex.*

As to the South Saxons the *Saxon Chronicle* contains one entry which may perhaps be reliable: 'A.D. 491. This year Ælla...besieged Andredesceaster, and slew all that dwelt therein, so that not a single Briton was there left'. The complete absorption of the Britons is confirmed by the fact that the name Anderida or Andredesceaster has been replaced by Pevensey. This relatively late date for the conquest would agree with the evidence of the survival of the British or Roman language for a considerable time in Kent, and also with the evidence of the archaeological finds in Sussex, the earliest of which date from about A.D. 500. But we dare not put much confidence in this isolated entry.

It is certain that a whole series of entries in the *Chronicle* concerning the conquest of the south coast are fictitious (see Zachrisson, *l.c.* 18, cp. Taylor, *Words and Places*, 208). Cymen (A.D. 477), who comes to land at Cymenesora, may have been postulated from Cumenes hora mentioned in the boundaries of Wittering in Sussex (Birch, *Cartular. Saxon.* 64). His brother Wlencing may represent Lancing, Sussex, transliterated by the Normans because it was thought to contain the common continental name Lanzo. The third brother, Cissa, whose name is probably Celtic, seems to originate from Cissanceaster, Chichester. Port, A.D. 501, has been coined from Portus Magnus, Portsmouth, and his companion Mægla may also originate from the Latin name of this harbour. The British King Natanleod, who falls at Natanleog A.D. 508, is the eponymous hero of this place, now Netley. Wihtgar, who is buried in Wihtgara-byrg A.D. 544, seems to embody the toponymic of the Isle of Wight. If we pay attention to the dates, we shall notice that they form a regular series running from A.D. 477 to A.D. 544, while the places mentioned are situated quite as regularly on a line from the east to the west. Such criteria betray the falsification. The West Saxon King Cerdic operating with Wihtgar is also fictitious, as the name is Celtic (cp. Chadwick, 30).[1]

§ 222. The Conquest of Essex, East Anglia, Wessex and the North of England.

Nennius, § 38, records the expedition of Ebissa and Octha to the regions next to the Picts' Wall (cp. § 219). Otherwise, there are no legendary records of the first invasion.

There are the same repetitions of river names from Holstein as in Kent, only dispersed over a larger area: Stour in Essex, Swale in Northumberland, Wensum in East Anglia (cp. Wansbeck in Northumberland). They seem to mark the landing-places of the invaders and to show that the Saxon element was predominant, even in Anglian states. Although these conclusions are only hypothetic, they are at least sufficiently well-grounded to merit discussion.

For the conquest of the middle and north of England we have, besides these names, only the archaeological finds to go upon, and they prove that settlements were founded along the Icknield Way and along the rivers in Suffolk and Cambridge at quite an early date (cp. the map designed by Leeds, reproduced as Fig. 7).

According to Gildas (ed. Williams, I, 60), the progress of the Saxons into the interior of England was stopped for 44 years through the victory won by the Britons at Mons Badonicus. This statement agrees with the traditions of the invaders in so far as the *Saxon Chronicle* records no places conquered from the Britons in the entries from 514 to 552; there are even no forged conquests.

The following entries concern the West Saxons.

[1] According to Prof. Phillips, the racial type of Sussex is purely Saxon, cp. Grant Allen, *Anglo-Saxon Britain*, 57.

552. Cynric fought against the Britons at a place which is called Searobyrig and put the Britons to flight.

556. Cynric and Ceawlin fought against the Britons at Beranburg.

571. Cuthwulf fought against the Britons at Bedcanford and captured four villages, Lygeanburg, Aegelesburg, Bænesingtun and Egonesham.

577. Cuthwine and Ceawlin fought against the Britons and slew three kings, Coinmail, Condidan, and Farinmail, at a place which is called Deorham; and they captured three cities, Gleawanceaster, Cirenceaster and Bathanceaster.

587. Cutha is slain by the Britons at Fethanleag.

Chadwick, 31, says about the battles at Searobyrig (Sorbiodunum, Salisbury) and Beranburg (Barbury): 'With the latter year (552) there begins a new series of entries which differs from the preceding one through the entire absence of the etymological element. The first two entries of the new series record battles at Salisbury and Beranburg. The only objection that can be brought against them is that they probably fall within Gildas' forty-four years of peace'.

Zachrisson says on p. 20: 'No...serious doubts (have) been expressed concerning the fight that took place at Barbury Camp near Marlborough. We are hardly justified in doubting the evidence of the *Chronicle* on the capture in the year 571 of the towns of Limbury, Bedf., Aylesbury in Buckinghamshire, and Bensington and Eynsham in Oxfordshire....It seems to be generally accepted that the account of the capture of Gloucester, Cirencester and Bath after the decisive victory at Dyrham, a village in Gloucestershire about ten miles north of Bath, is a historical fact'.

Zachrisson only rejects the statement of the *Chronicle* that the invading West Saxons came from the south, from Hampshire. According to him, they came from the east, following the valley of the Thames. However, what is wrong regarding the West Saxons as a nation seems to be true if we limit the statement to the founder of the West Saxon dynasty personally. Cynric, as we know from his genealogy, was a descendant of Fréawine, i.e. the South Jutlandic earl Frovin (Saxo). Consequently, he may have come to Britain with the Jutes who settled on the Isle of Wight and in Hampshire. Moreover, the *Saxon Chronicle*, ad an. 514 and 534, in set terms states that the 'West Saxons', i.e. Cynric and his men came to Britain together with his nephew Stuf who became prince of the Isle of Wight. When Cynric is—erroneously—made the son of a king with the

British name Cerdic, we may assume that the invader has become mercenary of the natives in Dorset, as the Jute Hengest in Kent, before he obtained the royal dignity among the hitherto republican West Saxons.

Thurlow Leeds, *History*, x, 105, maintains that 'it is archaeologically certain that the district immediately south and west of Oxford was held by the Saxons at least three-quarters of a century before the alleged conquest of these places in the *Chronicle*, but...it is difficult to obtain safe dates for *permanent* settlements from archaeological evidence' (cp. Zachrisson, 15).

The absorption of the conquered Britons was accomplished more or less quickly in the different parts of England.

As we mentioned in § 219, the Anglo-Saxon colonisation of North-eastern England may already have begun during the time of Roman rule. Along the coast the British names of towns have entirely disappeared, and the kingdoms with the British names Deira and Bernicia may have been practically Saxonised before the Romans gave up their dominion over Southern Britain.

A quick absorption of the natives also took place in Essex and East Anglia. According to Prof. Phillips, Essex shares the purely Saxon racial type with Sussex (cp. Grant Allen, *Anglo-Saxon Britain*, 57). And, after the great victory at Bedford in 571, the Britons must have been rapidly absorbed, since the ancient names of all the conquered villages have disappeared.

The conquest in the year 577 was less complete: Gleva, Corinium survive as Gloucester and Cirencester. In Dorcinium, the ancient Dorchester, the Christian population was probably spared, as the town became later the see of a bishop. However, the defeat of 577 was a great catastrophe to the Britons in another sense, for as a result of it the Britons in Wales were cut off from their countrymen in Cornwall.

Lit. Chadwick, ch. II; W. Stevenson, *The Beginnings of Wessex* (*Engl. Hist. Review*, 1899, 32); E. Thurlow Leeds, *The West Saxon Invasion and the Icknield Way* (*History*, x, 1925, 97); Zachrisson, *Romans, Kelts, and Saxons in Ancient Britain* (*Skrifter utg. av Kgl. Human. Vetenskaps-Samfundet i Uppsala*, XXIV, 12, 3 seq.); Oman, *England before the Norman Conquest*; Ekwall, *Engl. Place-Names in -ing*, pp. 108, 152 (on Essex), pp. 110, 152 (on Wessex), p. 153 (on East Anglia); *Engl. Place-Name Society*, II, 2. Mawer and Stenton, *Buckinghamshire*; 3. *Bedfordshire*; 4. *Worcester*; 5. Smith, *North Riding, Yorks.*; 8-9, Gover, Mawer, Stenton, *Devon*.

§ 223. Later Conquests from the Celts.

Having in the preceding paragraphs fully investigated the important, but obscure, beginnings of Anglo-Saxon history, we shall select only some important incidents of the later development for which there is more authority and which is sufficiently well known in advance.

A North British King Urbgen advances to the North Sea, besieging the Northumbrian King Theodric (572–579) on the island of Lindisfarne (Nennius, § 63).

In A.D. 603 the invading Scotch King Æðan is repulsed by the Northumbrian King Æthelfrid at Dægsanstan (Bede, I, 34). Bede says that Æthelfrid 'conquered more territories from the Britons than did any other king, either making them tributary or driving the inhabitants completely out, and planting English in their places'. In 607 he storms the fortress of Chester on the Irish Sea, the Castra legionum or Caerleon; his successor Edwin (616–633) for a time even subjugates the islands of Anglesey and Man (Bede, II, 5).

After advancing to the western seas in 577 and 607 the invaders had split up the Britons into three sections: (1) the kingdom of Strathclyde or Stræþcled-wealas, from the Clyde to Mersey, i.e. South-west Scotland and Cumberland; (2) Wales; (3) Cornwall. Yet the struggle for supremacy in North England still went on.

In 633 the North British King Cadguallon or Cædwalla kills Edwin and conquers Northumberland, assisted by the Mercian King Penda. Cadguallon tries to exterminate the Anglo-Saxons; but he is slain one year after (cp. Bede, II, 20). This is the last time that the Welsh penetrate to the North Sea.

Gradually, the Britons and Picts in Southern Scotland are subjugated by the Northumbrians whose King Ecgfrid in 684 even raids Ireland. But next year he is totally defeated in Forfarshire by the Picts. The English power begins 'to waver and lose ground', says Bede, IV, 20; the Picts regain their lost territories south of the Forth, and even some of the North Britons become their own masters for about forty-six years.

About 780 King Offa of Mercia conquers the region of Pengwern west of the Severn and builds his famous frontier wall against Wales, Offa's Dike. Strathclyde and Cumberland are subjugated in the first half of the tenth century. In 946 the English King Edmund grants them to King Malcolm of Scotland as a fief; though parts of a Celtic state, these regions are soon denationalised, owing to immigration of Anglo-Saxons and Norwegians. Even the Anglo-Saxon colonies on the east coast north of the river Tweed become Scotch provinces, but they finally cause the whole of Scotland south of the Forth and Clyde to become Anglicised.

The Britons of Devonshire are also gradually absorbed, and in Cornwall their language dies out in the eighteenth century. Only Wales remains Welsh, even after the loss of independence in 1294.

Lit. **Oman,** *England before the Norman Conquest*; **Winkelmann,** *Geschichte der Angelsachsen*; **Hodgkin,** *The History of England...to the Norman Conquest.*

§ 224. Collective Anglo-Saxon Development.

Attempts at uniting all Anglo-Saxons under the rule of a 'Bretwalda' were repeatedly made by kings of various tribes, enumerated by Bede, II, 5. The first Bretwaldas were: Ælli, South Saxon; Ceawlin, West Saxon; Æthelbert, Jute; Redwald, East Anglian; Edwin, Oswald and Oswin, Northumbrians. A strong Anglian supremacy was established by the Mercian Offa, but it was reserved to the West Saxon Egbert to extend his sway over all Anglo-Saxon states without exception, in A.D. 829.

Christianity was introduced among the Jutes of Kent during the reign of Æthelbert, in A.D. 595 (cp. Bede, I, 25), perhaps its acceptance was rendered more easy by surviving British Christians (cp. § 220). The next centre lay among the Northumbrian Angles whose King Edwin was the son-in-law of Æthelbert. The archbishopric of York was established in 627 (Bede, II, 14). York probably still contained Christian inhabitants, to whom it owed the preservation of its surname of 'municipium' (Bede, III, 1, cp. § 218).

The mission in Northumberland was promoted by colonies of Irish monks, such as the one at Lindisfarne (cp. Bede, III, 3). Young Anglian priests after the seventh century studied in Ireland (*ibid.* 27). Thus the Anglian see soon rivalled Canterbury and quite outstripped it as regards fighting the obstinate Saxon paganism. The East Saxons were converted between 653 and 673 (Bede, III, 22, 30); the South Saxons and Wihtwære last in 681 (*ibid.* IV, 13, 16). Their deeply inrooted paganism may have been due to the complete extinction of the British population in Sussex and Essex (cp. §§ 221, 222), but was also bound up with the Saxon racial character.

After the close of the eighth century England became a prey to Scandinavian Vikings. The area north-east of a line from London to Chester was repeatedly overrun and settled by them and obtained the name of Dena-lagu, 'the Danes' Law'. From 1013 till 1042 the Danes governed England. Then the national English kingdom revived but only to be ruined in 1066 by the Normans who for centuries kept English culture in bondage to the French tongue.

Though under foreign dominion the English nationality was constantly advancing among the Celts, partly through political conquests, partly because it was more open to the influence of other civilisations. The Saxons had certainly not utilised their advantageous position on the south coast during the times of the Christian mission, leaving the lead to the Angles and Irish. But after the Normans had linked together both shores of the Channel the normal route by which European civilisation travelled to Britain was established. Henceforth the united Anglo-Saxons were the first to receive civilisation from the Continent and they could pass it on to the Celts. Norman military strategy especially assisted the spreading of English civilisation by means of conquest. The Norwegians also served as pioneers, for their colonies on the Orkneys, Shetlands, the Isle of Man, and in Cumberland, Ireland, and Caithness, have all been inherited by the English nationality.

The Normans began the conquest of Ireland in 1141: it was completed by the victory of the English on the river Boyne in 1688. Scotland and the Isle of Man were the only Celtic states which were not united with England by force of conquest. The Celts had even become the political masters of the Anglo-Saxon settlements between the Tweed and Edinburgh; but it was the English civilisation and not the Celtic, which profited by this union.

During the Middle Ages, Cymric died out in Cumberland, Gaelic in Southern Scotland; later, Gaelic on the east coast as far north as Aberdeen; Cromwell ejected the Irish Catholics from large parts of Ulster, replacing them by English-speaking protestants from Scotland. In the eighteenth century Cornish died out, in the nineteenth Irish in the larger part of Ireland. Since the seventeenth and eighteenth centuries English has been spreading in overseas countries, North America, South Africa, and Australia. Thus the Anglo-Saxons have become the most widespread nationality in the world.

Otto Jespersen says (*Growth and Structure of the English Language*, §249): 'Only two or three centuries ago, English was spoken by so few people that no one could dream of its ever becoming a world language....

In 1714 Veneroni published an Imperial Dictionary of the four chief languages of Europe, that is, Italian, French, German, and Latin'. Jespersen quotes various authors who state the small reach of the English tongue, viz. Richard Mulcester (1585), Florio, Ancillon, le Clerc (1718), and Shakespeare (*Merchant of Venice*, I, 2, 72).

In § 251, Jespersen illustrates the growing expansion of English, as shown by figures which represent the number of millions of people speaking each of the languages enumerated. (The numbers given are necessarily approximate only, especially for the older periods. Where the authorities disagree, Jespersen gives the lowest and in parentheses the highest figure.)

Year	English	German	Russian	French	Spanish	Italian
1500	4 (5)	10	3	10 (12)	8½	9½
1600	6	10	3	14	8½	9½
1700	8½	10	3 (15)	20	8½	9½ (11)
1800	20 (40)	30 (33)	25 (31)	27 (31)	26	14 (15)
1900	116 (123)	75 (80)	70 (85)	45 (52)	44 (58)	34 (54)

In 1918 the number of people speaking English is by Jespersen (*Salmonsens Konvers. Lex.*) estimated to be 160 millions. According to *The Publishers' Weekly* of 24 November 1921 the number would be 170 millions. The distribution is represented thus:

Great Britain	42,767,530
Ireland (1925)	4,052,886
Canada	8,835,000
South Africa (**Europeans**)	1,521,635
Australia	5,426,000
New Zealand	1,218,270
India (**Europeans**)	320,000
U.S.A.	105,683,000

Prof. Nelson in a wireless lecture lately calculated the Englishmen, Scots, Australians, etc., to be 67 millions, and the citizens of U.S.A. to be 120 millions; total: c. 190 millions.

The entire population of the states with English as the official language is about 540 millions.

Among the people using the English language are about 20 millions of negroes and mulattoes. 'The "worst English in the world" is said to be spoken by the Gullah negroes of the Georgia and Carolina coasts and islands....The dialects spoken by foreign populations have received attention by scholars, but more should be given them. To be taken into account are the French-Creole of Louisiana, French-Canadian, Spanish-Mexican of the south-west, Italian-English dialects, German, Yiddish, Swedish-, Norwegian-, and Danish-American, Jersey and Pennsylvania Dutch, Slavic-English and other hybrid tongues. The Chinook or trade jargon of the Pacific North-west (was) once widely used by Indian tribes and by the white men with whom they traded,...but it now has no utilitarian purpose and is fast dying out' (Louise Pond in *Encycl. Brit.* s.v. *English Language*).

In China the so-called 'Pidgin-English' is used as a means of communication between various populations that do not understand each others' idioms.

Lit. L. Tesnière, *Statistique des langues de l'Europe*, 328 seq. (in Ant. Meillet, *Les langues dans l'Europe nouvelle*, 2nd ed.); Cohen and Ant. Meillet, *Les langues du monde*; Meyer, *Indogerm. Forsch.* XII, 84; Otto Will, *Die Tauglichkeit und die Aussichten der englischen Sprache als Weltsprache*; Freeman, *The Norman Conquest*; Seeley, *Expansion of England*; Lucas, *Beginnings of English Overseas Enterprise*; Beer, *Old Colonial System*; Somervell, *The British Empire*; Williamson, *British Colonial Enterprise* 1488–1588; *idem*, *History of British Expansion*; Egerton, *Short History of British Colonial Policy*; *idem*, *British Colonial Policy in the Twentieth Century*; Keith, *Self-governing Dominions*; Edmundson, *Anglo-Dutch Rivalry*; Zachrisson, *Anglic, an International Language*.

§ 225. Legendary Traditions.

In Old Gothonic legends the Saxons play no prominent part.

The eponymous Saxi Sunnmanna gramr, 'Saxon, prince of the South-men' (*Goðrúnarkviða*, III, str. 6), rather represents the German Saxons than their English namesakes.

The genesis of the Saxon name is a favourite theme both in Britain and on the Continent. The invaders arrange a negotiation, and on the signal: 'Nimed eure saxes!'—'Take your saxes!'—treacherously murder the unsuspecting natives. Hence the murderers are called Saxons (Nennius, § 46; Widukind, I, 6 and 7). It is a poetical fable, but not far from real life, for a German-Saxon margrave Gero in the tenth century used exactly the same stratagem against the Slavs.

The tribe of Hugas, probably the Chauchi, appear in the legend of Hygelác's fatal struggle against the Franks and Frisians, A.D. 526 (*Beowulf*, l. 2354, 2502, 2914).

Procopius, *Bell. Goth.* IV, 20, records a curious ethnic myth from Britain. A high wall, he says, divides the eastern and western parts of the island. The parts east of the wall are inhabited by ordinary human beings, whereas the parts west of it are possessed by monsters and devils. The myth obviously reflects the hatred of the Anglo-Saxon invaders for the conquered natives who are obstinately and fervently trying to reconquer the lost country. The idea of a wall running north and south throughout England is of course fictitious, but we may perhaps trace it back to a historical origin. The Picts' Wall, running from the eastern to the western sea, was originally built to protect the civilised Roman Britons against the wild barbarian Picts and Scots. These detested enemies chiefly came from the north, but a large number also came from the west, i.e. from Ireland and Galloway. The defenders of the Picts' Wall originally were Romans, Britons, and Frisian and German mercenaries. After the Romans had given up North Britain, they would have been replaced by Saxons and Angles, and the open eastern coast would have become entirely Saxonised (cp. § 219). Thus the Anglo-Saxons might have inherited the tales of the natives defying and cursing the invading 'devils' from the north and west. And gradually the Pictish and Celtic *invaders* would have been confused with the Celtic *natives* defending the western parts of Britain against the Anglo-Saxon invaders. This way of accounting for the origin of the fable is quite natural and it helps in an interesting way to explain the origin of ethnic myths (cp. vol. I, §§ 4, 44).

Numerous details are recorded in local Saxon traditions dealing with the conquest of Britain (cp. pp. 265, 269).

The most famous tale of Saxon raiders appears in the *Nibelungenlied* (ch. IV). Here the Frankish hero Sigfrid repulses the allied Saxons and Danes who menace the states of King Gunther of Burgundy. This reflects the victories won by the armies of the Frankish King Sigebert against the allied Saxons and Danes in Friesland about 565, and against the Saxons who attack the states of King Gunthram of Burgundy in 572. The co-operation with the Danes seems to indicate that the tale belongs to the non-German Saxons rather than to those Germans who adopted the Saxon name.

Lit. Chambers, *Widsith*; Chadwick, *The Heroic Age*; Schütte, *Journ. Engl. and Germ. Phil.* xx, 319; Stenton, *Engl. Place-Name Society*, I, 1, 186 (on the survival of heroic names); Taylor, *Words and Places*, 208 seq. (*Historic sites, Hengist and Horsa, Anglian Kings*, etc.).

C. §§ 226–235. *THE FRISIAN BRANCH*[1]

§ 226. Name.

O.Fris. Frisa, Fresa; North Fris. Frasche; O.E. Frísan, Frýsan, Frésan; O.H.G. Frieson; M.Dutch Vriesen; Dutch Friezen, Vriezen; O.N. Frísir; Lat. Frisii (Pliny, Tacitus, first century A.D.), Frisei (*CIL.* VI, 3230), Frisiones (*CIL.* VII, 415); M.Lat. Frisones, Fresones (the form with *e* is not exemplified in classical sources); Gr. Φρίσιοι (Ptolemy, second century A.D.), Φρείσιοι (Dio Cassius, third century), Φρίσσονες (Procopius, sixth century). Country: Fris. Fryslan; North Fris. Fraschlönj. Region: O.G. Fresiono-feld. Place name: O.L.G. Fresiono-wic; Germ. Friesenheim; Friesen-strasse (Hildesheim, Strassburg); M.Lat. Frisione-curtis, Fr. Fri-court (near Amiens). Personal name: O.G. Friso, Freso, Fres-ger, Fris-bolt; Dan. noble family Frijs. Obscure; perhaps derived from the 'frisure' (cp. O.Fris. *frisle, fresle* 'frizzle', O.E. *frise* 'comatus', Engl. *frizz* 'to curl'). Zachrisson suggests 'those who live on the sea-border' (cp. Celt. Remi < **preim-*, and Lat. *primus*).

Lit. Schönfeld, s.v. (with lit.); Förstemann, s.v.; Much, *Stammeskunde*, 85; *idem*, in Hoops, s.v.; Zachrisson, *Studier tillägnade Ax. Kock*, 492; Löwenthal, *Beiträge*, XLV, 255; Sverdrup, *Festskr. Falk*, 326 seq.

§ 227. Sub-divisions.

A. Ancient division.

1. Lat. Frisii majores (Tac. *Germ.* 34), in the Dutch province of Friesland, identical with the mediaeval Middle and Eastern Frisians.

2 (*a*) and (*b*). Lat. Frisii minores (Tac. *ibid.*), the Lat. Frisiavones (Pliny, IV, 101). Cp. the matres, Lat. *Frisavae (*CIL.* XIII, 106, Trisavis). The name contains the suffix *-av* (cp. Batavi, Chamavi). Home: between Helinius and Flevus, Pliny, *l.c.*, i.e. between Waal and Vlie; this is the mediaeval West Frisian territory in North Holland.

Lit. Schönfeld, s.v. (with lit.); Förstemann, s.v.; Much in Hoops, s.v.; Kauffmann, I, 404.

B. Mediaeval division.

1. Middle Frisians, the ancient Frisii majores; in the Middle Ages called rather East Frisians; the modern inaccurate term West Frisians (!) should be avoided. Area: Oostfriesland, Oosterland, M.Lat. Frisia orien-

[1] The notes on literature in this section are chiefly supplied by Dr Schönfeld.

talis, now the province of Friesland; according to the *Lex Frisionum* situated 'inter Laubachi et Flevum', i.e. between Lauwers and Vlie. It embraces three districts:

(*a*) O.Fris. Wistr-achia, 'the Western Waterland', Dutch Westergoo.

(*b*) O.Fris. Auster-achia; Lat. Auster-auia (Pliny, IV, 97 and XXXVII, 42, an island), 'the Eastern Waterland', Dutch Oostergoo.

(*c*) O.Fris. Sutr-achi, 'the Southern Waterland'.

Lit. Buitenrust Hettema, *Nom. geogr. Neerlandica*, IV, 16.

2. West Frisians or Westlingi, the ancient Frisii minores or Frisiavones, in Frisia occidentalis. The north-eastern part of North Holland is still called West Friesland. The *Lex Frisionum* exaggerates the dimensions: 'inter Flehi et Sincfalam', i.e. between Vlie and Zwin (old name of a channel in Zeeuws Vlaanderen). The language is now Dutch.

3. East Frisians, according to the *Lex Frisionum* 'inter Laubachi et Wisaram', i.e. between Lauwers and Weser. The language is now Low Saxon, except in Saterland. There are about ten districts. We enumerate the populations with remarkable toponymics or with codes of law in the local dialect, etc.

(*a*) 'Humsters' in Hummerze, O.L. Hugmerke, now Humsterland, an old borderland of the Hugas or Chauchi minores (cp. § 215, A 6).

(*b*) Inhabitants of Emisga, O.L.G. Emsigo (Law).

(*c*) 'Brookmen' in Brōkmonnalond, now Brokmerland (Law).

(*d*) 'Hriustrings' in Hriustri, now Rüstringerland (Law).

(*e*) 'Wurthsetes' in Wurtsetenalond, now Wursten, Rüstringian colonists in N. Hanover since the twelfth century (Law).

(*f*) 'Harlings' in Herloga or Herlingalond, now Harlingerland, with a dialect still spoken by some few persons on the island of Wangeroog and in the colony Varel.

(*g*) Inhabitants of Segelteralond, now Saterland, Fris. Sealterland, where they settled in the thirteenth century; still speaking Frisian.

Lit. van Helten, *Altostfries. Grammatik*, VIII seq.; Siebs in *Grundriss*, 2nd ed. I, 1167 seq.

4. North Frisians or Strand Frisians, M.Lat. Strantfresones (twelfth century) in Heligoland and in Western Slesvig, including the islands south of Rømø.

The Frisian names of local populations normally end in *-ing*: Hunsings in Hunsingoo; Butjadings 'beyond the Jade'; Stedings in

Stedingerland; Pelwermings, Strandings, Föhrings, Amrings, and Sildrings on the North Frisian islands of Pelworm, Strand, Föhr, Amrum, and Sild, etc.

Lit. Spruner-Mencke, *Handatlas zur Gesch. des Mittelalters*, map 31; te Winkel in *Grundriss*, 2nd ed., dialect map of Holland; Much in Hoops, s.v. *Friesen*; van Ginneken, *Handboek der Nederl. taal*, with dialect map.

§ 228. Ethnic Position.

The separate nationality of the Frisians is not noted by the Romans, who regard them as 'Germani', i.e. 'Germans'.

Nevertheless, its individuality and non-German character are obvious.

1. The mediaeval Frisians are co-ordinate with Germans, Saxons, Northmen, etc., never—as a nationality—included among Germani, Deutsche, Dutch, Franks, Saxons, Inguaeones, etc. If they are incorporated with Germany, it is a political and geographical subordination, not national. Though inaccurate writers may classify the Frisian language as 'German', and though this wrong terminology may influence Frisians with insufficient philological education, the vernacular unprejudiced speech instinct has always recognised the Frisian nationality as non-German.

2. The Frisian language, though closely cognate with the Anglo-Saxon, differs in important points. Some instances may illustrate the divergences.

(*a*) Gothon. *ai* becomes *ē* in Fris., as in L.G. (only under certain conditions Fris. *á*), but *á* in O.E. (as also in some cases in Scandinavian).

O.Fris.	O.E.	
brēd	brád	'broad'
stēn	stán	'stone'

(*b*) Gothon. *au* becomes *ā* in Fris. (*ē*, when palatalised) but *éa* in O.E. (*íe*, when palatalised).

O.Fris.	O.E.	
āk	éac	'also'
āre	éare	'ear'

(*c*) Whereas Frisian shares the O.E. and Scand. Breaking of vowels in certain cases (cp. O.Fris. *riucht*, O.E. *reoht*, Goth. *raihts* 'right', and

O.Fris., O.Swed. *siunga*, Goth. *siggwan* 'to sing'), this breaking does not occur before *hs* or before *r* plus consonant:

O.Fris.		O.E.	
sex		seox	'six'
ferra	'dexter'	feorr	'distant'

We have mentioned some remarkable points of agreement between Frisian and English dialects: the Frisian and Kentish palatalisation $\breve{e} < \breve{u}$; the change of $\breve{\bar{æ}}$ to $\breve{o}$ before nasals in East Frisian and in Anglian. But we must abstain from drawing conclusions from such phenomena, as their explanation is still a matter of dispute (cp. § 216).

Lit. van Helten, *Altostfries. Grammatik*, 1 seq.; Siebs in *Grundriss*, 2nd ed. I, 1177 seq.; Bremer, 842 seq.; Heuser, *Altfries. Lesebuch*, 2 seq., 105 seq.; Steller, *Abriss der altfries. Grammatik.*

3. The language of the modern Frisians is separated from those of their German, Dutch, and Danish neighbours by distinct barriers (cp. § 232 on the river Tjonger). There is no really intermediate dialect, though half-denationalised Frisians sometimes speak a mixed jargon. Anglo-Saxon may have formed a bridge between Frisian and German; but the complete extinction of the pure Saxons or Chauchi in Northern Hanover has created a gap east of the Frisians. It is one of those cases which Joh. Schmidt has observed in his 'Wave Theory'. (Some of the Western Chauchi seem to have adopted the Frisian political nationality.)

4. Tacitus, *Ann.* XIII, 54, relates the well-known anecdote of those Frisian ambassadors who claimed the most distinguished senatorial seats in the theatre of Rome, because 'nullos mortalium armis aut fide ante Germanos esse' (cp. *ibid.* IV, 74: 'Clarum...inter Germanos Frisium nomen'). It is a manifestation of national pride which betokens the genesis of an ethnic individuality.

5. The Frisian deities Baduhenna and Fosite (Tac. *Ann.* IV, 73, and Alcuin, *Vit. Willebrordi*, 10) may represent a local national worship, corresponding to those among Saxons, Swabians, Marses, Vandals, and Angles.

6. The Frisians, as long as they are independent, are governed by kings (cp. Tac. *Ann.* XIII, 54, and O.E. Fréscyning, *Beowulf*, l. 2503). Herein they differ from their republican Saxon kinsmen, and also from the early Franks.

7. The Frisian law, according to Ficker, *Untersuchungen*, belongs to the Scandinavian-Gothic type, and differs from the Saxon. We are not in a position to criticise this observation.

8. Individual Frisian names of juridical offices are: *rēd-jeva, frāna, bon, hōdere, gret-man*, and *tale-man*. A typical Frisian name, corresponding to the Saxon 'shire', is *dēl*, i.e. 'deal', e.g. Franekera-dēl.

9. Co-operation with one another, respect for law and right and personal freedom are characteristic of Frisian life. This is an outcome of the marshlander's eternal struggle with the sea. The Frisians are the most legally-minded of the Gothonic nations. Whereas the Inguaeones depict the hero Scyld as dispenser of fertility and peace, the Frisian divine saviour, who likewise arrives in a magical ship, establishes the *law*.

10. The acknowledged influence of the marshes on the Frisian physiognomy appears from the proverb: 'Deus mare, Friso litora fecit'—'God made the sea, the Frisian made the coasts'. The Frisians generally avoid the 'geest' or dry land, as appears from the distribution of nationalities, e.g. in Groningen (cp. pp. 286–287), but they set out to cultivate marshes in remote countries. For these reasons, their expansion is to a great extent directly opposite to that of the Jutes and Saxons, who, evacuating the marshes of the Cimbric Peninsula, pass by the Frisian coasts on their way to Britain. We might expect collisions as the consequence of the opposite movements, but such conflicts are almost unheard of. The Frisian settlers seem to be imperceptibly spreading over the foreign marshes, as peaceful propagandists of their inherited methods of coast defence and cattle-breeding.

11. The national Frisian type of country house is a building which is in Holland called *stelphoeve*, in East Friesland *platzgebäude*, in North Friesland *hauberg*, a rectangular and high-roofed building, wherein the various rooms are distributed around the stock of corn as the centre of the whole.

K. Mühlke in *Das Bauernhaus im Deutschen Reiche*, p. 118, describes it as follows: 'Der Hauberg ist auch im Holländischen, namentlich in den Provinzen Ostfriesland und Westfriesland, heimisch und gerade in der letzteren Landschaft in seiner vielleicht ursprünglichen Gestalt als vollständig quadratischer Bau noch jetzt zu finden'.

'Um einen mittleren, quadratischen Raum, das Vierkant, welcher als Kornbehältnis, als Bansen dient, bauen sich vier Flügel herum, südlich das Wohnhaus, seitlich und nordwärts die Viehställe, der eine Flügel mit der breiteren Tenne, die zwei übrigen Flügel mit mittleren Längsgängen. Die Tenne und der seitliche Längsgang münden an der hinteren Umfassungswand. Das Ganze ist mit einem einheitlichen hoch hinaufragenden Zeltdach überdeckt, welches nur durch Giebel oder kleinere Aufbauten über dem Wohneingang, dem Scheunentor und den Stalltüren unterbrochen wird.'

'Wird...innen nicht bloss *ein* Vierkant hergestellt, sondern, was eigentlich die Regel im Eiderstedtschen ist, mehrere Vierkante aneinander gereiht, so entsteht ein mehr länglicher Bau, und an Stelle der Dachspitze tritt eine Dachfirst. Mit dem Sachsenhause verbleibt dann einige Ähnlichkeit insofern, als eine dreischiffige basilikale Anlage auch vorhanden ist. Gleichwohl bestehen die wichtigen Unterschiede, dass die Tenne seitlich des Mittelschiffes im Seitenschiff liegt, dass das Mittelschiff nicht mit einer Balkenlage abgedeckt ist, sondern hoch bis in den Dachraum hineinreicht, auch das Getreide vom Boden ab aufgestapelt wird, und dass schliesslich die Seitenschiffe eine grössere Breite und Selbständigkeit besitzen. Andererseits könnte man den Hauberg mit einer von allen vier Seiten umbauten Hofanlage, wie sie weiter nördlich in den friesischen Marschen, in Nordschleswig, Dänemark und Südschweden sich ausgebildet hat, vergleichen. Es wäre dann nur der Unterschied zu beachten, dass beim Hauberg der mittlere Hof mit überdacht ist, und die äusseren Dachflächen der das Innere umgebenden Flügel zu einem mächtigen Kegeldache zusammengezogen sind. Es ist nicht ausgeschlossen, dass als Vorstufe zu dem heute bestehenden Haubergbau eine Gebäudeanlage ohne Zuzammenziehung der vier Dächer in der Mitte bestanden hat. Nach Angaben des früher in Koldenbüttel bei Friedrichstadt ansässigen Geh. Regierungsrats Sass in Schleswig hat bis Mitte des 19. Jahrhunderts in jenem Dorfe ein sehr alter Hauberg bestanden, welcher einen etwa 2 m. im Quadrat grossen Mittelhof besass, nach welchem die Satteldächer der vier Flügel ihre Traufen hatten....Dass diese Anlage, wenn sie der Vorläufer der jetzigen gewesen, sich weiter bilden musste, ergibt sich aus den grossen Fehlern derselben, dem Eindringen des Regens in die Mitte des Hauses und der Schwierigkeit der Abführung der Niederschläge. Mitbestimmend für die Weiterentwickelung war jedenfalls auch das Bedürfnis nach grossem Speicher- und Bansenraum.'

However, Fr. Saeftels, in his important monograph *Haubarg und*

Barghus, does not agree with Mühlke. He maintains that the 'hauberg' must have been evolved in Eastern Friesland before 1400 on the basis of the Old Frisian 'compound house', being afterwards transplanted to Eiderstedt about 1550–1600, where it was fully developed. The construction of the Frisian roof-timber distinguishes the Frisian type of house from the Saxon (see quotation on p. 209). But, according to Zangenberg, it agrees with that of the 'compound house' in North Jutland and in the South Jutlandic region of Fjolde-Husum, and also with Icelandic constructions.

The 'hauberg' still characterises various Frisian regions which now speak Saxon, such as Ostfriesland and Groningen, and it has been adopted by the pure Saxons in Dietmarschen. It is, moreover, frequent in various regions which now speak Dutch, such as North Holland, parts of South Holland (Alblasserwaard, Ijsselmonde, Beierland, Voorne, het Dortsche eiland), de Zevenbergsche hoek, and Zealand (cp. Schrijnen, *Nederlandsche Volkskunde*, 2nd ed. I, 56).

The 'hauberg', however, is not the only type of house occurring among the Frisians. Various populations imitate the types of their non-Frisian neighbours. The North Frisians, as Mühlke remarks, often adopt the Danish quadrangle. The Saterlanders in Oldenburg, on the other hand, have a type of house which is closely akin to the Saxon. Cp. Addy, *The Evolution of the English House*, p. 82 seq.: 'In Saterland are buildings, said to be of the sixteenth century or a little earlier, which have the dwelling-house, cattle stalls, and store-rooms under the same roof. The side walls are so low that the thatch reaches nearly to the ground. The walls are made of timber framework filled in with bricks, or, in the smaller houses, with wattles and mud. They are thatched with straw and heather. There are upright pillars with beams stretched across them. Both rows of pillars are overlaid by horizontal beams extending the whole length of the building, which is about 65 feet long by 49 broad. Upon the oblong so made, which forms the inner room of the building, rafters are fixed. The garret or loft is called *bölke*. Now the low side walls are erected, and long rafters laid from them to the ridge of the roof. By this means a sort of outer room going round the building is obtained, divided by a floor. Under the floor are cattle stalls and rooms. The upper portion, lying immediately under the long rafters, is used as a place to store fodder for the cattle, and for a gallery....Entering the great door (at the one gable end, G. Schütte) we find ourselves on a spacious main "floor". The smaller partitioned rooms on both sides usually serve for cattle stalls. On the left of the entrance lies the turf nook where turf for the fire is stored, and by the side of it the calf-house. Then crossing over a little passage which leads to a side door in the building, we come to the cow-house. There, separated from the "floor" by the great pillars and by small posts, stand the cattle, their heads facing inwards. On the right of the entrance, divided from the "floor" by a narrow partition wall, is the stable, and next to it the pigstyes. Adjoining the pigstyes is the weaving-room, made light by a large window and containing a loom and weaving apparatus. A smaller apartment, used as a washing room, lies near, with an exit to the yard....The whole domestic life of the Saterlander is spent on the spacious "floor". In the background, about 6½ feet from the back wall, burns the open fire, the centre of domestic intercourse. It is continually kept burning, for there is no lack of turf. In many houses it even serves for giving light, and by its dark red glow people work and amuse themselves. The older dwellings have no chimneys. The smoke of the turf fire spreads through the whole building....On the opposite side of the "floor" are four alcove beds one over another....The corn harvest lies in the cock-loft or *balk*. For the hay an additional room is made, which in many houses has a separate entrance'.

Lit. Gallée, *Het boerenhuis in Nederland*, 17 seq. (*Das niederländ. Bauernhaus*, 18 seq.); Schrijnen, *Nederland. Volkskunde*, I, 38 seq.; Hilkema, *Het Friesche boerenhuis*; Fr. Saeftels, *Haubarg und Barghus, die friesischen Grosshäuser an der schleswig-holsteinischen Westküste*; Reche, *Der gegenwärtige Stand...der Rassenkunde der Friesen* (*Volk und Rasse*, IV).

§ 229. History of the Frisians up to the Close of Ancient Times.

The Frisians belong to the primary stratum of tribes with names of the Simplex type along the North Sea, as do their close kinsmen, the Chauchi and Saxons. Their German neighbours towards the south-east, the Amsivarii and Chasvarii, represent a secondary settlement.

The Frisii majores east of the Vlie form the nucleus of the nation, extending eastwards to the river Ems (Ptol. II, 11, § 7). The Frisii minores or Frisiavones west of the Vlie must be regarded as emigrants.

In 12 B.C. the Frisians submit to Drusus and they rescue his navy during his war against the Chauchi (Dio Cassius, LIV, 32). The chieftain Cruptorix serves as Roman mercenary (Tac. *Ann.* IV, 73).

In A.D. 28 the Frisians revolt against a governor levying exorbitant taxes and slaughter numerous Romans in the grove of Baduhenna (Tac. *Ann.* IV, 72–74).

In 47 Corbulo pacifies the Frisians (*ibid.* XI, 19). Rome organises 'cunei' of Frisians (cp. Bang, *Die Germanen im römischen Dienst*, 99 seq.).

Meanwhile the Chauchi begin raiding Belgium in A.D. 41 and 47 (cp. § 217), and they seem to have settled among the Frisians (cp. Pliny, IV, 101: 'aliae (insulae) Frisiorum, Chaucorum, Frisiavonum..., quae sternuntur inter Helinium et Flevum').

In 58 the Chauchi drive the Amsivarii from the Emsgau, and the same movement may have caused the emigration of the Frisians ruled by Verritus and Malorix, who ask Rome in vain for admission into the military borderland north-east of the Lower Rhine (Tac. *Ann.* XIII, 54).

The relations between Frisians and Chauchi, however, generally seem to have been friendly, for both nations form a 'flagrantissima cohors' in the army of the Batavian Civilis during his war against Rome, A.D. 70 (Tac. *Hist.* IV, 79). Besides the Frisians here co-operate with the Batavian tribe of Cannenefates (*ibid.* 15). The war ends with the re-establishment of Roman suzerainty.

In 83 the Frisians intern some shipwrecked Usipii who have deserted from Roman service in Britain (Tac. *Agricola*, 28).

Frisians who have taken a Roman lease of the fishery dedicate a votive inscription to the goddess Hludana near Beetgum towards the close of the first century (*CIL.* XIII, 8830). A Roman purchase deed has been found at Tolsum (cp. *De vrije Fries*, XXV, 71 seq.).

Frisians serve as Roman mercenaries in Roman Britain in the second and third centuries. Perhaps they had acted as pioneers of the Anglo-Saxon nationality in the regions south of the Picts' Wall (cp. § 219).

Roman coins and other antiquities become rare in Friesland after the third century. It is at this time that the rise of the Frankish federation destroys the Roman dominion beyond the Rhine.

In 293 Constantius I repulses the Franks. Frisians appear among the prisoners distributed throughout Gaul (*Paneg. Constantio*, V, 9; cp. Frisione-curtis near Amiens).

Some few Frisians may have accompanied the Anglo-Saxons to Britain, for Procopius, who does not know the Saxons of Britain, mentions

'Frissones' instead of them (*Bell. Goth.* IV, 20; yet cp. Hoops, *Waldbäume u. Kulturpflanzen*, 567).

Lit. Zeuss, 136 seq.; Müllenhoff, IV, 428 seq.; Ihm in Pauly-Wissowa, VII, 105; Bremer, § 845; Blok, *Gesch. des niederländ. Volkes*, I, 16 seq.; Schmidt, II, 74; Much in Hoops, II, 99; Boeles, *Friesland tot de 11de eeuw.*

§ 230. History of the Frisians during the Middle Ages.

For two centuries the Frisians are not noticed. This is because their national line of development does not bring them into conflict with other tribes. Still, they are not passive, but rather very active, gradually replacing the Saxons as seafarers and colonising remote marshlands both east and west.

Their expansion is not always quite clear: there occur true Frisian colonies side by side with areas which are only Frisian in name, owing to temporary political fusion.

For example, the Frisians of 'Dorestate Frigonum patria' (Anonym. Ravennas, IV, 24), i.e. in Wijk-by-Duurstede near Utrecht, are really Franks, as are the 'Frisones, qui vocantur Destarbenzon' (*Ann. Fuld.* ad an. 885; *Mon. Germ. SS.* I, 402), i.e. in Teisterbant, Betuwe. The alleged Frisians of Marsum and Kennemerland are the ancient Marsaci and Cannenefates; they had co-operated with Frisians or Chauchi as early as A.D. 47 and 69–70 and now escaped Franconisation by joining the Frisian federation. Thus the *Lex Frisionum* extended its sway to the Channel of Zwin in Flanders. Holland north of the Meuse for centuries uses the procedure called *aasdōm*, i.e. 'the doom of the *āsega*', the verdict of the Frisian judge (cp. the place name Abkou-in-Aasdom, s.v. *Woordenboek der Nederl. taal*, I, 599 seq.).

True Frisians settle chiefly in the marshes as far south as the Meuse. The Frisian type of house called *stelphoeve* extends beyond South Holland, as also do traces of the national dress.

Towards the east, the distinction is less striking. The Frisians absorb their close kinsmen, the Chauchi minores or Hugas in Hugmerke and farther east. Beyond the Weser, outposts of Frisian settlers are placed in Wursten and on Heligoland, and they finally reach the marshes in South-western Jutland, including all islands south of Rømø.

The Frisians, as we mentioned in § 228, 10, prefer the marshes and avoid the 'geests' or dry lands. This is brought out by a comparison between map No. 31 in Spruner-Mencke's *Handatlas des Mittelalters*, and the geological map in Berghaus, *Physikalischer Atlas*, 3rd ed. Fig. 2.

Mediaeval Friesland west of the Vlie almost coincides with the marshes of the Rhine Delta.

Middle Friesland is almost entirely marsh and low moor ('Niedermoor'), though it embraces 'geests' such as Gaasterland near Stavoren.

East Friesland begins with a narrow border of marshes; the 'geest', with the town Groningen, remains non-Frisian. Farther east the Frisians occupy all the marshes between the Ems and the Elbe, and also some of the inland moors.

In Holstein, this colonisation has been interrupted; Dietmarschen has not been colonised by Frisians. But they occupy nearly all the marshes in South Jutland, including the border of the 'geest', the district of Goes. Their northern limit is the limit of the continuous marshes at the mouth of the river Vidå. Misthusum in a marsh farther north and Juvre on the island of Rømø may be scattered Frisian outposts (cp. Joure in Friesland).

Whereas the Frisian expansion is quite peaceful, the collisions with Franks and Vikings are violent.

The struggle between Hengest and the Frisian King Finn (*Finnsburg Lay*) may be regarded as a prelude of the Viking inroads.

About 526 the 'Geatic' Viking Hygelác attacks Frisians and Hugas (*Beowulf*, l. 2503). He may have landed in Hugmerke, but he is slain in the Pagus Hattvariensis on the Rhine.

The Frankish Kings Chlotar I (d. 561) and Chilperic 'terrify the Frisians and Swabians' (Venant. Fortunatus, *Carm.* IX, 1, 75 seq.). About 565 a Frankish army operates on Bordaa, perhaps the river Boorne, and repulses invading Danes and Saxons (*ibid. Carm.* VII, 7, 49–60). The decline of Merovingian power again emancipates the Frisians.

In 678 King Audulf's son Aldgisl allows Bishop Wilfrid of York to preach in Friesland (Bede, V, 190).

King Rēdbad reconquers the lost Frisian regions south of the Rhine, but loses them again in 689, being defeated by the *major domus* Pippin (*Lib. hist. Franc.* 49; 'Fredegar', *contin.* 6). In his fury Rēdbad destroys the church of Utrecht (Bonifat. *Epist.* 109).

In 696 Pippin appoints the Anglo-Saxon missionary Willibrord as archbishop of Utrecht (Bede, V, 11).

In 716, however, Rēdbad defeats Pippin's son Charles Martel near

Cologne (*Lib. hist. Franc.* 51, 52; 'Fredegar', *contin.* 9), reconquers Western Friesland, and fiercely persecutes Christianity.

In 718 he is decisively conquered by Charles (Alcuin, *Vit. Willibr.* 13).

In 734 Charles subjugates Middle Friesland; Rēdbad's successor Bobba or Poppo falls near the river Bordena, i.e. the Boorne (*Ann. Petav., Nazar., S. Amandi,* ad an. 734).

In 754 the heathen East Frisians kill Boniface, the apostle of Germany, without being punished (*Vit. Bonifat.* II, 350).

After 772 Charlemagne converts the Saxons, and his warlike crusades prove fatal also to the East Frisians. After their rebellion in 775 they are definitely subjugated. Liùdger becomes their most famous apostle.

The Viking raids of 525 and 565 are often imitated after the eighth century. As allies of the Saxons the Danes harry the subjects of the Franks, i.e. chiefly the Frisians.

In 810 the Danish King Gudfred makes the Frisians tributary (*Ann. Loiselian.* ap.; Du Chesne, *Script. Hist. Franc.* II, 47; cp. Saxo, 437).

In 826 the Emperor Louis grants Hriustri in East Friesland to the Danish ex-king Harald Klak, who later also, together with his nephew Hrørik, obtains fiefs in the Rhine Delta. These relations probably caused the immigration of the North Frisians into Jutland (cp. *Ann. Fuld.* ad an. 857: 'Rorih Nordmannus, qui praeerat Dorestado, cum consensu domini sui, Hlotarii regis, classes duxit in fines Danorum et consentiente Horico Danorum rege partem regni, quae est inter mare et Egidoram, cum sociis suis possedit'). Cp. Jan de Vries, *De Wikinger in de lage landen bij de zee.*

After 888 all Frisians, except those subject to the Danes, become German subjects. Frisian traders spread to Birka in Sweden.

Numerous Frisians after the twelfth century take part in the German colonisations on the reconquered Slavonic soil, but such scattered colonies were soon Germanised. Cp. Helmold, I, 57, 64.

For some generations, the German Emperor's supremacy remained almost illusory. Yet the Frisian national unity was anything but solid. In the twelfth century the seven Frisian Sealands founded a league for mutual protection, with a central assembly at the Upstallisbām near Aurich. It embraced Middle and Eastern Friesland and probably the remnants of Frisians in North Holland (cp. *Annales Egmundani*, ad an. 1167, ed. De Geer van Juftaas, p. 69: 'comitatum Holtlandiae in duos populos plurimum diversos divisum, Holtlandensem scilicet et Fresonicum....Cujus utriusque populi confinium et quasi divisio est villa Egmundensis').

The league of Upstallisbām was the last relic of the ancient Gothonic constitution in the age of feudalism. But it never grew into a centralised state. Besides, floods and landslides about the Vlie and the Jade disintegrated the seven Sealands. Their common history is soon broken up into local fragmentary records.

Lit. Hooft van Iddekinge, *Friesland en de Friezen in de middeleuwen*; Blok, *Gesch. der Niederlande*, I, 35 seq. (transl. from Dutch); *idem*, *Friesland im Mittelalter*; van Blom, *Geschiedenis van Oud-Friesland*; Gosses, *Bijdragen voor vaderlandsche geschiedenis*, *4de reeks*, IX, 209 seq.; Gosses en Japikse, *Handboek tot de staatkundige geschiedenis van Nederland*, XXII seq. (with lit.); Schmidt, II, 80 seq.; Nyèssen, *The Passing of the Frisians*; Wadstein, *Norden och Västeuropa*.

§ 231. History of the West Frisians Proper.

Isolated by the greedy Zuider Zee, the West Frisians finally cannot resist their hereditary foes, the Hollandic counts. In 1256 Willem II certainly is killed at Hoogwoud, but his son Floris V completes the conquest in 1289. Though Dutch-speaking the people still betray some traces of Frisian origin, and the name of West Friesland adheres to a part of North Holland.

Lit. Boekenoogen, *De Zaansche volkstaal*, III seq.; Karsten, *Het dialect van Drechterland*, I, *Inleiding*.

§ 232. History of the Middle Frisians Proper.

The attacks of the Hollandic counts failed. In 1345 Willem IV suffers a shameful defeat at Stavoren and falls. But anarchy ruins the country. In 1457 Friesland is recognised as a republic directly under the Emperor ('reichsunmittelbar'), but in 1483 it is subjugated by the Imperial governor Albrecht of Saxony. In 1523 the Emperor Charles V receives the oath of allegiance. Henceforth Middle Friesland shares the fate of the Netherlands. Unlike their brethren the Middle Frisians vigorously maintain their idiom and even foster a noteworthy national literature and civilisation. The rural dialect or Land-Fries is most pure, whereas the town dialect or Stad-Fries is either Dutch with Frisian characteristics, or Frisian with Dutch characteristics. The river Tjonger forms a distinct south frontier against Low Saxon with no intermediate dialects.

Het Bildt is a Dutch enclave, an alluvial district diked by Hollanders in the sixteenth century. There may be c. 325,000 people speaking Frisian (of 402,241, census of 1931).[1]

Lit. (On Het Bildt and het Stad-Fries) Kloeke, *De Hollandsche expansie*, 61 seq.

§ 233. History of the East Frisians Proper.

The Frisians in the marshes soon lose ground to the Saxons who occupy the larger part of Overijssel and Drente. Groningen (in Frisian called Grins) is a powerful Saxon city, which gradually Saxonises the so-called 'Groninger Ommelanden' on the coast between Lauwers and the Dollard. South of Groningen there occurs only one place name of Frisian type, viz. Peize, earlier Pedge. East of the Ems enterprising neighbours exploit the Frisian lack of unity, as in Holland. For example, in 1234 allied princely robbers under religious pretexts subjugate the Stedings and induce the pope to authorise their action as a 'crusade'. Oldenburg obtains Butjadingen as part of the spoil; later, the Butjadings revolt and again join the free Frisian Sealands, but in 1514 they are definitely incorporated with Oldenburg.

Edzard Cirksema occupied a prominent position among the native 'havdings', a hereditary nobility which had sprung from the ancient 'skeltatas'; his name is typically Frisian (*dz*, *C*). In 1464 he was appointed hereditary Imperial count ('Reichsgraf') of Ostfriesland. When his family died out in 1744 Prussia inherited this last remnant of Frisian autonomy.

The East Frisians now all speak Low German except in Saterland, a thirteenth-century colony in the moors of Oldenburg (some 4000 people). On the island of Wangeroog and in the continental colony Varel the dying Frisian dialect is scarcely spoken by as many as two dozen persons.

Lit. Huizinga, *Driemaandelijksche Bladen, uitg. door de Vereeniging tot onderzoek van taal- en volksleven*, XIV, 1 seq.; Bos, *Het Groningsche gild- en stapelrecht*, 6 seq.; Siebs in *Grundriss*, 2nd ed. I, 1168 seq.; Paul, *Älteste Geschichte Ostfrieslands*; Lüpkes, *Ostfriesische Volkskunde*; Nyèssen, *The Passing of the Frisians*, 261 seq.; Boeles, *Friesland tot de 11de eeuw*; W. de Vries, *Nom. geogr. neerland.* VIII, 20 seq.

§ 234. History of the North Frisians Proper.

The Frisian settlers seem to have immigrated since the ninth century (cp. p. 288). In the south-western marshes and geests of Slesvig, which had been evacuated by the Angles, they have absorbed a sparse popula-

[1] Private communication from Prof. Kapteyn.

tion of Jutish settlers, as appears from Danish place names such as Horsæby, Lindholm, island of Lundingland, and the insular districts Lundæbyarg and Holmbo.

The inhabitants of the islands Sild, Föhr, and Amrum, gave up quite early the name of Frisians and, in popular speech, designate their nationality only as Sildringian, Föhringian, and Amringian respectively. This fact has caused the islands to be compared with Ptolemy's three 'Saxon islands', and Bremer, § 128, suggests that the three insular populations might be remnants of the West Saxons. But such conclusions are scarcely justified. Ptolemy's Saxon islands rather are Heligoland and the islets about Cuxhaven, and the loss of the national name is also known in other parts of the Frisian territory.

The dialects of Föhr, Amrum, and of the districts of Horsæby and Bøking, have adopted the West Jutlandic definite article beside the common Gothonic, as *a, at* or *æ, æt.* It is a case of secondary fusions which contribute to the effacing of the distinct limits between different groups. The adoption of the local Jutlandic article must have taken place at a relatively early epoch, for the rules for the use in Frisian are very different from those in West Jutland.

From the beginning of their history and till 1864 the North Frisians have always appeared as Danish subjects, but with a considerable amount of home rule. The islands, together with the districts of Eiderstedt, Horsæby, and Bøking, form the Utland, 'Outer land', which is not an ordinary Danish county ('Syssel'), but a separate royal domain; its inhabitants are called 'the King's Frisians'.

The North Frisians also zealously defended their rights against Danish and German potentates. In 1252 the Danish King Abel fell in the course of an expedition against them. Later, their territory was diminished by terrible floods, and Low German conquers Eiderstedt, the surroundings of Husum, the islands of Nordstrand and Pelworm, whereas Danish is advancing in the vicinity of Tønder. They may now number c. 16,000.

The North Frisians possess no common literary language and only feeble beginnings of a written literature in the local dialects dating from the nineteenth century. A league for the preservation of Frisian was formed only in the twentieth century.

Lit. Langhans, *Über den Ursprung der Nordfriesen*; Lauridsen, *Om Nordfrisernes Indvandring i Sønderjylland* (*Hist. Tidsskr.* VI R, 4 B, 318); Lyngby, *Om Nordfrisisk i Bøking og Hvidding Herreder*; Ernst Brandt, *Die nordfries.*

Sprache der Goesharden; Marius Kristensen, *Frisisk* (in la Cour, *Sønderjyllands Historie*, I, 101); E. W. Selmer, *Sylterfriesische Studien*; P. C. G. Jensen, *Die nordfries. Sprache der Wiedingharde*; F. Schmeisser, *Nordfriesland*; Holthausen, *Nordfriesland*, p. 397 seq. (with a survey of North Frisian literature). Anthologies: Bremer, *Ferreng en ömreng Stacken üb Rimen*; P. C. Peters, *Ferreng-ömreng Liedjinbuck*; *idem*, *Schong, völjkens, schong!*

§ 235. Legendary Traditions.

The proverb 'Frisia non cantat' is misleading. The *Lex Frisionum, iudicia Wuldemari*, X, mentions harpists. The blind songster Bernlef 'antiquorum actus rerumque certamina bene noverat psallendo promere' (*Vita Liudgeri, Mon. Germ. SS.* II, 412).

Frisian laws abound in poetical formulas and epic survivals; at best, the Swedish can but rival them (cp. our dissertation *Oldsagn om Godtjod*, 81, 90).

A mythical lawgiver, 'the thirteenth', has been mentioned in § 228, 9.

Three main enemies are emphatically denounced: the sea, the Normans, and the Saxons. So, for example, in the tenth *Kest* (see De Haan Hettema, *Het Fivelgoër an Oldampter Landregt*, 14: 'Thet we use londe bihalda machte with thene salta sē and thene nordscreda ridder and with thene hāga helm and thene rāda schild', i.e. 'that we may hold our land against the salt sea and the northern armed champion and the high helmet and the red shield'). High helmets and red shields are well-known metaphors for Saxons.

A curious reference to the Jutish hero Amleth (Hamlet) has lately been discovered in a Frisian runic inscription (cp. J. Kapteyn, *Twee runeninscripties uit de terp van Westeremden* (*Jaarverslag XII–XV van de vereeniging voor terpenonderzoek*, Groningen); *idem* in *Beiträge*, XLVII, 1 seq.). The inscription reads: 'Ophāmu gistada Amluþ. īwim ōst ān þukn. īwi ōs ūst dūkale'. Prof. Kapteyn translates (p. 84): 'At Opham Amleth took his stand. Before his runic yew-staffs the surge has fallen.—Before this runic yew-staff let the foaming surge fall!' The words allude to some runic incantation. In the Jutish legend, Amleth equally appears as an expert in rune-lore.

Most famous of Frisian heroes is King Finn, Folcwald's son (cp. *Widsith*, l. 27, and the *Finnsburg Lay*); his memory seems to survive on the island of Sild (cp. H. Möller, *Das altengl. volksepos*, 64 seq., 75 seq.). His opponents are the Hokings and the 'Dane' Hengest, probably the

Jutish conqueror of Kent (cp. our article *Vidsid og Slægtssagnene om Hengest*, *Arkiv*, XXXVI, 1 seq.).

Later, Rēdbad and Charles Martel become centres of epic legends, as taking part in the political struggles of ancient Friesland. But the parts they play are more radically changed than that of the Goth Theodoric, who, being an invader into Italy, appears in German poetry as a returning exile. Rēdbad, the stout defender of Frisian freedom, owing to his heathen fanaticism becomes a Danish conqueror. And the victorious Charles who conquers the free Frisians, becomes their generous saviour from Rēdbad's fury. Besides, he is replaced by his great successor Charlemagne, who equally conquered the free Frisians (cp. especially the text *Van da tweer koningen*, in Richthofen, *Altfries. Rechtsquellen*, 439). The fable has been decorated with learned fabrications, but may still contain an element of ancient folk-lore.

Numerous Frisian episodes of lesser importance appear in the Danish legends of Saxo. The most noteworthy is the report of King Gudfred's conquests and of his haughty way of making the Frisians pay tribute (Saxo, 437).

Lit. Bolhuis van Zeeburgh, *Kritiek der Friesche Geschiedschrijving*; H. Möller, *Das altengl. volksepos*; Siebs in *Grundriss*, 2nd ed. II, 523 seq.; Symons, *ibid.* III, 628; Borchling, *Poesie und Humor im friesischen Recht*, 55 seq.; Romein, *Geschiedenis van de Noord-Nederlandsche Geschiedsschrijving in de middeleeuwen*, p. 139 seq.

VI. §§ 236–248. THE ANCIENT INTERMEDIATE PENINSULAR SUB-GROUP OR BRANCH

§ 236. Name.

The section has no name, a fact which reflects the vagueness of all our ideas about it, though if we accept Joh. Schmidt's 'Wave Theory' we are compelled to assume that it once existed.

It is possible that the tribes concerned were once called Inguaeones and by the Romans Cimbri (cp. Tac. *Germ.* 2: 'proximi Oceano Inguaeones', and *ibid.* 37: 'proximi Oceano Cimbri', and Ptol. II, 11, § 2: 'Kimbrikē Chersonēsos' for the Jutlandic Peninsula). But the Inguaeones of Pliny, IV, 99, include the Chauchi in Hanover, and the Ingwine of *Beowulf* are the Danes. Hence it appears that the domain of the Inguaeones was not clearly defined. The Roman use of the name Cimbri seems to be merely geographical.

§ 237. Sub-divisions.

We shall begin with the south and continue towards the north, generally following the direction indicated by the lists of Tacitus and Ptolemy. But we shall deal with the Angles first, owing to their greater importance, and with the Jutes last, because they gave their name to the modern inhabitants of the peninsula (ethnic 'front stress' and 'back stress').

1. O.E. Engle (Alfred's *Orosius*, 19, 20, his *Bede*, I, 876, 880, IV, 3983, V, 917), Angel-þéod (Alfred's *Bede*, 5, 24; S. 645, 34, 37), Angel-cynn (*ibid.* Pref. S. 471, 23, S. 584, 13), Englisc-men; O.N. Englar (Hallfreðr, *Hskr.* I, 307), Englis-menn (*Hskr.* III, 202); Lat. Anglii (Tacitus, first century A.D.); M.Lat. Angli; Fr. Anglais; Ital. Inglesi; Gr. Ἀγγειλοί (Ptolemy, second century A.D.), Ἀγγίλοι (Procopius, sixth century); Cymr. Eingl; O.Russ. Agljane (Nestor, eleventh century). Eponymous hero: O.Dan. Angul (Saxo, 21); O.G. Angling (*Quedlinburg. Ann.* ad an. 445). Personal names: O.G. Angil-berht, Angil-bald, etc. (see Förstemann). Regions: O.E. Ongel (*Widsith*, l. 35); Dan. Angel (in South Jutland); O.G. Engilin (in Thuringia). The name is probably identical with 'angle', a hook, but the application of the word is uncertain: 'people from the Angle'? or (la Cour) 'people from the firth' (cp. O.N. *angr* 'firth'?). Home: South Jutland, where the name survives in Angel; colonies in the Thuringian Engilin, and in England.

Lit. Erdmann, *Über den Namen und die Heimat der Angeln* (with lit.); J. R. Tengberg and Erdmann in *Nordisk Familjebok*, s.v. *Angelsaxer*; Sach, *Das Herzogtum Schleswig*, I, 65; Schütte, *Sønderjydske Aarbøger*, 1900, 38 seq.; *idem*, *Arkiv*, XXV, 313; Detlefsen in Sieglin's *Quellen u. Forschungen*, Heft 18, suppl. 13; Chadwick, 104; *idem*, in Chambers' *Encycl.* s.v.; Schönfeld, s.v. (with lit.); Chambers, *Widsith*, 71, 246; Hoops, s.v. *Angelsachsen*; la Cour, *Gesch. des schlesw. Volkes*, I, 28; *idem*, *Sønderjyllands Historie*, I, 147; Löwenthal, *Arkiv*, XXXI, 153; Noreen, *Fornvännen*, 1920, 38; Bosworth-Toller, s.v. *Angel-*, *Engel-*, *Engliscman*; Wadstein, *On the Origin of the English* (*K. Human. Vetenskaps-Samf. Skrifter*, XXIV, 14).

2. O.E. Rondingas (beside the Werne and Eowan, *Widsith*, l. 24); Lat. Reudigni (beside the Auiones and Varini, Tac. *Germ.* 40, first century A.D.). Perhaps derived from a river or firth *Rand (cp. Jutl. Randr-ús, 'the mouth of Rand', and the Norwegian lake of Rǫnd, now Randsfjord). The agreement between the accounts of Tacitus and *Widsith* shows that Rondingas is not a fictitious name, as assumed by Chambers and others.

The Brondingas are known from *Beowulf*, ll. 499–606, to be a real people (cp. also Brond, presumably an eponymous ancestor in the Northumbrian pedigree). The spelling Rondingas may be as trustworthy as Reudigni; first, it rhymes with Brondingas, and, secondly, it could not be miswritten for *Roudingas, as the O.E. *o* indicates a following nasal, whereas the Lat. Reud-, which is not found elsewhere, could easily be a miswriting for *Rand- or *Rend-. Home unknown.

Lit. **Müllenhoff**, *Nordalbing. Studien*, I, 152; *Beovulf*, 58; **Chadwick**, 269, 284; **Chambers**, *Widsith*, 110 seq.

3. O.E. *Éowan (dat. Éowum, *Widsith*, l. 26); Lat. Auiones (Tacitus, first century A.D.). Personal name: O.E. Éawa (probably the same as Eaha, the companion of Sigeferð Secgena léod, *Finnsburg Lay*, l. 15). The name is derived from Gothon. *auj-* 'water, wet land, island', whence the O.N. tribal name Eynir in Eynafylki, on the lake of Øjeren, and on the island of Öland.[1] Zeuss and Schmidt compare the Obioi of Dio Cassius, but these are rather identical with the Ubii (cp. §195, 3). Bremer's identification of the Éowan with the Uwen of a North Frisian legend is, according to Herman Möller, impossible on phonetic grounds. The home of the tribe is uncertain; perhaps on the islands west of South Jutland. Detlefsen proposes the district Åbo Syssel on the Gudenå, the largest river of North Jutland; the toponymic is Åboinger or Åbutter, 'river-dwellers'.

Lit. **Müllenhoff**, IV, 464; **Siebs**, *Zur Gesch. d. engl. fries. Sprache*, 17; **Bremer**, *Zeitschr. f. deutsche Philol.* XXV, 129 seq.; **H. Möller**, *Anzeiger*, XXII, 158 note 1; **Detlefsen** in **Sieglin's** *Quellen u. Forschungen*, **Heft** 18; **Kluge**, *Zeitschr. f. deutsche Wortforsch.* VIII, 141; **Schmidt**, I, 432, II, 25; **Schönfeld**, s.v. *Aviones*; **Much** in **Hoops**, s.v. *Aviones*; **Chambers**, *Widsith*, 197.

4. O.E. *Werne, *Wærne (dat. Wernum, *Widsith*, l. 25, *Wærnum*, l. 59); Lat. Varinnae (Pliny, first century A.D.), Varini (Tacitus, first century A.D.); M.Lat. Varni (Jordanes, sixth century), Guarni (Cassiodorus, sixth century); Gr. *Οὐαρινοί (prototype of Ptolemy's three corrupt forms, Αὐαρινοί, Αὐάρποι, Οὐίρουνοι, second century A.D.),[2]

1 The Oeonae, Mela, III, 4, § 56, and Pliny, IV, 95, inhabit the North Sea islands and live on eggs. This Greek word, Oionai, 'egg-eaters', might look like a corruption of Auiones.

2 The Virunoi owe their distorted name to their capital Virunon, which has again been distorted after the model of the Celtic Virunum, an important town in the province of Noricum.

Οὐάρνοι (Procopius, sixth century). Eponymous representative: O.N. Varinn. Personal names: O.G. Warin-hari, Warne-caut, etc. (see Förstemann). Obscure (cp. the South German tribe of Varisti). Home: probably on the river Warnow in Mecklenburg, in the Middle Ages occupied by the Slavonic Warnabi; later in Thuringia.[1] A colony in the Netherlands.

Lit. Müllenhoff, IV, 465; *idem*, *Nordalbing. Studien*, I, 129; Bremer, § 130; Schütte, *Sønderjydske Aarbøger*, 1900, 17; *idem*, *Beiträge*, XLI, 6, 9, 16, 41; *idem*, *Arkiv*, XXXIII, 35; *idem*, *Ptolemy's Maps*, 25, 64, 132; Detlefsen in Sieglin's *Quellen u. Forschungen*, Heft 18, suppl. 13; Chadwick, 198; Schönfeld, s.v. *Varini* (with lit.); Much in Hoops, s.v. *Warnen*; Jordan, *ibid.* IV, 523; Löwenthal, *Beiträge*, XLVII, 291, LV, 317 seq.; *idem*, *Zeitschr. f. Ortsnamenforsch.* VI, 77; v. Grienberger, *Philolog. Wochenschau*, XVIII, 934 seq., 1181.

[1] The name of the district of Werenofeld in Thuringia is often derived from the Varines, e.g. by Chadwick, 112. But the *Chron. Moissac.*, *Mon. Germ. SS.* I, 307, writes it Hwerenofelda, see Förstemann, s.v. *Hwereno-*. The arbitrary assumption of Müllenhoff, *Nordalbing. Studien*, I, 129 (1844), is not worthy of discussion. Rejecting Ptolemy's evidence, he places the Varines at the so-called 'Warnitz' in South Jutland, which was as he says 'in bygone times' called Warnaes, to be read •Varna næs, 'promuntorium Varinorum'. This is repeated in a careless quotation by Seelmann, *Jahrb. f. niederdeutsche Sprachforsch.* XII, 23, and by Meitzen, *Siedelung u. Agrarwesen*, II, 14 (1893): 'Das promontorium Varinorum, Warnaes, im Erdbuche Waldemars von 1231'; also by Bremer, § 130 (1899). Thus Müllenhoff's conjectural 'promuntorium Varinorum' is summarily declared a 'quotation from the *Liber census Daniae* of 1231'. Müllenhoff's assumption is again echoed by Möller, *Altengl. volksepos*, 4 note 2; Schönfeld, s.v. *Varini*; Chambers, *Widsith*, 196; Kauffmann, I, 410; v. Friesen, *Röstenen*, 55. And Meitzen's fictitious quotation deceives Chadwick, *l.c.* 199, and at one time deceived the author of the present work, *Arkiv*, XXV, 318. We would point out that 'Warnaes' is not an 'obsolete' form, as Müllenhoff asserts and his copyists without criticism repeat; the Danish form Varnæs, with the toponymic Varnsninger, is still used by the natives. The suppression of such vernacular forms is a serious fault, which led Seelmann to make an anachronism of some 2000 years regarding a certain point in the history of the Varines, cp. my criticism in *Smaaskrifter udg. af Selsk. f. germ. Filologi*, No. 15, 29, and Mar. Kristensen, *Namn och Bygd*, XVI, 106 seq. Varnæs probably has nothing to do with the Varines, for the name reappears in Sweden and Norway, and consequently cannot be taken as a mark of original ethnic localisation, as Schmidt assumes, II, 24. Cp. our article in *Arkiv*, XXXIII, 47, where this mistaken but tenacious theory is refuted, and also our vol. I, p. 151. Other erroneous theories are caused by the distorted spelling of the Varines in Ptolemy's work. His fictitious tribe of Avarini 'east of the Weichsel' (though with a mark of interrogation) is still found in current maps of ancient Germania, e.g. Fig. 2 in Müllenhoff's *Altertumskunde*, II, drawn by H. Kiepert (1887); Fig. 75 in Gerland's *Atlas der Völkerkunde* (Berghaus, *Physikal. Atlas*, 3rd ed. VII, 1892); Fig. 5 in v. Erckert, *Wanderungen u. Siedelungen*, 1901; R. Kiepert's *Formae Orbis Antiqui*, 1911.

5. Lat. *Eudusii, Euduses (Sedusii, Caesar, *Bell. Gall.* I, 51, first century B.C., cited by Orosius, VI, 7, § 17, as Eduses, Euduses), Eudoses (Tacitus, first century A.D.); Gr. *Eudusioi (Φουνούσιοι, Φουνδούσιοι, with misreading of Lat. E as F, Ptol. II, 11, § 7). The name has been derived from Gothon. *euð-*, O.N. *jóð* 'kindred'; Zachrisson proposes a derivation from a root **euð-* 'water', alternating with *eut-*, as in the name of the Jutes. A geographical etymology is always preferable (cp. Langenfelt in *Anthropos*, XIV/XV, 303). The name may originally have been an *s*-stem, or it may contain the same termination as in Goth. *bērusjōs* 'parents', and Hellusii (Tac. *Germ.* 46; cp. the *-is* in Jutl. Rømis, toponymic of the island of Røm, Nordres 'a northerner', see Feilberg, *Ordbog ov. de jyske Almuesmål*, s.v. *Rømø* and *Nordres*). Home: in West Jutland, west of the Harudes (Ptol. II, 11, § 7); cp. the juxtaposition of both tribes in the army of Ariovistus in 58 B.C. (Caesar, *Bell. Gall.* I, 51), and the juxtaposition of Eudoses and Angles among the worshippers of Nerthus (Tac. *Germ.* 40). Those Eudusii who emigrated to South Germany perhaps survive as Euthungi, Iuthungi (cp. § 157, 6), whereas the assonance of their name with that of the Eudusianoi on the Black Sea (Loewe, *Reste der Germanen*, 19) may be accidental.

Lit. Schönfeld (with lit.); Seelmann, *Jahrb. f. niederd. Sprachforsch.* XII, 35; Loewe, *Indogerm. Forsch.* XIII, 80 seq.; Schmidt, II, 25; Much, *Beiträge*, XVII, 206; *idem*, in Hoops, s.v. *Eudoses*; Schütte, *Beiträge*, XLI, 8, 15, 16; *idem*, *Arkiv*, XXXIII, 34; *idem*, (Norw.) *Hist. Tidsskrift*, 1917, 21; *idem*, *Ptolemy's Maps*, 19, 59, 64; Zachrisson, *Studia Neophilologica*, I, 89.

6. Gr. Χάλοι (Ptolemy, second century A.D.). Never mentioned in other sources. The present form would be identical with O.N. *halir* 'men'; but with Werlauff we prefer to read *Challoi, i.e. the Hallinger in the East Jutlandic district of Hallæ Hæret (*Liber census Daniae*, A.D. 1231). The centre of the district, now Hald, lies on a prominent hill in the middle of the plain (cp. O.N. *hallr* 'hill'). Home: East Jutland, south of the Cimbri (Ptol. II, 11, § 7); the two districts of Northern and Southern Hallæ, south of Himber Sysæl, correspond as to situation. Hallæ certainly is not a 'Syssel' (county), but the two districts of this name, if we add the area between them, are about the size of a county, i.e. a tribal district.

Lit. Werlauff, *Ravhandelens Historie* (*Danske Vidensk. Selsk. Skr.* 1836, 276 note); Schönfeld, s.v.; Much in Hoops, s.v.; Chambers, *Widsith*, 194; Schütte, *Hist. Aarbog f. Skive*, 1915, 14; *idem*, (Norw.) *Hist. Tidsskrift*, 1917 14; Noreen, *Fornvännen*, 1920, 48; Karsten, *Die Germanen*, 226.

7. Gr. Σαβαλίνγιοι (Ptolemy, second century A.D.). Obscure. Perhaps the Salling-boer in Salling Syssel; so already Pontanus. *Sabl-* might become *sall-* (cp. Dan. *billing, gnalling, killing, kylling, ælling* < **bitling, *gnagling, *kattling, *kukling, *andling*, 'bit, morsel, kitten, chicken, duckling'). The modern *-lling* often occurs where earlier sources write *-ling*, e.g. Jelling < Jalyng. Wadstein suggests that Sabaling- might be miswritten for *Salaving-, and this might become *Salving- > Salling-. But it is questionable whether the orthography with one *l* in the *Liber census Daniae* (A.D. 1231) is not irreconcilable with the assumed origin both from Sab(a)l- and from *Salav-. Home: north of the Sigulones (Ptol. II, 11, § 7); if the identification with the Sallingboer holds good, Ptolemy has placed the Sabalingioi too far south, but the mediaeval territory of the Sallingboer extended at least towards the middle of Jutland.[1]

Lit. Pontanus, *Rerum Danicar. Hist.* 649; Detlefsen in Sieglin's *Quellen u. Forschungen*, Heft 8, 60, and suppl. 10; Schönfeld, s.v. *Savalingii*; Schütte, *Geogr. Tidskrift*, 1915, 17; *idem*, *Hist. Aarbog f. Skive*, 1915, 14; *idem*, *ibid.* 1927, 7 (on the Sallingboer: (1) name, (2) sub-division, (3) ethnic character, (4) toponymics, (5) dialect, (6) paganism, (7) national dress, (8) national dances, (9) type of houses, (10) professions, (11) list of native authors); *idem*, *Ptolemy's Maps*, 64; Much in Hoops, s.v.; Wadstein in *Minnesskrift utg. av Filol. Samfundet i Göteborg*, 1925, 192; Löwenthal, *Beiträge*, XLVII, 292; Karsten, *Die Germanen*, 226.

8. Jutl. Har-boer, Ha-søsel-boer, Har-sel-boer, Ha-ssel-boer (and a local toponymic Har-bo-øre-boer); Lat. Harudes (Caesar, first century B.C.), Charydes (Augustus, *Res gestae*, first century A.D.); Gr. Χαροῦδες (Ptolemy, second century A.D.).[2] County: O.N. Hǫrðr; M.Dan. Harthe Sysæl (*Liber census Daniae*, A.D. 1231); Jutl. Harsyssel, Hasøsel, Harrisel. District: M.Dan. Harz Hæret (*Liber cens. Dan.*); Jutl. Hadsherred (toponymic: Hadsherredere). Personal name: O.E. ('Geatic') Hæred; Gr. Ἀρούθ, Ἄορδος (Erulian; Procopius, Agathias, sixth century A.D.). Family name: Langobard Arodus. The tribal name reappears in Norway as O.N. Hǫrðar, Norw. Horer, Haringar, county, O.N. Hǫrða-land, O.E. Hæreda-land; eponymous representative Hǫrðr, cp. §§ 278, 281. The name probably originates from Gothon. *haruð-*, Germ. *hard, hart* 'wood', whence for example the Harz or Harzgebirge with toponymic O.G. Harudi (*Ann. Fuld.*, *Mon. Germ. SS.* I, 368); the three tribal names Harudes,

[1] Saling may be a toponymic originating from the parish of Sal, which is situated due south of Saling Syssel.

[2] Ptolemy's Φαροδεινοί is perhaps a corruption of *Χαροδεινοί.

Hǫrðar, and Harudi may be regarded as toponymics, formed independently of each other on the spot. Home: in East Jutland (Ptol. II, 11, § 7), thus coinciding with Harz Hæret, according to Werlauff. The main body of the Harudes, however, emigrated to West Jutland and there founded the Harthe Sysæl; its designation 'county' is a sign of tribal rank. Ptolemy's evidence is rejected by Grimm, Müllenhoff, and Bremer, without the least justification. The juxtaposition by Ptolemy of (1) Harudes, (2) *Eudusii, (3) Kimbroi, is confirmed in three places, viz. by Caesar, *Bell. Gall.* (1 and 2), by Augustus, *Res gestae* (1 and 3), and by modern geography (1 and 3).

Lit. Colding, *Dictionarium Herlovianum* (A.D. 1631); Pontanus, *Rerum Danicar. Hist.* 649; Werlauff, *Danske Vidensk. Selsk. Skrifter*, 1836, 271; N. M. Petersen, *Regesta geogr. Islandorum* (*Fornm. sögur*, XII), s.v. *Hörðr*; Feilberg, *Ordb. ov. d. jyske Almuesmål*, s.v. *Harboskræp*, *Harsyssel* and *Harsysselbo*; Much, *Beiträge*, XVII, 203; *idem*, in Hoops, s.v. *Haruden*; Detlefsen in Sieglin's *Quellen u. Forschungen*, Heft 8, suppl. p. 9; Chadwick, 214; Schönfeld, s.v. *Harudes* (with lit.); Magnus Olsen, *Hedenske Kultminder*, 10; Schütte, *Geogr. Tidskr.* 1915, 17; *idem*, *Hist. Aarbog f. Skive*, 1915, 14; *ibid.* 1927, 46 (on the Hardsysselboer; *idem*, *Beiträge*, XLI, 16; *idem*, (Norw.) *Hist. Tidsskrift*, 1917, 7 and 14; *idem*, *Ptolemy's Maps*, 64; *idem*, *Hardsyssels Aarbog*, 1928, 155; Wadstein in *Minnesskrift utg. av Filol. Samfundet i Göteborg*, 1925, 193; Noreen, *Fornvännen*, 1920, 27; Karsten, *Die Germanen*, 226.

9. Jutl. Himmer-boer, Himmel-boer, Him-boer; Lat Cimbri (*CIL.* I, E, XVII, 1, 7; Cicero, first century B.C.); Gr. Κίμβροι (Poseidonius, first century B.C.), Κίμβριοι (Polyaen. second century A.D.). Roman auxiliary troops: Lat. Cimbriani (*Not. dign. Occ.* V, 12 and 155). Personal name: Lat. Cimberius (Caesar, *Bell. Gall.* I, 37, a Swabian). God: Lat. Mercurius Cimbrius or Cimbrianus (*CIL.* XIII, 6404, A.D. 191; 6605, A.D. 212, about Miltenberg and Heidelberg). County: M.Dan. Himber Sysæl; Jutl. Himmer-land. Cp. various Scandinavian analogies: Himmer Fjärden, a large firth at Söder Telje in Södermanland; Himbra in Upland (A.D. 1400); Hymber in Nerke (1429); Himbrim in South Norway (1636); the island of Himmerøien (South Trondheims Amt). Noreen compares the bird *colymbus glacialis*, O.N. *himbrin*, Iceland. *himbrini* or *himbrimi*, Norw. dial. *hymber*, and Norw. dial. *hīm*, 'a thin, transparent crust'; Much in Hoops, III, 43, compares Germ. *schimmer* 'gleam of light'. Noreen suggests a geographical term meaning 'glade', the original sense being 'a bright spot'. It must have expressed an idea which may be as easily connected with a firth as with a district. At any rate, the frequent

occurrence shows that the stem is genuinely Scandinavian. Müllenhoff emphasises the constant classical spelling with *c* or *k*, and the words of Festus, p. 43, ed. Müll.: 'Cimbri lingua gallica latrones dicuntur'. These arguments are without value. The Romans first heard the name of the Cimbri from Celts who had no *h* in their language and therefore substituted their own *k*;[1] and, once introduced with *k*, the name could not be altered, because of its fame in history. The alleged Gaulish signification of Cimbri, 'robbers', is simply due to the historical career of that people (cp. our article in *Arkiv*, XXXIII, 28). Home: in the northern part of Jutland (Ptol. II, 11, § 7); on the 'promunturium Cimbrorum... Thastris (var. Chartris)' (Pliny, IV, 97), that is to say, in the mediaeval county of Himber Sysæl, the present Himmerland. The fact that it was a county indicates its ancient tribal rank. Müllenhoff, Bremer, and Feist treat Ptolemy's evidence as absurd in the case of the Cimbri, as in the case of the Harudes, and on similarly inadequate grounds. They prefer Strabo who places the Cimbri south of the Elbe and emphatically denies that the Romans ever went north of this river (VII, 291 seq.). Trusting this guide, Müllenhoff and Feist go so far as to accuse the Emperor Augustus of telling us lies in his *Res gestae* (*Monumentum Ancyranum*)! It is certainly no wonder that a man so ignorant of northern geography as Strabo dared to deny the Roman naval expedition to Himmerland in A.D. 5; but when Bremer in A.D. 1905 and Feist in A.D. 1929 repeat such assertions, it only shows that they and Müllenhoff have never taken the trouble to compare Ptolemy's Cimbric Chersonese with the mediaeval and modern map of Jutland. The identification of the unique and enigmatic name Cimbri with the similarly enigmatic Himber Sysæl (unique as a territorial name) is self-evident, and only hypercritical authors have called it into question. It is curious that so obvious a point, noted some three centuries ago by the Danish historiographer Lyschander, should still be disputed by Feist in the year 1929. The arguments of Feist are as inadequate as those of Müllenhoff and Bremer. In the first place he neglects important evidence from archaeology and folk-lore: the Cimbri, according to Plutarch, worshipped the bull, and, as far as we know, they are solitary among the Gothonic nations in that respect. Now the only archaeological trace of bull worship, viz. the vessel of Gundestrup, leads us precisely to Himmerland. And the only obvious hint existing in

[1] Even to-day, a Mrs Johanna Langballe from my vicinity in Sallingland was by Italian peasants obstinately called Jocanna.

modern folk-lore is the so-called 'bull of Himmerland'. On such grounds we conclude that no identification of ancient tribal names and modern toponymics could be more solid than that of Cimbri and Himmerboer. Apart from Feist, the latest contributors to the discussion, such as Marcks, Ihm, Detlefsen, Schmidt, and Much, also categorically reject the sceptical view. Schönfeld, who in his dictionary still accepts Müllenhoff's theory, has since altered his opinion. There exist two colonies of Cimbri, the one on the Main and Neckar (*CIL.* XIII, 6602, 6604, 6605), and the other near Tongern in Belgium (Caesar, *Bell. Gall.* II, 29). Concerning the learned term Cimbri, used for 'Gothonic nations' by Dutch, German, and Danish scholars in the sixteenth to seventeenth centuries, see vol. I, § 13.

Lit. Lyschander, *Origines et antiquitates Cimbricae* (Westphalen, *Mon. ined.* II, 698); Pontanus, *Rerum Danicar. Hist.* I, 649; Pontoppidan, *Theatr. Danicum,* I, 318 (1730); Werlauff, *Danske Vidensk. Selsk. Skrifter,* 1836, 275 note; Feilberg, *Ordb. ov. d. jyske Almuesmål,* s.v. *Himmelbo* and *Himmerland*; Müllenhoff, II, 116; Bremer, §§ 61, 122; *idem, Literaturblatt,* 1888, 442; Much, *Beiträge,* XVII, 214; *idem,* in Hoops, s.v. *Kimbern*; Zippel, *Die Heimat der Kimbern* (Programme, Königsberg, 1893, 9); Marcks, *Bonner Jahrbücher,* 1894, 29; Steenstrup, *Danmarks Riges Hist.* I, 66; Kossinna, *Indogerm. Forsch.* VII, 290; Ihm in Pauly-Wissowa, s.v.; Schütte, *Nordisk Tidsskr. f. Filologi,* 1896, 143; *idem, The Scotch Geogr. Magazine,* XXX, 65; *idem, Geogr. Tidskrift,* 1915, 17; *idem, Hist. Aarbog f. Skive,* 1915, 14, *ibid.* 1929, 112; *idem, Beiträge,* XLI, 2 and 16; *idem, Arkiv,* XXXIII, 28; *idem, Fra Himmerland og Kjær Herred,* 1916, 1 seq.; *idem, Ptolemy's Maps,* 64; *idem, Jubilee Congress of the Folk-Lore Society,* 167; *idem, The Origin of the Cimbrians* (*Acta Philologica Scandinavica,* 1930, 91); Noreen, *Fornvännen,* 1920, 23; Wadstein in *Minnesskrift utg. av Filol. Samfundet i Göteborg,* 1925, 193; Löwenthal, *Wörter u. Sachen,* XI, 62; L. Schmidt, *Zur Kimbern- und Teutonenfrage* (*Klio,* XXII, 95); Feist, *Das Volkstum der Kimbern u. Teutonen* (*Zeitschr. f. Schweizerische Gesch.* 1929, Heft 2, 129).

10. Jutl. Tyboer. County: M.Dan. Thythe Sysæl (*Liber census Daniae,* A.D. 1231), Thiuth; Jutl. Ty, Tyland. The territorial name seems to be the O.N. *þjóð* 'people', and thus derived from a tribal name. Ty lies directly opposite Himmerland, and this juxtaposition seems to reflect the companionship of Teutones and Cimbri in the famous migration of 113–102 B.C. However, the Teutones of Pytheas, cited by Pliny, XXXVII, 35, do not dwell directly on the coast, since they do not themselves collect the amber. Mela, III, 5, § 54, places them on the island of 'Codanouia' in the Codan Gulf, i.e. one of Ptolemy's Scandian islands, probably Zealand, where there exists a mediaeval district Thiuth. And two prototypes of Ptolemy, II, 11, § 9,

referred the Teutones alias Teutonoaroi to the south coast of the Codan Gulf.[1] Evidence such as this from tribal names and literature makes the localisation of the ancient Teutones uncertain. There probably existed two sections of them, one in Zealand and one in Jutland. The juxtaposition of Teutones and Cimbri is repeated in other countries; for instance, Toutoni appear beside Cimbri on the river Main, according to inscriptions. The Laeti Teutoniciani in the Roman militia (*Not. dign. Occ.* XLII, 33) may perhaps originate from such colonies. Concerning 'Teutons' as a learned synonym used by German, French, and English scholars for 'Germans' and 'Gothonic nations', see § 148, 1 and vol. I, § 21.

11. O.E. Wendle? (*Beowulf*, l. 348); O.N. Vendil-folk (*Knytlinga Saga*, ch. 46, MS *Skinnbókin*, No. 180 b; cp. *Fornmanna Sögur*, XI, 252), Vandils-byggjar, Vandilsbúar (*ibid.*); Jutl. Vendel-boer, pronounced Wǫ̨jəlboer; M.Lat. Vandili, Wendilenses (Saxo, 588, 807, 908). County: O.N. Vendill (Snorri, *Ynglinga Saga*, ch. 27); M.Dan. Wændle Sysæl (*Liber census Daniae*, A.D. 1231); Jutl. Vendsyssel, pronounced Wænsøsəl (cp. the East Gothonic Vandali, Vandili, the West Jutl. district of Wændlefolk, now Vandfuld Herred, and the Svionic county of Vendel, with a lake and river of the same name). The word O.N. *vendill*, Norw. *våndel*, means 'a twig' and may, by secondary development, be conceived both as a river and as a headland like the Skaw, O.N. Vendilskagi. Home: the county of Vendill with the Vendilskagi; the West Jutl. district of Wændlefolk is probably a colony.

Lit. N. M. Petersen, *Regesta geogr. Islandorum* (*Fornm. Sögur*, XII), s.v. *Vendilbuar*, *Vendilfolk*; Hellquist, *Etymol. Bemerkungen*, IX (Gefle, 1893); *idem*, *Arkiv*, XXV, 199; Stjerna, *Arkiv*, XXI, 71, *Essays on Beowulf*, ch. iii; Chadwick, 214; Feilberg, *Ordb. ov. d. jyske Almuesmål*, s.v. *Vendelboer* and *Vendsyssel*; Chambers, *Widsith*, 208 (with lit.); Schütte, *Danske Studier*, 1914, 33, 34; *idem*, *Arkiv*, XXXIII, 70; *idem*, (Norw.) *Hist. Tidsskrift*, 1917, 37; Noreen, *Fornvännen*, 1920, 26.

12. O.E. *Ýte (dat. Ýtum, *Widsith*, l. 26), *Ýtan (gen. Ýtena, Alfred's *Bede*, IV, 16), *Éotas (gen. Éota, *ibid.*), *Iotas, *Iutas (dat. Iotum, Iutum, *Sax. Chron.* ad an. 449), *Iutan (gen. Iutna cynn, *ibid.*), *Geatas (gen.

[1] The impossible form 'Teutonoaroi' found in Ptolemy is a learned construction, but must be interpreted otherwise than by Müllenhoff, II, 237. *-oaroi* is simply a misunderstood Latin correction 'Vari', intended to restore 'Varini' for the corrupt 'Viruni'. Cp. our monographs, *Beiträge*, XLI, 15, and *Ptolemy's Maps*, 17.

Geata, dat. Geatum, Alfred's *Bede*, I, 15);[1] M.Dan. Iutæ; Dan. Jyder, Jyde-karle, Jyde-batter, Jyl-lændere; Jutl. dial. Jyjer; N.Samsø dial. Iwe; S.Samsø Iweder; Swed. Jutar; O.N. Jótar (and poetical appellative *ýtar* 'men'); O.L.G. Iuddas (Adam. Brem.); L.G. Jüten; M.Lat. Eucii (letter of King Theodebert, c. A.D. 550), Iutae (Bede, I, 15), Iuti (Saxo, 442), Gioti, Giothi (Æthelwerd, Will. of Malmesbury); Finn. Juutilaiset. Family name: Dan. Yde. Country: M.Dan. Jutland; Dan. Jylland; O.N. Jótland, Reiðgotland; O.E. Gotland (Alfred's *Orosius*); Germ. Jütland. Place names: M.Dan. Jöthne-wath, A.D. 1245; Dan. Jynde-vad ('Juteford', in South Jutland, with normal *-nd* for *-tn*, as in Dan. *vand, bund* < O.N. *vatn, botn* 'water, bottom'); Jyde-bæk 'Jutebrook', twice in South Jutland, on the Frisian frontier and near the Saxon frontier; Zachrisson objects that Jydebæk may simply contain the root **eut-* 'water' and not the name of the people, but the position on the south frontier of the Jutes speaks in favour of the ethnic etymology; Swed. Jute-nabben near Kalmar, Jute-kärret in Vestmanland (places of battles between Swedes and Danes); Finn. Juutin-rauma (the Öresund, literally the Dane-stream). Wood: O.E. Ytene (sc. **wudu*, 'Nova Foresta, quae lingua Anglorum Ytene nuncupatur', Florence of Worcester). The name probably originates from a Gothonic root **eut-* 'water'; Schück compares the Swedish lake of Yten. Others combine Jutes and Eudusii; Much compares the alternating *t* and *ð* in O.N. *blautr* and *blauðr* 'weak'. Various phonetic theories try to explain the divergent dental; we might also suggest that the *t* originates from a diminutive or pet form of the name (cp. Jutl. Åbutter beside Åboer). But all this is mere guess-work. Möller, Erdmann, Kossinna, and Siebs erroneously distinguish 'Euts' in North Germany from 'Jeuts' in Jutland. The Danish *j* in Jyder is secondary, as in the dialect form *jyver* for *yver* 'udder'; initial *j* was lost in Scandinavian, and consequently an original form *Jeut- could not have survived. The ȝ in the Anglo-Saxon forms is also secondary, as is the confusion with Goths and Göts (cp. O.N. Reiðgotland, which originates from the Hreiðgotar in Prussia). The home of the original Jutes must have been South Jutland, as they co-operate with Angles and Saxons; their maritime base was probably the harbour of Hjerting near the present Esbjerg (cp. the South Jutlandic ford Jöthnewath with an old genitive of the name Jutes).

[1] The forms Géotas, Géotland, which are often cited, should be marked by an asterisk.

Colonies: Kent, Hampshire, and the Isle of Wight. Since mediaeval times Jutland has included the Cimbric Peninsula; in Swedish and Finnish 'Jutes' means 'Danes' (cp. § 258, 6); in the Swedish dialect of Helsingland it may even include the Norwegians (cp. § 277, 5 (*a*)).

Lit. N. M. Petersen, *Regesta geogr. Islandorum* (*Fornm. Sögur*, XII), s.v. *Jótar*; Zeuss, 500; Grimm, 735; Müllenhoff, IV, 464, 466; H. Möller, *Das altengl. volksepos*, 88; Erdmann, *Name u. Heimat der Angeln*, 40; Kossinna, *Indogerm. Forsch.* VII, 292; Olrik and Schütte in *Salmonsens Konv. Lex.* 1st ed. s.v. *Jyder*; Fritzner, *Ordb. ov. d. gamle norske Sprog*, s.v. *Jótar*; Feilberg, *Ordb. ov. d. jyske Almuesmål*, s.v. *Jyde* and *Jylland*; Siebs in *Grundriss*, 2nd ed. I, 1158; Noreen, *Spridda studier*, II, 91, 139; *idem*, *Fornvännen*, 1920, 41; *idem*, cit. by Schück (see below), p. 6 note 2; Schück, *Upsala Univ. Årsskrift*, 1907, *Progr.* II, 6 and 16; Chadwick, 106; Chambers, *Widsith*, 237 seq.; *idem*, *Beowulf*, 8 and 333; Much in Hoops, s.v. *Jüten*; Björkman, *Anglia, Beiblatt*, 28, 175.

Synopsis of types of tribal names.

(*a*) Simplex. Auiones, Yte, Chaloi, Harudes, Kimbroi (Teutones). Anglii and Wendle may be referred to the Simplex type, if they originate from territorial names, Angel and Vendill.

(*b*) Long Derivative types. Varini, Rondingas, Eudusii, Sabalingioi; the perhaps corrupt Ptolemaic Kobandoi in West Jutland may be added.

(*c*) Compounds. No instances.

The later development of toponymics introduces a variety of Long types.

Among the Derivatives *-ing* is most frequent: Åboinger in the county of Åbo (Auiones?), Lovringer, *Baringer in the counties of Lofræth Sysæl and Barnge or Barwith Sysæl. Such toponymics from lesser districts are especially numerous: Hallinger in Hallæ Hæret (i.e. Chaloi?), Hånninger in Hanæ H., Heingæ in the district of He, Rousinger in Rugsø (Roxæ) H., Fanninger and Morsinger on the islands of Fanø, Morsø. Rare local forms are those ending in *-ik* and *-is*: Fanniker on Fanø, Rømiser on Røm.[1]

Compounds, which are originally avoided, now occur in increasing numbers. The Scandinavian element *-bo* normally designates the inhabitants of counties: Å-, Salling-, Hard-, Himmer-, Ty-, Vendelboer, for Auiones (?), Sabalingioi (??), Harudes, Kimbroi, *Teutones, Wendle; so also Vard-boer in the county of Warwith, and Angel-boer in Angel, which

[1] In a diploma of King Frederic II (1586), the island of Mandø is called 'Mandøser'. This seems to be a toponymic corresponding to Rømiser.

does not form a separate county. These Jutlandic toponymics ending in *-bo* contrast with the East Danish ones in *-far*; yet the latter type occurs in one English name, viz. Lindis-faran, and must consequently have been used in a part of Jutland. An equivalent is *-folk* in Vendil-folk (cp. the Anglian Norð-folc and Súð-folc, and the Gautic Vi-folka härad). Secondary forms of a colloquial character are Jyde-karle and Jyde-batter (cp. Å-butter for Å-boinger).

Lit. Schütte, *Folkelig Hof- og Statskalender* (*Danske Studier*, 1914, 29, 1915, 61, 198); *idem*, (Norw.) *Hist. Tidsskrift*, 1917, 1 seq.; *idem*, *Hist. Aarbog for Skive*, 1921, 1 seq.

§ 238. Ethnic Position.

A section of 'Inguaeones' once existed, but the region over which it extended is open to question and it certainly varied. The inclusion of the Chauchi (Pliny, IV, 99) cannot be verified; later, the Danes form the nucleus of the section (*Beowulf*).

Only two points are clear: that their chief ancient representatives are the Cimbri, and that they are consistently distinguished from the Erminones-Swabians.

Their connexion with the Cimbri appears from Pliny and Tacitus.

(1) Pliny, IV, 99: 'Ingyaeones, quorum pars Cimbri'; *ibid.* IV, 96: 'gens Inguaeonum...mons Saevo ibi...ad Cimbrorum usque promunturium efficit sinum, qui Codanus vocatur'.

(2) Tac. *Germ.* 2: 'proximi Oceano Inguaeones'; *ibid.* 37: 'proximi Oceano Cimbri'.

A distinction between the Inguaeones and the Erminones-Swabians is made by a larger number of authorities.

(1) Pliny, IV, 99: Ingyaeones including Cimbri are distinguished from the Erminones including Swabians.

(2) Tac. A, *Germ.* 2: 'proximi Oceano Inguaeones' are distinguished from the Erminones.

(3) Tac. B, *ibid.* 37–38: 'proximi Oceano Cimbri' are distinguished from the Swabians.

(4) Strabo, VII, 290–291: the Kimbroi are distinguished from the Swabians.

(5) Mela, III, 3, § 32: the Cimbri are distinguished from the Erminones, 'ultimi Germaniae'.

(6) Ptol. II, 11, § 7: the Cimbric Chersonese is represented by tribes

only, like Skandia, but Germany by both tribes, towns, mountains, etc. Germany includes the Swabians.

(7) *Widsith*, l. 43: Offa establishes the frontier of Angel (South Jutland) against the Swabians.

Though our authorities agree on the general distinction, the details are not quite clear. Tacitus separates the Cimbri from the Eudoses, Angles, and Varines, whom he regards as Swabians. If he had known the geographical position of the Eudoses, he would have seen his error, for the Eudoses, i.e. the Fundusioi of Ptolemy, are North Jutlanders, consequently 'proximi Oceano' like the Inguaeones-Cimbri, and not 'medii', as Tacitus designates his Erminones, who include the Swabians, according to Pliny. Besides, the Swabians are Germans, and neither the Jutes, nor the ancestors of the Angles in Britain, ever belonged to the German nationality. As we mentioned in § 158, Tacitus' erroneous designation of the Eudoses, Angles, etc., as Swabians perhaps originates from a temporary political union between the Angles and the Swabian kingdom of Maroboduus in Bohemia.

The most prominent characteristic of the alleged 'Swabians' north-east of the Elbe is their common worship of Nerthus, 'Mother Earth' (Tac. *Germ.* 40). The solidarity of this religious community still appears in mediaeval times: with the 'Reudigni et Auiones et Anglii et Varini' we may compare the list in *Widsith*, ll. 24–26: 'Rondingas, Werne, Eowan', and the common '*Lex Angliorum et Werinorum, hoc est Thoringorum*'. The amphictyony of Nerthus in reality must embrace the whole of Jutland and include the Cimbri, though Tacitus excludes them. We may trace Nerthus worship in a place name some few miles south of the Cimbric district, viz. the rectory of Njær near Randers. This religious community, however, did not continue to be peculiar to Jutland and Mecklenburg: the male Nerthus is worshipped throughout Scandinavia.[1] Among Saxons, Frisians, and Germans, on the contrary, the name of this deity is unknown.

As regards their constitution, the Varines, Angles, and Jutes of the

[1] The change from a female to a male deity may be explained by the fact that the feminine *u*-stems were generally given up in Scandinavian, so that, if such a form survived, it would mechanically change its gender (cp. Mogk in Hoops, s.v. *Njǫrðr*). Besides, the Asiatic cult of fertility, from which Nerthus originated, was fond of androgynous deities, whereas the later Scandinavian religion preferred the male (cp. vol. I, § 97).

Migration Age are monarchists, like the Danes of their day, and like the Swedes from primitive times. Cp. on the kings of the Varines, Procopius, *Bell. Goth.* IV, 20 seq.; on those of the Angles, *Widsith*, l. 35, *Beowulf*, l. 1949 seq., Saxo, 160 seq. (after the fourth century A.D.); the Jutish King Amleth, Saxo, 150. We may certainly consider monarchy during the Migration Age as a symptom of the general political tendency; but it is characteristic that the Saxons who are alleged to have been close kinsmen of the Angles remained ardent republicans for centuries after that time.

If we search for more specific details of these affinities, it is natural to expect that relations with Saxons and Germans would prevail towards the south, and relations with the Scandinavians towards the north. This presupposition is, moreover, confirmed by facts.

The Varines only supply some few names of persons (see Schönfeld, 290): Ermegisl, Radigis, Theudibald, Vaccar; we add Agrivulf (Jordanes, 233). But though the selection is meagre it shows a pronounced national physiognomy: in accordance with their southerly position the Varines have a nomenclature of purely Saxon and German type. The elements *Erm-* and *-bald*, which characterise their names, are strictly avoided in Scandinavian; and *Theud-* is at last very rare in Danish, though it is more common in Swedish.

The Angles, as situated farther north, occupy a more intermediate position. The phonetic type of the names Vermund and Uffo seems to be Saxon (cp. § 216), and Vermund is a name of German character, still used as Wahrmund. On the other hand, Anglian princely names such as Hróðmund and Cueldgils are typically Scandinavian (cp. § 216). The Anglian sub-tribes Norð-folc and Súð-folc have names of a Scandinavian type, and the name Lindis-faran betrays special connexions with the insular Danes. The ancient Anglian epic literature is almost purely Scandinavian, celebrating the Danes and ignoring the Saxons. And Saxo begins his history by stating that Angul was the brother of Dan.

The Jutes, as far as we may judge from the meagre evidence afforded by their names, show no primaeval Saxon affinity (see § 216, p. 270). If we may draw conclusions from the earliest runic inscriptions, their language shows pronounced traces of Scandinavian (cp. Hlewagastiz Holtiŋaz, with no West Gothonic loss of *-z*). The Jutes of Kent do not share the Saxon type of wergeld (cp. Chadwick, 84).

The name of the Cimbri reappears in several Svionic and Norwegian place names (cp. § 237, 9). The Cimbric bull worship, at a time when the Germans had no deities in personified form (Caesar, *Bell. Gall.* VI, 21), betrays direct connexions with Gaul, originating from the amber trade. The existence of a body of trained priestesses, of huge sacrificial vessels, and of richly decorated carriages for religious purposes, are all features which separate Jutlandic civilisation from that of the contemporary Germans, as described by Caesar and Tacitus, and which point towards influence from Gaul.

History shows a Jutish-Saxon co-operation in the conquest of Kent, where the leaders are Jutes, whereas the majority of their followers seem to have been Saxons, according to the choice of the river names Stour, Swale, and Wantsumu. The participation of the Jutes in the maritime activity of the Saxons had as its base the harbour of Hjerting near the present Esbjerg. Cp. Vilh. la Cour, *Sønderjyllands Historie*, I, 128, 133, 148. But as the large majority of the harbours of Jutland lie on the east coast, the relations with the Danish islands and the Scandinavian Peninsula were more intimate, and these relations finally decided the position of the peninsular section: it ceased to be intermediate and joined the Scandinavian sub-group.

The Jutlandic house, as shown by excavations in Ty and Himmerland, from the Iron Age, belongs to the Danish 'compound house' type, with the gable ends placed east and west, and with main entrance from the long side, not from the gable end, as in the Saxon type. This primitive type even to-day predominates exclusively in the middle part of South Jutland and is frequent in Angel and Sundeved and on the islands of Røm and Als. Only the extreme southern parts of South Jutland have adopted non-Danish types of the 'compound house', viz. towards the east the Saxon, towards the west the Frisian. The coast of West Jutland, Ty, Vendsyssel, and North Himmerland, down to the close of the eighteenth century, partly even to the present time, prefer the Danish 'double farmstead' or 'parallel farmstead', also occurring in Bornholm. The main part of Jutland nowadays belongs to the domain of the Danish quadrangle. The map in *Der grosse Brockhaus* (1929, IV, 624–625), representing the whole of South Jutland as exclusively exhibiting the 'Saxon compound house', is seriously at fault; in the larger part of the country only the Danish 'compound house' or the Danish quadrangle is found. Cp. R. Mejborg, *Das Bauernhaus im Herzogtum Schleswig* (transl. from Danish by Prof. R. Haupt); A. Asmussen, *Das alte Angler*

Bauernhaus (in Martensen and Henningsen, *Angeln beschrieben von H. N. A. Jensen*, p. 416); Zangenberg, *Danske Bøndergaarde* (*Danmarks Folkeminder*, No. 34).

The well-known peculiarity in West Jutlandic of placing the definite article before the noun, *æ mand* instead of normal Scand. *mand-en*, 'the man', is merely a secondary phenomenon. The primitive Gothonic language uses no article at all, when the noun is not accompanied by an adjective. The introduction of the article before the noun does not take place in Jutlandic and East Danish until late in the Middle Ages. When it is introduced, local influences caused South and West Jutlandic to imitate the German and Frisian position of the article, and this late development has nothing to do with the division of ancient Gothonic sub-groups (cp. our monograph, *Jysk og østdansk Artikelbrug* (*Vidensk. Selskabs hist. filol. Meddelelser*, VII, 2)).

The theory of J. Grimm that the Jutish nationality ought to be distinguished from the Danish has still been maintained by F. Kauffmann in a public lecture *Deutsch oder Dänisch?* (1923), cp. our article in *Beiträge*, XLVIII, 141. Otherwise it is nowadays only advocated by dilettanti such as A. Sach, author of *Das Herzogtum Schleswig in seiner ethnogr. u. nationalen Entwickelung*, 1896–1907. In 1914 twelve German philologists publicly stated that 'Mit Bezug auf das Dänentum des Westjütischen besteht kein Streit zwischen der deutschen und dänischen Wissenschaft'; the declaration was signed by Behaghel, Collitz, Gebhardt, Gering, Heusler, Hirt, Jiriczek, Mogk, Much, v. Unwerth, Wrede, and later by Braune (cp. also Th. Siebs in *Schleswigsche Grenzpost*, 3 Nov. 1911, and de Boer in *Deutsch-nordische Zeitschrift*, I, 198 seq.).

Various contrasts between Eastern and Western Jutland in dialect, place names, and civilisation, are examined in our article *Færdselsskel* (*Hist. Aarbog f. Skive*, 1929, 43 seq., with maps).

Lit. (*a*) The case for Anglo-Saxonism or Anglo-Frisianism: Grimm, 828, 831, 837; *idem*, *Grammatik*, LI, note; Müllenhoff, IV (see Index, s.v. *Ingvaeonen*, *Angelsachsen*, *Angeln*, *Jüten*); *idem*, *Nordalbing. Studien*, I, 133, 136, 169; Seelmann, *Jahrb. d. Vereins f. niederdeutsche Sprachforschung*, XII, 28; Kögel, *Gesch. d. deutsch. Litt.* I, 57 note; Bremer, §§ 77, 81, 121 seq.; Schmidt in Pauly-Wissowa, s.v. *Inguaeones*. (*b*) A more intermediate theory: Grimm, *Gramm.* I, 247 (on the Anglo-Scandinavian 'Breaking' of vowels); Rieger, *Zeitschrift*, 1859, 177 seq.; Kossinna, *Indogerm. Forsch.* VII, 308; Hoops, s.v. *Angelsachsen*. (*c*) The case for pronounced Anglo-Danish relations: Grundtvig, *Haandbog i Verdenshistorien* (*Udvalgte Skr.* VII, 9); Schütte, *Var Anglerne Tyskere?* (*Sønderjydske Aarbøger*, 1900, 1 seq.); *idem*, *Anzeiger*, XXVIII, 9; *idem*, *Arkiv*, XXV, 314, 317, 319; *idem*, *ibid.*

XXXIII, 38 and 87; *Smaaskrifter udg. af Selsk. f. germ. Filologi*, No. 13, ch. iv; Chadwick, 296; *idem*, in Chambers' *Encycl.* s.v. *Angles, Jutes*; Steenstrup, *Jylland og Jyder* (*Hist. Tidsskr.* 1910–12, 1 seq.); P. K. Thorsen, *Den berømteste Dialektgrænse i Danmark* (*Artikler og Breve*, udg. af Byskov og Marius Kristensen, II); Marius Kristensen, *Den bestemte Artikel* (in la Cour, *Sønderjyllands Historie*, I, 36). On the difficult question of the epic *éotenas*, see Chambers, *Beowulf*, 261, 272. On the racial character, Feilberg, *Ordbog*, s.v. *Jyde*; Gravlund, *Dansk Folkekarakter*; Schütte, *Jyder*; *idem*, *Dansk Folkekarakter*.

§ 239. History of the ancient Jutlanders and Varines, collectively.

The history of Jutland begins (345–113 B.C.) with that of tribes with the Simplex names *Inguiones(?) or *Eutones(?) (MSS Guiones, Gutones), Teutones, Cimbri, together with the (Saxon?) Ambrones. The Chaloi due south of the Cimbri probably belong to the same primaeval stratum.

About 345 B.C. the (In)guiones (or *Eutones?), who collect the amber and sell it to the Teutones, are visited by Pytheas from Marseilles.

From 113 to 58 B.C. the Teutones, Cimbri, Ambrones, Harudes, and *Eudoses send out swarms of emigrants to Middle Europe, etc.

In A.D. 5 Tiberius, camping on the Lower Elbe, menaces Jutland. The Roman navy reduces the Cimbri and Harudes to a sort of subjection.

About the same time the Swabian King Maroboduus in Bohemia is extending his dominion to the vicinity of the Cimbric Chersonese, and the Angles (as 'Swabians', according to Tacitus and Ptolemy) seem temporarily to have joined it.

Between A.D. 70 and 98 Pliny and Tacitus mention the Inguaeonic section, which seems identical with the worshippers of Nerthus, embracing Angles, Auiones, Reudigni, Varines, Eudoses, etc.

About 286–289 the Saxons and the Scandinavian tribe of Erules begin raiding the Channel. They probably are accompanied by Jutes who raid unprotected, outlying British islands such as Thanet and Wight.

In the fourth and fifth century the Anglian King Viglek (Angl. Wihtlæg) conquers and kills a neighbouring King Amleth.

In the fifth century Frovin, identical with the royal ancestor Freawine in Wessex, is killed in South Jutland by an invading King Athisl, probably the King Eadgils of the Myrgings in North Germany, mentioned in *Widsith*. Frovin's son Vigo (West Sax. Wig) takes revenge. The Anglian King Offa, Wærmund's son, repulses invading Swabians and Myrgings.

The Nerthus community is still traceable in the list of *Widsith*.

The 'Dane' (Jute) Hengest fights the Frisian King Finn at Finnsburg.

In 445 seq. Hengest accomplishes the Jutish conquest of Kent. Other Jutes conquer the Isle of Wight and Hampshire. Cynric, a descendant of the South Jutlandic chieftain Frovin, establishes the dynasty of the West Saxons. Angles settle in Eastern and Middle Britain north of the East Saxons.

In 505 Danes appear as northern neighbours of the Varines.

Saxo's king Dan who succeeds the (Anglian) king Uffo, i.e. Offa, seems to symbolise the establishment of Danish suzerainty in South Jutland (cp. p. 316).

The place names ending in *-leif* (Dan. *-lev*, Germ. *-leben*) seem to suggest a Danish colonisation on the east coast of Jutland and the south-western coast of the Baltic.

About 526 so-called 'Danes', led by the 'Geatic' King Hygelac, raid Friesland. Saxo mentions Hugleth, i.e. Hygelác as king of Denmark.

In 531 the Franks, after devastating Thuringia, probably reduce the Varines to subjection.

In 550 seq. the Saxons and Eucii (Jutes) voluntarily pay homage to the Frankish King Theodebert. Varines serve as mercenaries of the Byzantine general Narses in Italy against the Goths. About 580 'Danus, Euthio, Saxo' are mentioned as enemies of the Franks by Venantius Fortunatus. Here the Jutes appear for the last time as an independent people beside the Danes.

In 594 the Frankish King Childebert, aided by the Slavs, subjugates the rebel Varines. Probably on this occasion remnants of Angles and Varines seek shelter in Thuringia.

About 800 the law of the Thuringian Angles and Varines is codified, probably after the diet of Aachen in 802. The title of this law is the last trace of the ancient Nerthus community which now disappears. On the Continent it is absorbed by Danish, German or Slav civilisation, and in Britain by the Saxon. The names Angles and Jutes survive; that of the Angles is generalised in Britain, that of the Jutes on the Cimbric Chersonese.

The name of Jutes thus comes to embrace all Jutlanders except the Frisians. It is easy to understand that the Germans generalised the first tribal name they met north of the Saxons, and the German use of the name was afterwards adopted by the natives themselves. This process took place so early that old Icelandic literature knows absolutely nothing of separate Jutish sub-tribes; it is only in O.E. sources that we still catch a glimpse of some of them, viz. the Engle, Eowan, Rondingas, Wendle, etc. When the descendants of such tribes happen to be mentioned in Scandinavian literature, they only appear as local populations, Angelboer, Vendelboer, etc., no longer as tribes. Finally, the name Jutes in Swedish and Finnish comes to embrace all Danes; in the Helsingland dialect of Swedish it even includes the Norwegians.

Lit. Allen, *Geschichte der dänischen Sprache im Herzogtum Schleswig*; Bennike and Marius Kristensen, *Kort over de danske Folkemål*; Olrik and Schütte, *Salmonsens Konv. Lex.* s.v. *Jyder*; Marius Kristensen, *Nydansk* (*Smaaskrifter udg. af Selsk. f. germ. Filologi*, No. 12); *idem*, *Danskens Omfang* (la Cour, *Sønderjyllands Historie*, I, 76); Schütte, *Smaaskrifter udg. af Selsk. f. germ. Filologi*, No. 13, ch. IV; *idem*, *Jyder* (*Flensborg Avis*, 11 May 1924); *idem*, *Færdselsskel paa langs af Jylland* (*Hist. Aarbog f. Skive*, 1928, 43); *idem*, *Arkiv*, XXV, 317 seq.; Steenstrup, *Jylland og Jyder* (*Hist. Tidsskrift*, 1910–12, 1 seq.); Schmidt, II, 1–33; Gravlund, *Dansk Folkekarakter*.

§ 240. History of the Angles Proper.

On the etymology 'angle' (a peninsula?) or 'firth' (i.e. the Sli) see § 237, 1.

The epic home of the Angles is Ongel, next to the Swabians (that is Semnones) (*Widsith*, l. 44); 'Angulus...inter provincias Iutarum et Saxonum', Bede, I, 15 (cp. the Ongul of Nennius, § 37); situated north of the Eider (Saxo, IV, 172, cp. his eponymous 'brothers' Angul and Dan, I, 21); the land of the Danes (*Quedlinburg. Ann.* ad an. 445)—the latter piece of evidence identifies Angel as a Danish dominion with the traditional Gothonic home (cp. vol. I, § 72, 7, § 73).

Tacitus, *Germ.* 40, and Ptolemy, II, 11, § 8, show that the Angles were neighbours of the Langobards, i.e. the inhabitants of Bardengau in Hanover; thus the Angles seem to have extended through a part of Eastern Holstein.[1] Their south-eastern neighbours were the Varines in Mecklenburg, who like the Angles belonged to the peninsular group, the worshippers of Nerthus.

The alleged 'Swabianism' of the Angles (Tacitus, Ptolemy) perhaps indicates that they were subject to the Bohemian King Maroboduus from A.D. 6 to 17, like the Semnones and Langobards (cp. § 158). Ptolemy

[1] Ptolemy's localisation of the Angles in the interior of Germany is as absurd as that of his Langobards on the Rhine (!!) and no weight should have been attached to it (cp. our monograph *Ptolemy's Maps*, 127).

seems to give the most accurate version of the original source—mentioning only the Angles, not the Varines, Eudoses, etc., among the Swabian tribes. Tacitus has as usually exaggerated by including all the peninsular tribes except the Cimbri.

English and Danish sources record the rise of an Anglian dynasty after the fourth century: Waþol-géat, Wihtlæg, Wǽrmund, Offa, Éomǽr. Waþol-géat has been turned into Ger-vendel (Saxo, 135). Saxo's Viglet or Viglek, 160 (Wihtlæg), kills the Jutlandic King Amleth, whose 'sepultura ac nomine campus apud Jutiam extat', 161; local traditions dating from the seventeenth century place the heath near Randers, at Ammelhede. This slaying was probably due to a dynastic feud which resulted in the extension of Anglian suzerainty. Vermund (Wǽrmund) defends South Jutland against Athisl who kills earl Frovin (*ibid.* 163) (the Fréawine of the West Saxon genealogy), but is in return slain by Frovin's sons Keto and Vigo (Fréawine's son Wig). Athisl appears as a 'Swede', owing to his confusion with his well-known Swedish namesake who fights the Danes. The Athisl actually referred to is no doubt the famous North German prince, O.E. Éadgils, king of the Myrgings (*Widsith*, l. 93). (The chronological difficulty will be discussed below.) The famous Offa, Wǽrmund's son (Uffo of Saxo), repulses the Swabians and Myrgings at Fifeldor, 'the terrible door' (*Widsith*, ll. 33–43). Saxo, 173, replaces the vanished Swabians (Semnones) by Saxons, and Fifeldor by the synonym Eidorus, O.G. Egidora; this idea of bringing the names 'up to date' was quite natural. Offa is celebrated in various places, e.g. *Beowulf*, l. 1955, *Vitae duorum Offarum*, etc.; it is to be assumed that he frustrated a Swabian attempt to check the expansion of the Nerthus community.

We must now discuss at what period he lived. The pedigrees of Mercia and Wessex regard Offa and Wig as contemporaries like Saxo's Uffo and Vigo. Cp. Chadwick, 134: 'Offa lies in the eighth generation above Penda; so if, in accordance with the usual standard of calculation, we allow thirty years for each generation, his birth should be dated about 240 years before that of his descendant. Therefore, if we are right in believing that Penda was born about the beginning of the seventh century (cf. p. 16), Offa's birth ought to be dated about the year 360. Again, if we apply the same process to the West Saxon genealogy and assume that Cynric was born about the year 470, the birth of Wig, his fourth ancestor, will have to be dated about 350'.

Chadwick further accepts the identification of Athisl with Éadgils, an alleged contemporary of the Gothic King Eormanric who died about 375. This identification would also place Offa in the fourth century.

Chadwick, however, is aware of the chronological unreliability of the genealogies. In *Oldsagn om Godtjod*, 151, we try to show that in these genealogies the interval between the continental ancestors and the invaders of Britain has been filled by eponymous names, viz. Angel-þéow of Mercia, i.e. Angel-þéod 'Anglian nation'; Icel, *ibid.*, the eponymous ancestor of the Iclings, the dynasty of Mercia; and Gewis of Wessex, the eponymous ancestor of the Gewissæ or West Saxons. Moreover, Chadwick has shown Cynric's 'father' Cerdic to be a native Briton (Chadwick, 30). As a matter of fact, *Beowulf*, l. 1960, ignores Angel-þéow and regards Éomǽr as Offa's *son*, not as his grandson. Thus some two generations ought to be left out from each genealogy, and the date of the birth of Offa and Wig would fall within the fifth century, about 410–420.

Now some references in *Widsith* and *Beowulf* would seem to suggest even a much later period. Éadgils marries a sister of the Langobardic King Albuin who died in 572 (*Widsith*, l. 98), and Offa marries the widow of Hygelác who fell about 526 (*Beowulf*, l. 1954).

There is a difference of about a century between the dates given by the genealogies and those in ancient poetry. One of these sources must be wrong, and we prefer the genealogies. For they at least make an attempt at chronology, whereas *Widsith* unhesitatingly makes Ostrogotha who lived about 250 shake hands with Albuin who lived about 550. Offa's great deed can scarcely be later than the fifth century; in the sixth century continental history knows of Varines, Jutes, or Danes, e.g. in the entries of 505, 525, 550, 565, 580, 594, but the Angles are conspicuous only by their absence.

Those Angles who did not go to Britain or Thuringia seem to have quietly joined the Jutes and Danes. Cp. Chadwick, p. 296:

'It is true that the Angli of Britain seem never to have included themselves among the Danes; but the reason for this may be that the name *Dene* (*Danir*) had not come into use as a collective term before the invasion of Britain. There can be no doubt that those who remained behind were subsequently known as *Dene*; indeed the name *Engle* must have disappeared very quickly. The case of the populations of the south coast of the Baltic was somewhat different. Partly, like the Angli, they migrated westwards, while whatever element remained behind was swallowed up by the Slavonic invasion. With these reservations however we may probably equate the Danes of the Middle Ages with the Inguaeones of the first century.'

Henceforth, Angel only contains a local population of Angel-boer, speaking the South Jutlandic dialect of Danish. Angel does not even become a county, like the territories of the Cimbri and Harudes. And almost every one of the ancient names of the settlements in Southern Slesvig has disappeared; the early mediaeval nomenclature is secondary, showing the usual Danish types such as *-by, -toft, -rød,* etc. Nowadays, Angel is almost completely Germanised.

A war between the British Angles and Rhenish Varines about 540, described in a somewhat legendary manner by Procopius, *Bell. Goth.* IV, 20, is the last political act of the Angles proper on continental soil.

The *Lex Angliorum et Werinorum* about 800 recognises the existence of Angles in Thuringia, but they are soon afterwards absorbed by the Germans.

Lit. **Zeuss,** 152, 495; **Grimm,** 494, 604, 641, 659; **Müllenhoff,** IV, 464; *idem, Nordalbing. Studien,* I, 161; **Grundtvig,** *Haandbog i Verdenshistorien* (*Udv. Skrifter,* VII, 9); *idem, Nordens Mythologie,* 562; **H. Möller,** *Altengl. Volksepos,* 26 seq.; *idem, Anzeiger,* XXII, 129; **ten Brink,** *Beovulf,* 197, 220; **Erdmann,** *Über den Namen u. die Heimat der Angeln*; **Tengberg and Erdmann in** *Nordisk Familjebok,* s.v. *Angelsaxer*; **Much,** *Beiträge,* XVII, 191; *idem,* **in Hoops,** s.v. *Angeln*; **Sach,** *Das Herzogtum Schleswig*; **Bremer,** §§ 131–135; **Schütte,** *Var Anglerne Tyskere?* (*Sønderjydske Aarbøger,* 1900); *idem, Smaaskrifter udg. af Selsk. f. germ. Filologi,* No. 13, ch. iv, §§ 1–21; *idem, Beiträge,* XLI, 38; *idem, Ptolemy's Maps,* 127; *idem, Angels Saga* (*Grænsevagten,* December 1918, January 1919); **Chadwick,** 103 seq.; **Chambers,** *Widsith,* 202 seq.; **Hoops,** s.v. *Angelsachsen*; **V. la Cour,** *Gesch. des schleswigschen Volkes,* I (with maps of the archaeology and tribal names of early South Jutland); *idem, Sønderjyllands Historie,* I, 146.

§ 241. Legendary Traditions.

The British Angles possess a rich epic poetry dealing largely with Scandinavian episodes.

The eponymous ancestor is: Angel-þéow (Mercian *Pedigree*); Angul, brother of Dan (Saxo, I, 21); Angling, leader of the emigration from the land of the Danes (*Quedlinburg. Ann.* ad an. 445).

Isung, 'Ice-man', is the conqueror of Britain in a German legend (*Thidrekssaga,* I, 255); he seems to belong to a Scandinavian ancestral kindred of ice-giants, Fornjót's sons (cp. I, 130, 141).

The Anglian ancestor Scéaf, 'sheaf', only appears in England, but is clearly connected with Scyld, the eponymous ancestor of the Danish dynasty of Skjǫldungar (cp. *Beowulf*, l. 1 seq.; Æthelwerd, ad an. 973; Will. of Malmesbury, II, 116 (173, ed. Hardy)).

As mentioned in § 240, four Mercian generations appear both in English and Danish legends, viz. (1) Waþolgéat, (2) Wihtlæg, (3) Wǽrmund, (4) Offa. Three of the princes concerned are victorious in memorable wars, according to Saxo: Viglek against Amleth, Vermund against Athisl, Uffo against the Saxons (i.e. the Swabians of *Widsith*). Even the Icelanders celebrate Vármundr the Wise and his son 'Óláfr' (Offa). Anglian traditions continue with Éomǽr, 'the brave protector of heroes' (*Beowulf*, l. 1960); he, being an emigrant, already belongs to Britain. With Offa the true continental Angles come to an end, both in England and Denmark. Emigration of legends from Scandinavia to England entirely ceases at the close of the sixth century (cp. Chadwick, 213, and Schütte, *Arkiv*, XXV, 313). And in Denmark the ancient Anglian kings come to be regarded as native Danes.

The eponymous King Dan, who succeeds Uffo (Saxo 175), represents the Danish occupation of the Anglian territory.

Lit. Chadwick, *The Heroic Age*; Chambers, *Widsith*; *idem*, *Beowulf*; Schütte, *Danske Studier*, 1930, 78. The entire stock of Anglian epic geography is examined by Schütte, *Journ. Engl. and Germ. Phil.* XI, No. 4, 19 seq.

§ 242. History of the Varines Proper.

Though without political history in the first centuries A.D., the Varines must have had a certain importance, since they are mentioned both by Pliny, Tacitus, and three of Ptolemy's sources (cp. also the frequent occurrence of the element Warin- in West Gothonic names of persons).

The agreement between Ptolemy's Virunoi and Auarpoi shows that their home was in Mecklenburg, probably near the river Warnow.[1]

During the Migration Age they founded a colony in the Rhine Delta.

In 456 the Varine Ag(r)ivulf becomes Gothic governor of the annexed Swabian state in Galicia; next year he rebels and is executed (Jordanes, XLIV, 233; Hydatius, 180).

The Visigothic King Euric aids the (Rhenish) Varines against (Frankish) enemies (Cassiodorus, *Variae*, III, 3; cp. Schmidt, I, 266).

[1] On the '*promuntorium Varinorum', which Meitzen and Bremer imagine to have read in the *Liber census Daniae*, see p. 296.

About 500 the Ostrogothic King Theodoric summons the Erules, Varines, and Thuringians to ally with him against the aggressive Franks. Cassiodorus, *l.c.*, Hoops, *Waldbäume*, 583, and Schmidt, II, 28, maintain that again the Rhenish Varines are meant; we believe that they were too insignificant to be summoned thus.

About 510–526 there are relations with Langobards and Goths, and Varines serve in the East Roman army. The Frankish conquest of Thuringia in 531 seq. probably caused the neighbouring Varines to submit.

About 540 King Radigis of the Rhenish Varines is attacked by the bride he has repudiated, an Anglian princess from Britain (Procopius, *Bell. Goth.* III, 35). Soon afterwards these Varines submit to the Franks.

In 594 the rebellious Varines of North Germany are subjugated by the Frankish King Childebert and his Slavonic allies ('Fredegar', IV, 15). Mecklenburg falls to the Slavs (cp. the Slavonic tribe of Warnabi). Exiled Varines and Angles settle in Thuringia where the *Lex Angliorum et Werinorum* was codified about 800 (cp. Schmidt, II, 329, 340). On the questionable form Werenofeld see § 237, 4. Perhaps the name of the river Warnow was copied by the Varines in the name Wern in the Werngau. After the political catastrophe the small remnant of the Nerthus worshippers was soon absorbed by the Germans.

Lit. **Zeuss, 132, 360; Grimm, 604, 607; Müllenhoff, IV, 465; Much, *Stammeskunde*, 97; *idem*, in Hoops, s.v. *Warnen*; Chadwick (see Index, s.v. *Varini*, *Warni*); Schmidt, II, 22; Chambers, *Widsith*, 196.**

§ 243. Legendary Traditions.

The Varines are much less famous than the Angles.

An eponymous (?) Varinn emerges on the East Gautic runic inscription of Rök and in Snorri's *Heimskringla, Saga Ol. Tryggv.* ch. 64, and is besides echoed by the epic place names, Varinsvík and Varinsfjǫrðr, *Helgakviða Hundingsbana* (cp. Bugge, *Home of the Eddic Poems*, 135).

Billing, king of the Varines, appears in *Widsith*, l. 25, and in fragmentary Scandinavian lists.

King Radigis' breach of faith with his Anglian bride is recorded by Procopius with romantic features of a legendary character (*Bell. Goth.* IV, 20).

Lit. **Chadwick, *The Heroic Age*, 97; Schütte, *Arkiv*, XXXVI, 23.**

§ 244. History of the Harudes and Eudoses—*Eudusii Proper.

The Harudes (probably 'Foresters') dwelt in East Jutland, south of the Cimbri, east of the *Eudusii, according to Ptolemy, II, 11, § 7. His Φαροδεινοί (*ibid.*) may be *Harodini, 'the smaller Harudes'. The Norwegian Hǫrðar need not be a branch of the same tribe. There were Harudi at the German mountain of Harz; a territorial name *Haruð- anywhere might create a toponymic of this sort (cp. the three Eynir in various parts of Scandinavia, 'people of the island (*ey*)' or 'people of the Lake Øjeren').

In 58 B.C. 24,000 Harudes appear in Gaul, probably encouraged by the Cimbric raid, and join their Eudusian neighbours in the army of the Swabian invader Ariovistus, but the attack is repulsed (Caesar, *Bell. Gall.* I, 37 and 51).

In A.D. 5 a Roman navy reduces the Harudes and Cimbri to a sort of subjection (Augustus, *Res gestae*, p. 104; cp. Strabo, VII, 294).

The Eudoses are mentioned as worshippers of Nerthus (Tac. *Germ.* 40). On the possible survival of Eudoses as Euthungi in Southern Germany see § 157, 6.

Widsith shows no trace of either Harudes or Eudoses. The latter completely disappear. A royal family of the Langobards, the Harodos, may be descended from the Harudes, but equally well from the German Harudi at the Harz. Harz Hæret, in East Jutland, is a reminiscence of the Harudes in the position given them on the Ptolemaic map; but they seem to have left this region, which belongs to the area of the place names ending in *-lev*—a type probably introduced by the Danes during the Migration Age. The present Hardboer or Hardsysselboer, the descendants of the Harudes, inhabit the West Jutlandic county of Harthe Sysæl, now Hardsyssel, which is almost completely untouched by the names ending in *-lev*. The names of parishes in this county are of a most antique type (cp. our map Fig. 4 in vol. I).

Saxo's Jutlander Hor-vendil (I, 135) might be taken as a collective eponymous representative of Hardboer and Vendelboer. If so the defeat and death of his son Amleth in the war against Viglek (*ibid.* 161) (at Ammelhede in East Jutland?) would represent an Anglian conquest of the Harudes. There is also a modern tale of an Anglian attack at Anglands Moor in the territory of the Hardboer (cp. E. T. Kristensen, *Danske Sagn*, IV, No. 214).

The tribal rank of the Harudes is still indicated by the size of their county, which is the largest in Jutland. They possess their own local measure of butter, 'Harbo pund' (cp. Arent Berntsen, *Danmarks fructbar Herlighed*, 173, 225), and a national dance called 'Harbo Skræp' or 'Charudum saltatio' (cp. Grüner-Nielsen, *Vore ældste Folkedanse* (*Danmarks Folkeminder*, No. 16, 16)).

Lit. Feilberg, *Ordb. ov. d. jyske Almuesmål*, s.v. *Harboskræp*; Much in Hoops, s.v. *Eudoses* and *Haruden*; Ihm in Pauly-Wissowa, s.v. *Charudes*; Schmidt, II (see Index, s.v. *Charuden*); Storgaard-Pedersen, *Hardsyssels Historie*; *Hardsyssels Aarbog* (Publ. of Ringkøbing Amts hist. Samfund); la Cour in Linwald, Friis and Mackeprang, *Det danske Folks Historie*, 269; *idem*, in *Sønderjyllands Historie*, I, 147; Gravlund, *Hardsyssel* (*Turistforeningen for Danmark, Aarbog*, 1927, containing articles by Zangenberg on the type of houses, and by Elna Mygdal on the national dress); Schütte in *Hist. Aarbog f. Skive*, 1927, 46 ((1) name, (2) subdivision, (3) ethnic character, (4) toponymics, (5) dialect, (6) paganism, (7) national dress, (8) national dances, (9) type of houses, (10) professions, (11) list of native authors); *idem*, in *Hardsyssels Aarbog*, 1928, 155.

§ 244 *a*. The Ommerboer.

On the Ommerboer, inhabitants of Omungær Sysæl (between Himber and Åbo Sysæl), see Schütte and Bjerregaard in *Hist. Aarbog f. Skive*, 1930, 192 seq.

§ 245. History of the Teutones and Cimbri Proper.

Pytheas' visit to the Teutones, about 345 B.C. (Pliny, XXXVII, 35), is the first recorded event in the history of the Gothonic nations. We have seen in § 237, 10, that they were at that time not situated actually on the coast, since they did not themselves collect amber. But the mediaeval county of Thiuth, now Ty, at any rate lies on the north-west coast of Jutland, opposite the home of the Cimbri.

A Cimbric headland is mentioned by Strabo, VII, 292, and Pliny, II, 168, IV, 96. The expression of Tacitus, *Germ.* 2 and 37, 'proximi Oceano Inguaeones', 'proximi Oceano Cimbri', similarly indicates a headland, not simply a maritime position. Ptolemy, II, 11, § 7, makes the Cimbric Chersonese embrace the whole of Jutland, but places the Cimbri proper in the northern extremity, i.e. in the mediaeval Himber Sysæl, three sides and a half of which are surrounded by water. If the Ptolemaic Chaloi south of the Cimbri are the present Hallinger in Hallæ Hæret, the Cimbric territory cannot have extended farther south than it does nowadays.

The amber trade described by Pytheas connects the Teutones quite early with Gaul, and must also have influenced the Cimbri. Hence we derive the Cimbric bull worship, of southern origin (Plutarch, *Marius*, 23); also the body of trained priestesses (Strabo, VII, 294); the use of large sacrificial bowls (*ibid.*; cp. the Cimbric bowl of Gundestrup, executed in Gaulish style); and finally the use of helmets with images of wild beasts (Plutarch, *Marius*, 25).

The famous raid of the Teutones, Ambrones, and Cimbri in the second century B.C. was recorded by Poseidonius and Livy whose descriptions have unfortunately been lost. Extracts are given by Strabo, Plutarch, Orosius, and others. It is superfluous to describe the well-known migration at length, as it left so few lasting traces. We will only mention some points of ethnic importance.

A great flood caused the exodus, according to an old Greek author (Ephorus?) whom Strabo ridicules (VII, 292). An additional reason was probably a great ethnic movement which carried the Bastarnae and Sciri to the Black Sea about 200 B.C. (cp. §§ 130 and 144). That the Cimbri stayed some decades in North Germany may be deduced from the fact that their chieftains Boiorix and Lugius, who fell in 101 B.C., were named after the neighbouring Boji and Lugians respectively.

The emigrants first unsuccessfully attack two vigorous Celtic tribes, the Boji in Bohemia, and the Scordisci in Illyricum, named after the mountain Skardos, the present Shar Dagh (cp. Strabo, VII, 292). In the region of the Celtic Taurisci, about the Hohe Tauern, the Romans try to stop the invasion, but are defeated, in 113 B.C. (Livy, *epit.* 63; Strabo, VII, 293; Velleius, II, 12; Plutarch, *Marius*, 16; Appianus, *Celtica*, 13). This is the first collision between Gothonic nations and Romans, and thus it affords us a *terminus a quo* for the Gothic word Rūmōneis, which shows the ancient Gothonic change of ā into ō. The victorious barbarians then visit Helvetia, where they ally with the vigorous Celtic tribe of Tigurini (Strabo, VII, 293). They invade Gaul, unsuccessfully attack the Belgians, and in Spain the Celtiberians, and after many times defeating the Gauls and Romans with great slaughter, they are finally overthrown by the Roman general Marius—the Teutones and Ambrones at Aquae Sextiae in South-eastern Gaul in 102 B.C., and the Cimbri at Vercellae in Northern Italy in 101 B.C. (cp. Plutarch, *Marius*, 18 seq., 23 seq.; Orosius, V, 16, §§ 11 and 14; Velleius, II, 12, §§ 4 and 5; Florus, I, 38, §§ 10 and 14; Eutropius, V, 1).

Whereas the large majority of the emigrants were annihilated, a detachment of 6000 men had been left in Belgium in 102 B.C., in order to guard the heavy baggage (Caesar, *Bell. Gall.* II, 26); they succeeded in maintaining themselves and forming a vigorous tribe. Their original name is somewhat uncertain; Caesar, *l.c.*, calls them Aduatuci, but in VI, 32 attributes the fortress of Aduatuca to the Eburones. The later owners of Aduatuca are the Tungri and it owes to them its present name, Tongern; Tacitus, *Germ.* 2, emphasises their Gothonic origin and their character as invaders, whence it appears that the descendants of the Cimbri and Teutones are meant. It is not impossible that the Τωυγενοί, mentioned by Strabo, VII, 293, as companions of the Cimbri, are the Tungri, the form of the name being corrupt. It is superfluous to add that the small Gothonic minority was soon completely absorbed by the surrounding Celts. In the Middle Ages the Gothonic nationality was re-introduced by the Franks; nowadays the people of Tongern speak Dutch.

Other colonies of Teutones and Cimbri remained near the rivers Main and Neckar, and are traceable in inscriptions. They may have become partly Celticised, but nowadays speak German. It is possible that the last trace of them is found in the Roman soldiers named Laeti Teutoniciani and mentioned as the garrison of Chartres about 400 A.D. (*Not. dign. Occ.* XLII, 33).

The Celtic companions of the Cimbri, the Tigurini, have left their name in the Lacus Tigurinus in Southern Bavaria, now Tegernsee. As the Cimbri went this way on their expedition against Italy, the name must be mentioned among the reminiscences of the migration.[1]

In 69 B.C. the Scythian King Mithradates summoned the Cimbri of Himmerland to ally with him against Rome, if Justinus, XXXVIII, 3, § 6, is to be trusted.

In A.D. 5 a Roman naval expedition to Himmerland caused the Cimbri and Harudes to ask for the friendship of the Emperor (Augustus, *Res gestae*, 104). The Cimbri sent him their most holy sacrificial bowl and thus obtained amnesty for the Roman blood shed a century earlier (Strabo, VII, 293). This is the last entry regarding the history of the Cimbri.

[1] The present so-called Cembri or Cimbri in the vicinity of Verona and Vicenza are mediaeval German colonists who have nothing to do with the emigrants from Himber Sysæl—though the Danish King Frederic IV, on his passage in 1708, was hailed as their sovereign, owing to their imaginary identification with the ancient Cimbri.

The tribal districts form two mediaeval counties: (1) Thythe Sysæl or Thiuth, now Ty; (2) Himber Sysæl, now Himmerland; their inhabitants are the Tyboer and Himmerboer, respectively. The place names ending in *-lev*, marking Danish settlements of the Migration Age, form strong colonies in Himmerland and also appear in Ty. In Himmerland they are accompanied by several barrows of the legendary Kings Dan and Skjold (cp. Olrik, *Danmarks Heltedigtning*, II, ch. 36). Due south of the county a barrow of King Dan lies beside an old frontier wall called Dan-diget, 'the Dane-dike'. The area with place names ending in *-lev* in Eastern and Northern Himmerland exclusively uses toponymics ending in *-ere*. The western part, which has no names ending in *-lev*, preserves the Old Gothonic toponymics ending in *-ing*: Nibinger or Nivninger in Nibe; so in Staven, Blære, Ilris, Rind, Skals, and Kvols; the same is the case south of the Dandige, especially in Hallæ Hæret, the region of the Hallinger (the ancient Chaloi?). It is obvious that the region with names ending in *-lev* and toponymics ending in *-ere* has been largely colonised by Danes, whereas the people with toponymics ending in *-ing* represent the more pure descendants of the ancient Cimbri and Chaloi.

The dialect of the Tyboer is West Jutlandic (*æ mand* 'the man'). That of the Himmerboer is East Jutlandic (*manden* 'the man'); but Western Himmerland sometimes uses the West Jutlandic position of the article in ethnic names: de Lovns Folk, etc.

In *Danske Studier*, 1913, 178, we have suggested the survival of a famous Cimbrian in epic traditions, viz. Boiorix, Goth. *Bajareiks, later pronounced *Bērīk, possibly the same as the alleged 'Gothic' hero Berig, who was celebrated in the sixth century as the leader of the first migration from Scandinavia (Jordanes, IV, 25). Our suggestion has not been considered worthy of discussion, but it deserves some attention, because, if it were accepted, Boiorix would be the very earliest historical hero of Gothonic traditions.

Lit. (*a*) Teutones, Tyboer: Müllenhoff, II (see Index, s.v. *Teutonen*); Much, *Beiträge*, XVII, 5; *idem*, in Hoops, s.v. *Teutonen*; Schmidt, II, 1; *Hist. Aarbog for Thisted Amt*; Djörup, *Beskrivelse af Thisted Amt* (udg. af d. kgl. Landhusholdningsselskab, 1842). (*b*) Cimbri, Himmerboer: Zeuss, 141, 151; Müllenhoff, II (see Index, s.v. *Kimbern*); Ihm in Pauly-Wissowa, s.v. *Cimbri*; Much, *Stammeskunde*, 95; *idem*, *Beiträge*, XVII, 6; *idem*, in Hoops, s.v. *Kimbern*; Detlefsen in Sieglin's *Quellen u. Forschungen*, Heft 8, 28 seq. and suppl. 9; Schmidt, II, 1 seq.; Kauffmann, I, 231; Schütte, *Geogr. Tidskrift*, 1915, 17; *idem*, *Himmerlands Tyr* (in *Danske Studier*, 1927, 183); *idem*, *Fra Himmerland og Kjær Herred*, 1916, 1 seq.;

ibid. 1929, 533 (on Cimbrian paganism); *idem*, in *Hist. Aarbog f. Skive*, 1929, 110 seq. (the same series of paragraphs as in the article on the Harudes); *idem*, in *Jubilee Congress of the Folk-Lore Society*, 167; *idem*, *The Origin of the Cimbrians* (*Acta Philologica Scandinavica*, 1930, 91); Norden, *Die germ. Urgeschichte in Tacitus Germania*, 67 seq.; Sigm. Feist, *Das Volkstum der Kimbern u. Teutonen* (*Zeitschr. f. Schweizerische Geschichte*, 1929, Heft 2, 129); Zangenberg, *Gammel Byggeskik* (in Himmerland, *Hist. Aarbog f. Skive*, 1930, 1 seq.).

§ 246. History of the Wendle or Vendelboer Proper.

They are not mentioned by classical writers. Pliny with his Cimbrorum promunturium, II, 168, IV, 96, seems to attribute the Skaw to the Cimbri.

Beowulf, l. 348, mentions the chieftain 'Wulfgár, Wendla léod', among the subjects of the Danish King Hróðgár in the sixth century. We agree with Grundtvig, and with Chambers, *Widsith*, 208, that the Vendelboer are meant, and not the Vandals who had left Germany centuries earlier. The line in *Beowulf* thus shows the beginning of the extension of Danish dominion in Jutland. It agrees with the fact that Western Vendsyssel has a considerable number of the typical Danish place names ending in *-lev*, dating from the Migration Age. The founders of the Danish settlements generally abolished the ancient toponymics ending in *-ing*, though there exist survivals such as Bjesinger in Biersted (cp. Feilberg, *Ordbog ov. d. jyske Almuesmål*, s.v. *Birsted*).

The Vendelboer or Vendilfolk (*Knytlinga Saga*, ch. 46, MS *Skinnbókin*, No. 180 *b*) were a sturdy race. A mediaeval ballad in *Danmarks G. Folkeviser*, III, No. 162, praises their heroism during an unfortunate social rebellion of Jutlandic peasants:

> Alone stood the Vendelboer.
> They would not fly.

We have mentioned Saxo's Hor-vendil as a possible collective eponymous representative of Harudes and Vendelboer (cp. § 244).

The present dialect of the Vendelboer is East Jutlandic, but like Western Himmerlandic it often uses the West Jutlandic position of the article in ethnic names, de Vendelbo piger, etc.

Lit. Müllenhoff, *Beovulf*, 89; Bugge, *Beiträge*, XII, 7; Much, *ibid.* XVII, 210; Chambers, *Widsith*, 208; Schütte, *Jysk og østdansk Artikelbrug*, 136.

§ 247. History of the Jutes Proper.

Pliny's corrupt form 'Gutones' (XXXVII, 35) seems to ask for correction, and it is natural to read *Eutones. If the conjecture is accepted, the *Eutones or Jutes would have been situated on the amber coast, and Pytheas would have visited them there about 345 B.C.[1]

During the Migration Age the Jutes must have occupied the coast near the harbour of Hjerting (Esbjerg) (cp. Jöthnewath, 'Juteford', in North Slesvig (Vilh. la Cour, *Geschichte des schleswigschen Volkes*, I, 56)). When the Erules from Scandinavia and the Saxons begin raiding the Channel after A.D. 286 Jutes must have joined them; Bede, I, 15, names the Jutes as the first invaders of Britain, and their position gives support to his statement, as they possess all the outlying islands along the Channel: Thanet, Sheppey, Dungeness, and the Isle of Wight.

Yte (Jutes), with their King Gefwulf, appear in *Widsith*, l. 26, beside the Rondingas, Eowan, Wærne of the Migration Age (who correspond to the Reudigni, Auiones, Varini among the Nerthus-worshippers of the first century A.D.; Reud- may be a misreading for *Rend- or *Rand- (cp. § 237, 2)). Thus after four centuries the ancient religious community still proved its power of holding together.

Amleth's defeat and the Anglian King Viglek's victory (Saxo, 161) seem to indicate an Anglian expansion into North Jutland. But the subsequent emigration of the Angles left the supremacy with the Jutes. The exploits of a 'Danish' chieftain Hengest are dealt with in the *Finnsburg Lay*. This must be the famous Jutish conqueror of Kent. The name Hengest, 'Stallion', is unique, and two famous Hengests from Denmark, operating on North Sea coasts during the Migration Age, are as inconceivable as would have been two contemporary Julius Caesars in Rome (cp. our article *Vidsid og Slægtssagnene om Hengest*, *Arkiv*, XXXVI, 1 seq.).

Hengest's companions are Hnæf the Hocing (*Beowulf*, l. 107), described as a 'Half-Dane'; Sigeferð, ruler of the Secgan (*Finnsburg Lay*, ll. 15 and 24), i.e. Sæferð, ruler of the Sycgas (probably a Saxon tribe) (*Widsith*, l. 31); Húnláf, Ordláf, Gúðláf (*Beowulf*, l. 1143; *Finnsburg Lay*, l. 18), whom Chadwick rediscovers in three of the epic Danish King Leif's seven sons, viz. Hunleifus, Oddleifus, and Gunnleifus (in Arngrim Jónsson's *Skiöldunga Saga*, *Aarbøger*, 1894, 104; see Chadwick,

[1] But another reading is Guiones, perhaps for Inguiones.

52 note). The element *-láf, -leif* is a favourite Scandinavian type. We must assume that Hengest's battles with the Frisian King Finn took place before the conquest of Kent, i.e. before A.D. 445.

The Jutes after the migration of the Angles spread throughout the whole of Southern Slesvig, except the moors and dense woods along the frontier. Evidence of their advance is found in the name Jydebæk, 'Jutebrook', occurring near the town of Slesvig, and again near Bredsted in North Friesland.[1] The type of the name is later than that of the above-mentioned Jöthnewath. The Angles in their emigration seem to have left the country almost bare of inhabitants; at least there are very few place names of the ancient Simplex type, such as Fjolde with the toponymic Fjoldinger; the nomenclature nowadays generally contains the ordinary Scandinavian elements of the secondary stratum, *-by, -toft, -rød,* etc. Along the east coast and more sporadically along the north-west coast, there are groups of places ending in *-lev* which indicate that Danes settled there during the Migration Age, but were absorbed by the surrounding Jutes, who were more numerous. Towards the south-west, on the other hand, the Jutish population was so sparse that it was absorbed by the later immigrating Frisians. Still the Jutish occupation has left various traces in the nomenclature, not only place names and district names such as Lundæbyargh Hæret, but even typical Scandinavian toponymics ending in *-bo,* e.g. in the name of the district of Holmbo Hæret at the mouth of the Eider.

The Frankish King Theodebert about 550 boasts of being the lord of Saxons and 'Eucii', owing to their voluntary submission. Venantius Fortunatus about 580 describes the 'Danus, Euthio, Saxo' as terrified enemies of the Franks (*Carm.* IX, 1, 73). Here, the Jutes appear for the last time side by side with Danes and Saxons. Already *Beowulf* represents Hengest's people as 'Danes' or 'Half-Danes'.

The process of amalgamation is nowhere described. Temporary hostility between North Jutlanders and Danish settlers may be concluded from the existence of a frontier wall Dan-diget south of the Cimbri (see § 245), and we may imagine similar conflicts on the frontier of the Jutes proper. But the conflicts cannot have been serious and they are entirely ignored by legendary and historical traditions. On the contrary, the

[1] As we mentioned on p. 303, we do not agree with Zachrisson who maintains that Jydebæk might simply mean 'Waterbrook'. The position on the national frontier makes an ethnic signification most likely.

Danish Chronicle of Lejre in the *Ann. Esrom. Script. rer. Dan.* I, 223, emphasises the peaceful nature of the alliance of Jutes and Danes against German invaders. And South Jutland preserves legendary traditions of a more pronounced national Danish character than any other region of Denmark, e.g. a ballad in *Danm. g. Folkeviser*, III, No. 115, contains a mythical royal pedigree which is unique in Danish literature. The idea of a hereditary national animosity between Jutes and Danes, as depicted by Jacob Grimm and his followers, is pure fancy. The Jutes from this time onward are simply a Danish tribe, and their language in popular speech is not called 'Jutish', but exclusively 'Danish'. In German dialect the Jutes of the peninsula Svans or Schwansen are called 'Steert-dänen', 'Tail-Danes', the word *steert* being a Low German synonym of Germ. *schwanz*, 'start, tail'; consequently, their Danish nationality is emphasised (cp. § 259, B 2).

On the development of the name Jutes into a general term embracing all Jutlanders or Danes see § 239.

Lit. **Zeuss**, 499; **Müllenhoff**, IV (see **Index**, s.v. *Jüten*); *idem*, *Nordalbing. Studien*, I, 133, 136, 169; **Grimm**, 736; **H. Möller**, *Altengl. volksepos*, 88; *idem*, *Anzeiger*, XXII, 154; **Siebs**, *Zur Gesch. d. engl. fries. Sprache*; **Bremer**, § 135; **Much**, *Stammeskunde*, 99; *idem*, in **Hoops**, s.v. *Jüten*; **Chadwick**, 133, 163; **Björkman**, *Engl. Studien*, XXXIX, 356; **Jordan**, *Verh. d.* 40 *Versamml. deutscher Philologen*, 138; **V. la Cour**, *Geschichte des schleswigschen Volkes*, I; *Sønderjyllands Historie*, I, 148.

§ 248. Legendary Traditions.

Jutes often occur in local epic legends, but it is difficult to say whether Jutes proper or simply Jutlanders are meant.

The earliest Scandinavian ancestor Forn-jótr is perhaps 'the primaeval Jute' (cp. vol. I, pp. 10, 130, 141).

Hengest's exploits in Friesland must have been sung both in Scandinavia and in England, as we may conclude from the survival in epic on both sides of the North Sea of his followers Hunleif, Oddleif, and Gunnleif. Hengest's conquest of Kent and similar Jutish exploits in England, on the other hand, only grew famous among the people who had emigrated, and among the Welsh and Normans.

Saxo's first books abound in Jutish episodes, and so does the Chronicle of Lejre. The story of the peaceful union between Jutes and Danes in the latter source is important.

VII. §§ 249-281. THE SCANDINAVIAN OR NORTH GOTHONIC SUB-GROUP

A. §§ 249-253. *THE SUB-GROUP AS A WHOLE*

§ 249. Names.

1. Engl. Scandinavians; Scand. Skandinaver. The name means 'people of Scandia', as also the 'Scandzae cultores' of Jordanes, sixth century A.D. It is a modern academic derivative formed from the territorial name, Lat. Scandia (Mela, first century A.D.), Gr. Σκανδία (Ptolemy, second century A.D.), which is also found in the Compound form, Lat. Scadin-auia (Pliny, first century A.D.), O.E. Sceden-ig (*Beowulf*, l. 1686; cp. Scede-land, *ibid.* l. 19), Scon-eg (Alfred's *Orosius*), Langobard Scaten-auga (*Chron. Gothanum*, eighth century), L.G. Schonen; O.N. Skán-ey; Dan. and Swed. Skån-e; Lapp. Skadesi-suolo. Cp. the eponymous goddess of Scandinavia, O.N. Skaði (with masculine declension!). The name Scandia, generally conceived as 'Scania', was first noted down by the Roman admiral who discovered Denmark in A.D. 5. He probably distorted it, as it was to him difficult to pronounce; the real form he heard would have been something like *Scaðnjō. The form Scandinavia is an incorrect compromise between Scandia and Scadinauia. This bastard form already appears in the *Origo Langobardorum*, eighth century, as Scandanan, and a toponymic corresponding to Scandinavians occurs in the *Passio S. Sigismundi*, Scanadabii, meaning Burgundians. The *Origo* gives an etymology: 'Scandanan, quod interpretatur in partibus aquilonis'. This interpretation probably conceives Scadin-auia as the 'island of shadow', referring it to Goth. *skadus* 'shadow', Gr. σκότος 'darkness'. Cp. the Irish goddess Scāth in a north-eastern kingdom of shadows; she may have some connexion with the eponymous Skaði, the goddess of the Scandinavian winter sports. With Much we are inclined to prefer the etymology of the ancient chronicle to the proposals of modern philologists, such as Bugge's 'island of shepherds' (cp. O.Slav. *skotu* 'cattle'), or Schrader's 'island of the fish called shad' (O.E. *sceadd*, cp. O.Irish *scatán* 'herring'). It must be noted that, geographically, Scandia is not an island, but a peninsula. However, the Gothonic migration legends constantly and emphatically represent the Scandinavian cradle of the Gothonic nations as an island. And the primitive Gothonic language, as a matter of fact, possessed no specific

term for a region like Scandia. It may say 'nose', 'neck' or 'headland', but such expressions only meant small capes. A large peninsular region could only be expressed by the word **aujō*, which consequently meant indiscriminately 'insular or peninsular district'; cp. the peninsula of Svans-ø in South Jutland, the 'island of Svan'. The identification of Scandia, Scadinauia and the modern Scania has been advocated by Axel Kock, but Lindroth shows in *Namn och Bygd*, 1932, that it cannot be regarded as proved.

Lit. **Zeuss**, 157; **Müllenhoff**, I, 385, II, 357 seq.; **Much**, *Zeitschrift*, XXXVI, 125; *idem*, *Stammeskunde*, 24; *idem*, in **Hoops**, s.v. *Scadinavia*; **S. Bugge**, *Beiträge*, XXI, 424; **Schrader**, s.v. *Codanus*; **Axel Kock**, *Är Skåne de germanska folkens urhem?* (Swed. *Hist. tidsskrift*, 1905, 1 seq.); *idem*, *Arkiv*, XXXIV, 71; **Lindroth**, *Namn och Bygd*, 1915, 10, 1917, 39, 1932, 124; *idem*, *Anthr. Tidskr.* XX, 4, 1 seq.; **Noreen**, *Fornvännen*, 1920, 29; **Svensson**, *Namn och Bygd*, 1921, 64; **Schütte**, *Maal og Minne*, 1924, 199 (on Skadesisuolo); **Hellquist**, *Svensk etym. ordbok*, s.v. *Skövde*; **Kretschmer**, *Glotta*, XVII, 148; **Magnus Olsen**, *Arkiv*, XXXVIII, 94.

2. Germ. Nord-germanen, i.e. 'North Gothonic nations'. An academic term, formed in the nineteenth century; sporadically copied in English: North Germans (Chambers).

3. O.N. Norð(r)menn; O.E. Norðmenn (Alfred's *Orosius*, 16, 36); M.Lat. North(o)manni; Fr. Normands; O.Irish Nortmanar, Normanaig, i.e. 'North-men', but also, with restricted meaning, 'Norwegians' (cp. § 277, 1).

4. Engl. Northerners; O.N. Norðr-lendingar; Dan. Nord-boer. Name of language: O.N. norrœn tunga; Engl. Norn, Norse. All these terms, which may still be varied, denote the 'people and language of the North'.

5. M.Lat. Dani, i.e. 'Danes'; O.N. Dǫnsk tunga, i.e. 'the Scandinavian nationality'. In mediaeval ecclesiastical terminology, Dacia, i.e. Denmark, includes Sweden and Norway (cp. § 258, 1).

6. Arab. Waseng (read: *Wareng; Ibn Fadhlan, ed. Frähn, p. 178); M.Gr. Varangoi; Russ. Varjaži, i.e. O.N. Væringjar, 'the Scandinavians in Russia and Greece' (chiefly of Swedish nationality). Place names: Pol. Warężyn?; Pruss. Warengen? The Russian Nestor in the eleventh century uses Varjaži to mean 'Gothonic nations'. The etymology is perhaps 'people who go beyond the sea' (cp. vol. I, § 15).

Lit. **Stender-Petersen** in *Minnesskrift utg. av Filolog. Samf. i Göteborg*, 1925, p. 51 (on place names).

7. M.Gr. Rhōs; Arab. Rōs; Russ. Rus, Rusi, < Finn. Ruotsalaiset 'Swedes' (cp. § 272, 4).

8. Lapp. Darolažak? As the name may mean both 'Swedes' and 'Norwegians', it perhaps included all Scandinavians (cp. § 272, 6, and § 277, 7).

9. Finn. Pohjolaiset, Pohjois-maa-laiset, i.e. 'North-people, North-land-people'. A modern literary translation of Dan., Norw., Swed., Nordboer, Nordbor. It may also include the Finns and is thus more of a geographical than an ethnographical term.

Lit. Lönnrot, *Finskt-svenskt lex.*, s.v. *Pohjolainen*; Cannelin, *Svenskt-finskt lex.*, s.v. *Nordbo.*

10. O.Irish Lochlannaig, Lochlannacha. Cp. Cymric Lochlyn, 'Scandinavia' or 'Denmark' (*Taliesin*). Perhaps meaning 'seamen', or a corruption of 'Rogalanders' (i.e. Norwegians). It is generally used to designate Vikings of Norwegian origin, but may also include the Danes; e.g. in the Irish Nennius, p. 84, the Jutish conqueror Hengest is said to come from Lochland. In the translation of the *Civil War* of Lucanus, Lochlannacha means 'Gothonic nations' (cp. vol. I, § 14, and § 277, 6).[1]

11. O.Irish Gaill, tuatha Gall, 'foreigners', originally the Gauls, then transferred to the Scandinavian Vikings. Insi Gaill are the Hebrides, a Norwegian earldom. Finegala, now Finghall (Yorksh.), according to Bugge, *Vikingerne*, II, 278, is a *Fine na n-Gall, 'district of the North-men'.

Lit. Zimmer, *Zeitschrift*, XXXII, 236 note, XXXV, 62.

12. O.Irish Fiann, Fē(i)nnid, Fēnnid, tuatha Fēne, according to Zimmer, < the O.N. *fíandr* 'foes', i.e. Scandinavian Vikings; it is the same word as the modern Fenians. A legend assumes the presence of these Fenians at the arrival of St Patrick and mentions their individual language.

Lit. Zimmer, *Zeitschrift*, XXXV, 53, 98 note.

13. O.Irish All-maraig, i.e. 'foreign maritime people'.

Lit. Zimmer, *Zeitschrift*, XXXII, 245.

14. O.Irish For-tuatha, i.e. 'the people from abroad', eleventh century.

Lit. Zimmer, *Zeitschrift*, XXXV, 89.

1 Zimmer, *Zeitschrift*, XXXV, 140, derives the geographical name Lochland or Lothland from the Danish island of Låland.

15. O.Irish Echtar-chenēl, i.e. 'foreign tribes'.

Lit. Zimmer, *Zeitschrift*, xxxv, 94.

The academic term Scandinavians, if the *Origo Langobardorum* gives the right etymology, would characterise the peoples of Scandia as a northern race. The same idea stamps expressions like Northmen, Northerners, Norðrlendingar, Nordboer.

Various synonyms are created by foreigners who generalise the names of their nearest neighbours, 'Norwegians', 'Danes', or 'Swedes'.

The Gaelic Celts use numerous individual terms which designate the Scandinavians vaguely as 'seamen', 'foreigners', etc.

The German 'Nordgermanen' is not suitable for literal translation into English. The 'North Germans' of Chambers in his *Widsith*, 157 (1912), must be considered an exceptional form, due to its particular context (cp. Clark Hall's transl. of Stjerna's *Essays on Beowulf* (1912), 66: 'Scandinavian and Continental East Germans').

The best English form is 'Northerners'.

§ 250. Sub-divisions.

A. Ancient division. Ptol. II, 11, § 16, the inhabitants of Scandia.

1. South. 'Daukiones', a corruption of *Daneiones ?? Wadstein suggests *Dapriones in the district of Dapræ, Scania. At any rate, they are located in the country of the Danes.

Lit. Schütte, *Ptolemy's Maps*, 137; Wadstein, *Namnet Danmark*, 9 footnote, and 39; *idem*, in *Minnesskrift utg. av Filolog. Samf. i Göteborg*, 1925, 198; Svensson, *Namn och Bygd*, 1919, 1 seq.; Noreen, *Fornvännen*, 1920, 42; Karsten, *Die Germanen*, 227.

2. South. Goutai, i.e. Gauts or Gotlanders? Cp. Procopius, *Bell. Goth.* II, 15, § 26; Jordanes, III, 19.

Lit. Wadstein, *Minnesskrift*, 197; Svensson, *l.c.*; Langenfelt, *Anthropos*, XIV/XV, 309.

3. Middle. Leuonoi, O.E. *Léon? (*Widsith*, l. 80). Various locations have been proposed: about Ljuna or Linköping in Gautland, or in the district of Liugnæs in Southern Scania (cp. § 264, 2).

Lit. Svensson, *l.c.* 1918, 72; Noreen, *l.c.* 1920, 37; Karsten, *l.c.*; Langenfelt, *l.c.* 310.

4. East. Firaisoi. The identification is doubtful. Zeuss has proposed to identify them with the Finn(h)aithae of Jordanes, i.e. the inhabitants of Finveden, but then their situation would be southern rather than

eastern. Wadstein takes them to be the Færsingar, in the district of Færs in Eastern Scania; even this interpretation places them towards the south.

Lit. Zeuss, 159; Schütte, *Ptolemy's Maps*, 137; Wadstein, *Namnet Danmark*, 39 footnote; *idem*, in *Minnesskrift*, 197; Svensson, *l.c.*; Karsten, *l.c.*

5. East. 'Fauonai', a corruption of *Souionai? At any rate, they are in the position occupied by the Sviones, who form a powerful state, the only North Gothonic nation mentioned by Tacitus, *Germ.* 44. Wadstein would read *Feuonai, 'inhabitants of Funen'.

Lit. Schütte, *Ptolemy's Maps*, 137; Wadstein, in *Minnesskrift*, 196; Karsten, *l.c.*

6. West. Chaideinoi, the O.N. Hei(ð)nir, Norw. Heidmerkingar, in Heiðmǫrk, representing the Norwegians, the name of a part of the race being used for the whole. Some modern scholars, however, reject this interpretation (cp. § 279).

Wadstein's theory is supported by the fact that three of the peoples he locates, viz. Daukiones, Leuonoi, and Firaisoi, are in Southern Scania, that is to say, in a region which might easily be explored from the Roman factories in Prussia. On the other hand, names such as Goutai and Chaideinoi seem to show that Ptolemy's list mentions chiefly important tribes, generally corresponding to the leading nations of Scandinavia in later times. This makes it rather doubtful whether he would have noted the inhabitants of small subordinate districts. Svensson, like Wadstein, refutes the identification of Chaideinoi and Heinir, but in other respects gives a quite different interpretation transferring several names to Finland. His arguments, in our opinion, are not convincing.

To Ptolemy's fragmentary list we must add the Erules who do not appear in any ancient survey of Scandinavian tribes before the sixth century, but who in reality take part in the political life of Europe earlier than any other inhabitants of the Peninsula.

Lit. Zeuss, 153; Müllenhoff, II, 10 footnote; Läffler, *De östskandinaviska folknamnen hos Jordanes* (*Svenska landsmålen*, XIII, 9); Svensson, *Ptolemæus' redogörelse för folken på ön Skandia* (*Namn och Bygd*, 1919, 1 seq.); L. Weibull, *Skandza in der Darstellung des Jordanes* (*Arkiv*, XLI, 215 seq.); Noreen, *l.c.* 39; Karsten, *l.c.*

B. Early mediaeval division.

1. Danes, including the Jutes, inhabitants of the Dane-law in England, and some sections of the Norman population.

2. Swedes, including the Gauts, Gotlanders, and their colonies in Finland and Russia.

3. Norwegians, including the Icelanders, Faroese, Shetlanders, Orkney people, Greenlanders, and their colonies on the Hebrides and the Isle of Man, in Northern Gaul, Cumberland, Scotland, and Ireland.

The Gotlanders might make a fourth division from the linguistic point of view, owing to their marked individuality.

C. Modern division.

List of nationalities with separate literary languages.

1. Danes, including the Jutes.

2. Swedes, including the Gauts, Gotlanders, and Swedish Finlanders and Esthonians ('Eibofolke').

3. Norwegians, with two official literary languages, the 'Rigsmål', of Dano-Norwegian type, and the 'Landsmål', of chiefly West Norwegian type. There exists besides a special East Norwegian literary language.

4. Icelanders.

5. Faroese.

From the point of view of race, dialects and types of houses we ought really to place the West Norwegians apart and all other continental Scandinavians under one heading (cp. § 279, points 1–17). But as West and East Norwegians are united into one nationality we shall have to consider them in one chapter.

From the point of view of ethnic history, none of the above divisions may serve as a basis for detailed description, but we shall have to deal with (1) Erules, (2) Danes, (3) Gauts, (4) Gotlanders, (5) Sviones, (6) Norwegians.

Lit. For particulars concerning Scandinavian dialects see Lundell, *Grundriss*, 2nd ed. I, 1483.

§ 251. Ethnic Position.

The Scandinavian ethnic individuality is a recognised fact. Some of the proofs of this may be enumerated.

1. Collective names—Northerners, Rōs, Danes, etc.—are used by natives or foreigners (cp. § 249).

2. The O.N. expression *dǫnsk tunga*, i.e. 'Scandinavian nationality', emphasises the Scandinavians' possession of a common language as a mark of their common nationality.

3. Some typical marks of linguistic individuality are: (*a*) Preservation of final -*z*, later altered into -ʀ, run. *gastiʀ*, O.N. *gestr* 'guest'; plural in -ʀ > -*r*, O.N. *gestir*, Dan. *gæster* 'guests'. (*b*) Loss of initial *j*, O.N. *ár*, Dan. *år* 'year'. (*c*) Loss of initial *w* before *u* and *o*, O.N. *ulfr*, Dan. *ulv* 'wolf'. (*d*) Loss of final -*n*, O.N. *gęfa*, Dan. *give*, O.E. *giefan* 'to give'. (*e*) Definite article *hinn* alternating with 'the'.[1] (*f*) Suffixed article, O.N. *hús-it*, Dan. *hus-et* 'the house'. (*g*) A passive verb formed by adding the reflexive *sik*, O.N. *gęfask*, Dan. *gives* 'to be given'. Point (*f*) is not shared by West Jutlandic.

4. No linguistic barrier exists between the North Cape and South Jutland. By a barrier we mean a definite line separating the languages of neighbours who do not understand each other, if they are not taught each other's idioms. Such barriers separate the Scandinavian Jutlanders from the Frisians and Germans.

5. The Scandinavian juridical solidarity may be illustrated by a paragraph in the Icelandic codex called *Grágás*, 'Grey Goose'.

'Norrœnir menn oc danskir oc sœnskir eigo her arf at taca eptir frændr sina þridia brœðra oc nanare. En at frændsemi af öllum avdrum tungum·en danscri tungo scal engi madr her arf taca nema faþir eþa sonr eda broþir.'

'Norwegian men and Danish and Swedish in this country are entitled to inherit from their fifth cousins and still nearer relations. But in the case of kinship in all other tongues than the Danish tongue, no man shall inherit here except a father or a son or a brother.'

6. The Norwegian territorial division *fylki* 'county' has analogies in Gautland and Jutland: Vifolka härad, Wændlefolk Herred.[2] The term *sýsla* 'county' occurs in Norway and Denmark (cp. O.Swed. Sýsla, the island of Ösel). The term *herað* 'smaller district' ('sheriffdom') seems to originate in Denmark, but during the Middle Ages spreads to Sweden and Norway (cp. Tunberg, *Studier rörande Skandinaviens äldsta politiska indelning*). The German, Saxon, and Gothic *gawi* 'county' is never found. This different scheme of territorial division is one of the most conspicuous

1 However, in some Low and Middle Frankish dialects there is an article *jener* alternating with 'the'. The former occurs after a preposition, e.g. *en jənə wēntər* 'in the winter'. Cp. Lecoutere and Grootaers, *Inleiding tot de Taalkunde van het Nederlandsch*, p. 312, and our article in *Danske Studier*, 1932, 182.

2 The Anglian Norfolk and Suffolk must be regarded as showing Scandinavian affinity.

marks of contrast between Scandinavian and German borderlands: Jutland has *sýsla* and *herað* from the Skaw to the Eider; scarcely have we passed the Eider, when the element *gawi* appears: Dietmarschgau, Bardengau, Hellangau, etc.

As there is no uniform type of house in Germany, so also there is none in Scandinavia. The main types may be summarised as follows.

1. The 'compound house', uniting the dwelling-house, cattle-stalls, and granaries under the same roof, with the gable ends situated east and west, and with entrance from one of the long sides, appears throughout the whole of Denmark. In the middle part of South Jutland it is the only type existing. It also predominates in Sundeved, in the now German-speaking region of Angel, and on the islands Als, Røm, Ærø, and Møn. The oldest Danish houses, dating from the Roman Iron Age, are of this kind. A similar type, but consisting of dwelling-house and stable only, occurs on the Faroe Islands.

2. The 'double farmstead' or 'parallel farmstead' is another primitive type in Denmark. It is frequent north of the Limfjord, in North Himmerland, along the west coast of Jutland, and in Bornholm. We may compare the parallel rows of certain West Norwegian 'row farmsteads'.

3. The 'gamma house', built in the shape of a Γ, occurs on the Gautic island of Öland in the Iron Age; it is frequent in Denmark.

4. The irregular farmstead predominates in West Gautland, Vermeland, and in Helgeland north of the Firth of Vefsen; there are also traces of it in Denmark.

5. The collective village ('klyngebosættelse') is a settlement of various owners, dwelling-houses in one group, cattle-stalls in another, granaries in a third, and so on. The various houses of different owners are often combined in the same way as the 'row farmsteads'. This type predominates in West Norway between Söndmöre (incl.) and Agder (excl.).

6. The 'row farmstead' may be regarded as a development on the basis of the Danish 'compound house', substituting for the row of single rooms a row of combined houses with separate roofs. The single houses of the Icelandic 'row farmstead' have a shape similar to that of the English 'cruck' (cp. p. 245). This type occurs in very old Gotlandic houses. It predominates in two Norwegian regions, viz. Romsdal and a district consisting of Setesdal and West Agder. There is also a tendency towards the same arrangement in West Gautland and Dalsland.

7. The farmstead with three ranges (⊓ or ⊓) is frequent in Denmark.

8. The quadrangle (□), often wholly surrounded by buildings (□), with no separate court for men and court for cattle, is a characteristic Danish type. It may be found throughout the present length and breadth of this state, except the middle of South Jutland, and also occurs in the ancient Danish provinces Scania and Halland. A similar type predominates in Northern Sweden, in Finland, and in Eastern Norway. A main difference is that the midden is inside the Danish quadrangle, but outside the North Scandinavian one.

9. The rectangular farmstead with two courts, one for men and one for cattle, is the normal type in East Gautland, Central Sweden, and the Norwegian region of Gudbrandsdal. There are two varieties: the Gautic type separates the two courts by means of a fence, whereas the Central Swedish and Norwegian separates them by means of a range of buildings or divides the farmstead into two separate courts.

The houses in Sweden and Norway often have two storeys, in Denmark never. The walls of Danish houses in the Iron Age were often made of clay. A later type is the 'half-timbered' construction (Dan. 'bindingsværk', Swed. 'korsvirke') which, in Scandinavia, is not found outside the ancient limits of Denmark. On the Faroe Islands the houses are made of stone, in Iceland of turf. The material of the houses in Sweden and Norway is chiefly wood. In Sweden and East Norway the beams forming the walls are always placed horizontally (log houses), whereas in West Norway buildings with vertical beams are preferred (cp. the famous Norwegian 'stav-kirker'; see Sigurd Erixon in *Fataburen*, 1917, p. 117).

Lit. Mejborg, *Gamle danske Hjem*; Sigurd Erixon, *Fataburen*, 1917; *idem*, *Ymer*, 1922; *idem*, in *Svenska kulturbilder*, v, parts IX–X, p. 9 seq.; Vreim, *Aarsberetning for Foreningen til norske Fortidsmindesmærkers Bevaring*, 1929, 1 seq.

It remains for us to examine how early the Scandinavian ethnic individuality was noted.

Classical authors never mention it. Most ethnologists, from Zeuss to Bremer, certainly assume that Pliny's 'Hilleviones', IV, 96, correspond to the Scandinavian sub-group. But the assumption is arbitrary; for if Pliny regarded the Hilleviones as a sub-group, co-ordinate with Inguaeones, etc., why did he not add it to his list of the 'Germanorum genera',

IV, 99? An isolated name like 'Hillevionum gente' cannot be used in a methodical scheme of classification. We have suggested in *Salmonsens Konv. Lex.* 1st ed. that it is simply a corruption of 'illa Svionum gente'. Grienberger has set forth the same suggestion (*Zeitschrift*, XLVI, 152). Though it is rejected by Svensson, *Namn och Bygd*, 1921, 88, the idea seems quite relevant, since it is suggested independently by various authors. At any rate, it is most unsatisfactory to enlarge our scheme of classification with forms such as Hilleviones, which cannot be verified.[1]

Tacitus shows that the Roman ideas about the Scandinavians were very vague. Misled probably by the similarity in the sound of the names, he imagines the Sviones to be 'Swabians', i.e. members of a German branch! Cp. Frahm in *Klio*, XXIII, 181 seq. and our § 158.

Ptolemy, II, 11, §§ 7 and 16, is the first to make a distinction. His Scandia and his Cimbric Chersonese contain only tribes, whereas his Germany contains tribes, towns, mountains, etc. According to this arrangement of his statistical data, Scandia embraces the Cimbric Chersonese. But his manner of separating Scandinavia from Germany is due rather to his private theory than to his ethnological knowledge.

Jordanes, *Getica*, II, 24, is the first author who definitely notes a national contrast. He says that all the nations of Scandia are more wild and warlike than the Germani. His authority is probably the Norwegian King Hrodulf who visited the Gothic court in Italy (*ibid.*).

The first reference to the linguistic difference between Scandinavian and German appears in A.D. 942 (Dudo, *Mon. Germ. SS.* IV, 98). Duke William of Normandy asks the Saxon Duke Herman: 'Quis tibi Daciscae regionis linguam, Saxonibus inexpertam, docuit?' Herman answers that a captivity among the Danes has given him the opportunity of learning their language which is, as William says, not understood by the Saxons.

The knowledge of Scandinavian among western and southern nations resulted from the Viking raids which made the peoples of Europe familiar with the nationality afterwards called 'the Danish tongue'.

At the same time, ethnic changes due to emigration destroyed the link formed by the 'peninsular sub-group' of dialects which hitherto had bridged the gap between North and West Gothonic. The Angles emigrated, while Danes from the islands settled in parts of South Jutland,

[1] To keep Pliny's spelling unaltered and to declare this unverified and isolated name to be the common denomination of the Scandinavian sub-group is not sound criticism, though this arbitrary theory is found in numerous works.

as appears from the place names ending in *-lev*. Charlemagne decimated the Saxons in Holstein, introducing German settlers in their place. In 804 he gave Eastern Holstein to an entirely foreign people, the Slavs. In 857 the Dane Hrørik returned from Duurstede in Holland to Denmark and settled in South Jutland near the Eider, accompanied by Danish remigrants and by Frisians from the Netherlands or from Rüstringerland. About the same time the north-eastern bank of the Eider was occupied by invaders from the Swedish Uppland. To sum up, the emigration of the Angles and the decimation of the Saxons left a vacant space, and the Eider region became in a short time a meeting-place of nations from very distant quarters: Danes from Zealand, Swedes from Uppsala, Slavs from the Weichsel, Franks and Frisians from the Netherlands. It followed necessarily that the former gradual transition of dialects was from this period onwards replaced by a definite linguistic barrier. For further particulars concerning the position of the Jutlanders see § 238.

§ 252. History.

Scandinavia has a unique position in Europe: it is the only part of this Continent which has escaped foreign conquest. There has scarcely been any attempt to conquer it. As Tacitus says of the whole of his Germania, *Germ.* 2: 'Quis porro peteret?' 'Who would set out for such a rough country, under a severe sky, and badly cultivated?'

But though untouched by the expansion of foreign nations, the Scandinavians themselves have spread widely abroad. The sea sheltered them, but did not handicap their expansion—nay, rather promoted it.

On native soil an expansion towards the north has been going on steadily for some 4000 years. But this is not the chief direction. The north was too little attractive: 'quis porro peteret?'

From the time of the Cimbric raid to the Viking Age, or to the wars of Gustavus Adolfus and Charles XII, the great attraction is the south, and even the maritime expansion east and west has a southward trend.

But if the seas invited the Vikings to cross their waves, they also formed barriers which prevented a lasting increase of Scandinavian territory. In contrast to the Anglo-Saxons, who spread from the Cimbric Chersonese to England, from England to Ireland, from Europe to America, etc., the Scandinavians have failed to establish their language in large areas abroad: in Russia, in Germany, in the Netherlands, in Normandy, in Britain, in Greenland, and in the Nya Sverige (New

Sweden) of the United States, they are always absorbed by other nationalities. They always remain unconquered in their ancestral home, but inferior in political importance.

The languages and civilisations of the Scandinavian nations are limited in extent not only abroad, but also at home. Their attempts at political union have proved failures and their literary languages, instead of tending towards more uniformity, are constantly differentiating from each other: Norway in the present century has no less than three separate written languages.

The political southern frontier of Scandinavia once established at the Eider in A.D. 811 has remained extraordinarily steady. Jutland for 1000 years never belonged to Germany, whereas Holstein, though in dynastic union with Denmark for 500 years, did not cease to be a fief of the German Empire. As the result of various Danish-German conflicts, the political frontier of Scandinavia has been withdrawn from the Eider to the Firth of Flensborg. South-west of this frontier a non-Scandinavian nation, the Frisians, were settled in mediaeval times, and the region south of the Firth of Flensborg has for centuries been subject to German civilisation; but this is only a very small change in the arrangement of nationalities, in comparison with the enormous conquest Germany has made on Slavonic soil, extending from the Eider to the Weichsel.

The evidence of archaeology has been used to throw light on the origin of the Scandinavians. About 1900 it seemed to be generally assumed that the Megalithic people were of Gothonic origin. But Sophus Müller, *Aarbøger*, 1913, 254, holds that the first vestiges of Gothonic peoples are to be found towards the close of the Megalithic Period, in the low earthen barrows containing single corpses; they would represent the expansion of the Gothonic nationality from North-western Germany.[1] Thus it is at present safest to say that our Gothonic ancestors are to be traced in Scandinavia at least from the beginning of the Bronze Age.

The northern limit of the Bronze Age archaeological finds is represented on Bremer's map in his *Ethnographie* between pp. 830 and 831, based on the researches of Montelius. The Scandinavians have extended furthest on the Norwegian side, reaching the Firth of Vefsen in Southern Helgeland; in Sweden, their most northerly district is Helsingland.

[1] Cp. Vilh. la Cour in *Sønderjyllands Historie*, I, 120.

The question now arises whether it is possible to discover a stratum of tribal and place names which correspond either to the Megalithic area or to that of the Bronze Age.

At the present preliminary stage of investigation we can only answer that the Megalithic Age seems to have left no clear traces in the place names of Scandinavia. West Gautland, e.g., belongs to the most densely peopled areas of Sweden in the Megalithic Age, whereas Norway belongs almost entirely to the desert regions; but there is no trace of a corresponding contrast in the old tribal names and river names. If we turn to the Bronze Age we find various noteworthy indications of a correspondence between archaeological and onomastic facts. The larger part of Norway belongs to the Bronze area and is correspondingly covered by tribal names and river names of the most archaic Simplex type. The northern outpost of the Simplex tribal names is Skeynir in Skeynafylki or Skaun, 'the beautiful region', at the head of the Trondheim Fjord, a little south of the boundary of the Bronze area. There is another Skaun near the head of the Christiania Fjord, and six other instances occur in the intervening district, normally only one in each county and in favourable positions on lakes or fjords.[1] Finally, there is a district ('tinglag') of Skön <*Skaun in the Swedish county of Medelpad, comprising the harbour of Sundsvall and the island of Alnö; it lies a little north of the boundary of the Bronze area. It is obvious that this series of 'Skaun' or 'beautiful regions' represents a tribal expansion of a definitely primary character, and it seems to be closely connected with the Bronze Age.

In South Jutland the extension of the population during the Bronze Age has been accurately examined by Sophus Müller, *Aarbøger*, 1914, 195 seq. (cp. the sketch map drawn by V. la Cour in *Gesch. des schleswigschen Volkes*, I, 16, *Sønderjyllands Historie*, I, betw. 127 and 125), and it seems as if the most important centres coincide with settlements with Simplex names, e.g. æt Hæðum ('at the Heaths'), the modern Slesvig, and Gramæ, the centre of a large district ('herred').

During the Bronze Age strong influences from the south-east reach Scandinavia, being passed from nation to nation along the mercantile road from the Black Sea to the Prussian amber coast; such, for example, are the fashion of spiral ornaments, and the rites of sun worship, the south-eastern origin of which is revealed in the dipylon style of the

[1] See A. Bugge's maps in *Norges Historie*, I, 2, 21, 49, 55.

image found at Trundholm on the island of Zealand (cp. Sophus Müller, *Urgeschichte Europas*, 116).

After the fifth century B.C. these south-eastern influences give way to south-western, originating from the Celts to whom we owe the introduction of iron (Celt. **īsarnon*) (cp. § 245 on the Celtic influence upon the Cimbri).

The Goths emigrate from Scandinavia to Prussia according to their legendary traditions (Jordanes, IV, 25). Berig, the alleged leader of the migration, seems to be the famous leader of the Cimbric raid, Boiorix, who fell in 101 B.C. (cp. § 245). We may also compare the legend of the Gothic migration with the historical fact that the Sciri and Bastarnae appear on the Black Sea about 200 B.C. It seems to have been a great ethnic movement shared in by the Scandinavians.

The worship of fertility deities—Nerthus, Freyr, etc., originating from the south-western Orient—is probably common to Scandinavians and Angles about the beginning of our era.

In A.D. 5 a Roman navy visits the Baltic and the first map of Denmark is drawn. Pliny records the name Scadinauia; the Scandian islands are mentioned by Pliny and Ptolemy. The Celtic influence on the Scandinavian Iron Age comes to an end and is replaced by Roman influence. After the increase of the amber trade between Italy and Prussia during the reign of Nero (cp. Pliny, XXXVII, 45), the Scandinavian-Roman relations grow stronger and more extensive, as appears from the numbers of coins found. The traces of Roman influence in some parts of Zealand, says Kjær in *Bornholmske Samlinger*, 1907, 111, are so numerous that a fanciful ethnographer might feel tempted to assume a Roman colonisation. The Baltic islands of Bornholm, Öland, and Gotland, become the principal centres for the importation of Roman goods. An interesting couple of loan words, showing the route of the importation, are Gotlandic *lucarn* and *lucarna-staki* 'candle' and 'candlestick', < Gothic *lukarn* and *lukarna-staþa* < Latin *lucerna*. On the continental Scandinavian coasts of the Baltic, e.g. among the Sviones, the traces of Roman influence are much more sparse, and in Norway they become almost negligible. Tacitus, however, in his *Germania*, 17, mentions the import of furs from the far north.

This mercantile intercourse gives rise to the first description of the Scandinavian Peninsula. Pliny, IV, 96, mentions the numerous 'Hillevionum gens', perhaps a corruption of 'illa Svionum gens' (cp. p. 407).

Tacitus, *Germ.* 44, emphasises the royal power of the Sviones and their strong navies—a remarkable fact, as he mentions no other Gothonic navies in the whole of his *Germania*, and evidence of Gothonic maritime activity is very rare before his time. (There were: Scandinavian rock carvings of ships in the Bronze Age; a naval fight of the Bruchteri in 12 B.C., and raids of the Chauchi from A.D. 41 to 47.) Ptolemy, II, 11, § 16, produces the first general survey of Scandinavian tribes, a knowledge which the Romans had acquired through their mercantile connexions with the Prussian amber coast.

The increase of maritime intercourse results in the 'preliminary Viking Age', in the third century A.D. After 256 or 267 the Scandinavian tribe of Erules begins ravaging the coasts of the Black Sea, and in 289 also appears on the Atlantic shores. It is not impossible that the later Erulian raiders on western shores are not always Erules proper; the name may have been used collectively for 'Scandinavian Vikings', as were the names 'Danes', 'Northmen', and 'Rōs' in later times.

In the early sixth century a Norwegian King Hrodulf on a voyage to Italy gives a valuable ethnological survey of Scandinavia (Jordanes, *Getica*, III, 24). Here we notice first of all that the Scandinavians about that time have not yet absorbed a population near the Christiania Fjord called the 'Finni mitissimi', 'Scandzae cultoribus omnibus mitiores', 'the highly civilised Finns, more civilised than any other inhabitants of Scandinavia'. Andreas M. Hansen, *Landnåm i Norge*, 172 seq., denies that this can refer to the same people as the present Finns or Lapps. We must leave the question undecided; it is sufficient here to note the existence of a non-Gothonic race, which is also traceable in Norwegian epic traditions. If such survivals could persist in Southern Norway as late as the sixth century A.D., it seems also credible that the Finn(h)aithae of Jordanes, III, 22, the modern Finvidingar in Southern Sweden, may represent the same originally non-Gothonic nation, though in Hrodulf's time they may already have spoken Scandinavian.

Another interesting observation of Hrodulf is that the inhabitants of the rough Gautic mountains are constantly making inroads into the more fertile districts along the coast; compare the remark of Jordanes that Scandia is a 'vagina gentium'. This is part of the same primitive ethnic current which had caused the Cimbri, Eudoses, and Harudes to emigrate from Jutland some six or seven centuries earlier.

At the same time he notices the ambition of the Sviones and Danes to be taller than any other Scandinavians—a symptom of their aspirations to political hegemony—and he relates that the Danes have conquered and driven out the Erules. The Danish victory mentioned probably took place after the return of those Erules who had previously been conquered on the Danube by the Langobards about 505. It is the first historical instance of those inter-Scandinavian feuds which preceded the establishment of the states of Denmark, Sweden, and Norway, and which ended with the battle of Hafrsfjord in 872.

Both in Sweden and in Denmark the rise to political power is strengthened by the religious authority of the dynasties who were responsible for the great central sanctuaries of Uppsala and of Hleiðr respectively. And it is accompanied by propaganda for new deities, Thor and Odin, who, immigrating from the south-west, embody the warlike spirit of the great Migration Age.

The Swedes, i.e. the Sviones proper, emphasise their political rank by the element *þjóð* 'nation' added to their name: Sví-þjóð, Hrodulf's Sve-thidi. Odin, surnamed Sigi, had a great temple at Sigtuna near Uppsala. A circle of districts dedicated to Frey, Ull, and Thor indicates that the religious centre lies in the vicinity of Uppsala. Owing to maritime intercourse with the Saxons, the Sviones adopt Saxon onomastic elements, such as 'hundred' for O.N. *herað* 'district', and 'town', Swed. *-tuna*. The place names ending in *-tuna* mark the spread of Svionic settlements towards the west and south; the type is moreover adopted by the Norwegians. In Denmark it only occurs sporadically.

The Danes carry the cult of Odin to Northern and Eastern Jutland. One name frequently used for hills on which their law courts were held (*målhøg*) is probably an imitation of the Frankish *mahlberg*. The place names ending in *-lev*, a type of local origin, are the most characteristic marks of the Danish expansion during the Migration Age; they extend from Southern Sweden and Norway to parts of Western Jutland and of Northern Germany (cp. H. V. Clausen's maps in *Aarbøger*, 1916, and the author's map in *Frem*, 1926, 407).

While the overthrow of the Erules by the Danes is only an inter-Scandinavian change of dominion, Scandinavia at the same time expands towards the south and west. The Danes conquer the Bards, a North German tribe, and seem temporarily to have occupied their territory south of the Baltic. The Jutlandic tribes—Jutes, remnants of Angles, etc.—join the Danish state and from the point of nationality are absorbed by the Danes.

The Erulian Vikings in the Channel are from this time replaced by 'Danes'. The first of the so-called 'Danes' on western shores are the famous 'Geats', the followers of King Hygelác whose unfortunate expedition to Friesland about 526 is reported by Gregory of Tours. In 565 Danes and Saxons are repulsed from the same regions; here real Danes are meant.

About the same time the first Svionic raids beyond the Eastern Baltic are recorded in Þjóðolf's *Ynglingatal* (cp. § 275).

After the close of the sixth century dynastic feuds seem to have checked Scandinavian expansion. Meanwhile, the Franks are advancing by stages towards Scandinavia, conquering the nations of North Germany and Friesland, viz. from 531 to 534 the Thuringians, in 594 the Varines, in 734 the Middle Frisians, in 775 the East Frisians, from 772 to 804 the Saxons. In 804 the Franks reach Holstein and grant its eastern district to the Slavs who have previously conquered the south coast of the Baltic. In 811 the Eider is recognised as the frontier between Denmark and the Frankish Empire; it remains the political south frontier of Scandinavia from this time till 1864. (The present frontier, of 1920, runs a little farther north.)

The Danish Viking raids begin again in 787, as a counter-attack against Frankish expansion. Viking raids of 'Northmen from Hærethaland' are recorded in the *Saxon Chronicle* in the same year. The raiders are called 'Danes', but were rather Hǫrðar from Norway. There may have been some sort of co-operation between Danes and Norwegians. These raids, with interruptions, go on now for about 150 years. Emigration and Viking raids are largely stimulated by Harold Fairhair's struggle for supremacy, which ends in the victory in Hafrsfjord in 872.

In 876 the Dane Halfdene 'portioned out the land of the Northumbrians, and they tilled it and made a livelihood by it' (*Saxon Chronicle*). This is the first recorded settlement of Scandinavians in England.

Owing to the vigour of maritime activity the Scandinavians spread in all directions. Their spheres of operation will be sketched individually below.

To the north-east the Norwegian Ottar sails round the North Cape and visits the Permians on the White Sea.

To the east and south-east Swedish settlers enter the opposite coasts of Finland and the Esthonian islands. Others, the so-called Russes, become rulers of the whole of Russia. From the shore of the Caspian Sea they temporarily invade Northern Persia. Emigrants from all Scandinavian countries form the body-guard of the Byzantine Emperors, and fight in Sicily and other Mediterranean regions.

To the south Danes establish themselves in Prussia, in Jomsborg on the Wendic coast, and temporarily subjugate Holstein.

On the south-west Danes subjugate Friesland and establish themselves at Duurstede in Holland and on the island of Walcheren. Danes together with Norwegians found the state of Normandy in Northern France. Norwegians occupy the island of Noirmoutier at the mouth of the Loire, an ancient haunt of the Saxons. Danes and perhaps also Norwegians raid the coasts of Spain and venture into the Mediterranean Sea.

On the west Danes conquer the whole of England and invade Eastern Ireland. Norwegians colonise Shetland and the Orkneys, parts of the Hebrides and the Isle of Man, of Scotland and of Ireland.

To the north-west Norwegians colonise the Faroe Islands and Iceland. The Icelanders again reach Greenland, and even the North American continent.

With the rule of the Danish Kings Swain and Canute the Great in England, 1013–1035, the Viking Age culminates. Canute's death marks the beginning of the decline. Already some years before, in 1014, the Irish defeated the Norwegians at Clontarf. Scandinavian preponderance in England is finally checked by the victory of the Romanised Normans in 1066. Norway loses the Hebrides in 1266, Shetland and the Orkneys are pawned to Scotland in 1469. The Scandinavian nationality gradually disappears completely from Britain, and is also absorbed by the Slavs in Russia and by the Esquimaux in Greenland.

Meanwhile, the Scandinavians renew their attempts at expansion beyond the seas. The Danes conquer Rügen in 1169, Esthonia in 1219, re-establish the Scandinavian dominion over Greenland, and acquire small colonies in India, Africa, and on the Antilles. About 1700 the Swedes are ruling almost the entire East Baltic coast from Finland to Pomerania inclusive, and in the seventeenth century they found a colony, Nya Sverige (New Sweden), in the place now occupied by New York. But all these transmarine possessions except Greenland are now lost or sold. In Finland the Swedish colonists still number some 400,000 people, but they are losing ground to the Finns. In North America the original colonists of New Sweden have been absorbed, but are being replaced by large numbers of immigrants from all the Scandinavian countries, together numbering some million people. Of ancient Scandinavian territory, only the region between the Eider and the Flensborg Fjord has been lost.

The entire number of Scandinavians may be assumed to be some 15 millions, including the emigrants in U.S.A., etc., whose Scandinavian nationality is certainly questionable or disappearing. The single figures are: Swedes 7,300,000, Danes 3,700,000, Norwegians 3,676,000, Icelanders 140,000, Faroese 23,000.

Lit. **Worsaae,** *The Danes and Norwegians in England, Scotland, and Ireland*; **Steenstrup,** *Normannerne*; **A. Bugge,** *Vikingerne*; **Collingwood,** *Scandinavian Britain*; **Mawer,** *The Vikings*; **Björkman,** *Scandinavian Loanwords in Middle English*; *idem, Nordische Personennamen in England*; **Lindkvist,** *Middle English Place Names of Scandinavian Origin*; **Ekwall,** *Introduction to the Survey of English Place-Names* **(chapter on the Scandinavians); A. H. Smith,** *Danes and Norwegians in Yorkshire* (*Saga Book of the Viking Society, Proceedings,* **1925–27, 188 seq.); Smith,** *The Place-Names of the North Riding of Yorkshire* (*Engl. Place-Name Soc.* v); **Taylor,** *Words and Places,* **ch. viii; Axel Olrik,** *Viking Civilisation,* **transl. by J. W. Hartmann and Hanna Larsen.**

§ 253. Legendary Traditions.

Scandinavia has more epic traditions than any other Gothonic country, owing to the exceptional position of Iceland, which has become a treasury house of all the folk-lore of the race. The abundance of stories is so overwhelming that even a limited selection would exceed the space available in the present work.

We shall only mention some collective representatives of the Scandinavian sub-group.

One such is Ypper in Uppsala, the eponymous representative of that town, father of Nori in Norway, Østen in the eastern country (Sweden), and Dan in Denmark, according to the *Chronicle of Lejre* (*Script. rer. Dan.* I, 223).

Another is the giant Fornjótr, according to the *Orkneyinga Saga*, ch. 1 and the MS *Frá Fornjóti* (*Fornald. Sögur*, II, 1), *Flateyjarbók*, I, 24. He is represented as a Finn, and his descendants are giants of air, sea, and ice, of whom Snow the Old is the most popular. Various Norwegian and Icelandic families claim to be descended from Snow. His daughter Drífa and another member of Fornjót's family are ancestors of the Yngling dynasty in Sweden (*Yngl. Saga*, ch. 13). And Snow is a primaeval king of Denmark, according to the *Chronicle of Lejre* and Saxo, 415 seq.

Lit. Schütte, *Oldsagn om Godtjod* (on Fornjótr, pp. 130, 139, 190); *idem, Vor mytiske Kongerække* (*Studier fra Sprog- og Oldforskning*, No. 105); *idem, Dansk Kongetals tusendaarige Traad* (*Hist. Tidsskrift*, 1925); Olrik, *Danmarks Heltedigtning* (vol. I, transl. as *The Heroic Legends of Denmark*).

B. §§ 254–257. *THE ERULES*

§ 254. Name.

Lat. Eruli (Trebellius, *Hist. Aug.* c. A.D. 800), Eroli (*CIL.* v, 8750), Heruli (Jul. Honorius, fourth century; Sid. Apollinaris, fifth century; Jordanes, sixth century), Eluri (Jordanes); Gr. Αἴρουλοι (Eusebius, c. A.D. 300), Ἔρουλοι (Procopius, sixth century), Ἕρουλοι (Zosimus, fifth century), Ἔλουροι (Menander, sixth century), Ἕλουροι (Dexippus, third century).[1] The word Erul- is generally regarded as being identical with O.L.G. *erl*, O.E. *eorl* 'free man', O.N. *jarl* 'earl'; cp. the O.N. runic name ErilaR.[2] Nordenstreng and A. Noreen, on the other hand, suggest a derivation from an O.N. word *jara* 'struggle'; we believe that the first etymology is simpler and more probable. Schönfeld shows that the *h* cannot be verified and is parasitical, as in Herminones, Hermunduri, Herminaricus. A Gothonic *h* would inevitably have been written *ch* in Gaul, the constant scene of West Erulian operations; the fixed spelling *ch* survives in Modern French names such as Chabert, Chivert. The form Ἕλουροι is due to an arbitrary Greek etymology, connecting it with ἕλη 'swamps'. Bugge and other scholars have assumed that the name ErilaR, repeatedly found in the oldest Scandinavian runic inscriptions, is not a personal name, but a designation of nationality, 'the Erule'. But such a profession of nationality is not likely, as there is no analogy in other runic inscriptions. Elgqvist connects the name Erules with a dialect word *järul, järel*, in the South Scandinavian districts of Värend and Bleking. It means 'hardy fellow or warrior', but may also be a synonym

[1] Much suggests that the Austrian river Erlaff < Lat. Arelape may have contributed to preserving the legendary memory of the Erules in these regions owing to its erroneous derivation from the tribal name. Cp. *Rüdiger von Pechlarn* (*Vortrag in d. Akad. d. Wissenschaften*, Wien, 1913, p. 9).

[2] Grimm, p. 598, conjectures an O.E. *Eorlum for Eolum, *Widsith*, l. 87, and Chambers, p. 216, regards the suggestion as acceptable. But the name belongs to an obviously interpolated series of oriental names. We prefer the proposal *ibid.* to identify the Eolas with Aeoles, Aeolians.

for *värul* 'were-wolf'. It is, as a matter of fact, a strange coincidence that the word appears in just that part of Scandinavia which seems to have been the home of the Erules. But it is almost inconceivable that a medial, non-stressed *u* could have escaped the effect of that Scandinavian law of syncope which appears in such cases as Hǫrðar < Harudes, þrœndr < þrówende, Heinir < Chaideinoi, Vindr < Venethi. However, the form *järel* may perhaps agree better with Scandinavian sound laws, and Elgqvist suggests that *järul* might be due to imitation of the words *djävul* 'devil', and *värul(v)* 'were-wolf'. Home: (1) presumably in some South Scandinavian coast district; (2) later on the Black Sea; (3) on the Middle Danube; (4) in Italy; later still perhaps also somewhere on the Channel.

Lit. Zeuss, 475; Grimm, 470; Schönfeld, s.v. *Eruli* (with lit.); Much in Hoops, s.v. *Heruler*; Förstemann, s.v. *Heruli*; Bugge, *Norges Indskrifter*, Preface, 100, 192; A. Noreen, *Fornvännen*, 1920, 40; v. Friesen, *Röstenen*, 45, 76, etc.; E. Noreen, *Språkvetensk. Selsk. i Uppsala Förhandl.* 1916-18, p. 4; Magnus Olsen, *Norges Indskrifter*, III, 229; Marstrander, *De gotiske runeminnesmerker*, 95; Elgqvist, *Erulernas bosättning i Värend* (*Hyltén-Cavallius-föreningens årsbok*, 1930, extract p. 76 seq.); Langenfelt, *Anthropos*, XIV/XV, 312; Karsten, *Die Germanen*, 144; v. Premerstein, *Zeitschrift*, LX, 77.

§ 255. Ethnic Position.

The evidence at our disposal is very meagre.

1. The personal names, if not neutral or Gothic, seem to be Scandinavian.

Alvith, 'All-wood' or 'Sanctuary-wood', a name of a pronounced Swedish type, quite unique south of the Baltic.

Fara, cp. Burg. Burgundo-fara, Goth. Sende-fara; the element *-far* is Burgundian, Langobardian, Anglian, but above all East Danish.

Fulkaris, probably the same as O.H.G. Folch-heri; it is worth noting that there occurs a Fulcarslef on the Danish island of Falster.

Hariso (masc. *CIL.* v, 8750). Runic Hariso (fem.) occurs on a clasp found at Himlingøje on the island of Zealand. Cp. O.N. *hersir* 'sheriff', also used as a personal name. Cp. Zachrisson, *Festskrift t. F. Jónsson*, 206; *idem*, *Zeitschr. f. Ortsnamenforsch.* VI, 39.

(H)aruth, Geatic Hæred (*Beowulf*), Langobard family name Harodus. Cp. the tribal name, Jutl. Harudes, O.N. Hǫrðar. Haruth in the true Erulian form seems to be (H)aordos, with 'Breaking' as in English, cp. runic Tanmaurk for Denmark. As Procopius writes Aordos three times, he must have intended to spell it thus.

(H)rodvulf 'Honour-wolf', with contemporary namesakes in Norway (Jordanes) and Denmark (*Widsith, Beowulf*). The popularity of the name Rudolf in Germany is secondary, and may be due to the Erulian hero. The element *hrōð* is a privilege of early kings and priests in Norway and Denmark, and of the Geatic dynasty of Hreðlings, and may occur in East Anglian and Jutish dynasties: Hróðmund, a Skjǫldung name, (H)ro(ð)wena, daughter of Hengest. South of the Baltic there is only one early instance, the Visigothic (H)rothesteus, in the fourth century, father of the persecutor Atharid (*Martyr. S. Sabae, Acta Sanct.* 12 *April*, cp. Loewe, *Beiträge*, XLVII, 430). Cp. Schönfeld's *Wörterbuch*, where the Erule Rodvulf, a Roteldis and a Ruderich, sixth cent., and an undated Chrodebert, are the only representatives in a collection extending over six centuries.

The occurrence of pronounced Gothic types cannot prove original Gothic nationality, as the long time that the Goths lived in the vicinity of the Erules would necessarily result in a Gothic influence on the language.

2. The Erules from the beginning of their history are governed by kings like the Scandinavians and Goths; they are not republicans like the Langobards, Saxons, Franks, and Lugians.

3. The migration of the defeated Danubian Erules to 'Thule' (Procopius, *Bell. Got.* II, 15), in spite of Müllenhoff's denial, is a *re*migration, caused by their desire to assert their traditional right to their old homestead. It is emphasised that the natives along their road did not object to their passage; this peaceful conduct would be inconceivable if they had not had an acknowledged right of remigration. Their home was in the immediate vicinity of the Gauts, *l.c.*, and of the Danes (Jordanes, III, 23); consequently it must have been situated in Southern Scandinavia (cp. Freytag, *Bilder aus der deutschen Vergangenheit*, I, 66; Loewe, 29; Schütte, *Nord. Tidsskrift f. Filologi*, 1896, 143; *idem, Oldsagn om Godtjod*, 86; *idem, Arkiv*, XXXVI, 177; Bugge, *Norges Indskrifter*, Preface, 187; v. Friesen, *Herulernas bosättning i Skandinavien*, 494; Elgqvist, *Erulernas bosättning i Värend*, 13; L. Schmidt, *Beiträge*, LI, 103 seq.).

4. Procopius, *Bell. Goth.* II, 14, relates a characteristic custom of the Erules. When their aged people became decrepit, they themselves

claimed the right to be killed. The relations placed the victim on a high pile of firewood, and a man of foreign blood executed him with a dagger. Afterwards the pile was set on fire. Hyltén-Cavallius, *Wärend och wirdarne*, I, 128, II, 294, compares this rite with an ancient tradition in the district of Värend: it had been the custom to kill aged people by means of a club. The killing of the aged is also known in other parts of Scandinavia. In Gautland they used to throw themselves down from a high rock, the so-called *ætternisstapi* 'the family rock' (see *Gautreks Saga*, ed. Ranisch, *Palaestra*, XI, 5). In South Jutland, a steep cliff was used for the same purpose, the so-called Endrupskov Aftægt. However, in these cases the victims were killed by being thrown down a precipice, whereas among the Erules and in Värend a weapon was used. It seems to have been a common Scandinavian rite, but the actual mode of performance connects the Erules and the people of Värend (cp. Elgqvist, *Erulernas bosättning i Värend*, 74).

The Erules consequently were Scandinavians, and in their home country they spoke a pronounced Scandinavian dialect (cp. the newcomer (H)aord from Scandinavia with the 'broken' pronunciation of his name). But abroad they were more or less Gothicised. Hence we explain the alternative pronunciation of (H)aord's name, (H)aruth, without Breaking, and with the Gothic unvoiced *th*. The same Gothic *th* appears in Alvith. And Procopius definitely calls the Erules a Gothic nation.

Lit. Zeuss, 476; Müllenhoff, *Nordalbing. Studien*, I, 125, 126, 130, 155; *idem*, *Beovulf*, 30; Loewe, 25 seq.; Much, *Stammeskunde* (3rd ed.), 100; *idem*, in Hoops, s.v. *Heruler*; *idem*, in *Deutsch-nordische Zeitschrift*, 1929, 51; Schmidt, I, 334; Wessén, *De nordiska folkstammarna i Beowulf*, ch. i; Elgqvist, *Erulernas bosättning i Värend.*

§ 256. History.

The uncertainty of the localisation of the Erules is chiefly due to their absence from Scandinavian traditions. No doubt some hero represents them, but we cannot trace which.

Müllenhoff identified the Erules with the Hadu-bards of the Skjǫldung legends, placing their home on the isle of Zealand; but the sole fact that both these tribes were overthrown by the Danes is not a sufficient reason for identifying them. It is a mistake to separate the Hadu-bards from the Bards or Lango-bards of Bardengau, who have nothing to do with the Erules; the prefix in this case is merely an epic ornament (cp. our paper *Ethnische Prunknamen* (*Zeitschrift*, LXVII, 129)).[1]

In 1927 Wessén has set forth a theory which quite upsets the traditional distribution of nationalities. He regards the Danes of the Skjǫldung cycle as disguised Erules and, on the other hand, their Hadu-bardic opponents as disguised Danes. The final victory of the Danes alias Hadu-bards would have been forgotten by the legend which favoured the Erules. We regard this whole theory as too artificial, and the alleged 'partiality of the legend' seems to us an involuntary admission of a weak point (cp. our detailed criticism in *Danske Studier*, 1927, 65).

In our opinion the best evidence for the localisation of the Erules is the fact attested by Procopius that they were received by the Gauts and were situated in the vicinity of the Danes. Consequently they seem to have inhabited some place in the south of the Scandinavian Peninsula. The coast of Southern Scania and Bleking is the best position geographically—the one which would best explain their relations with the Goths in Prussia, the Rugians in Pomerania, and the Chau(g)iones in Hanover (?) or Friesland. Perhaps the existence of the word *järel* in Bleking and Värend (cp. § 254), and the rite of killing the aged people in Värend by means of a club (cp. § 255, 4), may be taken as evidence supporting this localisation.

Erules accompany the Goths to South Russia in the third century A.D. Both nations harry Asia Minor and Greece as pirates from the year 256 onwards (Zosimus, I, 32 seq.).

In 267, after a defeat in Macedonia, the chieftain Naulobatos enters the service of Rome (Syncellus, ed. Par. 382)—the first Scandinavian known by name.

In 269 the Erules, fighting on the side of the Goths, are with them defeated by Claudius at Nish (Trebellius, *Hist. Aug. v. Claud.* VII, 6; Eutropius, IX, 11).

In 289 Erules from the Baltic, accompanied by Chauiones or Caynones, appear in Gaul, where Saxon pirates have been operating since 286 together with Chauchi; we regard the Chau(g)iones as 'smaller Chauchi' (cp. §§ 215, A 6, and 217). Between 286 and 292 Maximian repeatedly drives the invaders beyond the Rhine (Mamertin, *Paneg.* 8,

[1] Much originally accepted Müllenhoff's view, but gave it up already in the first edition of his *Stammeskunde* (1900), p. 123; cp. his article in Hoops, s.v. *Langobarden*, § 9.

Genethl. 7). Captive Erules now often appear as mercenaries in Britain, on the Rhine, etc. The headquarters of these Western Erules are never mentioned.

In 456 their piratical bands invade Galicia and, about 459, they venture as far as the straits of Gibraltar (Hydatius, 171 and 194).

About 350 the Eastern Erules with their King Halaric are subjugated by the Gothic conqueror Ermanaric (Jordanes, XXIII, 117).

About 370 both Erules and Goths are forced to submit to the Huns, who gradually lead them to Middle Europe.

In 451 the Eastern and Western Erules are forced to fight each other in Gaul as mercenaries of the Hun Attila and of the Roman governor Aëtius respectively.

From 458 to 460 and from 476 to 480 the Erule Timotheos (called ὁ Ἔλουρος) was patriarch of Alexandria. He was the leader of the monophysitic party in Egypt (cp. Gelzer in *Jahrbücher f. protestant. Theologie*, X, 318).

In 480 the Erules destroy Joviacum, i.e. Schlögen, between Passau and Linz (Eugippius, *Vita Severini*, 24). Others, together with Rugians and Sciri, have entered the service of Rome in Italy and contribute to Odovacar's coup d'état in 476, when he dethrones the last Emperor (*Chron. min.* I, 309, 313; Ennodius, *Paneg. Theoderico*, 53).

In 489, however, the Ostrogothic King Theodoric conquers Odovacar and becomes King of Italy.

About 500 Theodoric's minister Cassiodorus summons the Erules, Varines, and Thuringians to ally with the Goths against the Franks (*Variae*, III, 3). Schmidt, I, 346, maintains that the Rhenish colonies are meant, because they were most often menaced by the Franks. Cp. *idem*, *Beiträge*, LI, 103 seq. But the existence of these colonies is questionable, and at any rate they must have been so insignificant that it was scarcely worth the trouble to form an alliance with them. On the other hand, we know that Theodoric actually allied both with Thuringia and with the Danubian Erules. The Erulian king, who cannot be anyone but Hrodulf, became his 'son-in-arms' (*Variae*, IV, 2).

All this is in vain. All emigrated Erules soon lose their independence and disappear from history.

In 505[1] King Hrodulf is conquered and killed by the Langobards

[1] The time is a matter of dispute. Schmidt places the incident about 505, other scholars about 512. The difference is of no great importance.

whom he has previously subjugated (Procopius, *Bell. Goth.* II, 14; *Origo Langob.* 4; Paulus Diaconus, I, 20). Some of the scattered survivors are received into the East Roman Empire; others (re)migrate to 'Thule', settling there in the vicinity of the Gauts (Procopius, *l.c.* 15).

After the Danubian Erules become Christian, about 530, the anti-Roman Arians quarrel with the pro-Roman Catholics. The chieftain Ochos is killed, and the Arians resolve to send for a royal prince from Thule. On their return, the messengers supply Procopius with important ethnic information. But the civil dissension goes on (cp. *Bell. Goth.* II, 14, 15, III, 34, IV, 25).

From 530 to 553 Erulian mercenaries are fighting everywhere in the Empire: against Slavs, Caucasians, Persians, Vandals, and Goths.

In 566 or 567 the Erules in Italy revolt, and their leader Sindval(d) is hanged (Paulus Diaconus, II, 3; Marius Avent. *chron.* ad an. 567; *Excerpt. Sangall.* ad an. 567), whereupon Justinian is hailed as Herulicus (Euagr. *Hist. eccl.* V, 4). After this, the Erules disappear from history.

Before 526 the Northern Erules are subjugated by the Danes, according to the Norwegian King Hrodulf who visited Theodoric in Italy (Jordanes, III, 23). The time of this incident is not quite clear: was it before or after the remigration of the Erules from the Danube to Thule about 505? The circumstance, emphasised by Procopius, that the Danes did not object to the passage of the Erules would seem to favour the assumption that it was before the conflict of the two nations. On the other hand, the returning Erules are not received by their countrymen, but by the Gauts; this circumstance again seems to show that it was after the ruin of the Erulian state. We must leave the question open.

Lit. Zeuss, 476, 489; Müllenhoff, *Beovulf*, 89; Much, *Beiträge*, XVII, 201; *idem*, *Stammeskunde* (3rd ed.), 100; *idem*, in *Deutsch-nordische Zeitschrift*, 1929, 43; *idem*, in Hoops, s.v. *Heruler*; Loewe, 5 seq., 29, 111, 165, 210; Bremer, § 110; Schmidt, I, 333 seq.; Wessén, *De nordiska folkstammarna i Beowulf* (*Kungl. Vitterh. Hist. och Antikv. Ak. Handlingar*, part 36, 2); Schütte, *Daner og Eruler* (*Danske Studier*, 1927, 65); Elgqvist, *Erulernas bosättning i Värend.*

§ 257. Legendary Traditions.

The tragedy of the Erulian King Hrodulf is vividly depicted in the Langobard legend. In the *Thidrekssaga* he is called Rodolf, but has an alter-ego 'Rodingeir of Bakalar', the faithful officer of King Attila.

Bakalar is Bechelaren or Pöchlarn in Austria, where the Erules dwelt as Attila's subjects. Rodingeir is identical with the 'Margrave Rüdeger of Bechelaren' in the *Nibelungenlied*, the faithful officer of King Attila and friend of the Ostrogothic King Dietrich von Bern. *Biterolf* places Rüdeger's home in Arabia, probably a mistake for the town Arrabona in Pannonia on the homonymous river, the present Raab. Cp. W. Grimm, *Heldensage*, 3rd ed. p. 109. Rüdeger's death plunges Dietrich into wild despair. Their intimate friendship seems to reflect the alliance between the Erulian King Hrodulf and his 'father-in-arms', King Theodoric the Great. There are several reasons for the substitution of Rüdeger for Rodolf; e.g. there was a Count Rüdeger of Austria in the tenth century, contemporary with Bishop Pilgrim of Passau and Margrave Gero of Saxony, who are both introduced without authority into the *Nibelungenlied*. As to the poetical background, Matthaei demonstrates the harmony of history and legend in one important point. Both emphasise the extraordinarily strong pledge of faith between the Gothic king and his sworn friend, and the tragic importance of the latter's fall. The ruin of Hrodulf was the collapse of the first wall of defence which the Ostrogothic king tried to build up against the enemies who menaced him—the first in a series of failures which resulted in the final catastrophe of Theodoric's reign. And Rüdeger's ruin foreshadows the successive destruction of all Dietrich's champions except old Hildebrand. It is really a wonderfully true reflection in epic form of the historical truth.

Lit. Henrik Bertelsen, *Didriks Saga af Bern*, 42; Bugge, *Home of the Eddic Poems*, 278 seq.; Matthaei, *Zeitschrift*, XLIII, 305; Schütte, *Journ. Engl. and Germ. Phil.* XX, No. 3, 309; Much, *Rüdiger von Pechlarn* (*Vortrag in d. Akad. d. Wissenschaften*, Wien, 1913).

C. §§ 258–262. *THE DANISH BRANCH*

§ 258. Names.

1. O.Dan., O.N. Danir (acc. Dani, written Tani, King Harold Bluetooth on the stone of Jelling, about A.D. 980); M.Dan. Danæ; Dan. Danske, Danskere;[1] N.Fris. Deanskan; O.E. Dene (Alfred's *Bede*, V, 921; *Orosius*, 19, 24, before A.D. 899; *Sax. Chron.* (see Index)), Denan (*Sax. Chron.* 943), Deningas (*Beowulf*, l. 465); M.H.G. Tene (*Kudrun*,

[1] The earliest examples of the form Danskere mean 'inhabitants of Danzig' (see Dahlerup, *Ordbog over det danske Sprog*, s.v. *Dansker*).

ed. Martin, str. 333); Germ. Dänen (L.G. form); M.Lat. Dani (Jordanes, III, 23, third century A.D.); learned Daci; Ital. Danesi; Fr. Danois; Gr. Δανοί (Procopius, var. Δακοί); O.Irish Danair, Danar (*Book of Leinster*, c. A.D. 1160); Lappish Dač (sing.); Finn. Tanskalaiset. Eponymous hero: M.Dan. Dan. Personal name: Ostrogoth. Danus; Visigoth. Danila; O.H.G. Tene-gar; O.E. Tene-berct. Country: run. Dan. Tanmaurk (Jelling, c. A.D. 980); gen. Tan-markaR (*ibid.* c. A.D. 940); Dan. Dan-mark; run. Norw. Tan-marku (Karlevi, c. A.D. 1000); O.E. Denamearc (Alfred's *Orosius*, p. 19, before A.D. 899); M.H.G. Tene-marke (*Kudrun*, str. 206), Tene-lant (*ibid.* str. 204), Tene-rīche (*ibid.* str. 354); Germ. Däne-mark (L.G. form); Ital. Dani-marca; O.Fr. Dani-marches (Rod. Glaber, *Coll. hist. Franc.* V, 14); Span. Dina-marca; O.Irish Danmargg (*Book of Leinster*); Finn. Tani-marku. Region: O.N. Dana-lǫg; O.E. Dena-lagu ('the Dane-law', in England). Place names: Engl. Denaby, Dan-by (W. Riding); Esthonian Tal-lin ('the Danish castle', i.e. Reval). Coronation stone: M.Dan. Danæ-rygh ('the Dane-stone', in Jutland). Parliament: M.Dan. Danæ-hof. Banner: Dan. Dane-brog.[1] Obscure. The name perhaps means 'Lowlanders'; cp. Engl. *den* 'cave', i.e. 'a low place'. Danir is not an abbreviation of Denmark, as Noreen, Schück, and Wadstein maintain; examples of the Simplex occur more than four centuries earlier than the Compound. The occurrence of a place name Danmark in Swedish provinces must be regarded as an accidental coincidence, as the element *dan-* is frequent in Swedish local nomenclature, and *-mark* is extremely ordinary. In the name Denmark the element *-mark* does not necessarily signify 'borderland', as Wadstein thinks; cp. the Norwegian territorial names Heið-mǫrk and Þela-mǫrk, which represent the *central* regions of the Heinir and Þilir; Wedermearc, *Beowulf*, l. 298, correspondingly seems to mean 'the entire land of the Geats'. On the use of 'Danes' as name of the 'Scandinavians' see § 249, 5.

Lit. Feilberg, *Ordb. ov. d. jyske Almuesmål*, s.v. *Danmark, dansk* and *Tillæg*, s.v. *Dansker*; Noreen, *Spridda studier*, II, 139, 142; *idem*, *Uppsala Univ. Årsskrift*, 1907, *Program*, 2, p. 5 note 2; Schück, *ibid.*; Anna Marie v. Liliencron, *Zeitschr. f. schlesw. holst. Gesch.* XLIV, 42; Wadstein, *Namnet Danmark* (*Göteborg Högskolas*

[1] The connexion with the name of the Danes is probably not original. In M.Danish there exists a word *dannebroget* 'with red and white stripes' (cp. Frisian *dan* 'red'). See Falk and Torp, *Etym. Ordbog*, and Dahlerup, *Ordb. ov. d. danske Sprog*, s.v. *Dannebrog*.

Rektoratsprogram, 1918–19, with lit. and numerous quotations); Much, *Stammeskunde*, 129; Meyer-Lübke in *S.B. d. Wien. Akad. phil.-hist. Kl.* CXLIX, 2, 22 (on Danila, Danildus); Dahlerup, *Ordbog over det danske Sprog*, III, 478–517; Brøndal, *Danernes Navn* (*Danske Studier*, 1920, 17 seq., with lit.); Schütte, *ibid.* 169 seq.; *idem*, *Arkiv*, XXXVII, 233 seq.; *idem*, *Atlantis*, 1923; Marstrander, *Norske Vidensk. Selsk. Skr. H.f. Kl.* 1900, pp. 5, 59, 90 (on Danair and Danmargg); Zimmer, *Zeitschrift*, XXXV, 133 (on Danair and Danmargg); Zachrisson, *Acta Phil. Scand.* I, 3; *Studier tillägn. Ax. Kock*, 494 seq.[1]

2. O.Irish Dan-marcaig.

Lit. Zimmer, *Zeitschrift*, XXII, 245 note.

3. M.Lat. Marco-manni (Ermenrich of Ellwangen, *Mon. Germ. SS.* II, 33, about A.D. 850; Rhabanus Maurus, *Opera*, VI, 334 (1624); *Annals of Massay*, ad an. 865 and 873; *Mon. Germ. SS.* III, 169, recording Viking raids in Gaul, etc.), meaning 'men from Den-mark'. Probably a learned term, alluding to the ancient German Marcomans. Notice the occurrence of Markamenn in Norway.

Lit. Steenstrup in *Indbydelsesskrift t. Kjøbenhavns Univ. Aarsfest*, 8 April 1900, 56 seq.

4. O.E. Ing-wine (*Beowulf*, ll. 1044–1321). Eponymous hero: O.E. Ing...mid Éast-Denum (*Rune-song*, Grein and Wülcker, *Bibl. d. angelsächs. Poesie*, I, 335); eponymous heroine (?): M.Dan. Fru Inger (leader of the emigrating Langobards, *Danm. g. Folkeviser*, I, No. 21). Obscure. This name is that of the ancient sub-group of Inguaeones, later applied to the mediaeval Danes (cp. § 236).

Lit. Schönfeld, s.v. *Inguaeones* (with lit.); Chadwick, 296; Schütte, *Smaaskrifter udg. af Selsk. f. germ. Fil.* No. 13, IV, § 7.

5. O.E. Scyldingas (*Beowulf*, l. 53, Compounds, ll. 464, 596, etc.), Scyldungas (*ibid.* l. 2025). Eponymous hero: O.E. Scyld (*ibid.* l. 4); O.N. Skjǫldr. The name is derived from the Danish dynasty of Skjǫldungar. It is generally interpreted as 'shield-men'. But it is more probable that it means 'inhabitants of Skjold'. A village of this name exists in Jutland, and in the middle of Zealand there is a Skjoldnæs, situated on the border of a lake. Lappenberg, Arnold, Plummer, and Stevenson, have identified O.E. Scyldingas with the M.Lat. Scaldi (*Ann. Lindisfarn.* A.D. 911, *Mon. Germ. SS.* XIX, 506), Scaldingi (*Hist. de S. Cuthberto, Rer. Brit. Scr.* I, 200, etc.). But Björkman objects that the vowel ought then

1 On the O.E. epic surnames of the Danes such as Gár-dene see Schütte, *Zeitschrift*, LXVII, 129 seq.

to have been *e* or *y*, not *a*. He derives this name of Scandinavian Vikings from M.L.G. *schalde*, M.Dutch *schoude* 'boat', 'ferry', cp. O.E. *æscmen* 'Vikings' < *æsc* 'dromo'.

Lit. Much in Hoops, IV, 187, §§ 1 and 4; Lappenberg, *Gesch. v. England*, I, 212; Arnold, *Rer. Brit. Scr.* I, 200, footnote 1; Plummer, *Two of the Sax. Chronicles*, II, 85; Stevenson, ed. of *Asser*; Björkman, *Saga-Book of the Viking Club*, VII, 132 seq.

6. Swed. Jutar; Finn. Juutilaiset, i.e. the West Danish tribe of Jutes. Place names: Swed. Jutenabben near Kalmar, Jutekärret in Westmanland (places of battles between Danes and Swedes); Finn. Juutin-rauma, the Öresund.

Lit. Lönnrot, *Finskt-svenskt lex.* s.v. *Juuti.*

7. Cymr. Eingl; M.Lat. Angli (*Ann. Cambr.*), a term used in Welsh poetry right up to the fourteenth century to denote the East Anglian Danes who fought the battle at Buttingdon in Shropshire. (Kind communication from Prof. Davis, Univ. of Liverpool.)

8. O.Irish Dub-gaill, 'dark strangers', contrasting with Find-gaill, 'fair strangers', i.e. Norwegians. Personal name: M.Irish Dougal. Place name: O.Irish Inis Gaill duibh (island in the river Shannon); Engl. Duggleby (Yorksh.). Alluding to a racial contrast or to a difference of national dress or armour.

Lit. Zimmer, *Zeitschrift*, XXXV, 97; A. Bugge, *Skrifter udg. af Vidensk. Selsk. i Christiania, H. F. Kl.* 1900, No. 4, 7 and 11.

9. O.Irish Dub-lochlannaig, 'dark Scandinavians', contrasting with Finn-lochlannaig, 'fair Scandinavians', i.e. Norwegians.

Lit. A. Bugge, *Skrifter udg. af Vidensk. Selsk. i Christiania, H. F. Kl.* 1900, No. 4, 5.

10. O.Irish Dub-genti (*Book of Leinster*); Cymr. Do-gynt, 'dark gentiles', contrasting with Find-genti, 'fair gentiles', i.e. Norwegians. According to the *Mabinogion* the name alludes to the black colour of armour, weapons, and ships.

Lit. Zimmer, *Zeitschrift*, XXXV, 70 (note), 97, 132.

§ 259. Sub-divisions.

A. Eastern Danes, often characterised by the element *-far*.

(1) Danir proper, Skjǫldungar, Sjællands-farer, O.N. Sjólands-farar (*Knytlinga Saga*, ed. Petersens and Olson, 244), in Zealand.

(2) Låler, Lålliker, Lålands-farer, in Låland.

(3) Falstringer, O.N. Falstr-búar, in Falster.

(4) Langelands-farer (Lavinds-farer), in Langeland.

(5) Fynboer, in Funen. An original Simplex *Fyner seems to occur in the place name Fyna-gårde in Bornholm.

(6) Skåninger, O.N. Skánungar, in Scania, O.N. Skáney.

(7) Hallinger (Hallin, Jordanes, III, 22, i.e. *Hallir?), Hallands-farer, in Halland.

(8) Blekinger, O.E. *Blecingas, M.Lat. Pleichani (Adam. Brem. *Mon. Germ. SS.* VII, 371, High German form), Blekings-farer (*Xenia Lideniana*, 107), in Bleking, O.E. B(l)ecinga ég (Alfred's *Orosius*, 20).

(9) *Borringer,[1] in Borring-holm, 'the island of the Borringer' (Bornholm), O.E. Burgenda-land, 'the land of the Burgundians'. In O.N. the island is called Borgundar-holmr, 'the island of the steep hills'. Notice the Burgundian Burgundo-farones, a surname of the Burgundians, who are supposed to originate from Bornholm.

B. Western Danes or Jutes, characterised by the element *-bo*.

(10) Vendel-, (11) Ty-, (12) Himmer-, (13) Salling-, (14) Hard, (15) Å-, (16) Angel-, (17) Ommer-, (18) Vard-boer, (19) Lovringer or Skov-boer, (20) *Baringer. All of these populations inhabit counties, except the Angelboer whose territory has at least a corresponding size. The first seven have been identified with the ancient tribes of (1) Wendle, (2) Teutones, (3) Cimbri, (4) Sabalingioi, (5) Harudes, (6) Auiones, (7) Anglii; in the case of (1), (3), (5), and (7), the identity may be regarded as certain. The Åboer are also called Åboinger or Åbutter (noticed by Aage Sørensen in Mellerup) (cp. § 237).

The inhabitants of subordinate districts ('herreder') sometimes represent populations which are in early sources designated as tribes, or occupy areas corresponding to counties.

(*a*) Bergio(r), in Biærg Hæret, Scania (Jordanes, III, 22).

Lit. Läffler, *Svenska landsmålen*, XIII, 9, p. 7; v. Friesen, *Röstenen*, 66; Noreen, *Fornvännen*, 1920, 43; Jiriczek, *Engl. Stud.* LX, 221; Svensson, *Namn och Bygd*, 1917, 119.

(*b*) Liothida, probably for *Liothgida in Lyuthgud Hæret, Scania (*ibid.*). The authority for this is the Norwegian Hrodulf, whose dialect may have dropped the *g*, as in O.Norw. Hróarr, the O.E. Hróðgár.

[1] The Danish family name Borring is supposed to mean 'inhabitant of Bornholm'.

Lit. Läffler, *Svenska Landsmålen*, XIII, 9, p. 7; Schück, *Upsala Univ. Årsskrift*, 1907, *Progr.* 2, p. 12; v. Friesen, *Röstenen*, 66; Noreen, *Fornvännen*, 1920, 43; Svensson, *Namn och Bygd*, 1917, 118; 1925, 25; Lindroth, *ibid.* 1918, 41; Weibull, *Arkiv*, XLI, 233; Jiriczek, *l.c.* 221.[1]

(*c*) Φιραῖσοι (Ptol. II, 11, § 16), perhaps the Færsingar in Færs Hæret, Scania, according to Wadstein. We regard the identification as somewhat doubtful. The *s* in Færs may be genitival.

Lit. Wadstein, *Namnet Danmark* (*Göteb. Högskolas Rektoratskrift*, 1918–19), IV, 39 footnote.

(*d*) Gydingar (*Svenska medeltidens rim-krönikor*, II, 8731), now Göingar, Gønger, in the Scanian district of Gything or Guthisbo. The latter name seems to indicate 'inhabitants of a locality *Guthir' (cp. the Gautic district Vadsbo, 'people of the ford'). Perhaps *Guthir was the name of a lake (cp. Guden Sø and Guden Å in Jutland). The district of Gything Hæret is twice as large as the Jutlandic county of Jalyng, and larger than several other counties.

(*e*) Fervir (Jordanes, III, 22), in the Hallandic district of Fyæræ < *Ferwō, 'coast which is exposed to the tide'.

Lit. Läffler, *Svenska Landsmålen*, III, 9, p. 8; Schütte (Norw.) *Hist. Tidsskrift*, 1917, 5; Noreen, *Fornvännen*, 1920, 43.

(*f*) Χάλοι (Ptol. II, 11, § 7), probably the Hallinger in Hallæ Hæret, Jutland. The districts North and South Hallæ, together with the districts of Rugse and Styfring between them, form a territory as large as the county of Jalyng (cp. § 237, 6 (lit. *ibid.*)).

Survey of types of names. (*Toponymics of counties, districts, and larger islands.*)

(*a*) Simplexes: Danir, Fervir, *Hallir (Chaloi, Cimbri, Harudes in Jutland).

(*b*) Long Derivative types: Skåninger, Hallinger, Blekinger, *Borringer, Falstringer, Gydingar, Færsingar, Gærsingar, Tøsinger, Lålliker (Åboinger, Lovringer, *Baringer, Hallinger, Hånninger, Heinger, Morsinger, Samsinger, Alsinger, Fanninger or Fanniker, *Eudusii, Rømiser in Jutland or in its vicinity).

[1] The connexion with Lödde å and Löddeköpinge in Southern Scania, Läffler, *Svenska Landsmålen*, XIII, 9, p. 7, is scarcely correct; see v. Friesen, *l.c.*; but it is advocated by Palmér, *Namn och Bygd*, 1928, 20.

(*c*) Compounds: five names ending in *far-* in Eastern Denmark (cp. Burgundo-farones), seven ending in *-bo* in Jutland.

Lit. Steenstrup, *Danmarks ældste Inddeling* (*Danske Vidensk. Selsk. Oversigter*, 1896, with map); Schütte, *Folkelig Hof- og Statskalender* (*Danske Studier*, 1914–15); *idem*, *Nordens ældste Indbyggernavne* ((Norw). *Hist. Tidsskr.* 1917, 1 seq.).

§ 260. Ethnic Position.

Though the individuality of the Danish nation is obvious and though its political area remains the same from the ninth to the seventeenth century, it is not easy to point out definite ethnic criteria.

It is a matter of controversy whether the Danes are aborigines, or whether their appearance in Zealand may be traced back to an immigration in historical times.

As a matter of fact, two ancient authorities speak of an immigration from Sweden.

The *Chronicle of Lejre* (twelfth cent., *Script. rer. Dan.* I, 223), says: 'Fuit in Upsala civitate Svethiae rex quidam Ypper nomine, tres filios habens, quorum unus Nori, alter Østen, tertius Dan dicebatur. Quem pater suus misit in has partes, quae nunc dicuntur Dacia'. The *Chronicon Erici regis* (c. A.D. 1300, *Script. rer. Dan.* I, 149) replaces Ypper by Humli, who is Dan's father according to Saxo; the title 'King of Upsala' applies to both (cp. *Gesta Danorum* in Lorenzen, *Gammeldanske kröniker*, 2 seq., and the *Chronicon* from Ryd, *ibid.* 62 seq., 136 seq.). According to the Chronicle of Ryd, Dan originates from Gothia, i.e. Gautland. The derivation from the Swedish Uppland may also be the subject of the myth in *Gylfaginning*, ch. 1, describing how Gefjón ploughs out Zealand from the place where nowadays the Mälar Lake is situated. Finally the Norwegian King Hrodulf (cited by Jordanes, III, 23), after mentioning the Swedes, continues in these words: 'Dani...ex ipsorum stirpe progressi'.

On the basis of these pieces of evidence the Swedish origin of the Danes has been assumed by various scholars, especially Swedes; so Birger Nerman, *Härstamma Danerna ifran Svealand?* (*Fornvännen*, 1922); v. Friesen, *Rö-stenen i Bohus-län*, 48; Wessén, *De nordiska folkstammarna i Beowulf* (*Kungl. Vitterh. Hist. och Antikv. Ak. Handl.* part 36, 2); Neckel, *Die verwandtschaften der germanischen sprachen untereinander* (*Beiträge*, LI, 5); the latter author's lecture on Gefjón has not yet been printed.[1]

The agreement of the evidence from the ancient sources certainly is remarkable, but we believe that the conclusiveness of this corroboration has been somewhat overrated. It is not absolutely certain that Hrodulf derives the Danes directly from the Swedes; the words 'ex ipsorum stirpe' may also be referred to the 'Scandzae cultores' who have been mentioned by him at the beginning of the whole chapter. This was hitherto the usual interpretation.

As to the *Chronicle of Lejre*, and the *Chronicon Erici*, they undoubtedly regard the Danes as emigrants from Uppsala in Sweden. But we cannot summarily take it for granted that this genetic myth is more reliable than that of the Scandinavian ancestors Fornjótr and Snow who are assumed to come from Finland. Cp. the ancestor of the world, Ymir, who seems to be an Ymuman or inhabitant of Umeå Lappmark, N. M. Petersen, *Haandbog i den gammelnordiske Geographi*, I, 205; cp. also the Norwegian princely ancestor Sæming, who seems to be the eponymous representative of the Same or Lapps, etc. There must have been a certain tendency to exaggerate the arctical origin of the Northmen.

At any rate, even if we accept the evidence of the *Chronicles*, it gives us no particulars as to the time *when* the emigration of the Danes from Sweden took place. And the time is indeed a point of great importance in any discussion of the ethnic position of the nation. Neckel and Wessén argue that, because the Danes emerge suddenly about A.D. 500, they must have immigrated shortly before that time. Such reasoning, however, cannot be reconciled with all that we know of their position.[2] The Sviones by about A.D. 500 had developed their own distinctly national types, being partly of Saxon origin, such as place names ending in *-tuna* ('town'),[3] district names ending in 'hundred', etc. If the Danes emigrated from Sweden about A.D. 500, one would expect them to share these Svionic characteristics, but they do not: they develop quite distinct

1 Neckel's interpretation of the myth of Gefjón has been contradicted by the folklorist Ellekilde, *Nationaltidende*, 17 December 1929. Edv. Erslev has also pointed out that there exists a region called Sjóland on the shore of Lake Mälar. He assumes that the myth originates from an etymological theory connecting this Swedish Zealand with its Danish namesake.

2 The incorrectness of the *argumentum e silentio* will be shown below on p. 372.

3 The element *-tún-* is of Celtic origin, < *-dunon*; south of the North Sea it only occurs among the Saxons.

types of place names, e.g. ending in *-lev*, district names ending in *-herað*, not ending in 'hundred', and toponymics ending in *-far*. The latter type has an analogue, Burgundo-farones, among the Burgundians who had disappeared from the Baltic coasts some two centuries before 500.[1] Moreover, the Danes of A.D. 500 had inherited the name of the ancient Jutlandic Inguaeones, and they were celebrated in the most friendly terms by the Angles. Such facts harmonise badly with the assumption that the Danes were a nation of invaders who had lately arrived from distant Svionic regions, and had settled as conquerors among the Jutes and Angles.

Consequently, if the *Chronicles* are right in deriving the Danes from the Sviones, and if Hrodulf agrees with them, the alleged immigration to Zealand must have taken place in remote antiquity. The foundation of the Danish state is a movement which is not a direct continuation of the Svionic expansion of about A.D. 500. On the contrary, the Danish expansion would seem to start from a centre on the isle of Zealand, and to spread both east and west, and its eastward movement would be directly opposed to the movement of the Sviones, which started from the Mälar region.[2]

Even if the immigration of the Danes took place in more or less remote ages, it might have left a marked Scandinavian influence on the language, as Neckel assumes (*l.c.* p. 4). This tendency was perhaps increased by an additional immigration of Gauts, which seems to have taken place after A.D. 500, and which can be traced in North Zealandic place names such as Æse-rum, Viga-rum, Niarthe-rum, Martheme (see below on p. 391) (cp. the Annals of Ryd which derive the Danes from 'Gothia'). On the other hand, we believe that Neckel exaggerates somewhat the ancient contrast between 'Südisch' and 'Nordisch'. As the ancient dialects of Zealand, Funen, and North Jutland are entirely unknown, it is safer to avoid deciding whether the inhabitants spoke 'Südisch' or not. The idea that the Danish Belts and Sounds would

1 Neckel in a private letter compares these toponymics with O.N. personal surnames such as Dyflinnar-, Holmgarðs-, Jórsalafari. But he is mistaken. Dyflinnarfari means 'a foreigner who makes a journey to Dublin'. But Sjællands-far means 'a man who lives in Zealand', or perhaps rather 'a man of the tribe of Zealanders' (cp. Langobard *fara* 'family').

2 H. V. Clausen in *Aarbøger*, 1916, reprint p. 37, maintains that the lines of settlements ending in *-lev* appear in Scania as arrows projecting from the west coast towards the interior of the country.

necessarily be linguistic barriers is misleading. It is often categorically contradicted by the modern dialect map.

A quite individual theory is set forth by Wadstein who, like Noreen, regards the name of Danes as derived from Denmark. He interprets Denmark as 'the damp frontier region' and places its original nucleus on the northern bank of the Eider. As Noreen's genetic theory is a misconception, Wadstein's whole construction has no solid basis. No matter how we interpret the elements, Denmark is derived from Danes, not Danes from Denmark. The geographical name gives no hint as to the original cradle of the nation, and a localisation in South Jutland is directly contradicted by the legendary tradition which points towards Zealand. Had the Danes been situated on the Eider about A.D. 500 it would have been *their* name, and not that of the less important Jutes, which became the general designation of the Jutlandic tribes.

In the pages to follow, we shall try to point out some features which indicate the establishment of a separate Danish national individuality.

A. The island nucleus of the Danish people.

1. The insular kingdom of Witheslef (var. -slet) is the nucleus of the Danes proper. Cp. the *Chron. of Lejre, Script. rer. Dan.* I, 223: 'Dan..., quem pater suus misit...ad regendum insulas quatuor, scil. Sialand, Mön, Falster et Laland, quae omnes uno vocabulo nuncupabantur Witheslef'.

2. If Witheslef is the correct spelling, the name is significant. The element *-lev*, in the name of a state, is absolutely unique and seems to indicate that this typically Danish element originates in Zealand (cp. under B 5).

3. The religious and political capital of Witheslef is Hleiðr, a name also unique in character. It seems to indicate the tent or baldachin of the sanctuary. This unique term emphasises the individuality of the Danish community.

4. Hleiðr is the acknowledged residence of King Fróði Friðgóði, the god Frey disguised in typically Zealandic form. His authority in Witheslef was so deeply rooted that no district within this area was ever dedicated to his rivals, Thor and Odin (cp. I, 115, 225).

5. The Zealandic Law had after 1284 official validity for Mön, Falster, and Låland. As there is no mention of separate laws for these three islands, we may assume that the Zealandic Law is practically the primaeval 'Law of Witheslef'.

6. The ethnic element *-far* is towards the west scarcely found beyond the limits of Witheslef: this includes the Langelandsfarer on the island of Langeland, but not the inhabitants of Funen and Jutland).[1] Towards the east, certainly, its area is larger, including both Halland and Bleking.

B. The enlarged Danish nationality appears to be established from early mediaeval times. Its extent is indicated by the following characteristics.

1. The name of the Inguaeonic group, which in the terminology of Pliny and Tacitus chiefly indicates the Cimbri, i.e. Jutlanders, is during the Migration Age given to the Danes. Cp. the Ingwine of *Beowulf*, ll. 1044 and 1321, and the O.E. *Rune-song*: 'Ing was first among the East-Danes'; further 'Lady Inger' in a ballad as national representative of the Danes (see § 258, 4). Chadwick says, *Origin of the English Nation*, 296: 'At the time when history opens, the Teutonic peoples of the western Baltic are all included among the Danes. In *Beowulf* the terms Dene and Ingwine are apparently synonyms, though the latter seems to be becoming obsolete. Our discussion has led us to conclude that the Ingwine of the sixth century were the descendants of the Inguaeones of the first century, whether the two words are really identical or not'.

2. 'Danes' soon replaces the obsolete term Ingwine. Already in the *Finnsburg Lay* the (presumably) Jutish Hengest is called a 'Dane'. Adam. Brem. writes, *Mon. Germ. SS.* VII, 275: 'Dani, quos Iuddas appellant, usque ad Sliam lacum', 'those Danes who are called Jutes, extending to the Firth of Sli'. The statutes of Åbenrå, A.D. 1335, art. 45, distinguish 'Danish and foreign beer', thus characterising Danish as identical with 'indigenous'. The Jutish inhabitants of Schwansen in L.G. are called Steert-dänen, *steert* 'start' being a L.G. synonym of H.G. *schwanz* 'tail'; thus their Danish nationality is emphasised. The German family name, indicating descent from Jutes in the frontier district, is Deen, not Jüte. The spoken dialect especially is in popular speech always called Danish, never Jutish. For example, the chronicler Hamsfort, I, 270, from some lost annals cites these words of the Danish King Sven Estridsen concerning the church language of South Jutland: 'linguae patriae et Danicae', 'their native Danish

[1] Besides, there is a sporadical instance among the Angles: Lindis-faran.

tongue'. A series of statements in the vernacular of South Jutland appears in Sach's *Das Herzogtum Schleswig*, viz. III, 190, 257, 369, 421, 441 (cp. Schütte, *Smaaskr. udg. af Selsk. f. germ. Fil.* No. 13, IV, § 6).

3. The central Danish area, Witheslef, lies between two extensive stretches where great moor finds have been made, belonging approximately to the period between A.D. 250 and 450 (cp. Stjerna, *Essays on Beowulf*, 147). On the east the places where there have been great moor finds are: Finnestorp (West Götland), Sjöröd (Scania), Skedemosse (Öland), Römeremose and Balsmyr (Bornholm). On the west the places are: Thorslev (Vendsyssel), Hedeliskjær (Åbo Syssel), Porskjær, the lake of Dallerup, and the pond of Vingsted (Lofræth Syssel), Vimose, Illemose, Kragehul, Krogsbølle (Funen), Hjortesprings Mose (Als), Nydam (Ellum Syssel, 2 finds), Thorsbjerg (Angel, Istathe Syssel). It is generally assumed that these finds indicate votive sacrifices dedicated to the gods after great battles during the expansion of some conquering nation. If this explanation is correct, the distribution of the finds allows us to attribute the sacrifices concerned to one nation only, that is, the Danes. The area included is obviously almost the same as that where the typical Danish place names ending in *-lev* are found (cp. point 5). But the latter, as a rule, represent a more advanced stage of the expansion, apart from isolated exceptions such as Bornholm, where there are moor finds, but no place names ending in *-lev*. Notice especially the moor find in Öland, and Skärlöv (*ibid.*); moor find at Thorslev, Vendsyssel; moor find at Thorsbjerg in Angel, between Tollesleve, Masleve, and Kosleve, the extreme south-western limits of the district where the names ending in *-lev* occur in Jutland; on the other hand, there are no moor finds and no names ending in *-lev* in Bleking.

4. The term O.N. *herað*, corresponding to the Bavarian *heri-rait* 'military troop', in Denmark comes to be used for a district smaller than a county but larger than a parish, and penetrates the system of territorial division from Halland to the Eider, whereas its adoption in the other Scandinavian countries is later and less universal (cp. Tunberg, *Studier rörande Skandinaviens äldsta polit. indelning* and la Cour, *Sønderjyllands Historie*, I, 212). In § 251, 6, we have already mentioned the marked national contrast between the Danish *herað* north of the Eider, and the Saxon-German *gau* south of the same river.

5. The place names ending in *-lev*, *-löv* are the most characteristic phenomenon which accompanies the Danish expansion during the Migra-

tion Age. Doubtless these names originate in Zealand, as H. V. Clausen points out in *Aarbøger*, 1916, 137 seq. (cp. my preliminary observation of the same fact, *Danske Studier*, 1905, 55). We may also consider the political name Witheslef for Zealand and its surroundings. Hence this type of name spreads east and west, to the Swedish and Norwegian borderlands, to Jutland and North Germany. Only a few of the larger Danish districts do not share it. It is absolutely foreign to Bleking and Bornholm, and to the Utland in South Jutland; in the West Jutlandic county of Hardsyssel, there is only one isolated example, situated at the south-eastern edge. The three districts first named above occupy positions on the boundary line, and their incorporation with Denmark seems to have been of a later date. Bleking was Swedish in the ninth century, according to the Norwegian Wulfstan, cited by Alfred, *Orosius*, p. 20; as a matter of fact, its place names are of a pronounced non-Danish type, which appears for example in the characteristic Götlandic and Smålandic element *-måla*, and in the Swedish *-ryd* for Danish and Scanian *-rød*, *-röd*, 'clearing'. Bornholm in the ninth century had a king of its own, according to Wulfstan (*l.c.* p. 20); its place names show some marked differences from the Danish type, such as the Swed.-Norw. element *-myre* for Dan. *-mose* 'moor'. The Utland is occupied by a non-Danish nationality, the Frisians.

Lit. Steenstrup, *Vore Landsbyer og Bebyggelsens Historie* (*Hist. Tidsskr.* 6. R. v, 313 seq.); Schütte, *Danske Studier*, 1905, 54 seq., 1927, 65; *idem*, *Frem*, 1926, 310 (with map of the place names ending in *-lev*); H. V. Clausen, *Studier over Danmarks Oldtidsbebyggelse* (*Aarbøger*, 1916, with maps).

6. Towards the south, Danish is distinguished from Frisian and German by evident linguistic barriers. Towards the Swedish side there are no such distinctions, and it is scarcely possible to point out a single test which would even approximately afford a linguistic distinction between the nationalities.

The change of middle and final *p*, *t*, *k* into *b*, *d*, *g* is regarded as a typical mark of Danish after the later Middle Ages, but the same phenomenon occurs in many dialects of West Gautland, Småland, Dalsland, South Bohuslän, and South-west Norway (cp. the map, Fig. 16), and, on the other hand, it does not occur in Middle and Eastern Bleking, and only in certain cases affects the extreme southern dialect of Jutlandic. The Danish change of final *a* and *u* into *e* is a test which gives a limitation fairly coinciding with the present political frontier, but then the south-western extremity of Scania would remain Danish, and in return Bornholm, which has preserved the *a*, would belong to the Swedish side. Danish *det store hus* 'the great house', as contrasted with the Swedish-Norwegian redundant form *det stora huset* (literally 'the great house-the'), marks a boundary which approaches more nearly to the political one; but still Bornholm remains on the Swedish side, and the Swedish form even advances west of the Öresund, being shared by the dialect of Dragör on the island of Amager. One element which affords a fairly good means of determining territorial distinctions is the word for 'clearing'. In the modern Denmark it appears everywhere as *-rød*, and the same form, written *-röd*, is still used in almost the whole of Scania. Halland has the variation *-red*, which is only a secondary development. These types, *-röd* and *-red*, contrast with the Swedish variation *-ryd* in Småland and Eastern Götland, and with *-rud* in the ancient Norwegian province of Bohuslän. So far, the distribution corresponds to the ancient political frontiers of Denmark, Sweden, and Norway. But the old Danish province of Bleking has the Swedish type *-ryd* (cp. § 260, B 5), and, on the other hand, the type *-red* of Halland prevails also in the larger part of Western Götland. For particulars concerning the Danish dialects, we refer the reader to Marius Kristensen, *Nydansk*, in *Smaaskrifter udg. af Selsk. f. germ. Fil.* No. 12, Bennike and Marius Kristensen, *Kort over de danske folkemål*, and Brøndum Nielsen, *Dialekter og Dialektforskning*, maps Nos. 4–26. Whereas the maps of Bennike and Kristensen do not contain the Swedish provinces Scania, Halland, and Bleking, Brøndum Nielsen includes them; cp. Ad. Noreen, *Vårt språk*, p. 89, wherein the dialects of Scania and Halland are regarded as Danish, and it is stated that the Swedish nationality of these districts—from a linguistic point of view—depends exclusively on the use of the Swedish literary language.[1]

In England the element *-thorp* ('village') is the most reliable of the Danish test-words (cp. A. H. Smith, *Saga Book of the Viking Society, Proceedings*, 1925–27, p. 198). On *-thorp* in Denmark see Ussing, *Danske Studier*, 1917, 83 seq.

7. Danish farms are never built on the double-court plan, giving one yard for men and one for cattle, which prevails in Sweden, Norway, and

[1] Noreen also regards the dialect of Bleking as Danish, but according to Wigforss it has a non-Danish type, a fact which agrees with the occurrence of the Swedish element *-ryd*.

Finland (cp. Vreim, *Aarsberetn. f. Foreningen til norske Fortidsmindesmærkers Bevaring*, 1929, 2). It must be noticed, however, that this plan is often followed in Danish manor-houses. Danish rural houses never have two storeys.

The plans of Danish farm houses are described by Zangenberg, *Danske Bøndergaarde* (*Danmarks Folkeminder*, No. 34). We owe various particulars to private letters from the author.

A 'compound house' dating from the Roman Iron Age has lately been dug out in Ginnerup in the county of Ty. It was rectangular, with the gable ends east and west; the entrance was in the middle of the north side, and the fire-place in the centre.[1] The walls were made of clay. Other Iron Age houses with entrance from the south have been found in Ginnerup, in Aars (Himmerland), and in Solbjerg on the island of Morsø. The position east-west and the entrance in the middle of the long side are still normal features of Danish rural dwelling-houses. The entrance is on the north side or on the south side according to the position of the house in relation to the village street.

A similar type is described in a mediaeval Icelandic tale (Zangenberg, p. 17): 'In Denmark it is usual for the dwellings, both for people and for cattle, to be under one roof....Thus the cows stood in the room close to the *skáli* (dwelling room), separated from it by a wall, and at the opposite end of the *skáli* was the fire-house'.

This primitive type, originally with no chimney, occurs in all parts of Denmark. Maps drawn at the time of the dividing-up of the country, between 1780 and 1815–20, show it prevailing in entire villages, e.g. in Ty and on the islands of Als, Lyø, Ærø, and Stryn. In Als very large farms are often built in this way. In the middle heath regions of South Jutland it seems to be the only type existing (cp. P. Lauridsen in the (Dan.) *Hist. Tidsskrift*, 6. R. VI B, p. 68).

In the 'double' or 'parallel farmstead' the dwelling-house and the building containing cattle stalls and granaries are separate, and run parallel to each other on opposite sides of the yard. The dwelling-house is in Jutlandic called *sals*, i.e. *sal-hus*, or *rade-lang*, now *roling*, i.e. 'long row' (of 'bays', cp. p. 245). The Jutish Law (1241) mentions *salhus* and barn as the main buildings of the farm.

This type predominates in large districts along the west coast of

1 'Compound houses' with the entrance in the middle of the long side also exist on the Faroe Islands and in South-western Bavaria about Kempten.

Jutland from Vendsyssel and Ty to the environs of Ribe, and also in North Himmerland. Nowadays it does not occur in Zealand and Møn, but there are traces of it on the islands in the eighteenth century, e.g. in Zealand and Bornholm.

The 'compound farmstead' and the 'double farmstead' obviously are the most primitive types in the whole of the country. The other types originate from the addition of more buildings.

The 'gamma house' (Γ) may be regarded as a 'compound house' with the occasional addition of a side range. On the island of Ærø, several large 'compound houses' have been altered in this manner. The type occurs in all parts of the country, but cannot be said to predominate in entire villages. It is especially frequent among the larger farms in Ty and on the island of Als. Similar houses, dating from the Iron Age, are found on the Gautic island of Öland (cp. Stenberger, *Öländska bebyggelsesformer från järnålderen* (*Rig*, 1930)). The Low Rhenish 'T-house' or 'dwarshus' may also be compared, but can scarcely have served as a model.

An approximation towards the 'row farmstead' may be observed in Vendsyssel, where the ranges of the 'double farmstead' are in certain places arranged with the single buildings in continuation of each other, separated by small intervals. In Zealand there also exist villages where half a dozen farmsteads are built with continuous walls.

The irregular farmstead may also be traced in the ancient registration maps, though it does not occur in modern times.[1]

The farmstead with three ranges appears occasionally, in North Jutland mostly with the buildings separate, on the islands often with the walls and roofs joined together. It is very frequent on ancient Zealandic registration maps.

The quadrangular farmstead occurs in almost the whole of ancient Denmark. Towards the east it is found in the southern part of Bohuslän (originally Norwegian), Halland, Scania, Lister, and Bornholm. Along the west coast of Jutland it reaches the south frontier of the Danish language, on the east coast it is frequent as far south as Flensborg and even occurs in the Germanised district of Angel. Only in certain regions it has not developed, e.g. in the interior heath regions of South Jutland (cp. above on p. 308). In the Germanised district of Svans (Schwansen), the Danish types are replaced by the Saxon 'compound house'. As was

[1] We believe to have noticed it in the manor of Store Frederikslund in Zealand.

the case with the previous type, the buildings in North Jutland are generally separate, on the islands often joined together. In Funen, when the buildings are so joined, the corners are often rounded. In Western Jutland there is generally a fixed scale of height: the barn is highest, the 'sals' of middle height, the intervening stables lower. The midden is generally placed inside the court, not outside as in Northern Scandinavia.

The quadrangle in Zealand as in Sweden seems to be of mediaeval origin (cp. Vreim, *l.c.* p. 5). According to Zangenberg (p. 55) the type with the buildings joined seems to be rather late, though occurring before 1688.

Mich. Haberlandt in *Die Völker Europas*, p. 498, maintains that the Danish quadrangular farmsteads are of Frankish origin: 'Die regelmässigen, viereckigen Hofbildungen Dänemarks, in Flachlandschaften Norwegens, aber auch im Umkreis der alten Landesmittelpunkte (Uppland), werden so wie die entsprechenden Dorfbildungen auf die Einflüsse des "fränkischen" Hofsystems seit dem Mittelalter zurückgeführt'. So also Sigurd Erixon, *Ymer*, 1922, 261. Zangenberg rejects this theory, because the domain of the Danish quadrangle is widely separated from that of the Frankish type.

The agreement between dialect and type of building is worth noting. Halland and Scania have Danish dialect and Danish quadrangles; Bleking has non-Danish dialect and to a great extent Gautic or Middle Swedish types of buildings. The Danish type only prevails in the western district of Bleking, though it seems to have extended further in earlier times (cp. Erixon in *Ymer*, 1922, 284, and a résumé of his lecture at the Congress of Scandinavian Folk-lorists in Copenhagen, *Danske Studier*, 1924, p. 157).

The various types of construction, 'syles', 'foot-timber', 'højrem', etc., are shown by Zangenberg on a map in *Danske Bøndergaarde*, 87. The use of the 'half-timbered' type (Dan. 'bindingsværk', Swed. 'korsvirke') does not extend as far east and north as the quadrangle. The east frontier runs through Scania, from the Bay of Skelder Vik towards Kristianstad. It is worth noting that several of the dialect maps drawn by Brøndum Nielsen (*l.c.*) show a similar line of demarcation, but as a rule running a little south of the Skelder Vik (cp. the maps Nos. 8 (four phenomena), 10, 12, 17, 19). Here again the close connexion between dialect and type of building is obvious.

A racial theory may finally be suggested to explain the genesis of the frontier between the Danish and Swedish nations. If we look at the political frontier before 1659, we notice on the Swedish side a right-angled projection at the point where Halland and Scania meet. This is caused by the district of Finveden which projects like a wedge between the two ancient Danish counties. The barrier was once occupied by a separate tribe called Finn(h)aithae by Jordanes, III, 22. If we are bold enough to assume that they were descendants of 'Finns', i.e. of non-Scandinavian aborigines, it becomes easy to conceive how it came to pass that a national frontier developed at this very place. The original contrast was between Scandinavians and non-Scandinavians; after the latter had been absorbed, the idea of a racial contrast still survived, and thus contributed to creating the distinction between Danes and Swedes.

Lit. Gravlund, *Dansk Folkekarakter*; Schütte, *Dansk Folkekarakter*; Wigforss, *Svenska landsmål*, 1917, 607 seq. (French résumé, p. 729).

§ 261. History.

The rich civilisation on the Danish islands during the Stone Age depended on free access to the chief raw material, flint, which was exported to Sweden and Norway on a large scale (cp. K. Weibull, *Sveriges och Danmarks äldsta historia*, 42).

During the Bronze Age the Danish islands were still a leading factor in Scandinavian civilisation. And influence from the far south-east is shown by the Greek style of the image of the sun, found at Trundholm in Zealand (cp. Sophus Müller, *Urgeschichte Europas*, 116).

Whether the Teutones of the great migration 113–102 B.C. included people from the Zealandic region of Thiuth, we do not know, but the possibility must at least be mentioned.

The worship of Nerthus and other vegetation deities of West Asiatic origin, found among the Angles and Jutes in the first century A.D., had undoubtedly an important centre on the fertile plains of Zealand (cp. Schütte, *Dänisches Heidentum*, 96, 97, etc.).

In A.D. 5 Zealand and the neighbouring islands were discovered by the Roman naval expedition which also noted Scandia, i.e. Scania. But the existence of inhabitants does not seem to have been recorded, except perhaps the Teutones on the island of 'Codanouia' (Zealand), Mela, III, 6, § 54.

Classical authors never mention the Danes—or at least never mention their name in an uncorrupted form. The question arises how we are to explain this silence. Does it mean that there were no Danes in the regions which were their headquarters in the early Middle Ages, that is, in Zealand and its surroundings?

This conclusion 'e silentio' is actually drawn and, on the basis of the *Chronicle of Lejre* and Hrodulf's report (Jordanes), various authors assume an immigration from Sweden about A.D. 500 (cp. above p. 359).

Such arguments, however, are not by any means conclusive.

The *argumentum e silentio* ignores the conditions under which Roman geographical knowledge was gained and by which it was limited. The Romans had frequent dealings with the continental tribes on both sides of the Elbe, and after Nero's time they had factories also on the Prussian amber coast. Hence they got to know the Jutlanders on the one hand and the Scandinavian tribes facing Prussia on the other. But the intervening district was but little known. Tacitus, for example, ignores an important tribe like the Burgundians in Pomerania, and Zealand is to him a *terra incognita*.[1]

About A.D. 150 Ptolemy, II, 11, § 16, mentions the Daukiones whom he places in the southern part of the larger Scandia, that is to say, in Scania. The reading is corrupt; we have proposed to correct it to *Daneiones, whereas Wadstein reads *Dapriones, i.e. inhabitants of the Scanian district of Dapræ. It must be one of the two, as tribal names beginning with Da- are extremely rare in Scandinavia. We do not think it likely that the Romans can have heard the toponymic of a comparatively small district like Dapræ. A tribe which is ranked with the Gauts would rather correspond to the Danes, whose name probably goes back to primitive times. The position given by Ptolemy, however, is not reliable. His scheme was arbitrary, and, wishing to create an impression of beautiful symmetry, he distributed the names which occurred as seemed best to him (cp. our monograph *Ptolemy's Maps*, 14). So, if a source mentioned Danes as living on a smaller Scandian island, i.e.

1 We have an analogy from South-eastern Europe. During the Middle Ages the neighbours of Roumania knew the Daco-Roman people only as Wallachen, Vlaci, etc., i.e. the same name as Welsh. In modern times, however, a nation of Roumanians appears in this country. If we accept the argument concerning the sudden immigration of the Danes about A.D. 500, we must also conclude that the Roumanians entered Roumania as late as the nineteenth century. But the truth is that they have always called themselves Roumanians, though Western and Northern Europe were unaware of this fact.

Zealand, the tribe would automatically be transplanted to the greater Scandia. For his system required that all small islands should be left blank, and that all names should be referred to the larger countries where there was room enough for them to be in readable writing.

The supposed reference to the *Danes in the classical literature of the second century may be explained by the growing importation of coins and wares from the Roman factories on the Prussian amber coast. Among the most remarkable traces of Roman influence we mention the splendid silver vessels found in Låland (cp. *Hoby-Fundet* in *Nationalmusæets Bog om sjældne Fund*, 27).[1]

The *argumentum e silentio* certainly proves that the Danes played no actual part in the history and legends of classical times, but it does *not* prove that their sudden appearance about A.D. 500 is due to an immigration from distant regions. The Angles, for example, are equally unknown to the political history and the legends of the first centuries of our era. They suddenly appear about the fourth century, with kings of three generations (Wihtlæg, Wermund, Offa) who can be traced in both English and Danish sources. And this reference does not indicate an immigration to their continental home, for we know from geographical sources (Tacitus, Ptolemy) that they were already settled there in the first century A.D. All we learn is that the Anglian state must have developed gradually and silently during the intervening centuries, and at last have made its importance felt, in the fourth century, through a sudden explosion of power. This may have been the case with the Danes.

At any rate, if the Danes were known by the Romans, they were very unimportant in their eyes. And in the early records of the Gothonic nations the Danes are only conspicuous by their absence. The Erulian Vikings of A.D. 256 and 289 are accompanied by Goths and Chau(g)iones respectively, not by Danes. The ancient Baltic myth of the Hjaðningar, according to *Widsith*, ll. 21–22, deals with Rugians, Glommas, and Hælsingas, not with Danes. The Anglian King Viglek in the fourth (?) century fights with the Jutlander Amleth, not with the Danes. Viglek's son Vermund has relations with the 'Swede' Athisl and with Frovin, the ancestor of the West Saxon kings, not with the Danes. The Jutish conquerors of Kent and Hampshire (A.D. 445 or 449) are associated with the Saxons, not with the Danes. And before the fifth century there

[1] **Hoby is an original Hovby, 'Temple-place'; the treasure was found at Skibelund, 'Ship-grove', probably a sanctuary (Svend Aakjær).**

does not appear a single Gothonic personal name compounded with the element Dan (cp. Schönfeld's *Wörterbuch der altgerm. Personen- und Völkernamen*).

This survey of negative evidence is the necessary prelude to the discussion of the historical genesis of the Danes, which was first placed in its right light by Olrik in *The Heroic Legends of Denmark*, I, 2. After being ignored for some 850 years of Gothonic history the Danes suddenly appear about A.D. 500, and with remarkable brilliance. The fame of their deeds spreads to the most distant quarters of Europe, as may be judged from various authors: the Greek Procopius in a reference of 505, the Gallo-Roman Gregory of Tours in a reference of 526,[1] the Norwegian Hrodulf in Italy before 526, a Gothic geographer cited by the Anonymus Ravennas in Italy, three English poets, the authors of *Widsith*, *Beowulf*, and the *Finnsburg Lay*, relating between them actions which extend from the fifth century to about 550. The introductory lines of *Beowulf*: 'Lo! we have heard the fame of the kings of the Spear-Danes!' are the most impressive testimony. Such evidence shows that a great political change must have taken place—the foundation of the state of Denmark. It is not possible to give the exact date, but we may at least construct an approximate sequence of the chief events with their dates, though of course admitting the possibility of error.

In the fifth century the Danes as guardians of the famous central temple at Hleiðr seem to have become the leading nation in the amphictyony of Ingwine (cp. the identification of Ingwine and Dene in *Beowulf*, and the remarks of Chadwick cited in § 260, B 1).

About 420 the Danish King Alewih the Courageous is contemporary with King Offa of Angel (*Widsith*, l. 35). The Danish supremacy does not yet extend to Offa's kingdom.[2]

After 430 Halfdan founds the Danish dynasty of Skjǫldungar in Zealand. His most famous sons are Hróarr and Helgi (Hróðgár and Halga, *Beowulf*). Hróarr succeeds him.

About 505 the homeless Erules on their way from the Danube to 'Thule' (i.e. Scandinavia) pass the Varines in Mecklenburg. And 'after

[1] Severinsen in *Danske Studier*, 1919, 96, points out that the expedition of Hygelác cannot be dated earlier than 526.

[2] The words of the poem do not necessarily allude to a conflict between the two kings, as Müllenhoff and Möller assume (cp. Chambers, *Widsith*, 203).

them they passed the tribes of the Danes...and after arriving at the sea, they went on board ships' (Procopius, *Bell. Goth.* II, 15). These words show: (1) that the Danes consist of various tribes, (2) that they already possess a footing on the continent due north of the Varines, probably on the east coast of South Jutland.[1] At approximately the same time, Wulfgar, leader of the Wendle, is mentioned as a vassal of Hróðgár (*Beowulf*, l. 348). The Wendle probably are the Wendilenses in the northernmost county of Jutland, Vendsyssel, where numerous names ending in *-lev* betray early Danish settlements (cp. Thorslev, the place where a great votive sacrifice was offered).

The singular popularity of the legendary King Dan in the counties immediately south of the Limfjord seems to betray an early Danish occupation even of these regions (cp. Olrik, *Danmarks Heltedigtning*, II, 36). Dan is reputed to lie buried with his horse in various places in Himber Syssel or thereabouts, and he is elected king on a peculiar rock called Danærygh south of Viborg, according to the *Chronicle of Lejre*, *Script. rer. Dan.* I, 224; probably these details are a reminiscence of Danish hero worship. There must have been temporary struggles south of Himber Syssel, where the advancing Danes built the earthwork Dandiget as a fortification against the inhabitants of Ommer Syssel, the Hallinger (Chaloi, Ptol. ?). Farther south the remains of colossal sacrifices seem to mark the Danish expansion on the east coast of Jutland and on the isle of Funen.

The Bards who probably occupied the coast of Mecklenburg (Scoringa) are serious rivals of the Danes.[2] Their King Fróda is slain by the Danes (*Beowulf*, l. 2048). Hróðgár succeeds in establishing peace, but afterwards the feud is renewed by Fróda's son Ingeld (l. 2059). He seriously menaces the Danish headquarters at Heorot on the isle of Zealand, but his power is finally destroyed owing to the combined efforts of Hróðgár and Halga's son Hróðwulf (*Widsith*, l. 45 seq.).

Before 526 the Danes expel the returning Erules from their homes on the Scandinavian Peninsula, according to the report of the Nor-

[1] The period is between 491 and 512; we choose 505 in agreement with Schmidt, I, 337 note 3.

[2] We cannot accept Wessén's theory that the epic Danes are disguised Erules, and the epic Hadu-bards disguised Danes. The Hadu-bards are simply the Barden from Bardengau (cp. § 256 and our article *Ethnische Prunknamen*, *Zeitschrift*, LXVII, 129).

wegian King Hrodulf, cited by Jordanes, III, 23. We suppose that this incident leads to their conquest of Scania. The *Chronicle of Lejre* says that the Jutlanders assist King Dan in conquering Scania (*Script. rer. Dan.* I, 224). Hrodulf states, by the way, that the Danes claim to be taller than any other Scandinavians—a sign of their political ambition.

About 526 the 'Geatic' Viking Hugleik invades the Rhine Delta and is slain by the Franks. Gregor. Tur. III, 3, calls him a 'Dane'. As the first notorious Danish Viking raid is recorded about 565, it is difficult to understand why Gregory should have designated the 'Geats' of 526 as 'Danes', if there had not been Danish raids before that time.

About 550 ? Hrolf or Hróðwulf, who after Hróðgár's death has succeeded in depriving his son Hrørik (Hréðríc, *Beowulf*, l. 1189) of the throne, interferes in the dynastic feuds of the Sviones (cp. Olrik, *The Heroic Legends of Denmark*, I, 5). Being pursued by King Aðils (Éadgils, *Beowulf*) near Uppsala, Hrolf has a narrow escape and only owes his safety to the sowing of golden treasures on the plain of Fyrisvellir (*Yngl. Saga*, 29). The stereotyped poetical metaphor 'seeds of Fyrisvellir', meaning 'gold', must allude to some actual incident, which indicates that Hrolf's military operations led him to the capital of Sweden. Series of names ending in *-lev*, extending from the Cattegat to the regions east of the lakes Wener and Wetter, actually denote a contemporary Danish sphere of settlement of not much smaller compass (see H. V. Clausen's map XI, *Aarbøger*, 1916). However, all the splendour of the Skjǫldung power vanishes when Hrolf is treacherously slain at Hleiðr by his cousin *Hjarvarð (Hiarthvar, Saxo, II, 89; Heoroweard, *Beowulf*, l. 2160), who is represented by Saxo as his vassal in Scania. Hrolf's death is immediately avenged on his slayer, and so there seems to have survived no representative of the Skjǫldungar except Hrørik, who maintains himself provisionally as king of a part of Jutland (Saxo, VII, 350).

The throne of Zealand, after the overthrow of the Skjǫldungar, seems to have been occupied by kings of the family called Siklingar.[1] Saxo, VII, 330, calls them immigrants from Götland, and he is no doubt right, for the element *sig-*, occurring in the royal names Sigvald and Sigar, had previously been avoided by the Danes, as by the Jutes and Angles.

1 Siklingar is derived from *sig-*, as the Norwegian form Veklingar from Végeirr (cp. Bugge, *Home of the Eddic Poems*, 132 note).

It is a favourite type of name with the Sviones, being connected with their famous sanctuary of Odin, Sigtúnir; Sigi seems to have been Odin's Svionic surname. The Siklingar then would have been propagators of a cult of Odin on Svionic lines; their close connexion with him appears from the fact that he acts as Sigar's counsellor under the name of Bolvis, 'the bad wise', one of Odin's well-known disguises (*ibid.* VII, 343). The residence, 'Sigari oppidum' (*ibid.* VII, 346), is the present Sigersted, near Ringsted. King Sigar's fame reaches the Anglo-Saxons (cp. *Widsith*, l. 28: 'Sigehere lengest Sæ-Denum weold'). But even *his* dynasty soon fails, being destroyed in a feud with the family of the chieftain Hagbard (Saxo, VII, 347 seq.).

After an interregnum which dissolves Denmark into small principalities (*ibid.* VII, 350), the unity of the state is re-established by the heroic King Harold Hildetand, i.e. 'War-tooth', among whose victims we find a local Jutlandic King Hrørik, presumably the last surviving Skjǫldung (*ibid.* VII, 362). Harold also seems to have conquered parts of Southern Sweden, but he is finally slain by the Swede Hring in the famous battle on the plain of Brávellir, probably near the Firth of Bråviken in East Götland (cp. Olrik in *Salmonsens Konv. Lex.* s.v. *Braavallaslaget*).[1]

The last act of the Jutes as a separate tribe is recorded about 547. The Frankish King Theodebert in his letter to Justinian boasts of having become their lord owing to their voluntary submission (*Mon. Germ. Epist. Merow.* I, 133). Later, they appear simply as Danes.

About 565 Danish and Saxon invaders are repulsed from Friesland by the Franks (Venant. Fortunatus, *Carm.* VII, ll. 49–60). This is the first definitely Danish Viking raid, but it is not repeated for some time. Anarchy seems to have paralysed the Danes.

In 787 the raids begin anew, provoked by Charlemagne's conquest of the Saxons and the advance of Frankish and Wendic settlers into Holstein. King Gudfred fortifies the Danish frontier near Slesvig; his fortifications are enlarged by later kings and give rise to the famous frontier-wall Danevirke, 'the Danes' wall'.

In 811 the river Eider is acknowledged as the frontier between Denmark and Franconia (cp. Einhard's *Ann. Mon. Germ. SS.* I, 198).

[1] According to Nerman, *Det svenska rikets uppkomst*, 255, the battle would have taken place about A.D. 750. But if Harold was a contemporary of Hroar's son Hrørik, this date would be too late.

The Danish attacks on the coasts of England begin in earnest about 820.

About 900 Denmark is governed by a dynasty which later became famous under the name of Knytlingar. Adam of Bremen says of one of its earliest representatives: 'Hardegon veniens a Nortmannia'. From this statement Norwegian scholars have assumed that the Knytlingar were originally a Norwegian family. As a matter of fact, Adam's 'Nortmannia' normally means Norway; but it may quite as well mean Normandy. Consequently the sentence quoted may very well indicate that Hardegon returned from a Viking expedition to Normandy. One fact which is decisively in favour of this interpretation is, as Lis Jacobsen points out (*Svenskevældets Fald*, 51), that the favourite names of the Knytlingar (viz. Gorm, Svein, and Canute) are in the tenth century a distinct prerogative of Denmark. It is possible that they may occur in Sweden too, but certainly not in Norway, where they only appear some centuries later, owing to the historical fame of the Knytlingar. The theory of the Norwegian origin of this family must, therefore, be rejected.

During the rule of the Knytlingar, a Swedish invader Olaf founded a kingdom in South Jutland in order to control the large mercantile town Hedeby or Slesvig, which was of great importance as a connecting link between western and eastern traders. One of the Swedish kings of Slesvig is Gnupa who is mentioned in two local runic inscriptions. In 934 the German King Henry the Fowler compels him to receive baptism (cp. Widukind, *Mon. Germ. SS.* III, 435, and Adam. Brem. I, 50, where he is mentioned as Chnuba, resp. as Chnob). Finally his son Sigerich, i.e. Sigtrygg in the runic inscriptions, is conquered by Hardegon, Svein's son (Adam. Brem. I, 52). According to the *Saga Ólafs Tryggvasonar*, 63, it is Gnupa who is conquered by Gorm. This conception of the final struggle cannot be correct; but it is probable that both Hardegon and Gorm, and perhaps also Harold Bluetooth, had to fight the Swedish invaders till these were at last completely subjugated about 940 (cp. Wimmer, *De historiske Runemindesmærker*, 48 seq.; Lis Jacobsen, *Svenskevældets Fald*, 17 seq.; Vilh. la Cour, *Sønderjyllands Historie*, I, 263 seq.).

Danish Vikings settle in Prussia, Pomerania, Friesland, Normandy, Northern and Eastern England, and parts of Eastern Ireland. Hrolf or Rollo, the conqueror of Normandy, has been a subject of dispute; Snorri,

Heimskringla, I, 131, calls him a Norwegian, whereas the French contemporaries of Rollo only knew him as a Dane. Though perhaps the French sources may have been inaccurate as regards the leader's birth, there is no doubt that the majority of settlers in Normandy were Danes, as appears from place names and other linguistic phenomena (cp. Anders Pedersen in *Danske Studier*, 1911, 75, and the Faroese scholar Jacob Jacobsen, *ibid.* 58). This is also admitted by A. Bugge in *Norges Hist.* I, 2, 273.

Christianity is preached to the Danes by the great Frankish missionary Ansgar in 826, and afterwards spreads gradually without meeting with fanatic resistance; this fortunate circumstance has saved Denmark from becoming the victim of such disastrous crusades as those which destroyed the freedom of the heathen Wends. Christianity is especially promoted by the Knytling King Harold Bluetooth (d. 985), as he himself states in the runic inscription on the huge stone of Jelling.

An attempt of the German King Henry the Fowler to found a margravate of Slesvig in 934 (Adam. Brem. I, 59) had no consequences. A similar attempt of the Emperor Otto II is frustrated by the Danes in 982, when the German castle is stormed and burnt down (Thietmar, *Mon. Germ. SS.* III, 24; cp. Steenstrup, *Danmarks Sydgrænse* (*Indbydelsesskrift til Kjøbenhavns Univ. Aarsfest*, 1900, 66) and Brandt, *Geschichte Schleswig-Holsteins*, 17).

The culmination of Danish power in the Viking Age is the union of Denmark, England, and Norway, under Canute the Great, but Norway a few years afterwards becomes independent and soon after Canute's death in 1035 all his conquests are lost. Denmark for some decades is subjected to Norwegian rule, and for more than a century suffers from the inroads of the heathen Wends, who continue the Viking raids after the pacification of the Danes. The Norwegian, Magnus the Good, repulses a great Wendic invasion from South Jutland in 1045, but the Wendic peril continues till the Danish conquest of Rügen in 1169. Then follows the crusade to Esthonia in 1219; the two conquests inaugurate a short period of Trans-Baltic expansion. After a century of German political and mercantile supremacy, a new period of Danish expansion follows, culminating in 1397, when Queen Margaret establishes the Union of Kalmar, which united the three crowns of Scandinavia. The union with Sweden soon breaks down; Denmark in the wars of 1645 and 1658 loses her provinces east of Øresund to Sweden, with the exception of Bornholm;

in 1814 she is separated from Norway, and in 1864 loses the southern part of Jutland to Germany. The only expansion after 1600 is the gaining of Greenland, which was rediscovered in 1605. The political change has made the Swedish literary language predominant in the old Danish continental provinces east of the Øresund, though the rural dialect and the types of houses have not altered and still keep their Danish nature. In Norway, where the Danish literary language predominated after the Union of Kalmar, the political separation in 1814 made for the time being no difference, but since a national movement has created a literary 'Landsmål' on the basis of the West Norwegian rural dialects, the Dano-Norwegian 'Riksmål' is continually developing more and more on non-Danish lines. In South Jutland, most of the southern regions between the Sli and the Firth of Flensborg have been Germanised, but the northern part has maintained the Danish idiom and even under German rule from 1864 to 1920 kept its Danish church language; the district was restored to Denmark in 1920.

The number of Danes is now about $4\frac{3}{8}$ millions. The figures from abroad given below represent the first generation of emigrants.

Denmark (1926)	3,454,500
Norway	7,200
Sweden	8,700
Finland	300
Great Britain and Ireland	7,400
Holland and Belgium	600
Switzerland	500
Germany and Austria	6,100
France, Italy, Spain, Portugal	2,500
Czechoslovakia, Poland, Baltic States	800
Balkan	100
Russia and Serbia	500
China	800
Japan	100
Siam	200
Holl. India, Malaya, etc.	500
North Africa	200
West Africa	100
South Africa	500
U.S.A.	190,000
Canada	7,200
Mexico, Central America, West India	300
Argentina	7,000
Brazil	600
Other South American States	500
Australia	6,000
New Zealand	2,000

Sum total of emigrants: 250,700.

Lit. Dahlmann, *Geschichte von Dänemark*; Allen, *Geschichte der dän. Sprache im Hzgt. Schleswig*; Steenstrup, *Normannerne*; *idem*, *Danmarks Riges Historie*, I; Sophus Müller, *Vor Oldtid*; K. Weibull, *Sveriges och Danmarks äldsta historia*; *idem*, *Sverige och dess nordiska grannmakter* (*Hist. Tidsskr. f. Skåneland*, 1921, 353); Linwald, Friis and Mackeprang, *Det danske Folks Historie*; V. la Cour, *Sjællands ældste Bygder*; *idem*, *Sønderjyllands Historie*, I; Sofus Larsen, *Jomsborg* (*Aarbøger*, 1927, 1928, 1931); Arup, *Danmarks Historie*.

§ 262. Legendary Traditions.

The fame of the Danes is great in epic, though no evidence of it survives in the old vernacular tongue. We can only enumerate some few representatives of the epic heroes.

Ing, the eponymous hero of the Inguaeones, appears as a Dane in the O.E. *Rune-song* (Grein and Wülcker, *Bibl. d. angelsächs. Poesie*, I, 335): 'Ing was first among the Eastern Danes'. Lady Inger in the ballad of the emigration of the Langobards (*Danm. g. Folkev.* I, No. 21) is presumably the female counterpart of Ing (cp. § 258, 4).

King Scyld or Skjǫldr, the genius of the Skjǫldungar, is celebrated by the Angles and Scandinavians, e.g. in *Beowulf*, in an English royal pedigree (see our monograph *Oldsagn om Godtjod*, 187), and in Saxo. His female counterpart, Skuld, who acts as the evil genius of the Skjǫldungar in the legend of Hrolf Kraki (Saxo, II, 89), in Iceland becomes one of the three weird sisters who govern the destinies of the world (cp. our monograph *Dänisches Heidentum*, 40).

King Dan's fame is limited to Scandinavia; he is especially popular in Himmerland (cp. Olrik, *Danmarks Heltedigtning*, II, 36).

The god Fróði Friðgóði becomes a famous champion of Denmark in Danish, Norwegian-Icelandic, and German legends. He is adopted into the Skjǫldung family and confused with the Bardic King Fróda (cp. p. 148).

Among the mortal heroes the Skjǫldungar are the favourites. England and Scandinavia resound with their fame. Some Jutlandic families only can rival them, in that they are earlier epic figures. The *Bjarkamál* dealing with the Skjǫldung King Hrolf Kraki was once the most renowned poem in Scandinavia and was even recited by an Icelandic skald before the battle of Stiklestad in Norway in 1030. *Beowulf* begins with the praise of Hrolf's family. Norwegian genealogies try to derive all Scandinavian or rather all Gothonic princes from the Skjǫldung ancestor, Halfdan the Old. In Sweden the Skjǫldung names are much more popular than some of the names of the contemporary native kings, as appears from runic inscriptions; e.g. the name of the famous Ongenþéow has not yet been found on runic stones, that of Aðils only once.

King Alewih the courageous (*Widsith*, l. 35) seems to be Alrekr enn frœkni ('the courageous') of Scandinavian poetry. King Sigar is similarly known both in England and Scandinavia (cp. *Widsith*, l. 28 and Saxo, VII, 334). The name of his family, Siklingar, becomes a poetic metaphor for 'princes'. The unhappy fate of Sigar's daughter Signe and her lover Hagbard is the theme of a Danish ballad and furnishes the Scandinavian poets with their favourite metaphor for the gallows: 'Hagbard's horse' (cp. Olrik in *Salmonsens Konv. Lex.* 1st ed. s.v. *Siklinge-Slægten*).

The fall of the famous King Harold War-tooth at Brávellir brings the early Heroic Age to a close. A Norwegian poet of the eleventh century depicts this event as a great assembly of Scandinavian heroes from all regions and ages.

The defeat of Danes and Saxons fighting against the army of the Frankish King Sigebert in 565 is described in a special chapter of the most famous German epic poem, the *Nibelungenlied*.

The admiration of Danevirke, 'the Danes' wall', that protects the south frontier of Denmark, gives rise to the legends of Queen Thyre Danmarkarbót, 'the help of Denmark', to whom the construction of that huge wall and also other beneficial works are attributed (cp. Ussing, *Sagnene om Thyre Danebod*).

A whole cycle of legends dealing with famous Danish Vikings is collected in the Icelandic *Jomsvíkinga Saga*.

Charlemagne's champion Ogier le danois, a creation of French epic poetry, is introduced into Danish ballads as Holger Danske, becoming a sort of national symbol.

Lit. Numerous legends dealing with the Danes are collected in the *Chronicle of Lejre* (*Script. rer. Dan.* I); Saxo's *Gesta Danorum*; *Skjǫldunga Saga* (lost; Latin extract by Arngrímur Jónsson); *Knytlinga Saga*; *Jomsvíkinga Saga*; *Fornmanna Sögur*; *Fornaldar Sögur*; *Danmarks gamle Folkeviser*; Evald Tang Kristensen, *Danske Sagn*. Criticism: Olrik, *Kilderne til Sakses oldhistorie*; *idem*, *Skjoldungasaga* (*Aarbøger*, 1894, 83); *idem*, *Danmarks Heltedigtning* (vol. I translated as *The Heroic Legends of Denmark*); Finnur Jónsson, *Old-norsk-oldisl. litteraturs historie*, II, ii, 665; Schütte, *Vor mytiske Kongerække* (*Studier fra Sprog- og Oldforskning*, No. 105); *idem*, *Dansk Kongetals tusendaarige Traad* (*Hist. Tidsskrift*, 1925).

D. §§ 263–267. *THE GAUTIC BRANCH*

§ 263. Name.

O.N. Gautar; Swed. Götar; M.Dan. Gødinger (*Rimkrønike*), Gydinger (Vedel's *Saxo*, 273); O.E. Géatas; L.G. Gōten; M.Lat. Gauthi-goth (Jordanes, sixth century); Gr. Γοῦται (Ptolemy, second century A.D.), Γαυτοί (Procopius, sixth century). Eponymous god: O.N. Gautr, Gautatýr (generally identified with Odin). Personal names: e.g. O.N. Gautrekr, Al-gautr; O.G. Sui-gaut. River: O.N. Gaut-elfr. Sanctuary: Swed. Göte-ve (cp. Lundahl, *Falbygdens by- och gårdnamn*, 170). The name Gutar, i.e. Gotlanders, may be a gradation ('Ablaut'). The stem *Gaut-* is commonly referred by all scholars to the verb Goth. *giutan, gaut, gutans* 'to shed'; yet the interpretations of this differ. Finnur Jónsson maintains that Gautar cannot be derived from the name Gaut-elfr which means simply 'the Gautic river'. If he is right, the tribal name must mean something like 'shedding seed', i.e. 'men'. Cp. Oscar Almgren, who interprets Gautar as 'penes magni', i.e. 'grown-up men', and Gutar as 'penes parvi', i.e. 'boys'. He compares the latter word with Modern Norwegian *gut* and Modern Swedish *gosse* (< **got-se*) 'boy', and with O.N. *goti* 'stallion'. The emigrants, mainly consisting of young men, would have called themselves Gutar, while the remaining older generation would have kept the name of Gautar. However, the arguments for the existence of such tribal names in Gothonic are rather weak (see Langenfelt, *On the Origin of Tribal Names* (*Anthropos*, XIV/XV, 295 seq.)). We have, in reality, hardly one clear Gothonic analogy, whereas there are dozens of Scandinavian names of tribes or local populations which are toponymics. This is also the opinion of R. Zachrisson, *On the Meaning of Early Teutonic Tribal Names* (*Studier tillägnade Axel Kock*, 490 seq.). So we should like to agree with v. Grienberger, Tamm, Noreen, Brate, Wadstein, and Zachrisson, that the Gautar are probably 'dwellers on the Gaut-elfr', if there were any evidence of that river being called Gaut. This, however, is not the case; the nearest that can be adduced is the lake Göten in Kalmar Län, Misterhult parish (see O. Rygh, *Norske Elvnavne*, 67). So the meaning of the tribal name remains obscure. In modern poetry the name Götar is used to mean Swedes.

Lit. Noreen, *Spridda studier*, II, 139; *idem*, *Fornvännen*, 1920, 44; *idem*, *Upsala Univ. Årsskrift*, 1907, *Progr.* 2, 5 note 2; Schück, *ibid.*; v. Grienberger, *Zeitschrift*, XLVI, 131; Stjerna, *Essays on Beowulf*, ch. IV; Schönfeld, s.v. (with lit.); Finnur Jónsson, *Danske Studier*, 1921, 41; Much in Hoops, s.v. *Gauten*;

Kalkar, *Ordb. t. d. ældre danske Sprog*, s.v. *Gøding*; Tamm, *Svensk etym. ordbok*, s.v. *Götar*; Hellquist, *Svensk etym. ordbok*, s.v. *Göt*; Almgren, *Hällristningar och kultbruk*, 283 seq.; Brate, *Zeitschr. f. deutsche Wortforschung*, 1910, 111; Svensson, *Namn och Bygd*, 1919, 2; Wessén, *Studier till Sveriges hedna mytologi och fornhistoria*; Wadstein, *Sveriges namn* (*Fornvännen*, 1930, reprint p. 3 note 2); Kemp Malone, *King Alfred's 'Geats'* (*Mod. Lang. Rev.* xx, No. 1).

§ 264. Sub-divisions.

A. Ancient division.

If Ptolemy's list of Scandian tribes includes some subordinate populations—such as Firaisoi, the Færsingar in the district of Færs?—we may possibly assume a division of the Gauts into two tribes.

1. Gr. Γοῦται, or the Gauts proper.

2. Gr. Λευῶνοι, perhaps the O.E. *Léon (mid Léonum, *Widsith*, l. 80). Original home: Middle Scandia (Ptol. II, 11, § 16), perhaps near Ljuna in Eastern Götland, or Liongaköping, the present Linköping. However, the name and position of the tribe in question are problematic. Bremer, § 105, proposes to read *Σουεῶνοι, Swedes, whereas Wadstein refers the name to the district of Liugnæs in Scania, the present Ljunits.

Lit. Müllenhoff, *Zeitschrift*, XI, 290; Schönfeld, s.v. *Leuoni* (with lit.); *idem*, in Pauly-Wissowa, s.v.; Lindroth, *Namn och Bygd*, 1917, 36; Wessén, *ibid.* 1921, 33; Wadstein, *Göteborgs Högskolas Årsskrift*, 1918, 5; *idem*, *Minnesskrift utg. av Filol. Samfundet i Göteborg*, 1925, 197, 198.

B. Early mediaeval division, according to the Norwegian King Hrodulf, cited by Jordanes, III, 19 seq., sixth century.

1. M.Lat. Gauthigoth (?), Western Gauts. According to v. Friesen (*Röstenen*, p. 134) Gauthigoth is an erroneous Compound made by a copyist. He thinks that the original MS had Gauthi, to which a copyist added Goth in an interlinear or marginal note; a later scribe then took this note to be part of the text and combined it with Gauthi. It is perhaps also possible that Gauthigoth stands for *Gaut-thioth, 'the people of Gauts'. At any rate, Gauthigoth is a corrupt form. Home on the Gaut-elfr.

2. M.Lat. Ostro-gothae, Eastern Gauts. Home on the Baltic.

3. M.Lat. Evagre. Obscure. See the next name.

4. M.Lat. Otingi. Obscure. Jordanes writes: 'dehinc mixi evagre otingis'. Müllenhoff reads: 'mixti Eva-greotingis'. However, a Compound of this sort is not likely. In the first place, such descriptive Compounds are almost exclusively poetical, while Hrodulf gives the

ordinary prosaic denominations. And secondly, the descriptive elements emphasise prominent ethnic rank, while the alleged *Greotingi are a population of inferior rank, mentioned nowhere else (cp. our article *Ethnische Prunknamen* (*Zeitschrift*, LXVII, 129)).

Lit. **Müllenhoff,** II, 63, 397; **Schönfeld,** s.v. *Evagre* and *Otingis* (with lit.); **Härje,** *Namn och Bygd*, 1912, 177; **Jiriczek,** *Engl. Studien*, LX, 220; **Weibull,** *Arkiv*, XLI, 215.

5. M.Lat. Theustes. According to v. Friesen (cit. by Langenfelt), the name is derived from a local lake Tjóstr 'the roaring'. Home in the district of Tjust, O.Swed. þiust, which forms the north-eastern border of Småland. However, the reading Theustes is not unquestioned; some MSS write Theutes, Teuthes.

Lit. **Zeuss,** 503, 506; **Müllenhoff,** II, 62, 398; **v. Grienberger,** *Zeitschrift*, XLVI, 153; **Schönfeld,** s.v.; **Noreen,** *Fornvännen*, 1920, 42; **Langenfelt,** *Anthropos*, XIV/XV, 307, 312.

6. M.Lat. Finn-(h)aithae, the Finnedi (Adam. Brem.), Finnenses (Saxo), i.e. 'inhabitants of the Finnish heath'. Home: O.N. Finn(h)eiðr, Swed. Finveden, in South-western Småland.

Lit. **Zeuss,** 158, 504; **Müllenhoff,** II, 50, 395; **Noreen,** *Spridda studier*, II, 138; **Schütte,** *Maal og Minne*, 1924, 195; **Karsten,** *Studier i nord. fil.* IX, Heft 3, 6; *idem*, *Die Germanen*, 130; **Löwenthal,** *Beiträge*, XLIX, 415.

As a seventh division the Vagoth (?) of Jordanes, III, 22, may be added, if they are to be interpreted *Vag-gothi, 'maritime Gauts', i.e. inhabitants of the East Gautic peninsula called Vikbolandet. But the name may also mean the Gutar (see § 268), or it may be entirely miswritten.

Lit. **Schönfeld,** s.v. (w. lit.); **Noreen,** *Fornvännen*, 1920, 44.

C. Later mediaeval division.

1. Swed. Västgötar, Western Gauts, in W. Götland.
2. Swed. Östgötar, Eastern Gauts (Ostrogothae, Jord.), in E. Götland.
3. Swed. Smålänningar in Småland, 'the small lands'.

(*a*) Inhabitants of Tjust (Theustes Jord.).

(*b*) Finvidingar (Finnaithae, Jord.), in Finveden.

(*c*) *Korungar in the district of Korunga. Obscure (cp. Hellquist, *Ortnamn på inge*, 80, 81).

(*d*) Virdar, O.N. Virðar, in Värend. Obscure.

(*e*) Swed. Öningar, O.N. Eynir, 'islanders' (with suffix *-īn*), on the island of Öland.

Lit. **Bugge in Gjessing's ed. of Arngr. Jónsson's** *Jomsvíkinga Saga*, **Preface, XIII; Schütte, (Norweg.)** *Hist. Tidsskrift*, **1917, 16.**

(*f*) Swed. Värmlänningar, O.N. Vermir, M.Lat. Vermilani (Adam. Brem.), in Värmland. According to Noreen, the tribal name is derived from the lake of Värmeln; we believe that both Vermir and Värmeln derive their names from a river Varmá; there are several such, and this may also have been the name of the present Klarälven, the main river of Värmland.

Lit. **Noreen,** *Spridda studier*, **II, 59.**

§ 265. Ethnic Position.

The Gauts at the beginning of their history seem to have occupied a position co-ordinate with that of the Sviones, Danir, etc. However, their importance was declining and therefore there is not much evidence, and that not very clear, concerning their ancient rank.

1. Ptolemy, II, 11, § 16, co-ordinates the Gauts with the Chaideinoi who represent, in our opinion, the Norwegian branch.

2. Procopius, *Bell. Got.* II, 15, § 26, mentions the Gauts as an ἔθνος πολυάνθρωπον, 'a large nation', as it seems, co-ordinate with the Danes, and not subjected to the Sviones.

3. The mediaeval and present division of Swedish provinces has a Götarike, or 'realm of Gauts'—embracing the sub-divisions 1–5—co-ordinate with the Svearike.

4. The Gautic language forms an individual dialect group side by side with the Svionic.

5. The Gautic name for district, *kind*, is in contrast to the Svionic substitute 'hundred', and to the Danish *herred*. *kind* agrees with Gothic *kindins* 'governor'.

6. The Gautic type of law, according to Kjer, *Edictus Rothari*, p. 150, often differs from the Svionic type and agrees with the Danish. We are not able to criticise this observation.

7. The Gauta-týr, or 'Gautic god', may indicate some local form of worship.

8. The Gautic farm houses belong to various types, viz.: (1) the 'gamma house' (Γ), occurring in Iron Age villages on the island of

Öland (cp. M. Stenberger, *Öländska bebyggelsesformer från järnåldern* (*Rig*, 1930)); (2) the rectangular farmstead, frequent in East Gautland; (3) the irregular group farmstead, frequent in West Gautland; (4) a separate Värmelandic variety of the same type, corresponding to the individual dialect of that region (it is also found in Northern Norway); (5) a West Gautic type which approximates to the West Norwegian and Icelandic 'row farmstead'. According to Sigurd Erixon (*Ymer*, 1922, p. 262 seq.) the second type may be regarded as a characteristic of the Gauts.

'In the Gautic type...the two courts (the one for men and the one for cattle) are separated by a fence. The form is rectangular, whereas the Danish-Scanian farmstead is rather square. This type...is frequent in Kalmar Län and Eastern Gautland. It is not rare...in Småland, West Gautland, Södermanland, and the eastern Uppland, and may also occur sporadically in other Swedish provinces.'

p. 263. 'In Gautland the farmsteads are often very irregular and not connected by any definite form. This character becomes always more predominant towards the west.'

p. 264. 'Moreover there is a distinct tendency towards arranging the stalls for cattle in one row and the rooms for men in another. This sort of "row farmstead" is frequent in Norway and also occurs in the western parts of Dalarna and in the Härjedal.'

The frontier between Gauts and Sviones in historical times is formed by the Firth of Bråviken in the east, and by the holy wood of Tiveden in the west. The Finn(h)aithae in South-western Småland, probably descendants of non-Gothonic aborigines, divide the Gauts from the Danes of Scania and Halland (cp. p. 370). Dense woods, the Markir, partly separate the Gauts and the Norwegians.

§ 266. History.

Even if the derivation of Gautar from the Gaut-elfr is not a proved fact, the archaeological and onomastic centre of the Gauts seems to lie near the Cattegat, not near the Baltic.

Districts with archaic Simplex names are thickly grouped around the Gaut-elfr. Along the coast, which in historical times belongs to Norway, we notice: Kville, Lane, Fräkne, Tjörn; then follow, on the West Gautic border of the river: Ale, Flundre, Bjärke, Barne, Viste, Åse, and, where the river leaves Lake Wener, Väne. Another series starts from the

Danish district of Fyæræ (with the tribe of Fervir, Jord.): Mark, the East Gautic Mo, and (east of Lake Wetter) Tveta, Vista, Dal, Aska. Farther east Simplexes are less predominant. The distribution shows that the surroundings of the Gaut-elfr are the primaeval centre of the tribe, East Gautland only the secondary field of growth.

About A.D. 180 the Gauts appear in Ptolemy's description of Scandia, a fact which shows their nation to have been of some importance. But the Sviones already seem to have eclipsed them, if we may judge from Tacitus.

At the beginning of the sixth century the Gauts are mentioned as a numerous nation by Procopius, *Bell. Got.* II, 15. They seem to have received without objection the Erules when they remigrated.

The Norwegian King Hrodulf about the same time mentions a series of tribes in the present Gautic lands (Jordanes, III, 19 seq.): 'Gauthigoth, acre hominum genus et ad bella promptissimum; dehinc mixi Evagre Otingis. Hi omnes excisis rupibus quasi castellis inhabitant ritu beluino. Sunt et his exteriores Ostrogothae...Theustes...quorum sedes sub humo plana ac fertili, et propterea inibi aliarum...gentium incursionibus infestantur'.

The importance of the Western Gauts is here emphasised. The 'rocky castles' may be identified with the fortified places of refuge found frequently in the Gautic countries, e.g. round the Firth of Bråviken. The Gauts of the interior are described as far below the standard of civilisation of the 'Finni mitissimi' in Southern Norway. We catch a glimpse of their warlike expansion, which carries them into the fertile coast regions, probably as a rule towards the south.

The wars of 'Geats' and Sviones in the early sixth century, and the unfortunate Viking raid of a 'Geatic' King Hugleik to Friesland about 526, as described in *Beowulf*, have been thought by Müllenhoff, Schück, Stjerna, Nerman, and others to refer to the Gauts on the Scandinavian Peninsula, because Géatas is the normal O.E. name for Gauts. The events described by the poem would represent episodes immediately preceding the Svionic conquest of Gautland in the sixth century. An especially important point is the fact that the Svionic King Éadgils or Aðils, who with the help of a Geatic army attacks his uncle Onela or Áli, meets the hostile army on the ice of Lake Wener (*Ynglinga Saga*, 29). The Geats here mentioned must have been situated in Western Gautland; it is inconceivable that they had come over from Jutland.

On the other hand, Fahlbeck has interpreted the Geats of *Beowulf* as Jutes, because the latter name is spelt thus in certain O.E. sources, and because such a localisation seems to be favoured by the fact that the Geats are represented as almost immediate neighbours of the Franks. So also Olrik, H. V. Clausen, and others. They have lately been supported by Kurt Weibull with fresh arguments.

The decisive circumstance, in our opinion, is this: how far are we able to recognise the persons and nationalities mentioned by *Beowulf* in genuine Scandinavian traditions?

In *Journ. Engl. and Germ. Phil.* XI, No. 4, we tried to support Fahlbeck's view, but we must confess that one circumstance has made us sceptical. The Svionic King Óttar, the Óhthere of *Beowulf*, according to the *Ynglingatal*, was defeated and slain by the Danes in Vendel, i.e. the Jutlandic county of Vendsyssel, and Snorri in ch. 27 adds that the Danes, because of that, gave him the opprobrious epithet Vendilkráka, i.e. 'Vendel Crow'. However, as Stjerna and Schück show, the scene is no doubt misrepresented. The Vendel in question is the Svionic one, the central district of Svíþjóð. Here, King Ottar's Mound was still known in the seventeenth century, and, moreover, Vendelkråka is still used as a playful toponymic meaning 'inhabitant of Vendel'. It hence appears that Thjodolf, the author of the *Ynglingatal*, and Snorri have like Fahlbeck identified the 'Geatic' opponents of Óttar with the Jutes, but that the identification is in this case wrong (cp. Stjerna, *Essay on Beowulf*, 53 seq. (and Almgren, *ibid.* footnote 62); Schück, *Uppsala Univ. Årsskrift*, 1907, *Progr.* 1, 124; Nerman, *Ottar Vendelkråka*).

However, the correction of this error does not at once solve the problem. There still remains one riddle to which we have tried to draw attention, but which has not hitherto been sufficiently considered: why has the famous Ongenþéow of *Beowulf* disappeared from the *Ynglingatal*? Why does a spectre of his epic fame seem to haunt the Jutlandic coasts? It is true the *Ynglingatal* has in his place in the royal pedigree an Egil. But this wretched coward has nothing to do with the famous hero of *Beowulf*. The true counterpart of the latter, from an epic point of view, is the gallant Viking Angantýr, who, according to the *Hervararsaga*, falls on Samsey fighting against Hjalmarr and Ǫrvaroddr. The scene has some resemblance to the death of Ongenþéow who is slain by the Geatic brothers Eofor and Wulf. But the fate of Ongenþéow has an even closer parallel in the death of a namesake of his grandson, King Athisl (Saxo,

169). Being challenged by two Jutish brothers, he is on the point of killing the one, when the other, breaking the rules of single combat, comes to his brother's aid and cuts down the aged king. The exploit gave rise to a Danish proverb, partly owing to the slain king's fame, partly owing to his slayers' manifest breach of the rules of chivalry. It would seem, therefore, that the situation was very rare. There is no other exact parallel than the death of Ongenþéow (cp. Heusler in Hoops, IV, 576, who recognises also the identity of the two epic dramas). Further, we have shown in *Arkiv*, XXXVI, 1 seq., that Angantýr's so-called 'brothers' are only the princes in the list preceding Ongenþéow in *Widsith* in another form. Here, the identity of the two famous epic figures becomes manifest.

To sum up, the negative evidence of the *Ynglingatal*, together with the positive evidence of the legends of Angantýr and Athisl, seems to show that Ongenþéow had emigrated from Sweden. The localisation of his death on the island Samsø near Jutland need not be taken as literally correct; Nerman has tried to show that Samsey has been substituted for Samland, i.e. East Prussia (see *Studier över Svärges hedna litteratur*, 140). But anyhow it indicates a scene south of Sweden and in the vicinity of Denmark. As a precursor of the Svionic invaders in the ninth century, Ongenþéow may have made expeditions against the great mercantile centre Hedeby in Southern Slesvig. Perhaps the Gauts rivalled him as emigrants here and on the Danish islands; we cannot deny the possibility, as we know practically nothing of the fate of these regions during the Migration Age. H. V. Clausen has pointed out a possible trace of the Geatic King Hygelác in South Jutland, viz. Huglæstath, where mercantile goods, after being carried on ships up the rivers Eider and Trene, had to be transhipped in order to reach Hedeby (see *Danske Studier*, 1918, 141). The place Earnanæs, where Beowulf is killed by the dragon, may also be found near Hedeby, viz. in the present Arnæs or Arnis on the northern shore of the Firth of Sli.[1] Finally, as Olrik remarks, Saxo, 175, mentions a 'Danish' King Hugleth who fights a Swedish chieftain Hømoth; this seems to reflect the Geatic King Hygelác whose country was harassed by the emigrated Svionic prince Éanmund. The entry concerning Hugleth follows immediately after a series of legends

[1] The name is not found elsewhere in Denmark, nor is there any *Ørnnæs or *Ørnsnæs; there is only a single Ørsnæs, which can scarcely be derived from the word *ørn* 'eagle' that appears in Earnanæs.

located in South Jutland: (1) the story of Vermund and Uffo, kings of Angel; (2) that of Frovin and Vig, ancestors of the West Saxon dynasty; (3) that of King Dan as successor of Uffo, i.e. the eponymic expression of the Danish suzerainty established on the ancient Anglian soil. The same section also contains the account of the battle between Athisl and two Jutish brothers (i.e. Ongenþéow against two Geatic brothers). In such surroundings the legend of Hugleth does not appear as a foreign element interrupting the natural sequence of events, but as the organic continuation of a drama played for some generations on Jutlandic ground.

Consequently, various Scandinavian sources, independent of each other, seem to indicate that the struggle between 'Geats' and Sviones was not exclusively fought on the Scandinavian Peninsula, but was continued in South Jutland. Until these points have been thoroughly discussed, the identity of the 'Geats' of *Beowulf* must remain open to question (cp. our article *Geaterspørgsmaalet* in *Danske Studier*, 1930, 70).

Generally speaking, the Gauts do not seem to have played a prominent political part during the Migration Age. *Widsith*, for example, mentions a king of the Sviones, a king of the Jutes, and four kings of the Danes, but no king of the Gauts, though this nation is mentioned in the second part of the poem. Similarly, Snorri in his *Ynglinga Saga* records but a few names of Gautic kings which may, or may not, be trustworthy. A Norwegian legend related by Saxo, 242, deals with a 'Gautic' King Gestiblindus who is simply Odin disguised.

Trustworthy evidence concerning the Gauts appears only in the traditions of their Danish neighbours. Saxo, VII, 329 and 334, records two contemporary Gautic dynasties, viz. Unguinus, Sygrutha, Syritha, Sigarus, Syvaldus, Sygne, Alf, Alger, and Syvardus, Wemundus, Ostenus, Alvilda (i.e. Alfhild). The common use of the elements *sig* and *alf*, together with the marriage of Alf and Alvilda, indicates that the two families are closely connected by kinship or friendship. Their names are, however, not characteristically Gautic, but Svionic, a consequence of the Svionic political and cultural superiority. (It must be noticed, at the same time, that the type is entirely different from that of the Geatic names in *Beowulf*, and also from that of the Gautic warriors in the list of combatants at Brávellir. This is quite natural, Saxo's Gautic kings being East Gautic, whereas the kings in *Beowulf* and the warriors at Brávellir are West Gautic.)

The family of King Sigar according to Saxo, 330, emigrated to Zealand.

Perhaps he and his people belonged to those Gautic auxiliaries who helped Hjarvard to conquer the Skjǫldung King Hrolf at Hleiðr (*Bjarkamál*). As Hjarvard was killed immediately after his victory, it is not unlikely that the leader of his Gautic auxiliaries inherited the throne thus vacant. But Sigar's family was soon exterminated in a feud with a native family.

The tradition of Gautic immigration to Denmark makes it necessary to consider whether we can discover any onomastic traces of it. Here it seems natural to pay attention to some North-east Zealandic names ending in *-rum*, viz. Wigarum, Æsarum (and Niartherum ?). Lindroth has tried to prove that they originate in Zealand and are transplanted to the Scandinavian Peninsula owing to a Danish invasion or influence (cp. *De nordiska ortnamnen på -rum* (*Göteborgs K. Vet. och Vitterh. Samhälles Handl.* 4, XVIII, 1)). We cannot accept this view, for the instances in Denmark are quite sporadic, whereas the use of this type of name has its centre in Gautland and more particularly in Småland. There is a large number of names ending in *-rum* in Eastern Scania, evidently starting from a base in Småland. One of the Scanian names concerned is Viggarum which is echoed by the Zealandic Wigarum. As Viggarum in Scania lies directly east of Wigarum, we must consider whether the name has not been transported by emigrants from the eastern side of the Øresund to the western. There is one manifest analogy in the same regions: Gladsax in Eastern Scania has given its name to a Zealandic Gladsaxe. According to Langenfelt, *Anthropos*, XIV/XV, 311, Gladsax is situated on a very steep hill (rising abruptly to 294 ft. from a level of about 100–120 ft.), and the element *-sax* must mean 'rock, hill', as in the Swedish Saxeknut, the name of a high mountain. But the Zealandic Gladsaxe is situated in an absolutely flat district; consequently, the name *must* be taken from the Scanian Gladsax. The relative positions are the same as in the case of Viggarum-Wigarum: one on the eastern side of the Øresund, the other directly opposite on the western side. Another trace of Gautic immigration is the name of Martheme (Mårum) in North-eastern Zealand, situated in the middle of large woods. It corresponds to Kolmården and Ödmorden, names of the frontier woods of Eastern Gautland and Sweden (cp. the place name Marþbækker in the law of Helsingland). *marþ* seems to be a typically Gautic and Svionic name for 'wood', at any rate foreign to the Danes (cp. Sahlgren in *Namn och Bygd*, 1929, 117). Thus the place name Martheme ('Wood-home') in the Zealandic woodlands supplements the traces of Gautic immigration which appear in the various names ending in *-rum*. We suppose that the presumed Gautic settlers were introduced as a consequence of those political revolutions which resulted in the establishment of the Sikling dynasty (cp. p. 375). The Gautic colony in South Jutland would be a continuation of the same movement.

Stjerna in his *Essays on Beowulf* points out that Öland, like Gotland, had in the fifth century become a prominent mercantile centre. But after the beginning of the sixth century, gold suddenly ceased to be abundant in Öland, but became more so among the Sviones. He concludes that this change indicates a Svionic conquest.

In the great battle at Brávellir, the monster meeting of northern Heroic Age, the Eastern Gauts sided with the Danes, the Western with the Sviones. The result of the struggle was that the Svionic suzerainty was firmly established. The battle marks the close of the Heroic Age; according to the chronology calculated by Nerman, *Det svenska rikets uppkomst*, 255, it took place in the middle of the eighth century.

During the Viking Age, the Gauts only play a small part. Their runic inscriptions mention only a few Viking expeditions, whereas the Sviones constantly appear as the leading maritime power.

Kurt Weibull in *Sverige och dess nordiska grannmakter*, p. 25 seq., maintains that there is no trace of a definite Svionic suzerainty till the eleventh century. Perhaps he overstates the negative evidence a little. He emphasises the fact that the early Norwegian poets, when mentioning their eastern neighbours, constantly speak of Gauts, never of Sviones. It is not till the reign of Olaf Skötkonung that the skalds and Adam of Bremen describe Gautland as united with Sweden.

But, from the Norwegian point of view, there was little occasion to mention the Sviones proper, as they were not neighbours of the Norwegians except in the northernmost parts of their country. And if the Gauts are still mentioned under their ancient national name, this fact does not prove more than that Gauts and Sviones were still two different *peoples*, as they were even much later. It does not prove anything concerning their political position. They may very well have formed two different states in one realm and under one king—the Swedish one.

During the eleventh century the incorporation with Sweden at last takes place. Adam of Bremen, for example, records the Eastern and Western Gauts among the 'populi Suediae' (IV, 23).

Henceforth the territories of the Gauts are simply self-governing states, each with its own legislation, forming part of the Swedish kingdom. It was not until the year 1350 that all the different Svionic and Gautic states were combined into one by the common *Landslag* ('law of the land') issued by Magnus Eriksson. 'Göta rike' nowadays is merely a name.

Lit. Zeuss, 158, 500, 511; Grundtvig, *Beowulfes beorh* (Preface, XXXIV); Fahlbeck, *Beovulfsqvädet* (*Antikvar. tidsskrift f. Sverige*, VIII, 2); *idem*, *Den såkalte striden mellan Svear och Götar* ((Swed.) *Hist. Tidsskrift*, IV, 105 seq.); *idem*, *Beowulfskvädet* (*Vitterh. hist. ant. handl.* 13, 3); ten Brink, *Beovulf*, 19; Müllenhoff, *Beovulf*, 13; Schück, *Folknamnet Geatas* (*Uppsala Univ. Årsskrift*, 1907, *Progr.* 2); Stjerna, *Essays on Beowulf*, ch. iv; Schütte, *Journ. Engl. and Germ. Phil.* XI, No. 4; *idem*, *Vidsid og Slægtssagnene om...Angantyr* (*Arkiv*, XXXVI, 1 seq.); *idem*, *Geaterspørgsmaalet* (*Danske Studier*, 1930, 70 seq.); Much in Hoops, s.v. *Gauten*; Chambers, *Beowulf*, 2, 8–10, 333–345; K. Weibull, *Hist. tidsskr. f. Skåneland*, 1921, 353; *idem*, *Sverige och dess nordiska grannmakter*; Eric Elgqvist, *Studier i södra Smålands bebyggelseshistoria* (*Hyltén-Cavallius-föreningens årsbok*, 1931, with archaeological map of Värend); Lundahl, *Falbygdens by- och gårdnamn* (*Göteborgs Högskolas Årsskr.* 1927, 2).

§ 267. Legendary Traditions.

The most famous eponymous representatives of the Gauts are the god Gautr and the epic King Gautrekr, the hero of *Gautreks Saga*.

Though some of the dynasties of the Gauts are famous, the nation does not count among the great powers of the Gothonic epic tradition. The Danish mythical ethnogony records three heroes, the Norwegian Nori, the Swede Østen, and the Dane Dan, but leaves out the hero of the Gauts. The list of princes in *Widsith* mentions no king of the Gauts, only a Sigehere, who was really of Gautic origin, but appears as king of the Danes. *Beowulf* constantly gives the Danes and Skilfings (Sviones) honorary prefixes, but it is only rarely that similar prominence is given to the 'Geats', even when their most famous heroes are mentioned (cp. our article *Ethnische Prunknamen* (*Zeitschrift*, 1930)).

Saxo mentions some Gautic dynasties, but the most famous of them, the family of Unguin and Sigar (Sigehere), has emigrated to Denmark (cp. § 266). The renown of Sigehere, as we mentioned above, reached England. The name of his dynasty seems to be 'Siklingar', formed like O.N. Veklingar, the descendants of Vęgeirr (cp. Bugge, *Home of the Eddic Poems*, 132 note). It gave rise to an O.N. poetical synonym for 'king', viz. *siklingr*. The unfortunate fate of Sigar's daughter Signe became the theme of a famous Scandinavian lay.

Snorri introduces into his *Ynglinga Saga* an alleged East Gautic King Hǫgni who is also known from the *Helgakviða Hundingsbana*. Hǫgni's companion, Granmar of Suðrmannaland, is interpreted by Snorri as king of the Svionic Södermanland, but the 'country of the Southmen' might also mean Germany. Several scholars regard Hǫgni as an East Gautic king who for a time held his own against the Sviones (cp. Hederström, *Fornsagor och Eddakväden*, II; Nerman, *Det svenska rikets uppkomst*; Nordén, *Östergötlands järnålder*, I).

The main literary and historical interest is connected with the dynasties of the 'Geats' of *Beowulf*. The keen interest taken by the Angles in their fates can hardly be understood except on the presupposition that the Gauts concerned had established colonies in the immediate vicinity of the Angles. The first king mentioned is Hréðel, and his descendants are called Hréðlingas. The most famous of them is Hygelác, who falls fighting against the Franks and Frisians on the Lower Rhine, and whose fame is echoed in Danish, Frankish, Frisian, and Welsh records. Then follows the originally Svionic dynasty of Wǽgmundingas, to which the hero Beowulf and his successor Wigláf belong. Their popularity in England appears from the fact that the name Wigláf was given to one of the Mercian princes.

Several subordinate Gautic heroes are enumerated among the combatants at Brávellir (*Sögubrot*, *Fornaldar sögur*, I, 384, and Saxo, VII, 391), but none of them seems to be known from any special saga or poem. Saxo, 372, records a Norwegian tale of two rascal brothers, Hialli and Scati, whose names appear combined in the name of a barrow. The place mentioned is Hjälleskata in Värmland, and the brothers thus seem to be its eponymous heroes. There seem to be no other noteworthy representatives of the Gauts in Scandinavian sagas.

Lit. See Heusler in Hoops, s.v. *Beowulf*; Nerman, *Studier över Svärges hedna litteratur*; works of Hederström and Nordén cited above; Stjerna, *Essays on Beowulf*; Schück, *Uppsala Univ. Årsskrift*, 1907, *Progr.* 2; lit. cited in § 266.

E. §§ 268–271. *THE GOTLANDERS*

§ 268. Names.

1. O.Gotl. Gutar; O.N. Gotar; Swed. Gotlänningar; Dan. Gullændinger; M.H.G. Goten. Adj. O.Gotl. gutniscr; Swed. gutnisk, gotsk, gotländsk; O.N. gotneskr; M.H.G. gotnisch, götnisch. Lindroth derives the name

from the little river Guteån near the farm Gute in Gotland, but like Hellquist we do not believe that the name can be separated from those of the Goths and Gauts (see §§ 116 and 263). However, even if this connexion is admitted, a derivation from a river name meaning 'shedding' remains possible.

Lit. N. M. Petersen, *Regesta geogr.* s.v. *Gotar*; Lindroth, *Namn och Bygd*, II, 75; Hellquist, *Svensk etym. ordbok*, s.v. *Göt.*

2. Finn. *Vuojolaiset, Wiolaiset (A.D. 1598), Woiolaiset (A.D. 1602). Country: Finn. Vuojola (? *Kalevala*); Esthon. Oja-mā, Oju-mā. Cp. the ordinary name of the Gotlandic sand-stone, Finn. *vuojo-kivi, vuojon-kivi* (dictionary of Juslenius, A.D. 1742). The localisation of the poetical country Vuojola is somewhat uncertain. Cp. Kaarle Krohn in *F.F. Communications*, XVI, No. 53, 122: 'Wie K. Grotenfelt nachgewiesen hat, werden in den alten finnischen übersetzungen des schwedischen landrechtes zwischen den *Suomalaiset* und "männern von Åland" oder dem inselvolke (*luoto cansa*) die *Wiolaiset* (1548) oder Woiolaiset (1602) den *guta* "Gotländern" entsprechend erwähnt. Im lexikon von Juslenius (1742) kommt das Wort *vuojonkivi* in der bedeutung "lapis sectilis" vor, auf Ösel wird das schleifrad *ujukāi* genannt. In Lönnrots lexikon ist *Voionmaa* mit "Öland" übersetzt, aber nach Wiedemanns estn. wörterbuch bedeutet *Ojamā* oder *Ojumā* "Gotland"'. Mikkola says: 'Zum Ausgangspunkt ist **vōja* oder **vōjo* zu nehmen. Man weiss nicht genau, wie dieses Wort etymologisch zu erklären ist. Wenn wir eine ursprüngliche Form *vōhja-* oder *vōhjo-* annehmen dürfen, so liesse sie sich mit dem baltischen Wort, das "deutsch" bedeutet, verbinden: litauisch *Vōkė* "Deutschland", *vokėtis* "Deutscher", lettisch *vācis* "Deutscher". In den baltischen Sprachen gibt es kein *h*, in Fremdwörtern wird es durch ein *k* ersetzt'. Whereas Mikkola derives the Baltic word from Finnish, Setälä[1] denies that a form like **vōhja* could have existed in primaeval Finnish, as that language had no *h*. He assumes a primaeval Baltic word **vōki̯ō* (**vāki̯ā*) which was introduced into Finnish and was subjected to the 'gradation' ('Stufenwechsel') of this language: the 'strong grade' ('Starkstufe') would be **vōki̯o-*, and the 'weak grade' ('Schwachstufe') **vōγi̯o-*. Both Finn. *vuojo, vuoja*, and Esthon. *oju-*, *oja-* are regular forms of the 'weak grade'. They would represent the oldest Finnish synonym for Gothonic. But, allowing for assonance, the word Vuojonmaa may also signify Gotland, and according to the most

[1] In a letter to the author.

ancient sources even Öland. Correspondingly, Vuojolaiset may mean Gotlanders and Ölanders. Buga assumes that Lithuanian Vokëtis may be referred to the ancient Vagoth, who according to Jordanes, III, 22, are situated between the Theustes in Tjust and the Bergio in the Scanian district of Biærg and may, consequently, be taken as occupying the modern Gotland (cp. also the ocean Vagus, *ibid.* III, 17, which seems to be the Baltic). Karsten, however,[1] rejects these derivations entirely and regards Finn. *vuojo-*, *vuoja-*, and Esthon. *oju-*, *oja-*, as the Gothonic *auja-* 'island', which appears in the Swed. Öland with toponymic O.N. Eynir. It must be borne in mind that the O.Gotl. form of the word for 'island' was *oy* and that Öland must consequently in the Gotlandic language have been called Oyland, a form rather close to Voionmaa and Vuojola. The ancient Gotlanders are likely sometimes to have called themselves *Oygutar to prevent confusion with the mainland Gauts. This *Oygutar can hardly be separated from Esth. Ojamā and Finn. Vuojolaiset.

Lit. **Kaarle Krohn**, *F.F. Communications*, XVI, No. 53, p. 122; **Mikkola**, *Sitz. Ber. der Finn. Akad. d. Wissensch., phil.-hist. Kl.* 1908, 14; **Wiedemann**, *Esthnisch-deutsches Wörterbuch*, s.v. *Ojamā*; **Setälä**, *Der älteste Germanen-name im Finnischen* (*Ann. Acad. Scient. Fenn.* Ser. B, Tom. XXVII, 396 seq.).

§ 269. Ethnic Position.

The isolated position of Gotland justifies the claim of its inhabitants to be regarded as an originally separate nationality co-ordinate with the Sviones and Gauts. Its individuality is emphasised by the fact that the Gotlanders possess a 'saga' of their own—the *Guta Saga*—a phenomenon which is quite unique in Eastern Scandinavia.

The phonology of the Gotlandic language gives it a claim to be regarded as a separate branch co-ordinate with Swedish and Danish. We may notice the following points.

1. The Gothonic diphthongs *ai*, *au* are preserved, whereas Gautic and Danish and most of the Svionic dialects develop monophthongs at an early stage. Cp. Gotl. *gait*, O.N. *geit*, Swed. *get* 'goat'; O.Gotl. *laupa*, O.N. *hlaupa*, Swed. *löpa* 'to run' (lit. 'to leap'). The palatalised *au*, O.N. *ey*, appears as *oy*: Gotl. *droyma*, O.N. *dreyma*, Swed. *dröma* 'to dream'.

2. The Gothonic diphthong *eu*, O.N. *jó*, *jú*, Swed. *ju*, Dan. *y*, becomes

[1] In a letter to the author.

a triphthong *iau*: O.Gotl. *diaupr*, O.N. *djúpr*, Swed. *djup* 'deep'; O.Gotl. *þiaufr*, O.N. *þjófr*, Swed. *tjuv* 'thief'.

3. O.N. *ǣ*, *ǿ* become *ē*, *ȳ*, cp. O.Gotl. *clēþi*, O.N. *klæði*, Swed. *kläde* 'clothes'; O.Gotl. *dȳma*, O.N. *dœma*, Swed. *döma* 'to deem'.

4. Gothonic short *u* is generally preserved (or re-established?): Gotl. Gutar, O.N. Gotar 'Gotlanders'; Gotl. *fulc*, O.N., Swed., Dan. *folk*. *o* only appears in the prefix *for*, and before *r* + cons.: O.Gotl. *horn* 'horn'; O.Gotl. *orþu*, O.N. *urðu* 'they became'; even in this case, however, *u* is kept after *b*: O.Gotl. *burg*, O.N. *borg* 'borough'. The distribution of *u* and *o* in Gotlandic is similar to that in Gothic; cp. Gothic Gutþiuda, but *faur*, *haurn*, *waurþun* (pronounce: *fŏr*, *hŏrn*, *wŏrþun*). The likeness between Gotlandic and Gothic becomes still more striking when we notice that the Gothic short *o* before *h*, e.g. in *drauhtin*- 'lord', is represented in Gotlandic (as in the other Scandinavian languages) by a long *o* which replaces a previously existing short *o* + *h*: *drōtin*, earlier **drohtin*. But Gothic certainly differs from Gotlandic in so far as the *o* appears before *r* without any exception: Gothic *baurans*, Gotl. *burin* 'born', etc.

5. Gotland has its own Law Codex, Guta Lag.

6. The Gotlandic type of farm houses according to Erixon is (East) Gautic. Besides, there occur traces of the 'row farmstead'. Cp. Mich. Haberlandt, *Die Völker Europas*, p. 444: 'In Norwegen...und auf Island (findet man) die Nebeneinanderstellung von Häusern mit ihren Traufwänden, was neuerdings auch für ganz alte Häuser mit aufgesteinten Wänden auf Gotland nachgewiesen ist und vielleicht als dessen altem Erdhaustyp angemessen angesehen werden muss'.

Lit. Söderberg, *Forngutnisk ljudlāra* (*Lunds Univ. Årsskrift*, xv, vi, 15); Ax. Kock, *Svensk ljudhistoria*, II, 105; E. E-ff in *Nordisk familjebok*, s.v. *Gottland*.

§ 270. History.

In the early annals of history, Gotland is little heard of. Its development is chiefly mercantile.

During Roman times there must have been a close connexion with the Goths in Prussia. Striking evidence is furnished by the Gotlandic words *lucarn* and *lucarna-staki* 'candle' and 'candlestick', identical with Gothic *lukarn* and *lukarna-staþa*, which in turn are derived from the Latin *lucerna*. Of 7000 Roman denarii found in Scandinavia, 5000 were found in Gotland.

During the Migration Age Gotlandic trade was still flourishing. Solidi from the time of the Emperor Anastasius (491–518) are frequent, whereas such coins are rare in other parts of Scandinavia. At the same time the island must already have been reached by West European trade. This fact appears from place names like Haborling-bo, Elingia-hem and Eskil-hem. Compounds containing a patronymic + *heim*, as in Elingia-hem, are a favourite type among the Saxons (cp. Walsingham), but almost unknown in Scandinavia. The combination of a human personal name with *heim* as in Eskil-hem seems also to be foreign to Scandinavia, whereas it is normal among Saxons and Germans.

The *Guta Saga* mentions a migration with the successive stations Thorsburg—on the east coast of Gotland—island of Fårö, island of Dagö, and the continent beyond the Baltic. According to Nerman, Thorsburg is the largest old fortress (*bygdeborg*) in Sweden. It is scarcely older than c. A.D. 400. The occupation of the islands Fårö and Dagö may be in accordance with historical fact. But the reference in the *Saga* to Gotlanders settled in Greece and still speaking their old tongue (c. A.D. 1300) is probably due to confusion with the Goths in the Crimea and Taman.

After 500 the fortunes of Gotland are at a very low ebb. About 500 new archaeological types appear, and these, according to Nerman, are of evident Svionic stamp. The development of Öland, Bleking, and Bornholm, betrays no similar break in continuity. Nerman thence concludes that a Svionic conquest, or at any rate a union with the Svionic state, had taken place about that time. The *Guta Saga* mentions attacks on the island and a final peaceful fusion with the Sviones, but gives no chronological data. Wulfstan, whose report was written before 899, regards Gotland as a part of Sweden (see Alfred's *Orosius*, p. 20).

Later, according to the *Saga*, the Norwegian King Saint Olaf visited the island and converted several of its leading men to Christianity.

During the Viking Age the trade of Gotland was again flourishing. Half of the 20,000 Arabian silver coins found in Scandinavia come from this island and there are also numerous Anglo-Saxon coins.

The capital Visby, the ancient Vi ('sanctuary'), became a member of the German Hanse League, and then together with the whole island was annexed by Denmark; finally, in 1645, Gotland was reunited with Sweden.

Lit. Nerman, *En utvandring från Gotland* (*K. Vitterh. Akad. Handlingar*, XXXIV, följden 3, del 1, häfte 4); E. E-ff in *Nordisk familjebok*, s.v. *Gottland*.

§ 271. Legendary Traditions.

The position of Gotland is unique in so far as it is the only East Scandinavian country which has produced a real saga of the well-known Icelandic-Norwegian type (written before 1285, see Lis Jacobsen, *Guterlov og Gutersaga*, p. 123). But this story was not taken up, and there is no echo of the *Guta Saga* in other literatures.

In the *Saga* the discoverer of Gotland is called Þielvar; he is perhaps a reflection of Thor's companion Þjalfi in the Norwegian myth (cp. our monograph *Oldsagn om Godtjod*, p. 194). He delivers the island from the power of elfish spirits. His son is Hafþi who marries Huitastiarna ('White star') and begets three sons, representatives of three districts, viz. Guti, Graipr, and Gunfiaun.

Further, the narrative records some episodes of Gotlandic history. First, there is a short story of a migration which leads the Gotlanders to Dagö near Esthonia and to Greece where the emigrants (really the Goths of the Crimea, see p. 24) still speak the Gotlandic tongue. Then follow the stories how Awair Strabain negotiated peace with the Sviones admitting their suzerainty, further how Ormica of Hainaim was baptised by Olaf the Saint, and how Botair of Acubek defended Christianity against his own heathen countrymen.

Lit. Lis Jacobsen, *Guterlov og Gutersaga, udg. af Selskabet til hist. Kilde-skrifters Oversættelse*, Preface, 11 and notes, p. 115 seq.

F. §§ 272–276. *THE SVIONIC BRANCH*

§ 272. Names.

1. O.N. Svíar, Sví-þjóð; O.Swed. Swear, Sve-þiuþ; Swed. Svenskar; O.Dan. Swe-thiuthæ (*Script. rer. Dan.* v, 623); Dan. Svenskere, Svenskinger; Goth. Suehans (Jordanes, III, 19, sixth century A.D.); O.E. Swéon (dat. Swéom, *Widsith*, l. 58), Swéo-þéod (*Beowulf*, l. 2922); Engl. Swedes; Germ. Schweden; Lat. Sviones (Tacitus, first century A.D.); M.Lat. Sveones, Svenones, Sve-thidi (Jordanes, quoting the Norwegian Hrodulf, sixth century), Svecones; Fr. Suédois; Gr. *Σουίωνες (Σούλωνες, Ptol. III, 5, § 8); O.Russ. Sviye (Nestor, eleventh century), Svei, Sviyane; Pol. Szwedy. Eponymous representative: M.Lat. Sve-thedus (genealogy of the sons of Boerinus, Kemble, *Translation of Beowulf*, Preface, vii).

Sacrificial ring: O.N. Svíagríss, 'pig of the Swedes'. Country: O.N. Sví-þjóð, Svía-veldi; Swed. Svea-rike, Sverige, Svärge; O.E. Swíoríce (*Beowulf*, ll. 2383, 2495); M.Lat. Suigia, Svetia, Svecia; O.Fr. Suane; Pol. Szwecya. Noreen derives the name from **swīo*, O.H.G. *geswio*, the stem being the same as in Lat. *suus* 'his own' (cp. O.N. *svéddï* 'dead without being killed', literally 'dead of itself'). Wadstein, however, rejects this interpretation and regards Svíar as a toponymic derived from a stem which he finds in the place names Svinnegarn near Enköping and Svia near Vaksala in Uppland. The root *swi-* would mean 'to dwindle', and names like Svia would indicate places where water has been drained away. This geographical etymology is *a priori* to be preferred (cp. Langenfelt in *Anthropos*, XIV/XV, 295; though he himself accepts the etymology 'our own'). The final *d* in Engl. Sweden originates from the element O.N. *þjóð* 'nation.'

Lit. Noreen, *Spridda studier*, II, 146; Schönfeld, s.v. *Sviones* and *Svethidi*; Läffler, (Swed.) *Hist. tidskrift*, XXVII, 169; Much in Hoops, s.v. *Schweden*; Söderwall, *Ordb. ö. svenska medeltidsspråket*, s.v. *Svear*, *Svänsker*; Hellquist, *Svensk etym. ordbok*, s.v. *Svear*, *Sverige*, *Svensk*; Tamm, *Svensk etym. ordbok*, s.v. *Svenskar*; Güntert, *Wörter u. Sachen*, IX, 131; Karsten, *Die Germanen*, 147; Sahlgren, *Svearna och Svia* (*Sydsvenska Dagbladet*, 22 February 1930, *Uppsala Tidning*, 19 July 1930); Wadstein, *Sveriges namn* (*Fornvännen*, 1930, with collection of quotations); Schagerström, *Namn och Bygd*, 1931, 144.

2. M.Lat. Gothi. A learned and poetical name, borrowed from the Gauts.

3. O.E. Scylfingas (*Beowulf*, l. 2603, etc.). Eponymous dwarf: M.H.G. Schilbunc (*Nibelungenlied*). A dynastic name, with eponymous female spirit Skjalf. Probably derived from a geographical element *-skjalf* which appears in the name of Odin's seat, Hliðskjalf.

Lit. Björkman, *Skialf och Skilfing* (*Namn och Bygd*, 1919, 163).

4. O.N. (in Eastern Norway) Austmenn 'eastern men' (*Landslov* af Magn. Haakonssøn, 7, 609). Cp. Østen as representative of the Swedes in the Danish genealogical myth. The same name in Iceland designates the Norwegians, and in Western Norway the Eastern Norwegians.

Lit. Fritzner, *Ordbog*, s.v. *Austmaðr*.

5. Finn. Ruotsalaiset; Esthon. Rōtslazed; Lapp. Ruotalažak; O.Russ. Rus'; M.Gr. Rhōs; Arab. Rōs. Country: Finn. Ruotsi. Place name: Esthon. Rōtsi-küll (Esthonia and Ösel). Generally derived from the Rodskarlar in the district of Roden or Roslagen, O.Swed. Rōþin, 'rowing district',

which faces Finland. Wiklund, however (in a letter to the author), rejects this etymology and maintains that Ruotsalaiset is of pure Finnish origin.

Lit. Friis, *Lapp. Ordbog*, Pref. xi; Cannelin, *Svenskt-finskt lexikon*, s.v. *Svenskar*; Wiedemann, *Esthn. deutsches Wörterb.* s.v. *Rõtslazed*; Hellquist, *Svensk etym. ordbok*, s.v. *Ryss*, 2.

6. Lapp. Darolažak, Tarolažak. Language: *tārru* (verb *tāruste* 'to speak Swedish'). Obscure. Setälä assumes that the name originates from Finn. *taro* 'village, cultivated place'; it designates the Scandinavians as agriculturists, in contrast to the nomadic Lapps.[1]

Lit. Lindah land Öhrling, *Lexicon lapponicum* (1780), s.v. *Taro*; Friis, *Ordbog ov d. lapp. Sprog*, Pref. xi; Wiklund, *Lule-lappisches Wörterbuch*; Halász, *Pite lappmarki szótár*; *idem*, *Deli-lapp. szótár*.[2]

7. Lapp. Laddelažak. Country: Ladde. Laddelažak may also mean Finns, and Ladde Kvenland (cp. Finn. Lantalaiset, i.e. Finns). The name means 'inhabitants of the land', i.e. 'agriculturists' (cp. No. 6).

Lit. Friis, *Lapp. Ordbog*, Pref. xi; Konrad Nielsen, *Det norske Sprog.*

§ 273. Sub-divisions.

1. O.N. Upp-svíar, Swed. Upp-länningar, in Uppland, a province formed in 1296 out of the four districts Tiundaland ('Tenhundredland'), Attundaland ('Eighthundredland'), Fiæþrundaland ('Fourhundredland'), and the northern Rōþin ('Rowing district') or Sioland ('Sealand'). There seems to have been a narrower district with the name of Uppland already in an earlier period, as we may conclude from the fact that the Yngling King Áli (identical with *Beowulf's* Onela, sixth century) is called Áli hinn upplenzki. This original Uppland, as the name indicates, would have been the interior part of the present province, fairly corresponding to the Tiundaland.

2. O.N. Suðr-menn in Södermanland 'Southern men'.

3. O.N. Vest-menn in Västmanland 'Western men'.[3]

4. O.Swed. *Nærikiar, Swed. Nerkjar, Närkingar, När-boar, in Nerike, Närke. Perhaps a derivative in *-k*, as Dan. Fanniker, Lålliker, Lyviker.

Lit. Sahlgren, *Festskrift til Feilberg*, 285 seq.; Hellquist, *Svensk etym. ordbok*, s.v. *Närke* (with lit.).

1 Private communication from Prof. Setälä.

2 We owe the notes on literature chiefly to Prof. Setälä.

3 Snorri in his *Ynglinga Saga* erroneously identifies Västmanland with Fiæþrundaland.

5. O.N. Helsingjar in Helsingland. Derived from O.N. *hals* 'neck', which may also mean both 'ridge', 'headland' and 'narrow water' (cp. two Zealandic districts ('konunglef') Hals, with neighbouring parishes Helsinge).

Lit. Hellquist, *Svensk etym. ordbok*, s.v. *Hälsing-*.

6. O.Swed. Gestringiar, Swed. Gästrikar in Gestrike or Gästrikland. Probably derived from the town Gestereke, now Gästre, in Uppland. Suffix *-ik* as in Nerkjar?

Lit. Sahlgren, *l.c.* 289; Hellquist, *l.c.* s.v. *Gästrikland.*

No general collection of Svionic toponymics has been made, but several of them occur as personal surnames (see Hellquist in *Xenia Lideniana*, 106). We noticed above the frequence of the suffix *-ing* in names of tribes of the superior rank: Upplänningar, Närkingar, Gestringiar (cp. also Ålänningar); toponymics of an inferior rank: *Ekshäringar or 'Sexöringar' in Ekshärad, Fensbolingar in Fensbol (see Sahlström, *Fryksdalsmål*, in *Svenska landsmål*, 1915, 11). The suffix *-ung* occurs in some toponymics: Kilungar in Rasbokil, Töibungar in Töibo, etc. (see Saxén, *Finska fornminnesfören. tidsskrift*, XXI, häfte 3).

The suffix *-ari* occurs in Øslare on the island of Ösel, name of a non-Swedish population, *Xen. Liden.* 106.

The suffix *-folk* in the village of Teir-folk (Saxén, *l.c.*) (only in Österbotten; cp. East Gautic Vifolka härad).

The suffix *-fari* in Bofara(r) in Hanebo (Helsingland, *Svensk diplomatarium*, Nos. 2 and 248 (1410)).

The suffix *-karl* in Rodskarlar in Roslagen or Roden, Botnekarlar in Botten, Dalkarlar in Dalarne, with fem. Dalkullor (*Xen. Liden.* 106). The place names Forkarby (< Fore-karla-by) and Älvkarleby, both in Uppland, contain the same word.

The suffix *-bo* as in Närboar; also in the personal surnames Brabo, Chilbo, Ginbo (?), Habo, Halbo, Holmbo, Hørbo, Larabo, Lerbo, Mar(k)bo, Sunbo, Trøbo, Trøgdebo, Tynderbo (*Xen. Liden.* 106).

§ 274. Ethnic Position.

Though the evidence afforded by archaeology and by the primary tribal names places the Scandinavian centre of civilisation on the coasts of the Cattegat and makes the coast of the Eastern Baltic only the external boundary of the sub-group, yet the Sviones even at the beginning of their history seem to have outstripped the Gauts and to occupy the position of a prominent separate branch.

1. The Sviones are the only representatives of 'Scandinavians proper' mentioned by Tacitus, *Germ.* 44 (first century A.D.). It certainly must be added that the author's knowledge is very fragmentary. He evidently got it from the knight sent by Nero to establish a Roman amber trade on the Baltic (Pliny, XXXVII, 45). This man may have met some Sviones, but not any other Scandinavians.

2. Tacitus, *Germ.* 44, mentions 'Svionum civitates' in the plural. It is uncertain whether this refers only to the ten 'hunds' (districts) of Tiundaland, or whether the union between Tiundaland, Attundaland and (?) Fiæþrundaland had already been established. The former alternative is not likely, cp. 3.

3. The political power of the Sviones and their large navies are emphasised (*ibid.*).

4. The name Sve-thidi in Hrodulf's report (Jordanes, III, 56) (before A.D. 526), O.N. Sví-þjóð, O.E. Swéo-þéod (*Beowulf*; cp. the eponymous figure Sve-thedus), contains an element denoting the high rank or 'great power' of the Sviones. Tacitus already seems to have known the Compound and to have translated it by the expression 'Svionum civitates'. From its constant use originate the modern forms, Engl. Sweden, Germ. Schweden (cp. M.Lat. Svethia).

5. A Svionic-Norwegian-Saxon element in the place names, more or less completely foreign to the Gauts, Danes, and Jutes, is *-tuna*. Though the word itself may have occurred in Gothonic, its use in Compounds seems to be due to Celtic influence (cp. the Celt. place names ending in *-dunon*).

6. A local Svionic type of marked South Gothonic origin is the 'hundred' (Saxon, German). The Gautic substitute is *kind*, the Danish is *herað*.

7. An Old Gothonic term for 'district', viz. **hunda-*, which occurs in Gothic and O.L.G., has formed a typical series of Compounds near Lake Mälar, e.g. Ti-(h)unda-land, districts of Lagunda, Hagunda, Åsunda, Norunda (see § 273, 1). Such Compounds were adopted by the Finns at a very early date, e.g. Sata-kunta (cp. Karsten, *Die Germanen*, 106).

8. A peculiar local Svionic element is *-garn* 'island'. It has been adopted by the Gotlanders (cp. Lindroth, *En omdebatterad önamngrup* (*Fornvännen*, 1914, 125)).

9. The Svionic district chief is called *domare* 'judge', a name which implies that his power was only judicial. Cp. also Dómarr, a mythical Svionic king, son of Dóm-(v)aldi, i.e. 'Doom-wielding' (*Ynglingatal*).

10. The Svionic territorial laws form an obvious unity, according to Fahlbeck in the Swedish *Hist. Tidskrift*, IV, 123.

11. The Svionic farmstead has its own type which Erixon calls the Central Swedish. Cp. *Ymer*, 1922, p. 263: 'The Central Swedish farmstead...is rectangular in form, but as a rule the different buildings are more closely connected than in the Gautic, and it has a separating wing with a doorway between the yard for men and the yard for the cattle. It is predominant in Västmanland, Uppland, and Närke, and also frequent in Gästrikland, the southern part of Dalarna, and in Södermanland. Farmsteads in the outlying parts of Svealand and Götaland are often sub-divided into two separate groups, each of which may appear as a complete square. This more sporadical type may be called the Middle Swedish'. Both the Central Swedish and the Middle Swedish types are also found in the Norwegian region of Gudbrandsdal.

A comparison with Noreen's map of Swedish dialects in *Vårt språk*, I, 98, shows that the Central Swedish type of farmstead corresponds fairly to a central Swedish area of dialects. Cp. our maps, Figs. 12 and 20.

p. 264: 'Dalarna and Norrland have a generally homogeneous type of farm, which consists of a simple quadrangle. In this the cattle-sheds may be comprised, but the cattle do not enter from the yard, as in Scania (and Denmark, G. Schütte); they enter directly through doors from the outside. This type also occurs in Finland', and, according to Vreim, in most parts of Eastern Norway. It may be called the North Scandinavian.

In historical times the south frontier of the Sviones was formed by the Firth of Bråviken and the dense woods of Kolmården and Tiveden. The northern borderlands were rocky woodlands with scattered settlements of hunting Finno-Ugrians.

In the course of their history the Sviones have absorbed the Gauts, Gotlanders, Smålanders, and sections of Norwegians, Danes, Finns and Lapps.

§ 275. History.

The old Svionic regions in the vicinity of Lake Mälar were within the area of Scandinavian settlements from the very first period of immigration down to the centuries immediately preceding our era. Civilisation in pre-Christian times had its centre in those peninsulas and islands round the Cattegat which later became the nucleus of the Danish state. Large areas which were destined to become Svionic agricultural countries were still submerged. The country lacked flint—the raw material which gave Denmark its industrial and mercantile superiority during the Stone Age. Neither had the Sviones any material to export, such as amber which enabled Denmark to import bronze in the following epoch. It was only during the course of a development which required almost a thousand years to mature, that the centre of activity gradually moved towards the Baltic coast.

In order to find out which area was first occupied by the Sviones, we must pay attention to a stratum of territorial Simplex names extending from the frontier-wood of Tiveden to the eastern extremity of *Laguz, i.e. Lake Mälar (O.N. Lǫgr). It comprises the districts of Kumla, Asker, two Åker, Daga, Bro, *Tjur (Tjurbo), Tör (O.N. Taur), and the island of Sili, now Selö. Some of the longer types of names are also archaic, viz. the territorial name Vendel, and the name of the island of Lofund, mentioned in *Ynglingatal*, str. 32. From this primitive nucleus the population has spread both north and south. Åker founded the district of Åkerbo north-west of Lake Mälar. The inhabitants of Selö founded the district of Selebo south of Lake Mälar; and the parish of Hölö farther south has founded the district of Hölebo which extends in a southward direction towards the Baltic.

In the same regions, several villages or towns with archaic names are also distinguished in various ways. Svia, near Vaksala, seems to stand in genetic relationship to the name of the Sviones (cp. the articles of Sahlgren and Wadstein cited in § 272, 1). Vendel, Lena, and Tuna contribute large archaeological finds. Mora is the king's ancient place of election. Lunda 'sacrificial grove' is the meeting-place of a folkland 'thing'.

It is worth noticing that the immediate surroundings of Lake Mälar seem to play a prominent part in the earliest legendary topography. Gefjon starts her famous ploughing from the Lǫgr, that is, Mälar. The mythical King Dag (*Ynglingatal*, str. 13) seems to be the eponymous hero of Daga härad. His perhaps eponymous successor Agni, according to str. 16 and Snorri's commentary, is killed in Taur at Agnafit on the shore of Stoksund, i.e. about the present Stockholm.[1] Eystein is killed on the island of Lofund, and his family in str. 42 is called 'Lofða kyn', i.e. 'inhabitants of Lofund'. Ingjald is killed at Ræning on an island in Lake Mälar (str. 39), and Snorri's prose mentions Sili (Selö, str. 39). Óttar's epic surname Vendilkráka signifies 'inhabitant of the Svionic Vendel'.

The character of the Mälar region was extremely favourable to the development of seafaring. In *Sydsvenska Dagbladet Snällposten*, 22 February 1930, Sahlgren shows that in the centuries immediately preceding our era the present Uppland was to a great extent submerged, Lake Mälar covering its lower part. The ancient Sviones consequently inhabited islands of an archipelago. On one of these islands was a hamlet, now called Svedja, but in 1365 written Swiya. Sahlgren is inclined to believe that this place was the centre from which the Svionic expansion started. Wadstein, on the other hand, assumes that 'Swiya' means a place which has become dry owing to the lowering of the water level, and the name 'Sviones' would then mean people living in such places (see *Sveriges namn* (*Fornvännen*, 1930)). As a matter of fact, the falling water level considerably increased the inhabited area, and it was just this circumstance which favoured the establishment of Svionic power. The soil, moreover, according to Kurt Weibull, contained large quantities of easily accessible bog-iron which afforded a means of developing industrial and mercantile activities, as soon as the Sviones had learnt to practise the art of smelting and working the raw metal—a process carried on on a large scale, at any rate after the Migration Age (cp. the territorial name of Jarnberaland 'Iron-transport-land', used for a part of Västmanland and Dalarna). At the same time the making of steel weapons was a main condition of that military superiority on which the Svionic expansion depended.

The Sviones first appear in the historical records of the first century

[1] Noreen certainly refers the words 'við taur' to the king's death 'owing to witchcraft' and so does Schück, *Upsala Univ. Arsskrift*, 1906, *Progr.* 1, 71. But this interpretation does not really contradict Snorri: the poet probably used an ambiguous expression on purpose, and Snorri's detailed threefold localisation seems to originate from exact local traditions.

A.D. At their first introduction into literature they show conspicuous marks of established political power.

A questionable entry in Pliny's *Natural History*, IV, 96, opens the evidence. After describing the situation of Scadinauia, he says that her enormous dimensions appear from the fact that 'portionem tantum, quod notum sit, Hillevionum gente quingentis incolente pagis, quae alterum orbem terrarum eam appellat'. 'For only a part of it, as people know, is inhabited by the nation of Hilleviones who possess 500 counties and call Scadinauia a separate continent.' His 'well-known' name Hilleviones does not appear elsewhere; in *Salmonsens Konvers. Lex.* s.v. we have proposed to read 'illa Svionum gente'—a suggestion which has also been set forth by v. Grienberger, *Zeitschrift*, XLVI, 152, and, we believe, also by Läffler. For only if the 'Hilleviones' are identified with a really well-known nation like the Sviones, does the position of that nation with the 500 counties become credible.[1] But the suggestion is rejected by Svensson, *Namn och Bygd*, 1921, 88.

Lit. Schönfeld, s.v. *Hilleviones* (with lit.); Löwenthal, *Beiträge*, XLV, 254; *idem*, *Arkiv*, XXXII, 269; Schrader, *Reallexikon d. indogerm. Altertumskunde*, s.v. *Germanen.*

Tacitus, *Germ.* 44, affords the first incontestable evidence as to the Sviones. They occupy a prominent position within his work, as sole representatives of the Scandinavian sub-group, and as sole representatives of Gothonic maritime power. He also emphasises their strong armies and their mighty kings, who may assume almost absolute power (i.e. owing to their function as supreme priests during the great feasts). But as Tacitus speaks of a plurality of 'Svionum civitates', it is obvious that the various 'hunds' (districts) possessed still a considerable amount of self-government and so, of course, did the 'folklands', if the union between them had already taken place. The religious function of the king, to which Tacitus seems to allude, no doubt concerned the worship of the Vanir or fertility deities. It was connected with the cult of the ancestral hero Ingvi, who was besides a favourite of the Angles, Jutes, and Danes. As proselytes to this religious community the Svionic dynasty of Skilfingar adopted the additional name of Ynglingar.

The reports of *Pliny (?) and Tacitus on the Sviones can only be

1 An identification with the Leuonoi of Ptolemy cannot be recommended, as even this name is unique and has absolutely no claim to the prominent position occupied by the 'Hilleviones'.

understood as being the result of mercantile connexions between Sweden and the Weichsel region. An epic echo seems to appear in the legend of an expedition which King Dag—the eponymous representative of Daga härad?—undertook to Reiðgotaland, that is the lands of the Goths in Prussia (see *Ynglinga Saga*, 18). Anyhow, the contact of the far north with southern countries in the first centuries of our era was not very extensive. Of 82 Roman solidi, dating from the years A.D. 249–395, found on Scandinavian soil, the Svionic countries have only contributed some few pieces. Later, the numbers increase, especially in the three large islands in the Baltic, viz. Bornholm, Öland, and Gotland, in all of which more than a hundred solidi dated after 395 have been found. The Svionic Uppland certainly does not rival those three islands as to the number of coins of that period it possesses, but its participation in the trade must obviously have been increasing, for the number of solidi from the later epoch is 25.

The problem of Svionic immigration into South-western Finland must here be mentioned, but as opinions differ considerably we dare not set forth any definite view. The islands of Åland seem to have had a population of Nordic race and Gothonic culture already at the end of the Stone Age, and so had the south-western coast of Finland. We are, however, not able to state whether this population came from Sweden or from the southern shore of the Baltic. Both opinions are advanced, and both may be right. It should be noted that Ptolemy, III, 5, § 8, has the following series of nations along his so-called 'river Vistulas', which represents in reality the *eastern* coast of the Baltic (cp. our monograph *Ptolemy's Maps*, 31): Finnoi, Sulones, Frugundiones, to be read Finnoi, Suiones, Burgundiones (cp. C. Müller's edition of Ptolemy, p. 424 footnote). It is certainly possible that Ptolemy's source had mistaken the western coast of the Baltic for the eastern, but it is also quite possible that his source was based on actual observation and that Svionic colonies were known to exist in Finland. The fact that the Finnish shore was in mediaeval times subject to the *ledung* ('levy'), indeed, seems to indicate that the Sviones had established their power in this country at a very early date, because the levy had probably existed already at the time of Tacitus. Snorri's *Ynglinga Saga* reports that several Yngling kings, beginning with Agni, made raids into different parts of Finland and exacted tribute. According to Karsten, *Die Germanen*, 103, the West Finnish archaeological finds from about the second century A.D. are chiefly or almost exclusively Gothonic: 'Mit grosser Wahrscheinlichkeit umfassten daher die neu angekommenen finnischen Stämme auch germanische Volks-elemente, und dieses germanische Volkstum wurde während der ganzen folgenden Eisenzeit durch rege Verbindungen mit Schweden verstärkt' (cp. the literature cited, *ibid.* p. 105).

After 500 Uppland suddenly outstrips all the neighbouring regions, both West Gautland and the islands in the Baltic. Huge treasures of gold were accumulated there, e.g. in Turebyholm, where was the largest collection of gold that has been found in Sweden, and one of the largest in the whole of Europe. The most imposing grave finds of Sweden have been made in the parish of Vendel, where the dead are buried in their ships together with splendid furniture. The economic revolution to which the buried treasure bears witness chiefly originates from progress in industrial technique: the Sviones have by this time, as we mentioned above, become familiar with the art of smelting and working bog-iron. Whereas in the world's trade they had previously been consumers only, they could after this take their part as producers (cp. Weibull, *Sveriges och Danmarks äldsta historia*, 82). At the same time, the rising level of the dry land increased the opportunity of farming. According to Gunnar Ekholm there was great progress in agriculture in the fifth century.

The Svionic overseas trade was still to a great extent carried on with Bornholm, Öland, and Gotland; but it is a marked feature of this new epoch that Svionic seafarers opened direct communications with nations beyond the Baltic.

For instance the Saxon and German territorial term 'hundred' became a standard type in the surroundings of Lake Mälar. Another type of southern origin was 'path', as in the territorial name Medelpad north of Helsingland.

A religious movement which accompanied this borrowing of names was the adoption of the worship of the Æsir, chiefly represented by the gods Thor and Odin. According to Snorri, *Ynglinga Saga*, 5, the new belief came from Saxland, and from the Danish islands spread directly to Sigtuna in the Svionic Uppland. We have no reason to doubt this report that the religion of Odin followed the road of maritime trade. In Sweden, again, it advanced not only towards the north and west, but also to the south, as a consequence of the Svionic expansion.

That mercantile relations between the Sviones and the Weichsel were continued into the sixth century is apparent from the fact that Jordanes, III, 19, refers to the Sviones by the Gothic form of their name, Suehans.

The Norwegian King Hrodulf (*ibid.*) mentions them as Svethidi, 'cogniti in hac gente reliquis corpore eminentiores', a statement which fits in very well with the views of the Norwegian anthropologist Bryn. The addition of the element *þjóð* 'nation' emphasises their political rank (cp. § 274, 4), and their claim to be pre-eminently tall of stature shows that they were ambitious to gain the leadership among the East Scandinavian tribes.

At the same time the Swéon and their King Ongenþéow appear in the Old English epic (*Widsith*, l. 31), next to the Saxon tribe of Secgas. A whole group of Svionic heroes is celebrated in *Beowulf*, and a number of the same persons—Ongenþéow, Éadgils, Éanmund—appear in Norwegian and even more conspicuously in Danish legends. Whereas the reports of Pliny (?), Tacitus, Jordanes, and Hrodulf, reflect only the general mercantile activity of the Sviones, the epic legends celebrate individual heroes and their political actions. But the question is: where did these actions take place? Was it exclusively on the Scandinavian Peninsula, or only partly there and partly on the southern shores of the Baltic? As we have discussed this problem fully in § 266, we may refer to that paragraph and only state our conclusions here. The stories in *Beowulf*, we believe, certainly illustrate the struggle of the Sviones for supremacy over the Gauts. But part of the conflict must have been fought on the southern shores of the Baltic, in South Jutland or in its vicinity. The localised Jutish traditions allow of no other interpretation. Both Gautic and Svionic emigrants must have been operating in the vicinity of the mercantile centre æt Hǽðum, in anticipation of the Svionic occupation in the ninth century.

Many scholars have been unable to realise the possible connexion between the Sviones of the Migration Age and Jutland. But Weibull has shown that to deny a connexion argues insufficient insight into the history of Svionic expansion (cp. *Hist. tidskr. f. Skåneland*, 1921, 317). The Svionic navies were prominent as early as the time of Tacitus, and the islands Gotland, Öland, and Bornholm, facilitated the progress of their activity towards the southern parts of the Baltic. There are archaeological traces of Svionic colonies in Northern Bornholm, and in the same region we observe a place name of a Svionic type, Saltuna. The probable goal of the expeditions was the southern part of Jutland with the port æt Hǽðum (near the present Slesvig) which was used as a centre for goods passing between Scandinavia and Western Europe. But the Svionic pioneers seem also to have reached the northern shores of the Cattegat.

The Norwegian poets Thjodolf and Eyvind in the Viking Age record early raids of Svionic invaders in the regions round the Cattegat. Eyvind's *Háleygjatal*, str. 7, relates that the Svionic Kings Jörund and Eirik captured the Norwegian King Goðlaug of Hálogaland somewhere in Denmark and hanged him at a place called Straumeyjarnes. Thjodolf's *Ynglingatal*, str. 22, confirms the story by calling Jörund 'the slayer of Goðlaug'. There is no Danish or Swedish island nowadays called Strömö, and even the Simplex Ström, Strömmen is extremely rare in Denmark. Later, Goðlaug's son Gylaug avenged his father's death by capturing Jörund in the Limfjord and hanging him (*Ynglingatal*, str. 22). We notice that the Sviones are here operating in a part of Jutland which belonged to the Norwegian sphere of interest rather than the Anglo-Saxon. This is the reason why the episodes concerned are told by Norwegian skalds, and not by *Widsith* or *Beowulf*.

The somewhat later King Ongenþéow, about the beginning of the sixth century, is the first Swede known to Anglo-Saxon tradition. In *Widsith* he is the sole representative of the Sviones, and his fame resounds in the pages of *Beowulf*. As we have pointed out in *Arkiv*, XXXVI, 8, *Widsith's* catalogue of kings and nations is the source of a well-known Danish and Norwegian list enumerating Angantýr's nine or twelve 'brothers'. Hence it appears that the famous Viking Angantýr is simply a reflection of Ongenþéow. The name is rare in historical Scandinavian nomenclature (see Lind, *Norsk-isländska dopnamn*, and Lundgren-Brate, *Personnamn från medeltiden*). The only cases in which the use of the name can be verified historically are those of a Danish king (eighth century), a Danish nobleman (A.D. 811), and an earl of Orkney, all of whom undoubtedly were named after their famous epic predecessor. Under such circumstances, the identification of the epic heroes Ongenþéow and Angantýr cannot be regarded as open to question. As to Angantýr, he is located 'í Bolm austr' (*Hyndluljóð*, str. 24 (B) and *Hervararsaga* (*Fornm. sögur*, II, 212)), that is to say, on the Bolms-ö in Lake Bolm, due east of the Danish frontier; the parish of Angelstad on this lake may have been regarded as 'the place of Ongenþéow' (on the other hand the substitution of the name 'Egil' for 'Ongenþéow' seems to show that a shortened form was used, which might be the 'Angel' found in 'Angelstad'). Ongenþéow, after killing the 'Geatic'

King Hǽðcyn (*Beow.* l. 2931), was overthrown by Hǽðcyn's brother Hygelác and killed after a desperate struggle by the brothers Wulf and Eofor (ll. 2487, 2962). The Norwegian echo of the drama refers it to the island of Samsø near Jutland, which Nerman regards as a mistake for the Prussian Samland (see p. 389). Jutish traditions point towards South Jutland. At any rate, it was at the southern limit of Svionic operations, far from Sweden, where Ongenþéow's fame had been entirely forgotten.

Ongenþéow's son Óhthere, O.N. Óttarr, according to the *Ynglingatal* was killed in Vendel by the 'Danes'. As the Svionic Vendel is meant, the 'Danes', i.e. Jutes, must here be regarded as disguised Gauts (cp. p. 388).

Óhthere's brother Onela is the O.N. Áli hinn upplenzki (*Ynglinga Saga*, ch. 29), and Óhthere's sons Éanmund and Éadgils appear as Hømoth and Høgrim, defeated Svionic opponents of Hugleth, i.e. Hygelác (Saxo, IV, 175). (The alliteration in *h* is introduced by analogy with Hugleth.) Éadgils is also known in Norwegian and Danish legends as Aðils or Athislus. The drama described in *Beowulf* is quite differently interpreted by various critics. It is sufficient to state that Éadgils and Éanmund revolt against Onela and emigrate to the Geats whose King Heardréd, Hygelác's son and successor, is killed by Onela (ll. 2202 seq., 2385). Then Éanmund is slain by the Geat Wéohstan who belongs to the emigrated Svionic family of Wǽgmundings (l. 2612). Éadgils succeeds in killing Onela and becomes king of the Sviones (l. 2393). Onela's defeat is described by Snorri (*Skaldskaparmál*, ch. 51, and *Ynglinga Saga*, ch. 29); here, however, Áli hinn upplenzki is by mistake transplanted from the Svionic Uppland to its Norwegian namesake. The battle took place on the ice of Lake Wener; according to the *Skjǫldungasaga*, Aðils was assisted by some champions of the Danish King Hrolf Kraki; they seem to have replaced the Gauts of the earlier legend. Afterwards King Hrolf rashly undertook an expedition to Uppsala, but had a narrow escape and had to save himself from the pursuing army of Aðils by 'sowing gold on the plain of Fyrisvellir' (*Ynglinga Saga*, ch. 29).

Eystein, the son of Éadgils, was killed by 'Jutish' (Gautic?) men on the island of Lofund in Lake Mälar (*Ynglingatal*, str. 33). His son Yngvar was killed by the Esthonians on the island of Sýsla, i.e. Ösel (*ibid.* str. 35). Yngvar's son Önund continued to raid Esthonia (*Ynglinga Saga*, ch. 33). These entries are the first indications of Svionic expansion into Russia.

Yngvar's grandson, Ingjald the Ill-ruling, by treacherously killing the vassal kings obtained direct rule of the Svionic folklands Fiæþrundaland and Attundaland and of the (Gautic?) kingdom of Næriki. According to the *Ynglinga Saga*, ch. 36, he also killed King Granmar of Suðrmannaland (the present Södermanland), and annexed his land, which seems to have been independent. However, some scholars doubt Snorri's report and think that he has confused the Transbaltic Suðrmenn (i.e. Germans) with the Suðrmenn in Sweden.

About a century later, c. A.D. 750 (according to Nerman, *Det svenska rikets uppkomst*, 255),[1] Svionic forces under a king called Hring, with the aid of the Western Gauts, attacked the Danish King Harold Hildetand and his East Gautic vassals. The armies met at Brávellir near Bråviken. King Harold was killed, his army defeated and East Gautland was conquered by the Sviones.

The expansion of the Sviones may be traced by means of personal names in runic inscriptions and by means of place names ending in *-tuna*, *-sättra*, *-garn*, etc., but no comprehensive investigation has yet been made. It is, for instance, noteworthy that the personal names in the runic inscriptions in the Jutish district of Djursland and near Randers have a marked Svionic sound, such as Asvid, Eystein, Freystein, Sigvaldi, Thorgny; no other part of Denmark offers anything like this. There is a Ram-tun in Djursland. Svionic runes are found at Gunderup in Himmer Syssel (Wimmer, No. 247), and at Laurbjerg in Åbo Syssel (No. 248). Cp. the stone of Karl the Good at Hobro with an exactly similar stone in Western Gautland. The rune-stone of Sæddinge on Låland (Wimmer, No. 85) mentions a local population of Sundr-svíar, i.e. 'Southern Sviones' (or 'separate Sviones'? as Lis Jacobsen interprets it, see *Svenskeveldets Fald*, 134 seq.).

In order to obtain statistics for a comparison between the Svionic 'vestrvíking' and 'austrvíking'—Viking expeditions to the west and to the east—the rune-stones ought to be examined. A rough examination seems to show that at least a third of the expeditions were to the west; several of them reached England.

The Sviones about 865 formed one state (regnum), according to Rimbert, *Vita Anskarii*, *Mon. Germ. SS.* Their expansion along the Baltic can be traced in historical and archaeological sources. According to Icelandic traditions, King Eirik Önundsson in the ninth century sub-

[1] But see on p. 376.

jected South-western Carelia, but the Svionic element was for a time almost absorbed by the Finnish (see Karsten, *Die Germanen*, p. 104). Wulfstan says that the Svionic territory included Gotland, Öland, Möre, and Bleking, whereas Bornholm had a king of its own (Alfred's *Orosius*, 20). Those Sviones who migrated furthest went first to Låland, and finally reached South Jutland, which was a most attractive goal. This region, with its capital æt Hǽðum, was not, as we regard it in the later Middle Ages, a subordinate borderland, but, owing to its command of the trade between Western Europe and Scandinavia, was of enormous importance: the possession of it in reality implied dominion over Denmark. Therefore, Svionic invaders for centuries aspired to conquer it. Towards the close of the ninth century a Svionic King Olaf occupied South Jutland; he was succeeded by his son Gnupa (Chnob) (Adam. Brem. I, 50). Gnupa (Chnuba) made raids on Friesland, but was conquered by the German King Henry the Fowler in 934 and compelled to receive baptism (Widukind, *Mon. Germ. SS.* III, 435). Gnupa's son Sigerich, i.e. Sigtrygg, was conquered by the Danish King Hardegon (Adam. Brem. I, 52), and later emigrated to Normandy where he fell in battle against the Franks 943 (see Flodoard's *Annals*). Both Gnupa and Sigtrygg are commemorated by the former's wife Asfrid on rune-stones near æt Hǽðum (Wimmer, *Runemindesmærker*, I, 78). Cp. K. Weibull, *Sverige och dess nordiska grannmakter*, p. 36 seq.; Lis Jacobsen, *Svenskevældets Fald*; Vilh. la Cour, *Sønderjyllands Historie*, I, 263 seq.

Svionic Vikings co-operated with the Danes in raids on Hanover about 994 (Adam. Brem. II, 29 seq.). On his expedition to England in 1015 Canute the Great also had Svionic auxiliaries. Four runic monuments in Uppland and Södermanland mention Svionic warriors as recipients of 'Danegeld' in England (cp. v. Friesen, *Fornvännen*, IV, 57 and VI, 104 seq.).

The exploits of the Sviones towards the east, however, were still greater than those towards the west. Svionic graves and antiquities in the interior of Russia, as well as East European and Arabian coins and articles from the Orient found in Sweden, show a growing intercourse in the ninth century. After the expeditions of Yngvar and Önund to Esthonia, Curland was the chief object of the Viking activity. The earliest deposits of Svionic antiquities in the Baltic provinces, and also the most numerous, come from this country. After being subjected the

Curlanders had rebelled before Ansgar's visit to Sweden in 853 (cp. *Vita Ansk.* ch. 30 (*Mon. Germ. SS.* II, 714)). However, the Sviones soon subjugated them again. At the beginning of the ninth century the Svionic settlements spread to the regions south-east of Lake Ladoga. According to Nestor, chs. 14 and 15, the Varjaži (Sviones) became masters of Russia in 859, were ejected in 862, but soon afterwards returned. 'Three brothers came;...the oldest, Ruric, settled in Novgorod; the second, Sineus, at Bjelo-Jezero; and the third, Truvor, at Izborsk. After these Varjaži the Russian Empire was named....Two years afterwards, Sineus and Truvor died. Ruric inherited their dominions and distributed their cities to his men—Polotsk, Rostov, Bjelo-Jezero etc.... The previous inhabitants were: in Novgorod Slavs, in Polotsk Kriviči, in Rostov Meres, and in Bjelo-Jezero Vesi.'

The Kriviči perhaps were Balts, the Meres and Vesi were Finns.[1] The power of the Russes was immediately extended to the shores of the Black Sea, and in 865 they undertook a great Viking raid against Constantinople (see Nicetas, *Vita S. Ignatii* (Haduin, *Act. Concil.* v, 966)). At the same time, they began to harry the dominions of the Chazares, Bulgares, and Burtases; according to the Arabian author Ibn-Fadhlan, they made a raid over the Caspian Sea to Persia as early as about 912 (see Zeuss, 550). From this time forward there were large bands of Sviones among the Imperial body-guard in Constantinople.

In the tenth century the Svionic colonies in Russia reached the height of their prosperity; most of the East European and Arabian coins found in Sweden date from before 975. After the middle of the tenth century the number of Swedish personal names declines in Russia, and after 970 Arabian coins in Sweden become rare, the latest date being 1010. About 1000 the grave finds in Russia show that Swedish influence is waning. Princes of Ruric's blood ruled Russia till 1598, but the Swedes had been absorbed by the Slavs long before that time (cp. Weibull, *Hist. tidskr. f. Skåneland*, 1921, 353).

The decline of Svionic activity in the east is balanced by increased activity in the west during the last part of the Viking Age. And if Arabian coins in Sweden become rare, Anglo-Saxon ones become plentiful. At the same time Sweden begins to interfere in Norwegian politics. This shifting of interest from the east to the west was so marked as to provoke discussion, and Snorri attributes to Thorgny

[1] Cp. Schönfeld, *Appendix* s.v. *Merens.*

Lawman a speech protesting against the new course inaugurated by King Olaf Skötkonung (cp. Weibull, *l.c.* p. 356). Concerning the annexation of Gautland see § 266.

Olaf Skötkonung in the eleventh century successfully raided Finland, and, after a series of so-called crusades in the twelfth and thirteenth centuries, that country was incorporated with Sweden. Swedish dominion was constantly being extended on Lappish ground, and Småland also was incorporated. Gotland was lost, but only temporarily, to the German federation of the Hansa and afterwards to the Danes. Sweden gradually conquered Halland, Scania, Bleking, Bohuslän, Härjedalen, Jämtland, Western Pomerania, Curland, Livland, Esthonia, and Ingermanland, transforming the Eastern Baltic into a Swedish sea. The Transbaltic dominions, however, were all lost again. Only in Finland do Swedish nationality and civilisation hold their ground east of the Baltic, and even there they are menaced by the native influences.

The number of Swedes in 1750 was calculated to be 1,780,678; nowadays it is some 7,300,000.

Sweden (1930)	c. 6,120,000
Finland (1920, Finlänningar)	340,963
Finland (1920, Swedish subjects)	6,901
Denmark	36,142
Norway	47,216
England and Wales	4,557
Scotland	290
Germany (1910)	13,000
South Africa (1920)	1,081
U.S.A.	625,585
Canada	27,700
Australia	5,025
New Zealand	1,206

Lit. Vilh. Thomsen, *The Relations between Ancient Russia and Scandinavia and the Origin of the Russian State*; Hildebrand, *Forntiden* (*Sveriges hist. intill 20de seklet*); Montelius, *Forntiden* (*Sveriges hist. till våra dagar*); Schück, *Forntiden* (*Svenska folkets historia*); K. Weibull, *Sverige och dess nordiska grannmakter*; Nerman, *Vilka konungar ligga i Uppsala högar?*; *idem*, *Ottar Vendelkråka och Ottarshögen i Vendel* (*Upplands Fornminnesförenings tidskrift*, VII); *idem*, *Ynglingasagan i arkeologisk belysning* (*Fornvännen*, 1917); *idem*, *The Foundation of the Swedish Kingdom* (*Saga Book of the Viking Society, Proceedings*, 1919–24, p. 113); Noreen, *Vårt språk* (§ 13, *Nysvenskans språkområde*); Gustav Andreen, *Det svenska språket i Amerika* (with map, reprinted by Noreen, *Vårt språk*, p. 92).

§ 276. Legendary Traditions.

In epic legends the Sviones play a considerable part, though almost all the traditions concerned are recorded by foreign nations, viz. Angles, Danes, Norwegians or Icelanders.

The eponymous Svethedus only appears in the English pedigree recording the 'sons of Boerinus' (cp. Kemble, *Translation of Beowulf*, Preface, viii). Otherwise the mythical representative of the Sviones is either the ubiquitous 'king Snow' (*Ynglinga Saga*, ch. 16), or a daughter of his kinsman 'Frost', the eponymous Skjalf, the spirit of the Skilfingar (*ibid.* ch. 22). The Danish genealogical myth (*Script. rer. Dan.* I, 223) introduces the eponymous Ypper of Uppsala as ancestor of all the Scandinavians, and his son Østen as ancestor of the Swedes; Østen is the Danish and Swedish form of the favourite Svionic name Eystein, but at the same time it may indicate the home of the tribe, as Dan. *østen* means 'east', O.N. *austan, austr.* In addition, various local eponymous figures occur among the early mythical kings of the Yngling dynasty: Vanlandi, symbolising the 'land of the Vanir'; Dag the Wise, probably the hero of the district of Daga; Yngvi, according to Noreen (*Namn och Bygd*, VIII, 1 seq.), a shortened form of Yngvin, 'Ing's friend', the chief worshipper of Ing, i.e. Freyr.

The most famous Svionic kings are those recorded in *Beowulf* and in the Skjǫldung legends, such as Ongenþéow, Óhthere, and Éadgils or Aðils (cp. § 275).

The Norwegian kings claimed to be descendants of the Ynglingar, and therefore Thjodolf of Hvin dedicated to them his poem *Ynglingatal*, a collection of short lives, the first of which seem to be mere reflections of sacrificial ceremonies.

Lit. **Schück**, ***Studier i Ynglingatal***, I–IV (*Upsala Univ. Årsskr.* 1905–10 and 1910); *idem*, *Studier i Beowulfsagan* (*ibid.* 1909); *idem*, *Illustrerad svensk litteraturhistoria*, 3rd ed. vol. I; **Stjerna**, *Essays on Beowulf*; Nerman, *Studier över Svärges hedna litteratur.*

G. §§ 277–281. *THE NORWEGIAN BRANCH*

§ 277. Names.

1. O.N. Norð(r)-menn; Norw. Nord-menn; Dan. Nord-mænd; O.E. Norð-men; Engl. Norse-men; M.Lat. North(o)-manni; O.Irish Nortmanar, Nor-manaig; Russ. Mur-man'. Eponymous hero: O.N. Nori (*Script. rer. Dan.* I, 223), Nor (*Flateyjarbók*, I, 24). Adjective: O.N.

norrœnn; Norw. norsk; Engl. Norse. Language: O.N. norrœna; Scotch Norn. Country: O.N. Norð-vegr, Nor-egr, Norð-manna-land; Norw. ('Landsmål') Noreg, Norig; Norw. ('Riksmål'), Swed., Dan. Norge; O.E. Norð-weg (Alfred's *Orosius*, p. 19); Scotch Norro-way; Germ. Norwegen; M.Lat. Nor-vegia, Nor-wagia, Nor-bagia, Nord-mannia; Finn. Norja. Place names: Engl. Nor-man-ton, Nor-man-by (West and North Riding, etc.). The name of the nation means 'North-men', inhabitants of the 'northern way'; cp. vol. I, § 80 on 'North-way', as an ancient Gothonic expression for the northern zone. On the use of North-men to mean Scandinavians see § 249.

Lit. **Feilberg,** s.v. *Nordmand, Norge*; **Noreen,** *Spridda studier*, II, 144; **Kock,** *Arkiv*, XXIV, 195; **Hellquist,** *Svensk etym. ordbok*, s.v. *Norge* and *Norsk*; **Söderwall,** *Ordbok öfver svenska medeltidsspråket*, s.v. *Nornisker*; **Leiv Heggstad,** *Fornorskningsordbok*, s.v. *Norge*; **Gustav Indrebö,** *Noreg, ein polemik*; *idem*, in *Den* 17. *Maj*, 9/2, 10/2, 12/2, 13/2, 1925; **Seip,** *Norge, om navnet på vort land*; *idem*, *Norge, svar til dosent Indrebö*; *idem*, in *Den* 17. *Maj*, 23/2, 25/2, 1925.

2. Engl. Norwegians; Germ. Norweger; Finn. Norjalaiset. Derived from the name of the country, Norway, Norwegen, Norja.

Lit. **Cannelin,** *Svenskt-finskt lexikon*, s.v. *Norrmänn.*

3. Dan. Norskere. Derived from the adjective *norsk* 'Norwegian'. The name is little used before the nineteenth century, for similar names, such as Danskere, Svenskere, Tyskere, always designate 'sovereign nations', and Norway was not recognised as a separate state before 1814.

Lit. **Feilberg,** s.v. *Norsk.*

4. Dan. Nor-bagger; Swed. Norr-baggar. Personal surname: O.Dan. Nor-bage (A.D. 1080). It is a nickname, mentioned as opprobrious A.D. 1257; nowadays, Dan. *norbagge* means 'a Norwegian horse'. The origin is probably Norw. Nord-bygger (Peder Claussön, translation of *Heimskringla*). *-bygge* 'dweller' has been confused with Swed. dial. *bagge* 'youth' or 'he-goat'; cp. the Danish nickname Stevns-bagger for Stevns-boer. Noreen, however, derives Norbagger from M.Lat. Norbagus for Nor-vagus; this form, indeed, may also have contributed to the genesis of the name.

Lit. **Falk and Torp,** *Etym. Ordbog*, s.v. *Nord*; **Noreen,** *Arkiv*, VI, 308; **Hellquist,** *Svensk etym. ordbok*, s.v. *Norr*; **Kalkar,** *Ordbog t. d. ældre danske Sprog*, s.v.; **Dahlerup,** *Ordb. ov. d. danske Sprog*, s.v.

5. Icelandic Aust-menn; M.Lat. (in Ireland) Oust-manni, Ost-manni. Personal name: M.E. Oust-man (coins, York); Engl. East-man. Place

name: Engl. Ox-man-town near Dublin and Waterford. The name means 'eastern men'. In Western Norway, Austmenn signifies Eastern Norwegians (cp. § 279). In Eastern Norway, it signifies the Swedes (cp. § 272, 4).

Lit. Fritzner, *Ordbog*, s.v.

5 *a*. Swed. Jutar, 'Jutes'. According to Rietz, *Svenskt dial. lex.* s.v. *Jute*, this name is used in the dialect of Helsingland. But we suppose that it includes also the Danes, being a survival from the times when Norway and Denmark were united.

6. O.Irish Hiruaith. Country: O.Irish Hirōt(h)a, Hiruaith; M.Irish Iorruaidhe, i.e. the tribe of Hǫrðar from Hordaland.

Lit. Zimmer, *Zeitschrift*, xxxv, 131; A. Bugge, *Skrifter udg. af Vidensk. Selsk. i Christiania, H.F. Kl.* 1900, No. 4 (printed 1901).

7. Lapp. Darolažak. A name of uncertain origin and of varying signification (cp. § 272, 7). The Swedish Lapps give this same name to the Swedes, and the Russian Lapps apply it to the Russians. It may perhaps also mean Scandinavians (cp. § 249, 8 and (etymology) § 272, 7).

Lit. Friis, *Ordbog ov. d. lapp. Sprog*, Pref. x–xi; Konrad Nielsen, *Det norske Sprog*.

8. O.Irish Lochlannaig; Irish Lochlannacha. Country: O.Irish Lothlinn, Lathlinn (*Ulster Ann.*, *S. Gallen MS*); Irish Lochlann. This name also signifies Gothonic nations and Scandinavians (cp. vol. I, § 14 and § 249, 10).

Lit. A. Bugge, *l.c.*; Marstrander, *ibid.* 1915, No. 5, 56.

9. O.Irish Finn-lochlannaig, 'fair Scandinavians', contrasting with Dub-lochlannaig, 'dark Scandinavians', i.e. Danes (cp. § 256, 8).

Lit. Marstrander, *l.c.* p. 5.

10. O.Irish Find-gaill (*Ulster Ann.* ad an. 850), 'fair foreigners', contrasting with Dub-gaill, 'dark foreigners', i.e. Danes. Personal name: Irish Fingal (cp. § 256, 9).

Lit. Zimmer, *Zeitschrift*, xxxv, 97; Marstrander, *l.c.* p. 7.

11. O.Irish Find-genti (*Book of Leinster*), 'fair gentiles', contrasting with Dub-genti, 'dark gentiles', i.e. Danes (cp. § 256, 10).

Lit. Zimmer, *l.c.* 97, 131; A. Bugge, *l.c.* p. 9.

§ 278. Sub-divisions.

Hrodulf, a Norwegian king in the sixth century A.D., cited by Jordanes, III, 23, enumerates the following tribes west of the Gauts and Sviones: 'Raumaricii, Ragnaricii,...*Vingvilor (Vinoviloth),...Grannii, Aganziae (Augandzi), Eunixi,...Thel(æ?), (H)arothi, *Raumi (Rani, Rannii). Quibus non ante multos annos Roduulf rex fuit, qui contempto proprio regno ad Theoderici Gothorum regis gremio convolavit'. Perhaps we ought also to add Adogit in the land of the midnight sun, i.e. *Halogii?

Haukr Erlandsson, a Norwegian 'lawman' (d. 1334), gives an almost complete list of the Norwegian provinces or 'fylki' (*Hauksbók, suppl.* VIII):

'Filke i Norege'. (1) Haleigia filke. (2) Naumdæla f. (3) j þrandheime Eyna f. (4) Sparbijggia f. (5) Stiordæla f. (6) Skauna f. (7) Verdæla f. (8) Strinda f. (9) Gauldæla f. (10) Orkdæla f. (11) Nordmœra f. (12) Sunnmœra f. (13) Firda f. (14) Fiala f. (15) Signa f. (16) Horda f. (17) Rygia f. (18) Egda f. (19) Austur Egdir. (20) Vestfold. (21) Vingulmørk. (22) Ranrijke. (23) Rauma ryke. (24) Heidmørk. (25) Hadaland. (26) Ringaryke. (27) Gudbrandzdalir.

An almost identical list is given by Hauk's Icelandic secretary in *MS Arnemagn.* No. 415, 40, after a series of annalistic notes which end with the year 1313. According to Storm, the original must have been written before 1164. Another version is given by the Icelander Ari Einarsson, *hirðmaðr* under King Eystein (1103–1123); it is quoted by the Norwegian author Peder Claussön in *Norges Beskrivelse*, 16. Here the provinces Fiala f., Hadaland, and Austur Egdir are eliminated, whereas Ravmdæla fylki is added (cp. G. Storm, (Norw.) *Hist. Tidsskrift*, IV, 478, and Finnur Jónsson's ed. of *Hauksbók*, CXXXV).

It seems as if the ancient region of Vǫrs has sometimes been regarded as a *fylki* (cp. A. Bugge, *Norges Hist.* I, 234). On the other hand, the eight *fylki* of the Tröndelag are less than the normal size of such districts; they rather correspond in size to a 'herred' (cp. Bugge, *ibid.* 233, and P. A. Munch, *Det norske Folks Hist.* I, 99).

Various ancient tribes, e.g. the Thel(ae?) in Hrodulf's sixth-century list, do not rank as *fylki* in the oldest known division of the country. The status of such regions may have varied.

The *fylki* are united into larger juridical associations, which may be called *þinglǫg*; their names are compounded with the element *-þing*, 'law-court'. They are enumerated in the *Historia Norvegiae* (*Mon. hist. Norvegiae*, p. 76 seq.):

'Zona...maritima.... .x. ciuitatibus inclita est .iiij. patrias complectens .xxx. prouinciarum capaces. Prima patria Sinus Orientalis dicitur, a terminis Dacie oriens et usque ad locum qui Rygiarbit appellatur extendit .iiij. prouincias continens. Secunda Gulacia ad jnsulas que Media nuncupatur usque protelatur .vj. implectens prouincias. quarum vltima...Mor...Tercia patria Trondemia...et est sinus octo capiens prouincias in sua latissima receptacula .iii. etenim sinuens et fiunt .xi. Quarta Halogia....'

'De montanis Norwegie. Mediterranea zona...iiij patrias et xij prouincias complectens...Huius prima patria regnum Raumorum et Ringorum cum continuis prouinciis. Secunda Thelemarchia cum remotis ruribus. Tertia Heidmarchia cum conualibus Albie. Quarta Valles Gudbrandi cum Loariis...Sunt preterea perplures jncolatus jnter maritima et montana. vt Waldresia et Vallis Haddingorum ac ceteri qui Gulaticis subiacent legibus....'

This classification, however, is somewhat misleading, for the 'patria' in list 1 is a chief *þing*, but in list 2 only a subordinate one. In reality there were four chief associations, and each of them originally seems to have comprised three *fylki* (cp. the three Svionic 'folklands': Tiundaland, Attundaland, Fiæþrundaland).

The more exact distribution would be as follows:

1. Heiðsævisþing (Upplǫnd), comprising Heinafylki, Raumaríki, Haðaland. Corresponding to the 'prima patria montana' in *Hist. Norv.*

2. Borgarþing (Vík), comprising Ranríki, Vingulmǫrk, Vestfold. Corresponding to the 'Sinus orientalis' of the 'zona maritima' in *H.N.* (cp. the *Kristnurétt* of Borgarþing, ch. 4, where the three *fylki* are mentioned).

3. Gulaþing, comprising Sygnafylki, Hǫrðafylki, Firðafylki. Corresponding to 'Gulacia' of the 'zona maritima' in *H.N.* ('Mor', *ibid.* is the region of Mœri) (cp. *Egils Saga*, LVI, 42).

4. Frostuþing corresponds to 'Trondemia' (Þrándheimr) of the 'zona maritima' in *H.N.* The dimensions are not quite certain. Einarr Skálaglam in *Vellekla* mentions a levy of troops from 'four folklands' in earl Hakon's army, and Snorri in *Heimskringla*, II, 285, interprets the folklands as Þrœndalǫg, Naumudalr, Raumsdalr, and Hálogaland. It

must be noticed that Hálogaland used the laws of the Þrœndalǫg, but did not belong to its juridical association.

The relations of Hálogaland to the Frostuþing may perhaps be compared to that of a 'territory' beside the 'states' of the United States of America. Similar borderlands of the Þrœndalǫg were the Herdalr and Jamtland east of the mountain of Kölen (cp. *Heimskringla*, I, 183). We may also regard the inhabitants of the Northern Swedish provinces of Helsingland, Medelpad, and Ångermanland as partly originating from the same root. Similar borderlands accompany the other chief groups of states in Norway. Thus Heiðsævisþing later comprises Guðbrandsdalir and Þelamǫrk; Borgarþing comprises Grenafylki and Vestmarr, and Gulaþing Sunnmœri, Rygjafylki, and Egðafylki (cp. the older Gulaþingslǫg, ch. 3).

The *linguistic division* of Norway is threefold.

A. East Norwegian, comprising Heiðsævisþing, Borgarþing, Frostuþing, Herdalr, Jamtland, and some other regions in the present Northern Sweden.

B. North Norwegian, intermediate between A and C, comprising Hálogaland and the extreme northern regions.

C. West Norwegian, comprising Gulaþing, the Faroe Islands, Shetland, the Orkneys, Iceland, and Greenland.

Lundell is inclined to regard A and B as one, but Ross regards B as pronouncedly West Norwegian, and as most of the inhabitants of the extreme northern regions seem to be colonists from Western Norway, this scheme has been accepted in the present work. Cp. the arguments set forth under the heading 'Ethnic Position', § 279.

Lit.[1] P. A. Munch, *Det norske Folks Hist.* I, 98; A. Bugge, *Norges Hist.* I, 2, ch. iii–viii; Noreen, *Grundriss*, 3rd ed. IV, § 14; Lundell, *ibid.* 2nd ed. I, 1484; Seip, *Norsk sproghistorie*, 13 and 42; *idem*, *Østlandsk formlære*; Amund Larsen, *De norske bygdemål*; Hans Ross, *Norske Bygdemaal*, esp. ch. i (*Norske Vidensk. Selsk. Skr. H.F. Kl.* 1905, No. 2); Hægstad, *Gamalt trøndermaal* (*ibid.* 1899, No. 3, 9); *idem*, *Vestnorske maalföre fyre* 1350 (*ibid.* 1905, No. 7, 1907, No. 1, 1914, No. 5, 1915, No. 3, 1916, No. 4); *idem*, *Det norske maalet fyre* 1350 (Hægstad and Torp, *Gamalnorsk Ordbok*, pp. ix–xxvii).

The following synopsis enumerates the tribes within the separate juridical associations. For the sake of convenience the literature con-

[1] The literature is chiefly supplied by Docent Gust. Indrebö.

cerning the tribal history is also given here, as the space does not allow this history to be recorded separately.

A. Heiðsævisþing, comprising Nos. 1–6.

B. Borgarþing, comprising Nos. 7–10.

C. Frostuþing, comprising Nos. 11–15.

D. Gulaþing comprising Nos. 16–22 (23–28).

A. Heiðsævisþing. Nos. 1–6.

1. O.N. Heinir (Sighvatr, *Hskr.* II, 77); Norw. Heidmarkingar; O.E. Hæðnas (*Widsith*, l. 81); Gr. Χαιδεινοί (Ptolemy, second century A.D.). Adj.: O.N. heiðskr, heinverskr. *fylki*: O.N. Heiðr (? Hornklofi, *Glymdrápa*, str. 2), Heinafylki, Heið-mǫrk; Norw. Heid-mark, Hed-mark, Hede-marken. Temple: O.N. Hein-hof; Norw. Henu. Juridical association: O.N. Heið-sævis-þing. The Heinir are the 'people of the heath'. We do not agree with Svensson who denies that the ancient Chaideinoi are Norwegians and removes them to some unnamed heath of Eastern Sweden (cp. § 279, introduction). Wadstein proposes to identify them with the Finn-(h)aithae of Jordanes.

Lit. Zeuss, 158; N. M. Petersen, *Regesta geogr.* s.v.; Much in *Beiträge*, XVII, 188; A. Bugge, *Norges Hist.* I, 2, 50; Schönfeld, s.v. *Chaidini*; Chambers, *Widsith*, 214; Schütte, (Norw.) *Hist. Tidsskr.* 1917, 19; *idem*, *Maal og Minne*, 1918, 116; Refsum, *ibid.* 1925, 54; Svensson, *Namn och Bygd*, 1919, 8 and 11; Noreen, *Fornvännen*, 1920, 37; Wadstein in *Minnesskrift utg. av Filol. Samfundet i Göteborg*, 1925, 195; Karsten, *Die Germanen*, 227. History: Helland, *Norges Land*, IV, 1, 808.

2. O.N. Raumar (Þjóðolfr, *Hskr.* III, 183); Norw. Rome-rikingar, Rome-rik-væringar; O.E. *Réamas (with poetical prefix Heaþo-Réamas, *Widsith*, l. 63, *Beowulf*, l. 519); M.Lat. Rauma-riciae (Jordanes, sixth century). Adj.: O.N. raumskr. *fylki*: O.N. Rauma-fylki, Rauma-ríki; Norw. Rome-rike. The Raumar are probably the 'people on the river Raum-elfr'. *Raumr is the same as *straumr* 'stream' (cp. Rauma, the river of the Raums-dalr). Finnur Jónsson maintains that Raum-elfr is derived from the name of the tribe, but I cannot admit that he is right. The name Raums-dalr in Northern Norway obviously is not derived from that of a tribe, but from that of a river, *Raumr, alias Rauma, and, when once exemplified here, it must necessarily be the same river name that appears in Raum-elfr. The addition of *elfr* 'river' does not affect

the argument, as the development from Simplex to Compound is a most frequent one.

Lit. N. M. Petersen, *Regesta geogr.* s.v.; S. Bugge, *Beiträge*, XII, 55; Müllenhoff, *Zeitschrift*, XI, 282; *idem*, *Beovulf*, 89; O. Rygh, *Norske Elvnavne*, 186; A. Bugge, *Norges Hist.* I, 2, 50; Schönfeld, s.v. *Raumariciae*; Chambers, *Widsith*, 210; Schütte, (Norw.) *Hist. Tidsskr.* 1917, 13; *idem*, *Maal og Minne*, 1918, 117; *idem*, *Zeitschrift*, LXVII, 129 seq. (on Heaþoréamas); Grienberger, *ibid.* XLVI, 16; Lindquist, *Beiträge*, XLIII, 103; Langenfelt, *Toponymics in English*, 103; Finnur Jónsson, *Danske Studier*, 1921, 41; Refsum, *Maal og Minne*, 1925, 52. History: Vibe, *Norges Land*, II, 60.

3. O.N. Haðar (Snorri, *Hskr.* I, 91; Haða berserkr); Norw. Hadelendingar. Eponymous figure: O.N. Hǫðr (*Frá Fornjóte*, 5). *fylki*: O.N. Haða-fylki, Haða-land; Norw. Hade-land. The root is probably a place name (cp. the island of Hǫð in Sunnmœri).

Lit. N. M. Petersen, *Regesta geogr.* s.v.; A. Bugge, *Norges Hist.* I, 2, 51; Schütte, *Maal og Minne*, 1918, 116. History: Helland, *Norges Land*, V, 2, 567.

4. O.N. Hringar (Sighvatr, *Hskr.* II, 464); Norw. Ringe-rikingar. *fylki*: O.N. Hringa-ríki; Norw. Ringe-rike. The name is derived from the word 'ring', but it is not easy to say what it means in this case. (H)ringis-akr in Heiðmǫrk may perhaps indicate an eponymous figure *Hringir who has been worshipped as a protective spirit (cp. Magnus Olsen, *Hedenske Kultminder*, 214 seq.).

Lit. N. M. Petersen, *Regesta geogr.* s.v.; A. Bugge, *Norges Hist.* I, 2, 51; Schütte, *Maal og Minne*, 1918, 116; Refsum, *ibid.* 1925, 53.

5. O.N. Dœlir (Snorri, *Hskr.* II, 327); Norw. Gudbrands-döler (incorrectly written Guldbrandsdöler). Adj.: O.N. dœlskr. Region: O.N. Dalir; Norw. Gudbrands-dalen. Dœlir is formed by gradation ('Ablaut') and means 'people of the dale (valley)'; the name is also applied to the inhabitants of Österdalen (Snorri, *Hskr.* II, 385).

Lit. N. M. Petersen, *Regesta geogr.* s.v.; Finnur Jónsson, *Aarbøger*, 1907, 177; Schütte, (Norw.) *Hist. Tidsskrift*, 1917, 15 and 28; *idem*, *Maal og Minne*, 1918, 115.

6. O.N. Þilir (Snorri, *Hskr.* I, 122); Norw. Teler, Tela-merk(j)ingar, Tele-bönder, Tele-döler; M.Lat. *Thelae? (*MSS* aetel, ethel, etc., Jordanes, sixth century). Region: O.N. Þela-mǫrk; Norw. Tele-mark, Tele-marki, Tele-marken. Probably derived from O.N. *þel* 'bottom'.

Lit. N. M. Petersen, *Regesta geogr.* s.v.; Aasen, s.v. *Telebonde*; P. A. Munch, *Det norske Folks Hist.* I, 100; Schönfeld, s.v. *Taetel* (with lit.); Schütte, *Maal og Minne*, 1918, 118; Svensson, *Namn och Bygd*, 1919, 142. History: Helland, *Norges Land*, VIII, 1, 566, 572.

B. Borgarþing. Nos. 7–10.

7. O.N. Renir (Einarr Skúlason, *Hskr.* III, 375); M.Lat. Ragna-ricii (Jordanes, sixth century). *fylki*: O.N. Ran-ríki. Obscure. According to Finnur Jónsson, the metre requires a short vowel. Comparison with the majority of Norwegian tribe names favours the assumption that it is a toponymic.

Lit. N. M. Petersen, *Regesta geogr.* s.v.; Schönfeld, s.v. *Ragnaricii* (with lit.); Schütte, (Norw.) *Hist. Tidsskr.* 1917, 5 and 14; *idem*, *Maal og Minne*, 1918, 117; Svensson, *l.c.* 134; Noreen, *Fornvännen*, 1920, 44; Finnur Jónsson, *Danske Studier*, 1921, 41.

8. Archaic N. *Vingvilōʀ? (Vinoviloth, Jordanes, sixth century). Region: O.N. Vingul-mǫrk. The only phonetic assonance seems to be O.N. *vingull* 'genital member of a horse'.

Lit. Schönfeld, s.v. *Vinoviloth* (with lit.); Svensson, *l.c.* 135.

9. O.N. *Fyldir (Vest(r)-fyldir, *Sverris Saga*, 396, 403, etc.), Foldungar (*ibid.* 399), Fjǫllungar (*ibid.* 399); Norw. Földingar; M.Lat. Westfaldingi (*Ann. Engolism.* and *Chron. Aquitan.* ad an. 813). *fylki*: O.N. Vestfold; O.Germ. Westarfolda (Einhard, *Ann.* ad an. 813). The tribal name is derived from Fold, the name of fjords in Eastern and Northern Norway.

Lit. N. M. Petersen, *Regesta geogr.* s.v. *Vestfyldir*; Aasen, s.v. *Vestfoldinger*; Ross, *Ordbog*, *ibid.*; A. Bugge, *Norges Hist.* I, 2, 52. History: Helland, *Norges Land*, VII, 1, 17.

10. O.N. Grenir, Gren-lendingar; M.Lat. Grannii (Jordanes, sixth century). *fylki*: O.N. Grena-fylki, Gren-land, Gren-mǫrk; fjord: O.N. Gren-marr. The tribal name probably originates from the name of the fjord.

Lit. N. M. Petersen, *Regesta geogr.* s.v. *Grenmǫrk* and *Grenland*; Finnur Jónsson, *Aarbøger*, 1907, 176; Schönfeld, s.v. *Grannii* (with lit.); Schütte, *Maal og Minne*, 1918, 116; Svensson, *l.c.* 140; Noreen, *l.c.* 45.

C. Frostuþing. Nos. 11–15.

11. O.N. Þrœndr (Þorfinnr Munnr, *Hskr.* II, 461), Þrœndir (Snorri, *ibid.* I, 148); Norw. Trönder, Trond-heims-folk, Trond-heims-menn; O.E. Þrówendas (*Widsith*, l. 64). Adj.: O.N. Þrœndskr. Juridical association: O.N. Þránd-heimr, Þrœnda-lǫg; Norw. Trönde-lag. Name of chief town: Germ. Dront-heim. The tribal name is probably derived from a territorial

name *þrōwand-, 'thriving', formed like Dan. and Norw. Borgund, Dan. Selund, Swed. Värend. The consonantal inflection is a sign of age (cp. vol. I, § 79).

Lit. N. M. Petersen, *Regesta geogr.* s.v.; Finnur Jónsson, *Aarbøger*, 1907, 177; A. Bugge, *Norges Hist.* I, 2, 22; Chambers, *Widsith*, 210; Schütte, *Maal og Minne*, 1918, 118. History: Helland, *Norges Land*, XVII, 1, 857, 885.

11*a*. O.N. Skeynir (*Saga Ól. Helga*, ch. 104). Diminutive '*fylki*': O.N. Skaun or Skeyna-fylki; Norw. Skogn, belonging to the region of the Ind-trönder. The Skeynir are the people of the region 'Beautiful'; the same toponymic occurs in the district of Rakkestad (cp. *Norske Gaardnavne*, I, 130). On the typical East Norwegian element Skaun see vol. I, § 79, p. 169, and § 254.

Lit. N. M. Petersen, *Regesta geogr.* s.v.; Schütte, *Maal og Minne*, 1918, 115.

11*b*. O.N. Eynir (*Saga Ól. Helga*, ch. 104). Diminutive '*fylki*': O.N. Eyjin iðri or Eyna-fylki; Norw. Inder-öy; belonging to the region of the Ind-trönder. The Eynir are the 'insular people'; the toponymic reappears on Lake Öjeren and on the Gautic island of Öland (cp. *Norske Gaardnavne*, I, 51).

11*c*. O.N. *Strindir; Norw. Strindingar. Diminutive '*fylki*': O.N. Strind or Strinda-fylki; Norw. Strinden; belonging to the region of the Ut-trönder. The Strindir are the 'people of the edge'.

Lit. N. M. Petersen, *Regesta geogr.* s.v. *Strind*; Schütte, *Maal og Minne*, 1918, 118.

11*d*. O.N. *Stjórar, genit. *Strjóna?, Stjór-dœlir; Norw. Stjör-döler, Stjör-dölingar. *fylki*: O.N. Stjóra-fylki, Strjóna-fylki (*Saga Ól. Helga*, ch. 43), Stjór-dœla-fylki; Norw. Stjör-dalen; belonging to the region of the Ut-trönder. The *Stjórar are the 'people on the river *Stjór'.[1]

Lit. N. M. Petersen, *Regesta geogr.* s.v. *Stjórdœlir*; O. Rygh, *Norske Elvnavne*, 247; Schütte, *Maal og Minne*, 1918, 117; Refsum, *ibid.* 1925, 57.

12. O.N. *Raumar, Raum(s)-dœlir (Snorri, *Hskr.* I, 186); Norw. Roms-dölingar. Personal surname: O.N. Raumr. *fylki*: O.N. Raum(s)-dœla-fylki; Norw. Roms-dal. Obviously derived from the river *Raumr, now Rauma, 'stream' (cp. No. 2).

[1] Gothon. *Steur-, the same name as the Holsteinic and Anglo-Saxon Stūr, but with a different gradation ('Ablaut') of the vowel.

Lit. N. M. Petersen, *Regesta geogr.* s.v. *Raumsdœlir*; O. Rygh, *Norske Elvnavne*, 186; Finnur Jónsson, *Aarbøger*, 1907, 343; Schütte, *Maal og Minne*, 1918, 117. History: Helland, *Norges Land*, xv, 1, 36, 1220, 1256.

13. O.N. Mœrir (Snorri, *Hskr.* I, 186); Norw. Mör (sing.), Möra (fem. sing.), Möringar (pl.). Adj.: O.N. mœrskr. *fylki*: O.N. Mœri, Mœra-fylki, *Mœr (Mor, *Hist. Norvegiae*); Norw. Möre. Sanctuary: O.N. Mærina helg (*Landnámabók*, IV, ch. 6). The Mœrir are the 'borderland people'.

Lit. N. M. Petersen, *Regesta geogr.* s.v.; Aasen, s.v. *Mør*; Finnur Jónsson, *Aarbøger*, 1907, 176; Schütte, *Maal og Minne*, 1918, 117; Refsum, *ibid.* 1925, 56.

14. O.N. Jamtr (Snorri, *Hskr.* I, 184, II, 310), Jamtar (*ibid.* sing. Jamti, II, 309); Norw. Jamtar, Jamt-lendingar; Swed. Jämtar, Jämt-länningar. Region: O.N. Jamta-land; Norw. Jamt-land, Jemt-land; Swed. Jämt-land. Obscure. The consonantal inflection is a sign of age (cp. vol. I, § 79). The termination in *-t* seems to be unparalleled among Gothonic tribal names; the Rhenish Usipetes and the Nicretes on the Neckar are rather Gaulish than Gothonic types, but it occurs in Norwegian geographical names such as Kǫrmt, now Karmöen.

Lit. N. M. Petersen, *Regesta geogr.* s.v.; Aasen, s.v. *Jamt*; Finnur Jónsson, *Aarbøger*, 1907, 173; Schütte, *Maal og Minne*, 1918, 118.

15. O.N. Há-leygir (Eyvindr Skaldaspillir, *Hskr.* I, 212), Hǫ-lgar (Hornklofi, *ibid.* I, 127); Norw. Helge-lendingar; M.Lat. *(H)a-logii? (Adogit, Jordanes, sixth century). Adj.: O.N. há-leygskr. Eponymous hero: O.N. Hǫlgi (Snorri's *Edda*, I, 400). Goddess: O.N. Hǫlga-brúðr (*ibid.* I, 400, 552, II, 432, 471, 554; cp. Storm, *Arkiv*, II, 124). Region: O.N. Há-loga-land; Norw. Helge-land. The origin is uncertain. Perhaps -Leygir is a gradation ('Ablaut') of the classical East Gothonic tribe name Lugi. A connexion with O.N. *Lœir in Lom, 'the people of the woods', is also possible. The prefix is O.N. *hár* 'high'; the Compound, corresponding to Lango-bards as compared with Bards, is almost unparalleled among Scandinavian tribal names.

Lit. N. M. Petersen, *Regesta geogr.* s.v.; Finnur Jónsson, *Aarbøger*, 1907, 176; Halvdan Koht, *Om Haalogaland*, (Norw.) *Hist. Tidsskrift*, IV R., 6 Bd.; Schönfeld, s.v. *Adogit*; Schütte, *Maal og Minne*, 1918, 116; Svensson, *Namn och Bygd*, 1919, 145; Noreen, *Fornvännen*, 1920, 46. History: Helland, *Norges Land*, XVIII, 1, 32, 778, 800.

D. Gulaþing. Nos. 16–22 (23–28).

16. O.N. Sygnir (Sighvatr, *Hskr.* III, 30); Norw. Sygner, Sogningar. Adj.: O.N. sygnskr. *fylki*: O.N. Sogn, Sygna-fylki. Place name: Norw. Sogndal (with toponymic Sogn-dölingar). The tribal name originates from the name of the fjord of Sogn.

Lit. **N. M. Petersen,** *Regesta geogr.* s.v.; **Aasen,** s.v. *Sygna*; **Finnur Jónsson,** *Aarbøger*, 1907, 176; **Schütte,** *Maal og Minne*, 1918, 118. **History: Helland,** *Norges Land*, XIV, 1, 22, 774, 786.

17. O.N. Firðir (Snorri, *Hskr.* I, 369), Fjarðar-búar; Norw. Fjorde-folk, Fjorde-menn; sub-divisions Nord-fjordingar (from Nordfjord), Sunn-fjordingar (from Sunnfjord Fogderi), Fyrds-fjordingar (from the parish of Fyrde). Aasen has a Norw. form Fyr (sing.), with fem. Fyrdska, but Gustav Indrebö, who is a native of the region, denies that such forms are actually used. Adj.: O.N. firzkr. *fylki*: O.N. Firðir, Firða-fylki. The Firðir are the 'people of the fjords' (i.e. of Nordfjord, Dalefjord, Fyrdefjord).

Lit. **N. M. Petersen,** *Regesta geogr.* s.v.; **Schütte,** *Maal og Minne*, 1918, 115.

18. O.N. Filir, Fjalir. *fylki*: O.N. Fjalir, Fjala-fylki. The Filir are the 'people of the boards'.

Lit. **N. M. Petersen,** *Regesta geogr.* s.v.; **Schütte,** *Maal og Minne*, 1918, 115.

19. O.N. Hǫrðar (Hornklofi, *Hskr.* I, 127), Harð-eng(r)ir; Norw. Hor (sing.), Hordingar, Haringar, most frequently Hardingar; O.E. Hæreðas (*Widsith*, l. 81); M.Lat. *(H)arothi (Jordanes, sixth century); O.Irish Hiruaith. Adj.: O.N. hǫrzkr. Eponymous figure: O.N. Hǫrðr (inscription of Rök, cp. *Frá Fornjóti*, 5). *fylki*: O.N. Hǫrða-fylki, Hǫrða-fold, Hǫrða-land; Norw. Horda-land, in Compounds Hord-land; O.E. Hæreða-land (*Sax. Chron.* ad an. 787). The tribal name reappears in Jutland as Harudes, in North Germany as Harudi. Yet it is not justifiable to regard the one tribe as a colony of the other: the toponymic Harudes might arise anywhere from a territorial name *Haruð 'wood', like the toponymic Eynir from Ey 'island', and Skeynir from Skaun 'the beautiful region' (cp. Nos. 11 *a* and *b*).

Lit. **N. M. Petersen,** *Regesta geogr.* s.v.; **Aasen,** s.v. *Hord*; **Finnur Jónsson,** *Aarbøger*, 1907, 176; **Schönfeld,** s.v. *Harothi* (with lit.); **Chambers,** *Widsith*, 214; **Much in Hoops,** III, 344; **Schütte,** *Maal og Minne*, 1918, 116; **Refsum,** *ibid.* 1925, 56; **Wadstein,** *Die nord. Völkernamen bei Ptolemaios* (*Minnesskr. utg. av Filol. Samf. i Göteborg*, 1925). **History: Kiær,** *Norges Land*, XII, 65.

20. O.N. Vǫrsar (Bjǫrn hinn krepphendi, *Hskr.* III, 237), Versir; Norw. Vesse, Vossingar. Adj.: O.N. vǫrskr. *fylki* or subordinate district: O.N. Vǫrsa-fylki, Vǫrsa-veldi; Norw. Voss. The tribal name is the toponymic of an obscure territorial name. The ending *-us* is an archaic form—a sign of great antiquity.

Lit. **N. M. Petersen,** ***Regesta geogr.*** **s.v.; Aasen, s.v.** ***Voss*****; Finnur Jónsson,** ***Aarbøger*****, 1907, 177; Schütte,** ***Maal og Minne*****, 1918, 118.**

21. O.N. Rygir (Snorri, *Hskr.* I, 122; poet. Holm-rygir, Hornklofi, *ibid.* I, 127; Eyvindr Skaldaspillir, *ibid.* I, 212); M.Lat. Rugi (Jordanes, sixth century). Adj.: O.N. rygskr. Eponymous figure: O.N. Rug-alfr (inscription of Rök, cp. *Frá Fornjóti*, 5). *fylki*: O.N. Rygja-fylki, Rogaland; Norw. Ry-fylke (cp. Finn. Ruija, a name for Southern Norway). The tribal name reappears as Rugi, south of the Baltic. It probably originates from a territorial name *Rygr 'stone'. The headland of Rýgjar-bit between Agder and Grenland has been conceived as an ancient landmark of the Rygir (cp. Helland, *Den rygske folkestamme* in *Norges Land*, VIII, 1, 591, and Skulerud, *Telemaalet*, 73); but according to Gustav Indrebö the suggestion is not justified. The poetical form Holm-rygir is a copy from (H)ulme-rugi, belonging to the East Gothonic Rugi south of the Baltic (cp. our article in *Zeitschrift*, LXVII, 132).

Lit. **N. M. Petersen,** ***Regesta geogr.*** **s.v.; Finnur Jónsson,** ***Aarbøger*****, 1907, 176; Schönfeld, s.v.** ***Rugi*** **(with lit.); Much in Hoops, III, 344; Schütte,** ***Maal og Minne*****, 1918, 117; Gust. Indrebö,** ***Rýgjarbit*** **(*****Namn och Bygd*****, 1932, 147). History: Kiær,** ***Norges Land*****, XI, 85; Gust. Indrebö,** ***Kor gamall er grense millom Agder og Rogaland?*** **(*****Maal og Minne*****, 1925, 5).**

22. O.N. Egðir (Snorri, *Hskr.* I, 122; Þorðr Sjáreksson, *ibid.* II, 366); Norw. Egder, Flog-egder; M.Lat. *Agadii (Aganzi, Augan(d)zi, Jordanes, sixth century). Adj.: O.N. egðskr. *fylki*: O.N. Agðir, Egða-fylki, Agðasýsla; Norw. Agder. The tribal name is a toponymic of a territorial name probably meaning 'projecting shore'. If Müllenhoff, II, 395, is right in reading the Lat. form as *Agadii, the ending would be unparalleled among Gothonic tribal names.

Lit. **N. M. Petersen,** ***Regesta geogr.*** **s.v.; Aasen, s.v.** ***Egder*****; Ross, s.v.** ***Egd*****; Finnur Jónsson,** ***Aarbøger*****, 1907, 175; Schönfeld, s.v.** ***Augandzi*** **(with lit.); Schütte,** ***Maal og Minne*****, 1918, 115; Svensson,** ***Namn och Bygd*****, 1919, 141; Noreen,** ***Fornvännen*****, 1920, 45. History: Helland,** ***Norges Land*****, IX, 1, 16, 716, 722, X, 1, 592; Indrebö (cited under 21).**

Colonists beyond the seas, chiefly from the Gulaþingslǫg, are:

23. O.N. Fær-eyingar on the Faroe Islands.

24. Hjaltar (*Sverris Saga*, ch. 119), Hjalt-lendingar, on the Shetlands, now Anglicised.

25. Ǫrkn-eyingar on the Orkneys, now Anglicised.

26. Írar, 'Irishmen', e.g. in the Yorkshire place names Irton and Irby (cp. A. H. Smith, *Saga Book of the Viking Society, Proceedings*, 1925–27, p. 207); now Anglicised.

27. Ís-lendingar in Iceland.

28. Grœn-lendingar in Greenland, now absorbed by the Esquimaux.

Apart from the tribal names mentioned above there exist numerous characteristic toponymics, e.g. *Borgyndir in Borgund (Sogn), *Dyfrir in Dovre, *Engrir in Engra skipreiða, Eynir on Lake Öjeren, Danglingar on the fjord of Eidanger, Haddingjar in Hallingdal, Læsir in Lesje, *Lœir in Lom, *Nœrir in Norane, *Ryrnir in Ryrjar, Skeynir in Skaun (Rakkestad Herred), Solongi (Saxo, 242) in Sóleyjar, *Syrir in Surendal, *Þrymir in Þruma, *Valdresir in Valdres, *Víkir in Vik (Hardanger), *Yrnir in Yrjar. Norway abounds more in such forms than any other Gothonic country; her inaccessible valleys have become treasure-houses of archaic forms which have in other countries been abolished. But I must refer the reader to the collections made by me in *Maal og Minne*, 1918, and by Refsum, *ibid.* 1925.

Survey of the types of tribal names.

It appears from the above list that the large majority of provincial tribes have names of the Simplex type.

Later development normally tends to replace the short Simplexes by longer words, chiefly ending in *-ing*: Sygnir > Sogningar, Strindir > Strindingar, Versir > Vossingar.

There is only one single example of a Compound among the old tribal names: Há-leygir. In the sixth century A.D. some secondary Compounds crop up: Raumar becomes Rauma-riciae (now Rome-rik-ingar), Renir becomes Ragna-ricii. So also Hringar > Ringe-rik-ingar, Firðir > Fjardar-búar, Fjorde-folk, Fjorde-menn, Hǫrðar > Harð-engrir, Egðir > Flog-egder, Dœlir > Gudbrandsdöler, Þilir > Tele-merk-ingar, Tele-bönder, Tele-döler, Þrœndr > Trond-heims-folk, Trond-heims-menn, *Stjórar > Stjór-dœlir, Stjör-döl-ingar, Háleygir > He-lge-lendingar. The poetical name Holm-rygir stands apart, as it is copied from an East Gothonic name from south of the Baltic.

The Compound ending in *-verjar* 'men' (of West German origin) is not exemplified among the Norwegian tribal names enumerated by Hrodulf (Jordanes) in the sixth century. In the Viking Age there appears one example, O.N. Vík-verjar, 'men of the Vík (gulf)'; this includes some South Norwegian tribes, viz. Renir, Grenir, Fyldir, etc. The type has probably been introduced owing to mercantile intercourse with Denmark. In Snorri's *Heimskringla*, where Vík-verjar occurs frequently, there are only two additional examples from Norway, viz. *Hein-verjar and *Hvin-verjar (adj. hein-verskr and hvin-verskr). But after Snorri's time this element becomes extraordinarily frequent, and is moreover enlarged into *-væringar*. Names of this type in modern times abound throughout Norway and Iceland, and the same elements are often used to enlarge older forms. Thus for instance we get a development in four stages: Raumar > Rauma-riciae > Rome-rik-ingar > Rome-rik-vær-ingar (cp. our list of such secondary toponymics in *Maal og Minne*, 1918, 118, and Laugenfelt, *Toponymics in English*, 13 seq. (Icelandic examples)).

§ 279. Ethnic Position.

Ptolemy's Chaideinoi, II, 11, § 16, represent the western tribes of Scandia, in a position equivalent to that of the Goutai, i.e. Gauts. (The MS Vatic. 191 from a probably post-Ptolemaic source adds the Finns, another name of high ethnic rank.) There can be no doubt that Ptolemy's source contained exclusively or chiefly nations of a rank equal to that of the Gauts, and we must reject Svensson's sugggestion, *Namn och Bygd*, 1919, 8 and 11, that these Chaideinoi in *Western* Scandia are to be taken as the otherwise unknown inhabitants of some unnamed 'heath' in *Eastern* Sweden. Wadstein's identification of Chaideinoi and Finn-(h)aithae (*Minnesskrift utg. av Filol. Samfundet i Göteborg*, 1925, 195) is more plausible. The Finnhaithae are situated on the *western* side of Southern Scandinavia, and Jordanes mentions them as a tribe. But the phonetic identity of Chaideinoi and O.N. Heinir is a fact which it is difficult to account for unless the two names refer to the same people, and it is usually regarded as conclusive. And we also believe that the 'Heath' of the Heinir is more important than Wadstein admits. It is true the importance of this region is almost too much emphasised by Ptolemy, if we accept the usual interpretation, for the Chaideinoi are the only representatives of Norway in classical times and their name would here be a synonym for 'Norwegians'. But, as a matter of fact, there seem to be several arguments which might explain how it came to pass that the region of the Heinir obtained such a prominence in early times.

The Norwegian 'Heath', Hornklofi's *Heiðr* (?), later called Heiðmǫrk, extending along the large lake of Mjǫrs, is one of the most fertile provinces of Norway.[1]

Its inhabitants appear in one of the earliest mediaeval sources that mention people from this country, viz. *Widsith*; they are there accompanied by three other Norwegian tribes only, and consequently occupy a rather privileged position. When the Yngling dynasty emigrates from Sweden to Norway, it first establishes itself in Heiðmǫrk. Moreover, one of Norway's juridical associations, Heiðsævisþing, obviously originates in this province. It is the only *þing* which reflects a tribal individuality; the other three are called after ordinary place names (Borgar-, Gula-, and Frostuþing). Again one of the first old Norwegian tribal names to be enlarged with the South Gothonic element *-verjar*, later so popular in Norway, is Heinir > *Hein-verjar. Finally, we must consider the ancient place name Hein-hof in the neighbouring province of Romerike, the 'temple of the Heinir'. This use of the tribal name combined with the element 'temple' seems to be almost unique in Norway; Magnus Olsen, *Hedenske Kultminder*, has only one additional example from Norway, Vosse-vangen, p. 132, which is secondary (for an earlier Vangr[2]), and he asks, p. 222 footnote: 'should Heinhof...be explained as an indication of a religious expansion from the Heiðmǫrk?' Among the other Scandinavians also, such a use of a tribal name is extremely rare and always seems to imply sacrificial relations of the highest importance; cp. the ring called Svía-grís, the most holy jewel of the Sviones, and the stone Dane-ryge in Jutland, the coronation stone of the Danish kings. (Cp. further the Gothic golden ring from Pietroassa with the inscription: 'Gutaniowi hailag'.)

1 The name need not mean 'region with heather'. In the Danish islands Zealand and Funen it is used to indicate central and fertile plains. Svensson certainly objects that the distribution of archaeological finds does not show the presence of a dense population in the older Iron Age. Cp. *Namn och Bygd*, 1919, 6.

2 Perhaps we ought also to add the region of Mærina helg in Mœri, *Landnámabók*, IV, ch. 6 (cp. Magnus Olsen, *l.c.* 123 note).

When all this evidence is taken together, we cannot but conclude that the occurrence of the Chaideinoi in a classical source is by no means accidental. It indicates a temporary prominence of this ancient tribe which was, however, after the Viking Age superseded by other representatives of the Norwegian people.

Apart from the Chaideinoi, the Norwegians are in classical times conspicuous only by their absence, and the native King Hrodulf, who in the sixth century notes a series of tribal names, shows no knowledge of a common national or geographical name. The Old Gothonic language certainly knew the expression 'North-way', but this only meant the northern zone as a whole. And the name of 'Northmen' might embrace all Scandinavians.

The Irishman Dicuil, in his *De mensura orbis terrae* about A.D. 815, speaks for the first time of plundering 'Northmen' on the Faroe Islands in terms that evidently must refer to inhabitants of Norway. And about 880 King Alfred the Great in his translation of *Orosius* introduces the names 'Norðweg' and 'Norðmen' in obvious contrast to 'Denmark' and 'Danes' (cp. A. Bugge, *Norges Hist.* I, 2, 19).

After Harold Fairhair has in 872 united the states of Norway, the existence of a Norwegian nationality is a matter of established fact Yet we must add that it can only be strictly defined from the political point of view, as 'Scandinavian subjects of the Norwegian king'. There is no linguistic barrier between them and the Sviones and Gauts, and there exists scarcely a single test whereby the languages may be differentiated or any obvious sign of Norwegian as distinct from the other Scandinavian languages.

The tests that we have are only approximate.

1. The use of the names Norway and Norsemen, and of the adj. norrœnn (Scotch Norn).

2. The preservation of the diphthongs *ei* and *au* is a most conspicuous mark of Norwegian, distinguishing it from Svionic, Gautic, and Danish, but the same sounds occur in Gotlandic and in various dialects of continental Swedish. Cp. Fig. 13.

3. The tribal region is called *fylki*, a name which is not used in other countries. Yet the use of *fylki* does not seem to be truly popular in large parts of Eastern Norway which prefer such expressions as *ríki* 'realm' (also Swedish) and *mǫrk* (also 'Geatic' and Danish).

4. 'Fjord' is often called *angr*; the similar designation in certain

North Swedish regions must be regarded as originating in Norway. In South-eastern Norway the fjords called *-angr* are rare, e.g. Eidanger, but on the other hand there are various names of lakes with the same element (cp. O. Rygh, *Norske Fjordnavne* (*Festskrift til C. R. Unger*), and G. Indrebö, *Norske innsjönamn* (*Norske Vidensk. Selsk. Skrifter*, II, *H.F. Kl.* 1923, No. 7, p. 245 seq.)).

5. The characteristic poetry of the 'scalds' is exclusively Norwegian. It is, however, scarcely common Norwegian, but rather West Norwegian.

Whereas the application of tests for common Norwegian gives but a meagre result, it is much easier to point out the difference between the East Norwegians and the West Norwegians. There are certain features which give to both sections an absolutely individual stamp, whereas, on other points the East Norwegian regions betray an obvious inclination towards the East Scandinavian type. If we regard the maps of linguistic phenomena, of types of houses, and of the distribution of the literary languages, Figs. 13–18, we shall constantly observe this inclination towards the east. It is not possible to counterbalance it by a single phenomenon which unites East and West Norwegians as a pronounced West Scandinavian unity. Our observation is anticipated by the *Lay of Brávellir* which is supposed to have been made by a poet from Thelemark in the eleventh century. According to Saxo's extract the author opens his survey of King Hring's forces with the Gauts and the people from the environs of the Vík, among whom he places his own countrymen proper, the Thelemarkings. Then, on p. 382, he introduces a West Norwegian list starting from Northern Norway, and with these words: 'E Norwagia vero memorantur'. That is to say: only the West Norwegians are represented as belonging to 'Norwagia'. On the whole, the impression is gained that the East Norwegians might rightly be regarded as a separate branch, like Sviones, Gauts, and Danes, if they were not linked to their western neighbours by the national name Norwegians. The following points may be noticed.

1. The name Austmenn or Austlendingar in West Norwegian seems to indicate the East Norwegians, though no exact definition is given. The place name Austmannali is a local mark of the contrast between East and West.

2. East Norwegians generally are dolichocephalous, the West Norwegians contain a large brachycephalous population, especially along

the coast (cp. Planche VI in A. M. Hansen, *Landnåm i Norge* (*Kortskaller*)). Perhaps this racial contrast is hinted at in the Old Norse legend describing how the country is peopled by two ancestors, Nor and Gor.

3. Eastern Norway contains numerous temples of Odin, viz. in Vingulmǫrk (3), Raumaríki, Haðaland, Hringaríki, Orkdœlafylki (3), Gauldœlafylki. Western Norway has only two examples, in Sogn and Firðir (cp. the lists in Magnus Olsen, *Hedenske Kultminder*, ch. 2).

4. Various phonetic phenomena distinguish two main dialects, though the distinction is never completely exact.

(*a*) East Norwegian, like the larger part of East Scandinavian, partly or wholly replaces the ancient diphthongs and monophthongs; West Norwegian preserves them. But various East Norwegian dialects, especially north of the Firth of Trondheim, share the West Norwegian type (cp. map, Fig. 13; Brøndum-Nielsen, *Dialekter og Dialektforskning*, 65).

(*b*) East Norwegian, like North Swedish, alters final *-a* into *-æ*, *-ə* in certain cases; cp. the same alteration as the normal rule in Danish dialects west of the Øresund. The larger part of West Norwegian preserves the *-a* (cp. map, Fig. 14; Brøndum-Nielsen, *l.c.* 60 seq.).

(*c*) East Norwegian, like Swedish and Gautic, preserves the 'thick *l*'; West Norwegian, like Danish and the extreme North Norwegian dialects, substitutes the same *l* as in Engl. *like* (cp. map, Fig. 15; Brøndum-Nielsen, *l.c.* 80).

(*d*) East Norwegian does not share the West Norwegian labialisation ('U-Umlaut') of *a*; ancient texts have *gatu* for West Norwegian *gǫtu* 'street' (cas. obl.) (cp. Brøndum-Nielsen, *l.c.* 86; Hægstad, *Norsk maalsoga*, 21).

5. The Svionic expression 'folkland' in Frostuþing seems to replace the Norwegian *fylki* (cp. Einarr Skálaglam, *Hskr.* II, 285); on the whole the *fylki* of the Þrœndalǫg, though sometimes governed by kings, do not seem to be equivalent to those in the rest of Norway.

6. The Svionic territorial expression *hund* 'a hundred' seems to appear in the Þrœndalǫg (cp. A. Bugge, *Norges Hist.* I, 2, 27).

7. The Swedish territorial expressions ending in *-rike*—Svearike, Götarike, Askrike, etc.—reappear in South-eastern Norway: Ranríki sixth century, Raumaríki sixth century, Hringaríki.

8. 'Geatic' Wedermearc, Danish Danmark, have analogues in South-east Norwegian: Heiðmǫrk, Vingulmǫrk, Þelamǫrk, Grenmǫrk.

9. The most characteristic place name of Eastern Norway is *Skaun*, 'the beautiful region'; the place is always on fertile ground near a gulf or lake. Normally there is only one instance in each county. No. (1) near Lake Mjǫrs, Heiðmǫrk; (2) near Lake Öjeren, Raumaríki; (3) near the very broad river Glommen, Vingulmǫrk; (4) and (5) near Drammensfjord and Sandefjord, Vestfold (No. 5 perhaps originally belonging to Grenland?); (6) near the south-western edge of the fjord of Trondheim, Orkdœlafylki; (7) near the fjord of Levanger, Skeynafylki; (8) near Lake Snǫs, Sparbyggjafylki; (9) near the mouth of the river Indalselv, and near the fjord of Selånger, Medelpad (cp. O. Rygh, *Norske Gaardnavne*, VI, 286; A. Bugge, *Norges Hist.* I, 1, 224, and Maps, I, 2, 21, 49, 55).

10. A typical East Norwegian name for 'fjord' or 'lake' is *Fold*. It is applied to: (1) the fjord of Christiania (or Oslo); (2) a lake in Hitterdal, Telemark; (3) two fjords in Helgeland; (4) various 'lakes' in the Uplands, whence a toponymic Vestfoldingar is derived, used for example to designate 'the people west of the Randsfjord' (see Ross, *Ordbog*, s.v. *Vestfoldinger*; cp. Indrebö, *Norske innsjönamn*, I, 267 seq.).

11. The element *-mar* 'sea' is frequent in South-eastern Norway, e.g. Grenmar, Vestmar and Godmar, on both sides of the Vík. It reappears in Svionic and Gautic, e.g. Hraiþ-marr in the inscription of Rök.

12. The river name *Raumr appears both on the Vík and in Northern Norway, in Raumaríki and in Raumsdœlafylki respectively (cp. § 278, A 2).

13. 'Settlement' in East Norwegian is called *by* as in Swedish and Danish, in contrast with *bö* in West Norwegian. The North Norwegian form *bu* is more akin to *by* than to *bö* (*by* may also occur) (cp. the map, Fig. 17).

14. The court of a farmstead in East Norwegian is called 'gardsplass' (literally 'yard's place'), in contrast with *tun* in West Norwegian (the same word as 'town') (cp. H. Vreim in *Aarsberetning for Foreningen til norske Fortidsmindesmærkers Bevaring*, 1929, 1).

15. In Eastern Norway, especially in Gudbrandsdal, the double court plan, giving one yard for men and one for cattle, is observed, as among the Sviones and Gauts. Since the eighteenth century the quadrangular form prevailing in North Sweden and Denmark has been introduced. The West

Norwegian type is the 'collective village' ('klyngebosættelse'). Romsdal, Telemark, Setesdal, and West Agder prefer the 'row farmstead', which also occurs in Nordmöre, and which is the normal type in Iceland (cp. Vreim, *l.c.* p. 39). In Eastern Norway the timber of the walls is always placed in horizontal position, as in Sweden; in Western Norway it is often placed in vertical position ('Stavbygning'). Cp. Fig. 20.

16. A West Norwegian peculiarity is the poetry of the 'scalds'.

17. In modern times the individualistic East Norwegian dialect has been adapted for literary use, though it is not acknowledged as a literary language equivalent to 'Landsmål' and 'Riksmål'. 'Landsmål', on the contrary, has been built up chiefly, though not exclusively, on a West Norwegian basis. Whereas 'Riksmål' still predominates in the whole of Eastern and Northern Norway, 'Landsmål' has conquered Western Norway, apart from the towns. According to *Norges offisielle Statistik*, VIII, 66, *Skolevesenets Tilstand*, 1925–26, the distribution of the two languages among the school districts ('Kretser') of the various provinces is shown as follows (cp. our map, Fig. 18, drawn on the basis of the large map *Riksmaal og landsmaal i skolen*, published by Riksmaalsforbundet in 1920):

	School districts	
Province	**Riksmål**	**Landsmål**
Östfold	198	—
Akershus	215	—
Buskerud	260	6
Vestfold	142	—
Hedmark	332	12
Opland	250	50
Telemark	128	185
Aust-Agder	109	121
Vest-Agder	194	123
Rogaland	148	203
Hordaland	160	379
Sogn, Fjordane	44	417
Möre	182	310
Sör-Tröndelag	295	34
Nord-Tröndelag	159	78
Nordland	578	53
Troms	375	15
Finnmark	147	—
	3916	1986

According to provisional calculations for 1930 the figures would be:

Province		School districts	
		Riksmål	Landsmål
Oslo Bispedömme	... ...	819	8
Hamar	... ...	633	73
Agder and Stavanger	... ...	560	627
Björgvin	... ...	174	1033
Nidaros	... ...	614	219
Hålogaland	... ...	1080	60
		3880	2020

The following details concerning the types of Norwegian houses may be noticed.

The primitive 'compound house' exists on the Faroe Islands. Originally consisting of one room, it is nowadays divided into *stofa* (living room) and stables. Similar constructions may be found in Iceland.

In the collective village the dwelling-houses of various proprietors are collected in one place, the stables in another, the barns in a third, and so on. This type according to Vreim, *l.c.* p. 39, predominates in Western Norway. It was frequent in Romsdal and Möre and also occurs in the Tröndelag. Hallingdal, Österdal, and parts of Gudbrandsdal show 'collective villages' from later times. They also occur in Telemark and Numedal, though mixed with other types (p. 3).

The irregular farmstead of the Värmland type, with the buildings grouped in a haphazard fashion, is found over a small part of South-eastern Norway and in Helgeland. Vreim refers the type to the later part of the Middle Ages, but it seems to be hinted at in the definite references to the various separate buildings of a farmstead which appear in the Icelandic sagas. Cp. Guðmundsson, *Privatboligen på Island*, *Grundriss*, 2nd ed. III, 429 seq.: 'Den Berichten der Sagas zufolge hatte man auf jedem allgemeinen Bauernhofe (*bør, býr*) ausser einigen Nebengebäuden oder Vorratshäusern und Viehställen mindestens 3 bis 4 und oft mehr Wohnhäuser (*hús, herbergi*). Die gewöhnlichen vier waren (1) die Stube (*stofa*), (2) die Schlafkammer (*svefnhús, skáli*), (3) die Küche (*eldhús*), (4) die Speisekammer (*búr*). Da man nicht wie jetzt grosse Häuser aufführte, die in mehrere Zimmer eingeteilt waren, sondern statt dessen mehrere kleinere Häuser baute, von denen jedes einen einzelnen Raum in sich fasste, so sind diese Wohnhäuser im Hinblick auf ihre Anwendung jedes für sich als ein Zimmer in einem grösseren Bau aufzufassen'.

The 'row farmstead' places the above-mentioned houses in a long row, Norw. *lån*. This type seems to have been characteristic of Setesdal and Telemark from early times, but it is also of long standing in West Norway and West Agder, and about 1800 it was normal in North Möre and Romsdal and might also be found in East Norwegian valleys and lowlands (Vreim, p. 39). The 'row farmstead', moreover, is the normal type in Iceland. Cp. Guðmundsson, *l.c.*: 'Auf Island bildeten die Wohnhäuser einen Gebäudekomplex, am häufigsten so, dass sie in doppelter Reihe aufgestellt wurden, zu beiden Seiten eines unter eigenem Dache aufgeführten Ganges (*dyrr, bøjargǫng*), welcher quer durch den Gebäudekomplex hindurchging und zuweilen nach hinten mit dem Kuhstall (*fjós*) in Verbindung stand. Doch hat man auch eine Aufstellung der Häuser in einer einzigen Reihe gekannt, das eine in der Verlängerung des anderen, sowie eine Form der Zusammenstellung, die den Übergang zwischen diesen zweien bildet, wo einige von den Häusern hinter den andern gestellt werden'. The form of the single room resembles that of the English 'cruck' (cp. p. 245).

The 'row farmstead' is symbolised in the famous myth of Utgarða-Loki's glove, mistaken by Thor for a house (Snorri, *Gylfaginning*, ch. 46).

The 'double court type', with one court for men and one for cattle, either combined or separate, is frequently met with in Gudbrandsdal and also in the East Norwegian lowlands and in Tröndelag and Österdal; it occurs besides in certain rectories in West Norway, Möre, and Numedal (Vreim, p. 39). The type in which the two courts are connected is the oldest and most common; it is the one which Erixon calls 'Central Swedish'. The type with two quite separate courts corresponds to Erixon's Middle Swedish type (p. 12).

The North Scandinavian quadrangle, of a type similar to the Danish, but with the midden outside the court, not inside, was introduced into East Norway and the Tröndelag in the eighteenth century. It is also met with in the lower regions of Valdres, Hallingdal, and Numedal (p. 39); besides it predominates in the whole of Northern Sweden and in Finland.

Lit. H. Vreim, *Trekk fra byggeskikkens geografi i Norge* (*Maal og Minne*, 1933, 12, with maps).

§ 280. History.

The development of Norwegian settlements during the various archaeological epochs is illustrated in Gustafson's maps in *Norges Oldtid.*

As to the earliest history of Norway, we mentioned above on p. 338 that it is a matter of controversy whether the megalithic graves belong to the Gothonic inhabitants or not. But the problem has little bearing on Norway, as this type of grave is only found in the south-eastern extremity of the country (cp. Bremer's map, *Ethnographie,* pp. 830–831, based on the researches of Montelius).

The Bronze Age must be regarded as the period when Gothonic settlement began in Norway, and it is worth noticing that the area of the settlement coincides generally with the district where the archaic tribal names occur.

These archaic Simplexes as a rule are toponymics, created from some place name in that particular district; such as for example: Sygnir in Sogn, Firðir in 'the fjords', Skeynir in Skaun, 'the beautiful region', Hǫrðar in *Haruð, 'the wood', etc. To this stratum we may also refer Rygir (from *rygr* 'stone'); if we are right, the Rugi in Pomerania must be colonists from Norway, for Pomerania has no rocks which might account for the formation of the name.

Simplexes are specially numerous round the Vík and the fertile 'Heath' where we meet with the only Norwegian tribe recorded in classical literature, viz. the Chaideinoi of Ptolemy, c. A.D. 150.

During the Roman epoch of the Iron Age, Norway was hardly within the South European range of vision. Only some few Imperial denarii have found their way to Norway—a striking contrast to the c. 4000 pieces which have been found in Gotland.

The great Migration Age at last established a more effective contact with the centres of southern civilisation. Rich deposits of Roman antiquities have been found at Avaldsnes on the island of Kǫrmt and at Klep on the peninsula of Jæder.

Together with the products of industry ideas were imported.

The old deities of fertility—Nerthus, Freyr, etc.—were forced to submit to the warlike gods of the south-west, especially Thor and Odin. We must note, however, that the worship of Odin remained practically unknown in large parts of Western Norway (cp. A. Bugge, *Norges Hist.* I, 1, 167).

Runic letters were introduced into Norway as into the rest of Scandinavia and inscriptions in the older runic alphabet have been found giving the names of the earliest historical Norwegians.

At the same time, the first Norwegian makes his appearance in Latin literature, for a King Hrodulf left his home about A.D. 500 to visit the Gothic King Theodoric in Italy, an interesting example of intercourse between remote regions (cp. Jordanes, III, 23). We owe to this first known Scandinavian traveller a list of Norwegian tribal names along the coast from Ranríki to Helgeland.

We may assume that Hrodulf was the king of a single tribe, representing a *fylki*. Up to the Viking Age it was the general rule that each *fylki* should have a king of its own. The Þrœndalǫg formed an exception, as its *fylki* seem generally to have been governed by chieftains only, but these so-called 'provinces' really were little more than the 'herreder' in other Scandinavian regions.

Hrodulf's report shows that south-eastern tribes such as the Raumar and Renir had in the sixth century consolidated into *ríki* 'realms'; the names are of Celtic pattern (cp. I, 162, 175). But we do not yet observe any traces of Norwegian unity.

A statement which sounds extraordinary is made by Hrodulf when he speaks of a South Norwegian nation called 'Finni mitissimi', 'the most civilised Finns', 'omnibus Scandzae cultoribus mitiores', 'more civilised than any other inhabitants of Scandinavia'. The truth of this seems, however, to be confirmed by other evidence, e.g. the expression 'Finna bygðir' applied by the scald Skúli Þorðarsson in A.D. 1257 to the regions near the Vík (cp. P. A. Munch, *Det norske Folks Hist.* I, 340, and A. M. Hansen, *Landnåm i Norge*, 163).

The first Norwegian Viking raids would seem to have taken place as early as about the time of Hrodulf, if we may trust the scalds Þjóðolfr of Hvin and Eyvindr Skaldaspillir, cited by Snorri (*Ynglinga Saga*, ch. 23–24). The Kings Goðlaug and Gylaug from Helgeland are said to have raided the Cattegat and to have fought Svionic rivals there. Our authorities are somewhat doubtful, but the time fairly coincides with the first historically known Scandinavian Viking raid, the expedition of the 'Geatic' King Hygelác to Friesland, c. 526.

The Anglo-Saxons of the Migration Age are acquainted with tribes from almost the whole of Norway, cp. the catalogue of *Widsith*: Hæðnas, l. 81 (i.e. Chaideinoi Ptol.), *Hæreðas, *ibid.* (Hǫrðar), Þrówendas, l. 64

(Þrœndr), Heaðo-Réamas, l. 63 (Raumar, also in *Beowulf*), i.e. representatives from the southern boundary right up to Helgeland.

This early reference to the Þrœndr is not fortuitous, for their county was the most highly organised in Norway before Harold Fairhair united the country (cp. A. Bugge, *Norges Hist.* I, 2, 22).

The region of the Vík was a centre of mercantile activity. Its toponymic Vík-verjar is one of the first examples of the element *-verjar*, imported as a consequence of the intercourse with Germany. Many antiquities have been discovered near the old harbour Skíringssal. There was close intercourse with Denmark and in consequence there were frequent political unions; e.g. in A.D. 813, Westarfolda, i.e. Vestfold, appears as a part of Denmark, Einhard, *Ann.*, *Mon. Germ. SS.* I, 200.

From the seventh to eighth centuries onwards the enterprises of the Norwegian Vikings extend beyond the North Sea. In 616 or 617 Irish annals report that the island of Tory north of Ireland was ravaged by a 'fleet from beyond the sea'. In 617 a similar fate befell the monastery on Eigg, one of the Southern Hebrides. The assailants cannot have been Picts, as their nation had been converted to Christianity before the seventh century; we must assume that Norsemen are meant. And place names ending in *-heim* and *-vin* on the Shetland Islands seem to suggest that the Norwegian settlement here, as well as on the Orkneys, had begun in the sixth century. According to the *Færeyinga Saga*, ch. 1, the Faroe Islands were colonised in the time of Harold Fairhair, and here the names ending in *-heim* and *-vin* no longer occur (cp. A. M. Hansen, *Landnåm i Norge*, 22–24; A. Bugge, *Norges Hist.* I, 1, 119, 2, 102).

In 787 the *Saxon Chronicle* records a reconnoitring expedition of three ships from Heredaland (Hordaland) to Northumberland. In 793 the monastery of Lindisfarne is ravaged, probably by Norsemen. After this the attacks become continuous. About 826–830 the Norsemen begin to settle in the Hebrides and in parts of Scotland and Ireland. Hereafter the Hebrides are in Irish called Innsi Gaill, i.e. 'the islands of foreigners'.

In 843 the Westfaldingi from Vestfold ravage Nantes and conquer the island of Noirmoutier in the mouth of the Loire (cp. *Ann. Engolism.* and *Chron. Aquitan.* ad an. 843). In 844 they reach Bordeaux.

About the same time the Norsemen from Ireland and France enter into mercantile relations with the Spanish Arabs. Al-Ghazal and other

Arab writers describe voyages to the Norwegian colonies in Ireland. A Danish rival conquest of Eastern Ireland had no lasting results.

In the meantime the assimilation of the tribal kingdoms into a national unity is gradually brought about. The dynasty of the Vestfoldingar is the pioneer. Þjóðolfr in his *Ynglingatal* says that this dynasty is derived from the Svionic Ynglingar or Skilfingar, a statement which A. Bugge rejects (*Norges Hist.* I, 2, 62). But it is worth noticing that str. 46 calls the dynasty 'Gautic', and the princely names Ingjald and Eystein are inherited from the Skilfing family. King Halfdan the Black gained a strong footing in the 'Uplands', and his son Harold Fairhair after fifteen years of strife finally crushed the resistance of the West Norwegians in the famous battle of Hafrsfjord, 872 (cp. *Egils Saga*, ch. ix; Snorri, *Hskr.* I, 122; A. Bugge, *Norges Hist.* I, 2, 98). Soon afterwards he also subdued the Norwegians in the Shetlands and the Orkneys (Snorri, *ibid.* I, 128).

The threatened loss of independence caused many of Harold's foes to leave the country, especially those from Western Norway (cp. Bugge, *l.c.* I, 2, 157). Some went to the British Isles, others to the unpeopled islands of the Atlantic. The first settler in Iceland was Ingolf in 874 (cp. *Landnáma*, ch. 6–8); Greenland was first colonised by Eric the Red in 886 et seq. (*ibid.* ch. 77–80). The old eastern district of Greenland corresponds to the present Julianehåb, the western to Godthåb. Finally even the American continent was discovered (cp. Steensby, *The Norsemen's Route from Greenland to Wineland* (*Meddelelser fra Grønland*, 1918)).

Discoveries were also made towards the north-east. Óhthere from Helgeland before the close of the ninth century undertook an expedition to Bjarmaland on the White Sea, cp. his report to King Alfred (*Orosius*, p. 17).

As to the controversy concerning the conqueror of Normandy, Rollo, see pp. 377–378. A. Bugge admits that even if Rollo was a Norwegian, this circumstance does not affect the nationality of the settlers, the majority of whom were well known to be Danish (cp. *Norges Hist.* I, 2, 173).

The colonists of the various regions had various constitutions. The states in Ireland and on the Isle of Man were monarchies; Normandy in 911 became a duchy of the European feudal type under the crown of France; most of the islands north and west of Scotland became Norwegian earldoms as early as 875; the Faroe Islands were subjected to Norway in 1035; Greenland and Iceland remained republics till 1261–62 respectively, when Norway annexed these survivals of the primaeval Gothonic type of political organisation.

Though Harold Fairhair's Norwegian state was not yet assimilated into a national unity, it was never from his time on exposed to the danger of dissolution by exterior forces.

For centuries Norwegian settlers have continuously been advancing along the northern coasts, but Iceland and the Faroe Islands have developed separate Scandinavian nationalities with their own literary languages, and the other colonies across the seas have ceased to be Scandinavian. The colonies in France are Romanised. In Ireland, where the power of the Norsemen was shaken by the battle of Clontarf in 1014, they were first partly Celticised and then entirely Anglicised. On the Hebrides they are Celticised, on the Isle of Man, in Cumberland, Scotland, on the Orkney and Shetland islands they are Anglicised. In Greenland they have been absorbed by the Esquimaux. The loss of Herjedal, Jemtland and Bohuslän to Sweden, however, has only affected the political nationality, as the dialect spoken in these districts remains unaltered.

The O.N. literary language was replaced by Danish under the union with Denmark. A new Norwegian 'Landsmål' was created in the nineteenth century; it is mainly based on West Norwegian. Danish-Norwegian 'Riksmål' has in the course of time been influenced by Norwegian to such a degree that it must be called a separate language from Danish, though it still lacks typical Norwegian characteristics such as the diphthongs *ei*, *au*, *öy*, etc. In the present century the East Norwegian dialect has been adapted for literary use. Though not officially recognised as a literary language, equivalent to 'Landsmål' and 'Riksmål', it is actually used in printed periodicals, etc. Thus Norway exhibits the extraordinary phenomenon of a single nationality with three written languages.

In 1750 the number of Norwegians was calculated to be about 625,000. In 1931 it was about 3,676,000.

Norway (1929)	2,600,000
Sweden (1920–21)	11,950
Denmark	5,600
Iceland and Faroe Islands	150
Finland	400

Great Britain and Ireland	4,300
Holland and Belgium	400
Switzerland	200
Germany (1925)	1,650
France, Italy, Portugal (1920–21)	1,060
Czechoslovakia, Lettland, Esthonia	120
China	520
Japan	70
South Africa	1,350
Madagascar	150
U.S.A. (1st and 2nd generation)	959,000
Alaska (1920-21)	2,170
Canada (c. 1930)	80,000
Mexico, Central America (1921)	120
Argentina (c. 1930)	2,500
Chile (1920-21)	200
Australia	3,000
New Zealand	1,050
Hawaii	140

(Sum total of emigrants c. 1 million.)

Cp. Ragnv. Jonsberg in *Nordmands-Forbundet*, 1924, pp. 417 seq., 485 seq.

The number of Icelanders in 1801 was estimated to be 47,240. In 1928 it was about 104,000 in Iceland; there may be some 20,000 in U.S.A.

The Faroese in 1925 were 22,835.

Lit. **P. Munch,** *Det norske Folks Historie*; **A. Bugge** in *Norges Historie*; *idem, Contributions to the History of the Norsemen in Ireland* (*Skr. udg. af Vidensk Selsk. i Christiania, H.F. Kl.* 1900, No. 4); *idem, Vikingerne*; **Fridtjof Nansen,** *In Northern Mists*; **Andreas M. Hansen,** *Landnåm i Norge*; **Gustafson,** *Norges Oldtid*; **Haakon Shetelig,** *Vorgeschichte Norwegens*; **Magnus Olsen,** *Hedenske Kultminder* (*Skr. udg. af Vidensk. Selsk. i Christiania, H.F. Kl.* 1914, No. 4); *idem, Farms and Fanes of ancient Norway*; **J. Jakobsen,** *Det norrøne Sprog på Shetland*; *idem, Shetlandsøernes Stednavne* (*Aarbøger*, 1901); **George T. Flom,** *The Transition from Norse to Lowland Scotch in Shetland* (*Saga Book of the Viking Society, Proceedings*, 1919–24, p. 45); **Hugh Marwick,** *The Orkney Norn* (**Oxford Univ. Press**); **M. Mjelde,** *The Norse Discoveries of America* (*Saga Book of the Viking Society, Proceedings*, 1919–24, 57).

§ 281. Legendary Traditions.

No other Gothonic nations rival the Norwegians as regards abundance of epic traditions. The centre of these epics lies in Iceland, and the original contributions made by Norway are relatively small in comparison with the Icelandic.

The eponymous hero of Norway is Nor, i.e. 'North'. In the Danish genetic legend, Nori is brother of Østen (the Swede) and Dan, and son of Ypper in Uppsala (*Script. rer. Dan.* I, 223). This myth is still genuinely popular. But in the current Norwegian-Faroese-Icelandic traditions, e.g. in *Orkneyinga Saga*, ch. 1, and *Frá Fornjóti* (*Fornald. Sögur*, II, 1), the Family of Nor has been supplemented with a number of rather academic eponymous figures. At best we may discern reminiscences of original ethnic traditions, wherein Nor and his brother Gor represent two different racial elements, the former in the inland settlement, and the second along the coasts.

Sæmingr is another of the primitive ancestors. From him descend the earls of Helgeland (cp. Eyvindr Skaldaspillir's *Háleygjatal*, str. 3, and Snorri's commentary, *Ynglinga Saga*, ch. 8). Sæmingr seems to be an eponymous hero, Same, i.e. representative of the Lapps.

Hǫrðr and Rugalfr, the sons of Nor, are eponymous heroes of Hordaland and Rogaland (cp. *Frá Fornjóti*, p. 5). They seem almost to be creations of academic fancy, yet perhaps they originate from a popular source, as they appear together in the East Gautic inscription of Rök.

Among the persons mentioned in this inscription from South-eastern Scandinavia, we thus find representatives of Norwegian Vikings together with the East Gothic King Theodoric from Italy. But this kind of thing is seldom met with. It is exceptional for Norwegian heroes to play an important part in a genuine Danish or Swedish legend; only through literary channels such as Saxo's history have they been introduced amongst the favourite heroes of Danish readers. Not even the striking personality of Harold Fairhair has been able to resist the general epic current, running as it does from the south towards the north. In *Widsith* the Anglo-Saxon epic 'Who's Who', there appear Norwegian tribes as far north as Trondheim, but not a single obviously Norwegian person. The Norwegians are equally absent from German legend. The first Norwegian personality to assert himself was King Olaf, the national saint of Norway, who became a general Scandinavian saint, and whose fanatical struggle against Norwegian pagans, confused with reminiscences of the god Thor's fury against giants and trolls, grew popular in legendary ballads throughout Scandinavia.

Lit. **Olrik**, *Kilderne til Sakses oldhistorie*; **Asbjörnsen**, *Norske folke- og huldre-eventyr* (**ed. by Moltke Moe**); **J. Moe**, *Norske Folkeeventyr*; **Moltke Moe**, *Hellenske og norske folketraditioner* (*Nordisk Tidsskrift*, 1879); **B. S. Phillpotts**, *The Elder Edda and Ancient Scandinavian Drama.*

ADDENDA ET CORRIGENDA.

p. 55. On the Vandalic census of A.D. 429 cp. L. Schmidt, *Geschichte der Wandalen*, p. 37.

p. 67, 2, Engl. Germans (cp. vol. I, § 19). The following sentence occurs in the *Διαμερισμὸς τῆς γῆς*, cp. Müllenhoff, *Deutsche Altertumskunde*, III, 317: ‘Γερμανῶν ἔθνη καὶ ἀποικίαι εἰσὶν ε′, Μαρκόμανοι, Βαρδουλοὶ, Κουαδροὶ, Βεριδοὶ, Ἑρμονδουλοί.’

p. 95, 5 (*a*), Svebi Nicretes. The name may possibly reappear in the enigmatic Níarar, mentioned in the Eddic poem *Vǫlundarkviða* which deals with German legendary traditions. The name of the river Neckar, Lat. Nicer, in correct O.H.G. form must be Nehhar, a form which actually appears in old sources. And when the name was transplanted to Scandinavia, the *h* must have been lost.

p. 113. The river Kamp in Nieder Oesterreich in the Czech language is called Kuba, whereas the Cham, an affluent of the Regen, is in this language called Chub.

p. 114. The Gothonic name of the Sarmates must have been *Bainingōz, i.e. Pannonians. Cp. our article *Die Nationalität der Báninger* (*Beiträge*, LVII, 42).

p. 160 (*c*). The name of Flemings perhaps belongs to O.Fris. *flēma* ‘to carry off’, O.E. *flíeman* ‘to fly’. Cp. the *Lex Salica*: ‘*flemere* “si quis navem alienam moverit”, “si navem furaverit”’. Consequently, the name would have indicated ‘sea-robbers’.

INDEX

The figures generally refer to pages. The sign § indicates a chief subject of the paragraph in question.

LIST OF ABBREVIATIONS AND REFERENCES

Aarbøger = *Aarbøger for nordisk Oldkyndighed og Historie.* København.

AASEN = AASEN, *Norsk Ordbog.* Christiania, 1873.

Abh. = *Abhandlungen.*

Acta Phil. Scand. = *Acta Philologica Scandinavica.* København.

ADAM. BREM. = ADAMUS BREMENSIS, *Gesta Hammenburgensis ecclesiae pontificum* in *Mon. Germ. SS.* VII, 267 seq., ed. Lappenberg. Hanover, 1846.

Aethicus = *Cosmographia olim Aethici dicta* in *Geogr. Lat. min.* ed. Riese. Heilbronn, 1878.

AGATHIAS = AGATHIAS, Ἱστορίαι in *Hist. Graec. min.* II, ed. Dindorf. Leipzig, 1871.

ALCUIN = ALCUIN, *Vita Willibrordi* in *Mon. Germ. Poetae Latini aevi Carolini*, I, 27 seq., rec. Dümmler. Berlin, 1881.

ALFRED'S *Bede* = *The Old English Version of Bede's Ecclesiastical History*, ed. Miller. London, 1890—8. *König Alfred's Übersetzung von Bedas Kirchengeschichte*, ed. Schipper. Leipzig, 1899.

— *Orosius* = *King Alfred's Orosius*, ed. Sweet. London, 1893.

Allg. = *Allgemein(e).*

AMMIANUS = AMMIANUS MARCELLINUS, *Rerum gestarum libri*, rec. C. Clark. Berlin, 1910—15.

Annal(es) Amandi = *Mon. Germ. SS.* I, ed. Pertz. Hanover, 1829.

— *Engolism(enses)* = *ibid.* IV and XVI. 1839 and 1859.

— *Fuld(enses)* = *ibid.* I—III. 1829—39.

— *Loisel(iani*, or *Laurissenses majores*), *Nazar(iani)*, *Petav(iani)*, *Tiliani*, *Vedastini* = *ibid.* I. 1829.

Anon. Ravenn. = *Ravennatis Anonymi Cosmographia*, ed. Pinder et Parthey. Berlin, 1860.

Anz. = *Anzeiger.*

Anzeiger = *Anzeiger für deutsches Altertum* in *Zeitschrift.* Berlin.

APOLLINARIS SID. = APOLLINARIS SIDONIUS, *Carmina* in *Mon. Germ. Auct. antiq.* VIII, 173 seq., rec. Lüttjohan. Berlin, 1887. Ed. Mohr, Leipzig, 1895.

APPIANUS, *Celtica* = Ἐκ τῆς Κελτικῆς, ed. Bekker, I, 34 seq. Leipzig, 1852.

Arkiv = *Arkiv för nordisk filologi.* Lund.

AUGUSTUS, *Res gestae* = *Res gestae divi Augusti*, 2nd ed., Mommsen. Berlin, 1883.

BEDE = BEDA, *Historia ecclesiastica gentis Anglorum*, ed. Plummer. Oxford, 1896.

Bede, Alfred's, see ALFRED.

Beiträge = *Paul u. Braunes Beiträge zur Geschichte der deutschen Sprache und Literatur.* Halle.

Bell. Gall., *Goth.*, *Vand.*, see CAESAR, PROCOPIUS.

Beowulf = *Beowulf with the Finnsburg Fragment*, ed. by Wyatt, introduction by Chambers. Cambridge, 1914.

BIRCH, *Cartular. Sax.* = BIRCH, *Cartularium Saxonicum*. London, 1885—99.

BOLL. = *Acta Sanctorum*, ed. Bolland, etc. Antwerpen, 1643 seq.

BONIFAT. *Epist.* = BONIFATIUS, *Epistolae* in *Mon. Germ. Epist.* III, 207 seq., ed. Dümmler. Berlin, 1891.

BOSWORTH-TOLLER = BOSWORTH-TOLLER, *Anglo-Saxon Dictionary*. Oxford, 1882—98.

BREMER = BREMER, *Ethnographie der germanischen Stämme* in *Grundriss*, 2nd ed. Strassburg, 1899. Reprint, 1905.

Burg. = Burgundian.

CAESAR, *Bell. Gall.* = CAESAR, *Commentarii de bello Gallico*, ed. Klotz. Leipzig, 1927.

CASSIODORUS, *Var.* = CASSIODORUS, *Variae* in *Mon. Germ. Auct. antiq.* XII, 1 seq., ed. Mommsen. Berlin, 1894.

Celt. = Celtic.

CHADWICK = CHADWICK, *The Origin of the English Nation*. Cambridge, 1907.

Chron. Aquitan(icum), cp. Wattenbach, *Deutschlands Geschichtsquellen im Mittelalter*, I, 205.

— *Gall.* = *Chronica Gallica* in *Chronica minora*, I, 615 seq., ed. Mommsen. Berlin, 1893.

— *Gothan.* = *Chronicon Gothanum* in *Mon. Germ. SS. Langob.* 7 seq., ed. Waitz. Hanover, 1878.

CIG. = *Corpus inscriptionum Graecarum*. Berlin, 1828—77.

CIL. = *Corpus inscriptionum Latinarum*. Berlin, 1863 seq.

CIR. = *Corpus inscriptionum Rhenanarum*, ed. Brambach. Elberfeld, 1867.

CLAUDIANUS = CLAUDIANUS, *Carmina* in *Mon. Germ. Auct. antiq.* X, 1 seq., ed. Birt. Berlin, 1892.

Corp. scr. Byz. = *Corpus scriptorum historiae Byzantinae*, ed. Bekker et Niebuhr. Bonn, 1828 seq.

Dan. = Danish.

Danm. G. Folkeviser = *Danmarks gamle Folkeviser*, publ. by Sv. Grundtvig. København, 1853 seq.

DESSAU, *Inscr. select.* = DESSAU, *Inscriptiones Latinae selectae*. Berlin, 1892—1916.

DEXIPPUS = *Die Fragmente der griechischen Historiker*, II, ed. Jacoby. Berlin, 1926.

Diamerism = Διαμερισμὸς τῆς γῆς, ed. Müllenhoff, *Deutsche Altertumskunde*, III, 270 seq. Berlin, 1892.

DICULESCU, *Die Gepiden* = DICULESCU, *Die Gepiden*, I. Halle, 1923.

— *Die Wandalen* = *idem*, *Die Wandalen und die Goten in Ungarn und Rumänien* (*Mannus Bibliothek*, No. 34). Leipzig, 1923.

DIO CASSIUS = *Cassii Dionis Historiarum Romanarum quae supersunt*, ed. Boissevain. Berlin, 1895—1926.

DU CANGE = DU CANGE, *Glossarium mediae et infimae latinitatis*. Paris, 1840—57.

DUDO = DUDO, *Historia Normanorum* in *Mon. Germ. SS.* IV, 93 seq., ed. Waitz. Hanover, 1841.

Ed. Hrothari = *Edictus Hrothari* (*Rothari*) in *Mon. Germ. Leg.* IV, 3 seq., ed. Bluhme. Hanover, 1868.

Encycl. Brit. = *Encyclopaedia Britannica*, 14th ed. London and New York, 1929.

ENNODIUS, *Panegyr.* = ENNODIUS, *Panegyricus Theodorico* in *Mon. Germ. Auct. antiq.* VII, 203 seq., rec. Vogel. Berlin, 1883.

ERMOLD NIGELLUS = ERMOLD NIGELLUS, *Elegiae* in *Mon. Germ. SS.* II, 501 seq., ed. Pertz. Hanover, 1829. *Idem* in *Poetae Latini aevi Carolini II*, ed. Dümmler. Berlin, 1884.

Esthon. = Esthonian.

EUGIPPIUS = EUGIPPIUS, *Vita Severini* in *Corpus scriptorum ecclesiasticorum Latinorum*, IX, 1, 2, ed. Knoell. Wien, 1885.

EUNAPIUS = EUNAPIUS, *Breviarium ab urbe condita* in *Mon. Germ. Auct. antiq.* II, 1 seq., rec. Droysen. Berlin, 1879.

EUTROPIUS = *Hist. Graec. min.* I, ed. Dindorf. Leipzig, 1870.

FALK AND TORP = FALK OG TORP, *Etymologisk Ordbog over det norske og det danske Sprog*, Christiania, 1900—6 = *Norwegisch-dänisches etymologisches Wörterbuch* (*Germanistische Bibliothek*). Heidelberg, 1910—11.

FALKE, *Cod. Trad. Corbej.* = FALKE, *Codex traditionum Corbejensium.* Leipzig, 1752.

FEILBERG = FEILBERG, *Ordbog over jyske almuesmål.* København, 1886—1914.

F. F. Comm. = *Folk-lore Fellows' Communications.* Helsingfors.

FIEBIGER U. SCHMIDT = FIEBIGER UND SCHMIDT, *Inschriftensammlung zur Gesch. der Ostgermanen* (*Akad. d. Wissenschaften*). Wien, 1917.

Finn. = Finnish.

Finnsburg Lay, see *Beowulf.*

FLORUS = FLORUS, *Epitomae libri* II, ed. Rossbach. Leipzig, 1896.

Forsch. = *Forschungen.*

FÖRSTEMANN = FÖRSTEMANN, *Altdeutsches Namenbuch*, 2nd and 3rd ed., publ. by Jellinghaus. Bonn, 1900—16.

FREDEGAR = *Chronicarum quae dicuntur Fredegarii scholastici libri* IV in *Mon. Germ. SS. Merov.* II, 1 seq., ed. Krusch. Hanover, 1888.

Gael. = Gaelic.

Generatio regum et gentium = *Die fränkische Völkertafel*, ed. Müllenhoff, *Deutsche Altertumskunde*, III, 325 seq. Berlin, 1892.

Geogr. = *Geography, Geografi, Geographie.*

Geogr. Graec. min. = *Geographi Graeci minores*, ed. C. Müller. Paris, 1855—61.

Geogr. Lat. min. = *Geographi Latini minores*, ed. Riese. Heilbronn, 1878.

Germ. = German (in German quotations = *Germanisch*).

Gesch. = *Geschichte, Geschiedenis.*

Gesellsch. = *Gesellschaft.*

GILDAS = GILDAS, *De excidio Britanniae* in *Mon. Germ. Auct. antiq.* XIII, 1 seq., ed. Mommsen. Berlin, 1898.

Goth. = Gothic.

Gotl. = Gotlandic.

Gr. = Greek.

GREGOR. TUR. = GREGORIUS TURONENSIS, *Historia Francorum* in *Mon. Germ. SS. Merov.* I, 451, ed. Arndt. Hanover, 1885.

GREIN U. WÜLCKER = GREIN UND WÜLCKER, *Bibliothek der angelsächsischen Poesie.* Leipzig, 1883—98.

GRIMM = J. GRIMM, *Geschichte der deutschen Sprache.* Leipzig, 1848.

— *Gramm.* = *idem*, *Deutsche Grammatik.* Göttingen, 1819—37.

— *Heldensage* = W. GRIMM, *Deutsche Heldensage*, 3rd ed. Gütersloh, 1889.

Grundriss = PAUL, *Grundriss der germanischen Philologie.* Berlin u. Leipzig, 1891. 2nd ed., 1896 seq. Separate volumes in 3rd, 4th and 5th ed.

HELMOLD = HELMOLD, *Chronica Slavorum* in *Mon. Germ. SS.* XXI, 1 seq., ed. Lappenberg. Hanover, 1869.

H.G. = High German.

Hist. = *History, historical, Historie, historisk, historisch.*

Hist. Aug. = *Scriptores historiae augustae*, rec. H. Peter, 1884, ed. D. Magie. London, 1922 seq.

Hist. Graec. min. = *Historici Graeci minores*, ed. Dindorf. Leipzig, 1870—1.

HODGKIN = HODGKIN, *Italy and her Invaders.* Oxford, 1879—99. (Vols. I—IV, 2nd ed., 1892—6.)

HOOPS = HOOPS, *Reallexikon der germanischen Altertumskunde.* Strassburg, 1911—19.

Hskr. = SNORRI STURLUSON, *Heimskringla*, ed. Finnur Jónsson. København, 1898—1901.

Indogerm. Forsch. = *Indogermanische Forschungen.* Strassburg, later Berlin u. Leipzig.

— — *Anz.* = *Anzeiger*, *ibid.*

ISIDORUS = ISIDORUS, *Etymologiae*, ed. Lindsay. Oxford, 1911.

— *Hist. Gothorum* = *idem*, *Historia de regibus Gothorum* in *Mon. Germ. Auct. antiq.*

Joann. Lyd. Mag. = *Joannis Lydi de Magistratibus Pop. Romani*, ed. Wuensch. Leipzig, 1903.

JORDANES = JORDANES, *Getica* in *Mon. Germ. Auct. antiq.* V, i, 551 seq., ed. Mommsen. Berlin, 1882.

JULIANUS, *Ep. ad Athen.* = JULIANUS, *Epistola ad Athenienses*, ed. Bidoz. Paris, 1924.

JUSTINUS = JUSTINUS, *Epitoma historiarum Philippicarum Pomp. Trogi*, ed. Ruehl. Leipzig, 1886.

KARSTEN = KARSTEN, *Die Germanen* (*eine Einführung*, in PAUL'S *Grundriss*). Berlin u. Leipzig, 1928.

KAUFFMANN = KAUFFMANN, *Deutsche Altertumskunde.* München, 1913—23.

KEMBLE, *Cod. Dipl.* = KEMBLE, *Codex diplomaticus aevi Saxonici.* London, 1839—48.

KLUGE, *Etym. Wörterb.* = KLUGE, *Etymologisches Wörterbuch der deutschen Sprache*, 11th ed. Berlin, 1930.

Lat. = Latin.

LEEDS, THURLOW, *Archaeology* = THURLOW LEEDS, *Archaeology of the Anglo-Saxon Settlements.* Oxford, 1913.

Lex Alamannorum = *Mon. Germ. Leg.* I, 41 seq., ed. Merkel. Hanover, 1863.

Lex Baiuwariorum=*ibid.* III, II, 183 seq., ed. Merkel. Hanover, 1863.
— *Frisionum*=*ibid.* III, IV, 631 seq., ed. Richthofen. Hanover, 1863.
— *Salica*=*Lex Salica*, ed. Hessels, London, 1880. Ed. Geffken, Leipzig, 1898.
L.G.=Low German.
LIBANIUS=LIBANIUS, *Opera*, ed. Foerster. Leipzig, 1903—21.
Liber hist. Franc.=*Liber historiae Francorum* in *Mon. Germ. SS. Merov.* II, 341 seq., ed. Krusch. Hanover, 1888.
LIVIUS=LIVIUS, *Ab urbe condita*, rec. Madvig. Hauniae, 1873—82. Ed. Weissenborn—Müller—Heraeus, Leipzig, 1926—30.
LOEWE=LOEWE, *Die Reste der Germanen am Schwarzen Meere.* Halle, 1896.
— *Gliederung*=*Die ethnische und sprachliche Gliederung der Germanen* in *Festschrift der Gesellschaft für deutsche Philologie in Berlin*, No. 16. Berlin, 1899.
MABILLON=MABILLON, *De re diplomatica.* Paris, 1681.
— *Saec.*=*Acta sanctorum ordinis S. Benedicti in saeculorum classes distributa*, edd. Mabillon et Ruinart. Paris, 1668—71.
Mainzer Zeitschrift=*Zeitschr. des röm. germ. Centralmusäums.* Mainz.
MALCHUS=*Hist. Graec. min.* I, 383 seq., ed. Dindorf. Leipzig, 1870.
MAMERTIN. *Genethl.*=MAMERTINUS, *Genethlius* in *Panegyrici Latini*, ed. Baehrens. Leipzig, 1911.
— *Genethl. Maxim.*=*idem*, *Genethlius Maximiani*, *ibid.*
— *Panegyr. Maxim.*=*idem*, *Panegyricus Maximiano*, *ibid.*
M.Dan.=Middle Danish.
MENANDER=*Hist. Graec. min.* II, ed. Dindorf. Leipzig, 1871.
M.H.G.=Middle High German.
MIGNE, *Patr. Lat.*=MIGNE, *Patrologia Latina.* Paris, 1844—1912.
M.Lat.=Middle Latin.
Mon. Germ.=*Monumenta Germaniae historica.* Hanover and Berlin, 1829 seq.
— *SS.*=*idem*, *Scriptores*, ed. Pertz. Hanover, 1829 seq.
— — *Langob.*=*idem*, *Scriptores rerum Langobardicarum.* Hanover, 1878.
— — *Merov.*=*idem*, *Scriptores rerum Merovingicarum.* Hanover, 1884 seq.
Monum. Boica=*Monumenta Boica.* München, 1763—1893.
MUCH, *Stammeskunde*=MUCH, *Deutsche Stammeskunde* (*Sammlung Göschen*, No. 126), 3rd ed. 1920.
MÜLLENHOFF=MÜLLENHOFF, *Deutsche Altertumskunde.* Berlin, 1870—1908.
MÜLLER, SOPHUS, *Urgeschichte Europas*, Strassburg, 1905=*De forhistoriske Tider i Europa* (*Verdenskulturen*, II), København, 1906=*L'Europe préhistorique.* Paris, 1907.
Myvyrian Archaiology=OWEN JONES, EDW. WILLIAMS, WILLIAM OWEN PUGHE, *The Myvyrian Archaiology of Wales*, 2nd ed. Denbigh, 1870.
NAZARIUS=NAZARIUS, *Panegyricus Constantino* in *Panegyrici Latini*, ed. Baehrens. Leipzig, 1911.
NENNIUS=NENNIUS, *Historia Britonum* in *Mon. Germ. Auct. antiq.* XIII, 113 seq., ed. Mommsen. Berlin, 1898.
N.H.G.=New High German.

N.L.G. = New Low German.

Norges Land = *Norges Land og Folk.* Kristiania, 1885—1913.

Not. dign. = *Notitia dignitatum*, ed. Seeck. Berlin, 1876.

Not. gent. = *Notitia gentium initio saec.* IIII *conscripta*, ed. Müllenhoff, *Germania antiqua*, p. 157 seq. Berlin, 1873.

O.Dan. = Old Danish.

O.E. = Old English.

O.H.G. = Old High German.

O.L.G. = Old Low German.

OLSEN, MAGNUS, *Hedenske Kultminder* = MAGNUS OLSEN, *Hedenske Kultminder i norske Stednavne* in *Videnskapsselskapets Skrifter*, *Hist.-filos. Kl.* II, No. 4. Kristiania, 1915.

Origo Langobardorum = *Mon. Germ. SS. Langob.* 1 seq., ed. Waitz. Hanover, 1878.

— *Swevorum* = *Zeitschrift für deutsches Altertum*, XVII, 57 seq., ed. Müllenhoff.

OROSIUS = OROSIUS, *Historia adversus paganos* in *Corp. scr. ecclesiast. Latin.* V, ed. Zangemeister. Wien, 1882. *Ed. minor*, Leipzig, 1889.

— Alfred's, see ALFRED.

Oxf. Dict. = MURRAY, *A New English Dictionary.* Oxford, 1888—1928.

PACATIUS = PACATIUS, *Panegyricus Theodosio* in *Panegyrici Latini*, ed. Baehrens. Leipzig, 1911.

PAULUS DIACONUS = PAULUS DIACONUS, *Historia Langobardorum* in *Mon. Germ. SS. Langob.* 12 seq., ed. Waitz u. Bethmann. Hanover, 1878.

PAULY-WISSOWA = PAULY'S *Realencyclopädie der klassischen Altertumswissenschaft*, ed. Wissowa. Stuttgart, 1894 seq.

PLINY = PLINIUS, *Die geographischen Bücher der Naturalis Historia*, hrsg. von Detlefsen (*Sieglins Quellen und Forschungen*). Berlin, 1904.

PLUTARCH = PLUTARCHUS, *Vitae parallelae*, III, i, 232 seq., rec. Lindskog et Ziegler. Leipzig, 1914—26.

PRISCUS = *Hist. Graec. min.* I, ed. Dindorf. Leipzig, 1870.

PROCOPIUS, *Bell. Goth.* = PROCOPIUS, *Bellum Gothicum* in *Opera*, rec. Haury. Leipzig, 1905—13.

— *Bell. Vand.* = *idem*, *Bellum Vandalicum*, *ibid.*

PTOL. = PTOLEMY, *Geographia*, I, ed. O. Cuntz. Berlin, 1923.

RHABAN MAURUS = RHABAN (HRABANUS) MAURUS, *De inventione linguarum* in *Opera*, ed. Migne, *Patrologia Latina*, 112 seq. Paris, 1878.

Rhein. Museum = *Rheinisches Museum für Philologie.* Bonn.

ROSS, *Ordbog* = ROSS, *Norsk Ordbog.* Christiania, 1895.

Rune-song, see GREIN UND WÜLCKER, *Bibl. d. angelsächs. Poesie*, I, 335.

ŠAFARIK = SCHAFFARICK, *Slawische Alterthümer.* Leipzig, 1843.

Sax. Chron. = *Saxon Chronicle*, ed. Plummer. Oxford, 1899.

SCHMIDT = L. SCHMIDT, *Geschichte der deutschen Stämme.* Berlin, 1904—18.

SCHÖNFELD = SCHÖNFELD, *Wörterbuch der altgermanischen Personen- und Völkernamen* (*Germanische Bibliothek*, IV, 2). Heidelberg, 1911.

SCHRADER = SCHRADER UND NEHRING, *Reallexikon der indogermanischen Altertumskunde*, 2nd ed. Strassburg, Berlin, Leipzig, 1917—23.

Scr. Rer. Dan. = *Scriptores rerum Danicarum*, ed. Langebek. Hauniæ, 1772—1878.

SEQUESTER, VIBIUS = VIBIUS SEQUESTER, *De fluminibus* in *Geogr. Lat. min.*, ed. Riese. Heilbronn, 1878.

SIGISMUNDI, *Passio* = *Passio Sigismundi* in *Mon. Germ. SS. Merov.* II, 329 seq., ed. Krusch. Hanover, 1888.

Slav. = Slavonic.

SOCRATES = SOCRATES, *Historia ecclesiastica*, ed. Hussey. Oxford, 1853.

STATIUS = STATIUS, *Silvae*, recogn. Phillimore. Oxford, 1904. *Statius, with an English Translation* by Mozley. London, 1928.

STEINMEYER U. SIEVERS = STEINMEYER UND SIEVERS, *Die althochdeutschen Glossen*. Berlin, 1879—1922.

STEPHAN. BYZANT. = STEPHANUS BYZANTIUS, *Ethnica*, rec. Meineke. Berlin, 1849.

STOKE, *Rymchroniek* = MELIS STOKE, *Rymchroniek van Holland*, ed. Brill. 1885.

SUETONIUS = SUETONIUS, *De vita Caesarum*, ed. Ihm. Leipzig, 1907.

Swed. = Swedish.

SYNCELLUS = *Corp. Scr. Byz.*, ed. Dindorf. Bonn, 1829.

Tab. Peuting. = *Die Peutingersche Tafel*, herausgeg. von K. Miller. Stuttgart, 1906.

TAC., *Ann.* = TACITUS, *Annales. The Annals, with an English Translation* by J. Jackson. (*The Loeb Classical Library.*) London and New York, 1931 seq.

— *Germ.* = *idem*, *Germania*, ed. Schweizer, Sidler et Schwyzer, 1st ed. Halle, 1912.

— *Hist.* = *idem*, *Historiae. The Histories, with an English Translation* by Clifford H. Moore. (*The Loeb Classical Library.*) London and New York, 1925.

Taliesin = J. GWENOGVRYN EVANS, *Facsimile and Text of the Book of Taliesin*. Llanbedrog, 1910; *idem*, *Poems from the Book of Taliesin, translated*, *ibid.* 1915; WILL. F. SKENE, *The Four Ancient Books of Wales*. Edinburgh, 1868.

Tid(s)skr. = *Tidsskrift*.

Tribal Hidage = ed. Goodall. *Zeitschrift für Ortsnamenforschung*, I, 39.

VEGETIUS, *Mulomedicina* = VEGETIUS, *Digestorum artis mulomedicinae libri*, ed. Lommatzsch. Leipzig, 1903.

VELLEIUS = VELLEIUS, *Compendium of Roman History, with an English Translation* by F. M. Shipley. London and New York, 1924.

VENANTIUS FORTUNATUS = VENANTIUS FORTUNATUS, *Carmina* in *Mon. Germ. Auct. antiq.* IV, 1 seq., ed. Leo. Berlin, 1881.

Vergl. = *vergleichend*.

Vict. Not. Num. = *Victoris Vitensis Historia persecutionis Africanae et Notitia provintiarum Africae* (*Numidiae*, etc.) in *Mon. Germ. Auct. antiq.* III, 1 seq., rec. Halm. Berlin, 1879.

VICTOR, *Caes.* = SEXTUS AURELIUS VICTOR, *De Caesaribus*, ed. Pichlmayr. Leipzig, 1911.

Vita Ansk. = *Vita Anskarii auct. Rimberto* in *Mon. Germ. SS.* II, 683 seq., ed. Dahlmann. Hanover, 1829.

Vita S. Sigismundi, see SIGISMUNDI, *Passio*.

Widsith = CHAMBERS, *Widsith, a Study in Old English Heroic Legend*. Cambridge, 1912.

WIETERSHEIM-DAHN = WIETERSHEIM, *Geschichte der Völkerwanderung*, 2. Aufl. besorgt von Felix Dahn. Leipzig, 1880–1.

Yngl. Saga = *Ynglinga Saga* (in Snorri Sturluson, *Hskr.*).

Zeitschr. = *Zeitschrift*.

Zeitschrift = *Zeitschrift für deutsches Altertum*. Berlin.

ZEUSS = ZEUSS, *Die Deutschen und die Nachbarstämme*. München, 1837. Reprint, 1905.

ZONARAS = ZONARAS, *Epitoma historiarum*, ed. Dindorf. Leipzig, 1868—75.

ZOSIMUS = ZOSIMUS, *Fisci historia nova*, ed. Mendelssohn. Leipzig, 1887.

ILLUSTRATIONS

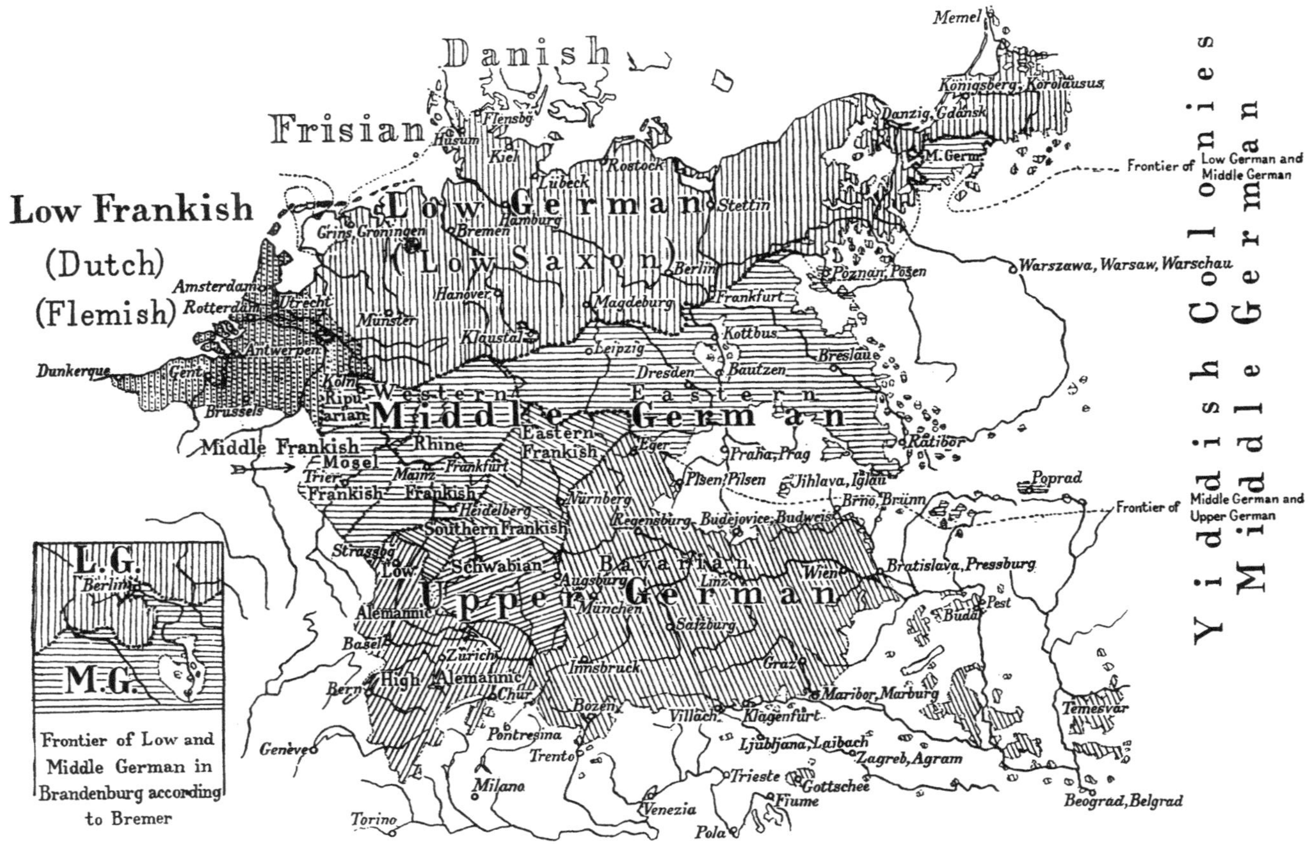

FIG. 1. German and Dutch dialects according to Behaghel.

Fig. 2

System of signs used on this map or on the map Fig. 20

Compound houses.

Houses with two wings.

Double farmsteads.

Row farmsteads.

Irregular farmsteads.

Collective villages.

Regular yards enclosed by buildings.

Double court plan (one court for men and one court for cattle).

Quadrangle (Danish and German types).

Danish compound house.

Frisian.

Frisian compound house ('hauberg', 'stelphoeve').

Saxon compound house.

'Dwarshus' or 'krukhuis'.

Frankish yard.

Frankish-Bavarian mixed type.

Bavarian compound house.

Alpine-Bavarian and Danish double farmstead.

Alpine-Bavarian irregular farmstead.

Alemannic-Swabian compound house.

Swiss 'länderbau' (double farmstead or group farmstead).

Territory of the German and Dutch languages.

Frontiers between Low German, Middle German, and Upper German.

Frontiers between Frankish, Bavarian, and Alemannic-Swabian.

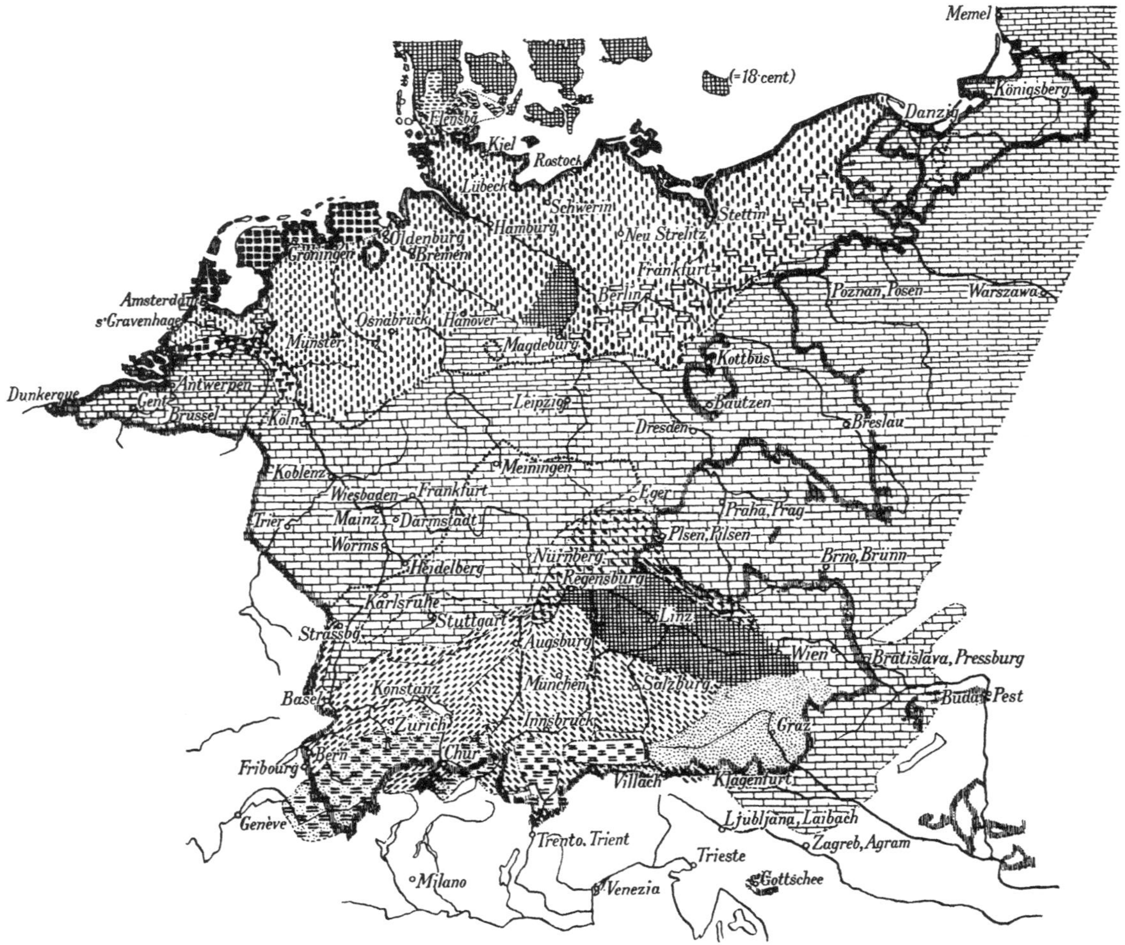

FIG. 2. Types of houses in Germany and the surrounding countries (chiefly according to A. Haberlandt)

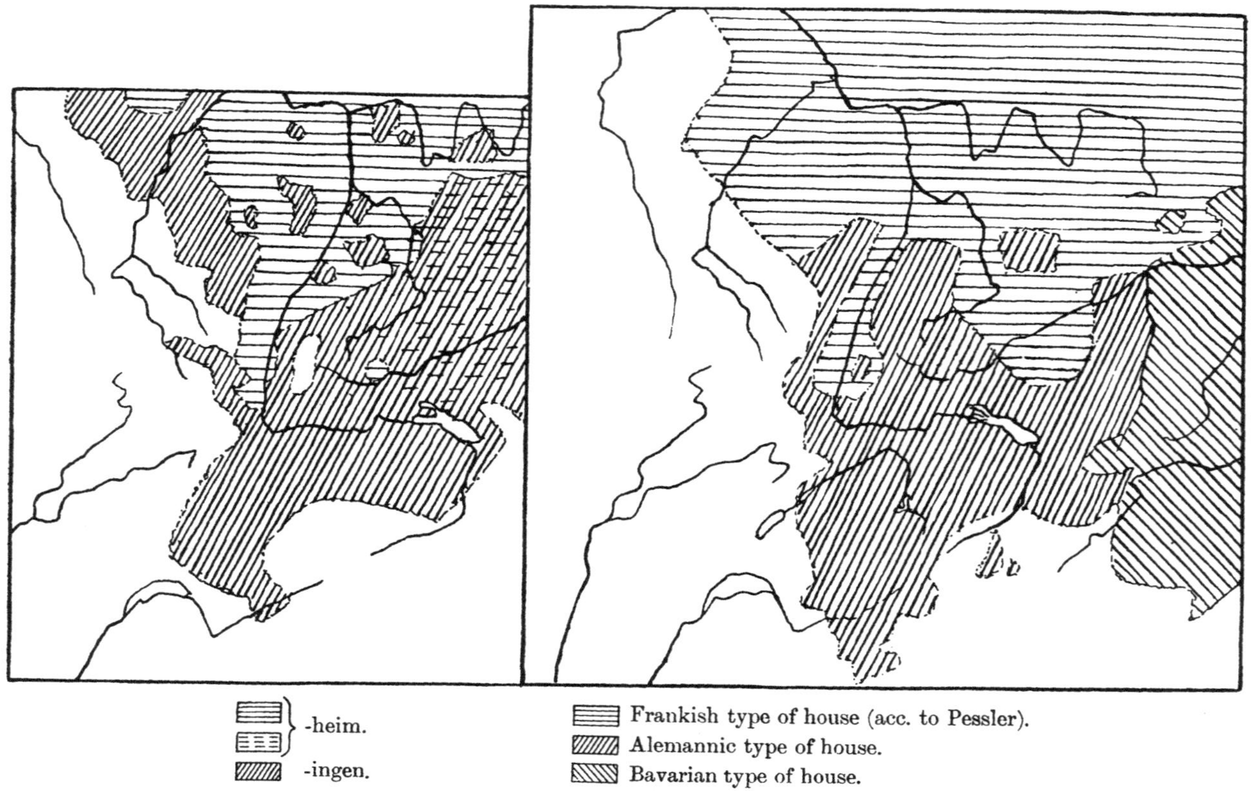

FIG. 3. South-western Germany and Switzerland

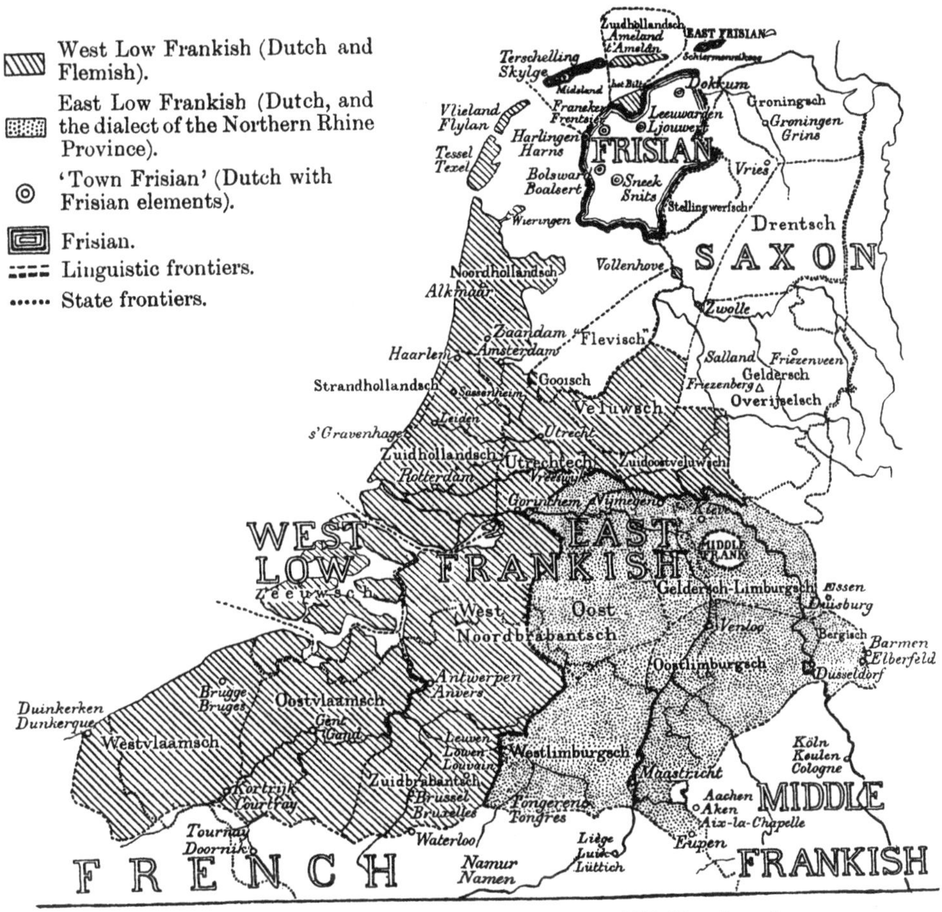

FIG. 4. Dutch and Frisian dialects of Holland and neighbouring countries

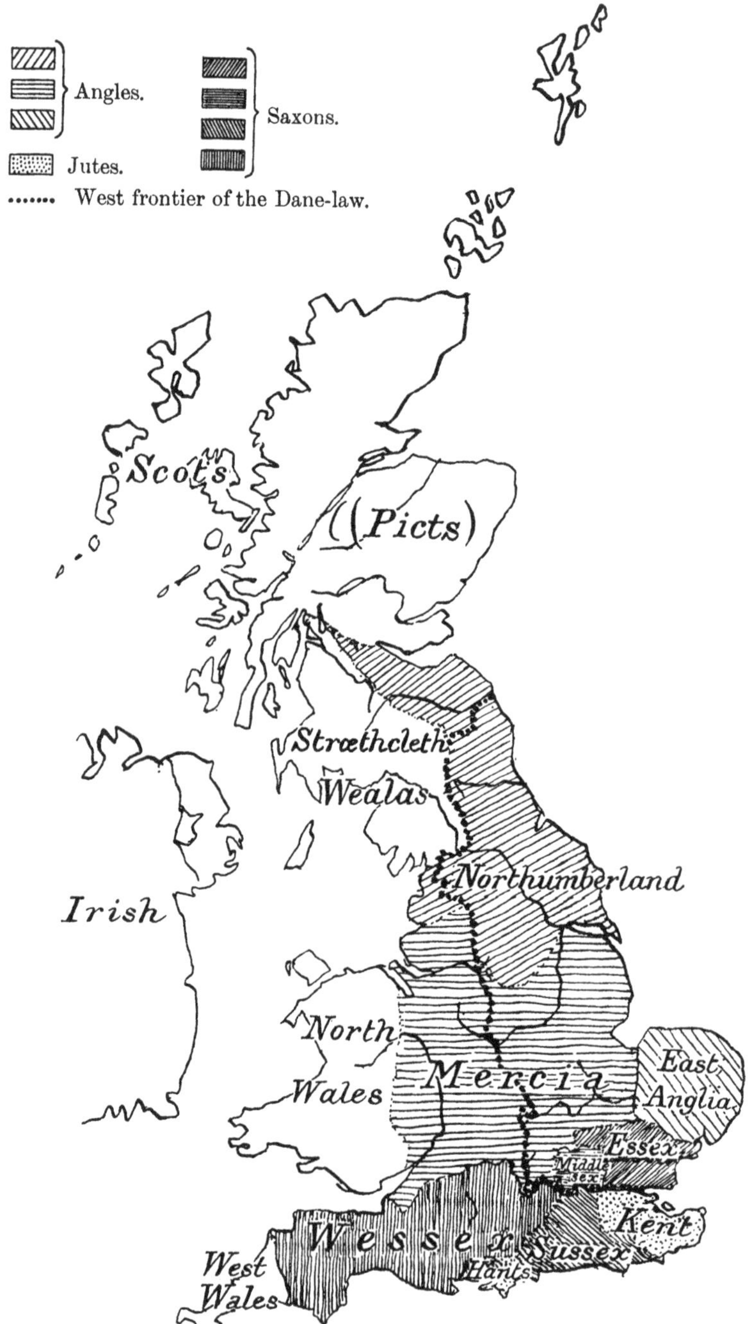

FIG. 5. Anglo-Saxon states according to Kluge (*Grundriss*)

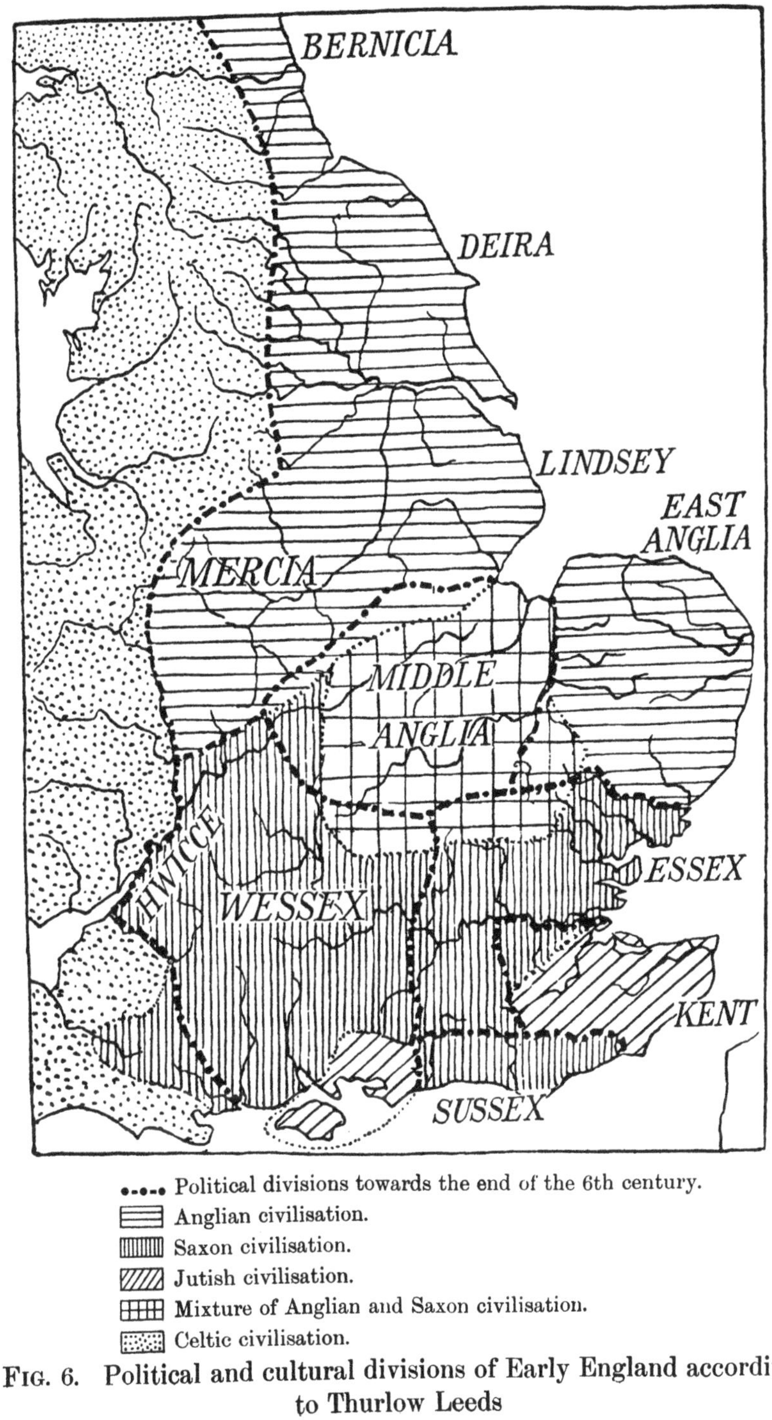

FIG. 6. Political and cultural divisions of Early England according to Thurlow Leeds

FIG. 7. English dialects according to Ellis

Fig. 8. Distribution of 'castra'

THURLOW LEEDS
ANGLO-SAXON
BURIAL PLACES
A.D. 450-650
Wansbeck
Skerne
Swale
Skerne
Wensum
Stour
Stour
Stour
Icknield Way
Wantsumu
Swale
Stour
Wansdyke
Bokerly Dyke
Stour

FIG. 9.

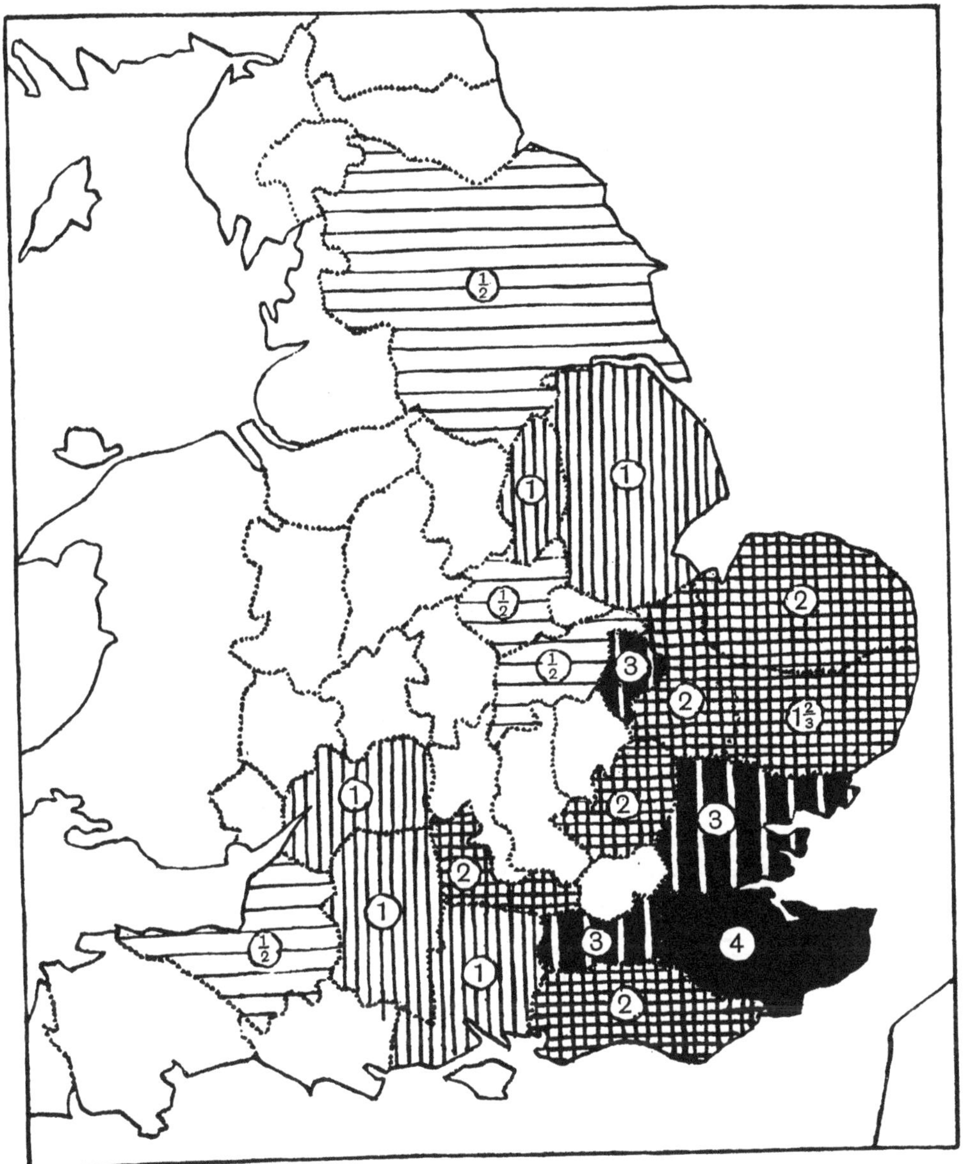

FIG. 10. Percentage of local names ending in *-ing* without further suffix (Domesday Survey) according to Seebohm

FIG. 11. Percentage of local names ending in *-ham* (Domesday Survey) according to Seebohm

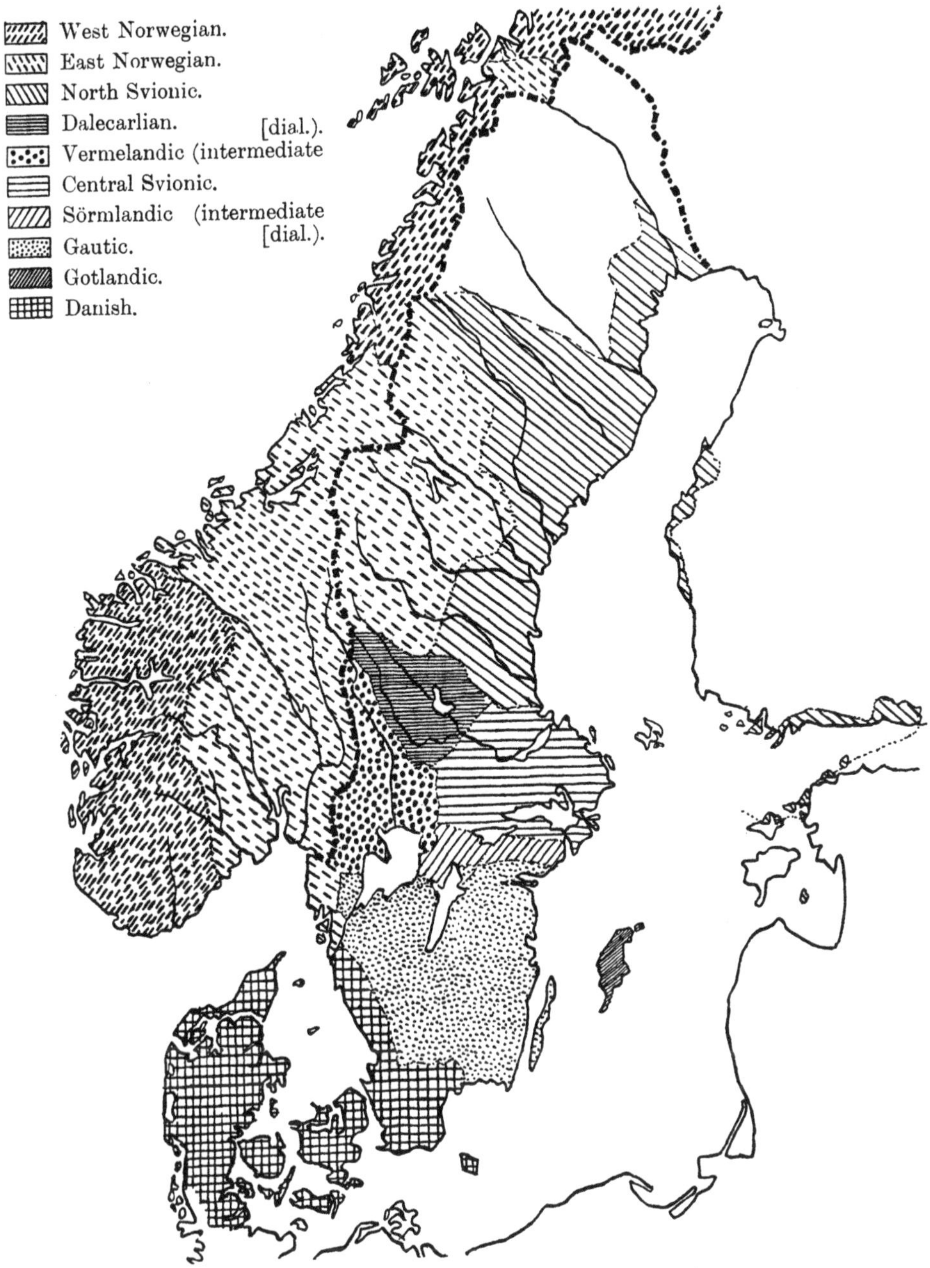

FIG. 12. Scandinavian dialects. (*a*) General survey

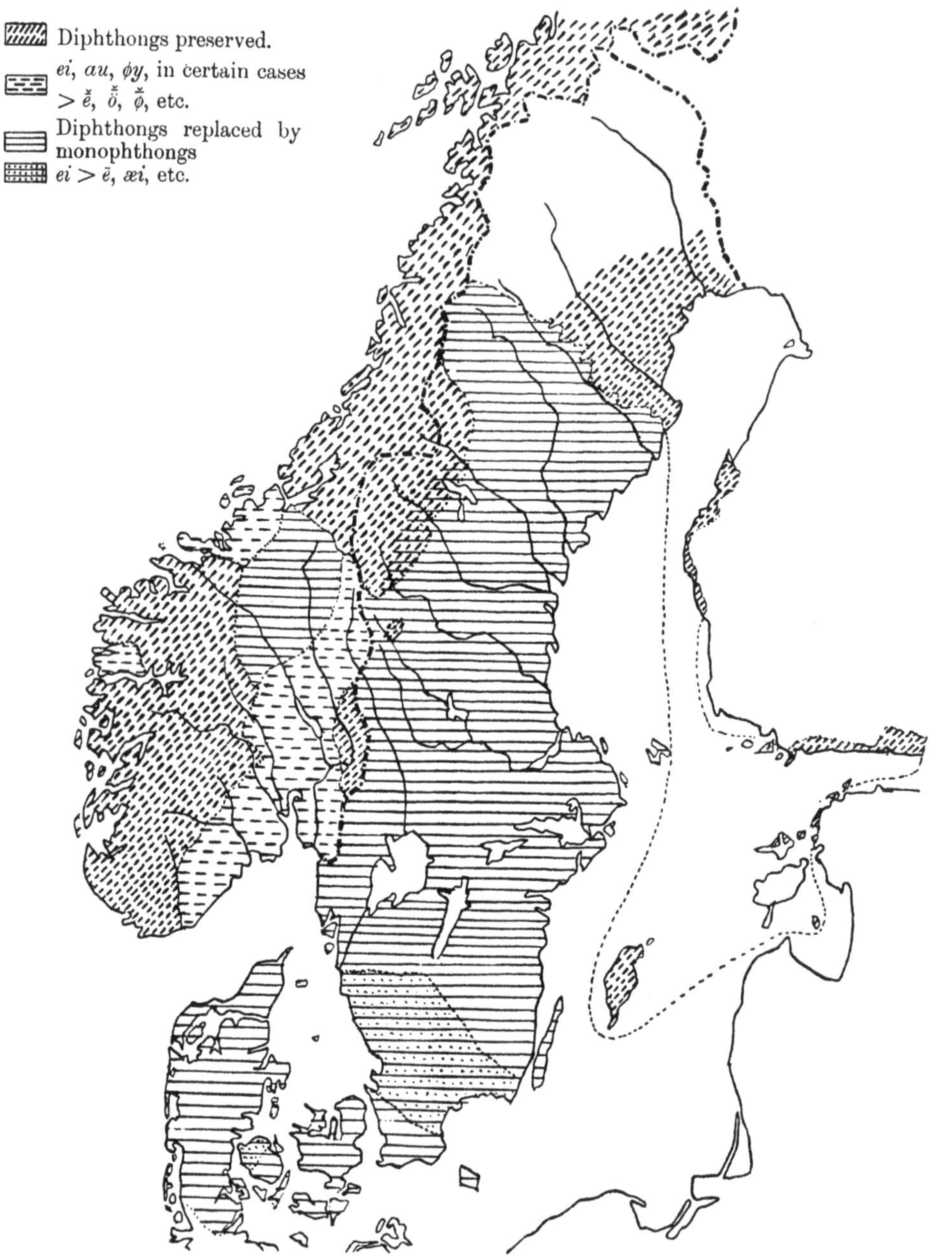

FIG. 13. Scandinavian dialects. (*b*) (According to Brøndum-Nielsen)

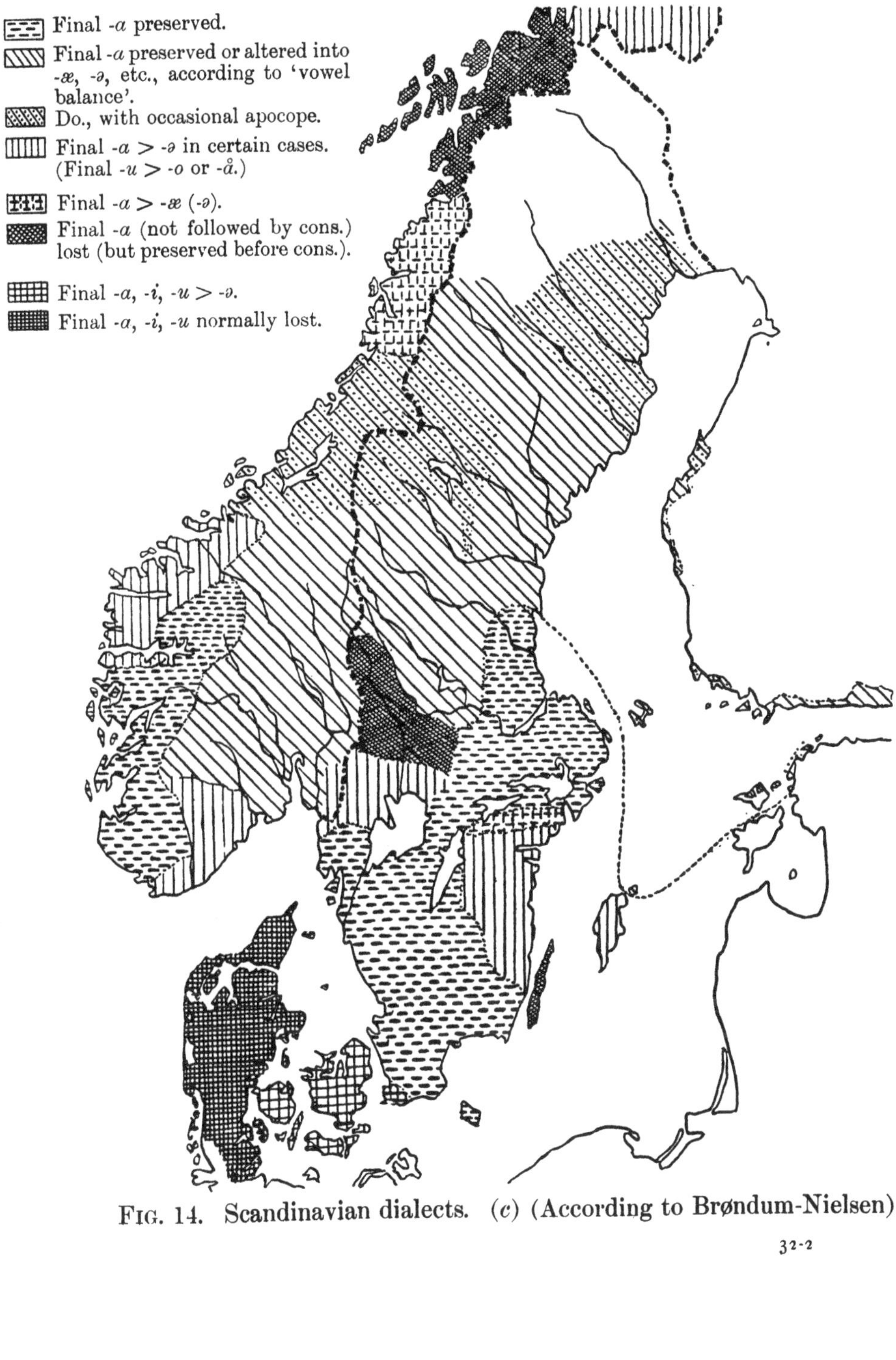

FIG. 14. **Scandinavian dialects.** (*c*) **(According to Brøndum-Nielsen)**

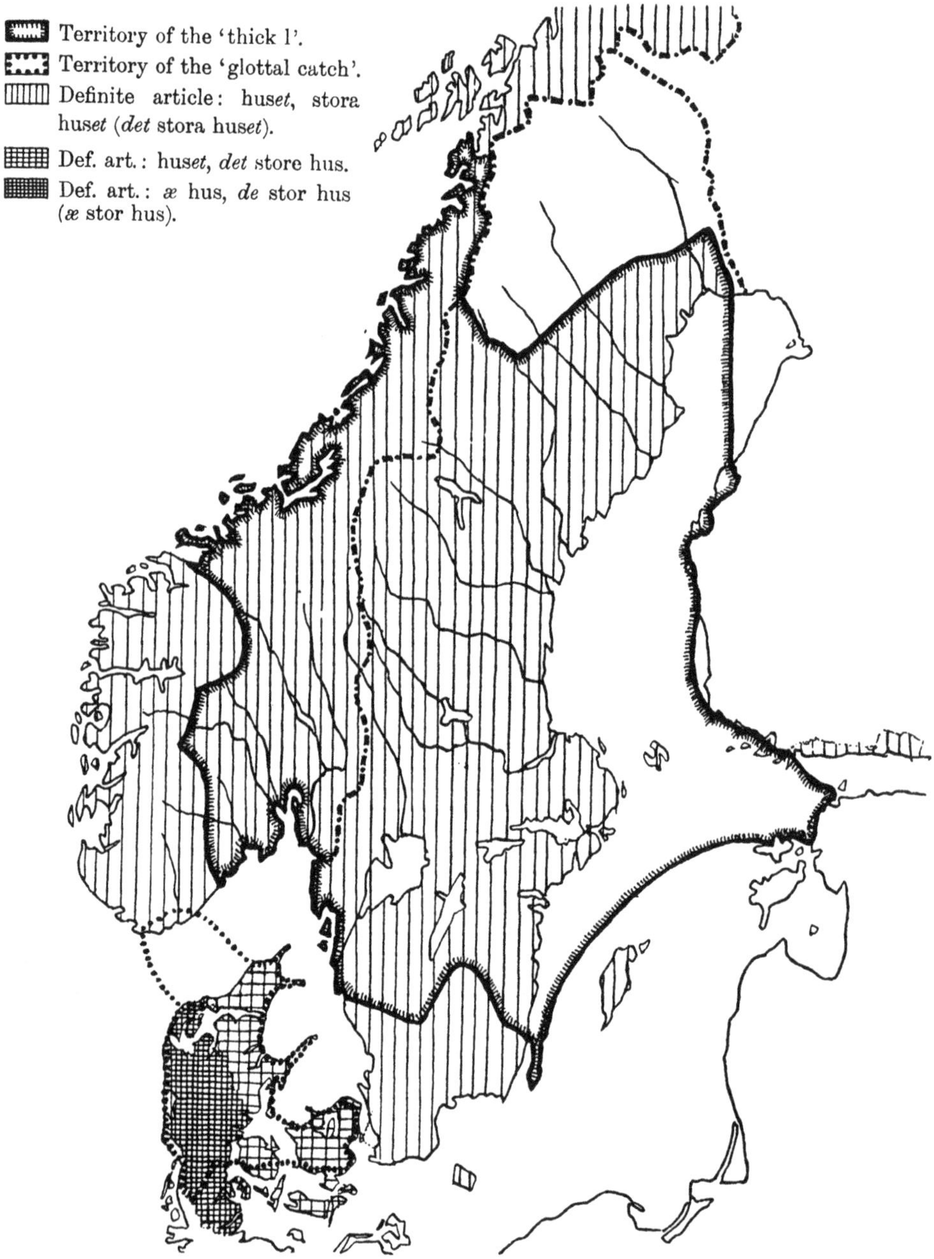

FIG. 15. Scandinavian dialects. (*d*) (According to Brøndum-Nielsen)

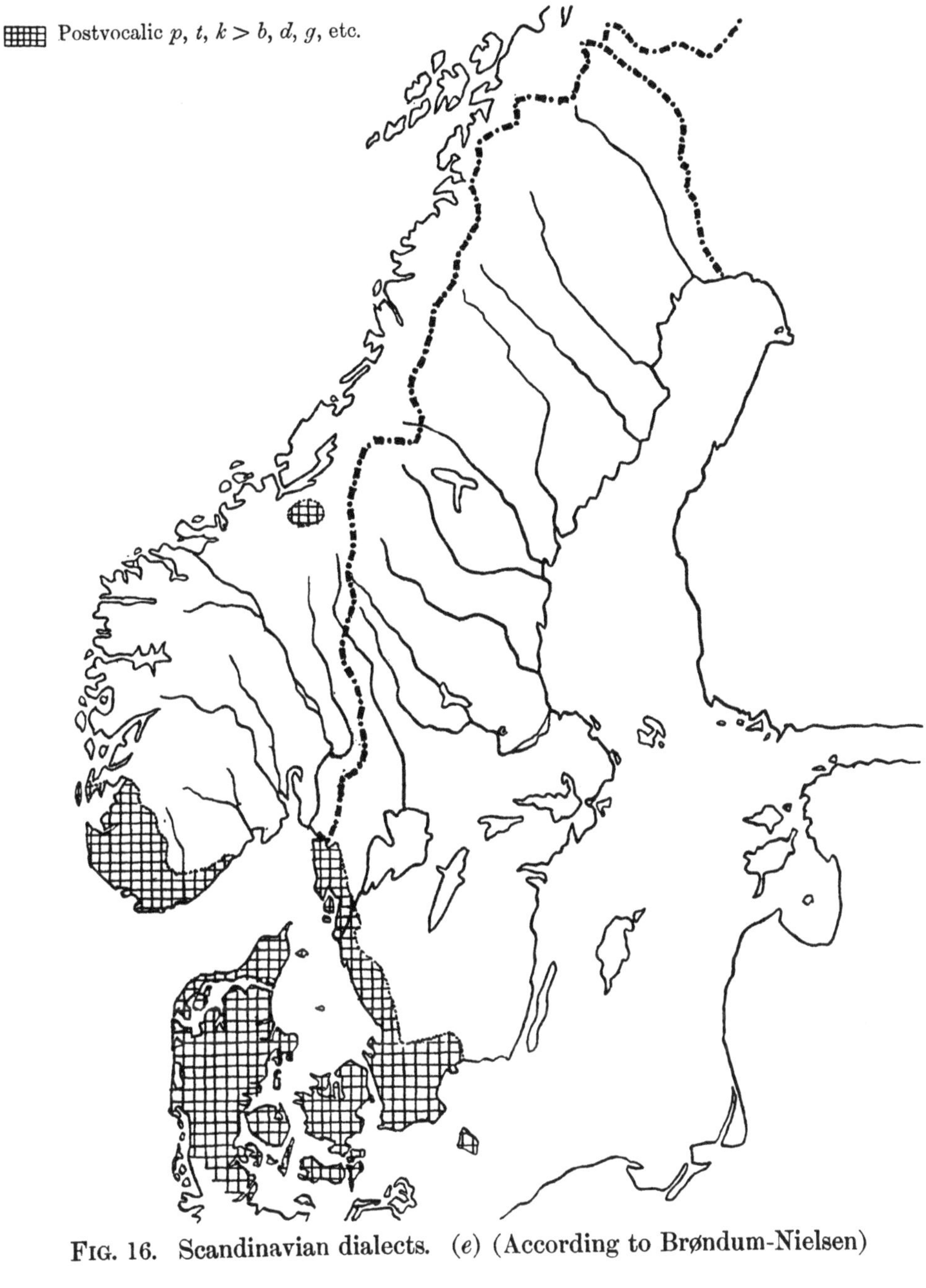

FIG. 16. Scandinavian dialects. (*e*) (According to Brøndum-Nielsen)

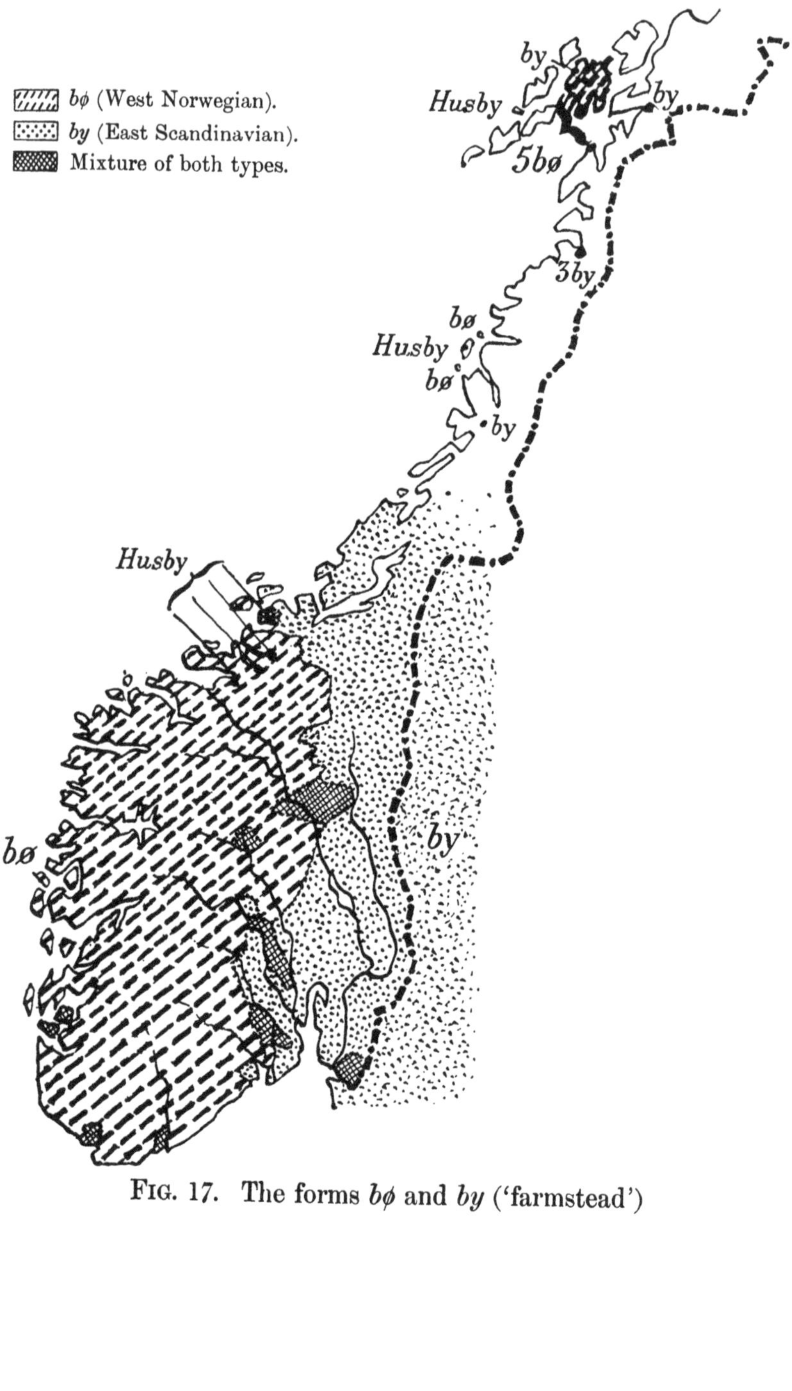

FIG. 17. The forms *bø* and *by* ('farmstead')

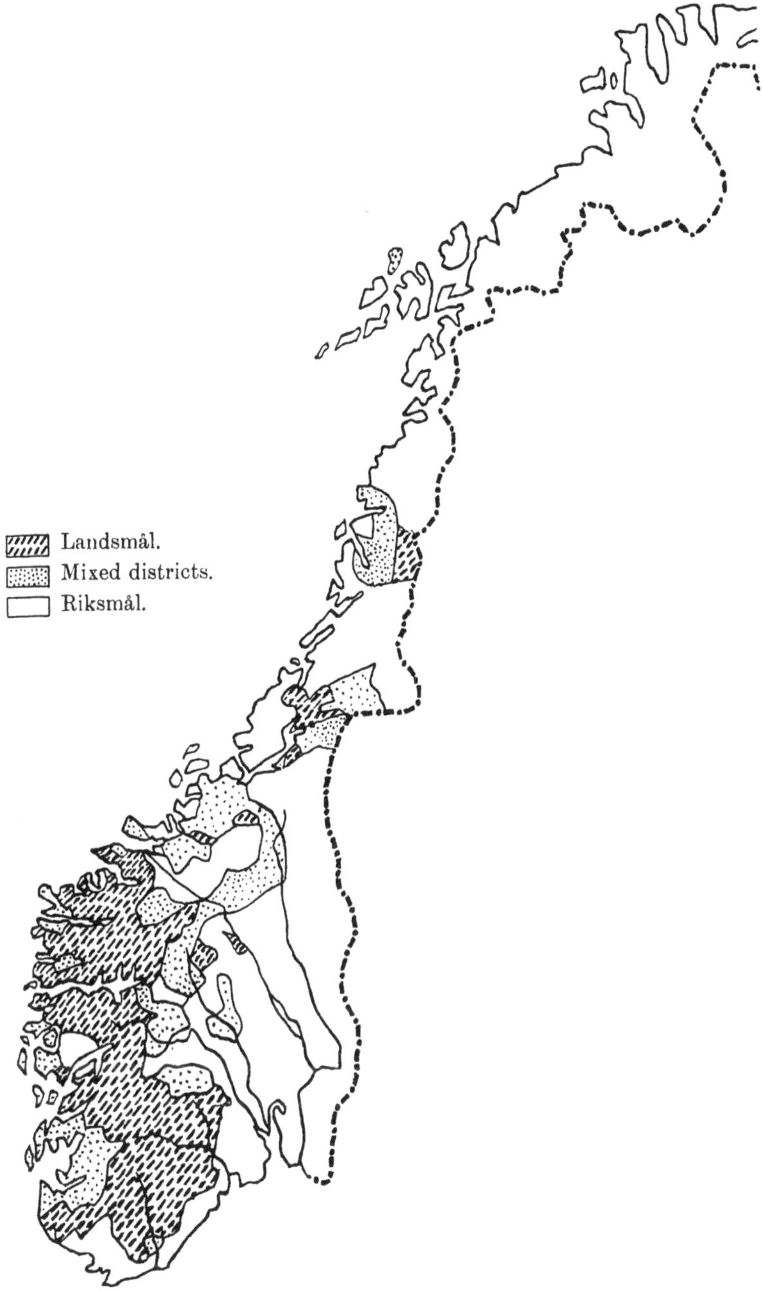

FIG. 18. The use of 'Landsmål' and 'Riksmål' in Norwegian school districts

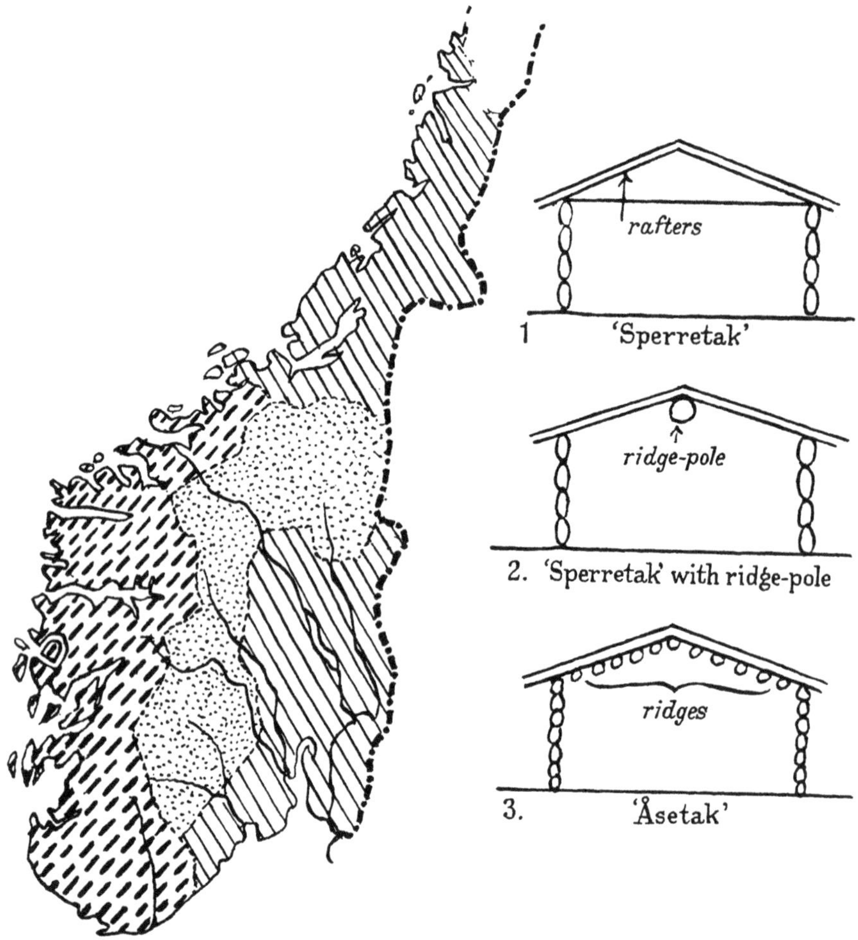

1. Rafters (sperretak). The pairs of rafters are wedged together in the ridge. The side-walls are their only support.

2. Rafters and ridge-pole (mönsåstak). The rafters are supported not only by the side-walls, but also by a thick ridge-pole from gable to gable.

3. Roof with ridges (åsetak). The roof is constructed by means of a series of ridges laid parallel-wise from gable to gable.

FIG. 19. Constructions of roof according to H. Vreim

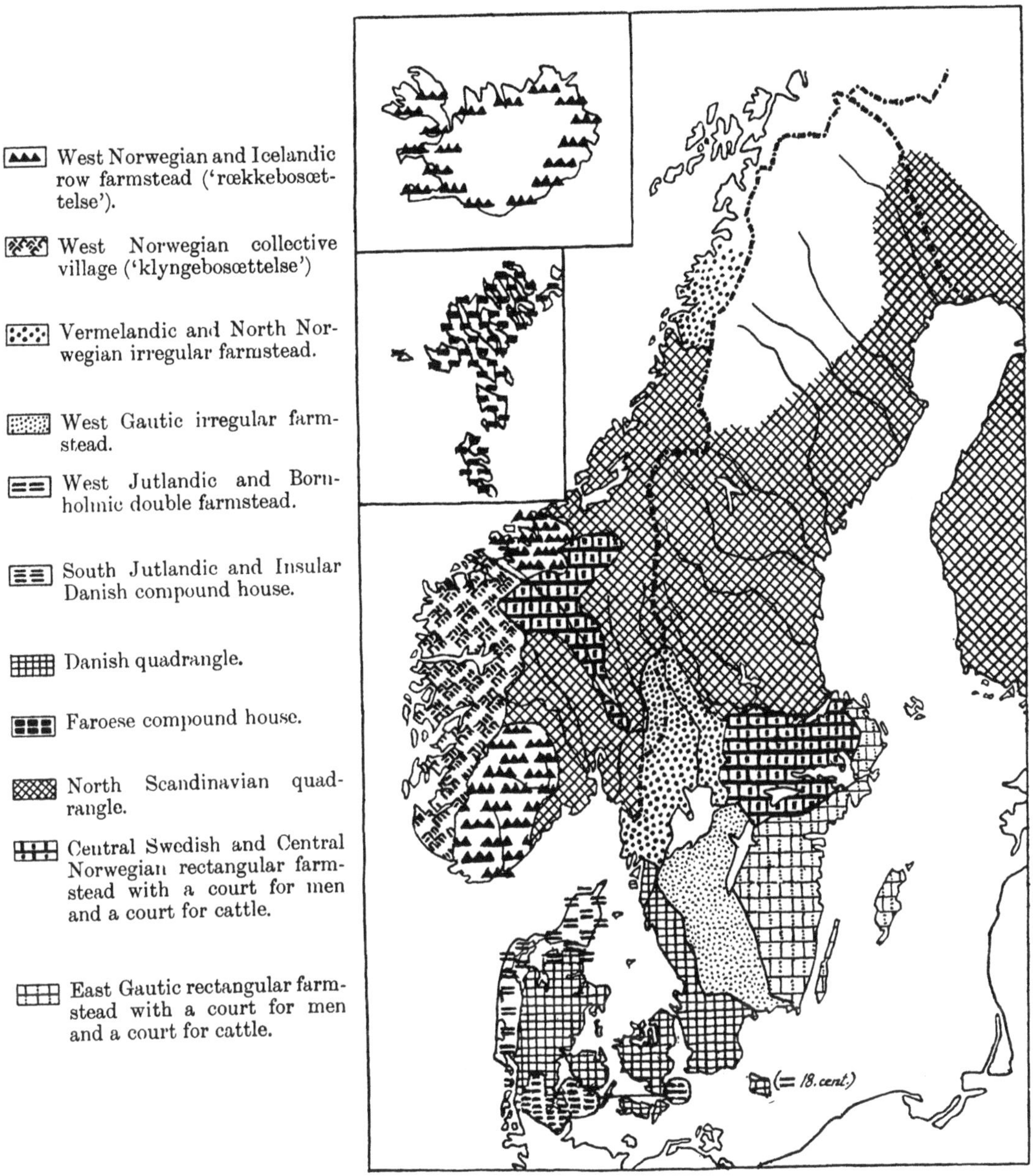

FIG. 20. Scandinavian types of farmsteads according to Erixon, Vreim, and Zangenberg

Lightning Source UK Ltd.
Milton Keynes UK
UKHW030705100121
376441UK00014B/376

9 781107 677234